John Scott Lidgett

John Scott Lidgett

Archbishop of British Methodism?

Alan Turberfield

EPWORTH PRESS

British Library Cataloguing in Publication data

A catalogue record for this book is available
from the British Library

0 7162 0571 8

First published in 2003
by Epworth Press
4 John Wesley Road
Werrington
Peterborough PE4 6ZP

Printed and bound in Great Britain by
Biddles Ltd, www.biddles.co.uk

Contents

Foreword

It is extraordinary that there has been no major biography of John Scott Lidgett, often called the greatest Methodist since John Wesley. Rupert Davies edited a symposium of essays about Lidgett in 1957, to which some of his later contemporaries contributed. A much more systematic and critical approach was needed based on the rich primary evidence now available. Alan Turberfield has produced this, drawing on his recent research. He conveys the extraordinary range of Scott Lidgett's 73 years of active ministry, featuring the work of the Bermondsey Settlement, which he pioneered, and over which he was Warden for over half a century. His political life and his contribution to education, nationally, locally, and in the University of London are carefully surveyed. How he achieved so much is remarkable, but Alan Turberfield shows that he was not a remote man. When once he made an appearance, no doubt robed, at a stone-laying event in Bermondsey, a poorly dressed local woman shouted 'That's our Dr Lidgett' – the man who was their friend and the friend of Randall Davidson, Archbishop of Canterbury.

Born in 1854 into middle-class Wesleyanism – his grandfather, John Scott, was Principal of Westminster College – he graduated from University College, London. Accepted for the Wesleyan ministry, he served for 15 years in diverse circuits – Tunstall, Southport, Cardiff, Wolverhampton and Cambridge. My working-class grandfather spoke glowingly of Lidgett's influence on him as a teenager. These were the days of the Forward Movement in Wesleyanism, with new attempts to bridge the gulf between the Church and the masses. Encouraged by W. F. Moulton, headmaster of The Leys School, to initiate work on the pattern of S. A. Barnett and Toynbee Hall, he set up the Bermondsey Settlement and lived there until his retirement. He was committed to the total development of people as individuals and in community. This was what today we would call a mission alongside the poor, though this particular style was very much of its era before the Welfare State.

Alan Turberfield shows that Lidgett's many interests in mission, ecumenism and politics stemmed from his theology. He was clearly the shrewdest Methodist theologian in the late Victorian and Edwardian period. While W. B. Pope was his early mentor, he was the first Methodist thinker to feature F. D.

Maurice's view of Christ as the Head of the human race. He questioned the old certainties, seeing love and holiness combined in the God and Father of our Lord Jesus. We have here a clear analysis of his writings from *The Spiritual Principle of the Atonement* (1897) to *God and the World* (1943). His vision of salvation builds on Wesley's doctrine of Christian perfection, seeing the whole of life as redeemable, not just religious aspirations. This was the vision he found in Ephesians and is by no means irrelevant today. Theology and life, reflection and action, were one for this immensely versatile man. He was editor of the liberal *Methodist Times*, at a time when cabinet ministers could not ignore its viewpoint, and a joint-editor and frequent writer in the *Contemporary Review*. Politically he remained a Liberal of Gladstonian persuasion, modified by the New Liberals and T. H. Green's assertion that the State should 'remove hindrances to freedom'. So he served on the London County Council, an Alderman for two spells and Leader of the Progressives from 1918 to 1928, suffering a disappointment when his style of Liberalism went into terminal decline despite Lloyd George, with whom he was active as late as 1935. This work is perceptively analysed here, as is his long support for London University of which, fortuitously, he became Vice-Chancellor in 1930.

Lidgett's support for Free Church unity led to his being President (1906) and Moderator (1923–5) of the National and Federal Councils of the Free Churches, though he never saw Free Church unity as an end in itself. He was clearly 'the man of the match' in securing the union of the three Methodist Connexions. He had been President of the Wesleyan Conference in 1908, and in 1932 presided over the first Methodist Conference. The important and surviving doctrinal clauses – orthodox yet flexible – of the Deed of Union bear Lidgett's clear stamp, asserting the Catholicity of Methodism and its evangelical and protestant heritage. In the year of Union he received an honorary DD from Oxford and was made a Companion of Honour, the only Methodist minister to receive it.

Lidgett was an enthusiastic supporter of the Lambeth Appeal for Reunion in 1920. 'Where there are no differences, our watchword must be union; where they are comparatively slight, federation; where they are serious but not destructive of the fundamental agreement of Christianity, co-operation . . .' That statement in 1908 echoed through a century! Lidgett was ahead of his time in some of these matters, trusted greatly by Anglicans as a positive Free Church spokesman.

Alan Turberfield is a clear guide through the controversies over the Education Act of 1902. Should there be a 'dual system' of State and 'Church' schools? Lidgett took a middle position between secularists and the powerful Anglican and Roman Catholic parties. He was never a denominationalist, schism was as abhorrent to him as secularism. The issue of 'Faith Schools' is with us again, a century later, in a multi-cultural society.

Scott Lidgett remained an active Methodist minister – Chairman of his District for some 39 years! – until after the end of the Second World War. This was a unique and possibly unwise achievement. The Roman Catholic historian, Adrian Hastings, a little naughtily wrote:

> When the World Methodist Conference met in Oxford in 1951, it was somehow symbolic that the Patriarch of British Methodism, Scott Lidgett, now ninety-seven years old, should preach from the pulpit of the University Church. He spoke for forty minutes and then collapsed into unconsciousness. Methodism had arrived – was it also about to pass away?

We give the warmest welcome to this important biography. It deserves a wide readership across the Churches. Lidgett's view of faith embracing theology, social and political action, 'the statesmanship of thought' and personal holiness is by no means irrelevant to the needs of the twenty-first century, though it has to be worked out in a context very different from that of Lidgett's heyday.

John Munsey Turner
February 2002

Preface

This biography aims to set John Scott Lidgett in the context of his times, a period of almost a century, and to appraise his stature as it emerges from his extraordinarily varied roles as Methodist theologian, educationalist, politician, ecclesiastical statesman and social reformer. It makes no attempt to assess rival claims for greatness among other Methodists or members of other churches: its focus is on those of Lidgett himself. It illustrates the struggle taking place in the Wesleyan Methodist Church to come to terms with new ideas, theological and social, and examines the ecumenical debate of his time: the impetus and obstacles to various forms of union between Protestant churches, the Faith and Order Movement, the Lambeth Appeal, the subsequent negotiations and the achievement of a united Methodist Church. Lidgett's contribution to educational, ecumenical, political and social developments and to Methodist theology is identified, together with ways in which all his activities derived from his theological and educational convictions. Many of the matters treated in the biography continue to have relevance to today and are therefore likely to be of interest to members of both the Anglican and Free Churches.

A symposium of essays on aspects of Lidgett's career was published in 1957, but no biography has yet been written. Doctoral or other theses and monographs, concentrating on specific topics or associated personalities, have not sought a rounded picture. The history of Methodism during this period has not been written from Lidgett's perspective nor with a detailed assessment of his participation in the larger historical scene. Hitherto there has been no systematic effort to draw on all the primary sources available. Though few of his letters survive, use is here made not only of Lidgett's autobiographies, *Reminiscences* (1928) and *My Guided Life* (1936), but also, *inter alia*, of a trawl of his family, friends, acquaintances and members of his congregations; the papers of Archbishops Davidson, Lang and W. Temple, and of Bishop Bell, in Lambeth Palace Library; *Annual Reports* and *Monthly Magazines* of the Bermondsey Settlement; the archives of the LCC, London University, the Methodist Church, and local London Boroughs; Methodist, Nonconformist and Anglican journals; and notably Lidgett's editorial contributions to the *Methodist Times*, a particularly valuable reflection of his thinking between 1907 and 1918.

Lidgett's overlapping autobiographies repeat one another, often verbatim: the second adds comments on the period between 1928 and 1936 and covers in particular the achievement of Methodist Union and his Vice-Chancellorship of London University. Conscious of his own importance and wide contacts, and writing clearly and logically from an assured position, he gave his outlook and activities an overall consistency. This might have made it difficult to trace the successive stages of his thought, or assess how far what he wrote some time after the events described was in fact an elaboration of his views and others' attitudes, perhaps adjusted and developed in the light of mature reflection and further reinforcements to his thinking. Contemporary sources, however, confirm his consistency and his account emerges as generally accurate. The author's view of his past was, perhaps understandably, laudatory, but though the autobiographies were flawed by omissions and inflated coverage of insignificant incidents, there were few mistakes.

This biography initially follows a roughly chronological sequence, often with considerable overlap between chapters, and then concentrates on themes which in turn interrelate with one another. Calendars of main events are set out in the Prefaces to Parts 1–7 and 9. Detailed notes to each chapter can be found at the end of the book, and there is a series of appendices. A full list of Lidgett's publications is included in the bibliography.

Acknowledgements

A biography inevitably incurs many debts. Mine are considerable, evident in the bibliography, the appendices, the notes to the text, throughout the text itself and in the list of individual people and institutions acknowledged below. I am very grateful for all this assistance and apologise for any inadvertent omissions. Every effort has been made to trace copyright ownership. The publisher would be grateful to be informed of any omissions.

The list of those to whom I am indebted includes: the supervisors of my initial doctorate thesis: the late Revd Professor P. B Hinchliff and the Revd Dr K. B. Wilson; other scholars consulted, who gave further encouragement and guidance: Drs Jane Garnett and Sheridan Gilley, the Revd Dr John Newton, Drs Peter Nockles and John Walsh, Professor W. R. Ward, and especially the Revd Dr Ralph Waller; writers of theses consulted, listed in the bibliography; others who gave interviews: Mrs Elisabeth Brewer, for example, 4 March 1993; Mrs Irene Brewer, for example, 12 February 1993; the late Revd Reginald Buckmaster, 11 September 1992; the late Revd Dr Rupert E. Davies, 19 March 1993; Mrs Elizabeth ('Libby') Fairweather, 14 August 1993; the late Revd Raymond George, 19 March 1993; the late Mrs Lorna Horstmann, 21 September 1992; Miss Elisabeth McDougall, for example, 21 August 1993; the late Revd the Lord Soper, 24 September 1992; others who commented, supplied information or answered enquiries by letter or telephone, including: Bishop J. Adams; John Beasley; Mrs Elisabeth Brewer; Mrs Irene Brewer; Mrs M. Bristow; Mrs S. A. Brooke; the Revd David Bryant; Prof. A. H. Bunting; Freidmann W. Burkhardt; Mrs Elizabeth Camp; the Revd F. W. Clifford; the late Revd Michael Edwards; the late Mrs Phyllis Flemington; Brian Frost; the Revd Reginald Frost; the Revd Dr Stanley B. Frost; Sister Muriel Gage; the Revd Richard Goldring; Dr Alan Hall; Donald Henry; Gary Hobbs; Ms Freda Jenkins; Mrs Jane Jones; Norman Jones; Dr Elaine Kaye; Arthur Kelsey; Leslie Kingsnorth; the late Revd Rex Kissack; Ms Petra Laidlaw; the Revd John Lampard; J. D. Lewis; Dr Gareth Lloyd; Mrs Ruth Marsh; Miss Elisabeth McDougall (genealogist); the Revd W. Motson; Harold Packington; Sister Lois Rands; Adam Rates; Mrs D. R. Rouse; Miss Joan Stampe; John Telford; Dr John Thompson CB CVO; the late Donald Tranter; Walter Veale; the late

Roy Wake; Dr Pauline Webb; Dozent Dr Michael Weyer; the Revd J. Wright; publishers and holders of copyright who kindly gave permission for the use of quotation and/or illustrations: principally, the *Methodist Recorder*, for the photographs of John Scott Lidgett; the Blackheath Society, for the photograph of one of Lidgett's family homes; the Revd Dr Leslie Griffiths, for the photograph taken from an unknown artist's portrait of Hugh Price Hughes; the National Portrait Gallery, London, for the portraits of Archbishop Davidson and David Lloyd George; the Witt Library, the Courtauld Institute of Art, for the portrait of Archbishop Cosmo Gordon Lang; Punch Ltd and the Southwark Annual for the poem and advertisement about the Bermondsey Settlement; Westminster Institute and the Wesley and Methodist Study Centre, for the picture of W. B. Pope; T. J. Brookes for the photograph of W. R. Nicoll; A. T. Nowell for the photograph of A. S. Peake; the Trustees, Librarians, Archivists and staff of the following: the Bodleian Library, Oxford; the British Library of Political and Economic Science; Colindale Newspaper Library; Lambeth Palace Library; the London Metropolitan Archive; the London Picture Library; the University of London Archive; the John Rylands Library, Manchester; the Southwark Local Studies Library; the Greenwich Local History Library; Lewisham Local Studies and Archives; the Wesley and Methodist Studies Centre at the Westminster Institute of Oxford Brookes University; Dr Williams's Library, London; and in particular Harris Manchester College in Oxford University which provided me with a base for my doctorate studies and a Fellowship for subsequent research; the Secretary of the Methodist Conference for permission to consult the *Wesleyan Conference Journal* 1918–32 and Methodist Union Committees' Minute Books; the Revd G. M. Burt, A.Ghagan, P. Forsaith, E. A. Rose, J. Coulter, J. O'Keefe, N. Rhind, J. Vickers, John Everson, Anna Hardman, Alex Knights, Stephen Rogers, Peter Andrews, Kathryn Wolfendale, Matthew Percival (Courtauld Institute of Art), Matthew Bailey and James Kilvington (National Portrait Gallery), for help variously with publication, word processing, checking of references, illustrations, and the compiling of the index; the Revd J. Munsey Turner for contributing his Foreword; and, above all, my wife for all her encouragement, support and endless patience.

References, abbreviations and terms

References

References to individuals are usually to ministers or clergy, unless the context makes it clear that the individual is a layman. Virtually all the people mentioned are men. As products of their age they spoke naturally of 'men' and 'mankind'. Such terms are retained. To do otherwise would distort history.

References to Methodism are usually to Wesleyan Methodism, unless the context is concerned with the Methodist denominations as a united whole.

References to the *Methodist Times* are usually to Lidgett's statements as Editor in either the leading article or his 'Notes and Comments', so that page references are not always required.

In the endnotes and bibliography, unless stated otherwise, books and pamphlets were published in London. The bibliography also includes unpublished sources such as university theses.

Abbreviations

Abp	Archbishop
b.	born
Bp	Bishop
BW	*British Weekly*
c.	about
CD	Contagious Diseases
CE	Church of England
COPEC	Conference on Christian Politics, Economics and Citizenship
CR	Lidgett, *Christian Religion*
d.	died
FCEFC	Federal Council of Evangelical Free Churches
FCFC	Free Church Federal Council
FCYB	*Free Church Year Book*
FG	Lidgett, *The Fatherhood of God*

GCCh	Lidgett, *God, Christ and the Church*
GCJ	Lidgett, *God in Christ Jesus*
Guided	Lidgett, *My Guided Life*
HistMethGB3	Rupert Davies, Gordon Rupp and A. Raymond George (eds), *A History of the Methodist Church in Great Britain*, Vol. 3, 1983
i/c	in charge of
LCC	London County Council
LEA	Local Education Authority
LPES	London: British Library of Political and Economic Science
LPSS	Library of Political and Social Science
LQR	*London Quarterly Review*
m.	married
M.Rec.	*Methodist Recorder*, sometimes just *Recorder*
MS	manuscript
MT	*Methodist Times*
n.d.	no date
NCEFC	National Council of Evangelical Free Churches
PM	Primitive Methodists
RC	Roman Catholic
Rem	Lidgett, *Reminiscences*
RTD	Randall Thomas Davidson Papers, Lambeth Palace Library
RTD:LC	Davidson's 1920 Lambeth Conference Papers in the above
S&S	Lidgett, *Sonship and Salvation*
SP	Lidgett, *Spiritual Principle*
Symp.	Rupert Davies (ed.), *John Scott Lidgett, a Symposium*, 1957
UM	United Methodists
VD	Venereal Disease
VT	Lidgett, *The Victorian Transformation of Theology*
WBU	Wesley Bible Union
wef	with effect from
WMMS	Wesleyan Methodist Missionary Society
WMUSS	Wesleyan Methodist Union for Social Service
WW1	World War 1
WW2	World War 2

The Papers of Bishop Bell, Bishop (later Archbishop) Lang, Bishop (later Archbishop) William Temple and Tissington Tatlow, all in Lambeth Palace

Library, are not abbreviated, but named as Bell Papers, Lang Papers, Temple or Tatlow Papers. Bell Papers are distinguished from his biography, *Randall Davidson, Archbishop of Canterbury* (3rd edn), 1952.

Terms

Circuit: group of churches supervised by a superintendent minister, usually with at least one assistant minister.

Committee of Privileges: Wesleyan Conference Committee concerned with public relations; empowered, with provisos, to take emergency action on public issues on behalf of the Conference when it was not meeting. Such action required ratification at the next Conference.

Conference: ruling body of the Wesleyan Methodist (from 1932 the Methodist) Connexion, meeting annually in July, often referred to simply as 'Conference'. The word may connote either the body of its members or the annual event and time of year. It elected annually a distinguished minister as President, an honour rarely granted more than once. There were two sessions, the 'Pastoral' for ministers only and the 'Representative' for ministers and laymen.

The Connexion: the whole of the Wesleyan Church, organised with its churches, Circuits and District Synods under overall Conference authority.

Districts: a regional group of Circuits. Each District's ministers and elected lay representatives met at specified intervals in 'Synods' under their District Chairman.

Fernley: an annual lecture, endowed in 1870 by layman John Fernley, delivered during the period of the Wesleyan Conference by a minister, and normally published, on a subject agreed by a specially designated Board.

Legal Hundred: until virtually all Methodist denominations united in 1932, 100 Wesleyan ministers (deemed to represent the original Conference of John Wesley) were required formally to ratify Wesleyan Methodist Conference decisions. Elections were held annually to fill vacancies.

London: references are almost wholly to the County (e.g., the London County Council), not to the City of London, separately administered.

Nonconformists: in this book the term excludes Roman Catholics.

Plan: each Circuit's Plan, issued quarterly by the Circuit Superintendent, records his deployment of ministers and local preachers to conduct worship in the individual Circuit churches.

President: unless specified otherwise, President of the Wesleyan Methodist (from 1932 the Methodist) Conference.

Social Purity Committee: Wesleyan Conference Committee concerned with issues of vice, notably prostitution, the white slave trade, the Contagious Diseases Act, etc.

Stationing, Stations: appointing ministers to their stations (Circuits); or an annual committee draft to be ratified by Conference.
Superintendent: the minister in charge of each Circuit.
Synod: see above on Districts.

Introduction

On 11 September 1951 a major service was held in the University Church of St Mary the Virgin in Oxford.[1] The World (hitherto called the 'Oecumenical') Methodist Conference, which had been convened variously in England and North America every ten years between 1881 and 1931, was holding its first meeting since 1939. Its Conference sessions met in various places including the University's Sheldonian Theatre or Wesley Memorial Church, but for its principal Conference service to commemorate John and Charles Wesley no church could be more appropriate than the one in which John, as Fellow of Lincoln College, had preached regularly over 200 years before. Little doubt existed in principle about who should be invited to preach, but there was considerable nervousness over his advanced age and deteriorating health. Moreover, he could only stand with assistance. Accordingly contingency plans for possible medical attention had to be made.

The credentials of the Revd Dr John Scott Lidgett, then aged 97, were impeccable. When he died less than two years later, Colin Roberts, the President of the Methodist Conference, called him 'in some respects . . . the greatest Methodist since Wesley'.[2] After entering the ministry in 1876, he had not retired until 1949. During 59 of those 73 years, throughout two World Wars, he had lived in the slums of London's dockland as Warden of the Bermondsey Settlement he had founded. The Wesleyan Conference had elected him its President in 1908/9. Having helped to unify the splintered branches of Methodism, he became First President of the Uniting Methodist Conference in 1932, the high point of his ministry. His theological writings and public prominence had gained him Honorary DD degrees from Aberdeen, Oxford and Edinburgh Universities. After service as its Vice-Chancellor, London University honoured him with the degree of Doctor of Laws, while in 1933 HM the King made him a Companion of Honour. Lidgett's vision of the Catholicity of the whole Church had engaged him in multiple ecumenical activities in relation not just to Methodism but to the Free Churches and the Anglican Church. He had been President/Moderator and Secretary of both National and Federal Councils of Evangelical Free Churches, and his friendship with Randall Davidson, the Archbishop of Canterbury, had resulted in his being consulted on major national, especially educational and ecumenical, issues and inclusion as one of Davidson's pall-bearers in 1930. As a member of the London School Board and then the LCC, he had been intimately involved in the educational progress of London's schools and become (uniquely as a Methodist minister) Leader of a political party, London's Progressives. He had served as editor of the *Methodist Times* and joint editor of the *Contemporary Review*, and he was to continue producing books until the year before his death. Throughout his long life his passions had been to promulgate the doctrine of Fatherhood of God, explore its implications in social action, and insist on the Wesleys' 'salvation' of England in the eighteenth century and Methodism's 'unfinished task'. No Methodist in 1951 could have matched his record, and Methodism owed a great deal to him.

A chair was provided for Lidgett near the reading desk, 'from which he commanded a view of the crowded assembly'.[3] Excused the need to climb the pulpit steps, he preached from there when the time came. Well before the reciting of his beloved Nicene Creed, he struggled slowly and painfully to his feet so that he could be standing for it. The microphone system had broken down during the service.[4] So when Lidgett came to preach, as he did for a full 40 minutes on 'The Modernity of John and Charles Wesley', one of his favourite themes, the strain of projecting his voice to such a large congregation must have been considerable. Many could not hear very much. Rex Kissack, then minister of Wesley Memorial Church in Oxford, recalled that:

> At the end of his sermon, he collapsed! I have a fleeting vision of the other scarlet robed and hooded figures catching him and bearing him out. I confess it seemed like a painting of the 'Deposition from the Cross'. The general impression was that this must be the end, and how utterly fitting for the greatest Methodist of his age.[5]

Eric Baker, Secretary of the Methodist Conference, commented[6] on how triumphant it would have been for him to die preaching in the very church from which John Wesley had been banned: Wesley's sermon on 'Scriptural Christianity' proved too outspoken for his academic peers in 1744.

Mercifully a doctor, Arthur Hill, was standing by for such an emergency, and after an injection the old man began to recover. According to Paul Sangster,[7] 'one hooded vulture's eye opened, looked at the syringe in the surgeon's hand, and his voice croaked softly, "That gave you a nasty shock, didn't it?"' Moreover, even in such circumstances, 'the old dog', as Sangster called him, was ready to utter an erudite witticism. According to Rupert Davies,[8] 'He was already becoming conscious as he was lowered on to a stretcher, and remarked: "*facilis descensus*". He did not add, as Vergil did in his Aeneid, "*Averno*" ("to the lower regions")'. A more appropriate translation for that situation would have been 'to Hell'! Kissack said that Gordon Rupp, the prime mover in inviting him to preach, who must have been feeling guilty, afraid of being cast as a regicide, 'told me how he reassured the reviving hero in the vestry . . . with "Dr Lidgett, you were terrific!" To which the answer came: "Terrific?! What do you mean? That I struck the congregation with fear?!"'

On regaining full consciousness Lidgett remarked: 'It is always said that preaching, if it is real preaching, ought to take it out of a man'. To attribute this aphorism to others was perhaps a gesture of modesty. More likely it was Lidgett's own.[9] It was certainly apposite and accurately reflected a deep conviction.

Responding to anxious enquiries next day, Lidgett insisted he had made a splendid recovery, and attributed his collapse to the heat and the long wait before he preached. Raymond George commented that on that same morning Wilbert Howard, 'that most punctual of men', came slightly late to preside at the Conference. 'He apologised, saying, "Lidgett sent for me" in tones of the deepest respect.'[10] That venerable figure is the subject of this biography.

Part 1

Background

This chapter explains Lidgett's family background (including his early life), the Wesleyan context, and the changes in attitudes and religious beliefs which faced the rebellious intellectual.

Calendar of main events 1854–90

1854	Born on 10 August, at Lewisham.
1865–70	Attended Blackheath Proprietary School.
1869	Father died.
1870	Felt call to Wesleyan ministry, while on holiday at Whitby.
1871–2	Left school, matriculated, worked in office of shipping and insurance brokers.
1873–5	Attended University College, London, and gained his BA and MA there.
1875–6	Home study prior to acceptance for ministry.
1876–8	Circuit Minister in Tunstall.
1878–81	Circuit Minister in Southport.
1881–4	Circuit Minister in Cardiff.
1884	Married Emmeline Martha Davies.
1884–7	Circuit Minister in Wolverhampton.
1885	Son, John Cuthbert Lidgett born on 18 August
1887–90	Circuit Minister in Cambridge.
1887	Daughter, Lettice Mary born in September.
1890–1949	Warden of Bermondsey Settlement.

I

Background 1854–90

John Scott Lidgett was born in 1854 into a comfortable, middle-class and thoroughly Wesleyan home in Lewisham. The family soon moved to Blackheath. John Jacob Lidgett (1828–69), an active Wesleyan layman to whom he looked up as a model father, was in the shipping business, while Lidgett's mother, Maria Elizabeth Lidgett (1824–1911), was the daughter of John Scott (1792–1868), first Chairman of the Wesleyan Education Committee (1843–67), and first Principal of the Westminster Normal Institution, the Wesleyan Teachers' Training College (1851–67), as well as being twice elected President of the Wesleyan Methodist Conference[1] (1843 and 1852). Lidgett was particularly fond of him: as a child, he had not only been visited by his grandfather but had stayed in the College when his grandmother, Maria Walker Scott, was ill. Throughout his adult life, he carried about with him the text of John Scott's 1862 address, 'The Working Class entitled to a Good Education', and even Scott's paisley dressing gown and plaid shawl. That family connection in itself, together with associated visitors, acquaintances and contacts, would almost have sufficed to support Lidgett's claim[2] to have been brought up in the inner circle of the Wesleyan ministry and to have discovered, when Wesleyan President himself in 1908, that he had already known personally 50 of the 91 Presidents since John Wesley's death.

John Scott had been 'a trusted lieutenant'[3] of the autocratic Jabez Bunting (1779–1858) who had given his own direction and leadership to the Wesleyan movement after Wesley's death. In his Introduction to the *Early Correspondence of Jabez Bunting 1820–1829*[4] W. R. Ward mentioned that Lidgett *was said* to have claimed his own place in the Wesleyan succession by affirming that as a child he had been blessed by the great Dr Bunting, 'as the young Jabez had been blessed by John Wesley'. But no such claim, Ward said, was made by Jabez himself in his autograph (*sic*), though if it were true it could have been expected to figure, for example, in Thomas Jackson's sermon at Bunting's funeral.

True or false, some such story was current in the folk-lore of the late 1920s, telling of Wesley's blessing of Jabez, not necessarily as an infant but some time before Wesley's death, and including Jabez's blessing of Lidgett. S. B. Frost, formerly Vice-Principal of McGill University, told me that as an adolescent, though received into Church membership, he deliberately refrained from receiving Holy Communion until he knew Lidgett was due to take the Communion Sunday Service at Southwark Park Methodist Church. He wrote:

> Rebelling mildly against my upbringing, I went 'High Church Methodist' and wanted to emphasise the line of descent from John Wesley himself. I received Holy Communion from the hands of one whom I knew to be in the true Wesleyan succession. I had read a bit of Methodist history by this time and felt that Lidgett – Jabez Bunting – John Wesley constituted a truly evangelical apostolic succession. Lidgett read the full 1662 Prayer Book Liturgy.[5]

The date of this incident appeared to have been *c.*1928. In his *Reminiscences* of 1928 Lidgett did not say Wesley gave a blessing to the infant Jabez, but he did boast of being 'taken as an infant to the deathbed of Dr Bunting to receive his blessing'[6] – a claim curiously omitted altogether from *My Guided Life* in 1936. If it were really true, he could hardly have failed to make it again. Perhaps by then he could afford to rely on the oral legend, and drop it quietly from his more substantial autobiography.

Lidgett did not mention Jabez at all in *My Guided Life*, nor strangely enough Jabez's relationship to Percy William Bunting (1836–1911), Lidgett's uncle,[7] married to his father's second sister, Mary Hyett Lidgett (1840–1919): Percy was Jabez's grandson. (These and other family relationships can be followed in the family trees[8] set out in Appendix 2.) Lidgett, however, praised Percy and Mary in their own right for their 'unfailing stimulus and the broadening of all my sympathies'. Perhaps the aura surrounding the Bunting name was sufficient. Lidgett's and Jabez's views were by no means identical, but two features of Jabez's career among others may have remained consciously in Lidgett's mind. One was the importance of legal advice and support. Theologically Lidgett had a deep respect for justice, as well as pragmatically for legal expertise, and his earliest ambition was for the Bar.[9] Percy's father had been a solicitor, and his experience had proved invaluable to *his* father, Jabez, during troubles in his career. Percy, Lidgett's uncle, was a barrister of Lincoln's Inn, knighted in 1908 no doubt for his professional, Wesleyan and Free Church Council distinction, and his advice would have been much appreciated by his nephew, often a Committee colleague. Lidgett's only son, John Cuthbert Lidgett (1885–1918), worked as a solicitor with Munro, Slack and Co. after graduation and became his father's 'right-hand not only in Bermondsey Settlement work, but in other directions'.[10]

The other 'lesson' of Jabez Bunting's career was the value of a London base. Jabez settled permanently in London as the powerful secretary for foreign missions in 1833. This kept him in continuous touch with developments in central government and the churches, and though the Wesleyan Conference venue changed annually, London was where committee work both of the Conference and other bodies took place. Lidgett might well have come to appreciate the value of retaining his base in the Bermondsey Settlement for this, among many reasons, even if it was not his initial motivation. He claimed[11] simply to have chosen 'the most neglected neighbourhood of poorer London'.[12] But he may also have wanted to follow the precedents set by John Scott and Samuel Barnett in the slum setting of Westminster College and Toynbee Hall, as well as perhaps to find a site accessible to his family home and close to the South Bank and East End, familiar to him from his boyhood.[13]

Lidgett's father's younger brother, George Lidgett (1831–1907), a strong Liberal, devout Wesleyan local preacher and prominent in Wesleyan Conference Committees, had cemented the relationship with John Scott in 1855 by marrying Sarah Ann (1830–97), Scott's other daughter. He was in the shipping and insurance business, at times chairman of the General Shipowners' Society and Lloyds Insurance Company, and director of the Star Life Assurance Society. Though Lidgett's own family household was not wealthy, they managed their affairs prudently and worked hard, and their wider family circle included some well-placed and successful commercial entrepreneurs. George's eldest daughter, Ellen Mary (1858–1952), became in 1883 the second wife of another Wesleyan, John McDougall, knighted in 1902, a director of the McDougalls' Flour Milling Company, and chairman of the *Contemporary Review* Company. Lidgett later became the co-editor of this journal, succeeded him as chairman, and served in the LCC alongside him. John Augustine Lidgett (1871–1948), George's son, built a house at Lidgetton,[14] a township in Natal, named after his grandfather who in 1850 had purchased the surrounding, hitherto undeveloped land. Wattle, used for tanning leather, was grown there using native labour, not very lucratively. The members of the whole Lidgett family had shares in the resultant industrial enterprise, the Lidgetton Land Company Limited, floated in 1907. The land was sold in 1963 and the company wound up in 1972.

William Henry Budgett (1827–1900), who married Ann Jacob Lidgett (1839–1936), Lidgett's father's sister, was a prosperous wholesale grocery merchant in Bristol. He was almost certainly the son of Samuel Budgett (1794–1851), the subject of *The Successful Merchant*, published in 1852 by William Arthur, Wesleyan minister and philosopher, to illustrate how Christian principles were applied to business practice.[15] Lidgett often stayed with the Budgetts, on holiday or when engaged in the locality. Lidgett also had reason to be grateful to Elijah Hoole (1837–1912), who married his favourite aunt Judith (1845–1932),[16] his father's youngest sister, in 1868. As an architect, Elijah Hoole had worked on projects for the social reformers Octavia Hill and Emma Cons, and built Toynbee Hall in 1884 for Samuel Barnett. This helped to inspire the concept of the Bermondsey Settlement which he began to build for Lidgett in 1890.

Elijah's father, a Wesleyan minister (1798–1872), provided a link with another notable family, the Chubbs. Elizabeth Chubb, his wife, was the sister of John Chubb (1818–72) whose second son, George Hayter Chubb (1848–1946), was a partner and Managing Director of Chubb and Son, Lock and Safe Company; he was knighted in 1885, made a baronet in 1890 and became the first Baron Hayter in 1927.[17] Lidgett's link with George Hayter Chubb was also through his aunt, Lady Mary Bunting: her sister-in-law, Elizabeth Bealey Bunting (1838–1903) was John Chubb's second wife. Sir George Hayter Chubb was one of the first laymen admitted to the Wesleyan Conference in 1878 and a prominent member of its committees thereafter, a Society Steward (along with R. W. Perks, another distinguished Methodist) of the Chislehurst Wesleyan Church in 1881. He was 'the leading spirit' in the Nonconformist Unionist Association.[18] On 15 June 1885, significantly the year before his knighthood, he had told Lord Salisbury that Wesleyans 'belong to a much higher social class than used to be the case'.[19]

Lidgett's family clearly came from the more prosperous Nonconformists. Mark Johnson argued that it was the Nonconformist 'attempt to achieve complete social, political and religious equality' and overcome social stigma which influenced 'their reception of new theological ideas and doctrinal changes'.[20] M. T. E. Hopkins,[21] however, regarded this judgement as incomplete: the old theology was abandoned because its unethical elements[22] were 'no longer acceptable in the religious market they were targeting'. But Johnson was right to refer to the struggle all Nonconformists had faced to remove civic and political disabilities, nor was the Wesleyan middle class exempt from envy of the Established Church's social status. J. J. W. Edmondson found among Methodists even by the middle of the nineteenth century 'a growing desire for increased "respectability" in the eyes of the nation', 'to preserve the place in the social order which they were then progressively winning'; they thought the label 'National Church' was 'more appropriate than "enthusiastic movement"'. This he saw as leading them 'to follow popular doctrinal trends rather than cleave to the conservative . . . theology of Wesley'.[23] Lidgett could have come to be affected by these factors, some consciously, some not.

But Lidgett's family had close Anglican connections. He had spent many holidays, both as boy and adult, in Appleton-le-Moors. There Mary Hyett Shepherd (1806–91), the childless sister of Ann Jacob Hyett (1804–79), Lidgett's paternal grandmother, had built a church and vicarage and endowed the living in memory of her husband, Lidgett's grandfather's partner 1841–5. Lidgett was present at the laying of the church's foundation stone in 1863. Joseph Shepherd, who died in 1862, had in 1854 built a National School[24] there in his native village, and in 1858 enlarged what Lidgett described as a 'hunting box' (a large cottage) into 'an imposing mansion', known as The Hall.

Mary Shepherd's home, he wrote in 1936:

> was frequented by the clergy of the immediate neighbourhood, and in particular by the respected vicar of Lastingham [the Revd Richard Easterby]. Hence I was brought up to be interested in the ecclesiastical history of its wonderful Church . . . came to sing in the choir . . . and eventually to read the lessons. Thus it came about that the sympathetic attitude towards the Anglican Church which prevailed among my Methodist relatives was strengthened by an early appreciation which led the Archbishop of Canterbury to say to me in comparatively recent years, 'You see, you understand us'.[25]

When Mary Shepherd died, the property was bequeathed to her nephews and nieces and their children. The family often visited the Hall both before and after her death.

John Lidgett, Lidgett's grandfather, had a house at Tunbridge Wells, and it was there Lidgett met by contrast the evangelical movement in the Anglican Church, perhaps also that of Selina, the Calvinistic Countess of Huntingdon. Speaking not of his parents or other relatives but of his father's two youngest sisters, Judith (1845–1932) and Elizabeth Sedman Lidgett (1843–1919), one who never married, Lidgett said they reacted against 'the narrowness and other-worldliness of the evangelicalism which at that time prevailed in the Church of England circles of Tunbridge Wells'.[26] Its exaggerated individualism, Calvinistic theology, narrow fundamentalism, and sharp distinction between the sacred and secular, he wrote, provoked their (albeit somewhat amused) antagonism.[27] Lidgett was careful to say his own family circle respected the evangelicals' piety and the quickening they had given to the spiritual life of the Anglican Church. But these evangelicals exhibited what his aunts, at any rate, thought a 'disproportionate, and as it now seems to me, somewhat unwholesome'[28] insistence on the Last Things.

In Lidgett's opinion their obsessive concern about eternal punishment in the after life prevented the full expression of Catholic truth, failed to satisfy men's spiritual needs, and proved inadequate 'to inspire the progress of the age'.[29] He remarked that his aunts' influence 'strengthened my natural tendency to reject the Pre-Millenarian pietism which prevailed at Tunbridge Wells . . . and to seek an interpretation of the Christian religion which gave ampler recognition to intellectual and social pursuits'.[30] Lidgett's autobiographies may have reflected his more mature outlook than his thinking at the time, but his comment on the 'terror' his form master inspired in expounding the Second Advent helped to justify his account.[31]

Protestant debate on the after-life in fact raged on beyond as well as before 1900. The Anglican, Frederick Denison Maurice (1805–72), had rejected the idea of endless punishment in 1853, and several books appeared in the seventies. In 1871 the Wesleyan, Marshall Randles, restated the traditional view in his *For Ever*, and published a fourth revised edition in 1895. In 1878 a revised edition of the Congregationalist Edward White's 1846 book on conditional immortality was issued; Canon Farrar advocated universal immortality;[32] and the Fernley Trustees refused to publish G. W. Olver's lecture,[33] rejecting the eternal duration and bodily torment of hell.[34] In 1898 and 1902 another Wesleyan, Agar Beet, was pursued for 'heresy' in asserting in his *Last Things* that the traditional view had gone beyond the assured teaching of the Bible, and that conditional immortality was at least a possibility.

Members of the Blackheath Wesleyan Church (which Lidgett's father helped to build and where his family worshipped), and leaders of the Wesleyan Church nationally, were far from free from Lidgett's strictures: Wesleyans were expected to confess 'a desire to flee from the wrath to come'. Lidgett admitted that, with the exception of his maternal grandfather, ministers[35] at Blackheath during his boyhood gave undue prominence to death, judgement, heaven and hell, overshadowing 'the graciousness of the Gospel' by the awakening of religious apprehension and fear.[36]

But the mean between these two extremes seemed to have been exemplified by the character of his father. His reference to 'My father's radiantly gracious fatherliness which transfused and directed his unquestionable authority' appears idealised, but the balance he thought his father achieved was in due course elevated into Lidgett's idea of God and his relationship to mankind.[37] He drew a convincing picture of a happy childhood, apparently free from the overpowering severities of the Victorian father as portrayed in Edmund Gosse's *Father and Son*.[38] It fitted his description of his father's breadth of outlook, the intellectual and artistic interests and talk in the family circle, and the lack of any 'hard and fast distinction between the sacred and the secular, the spiritual and the social'.[39] The family combined a stern pursuit of duty and righteousness, an unworldly, yet optimistic outlook on life, and a width of interests, political and social.

It was not only issues affecting the Christian faith and educational progress that were debated by his family and visiting friends. Each morning[40] *The Times* was read aloud and a keen interest taken in events both in Britain and abroad, the American Civil War, for example. Lidgett speaks[41] of walking across the Little Orme at Llandudno in his boyhood with his father and Henry Fowler (later Viscount Wolverhampton) when they discussed public as well as Wesleyan Methodist affairs. He was taken to such events in London as the demonstration[42] in honour of Garibaldi, fighter for Italian liberation. While still at school the young Lidgett took a firm stance[43] in favour of Liberal and against Conservative policies and overcame his father's initial hesitation over 'voting Liberal' in the General Election of 1868. The fervour of Gladstone's oratory and the majesty of his appearance proved so impressive that Lidgett even referred to 'my worship of him'[44] at this time, and to its being deepened by Gladstone's attitude, for example, to the current Bulgarian atrocities and his opposition to Disraeli's pro-Turkish policies.

Areas of social concern were the particular focus of Lidgett's aunts, Elizabeth Sedman Lidgett and Lady Mary Bunting. The former became a member of the St Pancras Board of Guardians for 40 years and campaigned against atrocities in Armenia. Lady Mary, in co-operation with Josephine Butler and others, was particularly active, among other things, in efforts to remedy the plight of young girls lured into prostitution and secure the repeal of the Contagious Diseases Acts; she visited the continent to inform her international outlook. Her sister-in-law, Sarah Maclardie Bunting (1841–1908), who in 1870 married Sheldon Amos, Professor of Jurisprudence at University College, London, became similarly involved both in the welfare of Armenian refugees in Cyprus and of women and girls at home. Clearly the Lidgett family were affected by the growth in ethical and humanitarian thinking, 'the moral sensibility of the times', which D. W. Bebbington[45] has called the chief solvent of Nonconformist theological conviction in the Victorian age.

Lidgett did not always make it plain whether his description of Wesleyan Methodism in general or the local Blackheath Wesleyan Church was true, in whole or in part, of his family also. Speaking of contemporary Methodism, Lidgett said that 'restrictions of conduct and amusements that may be called Puritan were practised and *inculcated*',[46] and Methodist teaching was concentrated 'on the exposition and *enforcement* of . . . Methodist doctrines'.[47] But whether the words I have italicised referred simply to an emphasis, or how far critical questioning was suppressed is unclear. In the family and Blackheath Wesleyan Church Circle there was approval for the philanthropic and social activities of the evangelical Lord Shaftesbury and his followers. Though they may not have shared his Millenarian motivation for preparing the world for Christ's coming, their focus was largely on individual salvation, a search for holiness and sanctification in personal terms, fitness for heaven. Despite its drawbacks, the Methodist class meeting was to Lidgett of value in preserving the intimate fellowship and unworldly temper of Methodism. Mention of 'gracious humanity' coupled with evangelical faith suggested that harshness was absent at least in his family. Yet he admitted[48] the theological outlook of Wesleyan Methodists was almost entirely self-enclosed, with relatively little contact with other non-episcopal churches.

Within Lidgett's family, debate was stimulated by their many visitors. One family friend was the medical adviser to Westminster College, W. Kitchen

Parker FRS, Hunterian Professor of Anatomy in London, an expert in embryology and collaborator with T. H. Huxley. Referring to the evolution controversy in his boyhood, Lidgett said, 'On his visits animated discussions always took place between him and my uncompromisingly fundamentalism[49] (*sic*) uncle, George Lidgett'.[50] It is reasonable to infer that Lidgett, as a boy, began to accept Darwin's hypothesis and adopt liberal views of Scripture.

Lidgett's own personal faith grew out of the family's practice of daily prayer, regular Bible reading and attendance at worship. Through the influence of his parents and notably his aunt Judith, from his earliest childhood he had been, he said 'the subject of deep religious feeling'. He had not previously spoken of it, but in early January 1868, when he was 13 years of age, a sermon[51] by his grandfather, John Scott, moved him to ask for Holy Communion at the Covenant Service that same afternoon. Although John Scott unexpectedly died of a stroke in the following week, to Lidgett that 'conclusion of his [John Scott's] ministry', marked by his own initiation into Church membership, 'eventually led me to the Christian ministry' and subsequently to carrying on 'the spiritual and educational work of which he was a striking and influential example'. At age 15 he entered his school's Lower Classical sixth form and became a Sunday School teacher. His Blackheath Wesleyan Church having decided to establish a Day School in the nearby 'parish' of East Greenwich,[52] where it had a Mission Church, Lidgett was appointed its secretary, helped to raise funds to equip it, and was active both in distributing religious tracts within its neighbourhood and open-air preaching outside Greenwich Park.

His 'call' to the Wesleyan ministry came[53] when the Budgetts took him on holiday to Whitby. It was another sermon, on this occasion delivered there by a preacher whose name he could not afterwards remember, which came as what he felt was an imperative and irrevocable divine summons to him personally. His decision to answer the summons was not disclosed immediately to his (by then widowed) mother, but when he mentioned it to his uncle (and now guardian) George, his uncle initially opposed it. The consequences in terms of his leaving school and later career are discussed later. At this point it is sufficient to record that by 16 he had preached his first sermon (on 26 March 1871), and become a local preacher. He acted as a District Visitor, went on to be a Class Leader at 18 and Sunday School Superintendent at 20,[54] and engage in a variety of philanthropic activities.

Despite attending a privately funded proprietary school in Blackheath (he had been to a preparatory school from age 7 to 11), Lidgett fully appreciated the bitterness of Nonconformist objections to Anglican influence through their National, denominational and non-Provided schools, not least in rural 'single school' areas with no Wesleyan or other Nonconformist or Provided school alternative. Anglican control over staff appointments and pupil teachers in their schools severely reduced the scope of Nonconformist aspirants to a teaching career and to the increased social status this could give. In Anglican schools where Nonconformist chapels and their Sunday schools were scorned, where the children of Nonconformist parents were required to attend the parish church and learn the Church catechism, there was predictable resentment.

At the same time, from his own experience, Lidgett could see the value of denominational education in principle, and throughout his life he regarded religious education as a vitally important part of the curriculum for all pupils: he disliked the concept of purely secular schools. Wesleyans had been building their own schools, though many fewer than the Anglicans, and he appreciated their reasons: desires, for example, to make a contribution to the welfare of local society, pass on their own distinctive ethos to their children, maintain a flow of adherents to their Church and entry to their teacher training college, and register their denominational identity in competition with the Established Church. His contacts enabled him to understand opposing positions and their complexities. But denominational rancour increasingly disturbed him, together with the tangle of the country's educational 'system'.

Further scope for making a balanced appraisal of sectarian differences came from Lidgett's contact with Anglo-Catholics. Wesleyans' reaction against 'Puseyism' and its increasing influence in the latter half of the nineteenth century tended to put severe strain on their original links with the Church of England. Lidgett and his family, however, firmly rejected the label of 'Dissent': to them Methodism was not a 'sect'. Lidgett's later career makes it clear that his ultimate aim was the reunion of Methodism with its 'parent' body, despite the spectrum of theology the latter embraced. Lidgett fully shared Wesleyan distaste for 'clericalism' and fears that Pusey's movement was leading Anglicans to Rome and reneging on the Reformation. The increasing emphasis on elaborate ceremonial, with its special vestments, incense and so on were bad enough, but the idea of priests offering sacrifice for the people was anathema. He resented Pusey's sneers at Wesleyan belief in 'Justification by feeling'.[55]

But this did not prevent him from acknowledging in his early ministry[56] the value of what Anglo-Catholics had written. Two relatives, he said, had interested him in Newman's writing: his grandmother Lidgett in the *Apologia*, and an aunt (perhaps Judith) in the *University Sermons*.[57] Lidgett himself became indebted to Newman for pointing him to Patristic Studies, the Nicene Creed and Church history, 'especially in regard to the development of doctrine'.[58] He was also grateful for Newman's influence on Maurice's Catholic view of the Church.

Another Wesleyan, his grandfather John Scott, had also shown an unblinkered outlook. He had written to congratulate H. P. Liddon, Pusey's successor as the leading High Churchman, on his Bampton lectures, *The Divinity of Our Lord and Saviour, Jesus Christ*[59] perhaps because Liddon had resisted views eroding Christ's status; Scott received an inscribed photograph in reply.

Lidgett himself quoted from Liddon's University sermon on *The Divine Victim* in his own *Spiritual Principle of the Atonement*.[60] His article in the *London Quarterly Review* of January 1899 on 'The Present [Ritual] Crisis in the Church of England' was at pains to produce a balanced picture, illustrating faults on both sides of the controversy. Bishop Adams told me[61] of a visit he, as Rector of Bermondsey, made to Lidgett at the Bermondsey Settlement in July 1947. Asked about his current reading, Lidgett said, 'I'm reading Liddon and John Henry Newman, not for their theology but for their assurance'. Throughout his career Lidgett was not averse to cultivating contacts with Anglo-Catholic clergy, not least at the highest level, and he warmed to the radical social stance evident among them.

Charges of 'High Churchmanship' and 'Ritualism' were levelled not only against the Anglo-Catholics within the Church of England, but within Methodism itself. There the words largely connoted fondness for the Prayer Book liturgy of Morning and Evening Prayer. The example of John Wesley *qua* High Churchman was not to every Wesleyan's taste, as is clear from George Osborn's revision of Wesley's poems and hymns, from an alternative book of public prayers and services made available in 1883, and notably from a publication dated 21 January 1886. Its author, 'an old-fashioned Methodist', was identified by Horton Davies[62] as George Walker of Eaglescliffe in Durham. Bemoaning the low spiritual condition of Methodism at this period, Walker attributed it not only to a greater consciousness of its human founder, Wesley, than of its divine founder, Christ, but also to an excessive eagerness to mimic High Anglican ritualism; in the author's view, formalism and ceremonialism crept into worship only when vital devotion (for which he seemed to think simple spontaneity and the pleading of extempore prayer were vital) had expired.

His evidence[63] was an evening service in Blackheath Methodist chapel, as described in the *Methodist Journal*. Clearly a wide spectrum of views existed within and across the various branches of Methodism about the style of worship derived from the Wesleys: there was controversy not just in 1886 but in previous (and future) years. The liturgical tradition had lost favour in Tunstall where Lidgett found 'fervid emotionalism' in 1876,[64] but it remained to Lidgett (and many other Wesleyans) spiritually satisfying. That preference did not conflict with his sincere Wesleyan conviction of consciousness of direct and immediate fellowship with God, bringing, as he put it in his *Fatherhood of God*,[65] 'joyous certainty, a deep and even exuberant spiritual satisfaction' through the experience of the Holy Spirit. As a (not uncritical) follower of John Wesley, he approved of appeals in worship for religious decision, provided they were 'tender'.[66] The Wesleyan evangelical drive to increase Church membership had his full support.

Lidgett's family and church background, his consequent awareness of controversy, and his University training[67] in Logic and Philosophy gave him confidence to question, if not immediately to challenge, received views of entrenched Victorian tradition. His meeting with people prominent in business, Wesleyan and Anglican churches, and academic circles enabled him to discuss with ease, unaffected by any sense of social inferiority or cultural or academic divide. He quickly learned to establish, develop and, where appropriate, make use of personal contacts. This asset was valuable in gaining information and opinion, reducing misunderstanding and suspicion, and assessing the most acceptable way forward when difficult decisions had to be made.

Yet for all that, as Rupert Davies said: 'He was not a man to whom intimate personal friendship came easily, nor one whose personality was a great incentive to it in others'.[68] He took pride, perhaps too much pride, in announcing the range of his contacts. From them he earned respect rather than affection. Mentioning their names in his autobiographies indicated not insecurity but determination to show that in his view he had achieved more than his peers. Success mattered to him personally, but he was proud of Wesleyan Methodism, its achievements and *raison d'être*. It was not simply a club where he could find encouragement and support.

His father's death in 1869 brought considerable frustration. Uncle George, taking over as his guardian, saw work with his shipping and insurance brokers as leading to a career like his own or at least as testing Lidgett's vocation for the ministry. He insisted he left his Classics Sixth form at 16. After two years' office work, Lidgett's resolve remained unshaken, and George permitted him to go to the university. But to Lidgett's annoyance, even though his father had 'contemplated' him going to Oxford or Cambridge,[69] George directed him to University College, London, within daily travelling distance, since in his opinion the older universities were 'not likely to strengthen, and perhaps likely to undermine, my Methodist convictions and sympathies'.[70] George's brother, Samuel Jacob Lidgett (1833–57), had had a distinguished Cambridge career; so too had Percy Bunting, George's brother-in-law, and he certainly emerged from Cambridge unscathed. Attitudes to religion in the college which George had chosen might have made him hesitate, but he seemed unaware of them. Lidgett did not argue. He entered University College in January 1873 and left with a First Class degree in Logic and Philosophy. In the course of his studies he all but decided to return to his uncle's firm as a result of the death of his friend and cousin Frank, George's eldest son, from typhoid in Naples, but his uncle urged him to continue his chosen career.

Lidgett was clearly an intellectual. The importance of paying close attention to the text of biblical documents would have been underlined by William Fiddian Moulton (1835–1898), tutor in Classics and New Testament subjects at Richmond College for Wesleyan ministerial students. Lidgett had met him as a weekend guest in his parents' home during his boyhood. He went to see him in 1870 when he had decided to enter the Ministry, and remained in constant touch for nearly 30 years. Moulton, a distinguished Greek scholar, published in 1870 his work as editor and translator of J. G. B. Winer's *Grammar of New Testament Greek*,[71] dedicated to Bishop Ellicott; for this in 1874 Edinburgh University awarded him an Honorary DD. He was one of the 17 non-Anglican members of the committees which produced the Bible's Revised Version. In 1875 the Wesleyan Conference appointed him as the first Headmaster of The Leys School in Cambridge. Elected to the Legal Hundred[72] in 1872 and to the Conference presidency in 1890, Moulton proved to be a champion of Higher Criticism and a valuable contact and confidant.

In 1875, George Lidgett took his nephew to the Wesleyan Conference in Sheffield, where he introduced him to William Burt Pope (1822–1903), Tutor in Systematic Theology at the Didsbury Ministerial Training College, and destined to be Conference President in 1877. With a year to wait before acceptance as a ministerial candidate, Lidgett was grateful for Pope's advice on what to read. It was Pope rather than Moulton whom Lidgett specifically mentioned as stressing the importance of systematic biblical study and strengthening his 'determination both to be a hard student and also to base all my sermons on accurate expositions of the Holy Scriptures'.[73] Lidgett learned to oppose 'arbitrary selection of particular texts . . . and one-sided insistence upon them'.[74]

Lidgett was a strong character who never wavered in his Christian conviction. But as an intellectual, 'essentially an exact and careful scholar' (W. L. Hannam's description of him when he became Conference President in 1908), he developed a keen appreciation of the case against, as well as the case for, Christian belief. At University College Lidgett came into contact with Professors Croom Robertson and W. K. Clifford.[75] The former caused an initially 'unresolved conflict between my religious convictions and my philosophical teachers',[76] and the latter carried on a campaign against Christianity. Then in 1875, or soon after, he would have read Pope's *Compendium of Christian Theology*, published in two volumes in 1875 and revised in three in 1879. This had included arguments for the existence of God, as well as a defence of the Gospels and Christ's personal character and status against the views of F. C. Baur and others at Tübingen.

During contacts with Lidgett, especially in Southport (Lidgett's transfer there from Tunstall, his first appointment, in 1878 had been owing to Pope's influence), Pope stressed the importance of intellectual rigour. This was, in fact, a characteristic of John Wesley himself. In *Reminiscences* Lidgett recalled being questioned about an (undated) lecture by F. W. Macdonald (1842–1928), Conference President in 1899, on 'The Modern Attack and Defence of the Faith'. Pope asked, 'Did he show that he felt the difficulties? If not, the lecture was no good'.[77] Lidgett implied he followed this advice, and wanted others to know! His *Guided Life* made the point more directly. Writing in 1936[78] about his *Christian Religion, Its Meaning and Proof*, published in 1907, Lidgett said, 'I did my best to look the difficulties in the face'.

During his ministry (1881–4) in Cardiff (his third appointment), he heard of anti-Christian lectures in London given by Charles Bradlaugh.[79] When Bradlaugh's associate, G. W. Foote,[80] was to give a lecture on 'The Case against Christianity' in 1893 at the Gladstone (Liberal) Club in Bermondsey, where Lidgett was the Settlement Warden, he claimed the right of reply. This led him to deliver a series of lectures in defence of Christianity, both inside and outside the Settlement, including lectures in the open air of Southwark Park. These were reported *in extenso* in the local weekly paper. But not all Wesleyans saw the value of such reasoned defence: an evangelical appeal for converts was, to some, all that was needed. At the 1907 Conference when the Revd F. Ballard was proposed for a special appointment to defend the Christian faith, Lidgett (with others) had to argue against strong opposition by Samuel Chadwick (1860–1932) and Dinsdale Young (1861–1938) to get the proposal adopted.[81] Lidgett's reputation for intellectual honesty, and its inheritance from Maurice and Pope, were recognised by Gordon Rupp in a sermon at Handsworth College in April 1956:

> There is in F. D. Maurice (and of this Scott Lidgett was a conscious heir) a hospitality towards truth, from the most diverse sources, in history, science and philosophy, – a hospitality . . . eager, welcoming, virile because stayed on the mind . . . of Christ, from whom all truth derives and in whom all wisdom rests.[82]

Pope exemplified that openness, Rupp said, by his robust defence in 1881 of science and philosophy in ministerial training.

Lidgett rebelled against the anti-intellectual outlook of evangelicals who insisted[83] that evangelism could only be on the basis of a 'simple Gospel', reluctant to tackle the 'big' questions and issues of the time, and afraid to allow debate on them. Narrow attitudes needed challenging and correction. In particular, as in his early ministerial years he appraised Conference debates and Wesleyan writing, he began to chafe at the climate of caution over the expression of unorthodox theological views. Wesleyans were prone to maintain conservative, traditional positions and avoid controversy – a stance, however, not unknown at that time in other denominations. But in *Reminiscences*, writing of the 1880s, Lidgett complained that 'the leaders of Wesleyan thought were inclined to practise too much "economy" in the interests of safety and owing to the undue influence of a masterful personality'.[84]

This referred to the autocratic George Osborn (1808–91), first a theology tutor and later Professor at Richmond College from 1868 to 1885, and twice

(1863 and 1881) Conference President. Like John Scott, he had been associated with Jabez Bunting, but Lidgett appears not to have met him before being taken to Sheffield. A formidable figure with a spade beard, Osborn dominated Conference debates like Bunting, enforcing discipline and adherence to inherited Methodist doctrine. A founder of the Evangelical Alliance, he was averse to new learning and new ideas, and resisted change. Throughout the 1870s and 1880s, Lidgett said, 'The chief concern of high politics for leading ministers was little else than the management of Dr Osborn.'[85] Lidgett smarted, first vicariously and then personally, from his dictatorial rigidity. He gave three examples.

The first occurred over support for the Darwinian theory. Owen Chadwick in effect described Frederick Temple's Bampton lectures in 1884 which 'assumed evolution as an axiom' as closing debate 'among educated Christians';[86] the magazine, *Punch*,[87] thought it was over on 8 December 1877. But internal division continued among Wesleyans well into the next century. Evolution 'did not disturb' the Didsbury College of 1892,[88] and opponents were still active in the Wesley Bible Union (WBU), begun in 1913. W. H. Dallinger LLD, FRS (1841–1909), set apart by the Conference to develop his work on micro-organisms, and soon to become President of the Microscopical Society from 1884 to 1887, was to deliver his Fernley lecture in favour of the theory during the 1880 Conference, but was prevented by Osborn's stubborn opposition. Another lecture had to be substituted at the last moment, and the Fernley Committee stated that, while Dallinger's views were probably acceptable, the time was not ripe for stating them. Eventually, in 1887 when Osborn had retired, the same lecture was permitted.

Scientific knowledge, variously interpreted, had been appropriated by Wesleyans of every status and class for polemical, social and political purposes. Wesleyan leaders had resisted whatever ideas appeared to threaten their authority, or encourage infidelity, secularism, working-class radicalism, and connexional indiscipline. Amid the Darwinian controversy Osborn would have reacted particularly sharply to Huxley's claim that theological concerns were intellectually irrelevant to professional scientific thought.[89] Nevertheless, by 1880 the Fernley Trustees judged that a sufficient number of Wesleyans, no doubt influenced by scholars like Pope, Arthur and Rigg,[90] had come to support Darwin's hypothesis. Having accepted during boyhood its implications for Scripture, Lidgett became convinced that it pointed to the activity and immanence of God, but in 1907 he revealed reservations about the principle of natural selection: to him, chance negated the reason and purpose behind the universe as a whole.[91]

Lidgett's second anecdote recorded Osborn's insistence that while the relationship of God to the justified and regenerate was that of Father, his relationship to the rest of mankind was that of holy, awful Sovereign,[92] consigning them to an eternity of conscious suffering. One evening in July 1881, before Lidgett left Southport, he met Pope who had just returned from London in jubilant mood. There the issue had been the revision of the First Catechism. Its first question had been, 'What is God?' and the answer 'An Infinite and eternal spirit'. But Pope had gained agreement for a change to 'Who is God?' and 'Our Father'. Osborn remained unmoved.

That and other conversations in Southport and in Pope's Didsbury house,[93] together with correspondence between them, proved highly significant. Writing in 1936, Lidgett acknowledged his debt to Pope: 'I came to enter, to a considerable degree, into his [Pope's] point of view, especially in regard to the primacy for Christian theology of the doctrine of the Fatherhood of God'.[94] But Pope put none of his own thoughts on that subject on paper, and it was the writing of F. D. Maurice, mentioned above, that became the dominant influence on Lidgett's theology. As Henry Rack stated, 'Lidgett's theology of the Fatherhood of God is almost entirely derived from Maurice'.[95] That was evident from Lidgett's very first publication. This he dedicated to W. F. Moulton. Pope had to wait until 1943 for Lidgett to dedicate a book to his memory.[96]

Certainly it was in 1881, about the time of the catechism incident, that Lidgett first learned about Maurice, perhaps initially in the biography written by his son, and then from Maurice's own writings. He may well have noticed the son's complaints about J. H. Rigg (1821–1909), President of the Wesleyan Conference in 1878 and 1892, whose *Modern Anglican Theology*, published in London in 1857, 1859 and 1880, was in effect a polemic against several thinkers, but principally against Maurice. The young rebel Lidgett, to whom Maurice had become an inspiration, refused to read Rigg's work (perhaps the 1880 edition), as (much later) he revealed orally to E. G. Rupp.[97] Absorbing the current, but misleading picture by Maurice's son and later admirers, of the ill-treatment and misunderstandings Maurice suffered in his lifetime,[98] Lidgett probably began in the 1890s to see himself as refusing, like him, to be deterred by criticism from the religious 'establishment'.

The third mention of Osborn's 'absolutism'[99] referred to his summoning Lidgett 'in his second presidency', that is in 1881/2, soon after Lidgett had moved to Cardiff. Osborn wanted him to take 'the appointment at Stuttgart'. Its nature and Osborn's reasons remain unclear. Lidgett might have been thought suitable to join J. G. Tasker who was spending 'a term' (probably four years, perhaps from 1880) at the Bad Cannstatt seminary nearby,[100] the Wesleyans' centre since 1875.[101]

Osborn's directive could have been a recognition of Lidgett's promise and ability; it could hardly have been fondness on Osborn's part for contamination by German theology. Pope had been accused of being corrupted by his interest in it, but escaped censure because he had concentrated on the more orthodox

German theologians.[102] Having recommended his namesake, Henry J. Pope (Conference President in 1893),[103] for service there, Pope could also have put Lidgett's name forward. By 1897 at any rate, Lidgett could read, if not speak, German.[104] Lidgett could have been seen, even at this early stage, as a potential irritant at home, questioning the judgements of his elders. Whatever Osborn's motivation, Lidgett refused, offering 'cogent' reasons, and stating that his judgement and conscience were against it. To this Osborn's reply was, 'Speak of your judgement, if you like, but not of your conscience. I hold that, when the Methodist Conference has spoken, no man has a right to have a conscience against it'. Lidgett did not record his reasons.[105] He may have already been thinking of the doctor/colliery owner's daughter whom he would marry in Cardiff in 1884. Whatever case he made, his defiance was successful. His Wesleyan pedigree would have been no disadvantage.

Recalling 60 years of active ministry in 1936,[106] Lidgett spoke of the seventies and eighties when it was easy to raise suspicions of unorthodoxy on comparatively trivial grounds and face severe discipline in Conference. Fears of 'heresy' charges from the Conference 'backwoodsmen' were making College tutors apprehensive about voicing or teaching[107] unorthodox ideas, still less supporting challenges to received doctrine. Henry Lunn MD (1859–1939, knighted in 1910), who found it necessary to resign from the ministry in 1893 because of objections to his criticisms of Wesleyan missionaries, dubbed the Wesleyan Mission House as 'the Acropolis of Methodism', from which its Secretaries held sway, together with the rest of the gerontocracy on the Conference platform. These were, Lunn declared, in dread of the 'Forward Movement', a pressure group of young ministers, led by Hugh Price Hughes (1847–1902), eager to grapple with the social and (internal) denominational problems of a new age. Lidgett had met Hughes[108] en route for Conference on the Liverpool landing stage in 1881, a significant year. There he learned Hughes was a convert to the value of Higher Criticism. He became his friend, and soon aligned himself to his 'progressive' approaches.

Lidgett was allowed no theological training in Didsbury, Richmond or Headingley, branches of the 'Theological Institution'.[109] Requirements in the 'field', his degree, and perhaps overcrowding in the colleges[110] meant he had to train himself. This he did by maintaining an intensive reading programme from the start of his first ('Home Immediate') appointment in Tunstall. In a wide range of authors he studied issues raised by evolution, positivism and the assaults on Christianity, for example.

He would not have regretted escaping from Richmond, with Osborn as his theological tutor. Though W. B. Pope held the same post in Didsbury at the same time, there would have been little other stimulus or progressive thinking then, or later. Comments on Didsbury College by J. E. Rattenbury,[111] a student some 14 years after Lidgett entered the ministry, disclosed 'no seething cauldron of intellectual life and struggle', but a seminary 'behind the times theologically', where ideas from German biblical criticism were described as 'German extravagances' and 'foolish', if neither John Wesley nor Adam Clarke had mentioned them. George Jackson left Richmond in 1887 without having heard of Robertson Smith and 'The Problem of the Old Testament'. Study of both Testaments was mainly a crawl by Greek and Hebrew beginners over a few chapters; and despite his knowledge, Jackson's tutor, W. Theophilus Davison (1846–1935), when faced by difficulties, infuriatingly sat on the fence.[112] Lidgett's reading, contacts with trained colleagues, and attendance at Conference, would have made him aware that, though there were some Wesleyan *textual* scholars, their theology remained essentially static.

Lidgett's comment in 1936 on Richard Watson, the only Methodist to write systematic theology before the 1870s, was contemptuous: 'His "Institutes", while comprehensive and lucid, were not characterised by any originality of thought. They represented the fundamentalism [always to Lidgett a pejorative word] of evangelical theology in its Arminian form as inherited from John Wesley.'[113]

Moreover, he went on:

> Scholarship in the strict sense of the term, was scarce, though the commentaries of Adam Clarke and Joseph Benson came up to the general standard of the early nineteenth century, and were held in high regard by the Wesleyan Methodist ministry . . . In my boyhood, however, men more eminent in scholarship . . . began to appear, and the Theological Colleges at Richmond and Didsbury were staffed by some of these.

Lidgett sought to be tactful, but in effect damned with faint praise. He picked out here as exceptions the two scholars who helped to shape his own personal career, Moulton and Pope. Speaking of his early days,[114] Lidgett acidly complained of the circuits' demands 'for gentlemanly ministers who could be counted upon not to shock the susceptibilities of their congregations', 'estimable but harmless men', 'a real Methodist peril'.

He would, moreover, also have known of the generally low educational standards of ministerial students in all colleges. Even in 1910 Samuel Chadwick was opposing any rise in entrance standards as learning was likely to shut out many who were 'called' to the ministry.[115] It would have been obvious to Lidgett that Colleges thought their *priorities* were to improve basic education, train preachers and teach Wesley's doctrines and the practices of the Connexion and its circuits.

Lidgett's own training and outlook explain his ambition. In 1936 he recalled that during the exacting studies of his early ministry 'the prospect of becoming eventually a theological teacher began to allure me'.[116] But he said the summons came instead to 'bury myself' in the Bermondsey Settlement, renouncing 'theological science'.[117] In fact what he did was far from 'burial', fitting the production of works of theology into a punishing programme of ministerial, ecclesiastical and civic duties. Only once did he allow his name to go forward for a Wesleyan theological post. At the 1902 Conference, surprisingly after the events of 1897, Randles proposed him for Agar Beet's post at Richmond.[118] He refused this nomination, no doubt because it was inspired more by hostility to Beet than by approval of himself. Lidgett did, however, let his name go forward for Handsworth, but the more experienced W. T. Davison was the successful candidate.

Lidgett's theological writing revealed a characteristic aim. He was above all an educator, an *expositor*, discerning educational tasks crying out to be done. He not only wanted to prove himself as an intellectual without ministerial training, able to more than hold his own with the best of his Wesleyan ministerial contemporaries. It seems from his writing he had also begun, during his early ministry, progressively to see that Wesleyan theology needed updating, and to that extent deficiencies had to be remedied in the output of Wesleyan theological colleges and denominational journals, and among circuit ministers at large.

Amid their family atmosphere Wesleyans took note almost solely of fellow Wesleyans, certainly if a Wesleyan lead was available. Wesleyans[119] had been slower than some Anglicans in absorbing the results of intellectual changes in the latter half of the century. H. D. Rack admitted that Methodism's 'lack of a tradition of strictly theological and philosophical scholarship comparable to that of the Anglican Church' had been a serious handicap.[120] The emphasis Lidgett sought, less on preparation for the future life and more on the meaning and values of the present life, had, he said, 'already made its mark outside our borders through the teaching of Frederick Denison Maurice, Charles Kingsley and their friends'.[121]

Fired by Maurice, who gave him a gospel to preach, and by ideas which were already beginning to crystallise on the wider national theological scene in the 1880s, Lidgett wanted to expound them in his own way. He appeared, perhaps he wanted to appear, to fellow Wesleyans much more radical than he really was. He may also have been influenced by a desire to raise Wesleyan respectability by proving to his contacts in other denominations that his Church was aware of current theological thinking.[122] In fact that became important as ecumenical contacts developed, access to universities widened, and, with educational standards rising, congregational expectations of ministers increased.

If the outlook of many of his ministerial colleagues had to be changed, Lidgett began to see that care, understanding and courage would be required. Theological understanding among laymen also needed to be improved. He had heard Henry Fowler (later Viscount Wolverhampton) first at the 1875 Conference when he advocated laymen's admission to Conference against

Osborn's opposition. They had risen in importance by becoming in 1878 members of the Conference 'Representative' Session and its committees on virtually equal terms with ministers. Yet the 'earnest, but somewhat uninstructed fundamentalism', which to him represented an inadequate presentation of Christian truth, was accepted by too many laymen as reflecting the belief of the Christian Church as a whole. Lidgett found, for example, that this mistaken stance was creating prejudices in Bermondsey against Christianity among the more intelligent working men[123] outside the Church. The Forward Movement's 'slogan' was that people had bodies as well as souls. Lidgett, deriving his response from Scott,[124] stressed the importance of *minds* also. Bermondsey was where he took his first major initiative.

Part 2

Coming to the fore

Chapters 2–6 refer briefly to the impact of Lidgett's circuit experiences on his call to Bermondsey before making substantial comment on his Settlement there, his theological trilogy (a major and complex enterprise) and his widening activity from 1890 to 1905.

Calendar of main events

1890	Bermondsey Settlement proposal officially ratified by Wesleyan Conference.
1892	Bermondsey Settlement opened. Poor Law Guardian elected each spring to 1906.
1893	Visited Lucerne (Grindelwald Conference).
1894	London School Board Circular controversy.
1896	Official launch of National Council of Evangelical Free Churches (NCEFC); Wesleyan Conference debate on recreation; elected to Conference Special Education Committee.
1897	Elected member of NCEFC Executive; *The Spiritual Principle*; London School Board Triennial November Election, held also 1900, not 1903.
1899	Elected Ministerial Secretary, Wesleyan Committee of Privileges; NCEFC Catechism; Boer War; Cockerton Judgement.
1900	Elected Progressives' Chief Whip.
1901	NCEFC Council Meeting in Cardiff; NCEFC Simultaneous Mission in London.
1902	Balfour's Education Bill; Passive Resistance Committee independent of NCEFC; election to Wesleyan Legal Hundred; *Fatherhood of God*; death of H. P. Hughes.
1903	London Education Act; Wesleyan Conference at Camborne; elected President of Metropolitan Federation of Free Churches; NCEFC committed to election of the Liberal Party.
1904	LCC Education Authority succeeded London School Board.
1905	Elected LCC Alderman to 1910.
1906	Liberals win majority in Parliament.

2

The Bermondsey Settlement – 1

Lidgett's reading programme and pastoral responsibilities in the first 11 years of his ministry[1] set the course of his future career. Posted first to working-class Tunstall in the Potteries (1876–8) with its noisy devotional meetings, he was then sent to genteel and affluent Southport (1878–81). This was followed by Cardiff (1881–4), rapidly growing commercially, where he became involved in establishing its University College, while helping to counter temptations in the docks and the military camps. Ministry in the working-class districts of Heathtown and Wednesfield in Wolverhampton (1884–7), his fourth appointment, brought him into contact, among others, with H. H. Fowler, its Liberal MP, and J. B. Paton, the Congregationalist social reformer, noted *inter alia* for his recreative evening classes for girls and boys. On being posted to Cambridge in 1887 Lidgett mixed with undergraduates and dons from the university, and The Leys School masters and boys. He also encountered the local Charity Organisation Society, pressures for evening continuation schools, and growing interest in College and University missions and Settlements. The Leys Headmaster, W. F. Moulton, his mentor for many years, in 1885 had encouraged Hugh Price Hughes to found the weekly *Methodist Times* as a vehicle for the Forward Movement and its social concerns. Moulton had also recently given his blessing to the venture by Old Boys and senior pupils in founding the Leysian Mission in London.

The strong contrasts of Lidgett's postings in diverse areas vividly illustrated pressing social problems and the disturbing gulf and dangerous estrangement between the rich and educated, and the poor, relatively uneducated, working class. The social divide had deeply affected Lidgett before he preached to his academic congregation at The Leys in November 1887. He chose the text, 'Whether one member suffereth, all the members suffer with it' (1 Cor. 12.26). He stressed: 1. the spiritual, *intellectual* and physical conditions which did so much to strengthen the temptation in crowded cities to intemperance; 2. the wholeness of society, *all* of its classes; 3. the spiritual *loss sustained by well-to-do*, educated and leisured people from their failure to *share* their advantages and co-operate with the industrial classes in remedying their adverse and demoralising conditions.

The impression this sermon made, coupled with what he called a 'clear and imperative call from God', led him to put forward a scheme for 'planting a colony, somewhat on the lines of Toynbee Hall, in one of the poorest parts of London'.[2] Toynbee Hall in Whitechapel had been established in 1884 with financial help from Oxford and Cambridge Universities. Social concern, evident over the previous 20 years, had led to the emergence of Christian Socialists, on whom comment is made later. Experiments, with college and public school missions, for example, had been made, notably in London which exhibited well-known problems and was accessible to Oxbridge. But the concept of a settlement like Toynbee Hall had arisen from its advocate and first Warden, Samuel Barnett, Vicar of St Jude's, supported by the views of such Oxford University thinkers as Benjamin Jowett, Thomas Arnold and Arnold Toynbee whose name was given to the Hall.

Lidgett was also influenced by Barnett's condemnation of attempts merely to palliate social evils through charitable help and remedial, not preventive, action. Toynbee Hall's emphasis was on social and educational work, while Oxford House, founded in the same year, firmly focused on proselytising. Evangelistic work, supported by a variety of social agencies, was also the feature of Wesleyan Missions, established during the eighties in London and elsewhere.

Moulton welcomed Lidgett's proposal, no doubt as a further initiative to reflect the Wesleyan Forward Movement, and Moulton's name was initially associated with it. The Wesleyan Conference took some persuading, but the 'Methodist Settlement in London' opened officially in Bermondsey on 6 January 1892. Lidgett remained there until he retired in 1949. That he stayed so long he owed, at least initially, to Hughes who persuaded the Conference in 1895, against predictable opposition, to allow judicious relaxations, in addition to those granted to Charles Garret in 1875 and Collier from 1885, of its rigid three-year itinerancy rule.

Lidgett[3] and Hughes[4] were indebted to the Oxford philosopher and local Liberal politician, T. H. Green, whose deep ethical concern and sympathy for Christians' belief in divine immanence they linked with an emphasis on the practical character of Christian life, self-sacrifice and the moral obligation of service not least to 'brethren' lower in the social scale. Though Hughes thought his concept of perfection to be attained was a philosophical expression of Wesley's doctrine of 'entire sanctification',[5] he was more impressed by Green's character than his ideas. Lidgett's respect for Green began at the university with his response to views, disturbing to the Christian, expressed by the philosophers David Hume, the two Mills and Alexander Bain.[6] He clearly valued Green's boost to the moral fervour of social activism, his concept of human fulfilment and his call to liberate the powers of the individual. Lidgett's thought, he acknowledged, was greatly influenced by Green's *Prolegomena to Ethics*.[7] His discussion of the ethical aspects of the Atonement quoted from it, and he would have seen that Green's ideas could contribute a religious and philosophical basis for social reform, education, and the development of Liberal political thinking.[8]

Though he did not separate theological reflection and thinking on social ethics, Lidgett's reading after 1876 led him in terms of action first to its social application, and later to the exposition of doctrine. Recording the current philosophical debates, controversies (such as those on evolution and higher criticism) and authors who principally engaged his attention, his list appeared to end with Green's *Prolegomena*.[9] As if this suggested *theoretical* stimuli to action 'to promote the common good', his next paragraph resumed with:

> On the more *practical side*,[10] the *Life of Charles Kingsley* . . . published in 1877, fed the flames of my social enthusiasms and stimulated me to various forms of social activity. Finally, and not least in importance, came the publication in 1881 of the *Life of Frederick Denison Maurice*.

This, Lidgett said, spurred him on to study 'the most important' of Maurice's writings. Maurice's theological ideas became the major influence on Lidgett's thinking, writing and action throughout his life, and the Fatherhood of God assumed for Lidgett overarching importance as the key to all theological understanding and its practical outcome. As Lidgett expounded it, this doctrine inescapably connoted the brotherhood of all men and women, and the importance of fellowship and co-operation, not competition, between them. The Incarnation, God's readiness to become man, showed, he believed, that every human life, of every class, in every part of its being, 'personal and social, spiritual and secular', was sacred.

Lidgett's discussions with W. B. Pope on the Fatherhood of God had also made an impact on him in 1881. His autobiographies paid tribute to Pope: he called him 'the greatest systematic theologian that Methodism has ever possessed'.[11] The Preface to the *Spiritual Principle* attributed to him 'any light given to me on the meaning of our Lord's death' and 'on the great Obedience', but not his (unpublished) discussion of the Fatherhood of God. Pope's *Compendium* had put the prime focus of his treatment of faith and ethics on the individual: he had said justice blended with love should mark the dealings of men with one another, but his doctrines were not applied to the problems of society. In contrast, Maurice had given the Fatherhood of God a wider reference. Lidgett emphasised the close Christian Socialist link between Maurice and Kingsley by bracketing them together in the context of social concern: there are three such references in *My Guided Life*.[12] Once absorbed, Maurice's views were bound to take precedence over those of Pope, but Lidgett remained in debt to Pope's initial stimulus.

Lidgett's discovery of Maurice's focus on the doctrine at an early and crucial stage in his career was duly recorded, but vanity often prevented him from acknowledging directly Maurice's all-pervading influence on his own writing until later in his life. Maurice was not acknowledged in the Preface to the *Spiritual Principle* in 1897, and he was given only four pages of text, though the Fatherhood of God was central to its thesis. His importance in nineteenth-century Church history was recognised in Lidgett's *Fatherhood of God*, but *Reminiscences* made no reference to him: speaking of the *Spiritual Principle*, Lidgett pointed simply to himself: 'I had come to see that as the Fatherhood of God, properly understood, is the highest, so it is the universal relationship in which He stands to mankind, however lacking may be the response of sonship'.[13]

In Lent 1934 Lidgett was delighted to be invited to deliver a eulogy in the second series of the Maurice memorial lectures, published as *The Victorian Transformation of Theology*. He paid strong tribute to Maurice in 1936, but even there, as he spoke of Maurice's ideas, the note of personal vanity crept in:

> In many ways of thought and practical endeavour my mind had been *independently* prepared . . . The teaching of Maurice *clinched* all these convictions and established them on a reasoned foundation, while the study of his heroic witness to and his fearless application of the Truth as he saw it drew me to him as the greatest prophet of the nineteenth century – a judgement which has never since been shaken.[14]

Lidgett no doubt hoped that 'heroic witness' had been mirrored in his own career.

Maurice's application of theology to social activity,[15] coupled with Lidgett's own experience, awareness of other initiatives, and almost certainly one other book and one other theologian, provided the context for his 'call' to Bermondsey. The theologian was James Baldwin Brown (1820–84), a Congregationalist minister in Lambeth and Brixton,[16] whose insistence on the Fatherhood of God and Brotherhood of Man and on their social and doctrinal application was owing to Maurice's influence. Stella Wood called Brown 'the primary interpreter of Maurice to Nonconformity'.[17] Brown also found implications for the Atonement, for 'stretching the hand' not down but 'across' to his brother men,[18] for improvements in sanitation, for increased educational opportunities and so on. There is little doubt that Lidgett would have heard of him. Close family contacts would have ensured that Percy Bunting, who attended Brown's funeral, talked about his ideas. Surprisingly, though involved in the National Council of Evangelical Free Churches (NCEFC) from its beginnings, Lidgett never acknowledged the contribution of a fellow Nonconformist of distinction who died 12 years later than Maurice. Perhaps it was because Brown had derived so much from Maurice, and so little had percolated into Methodism.

The book was by the Wesleyan, William Arthur, who in 1856 had published

The Tongue of Fire, about the Holy Spirit. The subject was dear to all Methodists, the book was popular, but the holiness it commended was not other-worldly:

> Fearful social evils may co-exist with a state of society wherein many are holy ... The most dangerous perversion of the Gospel, viewed as affecting community, is, when it is looked upon as a means of forming a holy community in the world to come, but never in this.[19]

That message would not have been popular with the great majority for whom the salvation of the individual soul was far more important than attention to the needs of society. But it continued to inspire Wesleyan progressives like S. E. Keeble (1853–1946), who in 1919 quoted Arthur on the title page of his own pamphlet, *Towards the New Era*:

> Have not those who see and feel the importance of first seeking the regeneration of the individual too often insufficiently studied the application of Christianity to social evils? . . . Nothing short of the general renewal of society ought to satisfy any soldier of Christ.[20]

Lidgett's own battle towards achieving this began in the slums of Bermondsey. His energies were directed more to taking public action than insisting on personal piety, though the latter never lost its importance.

In general a Settlement was an attempt by middle-class, not just rich, public school, university and professional men (and some women) to interest their own class in the welfare of the poor. Its particular feature was the (mainly short-term) presence of untrained Lay Residents within deprived areas, making personal contacts, in seeing slum conditions for themselves, and offering some contribution to alleviating them.

The aims of the Bermondsey Settlement, as of many settlements, may be broadly classified as theological/religious, social and educational. Standish Meacham has identified the first as, for *Lidgett*, the most important: 'The activities of the Wesleyans' Bermondsey Settlement . . . consisted primarily of religious work'.[21] Based on only one of Lidgett's comments,[22] this judgement is simplistic and misleading. All three strands, it is true, were intertwined and overlap, difficult to separate from one another. Deep religious conviction, repeatedly articulated, drove the Warden forward; he appealed for residents with a sense of religious obligation. But the activities of the Settlement *qua* Settlement were not in the strict, narrow sense religious or evangelical, but primarily educational, and social service by its students was intended to arise out of widening their intellectual and cultural horizons in a variety of educational, recreational and social activities, and from the example of the resident staff. The centrality of Lidgett's educational and social aims was emphasised early in his *Guided Life* account: 'The work which I started in January 1892 was, to begin with, chiefly *educational*'; and 'From the beginning, while *basing* my arguments on spiritual, and indeed evangelical grounds, I set social rather than ecclesiastical duties in the foreground.'[23]

Lidgett's Settlement was not a Mission.[24] Evangelical provision was to be made available in the 'Circuit' of two local churches with Sunday schools (Southwark Park and Silver Street), of which Lidgett was made Superintendent,[25] but not in the Settlement itself. The Warden's ministerial status, and his theological contributions to the Settlement's lecture programme and its *Monthly Record*, could not escape students' notice. Nor could the ways in which he and *most* of his residents were striving to give practical expression to the principles of their Christian faith, exhibiting (as in his *Third Annual Report*) 'in practice a large conception of what Social Christianity means', and seeking (as among his Aims, listed below) to bring 'attractiveness to Christian work'.[26] He hoped some students might develop friendships close enough to their teachers to 'become persuaded of the disinterestedness of their aims'; see 'the relation of the great Christian facts and truths to social order, well-being and progress'; and respond to the exposition of the Christian faith by recognising God as the Creator and source of all Truth, and coming 'to know the historic Christ'. But students were never asked or expected to attend a service of worship. Nor was an evangelical appeal made to them: that might have alienated many. The first priorities were 'to improve their gifts and then to use them for others'.[27]

In his view the Church had twin missions, to evangelise and educate. Helping his students to develop their educational potential was valuable in itself. It could bring them to recognise God as the Creator and the source of all truth, beauty and goodness. It could assist them to a better and up-to-date understanding of the Christian faith. This last aspiration might not be achieved; no 'leap of faith' might take place; no increased membership of his churches might occur; but Lidgett's educational imperative for the Settlement was not thereby invalidated.

In many respects Lidgett followed the precedent of Toynbee Hall. Before becoming its Warden in 1884, Samuel Barnett had expressed disillusionment with the effectiveness of the churches and poor popular participation in Church activities: he had little time for church administration, dogma, preaching and ritual. In November 1883 in St John's College, Oxford, his talk to dons and undergraduates on 'Settlements of University Men in Great Towns' contrasted Oxbridge College Missions with Settlements. The latter, he said, would have far broader aims, reconnecting lay men and women into the community and making them 'conscious of their brotherhood' – a better base on which to build bridges with the poor and deprived. A Mission, on the other hand, staffed by resident Anglican clergy, was, as Barnett put it, likely to last 'only until its district could become an independent parish'.[28] Missions were narrowly focused, simply foundations to proselytise. Ernest Aves saw church missions as stereotyped institutions without flexibility, 'where the men work under authority, are told off to this and that'. 'At Toynbee', he said, 'the method has been to find out what a man is good for, and let him do it in his own way.'[29] Lidgett adopted this policy.[30] He would have been well aware of Barnett's views, not least because Barnett's architect for Toynbee Hall, and later his own in Bermondsey, was Elijah Hoole.

Lidgett's 1891 pamphlet, *The Aims and Work of the Bermondsey Settlement*, setting out the need for Settlements, strongly criticised the churches, missions and their members. It warrants quotation *in extenso*:

> The growth of great cities . . . the concentration of manufactories and the increased facilities of railway travelling are fast sending the rich, educated and learned into the suburbs and the country. This fashion is being followed by the more successful artisans and tradesmen, till the central districts of London and great towns are left to the poorest and least capable . . . where social problems are acutest, there are fewest to solve them; where Christian worship, teaching and philanthropy should be most beautiful, they are weak and unattractive; where a united and persistent effort should be made to give healthy and happy colour to the monotony of life, and to open to toiling men and women the resources and enjoyments of God's World of Truth, Beauty and Goodness all around them, there is the total absence of those who can organise and lead it . . . multitudes who might, if they would, lead the people into the promised land, have either forgotten entirely that they are their brother's keepers, and that where much is given, much will be required, or seek to discharge their obligation by maintaining an army of Missionaries and Bible-women to minister just so much of the higher life as the poor are supposed to need.[31]

Clearly brotherhood needed leadership.

Lidgett followed this up in his first *Annual Report*:

> The Christianity which will win the people of this city will be the Christianity which sends its flower to minister to the *many-sided necessities* of such neighbourhoods as ours. The multitudes . . . will see *little* of His glory through *our poor half-starved Churches* which are struggling to do *a small fragment of the work*, while those who *could* 'humble' themselves to live among us take their ease afar off.[32]

W. F. Lofthouse, a former Settlement resident, described local congregations as 'clinging desperately to their respectability' and knowing 'as little of their neighbours as did the exalted dwellers in Streatham and Dulwich'.[33] Reversing his family's admiration for philanthropy, and echoing Maurice, Lidgett opposed the common policy of dispensing charity as merely eleemosynary,[34] feeble, unconstructive, rousing resentment, palliating results rather than grappling with causes.[35] His most stinging attack on the Churches' inadequacies for the comprehensive task he favoured was in his *Annual Report* for October 1894:

> Those [Churches] in the midst of them [working men] are, for the most part, too weak to help them – have so much to do to make ends meet that they have little leisure or energy to spare, or are officered and attended almost entirely by classes between which and the labouring population there is an almost total absence of sympathy. The suburban Churches belong to the 'swells'.[36]

Quite apart from the unattractive fabric of the churches, their 'officers' were often in his view narrow and inadequately instructed, lacking courage, strength and resources, and their congregations were very often served by the poorest men in the ministry. Most damagingly, to him their limitations included insufficient *intellectual* provision. In his *Second Annual Report* in 1893 he wrote:

> A great proportion of the labouring classes, at least, live in a world *entirely foreign to the appeals and efforts of the Churches*. Spiritual indifference is commonly given as the reason . . . But it is most important for us to realise that that to which they are indifferent is seldom the *full* Gospel of our Lord Jesus Christ . . . Preaching gives no *complete* idea of the Christianity of Christ . . . If we would fill the Churches, we must go *outside them* . . . We must remember that the working people have *minds*, are exercised about the perplexing mysteries of the world, and must be talked to as men, not indeed controversially [this seems to refer to denominational or political polemics], but plainly, sympathetically, and with *competent knowledge*.[37]

So the work of the Church was not rejected – far from it: his own church activities were complementary to the distinctive work of the Settlement. They accorded with his own convictions, but were, in fact, vital for his survival in the post. He would never have had permission for the Settlement under the objectives he set for it without undertaking responsibility for a Circuit, however small. In outlining his plans to Richmond College ministerial students in May 1890, he took care to offer 'bright, attractive religious services'.[38] Both Lidgett and Barnett were (later) honoured by their churches, but for some time neither was fully understood by his fellow clergy and church dignitaries.

Lidgett had to face initial and sustained opposition from within his own Church. His obituary for Moulton in 1898 acknowledged his 'powerful influence' in securing from Conference its formal approval, though 'there was very little real conviction behind that approval'. Some years later, Rigg, twice President of Conference, said he had been bound to support the scheme at the beginning 'owing to the advocacy of Dr Moulton', but had believed it 'foredoomed to failure'.[39]

Lidgett's fellow ministers, and many Wesleyans at that time, were afraid[40] of any preaching that could not be called evangelical, and of any meetings other than for Bible Study, Temperance advocacy and money-raising for mission at home and abroad. In 1883 they had been appalled by the situation described in *The Bitter Cry of Outcast London*.[41] But like their Southwark colleague, Forster Crozier, they retained their optimistic belief that evangelical effort alone could solve the social ills there described.[42] Conference addresses acknowledged the desperate needs of people in London, but focused on the '*spiritually* destitute'. Conference had set up Wesleyan Methodist Missions, but even so there was fear of 'politics in the pulpit',[43] and apprehension that 'a sudden call for political action, and too drastic a response, might follow'. Preaching the gospel was thought to be the paramount duty of the Church, and that meant aiming directly at conversion of individuals as the most vital of all priorities. For Lidgett to query this passionately held article of faith, not just orally but in writing, was bound to attract opposition, and the explicit way in which he relentlessly expressed his criticisms was a mark of his independence, courage and conviction.

In 1889 the Conference had sanctioned a settlement in London 'for *Religious and Social work* in connection with *our own Church*'. In the following year Lidgett and Moulton succeeded in adding to the terms of reference: 'The general object of the Settlement shall be to provide a centre in London for Religious, *Educational* and Social work to be carried on by resident and non-resident workers'.[44] Lidgett then published (and re-published annually without alteration) the aims of his Settlement,[45] aims mainly educational and social, not calculated to endear him to his evangelical critics:

1. to bring additional force and attractiveness to Christian work;
2. to become a centre of social life where all classes may meet together on equal terms for healthful intercourse and recreation;
3. to give facilities for the study of Literature, History, Science and Art;
4. to bring men together to discuss general and special social evils and to seek their remedy;
5. to take such part in local administration and philanthropy as may be possible;
6. and so to do all this that it shall be perfectly clear that no mere *sectarian* advantage is sought, but that it shall be possible for all good men to associate themselves with our work.

No reference here to evangelism, the Christian Church, or even the Wesleyan Connexion. On an underground train a minister asked him directly: 'What does Methodism get out of this?'[46] But Lidgett was bent on making the Settlement *non*-denominational. Strong protests from fellow Wesleyans may be inferred. Lidgett was defiant. The 1894 *Annual Report* stated:

> Much of what we are doing cannot in the nature of things bring us any ecclesiastical advantage or to the Settlement as a body any prestige. But of it all we can unhesitatingly say, 'It needs to be done', and . . . 'This would not be done in this neighbourhood but for us'.[47]

He insisted that the Settlement, as opposed to Missions, was based on Christian principles, not ecclesiastical organisation. His prime purpose was to proclaim via the Settlement's example a message, *a common duty*, not a special calling.

Such a disinterested attitude in its way reflected an Arminian, Catholic approach to mankind, but his particular application of it contrasted with that of the contemporary movement for Wesleyan Missions. He did not seem concerned that Settlements like his own were not promoted elsewhere in Methodism. He may well have been flattered to be thought unique.

Inevitably Lidgett was accused of setting the secular above the spiritual. Powerful friends protected him in the Committee established to oversee his work. Percy Bunting, editor of the *Methodist Times*, for example, strongly commended his work as unique in Methodism, and urged Conference to be patient: it would take time and much training before people in Bermondsey would listen to the gospel.[48] In 1902 Bunting was stressing the effectiveness of the Settlement 'in the wider sphere of evangelism which claims all life for the Kingdom of God'.[49] But Lidgett himself took care in composing his *Annual Reports* to provide a defence against his opponents. Each contained prominently placed headings, such as 'Evangelism', 'Our Evangelistic Work' and even 'The Aggressive Work'. He stressed here the work of his two churches; the training he offered in the Settlement for local Sunday school teachers; his lectures inside and outside the Settlement on 'Popular Christian Teaching'; open-air preaching (already in 1892 he was President of the newly formed Southwark Park Open Air Mission); and his reply to G. W. Foote's 'Case against Christianity'. Lidgett's lectures were not evangelical in the narrow sense, but his overall religious zeal and his energetic efforts spoke for themselves. They protected the educational and social work which he also proudly listed, guarded against any charge of misuse of Wesleyan resources, and muted, even if they did not completely silence, his Wesleyan critics.

In his 1893 *Annual Report*, the sentence concluding a list of his 'Aggressive' evangelical work contained a *double entendre* sting in the tail:

> But it must be illustrated by an intense, broad and practical Christianity and, as this Report goes on to describe *other*[50] enterprises of the Settlement, I ask my readers to keep in mind their bearing on the living interpretation of Christ to those, whose conception of His purposes is so poor.

His 1897 *Report*[51] was even more direct:

> It is given to them [Settlements] to show to the religious people with whom they are in contact, how broad and humane the Christian ideal is, and how closely bound up with the highest spiritual interests are the general educational and social activities which Settlements naturally create. There have not been wanting signs of sometimes imperfect sympathy between Churches and Settlements.

But initially he also faced opposition from other quarters. Local politicians and labour leaders found the expression of evangelical conviction in social service almost incomprehensible. The community suspected a sinister political or Church intrusion. Lidgett's reception by the local clergy and ministers was also far from warm:

> They assured me there was no demand in Bermondsey for such a scheme, and that I should meet with little response. They also seemed nervous lest I should bring financial support from outside to inaugurate a work which would damage their own struggling Churches.[52]

Being dubbed 'the poorest men in the ministry' would not have delighted them, nor his censure of conventional church work, and he admitted they had reason to object that the enterprise had appeared complete in the neighbourhood instead of springing from small beginnings.

Yet his public apologias for the faith were clearly unsectarian and won some of them over. In 1896 he even formed the Bermondsey and Rotherhithe District Council for the Evangelical Free Churches, and became its first President. Its 'headquarters' were in the Settlement. It aimed to develop a greater sense of union between the Nonconformist Churches of the District and achieve their more effective co-operation for both evangelical and social purposes. Already in 1891 Lidgett had been involved in what in 1896 became the National Council of Evangelical Free Churches. He also avoided rivalry with other Settlements; though they differed from one another in emphasis and provision, he was anxious to co-operate, not conflict, with them. Samuel Barnett, for example, was a Vice-President of his committee from the start, Barnett's wife lectured for him, and he praised both in his *Idea of God and Social Ideals*.[53] At least one Conference was held[54] for Settlement Wardens to discuss the multiplying of Settlements 'in the large provincial cities and towns of England', and Lidgett was there.

A further initial (and on-going) problem was financial. Apart from his ministerial salary, Lidgett never received any Warden's allowance; the Conference provided no financial support, in effect forcing him to rely for what he needed to open and maintain the buildings (the Settlement and the women's Alice Barlow House) and meet expenses[55] almost entirely on appeals to benefactors, and to supporters in Oxford, Cambridge, Edinburgh and Aberystwyth universities, and Methodist schools: in sum, the middle class. His visit in 1888 to Mansfield College, Oxford, to discover whether a joint Wesleyan/Congregational Settlement was possible, will have had economy as well as Nonconformist co-operation in mind. Fairbairn, the Principal, first promised his support, and then withdrew in favour of setting up the Congregationalists' own Mansfield House.[56] Lidgett endured a lonely campaign, obliged to travel 'like a mendicant' (as he put it)[57] all over the country to raise money for his building fund. His appeal competed with London Mission appeals and was suspected as intended for social, secular activities, not 'for the gospel and spirituality'.

As a somewhat academic figure, he faced doubts both about his own ability to act as a recruiting officer for Settlement staff volunteers and about recruitment prospects in general. His letter to the *Methodist Times*,[58] advertising for residents, claimed the neighbourhood was healthy, but a far less rosy picture was evident from the Borough Medical Officer's report and the death in 1910 of Joyce Salter from the third onset of a malignant form of scarlet fever.[59] She was the only daughter of Dr Alfred Salter, a Settlement resident in 1898, who after marriage in 1900 continued to live in the area. The Settlement was a grim, unattractive building, surrounded by decaying docks and drab dwellings for the many unemployed constantly seeking casual labour. Relatively few Methodists became residents, but he was fortunate in attracting several very able people: for example the benefactor, Alice Barlow of Edgeworth, a formidable sister of the Royal physician; W. E. Brunyate, later legal adviser to the Cairo Government; C. W. Kimmins from The Leys, later Inspector of Schools for the LCC; and Kimmins's friend, Boyd Carpenter, son of the Bishop of Ripon. Some Wesleyan parents would have resented his attempt to alter entrenched attitudes. He gained many fewer wealthy supporters than Barnett, and his social influence was less wide. One of the 'prosperous' people he approached, the Rt Hon. H. H. Fowler, later Lord Wolverhampton, 'scouted my plan as altogether Utopian and certain to prove futile. It was hopeless, he declared, to attempt to transplant University influences into working class districts'.[60] Though he was supported by Colonel S. B. Bevington, head of a major local leather company and later the first Mayor of the Borough, the other large firms in Bermondsey gave him a chilly response. Through shortage of funds the Settlement building was not completed until 1898, and rigid economy forced a modification to the architect's original plans. It was not until 1932 that a private appeal almost cleared the Settlement of debt, but financial worries never ceased.

Lidgett's educational philosophy has already been glimpsed from its application. Education, Lidgett thought, was valuable as training students for service to the community. That meant the *non*-Wesleyan community and *non*-sectarian provision, not least where competent social workers and administrators were lacking: 'We need', he said, 'to arouse the sense of social duty . . . the will to co-operate with unselfish bent for the common good. We therefore enlist our students on our cause'.[61] Lidgett believed the well-being of the individual could only stem from that of the community. And so a new sense of personal responsibility had to be stimulated, based on acknowledging membership of the community and developing a desire to serve and improve it. In his view, education should not be confined to provision for children and adults. Public interest needed to be aroused in health, nutrition, housing, sanitation, green fields and so on.

Though mainly working in London during the day, Settlement residents, with its staff, set the example.[62] Their social and administrative activities, further exemplified in Appendix 1, included a penny bank, an insurance branch, free legal advice to the poor, participation in the local community as Poor Law Guardians, School Board members, school managers, and LCC and Borough council members, with district nursing, a minor ailments and dental centre for children, a day nursery, schools for mothers, provision for the sick and lonely poor, and holiday funds for children and for women.

Lidgett steadily and quietly occupied strategic posts, as Lofthouse put it, and sought to attract all kinds of social work to make the Settlement their base. Taking risks by becoming involved in party politics for the Progressives, he offered himself for election as Poor Law Guardian in 1892 and as a member of the London School Board in 1897. In striving to see school places provided for every child, improvements made in school buildings, and biblical instruction retained, for example, he had to face opposition variously on financial, sectarian and secular grounds.

Lidgett's claim on retirement[63] in 1949 that 'no single feature of our up-to-date social administration was not forecast or anticipated by the voluntary efforts of the Settlement' was certainly an exaggeration. In fact few, if any, of the educational and social activities listed above were original to his Settlement. But these gradually became more widely practised in Borough and later State agencies as well as in continuing[64] voluntary enterprise, and that certainly delighted him. He was quoted as stating in his 1898 *Annual Report*: 'The most practical demand made upon the Christian faith is that it should leaven and transform the State.'[65] Implicitly he claimed this as the major success of his Settlement by naming the many influential civic and political figures as at one time or another associated with him as residents or in the LCC, and more generally by pointing to the Settlement's supply of workers in many spheres of local administration.[66] He said:

> For us the duties of Local Government are sacred, having to do with the environment which helps or hinders the higher life of those who are affected by it, and influencing for good or evil the moral tone of the community, according as they are faithfully or carelessly discharged.[67]

But Lidgett believed passionately in the fundamental importance of education, 'the opening of the mind to desire, to seek after and to enjoy knowledge *for its own sake*'.[68] Education, he was convinced, was needed to develop personality, to help people to rise above depressing, monotonous, squalid, even brutal and immoral surroundings, enjoy all God's creation, and practise creativity. Lidgett wanted his helpers and students to search for, value and share the highest values of truth, beauty and goodness as they apprehended them. Maurice had made the same point: 'We dare not refuse to any member of that family all mankind a share in the beauty, riches, and responsibilities of the world which God created'.[69] No doubt Maurice's 1854 Working Men's College had set a precedent for Bermondsey, as for Toynbee Hall. Neither Lidgett nor Maurice pressed people to recognise that it was God's world, and God was the source of all truth, beauty and goodness: they hoped that might result. In that sense all education was religious education. Unlike Wesley, Lidgett deliberately refused to direct it narrowly to preparation for eternity or enforce a tunnel vision on discerning God's working in the world. Scott's 1862 address, mentioned above, was Lidgett's 'Bible', with its tripartite exhortation to fit Mind 'for its duties to itself, to mankind, and to its Maker'.

Untrained as a teacher himself, Lidgett did not provide training or equipment for his residents: like him, they lectured, no doubt often over their students' heads, and learned teaching techniques *ambulando*. His grandfather's example was evident in his general call to teach students to think and *how* to think,[70] in the ideals he advocated and in the store he set by the friendship and influence of a dedicated personality.[71] He seemed to reflect the Oxford tutorial system when he said that knowledge for its own sake 'is only fully possible . . . where both social intercourse and the close bond between teacher and taught increase the elasticity and receptiveness of the mind.'[72]

In his view: 'We are to re-create one another . . . Many . . . pursue "the trivial round" . . . long after the living interest and enthusiasm are gone . . . Brain activities get to be like extinct volcanoes.'[73] Lidgett would have recognised that both teacher and taught needed to share a love of truth and creation, even if not of God.

Lidgett aimed to counter 'intellectual starvation'[74] among the poor. That was why he stood out against those Anglican clergy and middle-class people who objected to London School Board rate increases, enabling the children of the poor and industrial classes to compete for employment with their fee-paying sons in non-provided schools.[75] John Scott had convinced him that the working classes were entitled to a good education. Lidgett did not patronise: 'Never suppose', he said, 'that the population of Bermondsey must be treated as stupid and only capable of appreciating inferior gifts. Set before them pearls of great price'.[76] Human beings deserved to be treated as human, not as mere recipients of charity and wages. In education as in social care that meant attention to the handicapped, disadvantaged and less able. Lidgett helped in pioneering what was later called Special Education and promoting extended provision for secondary education via Higher Elementary and Central Schools.

The Settlement and its Women's House provided for both sexes. Students, mainly young adults, were 16-plus upwards, mainly 16–25. Over the years its educational provision was wide. The programme included 'Popular' and University Extension lectures, classes in academic disciplines (for example, science, mathematics, history, literature, languages),[77] as well as *practical*, manual and commercial subjects, music, choral concerts, art exhibitions, educational visits, physical exercise (in games, 'play', swimming, gymnastics and drill), and recreational activities, clubs and societies such as the Boys' Brigade, and the Debating Society, conducted on parliamentary lines. At the 1896 Conference Lidgett fought the cause of organised recreation on Wesleyan premises against Dinsdale Young (1861–1938) and others opposed to any form of 'entertainment'. Lidgett wanted non-sectarian religious instruction to be available in the Settlement, and for all pupils in the local schools. He became known as a strong champion of the welfare of children and young people. His support for the education of infants, of girls as well as boys, and adults, and for equal opportunities for women and men, permeated his own and colleagues' administration as school managers and in the wider sphere of local government. Speaking in 1949, he paid tribute to the assistance he received from 'very capable women', because (he said) 'I knew that men did not possess the full key to the social problems of London'.[78]

Education for Lidgett had intrinsic worth. It was not valued simply in terms of advancing careers or social status, nor did he ever mention any need for an educated work force to counter increased competition in world trade. He thought of the widening of the franchise as strengthening, rather than *making* his case: 'Even adult suffrage will not help the working classes much, except as it goes hand in hand with education', he said.

Lidgett was, nevertheless, a man of his age and social (middle) class. The French Revolution had led that class to fear unrest and far-reaching social change,[79] and Lidgett was disturbed by the activity of 'the representatives of "free thought" in clubs and workshops',[80] Radicals and Labour politicians. He was, nevertheless, himself suspected of radical sympathies in applying his theology. He found it necessary in his Presidential address of 1908[81] to defend the growing power of the State in securing conditions for the wider and more complete enjoyment of freedom. To some extent he shared in 'middle-class guilt'. Worried by growing divisions in society, what he wanted was social *harmony and co-operation* rather than social equality. He wanted no change in the social order. It was, however, for others to see education as of *simply secular* significance, merely as a means to counter among the lower orders the pursuit of pointless pleasure, gratuitous violence and crime, or the ignorant exercise of electoral power, or as a means to inculcate self-restraint, respect for tradition and authority. For Lidgett education had a *divine* sanction. It provided a spur to fulfilling each person's potential, satisfying scope for fellowship and co-operation, the powerhouse for steadily transforming social conditions and achieving social harmony.

The Fatherhood of God, from which Lidgett derived this 'divine sanction', had to be expounded, he decided, in published works.

3

The Spiritual Principle of the Atonement

The Spiritual Principle was Lidgett's first theological work and the best known to later generations.[1] His thesis was not summarised, but emerged in the course of a closely yet wordily reasoned exposition. This calls for detailed analysis to unravel the sequence of his thinking on the Atonement, and more importantly to illustrate his perspective across the whole field of doctrine.

Lidgett's work on the Atonement was published several years after arriving in Bermondsey. Such interest was unlikely during 1873–5, the period given by the *Methodist Recorder*:[2]

> While . . . a student at University College, London, the structure of the Christian doctrine of the Atonement took shape in his mind. As though by a flash of understanding, he saw through the eyes of his imagination all its complex relationships unified in one coherent design.

The story perhaps arose from a self-flattering oral account in his old age: no extant evidence is available for it. There was drama enough in what Lidgett wrote about the 'vivid intimation'[3] or 'voice'[4] in 1877, telling him to write on the Atonement. He visited Moulton that same week 'to report progress', in his circuit work no doubt, and to 'tell him tentatively that I felt something had to be done to restate the doctrine'.

Neither autobiography explains his *initial* interest in the Atonement or the interpretation he wanted. He admitted 'the concern slumbered for years'.[5] He made no special study of the doctrine and its history.[6] His wide reading programme continued, pastoral and social concerns preoccupied him, and he confessed that until the Foote incident in 1893 he felt too diffident to undertake any theological teaching except in preaching.[7] Then, his regular courses of public lectures in Bermondsey defending the Christian faith, their publication in the local paper, experience of public debate and a second 'intimation' overcame his 'diffidence and hesitation' about the project.

During the 1894 Wesleyan Conference in Birmingham, he said, 'an incidental remark'[8] on the Atonement, towards the end of G. G. Findlay's Fernley lecture on a different subject, sparked off 'a constraining influence',[9] inspiring him to make an immediate sketch of his future treatise. The lecture, 'Christian

Doctrine and Morals Viewed in Their Connection', attacked those whose 'New Morality' repudiated what Findlay saw as the essential connection between morals and Christian doctrine. But concepts and phrases used *throughout* could have triggered thoughts about the Atonement: reference to Christ's *filial* will, rather than his response to an *impersonal law*, was one example.

Next Monday, Lidgett again sought out Moulton. 'In a stammering way',[10] he said that he felt called to write on the Atonement. To his 'sober, yet joyful surprise' Moulton suggested he gave a Fernley lecture on it. This Moulton arranged with the Fernley Trustees, via C. H. Kelly (Connexional Book Steward), for the Leeds Conference of 1897. On 30 July Lidgett spoke from his book's Chapter 5 at Woodhouse Moor Wesleyan Church.

There seem to be several reasons for his choice of the Atonement. The first was the need for clarification. In 1877 Lidgett may simply have seen, in Tunstall and Methodism generally, a vital need to clarify the bewildering and competing literature on such an important doctrine. He expressed concern 20 years later[11] at the despair 'in many quarters' of arriving at a satisfactory conclusion, and quoted the Congregationalist R. F. Horton as saying 'We are entirely out of our depth in any discussion of the subject'.[12] Lidgett said: 'While the Christian Church has held from the beginning the faith that the death of Christ was an atoning sacrifice, no definite explanation of its precise meaning and method has ever been authoritatively given'.[13] The task of unravelling complexities and deepening understanding appealed to Lidgett's educational drive.

Many believers, he thought,[14] had developed other religious interests: the rediscovery of the historic Jesus; attempts to write his 'Life'; the application of his spiritual and moral principles to current problems; and Christianity's relation to other religions. To him these, though worthy, had contributed to a serious neglect of the doctrine. Scepticism and hostility to the Church also disturbed him: evolution led some to infer that men would gradually free themselves from evil; others, like George Eliot, thought atoning impossible: we just 'reap what we have sown'.[15]

A second reason for choosing the Atonement was his desire for coherence. Many church leaders saw scope for different interpretations of the Atonement and different ways of explaining it to the faithful. To Pope, all the leading versions were complementary, each representing a real aspect of the whole.[16] To Lidgett, however, they seemed 'mutually exclusive'. Theologians, 'hard-riding' on arbitrarily selected texts[17] to justify their chosen aspect,[18] had not discovered 'a living principle sufficiently supreme and comprehensive to unite and harmonise them all'.

Identifying comprehensive principles attracted him. Study of logic had led him to place the highest premium on *rationality* and *coherence*. He said, for example, 'As faith becomes rational . . . it must needs seek to apprehend, and therefore to represent, Reality as a consistent and coherent whole'.[19] Lidgett was no reductionist: his rationality connoted reasonableness, refusal to be ruled by the heart, but leaving room for the 'leap' of faith. As in 1902, he hoped he might 'help some who are seeking a view of Christian theology comprehensive enough to include and harmonise many elements of truth which, seen in isolation, become distorted and misleading'.[20] Here was a gap to be filled.

Lidgett found his comprehensive view sometime after 1881, when he discussed the Fatherhood of God with Pope, and when, perhaps after hearing of Maurice, he began to study his writings. He realised 'the doctrine of the Atonement which was generally held in my youth' was 'that which chiefly withstood the truth of the supreme and universal Fatherhood of God'.[21] He reasoned that if the Fatherhood of God was to be upheld as the overarching principle of theology, with nothing to limit or undermine its universality, then the *obstacle* of what he saw as inadequate,[22] unjustified and out of date concepts of God (essential to traditional interpretations of the Atonement) had to be removed. Looking back in 1935,[23] he spoke of the 'urgent need at that time [1894–7] to disencumber Methodist theology from outworn philosophical and legal conceptions so as to liberate the full significance of "our doctrines"'. This was what caused his resolve, finally in 1894, to write on the Atonement.[24] To choose such a minefield showed courage. Exposition of the Fatherhood of God generally had to wait.

Use of the Fatherhood doctrine in expounding the Atonement had another appeal to a Methodist, its link with spiritual experience. To Lidgett a proper understanding of the Atonement had to be intrinsically related to sinners' spiritual well-being. The idea of God, he insisted, had to be adequate to the unfolding content of spiritual life, 'so that God, as *spiritually and intellectually* apprehended (Lidgett stressed *both* aspects), may be the illuminant, and not the enigma and even stumbling block of men's highest ideals and efforts'.[25]

Lidgett's definition[26] of the Fatherhood of God, repeated[27] in his 1902 book, was that 'it necessitates our conceiving of the creation of mankind as the calling into existence by God, *out of His own life*, beings at once kindred with Himself and having a distinct individuality of their own.'

This calling into existence is

> motived (*sic*) by the love of God; introduces them into a world, a home, of love which environs their whole life; and has, as its end, that fellowship of mutual giving and receiving, that most intimate communion which can only be between those who are spiritually akin, a fellowship which it is the object of fatherly education to perfect. The motive as love, the end as fellowship, the method as the education of the home, all these are set forth when we speak of the Fatherhood of God.

Schemes hitherto had neglected this 'precious' relationship[28] and 'most intimate communion . . . between those who are spiritually akin'. Lidgett claimed an advance on the past.

In the *Reminiscences*, he declared that 'the Fatherhood of God, properly understood', should 'determine the spiritual principle of the Atonement, at once bringing it into line with the gracious purpose of God and calling into full and redemptive expression the true spiritual life of man.'[29] Spiritual values were 'part of the *original* equipment by which man entered into manhood'.[30]

Lidgett claimed that the Atonement had for some years received comparatively little attention: no work, he thought, had 'largely influenced' the religious world since the Congregationalist Dale's *Lectures on the Atonement* in 1875. Dale's revised version of Protestant orthodoxy retained its essence and proved widely acceptable especially among Nonconformists: it was already in its seventeenth edition by 1897. Lidgett, who was deeply indebted to Dale's thesis, paid him a very sincere tribute.[31] But work had continued to be done on the subject since 1875. Lidgett wanted to devise a Methodist 'Dale'.[32] He thought it timely to make Methodists aware of the major theories, provide his own lengthy critique, and offer an up-dated overall verdict in line with contemporary thought. His tortuous (and dull) style was perhaps owing to a display of learning, a wish to avoid challenge, and time spent doing so.

Lidgett's approach was to summarise specifically biblical teaching only briefly: detail was reserved for his next book. The appendix supplied, significantly for students, a 69-page background sketch of the doctrine in Church history. Acknowledging he had consulted available histories of the doctrine including Anselm, Lidgett's Preface claimed his appendix was the result 'for the most part' of independent reading. Such reading was clearly evident in the main text where his direct quotations are accurate and apposite. He may not have read in depth all the authorities to whom he referred, a few perhaps not at all, but the evidence of his research was daunting. Apart from those mentioned above, reference was made to some 54 theologians, by one who had had no ministerial training, occupied no theological college post, and whose responsibilities since 1876 could have justifiably been regarded as full-time! He quoted from the Greek. Some continental authors had become available in translation,[33] but he had read at least one in the original German. He made, for example, several references, paraphrasing parts of the text, to Volume 3 of A. B. Ritschl's *Rechtfertigung und Versöhnung*,[34] not translated into English[35] until 1900; his one quotation he translated himself. On a date unspecified, Lidgett expressed to Lorna Horstmann[36] regret about writing long, involved sentences. This he attributed to his 'training with' [study of] German philosophers and theologians. Even when disputing others' opinions, he sought tactfully to highlight some element of truth (as he saw it) in them. Lofthouse observed[37] that he never threw away what was valuable. His debts were considerable.

Lidgett set out to challenge current orthodoxies. First was the traditional doctrine. For much of the nineteenth century the churches' major test of orthodoxy was whether believers accepted *the doctrine of penal substitution*: that Jesus appeased the wrath of God at the sin of mankind by dying in their place, thereby paying the penalty God demanded and so achieving reconciliation (atonement) between man and God. In liberal opinion,[38] however, this was crude, harsh and morally repulsive, picturing God as a sadistic tyrant, ready to punish the innocent Christ instead of the guilty. Evangelicals nevertheless continued well beyond 1900 to cling to penal substitution as 'the unchanging substance'[39] of their faith, seeing Christ's death as an act demanded by God for the salvation of mankind as a whole.

In some churches the old orthodoxy began to fade, but most Wesleyans, including college tutors like J. S. Banks, Davison and Findlay, accepted it. Though shaken and increasingly bewildered by inroads into their cherished biblical and doctrinal beliefs,[40] traditionalists still upheld the 'Godward' (as L. W. Grensted[41] used the term), *objective* interpretation of the Atonement. They resisted the liberals' 'Manward' thesis, which stressed the moral transformation the Cross produced in the individual. On this *subjective* approach Christ's death was the greatest moral act, the highest manifestation of perfect love. Both opposing theories admitted of variations and different emphases.

Many Christians believed morality could only be preserved by adhering to traditional views and rejecting whatever might be suspected of a lax attitude to sin. Closely related to controversy on the Atonement were differences about the character of God and the after life. Though Wesley had rejected Whitefield's harsh Calvinism and insisted on man's freedom to accept *and* lose what God had done for him through the Cross, belief among Wesleyans in predestination died hard. Tenets similar to Osborn's (that God fore-ordained some souls to salvation, others to damnation) were carried into the new century by prominent figures like Dinsdale Young.

Lidgett was not alone in discerning that interpretations of the Atonement, varying through the ages according to their differing views of the nature of God, related to 'the dominant conceptions of the times in which they were written'. 'They reflect', he said, 'the prevalent organisation of society, whether feudal, monarchic or constitutional, in respect of law, government and even commerce'.[42] Words like 'demand', 'acquittal', 'buying back', 'transaction' and 'sovereignty' dominated theological thought. These analogues, assuming 'submission to constituted authorities, armed with executive force, guided by traditional precedents and sustained by inherited loyalties and habits of conduct',[43] were, he said, anachronistic amid the social changes of the late nineteenth century. But the churches' static conservatism regarded any revolutionary doctrine as subversive, and *varied* images from the past compounded people's confusion.

The doctrine of Sovereignty also needed to be challenged. Developments outside the Church were changing religious ideas. Thinking in science had also been static, dominated by acceptance of fixed natural laws. The theology of Western Christendom had similarly, in Lidgett's view, been ruled by the doctrine of God's majestic Sovereignty, which Augustine expounded 'with awful rigidity', and Calvin 'inculcated' with 'increased severity'.[44] Darwin's hypothesis had revolutionised not just men's views of the Universe: it had significantly challenged views of Man and God, showing[45] that 'the present situation, in every sphere of thought and life, was the result of a gradual and all-embracing process, immanently conditioned and still incomplete'. God could no longer be seen as remote but as working within his creation. Views of God's transcendence, 'otherness' and sovereignty had to be reconciled with the equally fundamental truths of his immanence, kinship[46] . . . and his Fatherhood.

Though literalist Wesleyans still opposed Darwin's view, evolution had made it 'increasingly clear' to Lidgett that 'the doctrine of Divine Sovereignty tended unduly to separate God from his creation, to make his relationship to it altogether external'. Sovereignty also tended to explain the spiritual life in inadequate, artificial and somewhat mechanical terms,[47] running counter to believers' spiritual experience of the loving tenderness of God.[48] Theories of the Atonement had concentrated on justice and sovereignty, specific and artificial *attributes* of God, on God as 'a notion' (Maurice's word) rather than as a person. This impersonalised, even *de*personalised the relations between men and God, and people wondered, Lidgett said,[49] whether regard for his own majesty or for abstract claims of justice could really be paramount in the heart of God. So concepts like Sovereignty, inherited from Calvinistic orthodoxy, had to give way to what was for Lidgett the original and more appropriate concept of fatherly love. In evolutionary terms God's love allowed nature its course.

That this love was applied to *all* erring humanity was the view in 1828 of Thomas Erskine of Linlathen (1788–1870), from 1847 a friend and mentor of Maurice, and an influence on Lidgett. Erskine's *Unconditional Freeness of the Gospel*[50] denied, for example, that God's pardon through the blood of Christ was offered only on condition of faith: for its effectiveness God's pardon depended instead on individuals, accepting it in faith and subsequently maintaining the necessary self-discipline. In 1856 McLeod Campbell of Row (1800–72), despite his Calvinist background, had challenged traditional views by stating in *The Nature of the Atonement* that all men are pardoned: if only they would realise it, all are already by the act of God himself his children. Lidgett's *Fatherhood of God* lauded Campbell for 'his great attempt to rescue the Atonement from Calvinist and governmental explanations and to interpret it in terms of Fatherhood – of the eternal relationship between the Father and the Son'.[51]

Lidgett, however, was fascinated by a variant of the 'governmental' and 'Sovereign Ruler' concept of God and chose the *Defensio Fidei Catholicae de Satisfactione Christi adversus Faustum Socinum senensem* for special discussion. Huig de Groot (1583–1645), or Grotius, its author, was an Arminian divine, a constitutional lawyer who pleaded for international law when Dutchmen were fighting for their independence. Predictably he advanced essentially a lawyer's theory. Lidgett did not acknowledge that Grotius was, like himself, a 'child of his time'.

Grotius regarded God, not as a judge administering justice, nor as Anselm's feudal monarch, but as a ruler concerned for the highest ends of his government. Forgiving sinners because of the death of Christ was, he suggested, a 'relaxation' of the law a Rector was competent to make; the death of Christ was exacted, not as the equivalent of punishing sinners, but as 'the most striking means of placing in a clear light the character of God, and heinousness of sin, and the authority of the law'.[52] God, therefore, combined both clemency *and* severity, hatred of sin *and* care for preserving the law. These attributes, he said, might be manifested through punishment of someone other than the sinner. As God incarnate and destined to be connected with the human race as its head, Christ fulfilled both provisos.

Lidgett's concept of Fatherhood in effect modified the governmental theory. He objected to Grotius' interpretation of God's sovereignty; moreover God's kingdom differed in substantial ways from human governments. For Lidgett the display of God's nature had to depend on being 'a *fulfilment* of all righteousness, and not a *relaxation* of it'.[53]

In essence Lidgett set out from a conservative base, but sought an acceptable modification of the objective theory. He insisted on the inescapable significance of human sin, the wrath and justice of God, and the salvific aspect of the Cross. To him subjective theorists had emasculated the Atonement. They had recognised 'the overwhelming appeal of God to man' by Jesus, but failed to couple this with Jesus' equally vital *Godward* activity in making 'an all-availing "sacrifice, oblation and satisfaction for the sins of the whole world" to God on behalf of man'.[54] But, in conscious opposition to many colleagues, the theory of Christ's death as *substitution*, *instead of* us, was to him unethical. He preferred, like Maurice,[55] to see Christ as acting *on behalf* of us, our 'actual representative'. In Lidgett's formulation, Christ secured the *satisfaction* of God by dying as our *representative*, 'putting away sin on our behalf'. This gave 'satisfaction' an emotional connotation absent from its original Medieval context.

Wesleyans had long maintained the substitutionary view. George Cubitt, a Connexional editor, for example, had firmly stated: 'Christ died in our stead, not only for our benefit'.[56] In his Fernley lecture of 1871 Pope, thinking it unsafe to concentrate on one theory, suggested a compromise: 'He [Christ] is not the Substitute of God, but His Representative; and not otherwise our Substitute than as our Representative also'.[57] Reading Hebrews taught him to see the resurrected Christ supremely as Mediator, the High Priest representing men before God and achieving their reconciliation. Pope's *Compendium* said this had to be 'wrought out by a SACRIFICE of OBEDIENCE in life and death, which has PROPITIATED God in respect to sin'.[58] Lidgett accepted his 'Sacrifice of Obedience', and the concept of propitiation quoted from Hebrews. He too believed the 'sacrifice' of Christ was the means whereby God took the initiative, sin was *punished*, justice was served and men were enabled to become 'at one' with God.

Lidgett's thinking on the 'satisfaction' of God through the sufferings and death of Christ contained a residual element of Calvinism. Maurice by contrast believed Christ's death was an expression of voluntary obedience, *not* the satisfaction of a demand by God's justice; the Atonement was an assurance that God really was self-sacrificing love, neither a bargain nor a matter of punishment and rewards. Lidgett, however, insisted that sin provoked the essentially altruistic wrath of God and required divine *punishment*. His God had 'a hard centre'. But God's wrath, to him,[59] was not Horace Bushnell's independent 'impulsive, indeed an explosive wrath-principle', which, as with all moral agents including God, Bushnell admitted had to be brought under the further control of Wisdom.

McLeod Campbell had argued that 'while Christ suffered for our sins as an atoning sacrifice, what He suffered was not – because from its nature it could not be – a punishment'.[60] His sufferings, he believed, were not externally imposed, but an act of *vicarious penitence* for the whole human race: Christ thereby showed to mankind both what sin means (what pain it gives) to an all-holy God and that he, as the loving son of that holy God, fully sympathised with God's condemnation of it.

Lidgett found that quite inadequate. In his view Campbell[61] had treated Christ's self-sacrifice as 'wholly relative to sin', as too exclusively the response to God's condemnation of sin, and not *primarily* the response to the demand of God for righteousness.[62] Moreover Christ's alleged attitude of repentance seemed incompatible with his attested sinlessness.[63] It was Christ's *death* that was vicarious, he argued, not as simple substitution, but in the sense that what Christ did for us was both necessary to be done and impossible for us to do.[64] For Lidgett God's characteristics included transcendence and justice requiring satisfaction; both should be reflected in any adequate theory of the Atonement.

Nevertheless Lidgett took Manward theories seriously. His belief in the immanence of God, each individual's spiritual experience, and the spiritual nature of the Atonement, revealed some sympathy for a psychological, subjective stance. He decided to comment on three subjective protagonists.

Lidgett chose to comment first on Bushnell and Ritschl as the most strenuous opponents of any doctrine of satisfaction on account of sin. Both interpreted the Atonement in terms of its moral influence. Lidgett readily acknowledged ethical factors had to be considered. Ritschl, for example, had, he agreed, rightly emphasised that 'the relations between man and God are ethical, that ethics belong to a higher realm than law and government, and that therefore legal and governmental necessities cannot be treated as the supreme grounds of the divine action'.[65] But Lidgett argued it did not follow that (in a civilised community) a command was unconnected with ethics. The necessities that Lidgett claimed were associated with God were not, he said, *imposed* on God, but part of his nature.

Several of Ritschl's concepts were expressed in the Bermondsey Settlement: the social nature of personality and the principle of self-sacrificial love, for example. But Lidgett thought Ritschl wrong to base on the former his thesis that the creation of a community unified by acceptance of the latter was the *principal* purpose of Christ's death. Forgiveness of sins was not achieved through the community for which Christ died. To be valid, Atonement had to have a Godward, not primarily a Manward focus.

Westcott's *Victory of the Cross* would have pleased Lidgett by rejecting theories of substitution and legal transaction, and by using the Fatherhood of God image.[66] But he objected to Westcott's thesis that: 'It is the subjective influence of the sacrifice first upon Christ, and then upon men, by which its end is interpreted'.[67] It was insufficient for Westcott simply to say, that[68] 'By dying to sin in the power of Christ's sacrifice, the believer is quickened to righteousness, and becomes a true son within the family of God, a son who is now ready to share in the discipline of Christ's sufferings for the sake of others'.

Lidgett agreed that Christ's sufferings 'did evoke [in him] a response in which lay the manifestation of his highest spiritual capabilities', which 'draws out the sympathy, aspiration and imitation of those who believe in him'.[69] He endorsed Westcott's comments on the disciplinary character of Christ's sufferings: Christ's incarnate nature grew to perfection and needed discipline for its growth. But Lidgett insisted on understanding 'Christ made perfect through sufferings' as 'a perfecting of character in order to (*sic*) His priestly ministry'. To Lidgett, Christ's victory in, through and over his sufferings 'was not only the means of His own and our perfecting; it was, above all, the consummation, and constituted the merit, of His satisfaction to God for sin'.[70]

Lidgett commended Fairbairn's *Place of Christ in Modern Theology*, but surprisingly made no comment on his (albeit brief) section on the Atonement. Lidgett would have been pleased that he strongly affirmed the love and justice (or righteousness) of God, reconciled them together, and objected to substitution and God's judgement as 'juridical'. Praise[71] was explicit for his treatment of the Fatherhood of God and of Christ as the Head, basis and symbol of a new mankind.[72] As 'growingly' accepted by Fairbairn and others, the doctrine of the Trinity was, as Lidgett said, 'the best justification of our faith in the personality, the reason, the love – in short in the whole spiritual life of God',[73] and Fairbairn had unequivocally exposed 'the nature and desert of sin'.[74]

Though Fairbairn's description of the Atonement 'appeared perfectly orthodox',[75] it was in fact unusual. He spoke of a sacrifice made by the Father in giving his Son to die for the world, thereby exhibiting 'God as a Being who does not need to be appeased or moved to mercy, but suffers unto sacrifice that he may save',[76] and then said the Atonement was:

> designed to create in man all the effects of corrective and remedial sufferings to do the work of restorative and reformatory penalties, only it accomplishes this in a more efficient mode than could the sufferings themselves. It burns into the soul of the sinner the sense of the evil and shame of sin, forces him to look at it with God's eyes, to judge it with his conscience, to hate it with his hate – in a word to change his own attitude to it for God's.[77]

The drift of Lidgett's argument shows he would have rejected such a subjective approach.

Lidgett was influenced by new thinking on the relation of the Cross to the Incarnation. Guided by Maurice and Kingsley, Lidgett found the clue to the Cross lay in shifting the focus to the Incarnation, a significant departure from orthodox Evangelical belief.[78] Christ's work on the Cross had been placed centre-stage both because of the vivid way it was experienced in conversion, and because Atonement offered by the Cross was seen as God's remedy for the Fall of Man. By contrast Maurice, Westcott and others had refused to accept the Incarnation as the direct result of the Fall: it was God's plan from the time of Creation itself.

On this basis the Incarnation was seen as *the way* to the Cross and the Atonement. For Lidgett the starting point for doctrine

> must not be with the Fall and its remedial treatment, but with the eternal purpose of the Father . . . Atonement and Redemption . . . set right what is wrong by the fulfilment *for* man and *in* man of what has ever been the constitutive . . . Truth of human nature.[79]

For Lidgett this had distinct advantages. Repellent technicalities, abstractions and illegitimate analogies could be overcome if the Cross was understood in the light of the Incarnation and the Fatherhood of God. Moreover, he could regard the Incarnation as the central answer to the fundamental question of the relationship between God and Man, from which guidance and understanding on the major issues of human life could be derived. Lidgett found it the

> supreme fact . . . not only the highest truth of theology, but the practical principle, divinely given and immanently real, for the understanding of man and for the ordering of human life in all its relationships and concerns . . . The Incarnation made manifest the spiritual structure of the Universe, revealed its originating motive and its final end . . . [80]

The consistent formula Lidgett sought now fell into place. The Incarnation provided wholeness, combining spiritual and social, family, nation and mankind, the Church and humanity in an indivisible whole.[81] Christ's life should be seen as 'a consistent whole of spiritual self-realisation in and through his filial obedience', and the 'costingness' of this sacrifice 'was due, not to the arbitrary exaction of God, but to the sinful imperfection of the world and its results, as conditioned by the constitution and discipline of human life'.[82]

But the changed emphasis, although evident elsewhere, was not without criticism. Apprehension had surfaced in the 1892 annual Conference address to the Methodist Societies, signed by Rigg as President:

> We rejoice in the prominence which is being given to the doctrine of the Incarnation, with all its solemn lessons and inspirations. But we must be careful lest the Cross passes into the background from which it is the glory of our fathers to have drawn it. Give to the *death* of Christ its true place in your own experience and in your Christian work – as a witness to the real and profound evil of sin . . . as the only effectual appeal to the general heart of men, and, above all, as the Atonement for our sins.[83]

Surprisingly, *The Spiritual Principle* contained no explicit reference to the kenosis theory, a major feature of theological thinking about the Incarnation over the previous decade. Its principal expositor was Charles Gore, who in 1889 edited *Lux Mundi*, subtitled *A Series of Studies on the Religion of the Incarnation*. But none of Lidgett's works until 1934[84] mentioned directly either the word 'kenosis' or Gore's theological views. Lidgett's applause for Fairbairn[85] did not include support for the self-emptying of Christ.

Lidgett, like Pope,[86] had rejected the kenotic theory. Remaining firmly wedded to the orthodox Christology,[87] he interpreted Philippians as simply stating that Christ humbled himself through his self-sacrificial life and death on earth, without any connotation of wider-ranging limits to his divinity. His comments were indirect: 'Deny the Divinity of our Lord, and the satisfaction to the deepest needs of men afforded by these words [John 14.9 and 10.30], or rather by the reality they set forth, is destroyed. God has not then entered into the sphere of humanity.'[88]

Lidgett's view was again implicit in the 1907 *Bermondsey Settlement Magazine*[89] and in 1915 in his *God in Christ Jesus*: Christ 'could not be what he is or achieve what he does were he not at once truly God and perfectly man'.[90]

Again derived from Maurice and others and central to Lidgett's thesis was also the notion of the Antecedent Christ, belief that Jesus was the 'Head of the Human Race' and we have kinship with him. As Jesus was the Son of the Father of mankind, so Jesus is related to *all other sons* who constitute the human race. Lidgett declared:

> His relationship with the Father carried with it His creatorship and His unceasing relationship, both to the Universe which He had created and to mankind as its culmination. And, on the other hand, Christ could not have taken up the place which He did in their spiritual life as Saviour, and effected what He did, had there not existed beforehand a natural relationship between Him and them – nay, had He not been the creator and eternal Lord of those whom He redeemed, and in whose hearts He reigned. His whole position relative to them implied Godhead, and not only that, but *Godhead in a special kinship to mankind.*[91]

This thesis was then linked with the Atonement:

> His relationship to the human race and His consequent Incarnation, enabled Him, and Him alone to *give complete expression* under our penal conditions, to the submission of mankind to God, to make reparation to His law and to put away sin from man. An atoner other than human, other than perfect, other than originally and universally related to the race, could not have effected this – the indispensable condition of Atonement.[92]

If Lidgett was to make the Fatherhood of God central to his thesis, it had to be properly understood. He had to counter false notions, not least the sentimentality the doctrine connoted for some of his contemporaries. Some theologians, Lidgett said, repelled by the severe and artificial doctrine generally held in his youth, had reduced it to 'the appeal of the Love of God, made pathetic and constraining by the Cross of Christ, to men to renounce the alienation and selfishness of sin and to be "reconciled to God" as his Sons.'[93] The biblical doctrine had been emasculated, he said, elements of spiritual and moral weakness had been apparent; and 'the sovereignty of God and the righteous ends which he seeks and demands in the life of man have been obscured'.[94] God's 'Fatherhood and compassionateness' were being treated as almost convertible terms.[95] Insisting on God's love and concern for the whole sinful race did not for Lidgett entail sentimental belief in God as an *indulgent* parent, too ready to forgive, too good-natured to inflict any punishment at all.

Moreover, Lidgett thought this interpretation put an exclusive focus on the Cross. Christ's 'two-fold deed', as Apostle (bringing God's appeal to man) and as High Priest (making an all-availing 'sacrifice, oblation and satisfaction for the sins of the whole world'), must, he felt, be 'our Lord's entire incarnate life'. It was 'consummated by the death of the Cross, but spiritually implicit from the first, not externally imposed at the end of his earthly course'.[96] The Incarnation and the Atonement, Christ's life and passion, our creation and redemption should, he thought, be regarded as a whole.

A further notion to be countered was that of an External Law, promoted for example by Bushnell and Dale. Lidgett admired Dale, not least for his 'robust manliness' (his virile grasp of the stern reality of the wrath of God), his 'ethical fervour' and 'evangelical faith'. Dale's convictions became Lidgett's: the objective stance on the Atonement; its ethical, not arbitrary or forensic aspect; the Cross as demonstrating the Love of God; the relevance to the Atonement of the Father/Son relationship. Lidgett like Dale rejected the Atonement as a *transaction* between Father and Son, and strongly insisted on the *penal* quality of Christ's death, giving it its saving power, and on Jesus' voluntary acceptance of the sacrifice of his own life as Head and Representative of humanity. Dale also dismissed Calvinists' view of Christ's death as saving the elect from hell.

Dale, however, attached juridical significance to Christ's death, treating the Cross as entailed by the need to satisfy and vindicate an impersonal 'Eternal Law of Righteousness'. Dale's Law was seen as *apart* from the divine being, and to its authority Christ was alleged to submit. Lidgett, however, like Maurice, could not accept the existence of any law in parallel, still less superior to God's (loving) Fatherhood. Moreover Dale lacked the spiritual emphasis: 'Surely all spiritual satisfaction for transgression of the law involves an act of spiritual adhesion to the law'.[97]

Bushnell had also posited an eternal law, independent of God, and with God as its first obedient subject. He said it was vital for Christ to honour the law by his obedience, incarnation and vicarious sacrifice, if his task, of re-establishing the power of the law in the hearts of mankind, was to be achieved. But 'externalising' the divine law was anathema to Lidgett,[98] Bushnell's even more grievous than Dale's

All this detailed discussion of the Atonement debate leads up to Lidgett's own thesis, a statement of the 'Spiritual Principle'. For him the real basis of penal satisfaction was not to be located in an 'Eternal Law', but in the nature of Fatherhood itself. In his view God's justice and wrath co-existed within his nature with his fatherly love for the human race; his holiness and love were uniquely combined; immanence and kinship should be seen to qualify and transform, not to displace his transcendence; Fatherhood and sovereignty were not mutually exclusive, neither were love and justice.

Lidgett justified this by a personal interpretation of the Atonement in terms of the relationship between a father and his son or sons. 'Typical' fatherhood, as he saw it in his *Fatherhood of God*, featured both a 'supremacy of love' which 'promotes the well-being of the child' together with the 'practical omnipotence' by which the father secures respect for his commands.[99] Lidgett's exposition in *The Spiritual Principle* warrants quotation *in extenso*:

> In dealing with a disobedient and rebellious child the father has to do justice to his own character and will as an authority over the child, – an authority representing the ideal of what the child should become and guiding him on the way to its realisation. He has to assert the sanctity of the law which has been broken and to secure its recognition. He has to bring home to the child the consciousness of wrong-doing. All this is the work of punishment . . . Satisfaction is made by an act which, in its various aspects, is at once a submission to the father's authority, an offering of homage and reparation to the law, an expression of agreement with the father's mind, and a surrender to his love. All this . . . can be expressed only . . . through that condition of punishment . . . entailed upon the child by his wrong-doing. The punishment . . . by the father is made the very means of uttering the conversion of the child.[100]

Lidgett thought Maurice right to say Christ's sacrifice did not change God's mind towards his creatures, and mercy was not wanting in the Father, but mistaken in failing to recognise that the claims of justice, demanding punishment, could not be denied before God's forgiveness could be given.[101] That called for a detailed description of the nature of a father's anger and forgiveness:

> And a father's forgiveness is more than the pardon of a King. The pardoned rebel goes free. His release from penalties, however, does not imply reception into favour. But the forgiveness of a child is his restoration to the fellowship of life and love. And the first condition of that restoration is that the sanctity of the parental and filial bond, – of the law and of the spirit which are based upon that bond – should be so effectively honoured, as to enthrone them in the heart of the child . . . The father, therefore, as the guardian of the family bond, of the law which is the condition of the life of the child, inflicts the punishment which vindicates them. He is wrath until the child comes to the true mind with regard to them. His anger has nothing of personal resentment . . . nothing of harsh exaction about it. It is in the interest of the child himself and is felt to be so by the child. It cannot be waived.[102]

To Lidgett what most influences the child to make satisfaction is the sense that the demand for righteousness is the demand of love. God was not primarily sovereign or judge, but by grace fundamentally our Father. Sonship and right relations can only be restored through such satisfaction; they are 'proved only by homage to the violated law, in submission to the punishment which expresses the mind of the father and asserts the supremacy of the law'.

Both father and son play their part: 'The fundamental condition of fatherly satisfaction is that it shall satisfy the fatherly by perfecting the filial . . . The satisfaction offered perfects the filial response of Him who offers it, and of them, in Him, for whom it is offered.'[103]

The Spiritual Principle of the Atonement, the principle containing all others, was therefore his version of the Fatherhood of God. Lidgett expressed his thesis thus:

> The satisfying principle in our Lord's death was none other than His complete surrender and obedience to His Father in manifesting His own life as the Son throughout His earthly life – but especially in death – under the penal conditions prescribed for him by His Incarnation and consequent union with the race of sinful men.[104]

Accordingly propitiation and reconciliation were gained not by Christ's sufferings and death in themselves, but by the spirit in which they were endured. Rupert Davies rightly called satisfaction as loving obedience 'an idea far removed from emphasis on the blood of the Lamb spilt to appease an angry God'.[105] Though not a subjective version of the Atonement, Lidgett's theory avoided 'the harshness of some transactional theories'.[106] As Lidgett explained in 1913, because Christ was 'related both to God and Man', his Atonement was 'the act of both'; it was 'an acceptance on behalf of man of righteousness as the principle of life'; and it offered 'eternal life in fellowship with God'.[107]

Lidgett's *Spiritual Principle* had a social message. Davison's review accurately predicted: 'The truths here expounded on Fatherhood and Sonship may well lead to a life devoted to enforcing the principle of Brotherhood'.[108] It was Lidgett's application of the Fatherhood of God to social, educational and ecumenical concerns, and his link between theology and action, that was to make the greater impact outside his denomination than his personal interpretation of the Atonement. A similarly apt verdict by W. Strawson has compared Lidgett's work with Wesleyan views then current, and called the social thrust, derived from Maurice, which Lidgett constantly impressed on others, especially his Wesleyan colleagues, 'an interesting departure from the individualism and "other-worldliness" which tended to vitiate contemporary theories of the Atonement'.[109] Lofthouse commented:

> There are no 'joins' to be seen where Mr Lidgett's theology passes into his exposition of the principles of human progress: both are sides of one and the

> same thing, Christ's headship of the race and Christ's purposes for the race.[110]

Lidgett did not acknowledge the importance for his own social message of Dale's last chapter on the Atonement, although there were obvious points of affinity. David Thompson pointed out that, having centred his understanding on the Incarnation, Dale had explained the significance of the Atonement 'in terms of the redemption of the race', ensuring that the gospel could not be presented as 'purely individualistic'.[111]

Lidgett's final chapter, 'The Principle of the Atonement and Social Progress', expressed *his* link between the Cross and all that 'Sonship' (a concept he found had a greater impact than 'Incarnation') implies. Talking of the believer's reception through Christ's Spirit of 'all which His Cross sets forth', he said:

> The renewal and perfecting of society is the task set before those whose life is rooted in Christ . . . The fuller realisation of the filial spirit will have its immediate effects upon political, social, and economic interests, ordering them in growing conformity to the mind of Christ . . . The keener apprehension of spiritual relationships may even lead some Christian men to concentrate their efforts upon political and economic reform, or upon the improvement of the general environment of the people . . . But ultimately the regeneration of individuals and the practical authority of the revelation of Christ are the essence of human progress . . . Only by the law of service, ungrudgingly rendered in free spirit to God on behalf of men, at the cost of the self-sacrifice which is the price of love and righteousness alike, can the progress of mankind be secured. The principle of the Lord's death is both the end and the way.[112]

Changes in theological views also exercised an influence on politics during the nineteenth century, but the extent and dominance of that influence is debated. Boyd Hilton[113] has controversially emphasised strong links between economic, social and theological thought in that period. The theologians' change of emphasis from the Cross to the Incarnation, from eternal and vicarious punishment to Christ's compassion and solidarity with mankind, he saw as connected with the shift from 'the aggressive individualism' of the earlier 'half' of the century (his 'Age of Atonement') towards sympathy with increasing government intervention and the growth of Christian social action (his 'Age of Incarnation'). To him the change in moral and theological perspective by 1870 was much more significant than any alteration in pure economic theory, or (*pace* Edward Norman)[114] Anglican concern to win over the lower orders or respond to the prevailing secular intellectual and economic culture. Hilton's argument is complex, and worked out principally in relation to Anglican, not Nonconformist, Evangelicals who were active 30 years or so earlier than Lidgett's preparation of his *Spiritual Principle*.

The political philosophy with which Hilton associates 'Moderate Evangelicals' in his period was, however, strong in Lidgett's early life. It featured a laissez-faire view, leaving individuals to work out their own salvation, exercise 'self-help' (the only way to both spiritual and economic salvation), and interpret temptation, pain and misery as working for inner improvement. It can be identified with the so-called 'Old Liberalism' pursued by Gladstone. Optimistically[115] this connoted belief that nothing was impossible to achieve by appealing to men's reason, by promoting general welfare through individuals' voluntary action, and by removing only such obstacles as would prevent their 'essential goodness' from 'functioning freely'. 'Individualism' and 'Voluntaryism' were the catchwords, and the State was to do nothing that individuals could do for themselves.

Lidgett came to oppose Christians' adherence to a purely individualistic gospel and reliance principally on personal philanthropy in response to it. Theological convictions, similar to those which led him to emphasise instead the importance of wider social concern, had been circulating among 'Christian Socialists' like Maurice for some time[116] before Lidgett found his own way of articulating them. The late Victorian revival of this concern sought to oppose individualism and shift the focus towards society and its urgent problems, ready to identify environmental causes of poverty and call on the churches both to act and persuade the State to act. For their contribution in expounding their views of the 'Social Gospel' evangelical Nonconformists (not least R. W. Dale, J. B. Paton, A. M. Fairbairn and H. P. Hughes) deserve as much recognition as Anglicans like B. F. Westcott, Scott Holland and Stewart Headlam.[117]

Undoubtedly parallel ideas and alarm on discovering the incidence of poverty can be found among secular thinkers and Christian Socialists of all denominations and types of churchmanship, but changes in popular thought and their effects were more complex than Hilton or Norman supposed. Theology clearly made an impact, but neither Evangelicalism nor Christian Socialists were alone in affecting approaches to secular politics at the end of the century: Utilitarianism (a continuing influence from early in the century), economic thought and theorists (not least J. A. Hobson) were also involved.

From these a New Liberalism[118] had begun to emerge, seeking to justify the free market by making it work 'fairly': adherents found 'voluntaryism' was not enough. New Liberals saw many national problems as having social, not personal, causes, and the way to improvement as through increased State action, removing obstacles to personal freedom and development, not relying on individuals' personal moral regeneration. Their aim was marginally to adjust the existing capitalist system by mitigating its harmful effects on people incapable of fending for themselves. Much influenced by fellow Nonconformists both in theology and its social application, Lidgett developed a natural affinity with the New Liberals. Their policies accorded with his belief in 'ordered progress', or, as Lofthouse put it, 'progress within certain limits which he had no wish to overstep',[119] and it was such policies that Lidgett decided to pursue within the London municipal context. But comment on his political involvement will come later.

4

Response to *The Spiritual Principle of the Atonement*

Lidgett was immediately suspected of heresy. Marshall Randles (1828–1904), Didsbury's Theology tutor and Conference President in 1896/7, upheld at proof stage charges by an unnamed 'clerical reviewer' that *The Spiritual Principle* 'did not take sufficient account of Divine Justice', and stated that 'if the Fernley lecture was established to support Methodist doctrines, then this lecture was not entitled to a place in the series'.[1] Thus *Reminiscences*. The later autobiography amplified the strictures: Lidgett had 'ignored the demands of divine justice and therefore the penal character of our Lord's sufferings' and 'shifted the emphasis from the Cross to the Incarnation, from the death to the life of Christ'.[2] The charge of Incarnationalism was to be expected, but criticism of Lidgett's treatment of God's justice and Christ's penal suffering was surprising. Randles's attitude, however, was predictable: he had already written[3] on substitution, retribution and the doom of endless suffering.[4] At Randles's funeral, W. L. Watkinson (1838–1925) said that Randles 'was not the man to reconcile us to a dark subject by poetic touches, and the severe style of treatment had offended some'.[5]

Randles, however, 'did not proceed to extremities'.[6] Evidently second thoughts, on whatever basis, prevented him from imposing a ban. Kelly went ahead and published the book. Lidgett did not alter his text, but took care to mention the honoured names of Pope and Moulton in his Preface. Dedicating the book to Moulton might also have been calculated to thwart or mitigate opposition to its publication and any subsequent attack. In his *Guided Life* he said that he offered to withdraw the dedication,[7] but Moulton refused, stating his readiness to defend the book in Conference, if necessary. In *Reminiscences*[8] Lidgett stated that he went to Leeds unsure whether his lecture would be delivered or his book published. His confidence would have been strengthened by knowing that Moulton had read and commented on his manuscript. In the event all was well, and Conference voiced no objection.

Lidgett escaped significant censure for several other reasons. Not least important were the length of his book (a 'record' for size, Hope Moulton, W. F. Moulton's son, called it),[9] and the complex density of its argument. Some reviewers were initially uncertain what to make of it; readers may well have been deterred from wrestling with it at all! Davison, then of Handsworth College, confessed he had to read the book several times, and could not decide 'on first impressions' whether Lidgett's insistence on Fatherhood being 'the sole relationship' with mankind was 'a success or failure'.[10] Even H. P. Hughes admitted the book was 'far too argumentative to enable anyone of lower rank than a professor of theology to pronounce at once on its merits'.[11] The *London Quarterly Review* suggested compression would have added to its effectiveness.[12] Time was clearly needed to plough through the work, summarise its arguments and appraise its significance. Hasty reading inevitably led to misinterpretation. Even in the Bampton Lectures 18 years later Hastings Rashdall[13] regarded Lidgett as a defender of substitution.

Lidgett would have remained apprehensive after the 1897 Conference that adverse comment, based on maturer reflection, might build up before the 1898 Conference. Fortunately for him another publication dominated attention instead. Agar Beet (1840–1924) of Richmond College caused a furore soon after July 1897 by publishing *The Last Things*,[14] which denied that the Bible taught an eternity of conscious suffering for unrepentant sinners. Though the Wesleyan Theological Committee decided against action, anger increased until, at the 1898 Conference, on a motion supported by two 'die-hards', Randles and Watkinson, the 1897/8 President, he was required to withdraw the book and promise not to issue another edition.

Though on the alert for damaging reviews, Lidgett found to his relief that these did not charge him with 'heresy'. Reviewers who objected generally damned him with faint praise.

The most hostile was W. R. Nicoll (1851–1923),[15] the Presbyterian editor of the *British Weekly*, no friend of Lidgett as later events showed. While calling Lidgett a competent scholar, many of whose words deserved serious consideration, Nicoll devoted almost all his article to a devastating attack on Lidgett's tedious style and lack of evangelical warmth; these he compared unfavourably with the work of McLeod Campbell. For example:

> It will not, we believe, be admitted that Mr. Lidgett is successful in his reconstruction of the doctrine . . . Nor is it likely that his book will make any impression on the religious mind. The extreme aridity of his treatment will prevent this.
>
> If there is any reflection of the glory of the Cross, it is at best lunar, without brilliancy, passion and warmth, though with occasional glimpses of a pale, but true beauty.[16]

Lidgett simply commented that Nicoll 'bore witness to the book's orthodoxy'.[17] In 1957 Lofthouse perhaps revealed Lidgett's true reaction: Lidgett, he said, was 'galled' by an unnamed reviewer saying 'he did not write like a sinner saved by grace'.[18]

Beet was the reviewer for the *Wesleyan Methodist Magazine* in October 1897.[19] He cordially commended the new volume, 'with an earnest hope that we shall hear much more from one whom God has evidently fitted to be a teacher in His Church'. Lidgett, however, would have resented the rather patronising tone of the college tutor. Beet viewed the book as 'a valuable addition to the literature of the subject, not in any way superseding or surpassing, but supplementing the great work of Dr Dale'. Where Lidgett attempted to correct Dale, Beet could not agree. Interestingly Dale, not Lidgett, was chosen by the Anglican, R. C. Moberly,[20] for comment in 1901.

Beet agreed that the Fatherhood doctrine, already in vogue, 'sheds light' on the Atonement. But he lamented Lidgett's decision not to provide an exhaustive proof that God's Fatherhood of all mankind was the characteristic revelation of Christ, or that 'the whole action of God towards man may be explained *along the lines* of the noblest human fatherhood'. Moreover, 'Neither he [Paul], nor any other writer in the New Testament ever connects the death of Christ with God's fatherly relation to mankind'. Beet could not 'conceive a father condemning his son to death except by bringing in a relation other than that of father'. Lidgett's thesis, he thought, went a long way to asserting universal salvation.

In the *Methodist Recorder*[21] Hope Moulton also expressed concern about the book's implications for the afterlife. He applauded theologians' rejection of a 'milk and water theology, degrading God to the level of a weak parent who spoils his children because he cannot bring himself to punish them for their good': Lidgett's feature was the systematic application of the fatherly relation of God as including and conditioning the other relations including his wrath. Yet he felt bound to record 'the one most serious problem . . . almost in deeper darkness than before', the prospect of eternal punishment as a direct consequence of divine Fatherhood: Scripture assigned 'endless doom' to the man 'who has proved hopelessly and finally unbrotherly', and this would be inflicted by his heavenly Father.

The unnamed reviewer in the *London Quarterly Review* impugned Lidgett's intellectual rigour:

> We do not see how the idea of satisfaction to God can be retained apart from the judicial character. Whatever repugnance there may be in the modern mind to judicial or forensic representations of God's dealings, they seem inevitable to logical thought.[22]

Banks of Headingley College took a similar view. He had supported the orthodox doctrine and opposed the Abelardian (subjective) theory and Maurice's views in his 1887 *Manual of Christian Doctrine*. In his eighth edition, partly rewritten in 1902, he felt obliged to refer, albeit briefly, to Lidgett's 'thoughtful volume', but viewed his attempt to incorporate the demand for satisfaction in the fatherly character of God as 'more daring and ingenious than successful'.[23] The two domains of Father and Ruler/Judge were, he maintained, quite distinct.

The *Methodist Times* review, commissioned by H. P. Hughes, was written by W. T. Davison.[24] Davison's support in his 1888 Fernley lecture for penal substitution[25] did not augur well; but in the event his review, though characteristically cautious, proved reassuring. Davison rightly decided that 'In a large part of his exposition Mr. Scott Lidgett coincides with the majority of evangelical theologians'. He had provided 'no new truth' but restated 'an old truth', 'free . . . from many excrescences which . . . had hidden its true beauty', and offered 'a new point of view'. An excellent service had been 'rendered . . . by pointing out the dangers of . . . dwelling on what is "due" to an abstract principle, instead of the living God'. Davison commented: Lidgett 'brings everything to the test of Scripture'. He had not explained 'substitution' away, 'though he rightly insists, as Dr Pope . . . on the dangers attending the use of this word and on the impossibility of regarding the vicarious work of Jesus Christ as substitution pure and simple'. Davison's reference to Lidgett's firm scriptural base and link with the much-respected Pope would have gone far to calm fears among the 'Old Guard'.

Lidgett was especially pleased that the *Spiritual Principle* was seen indirectly to refute slanders about his Bermondsey work. In 1936 the *Methodist Recorder*[26] quoted him as saying that *The Spiritual Principle* 'led many to realise that what was thought to be undue secularity of temper . . . was intended by me to be an expression of profound spiritual faith'. This secularity charge, voiced almost from the Settlement's beginning, was repeated in Nicoll's snide 1897 review. He had seen it as a hopeful sign that the book could come not only from a Methodist but also from one in charge of the London Settlement where 'it has often struck us with misgiving that the preaching of a Gospel for the sinner has been allowed to take a secondary place, if not altogether to disappear'. By 1898 Lidgett was able to take this criticism in his stride.

What then did Lidgett achieve? The significance of *The Spiritual Principle* lay largely among contemporary Methodists. Most reviewers had been impressed by his scholarship, and none of their reservations affected his thinking. The treatise staked his claim to be a theologian of some substance among his colleagues. In 1936 Lidgett was justified in saying it 'gave me a certain position in the Churches and in theological institutions'.[27] But his boast[28] that his lecture was used as a textbook in many theological colleges of denominations throughout the English-speaking world may well be unjustified. In 1910 the Wesleyan Book Steward was advertising *The Spiritual Principle* as 'the greatest book in modern times on the subject', but complimenting an outgoing President was predictable. The *Methodist Recorder*'s adulatory obituary exaggerated wildly by saying: 'Before he was 43 he had stepped into the front rank of British theologians with his Fernley lecture'.[29]

What he had done was to help Wesleyans and perhaps some Nonconformists to inform themselves about major theological ideas on the Atonement over the previous 50 years. He had indulged his passion to educate. It was Maurice's thinking, despite some reservations, that excited him and he wanted most to popularise. He showed courage. He had been, in Munsey Turner's words,[30] 'the one Methodist thinker to take Frederick Denison Maurice's view of Christ as the Head of the human race rather than John Wesley as his starting point', and get away with it! Circuit ministers may have heard of Maurice, but their reading tended to concentrate on the Bible, some commentaries and a few published sermons. Their energies had focused on preaching, pastoral work and, for many, on building new churches.

In effect Lidgett had said nothing really new. He was, however, satisfied to have humanised objective theories without exposing the Church to the dangers many had seen in relaxations of orthodoxy; and though he had reinterpreted the doctrine in several respects, most of their central convictions, including spiritual relationships with God, remained intact.

What had Lidgett achieved on the wider, national scene? His thesis depended on his choice of analogy, no doubt based on experience of his own father. F. W. Dillistone[31] reacted by commenting on the contemporary social context. Like Strawson in 1983,[32] he found Lidgett's (patriarchal, rather than paternal) image of the Father was even in 1897 becoming outdated, if not already obsolete. Family life was already changing: family members' personalities allowed to develop in their own right, and the father's former status in decline. In Dillistone's view:

> Lidgett is still living and writing within a context of law: the authority of a father to represent a transcendent law, to determine when and how it has been infringed, to judge what constitutes an appropriate reparation or punishment. A son's primary virtue is obedience, even submission. . . . These principles are taken for granted, and in consequence we really have a . . . humanisation of legal and penal concepts, not an altogether new exploration of the father–son relationship in the light of changing attitudes in the world of late nineteenth and early twentieth centuries.[33]

Lidgett could thus be described as a writer almost behind his time.

From his national perspective in 1957 Rupp said Lidgett's first three works had 'little survival value'.[34] Lidgett had presented a strong, personal version of much classical teaching on the Atonement without making any significant advance. Of Nonconformist treatises Dale's had made the greater impact. Complimenting Lidgett in January 1933[35] on seven editions of *The Spiritual Principle*, Lofthouse said few books on the Atonement had run into as many as three. Yet Dale had notched up 25 by 1909. Anglican writers on theology virtually ignored Lidgett's book.

In terms of theological trends at the time Lidgett was already out of date. Much nineteenth century theology was drifting strongly towards variations on the Manward doctrine, away from his own position. This was evident in many of the writers whose views Lidgett had found wanting.

Substitution, however, continued to be upheld by evangelicals, such as Bishop Moule,[36] and the Nonconformist James Denney.[37] Moule, for example, agreed substitution was not in the Bible, but various passages left him wondering how else to express their meaning. The fundamentalist journal the *Record* was advocating substitution in 1924. Theologians were reluctant to abandon the objective view altogether, though arguments for its alternative seemed compelling.

That was well illustrated, just over three years after Lidgett's book, by R. C. Moberly's *Atonement and Personality*. Retaining the objective theory was clearly an effort. Though he did not entirely succeed, his work gained more lasting and widespread fame than *The Spiritual Principle*. Moberly reacted to Dale's *over*emphasis on the Atonement as outside humanity and *under*emphasis on its impact through the Holy Spirit.[38] Without referring to Lidgett's analogy, his picture of a father was similarly patriarchal. Using ideas of personality emerging from the then embryonic science of psychology, he explored what perfect penitence, punishment and forgiveness might, and could not imply within a human family. Though, he maintained, perfect penitence was essential for forgiveness but impossible for sinful mankind, Christ, being identified with both God and Man, was uniquely able to unite perfect penitence, expressed on behalf of mankind, with the perfect forgiveness of God. Moberly thought Christ's mediation between man and God resembled a mother's mediation between a father and their naughty child.

Attempting to link objective and subjective theories together, he suggested the historical fact of the Atonement was objective, while its purpose was to become personal experience and subjective, to concentrate people's attention on the eternal present, and carry forward Christ's atoning work into the actual experience of the Church's sacramental life, a continuous offering of his sacrifice. Moberly considered his interpretation an appeal to accept the Holy Spirit, the perpetual inward presence of the incarnate Son, as the primary means of revealing him.

Moberly's argument clearly leaned heavily towards the subjective view. In *The Idea of Atonement in Christian Theology*,[39] strongly advocating an Abelardian doctrine, Hastings Rashdall described his fellow Anglican's work as an attempt to combine theories 'which, in spite of all his subtlety, still stand apart in his pages like oil and water'. Nevertheless Moberly's book was recognised as an original contribution, moving the debate significantly forward. A. M. Ramsey praised its influence practically in teaching, evangelism and the 'cure of souls'.[40]

How then did Lidgett react to such trends? The pattern of his theology was set in 1897. His views on the Atonement and the Fatherhood of God changed little before the First World War, and very little during and after it. Wesley had called himself *homo unius libri*. Lidgett, convinced that Fatherhood was the Key to all understanding of God, was *homo unius doctrinae*. His *Fatherhood of God* in 1902 and *The Christian Religion* in 1907, simply reiterated the fundamental lines taken in *The Spiritual Principle* and explored various ways of repeating them. His adopted theology not only satisfied him intellectually and morally but also had practical significance.

Writing his *Christian Religion* 'in a period of transition and uncertainty'[41] had not altered his own position. He aimed 'to give full effect to the truth of the immanence, while steadfastly maintaining the transcendence of God'. Maintaining the balance between opposing views was characteristic of Lidgett's thinking generally. He had rebelled against refusal to respond to the transformation of human thought, accept the primacy of God's Fatherhood over his sovereignty, or appreciate the significance of Higher Criticism, evolution and the social application of Christianity. But amid increasing responsibilities, as a chairman or participant in secular as well as religious debate, he began, despite his fixations, to gain something of a reputation for seeking balanced, compromise solutions to problems or issues. To work effectively as minister or politician called for tolerance of diverse convictions without compromising his own.

In theology, notably over the Atonement, this worked to his advantage. Feeling secure in his own modified orthodoxy, Lidgett was able to retain a considerable degree of consistency and occupy something of a centre ground, as the objective/subjective controversy turned this way and that. Calmly, though not uncritically, he accepted changing views, ready to work with them, even if they could not be accommodated into his scheme.

The subjective trend was soon reflected within Methodism itself. The stance adopted in 1906 by Lofthouse (1871–1965) in his *Ethics and Atonement* contrasted radically with what fellow Wesleyans had read before. Strawson admitted he did not know how he 'got away with it less than ten years after Lidgett had been threatened with a doctrinal charge for his much less revolutionary *Spiritual Principle*'.[42]

Warburton Lewis, for the *Methodist Times*[43] was prepared to call Lofthouse's book 'an advance on anything yet done', but complained Lofthouse was still 'not near enough to God': he would have preferred his presentation in a traditionally robust evangelical style. Lidgett would have raised an eyebrow at Lofthouse's stance, but he could recognise the strength of opposing views in areas of unresolved controversy, and in 1906 he was far too busy to comment. Lofthouse's Preface acknowledged *The Spiritual Principle*. Both advocated the social application of Christianity, respected one another's intellect, and remained life-long friends.

Lofthouse said Christ's death, described as a sacrifice in Scripture, should not be considered substitutionary: we should instead notice what the text frequently links with it, an appeal to sacrifice ourselves. The Atonement, he thought, was the result not of popular morality, unable to restore right relations once broken, but of a display of New Testament ethical principles. To Lofthouse 'contrition, not punishment or its absence, is the condition of forgiveness'.[44] Contrition, making the wrong-doer forgivable, was what Christ aroused by his self-sacrifice, not just on the Cross, but from Bethlehem to Calvary.[45] Reformation was a matter of personal influence. It was via the persuasive personality of Christ that we grow into our relationship with a personal God. This Abelardian and psychological approach, reiterated in his 1921 Fernley lecture, *Altar, Cross and Community*, was a far cry from *The Spiritual Principle*. Yet Lidgett, as editor (jointly with B. H. Reed) of *Methodism in the Modern World* in 1929, was ready to give Lofthouse the task of writing its chapter on the Atonement.

Another Methodist also contributed a view on the Atonement. A. S. Peake (1865–1929), a highly respected scholar and Primitive Methodist layman, had like Lofthouse emerged from Oxford with his Methodist beliefs unscathed. His *Christianity: Its Nature and Its Truth* (1908) reflected recent trends in liberal thought, brushing aside notions of propitiation, expiation and the wrath of God, and traditional doctrines of sacrifice and penal substitution. He criticised traditional views, even those of John Wesley where he thought necessary. But such was the respect in which his personality, scholarship and faith were held, that like Lofthouse he aroused no significant opposition. Lidgett did not comment.

Like others before him, Peake looked for illumination in human relationships and experience. But he decided punishment cannot properly be transferred, and vicarious suffering involved no transference of merit: a person's conscience can be aroused, but this did not lighten the guilt he had to bear. Christ's death was not 'substitution' or 'representation', but 'identification': 'It is possible', Peake said, 'for Jesus to suffer on our behalf, and for the benefits of that suffering salvation to be appropriated by us, because He is one with the race for which He dies'.[46] If Jesus was seen as substitute, Peake argued, he could not have endured the worst penalty of sin, alienation from God. If, however, he[47] 'identified himself to the utmost extent with his brethren', he must have known, as far as a sinless being could know, the evil of sin, the sharpest of all the pangs, namely, the separation it creates between men and God. But Peake stressed we need both the negative deliverance from sin and the positive life of holiness. We are saved by the power of Christ's life,[48] by union with him.

Peake's interpretation was subjective, implying, as Edmondson indicated,[49] that 'the effectiveness of the "racial" act is dependent not on the one Christ who was involved in the act, but on the follower'. Christ's death was therefore not effective by itself, but simply 'an example to be followed'.

The Atonement pendulum swung to its furthest subjective point in the New Theology which the Congregationalist R. J. Campbell (1867–1956) proclaimed in City Temple sermons and a book published with this title on 20 March 1907. To Campbell God's immanence meant God and his universe were essentially the same. He rejected a two-natures Christology: in Christ 'humanity was Divinity, and Divinity humanity',[50] and Christ did nothing for us which we are not also called to do for ourselves and one another. The Atonement was 'not such a great mystery after all'. He cited instances of Atonement in action: Keir Hardie 'pleading for justice to his order';[51] and 'many a noble wife' remaining by her husband's side, 'patiently accepting the disabilities caused by his wrong-doing'. Here, he said, 'All that love can do is to share to the uttermost in the painful consequences of sin, and by so doing break their power'. 'What other Atonement is needed than this?'.[52]

Reaction from fellow Congregationalists was strong. A symposium of sermons and essays attacking Campbell's views was published almost immediately as *The Old Faith and the New Theology*.[53] Lidgett, editor of the *Methodist Times* from March 1907, joined in the condemnation, for example, through his article on 28 March and Note on 17 October. But the most powerful critic was the Congregational Principal of Hackney College, P. T. Forsyth (1848–1921), whom Adrian Hastings has described as the 'greatest of Free Church theologians' in the Edwardian Age.[54] Forsyth expressed original, penetrating but complex views, sometimes difficult to grasp, often expressed in jerky phrases and paradox. His writing swung back the pendulum to a firmly objective stance on the Atonement. Liberal theology, he insisted, had no power.

Forsyth shared Lidgett's criticism[55] of Campbell's failure to give 'balanced assertion to the transcendence of God as well as to his immanence' and confront 'the terrible fact of sin', the human heart's deep-rooted enmity of God. Both rejected Campbell's reductionist Christology which regarded Christianity as simply human nature at its best. Lidgett would have agreed that, even at its most unselfish, self-sacrificial and heroic, human nature could not save itself or produce the effect of Christ's death; men needed redemption, and that had to be done for them.

Forsyth argued Man could not atone, so God himself atoned: 'In a theology of grace . . . Atonement has meaning and value only as offered by God to himself'.[56] Jesus, he said, was not punished by God; Christ's death should be regarded as penal in the sense that he bore God's penalty on sin.[57] The Atonement, to Forsyth, was substitutionary as well as penal, and the satisfaction of God a divine necessity, a practical recognition of God's wounded holiness.

Countering Lidgett, Forsyth said, 'The Incarnation has no religious value but as the background to the Atonement':[58] the Cross was more central, literally crucial for salvation. Lidgett, however, was intrigued by Forsyth's concept in *The Person and Place of Jesus Christ*,[59] of 'progressive incarnation', kenosis matched by plerosis. 'The less he [Christ] thought of prerogative, the more he grew in power'. Forsyth's stress on Christ's incessant obedience was welcome.[60]

Lidgett would have seen Forsyth's protest against 'current shallowness' in modern religion as helping to justify his own resistance to the allure of subjectivity. No doubt the impact Forsyth made reassured him that his own moderate, but generally orthodox position would survive the changes in fashion.

Lidgett's basic objection to Forsyth's theology was his tendency 'to disparage the constructive and unifying work of reason', 'to belittle rational consistency', and to go too far in magnifying the claims and needs of grace: 'While the Illumination cannot give us Redemption, Redemption will then satisfy that which is well-grounded in the Illumination'.[61] To him Forsyth had closed his eyes to 'the necessity of seeing life whole, of offering such an exposition of divine grace in Christ as, while preserving its transcendent features, will display its vital relations with every realm of life and truth'.

Reason, coherence and consistency remained Lidgett's watchwords. Having applied them, he felt secure.

5

The Fatherhood of God and *The Christian Religion*

Lidgett wrote a trilogy of major and interrelated works. The two following *The Spiritual Principle* require much briefer coverage.

The Fatherhood of God in Christian Truth and Life

The Fatherhood of God[1] aimed, Lidgett said, 'to establish the supremacy of the Fatherhood of God more systematically and to set forth its consequences on a broader scale than simply in relation to the Atonement'.[2] Rupert Davies called it Lidgett's most notable book,[3] perhaps because its subject was central to all his work. Though a substantial volume, it broke no new ground, but publication in Scotland in 1902 brought perhaps an unexpected reward in 1909, an Honorary DD from Aberdeen University. Its Professor of Dogmatic Theology, Dr Curtis, had used the treatise as his students' text book. It certainly reads like one, no doubt intended, like its predecessor, to serve a didactic purpose.

By his use in *The Spiritual Principle* of the Fatherhood of God doctrine and its subsequent full-scale exposition Lidgett was in effect the first nineteenth-century Methodist to affirm in print and in detail the new prominence of the doctrine and underline its importance. To him Wesleyans had been insufficiently aware of the contributions of Maurice and Pope, and neither, he implied, had given the doctrine adequate attention. He wanted to work out his own detailed exposition, support *The Spiritual Principle*, and continue educating his Wesleyan contemporaries. He was also anxious to demonstrate his abilities as a scholarly theologian well versed in the Bible as well as the history of doctrine. Moreover, he saw it as his duty to expound 'that conception of God's relationship to, and dealings with, mankind in Christ, which supplies, to me at least, the principles upon which social work should be based'.[4] Remarkably, the book was based on lectures 'for a small class of theological students' at the Bermondsey Settlement. These were obviously endowed with intelligence, enthusiasm and unusual resilience!

To establish a detailed case for the Fatherhood doctrine as rooted in the

Bible, Lidgett had to face complex problems, and overcoming them required subtlety and skill. The Old Testament, he said, had led readers to discern the sovereignty of God as his characteristic relationship to mankind; analogues in human society had then made sovereignty the guide to interpreting the New Testament. Now the Old had to be seen from the christocentric perspective of the New, 'the preparation in its connection with the fulfilment'.[5] The Old Testament focused on God's kingship, but fatherliness was evident, he argued, for example, in the Psalms,[6] and 'Without the previous revelation of God's righteousness and Kingship, the conception of the Fatherhood of God must sink to naturalism and sentimentality'.[7]

Lidgett's dialectical skills were also deployed in interpreting the 'forensic' elements in the New Testament epistles. His thesis was that:

> The work of justifying 'the ungodly' . . . is fatherly rather than forensic or even Kingly. Justification is forgiveness, but it is more. It includes re-instatement . . . 'Justification' and 'adoption' may be taken as practically equivalent . . . The former is judicial, but, by reason of its result in the reception of sonship, cannot be separated from its source in Fatherhood.[8]

Respect for the legal profession led Lidgett to value the way 'forensic' elements enabled believers 'to realise the vast and manifold functions . . . included under the Divine Fatherhood'.[9] As for the concept 'sacrifice', both Testaments seemed to him to emphasise its *spiritual* meaning and express the self-giving to God, applicable above all to the sacrifice and sufferings of Christ.[10]

Lidgett's work contained a historical overview. His thesis was that the Fatherhood doctrine was the original doctrine for which divine sovereignty had subsequently been substituted, above all by Augustine. In his review[11] H. B. Workman, a Church historian, alluded to 'numerous mistakes' in Lidgett's comment on the period between Augustine and the Reformation, though he applauded his coverage of subsequent developments.

The Methodist contribution was certainly more important to Lidgett's Methodist readers. He duly recorded the Methodists' Calvinistic inheritance,[12] but his defence of their relative lack of progress in theology was rather patronising:

> The practical aim of the great Methodists, and their absorbing concern in salvation as a process and experience, kept them from recasting the highest theological conceptions by the help of their spiritual experience and their universal sympathy. The time had not come for such a task, *nor were they the men to accomplish it*. They took the higher theological conceptions current in their time as they found them, though filling them with a new evangelical

> meaning and warmth. It fell to later teachers of the nineteenth century, in their conflict with Calvinism . . . to re-assert in its fullness the truth and supremacy of the divine Fatherhood.[13]

Lidgett proudly claimed that Methodism had saved England from revolution, but his forebears, he acknowledged, were not philosophers:

> Their experience and their teaching went towards the remoulding of the doctrine of the relation of God to mankind, and made that remoulding inevitable. Their work supplied both the necessity and the material. But the accomplishment waited for a season.

Methodist preachers, he argued, had presupposed the universal Fatherhood of God, which 'comes into sight once and again, especially in the Methodist hymnology. It was, however, for the most part, a deduction waiting to be made'.[14]

For Lidgett Wesley's essential doctrine in practice had been the 'assurance that all men, however sinful, were called to, might be rendered capable of, and could only be completed in the life of God's sons'.[15] Lidgett identified Methodism's distinctive doctrine as that of the Holy Spirit, in particular, the 'direct and immediate fellowship with God' which the Spirit provided, and 'the *direct* witness' of the Holy Spirit to our adoption as sons'.[16] Such filial experience presupposed and verified the universal Fatherhood of God as the supreme relationship of God to man, he said. His style almost became lyrical when he spoke of early Methodists describing their new experiences as 'stepping into liberty', a phrase which 'set forth the buoyancy, the spiritual power, the sense of heirship'.[17]

Comment on the intense vitality of Methodist zeal gave Lidgett scope to criticise both Calvinist Nonconformity and the Anglican Church. The former exhibited 'the immobile dependence of the evangelicals on scripture' and 'largely substituted confidence in the electing decrees of God for the evangelical content of its theological belief'. Anglicans abhorred 'enthusiasm' in religion, including any 'professed consciousness of, or belief in, direct and immediate fellowship with God';[18] they gave little attention to the spiritual side of human nature, a major argument for the divine Fatherhood. It was growing recognition of the depth and intensity of God's love, resulting from the Methodist revival, which to Lidgett had caused a revolt against the highly elaborated Calvinists' 'plan of Salvation' and concept of sovereignty, and a change from the time-hallowed starting point of the Cross. Nineteenth-century theologians had decided 'to go behind the Fall and beneath the fact of sin, to discern and set forth the original relations of the Godhead to mankind, out of which Redemption arose'.[19] What they thought fundamentally important was 'God's *original purpose*' in Creation, 'and not the remedy for its miscarriage through sin'.[20]

Lidgett did not speculate whether the concept of 'Creator' gave way to that of 'Father' as soon as the Church began to talk of God as the first person in the Trinity. The Father was Lidgett's prime focus, but the Trinity helped him develop his case for the Fatherhood doctrine:

> The source [of the Godhead] is in the Father; yet He never *became* Father, but is so eternally, His Fatherhood being in relation to His Eternal Son . . . The Father is the originating source of love, creating beings made in and for love; destined, therefore, for that sonship in which alone the life of creaturely love can be fulfilled.[21]

Christ, he said, first revealed the Fatherhood of God; St John's Gospel showed this original relationship as eternal, 'completed by the relationship of the Holy Spirit to the Father and the Son':[22] thus the threefold relationship, declared in the doctrine of the Trinity.

Lidgett applauded nineteenth-century theologians for restoring the pre-eminence of the Fatherhood of God, substituting sovereign love for arbitrary will. Maurice was highly praised as the most original and influential among them. Debts were acknowledged to Kingsley, Erskine of Linlathen and McLeod Campbell, but strangely not to Pope, though he had made a 'substantial advance'[23] towards re-establishing the Fatherhood doctrine. Lidgett preferred to treat many aspects of theology as 'too universal to be explained by individual influence': he listed them under 'the principal of these causes of theological change'.[24]

Reference in the Preface to his own social and administrative work might have led to reflection on the social application of Maurice's and Kingsley's thinking. Instead Lidgett contented himself with a brief comment on 'the ideal which the Fatherhood of God affords of the spirit in which human affairs should be administered'.[25] He simply advocated a compromise in public and private affairs between fatherhood and sentimentality:

> If our account of the Divine Fatherhood be true, its influence as a guide to human conduct will not encourage softness in policy or administration, either in public or in private affairs. Authority will be strengthened rather than weakened, while . . . exercised in full regard to the humane ends . . . it is intended to serve. The perfect union of the virile and the humane is one of the greatest needs.

Lidgett's book provoked no charges of 'heresy'. Reviews were generally approving. In the *Wesleyan Methodist Magazine* Davison called the work balanced and comprehensive, avoiding potential pitfalls, and original.[26] But 'original' outside Methodism it was not: Lidgett had repeated many widely-held views. Davison's major complaint was Lidgett's tendency to construe everything in terms of one doctrine, pressing every aspect of Christian doctrine to make it come under the one category, so that the treatment became positively misleading and some other doctrines hardly recognisable. In the *Methodist Times* Arthur Hoyle was enthusiastic, but criticised the inexorable plodding progress of Lidgett's style: 'The writer goes on like a steam-roller, but he is never noisy, and alas! one hardly ever gets even a breath of heat, but the result is plain and straight before you, an undiscovered country'.[27]

Lidgett would have been delighted when H. P. Hughes told him that his (by then two) books had 'finally disposed of the juridical view of redemption' and his recent sermon had been based on the *Fatherhood of God.* That sermon was his last,[28] and his daughter sent Lidgett the manuscript. Marshall Randles's reaction to Lidgett's treatise was a great surprise: in 1902 he proposed him for the Richmond College Theology chair, and in 1904 arranged for *The Fatherhood of God*, not perhaps *The Spiritual Principle*, to be placed in the Rylands library.

Lidgett declined Randles's nomination, perhaps because it was motivated by the plot by W. L. Watkinson (1838–1925) and Randles himself[29] to unseat the chair's occupant, with whom Lidgett might have had some sympathy. The 1902 Conference was notable for its furious debates over Joseph Agar Beet's publication of *The Immortality of the Soul: A Protest*,[30] which marked his refusal 'to remain silent about the doom of the lost' even after Conference had opposed his *Last Things* in 1898.[31] Watkinson, President in 1897, was known for strong conservatism, mordant wit and opposition to H. P. Hughes. Beet was defended by (among others) William Slater, whom Wilbert Howard called 'a pioneer' in theological outlook, and whose Conference speech 'revealed, as in a flash, the tension of those years when the battle for intellectual liberty had not yet been won'.[32] Though Beet survived, not least by younger ministers' votes in the Pastoral Session of Conference,[33] 'heresy hunting' was far from over in 1902. Perhaps political shrewdness kept Lidgett, elected to the Legal Hundred in that year, and not under any doctrinal attack himself, from involvement in the controversy. He was, nevertheless, for many years suspected by some as a 'dangerous' person.

But more important to Lidgett than Randles's approval was the response of the Anglo-Catholic Edward Talbot, then Bishop of Rochester, subsequently of Southwark (1905) and Winchester (1911). His contact, and later friendship with Lidgett, began in 1895 when Lidgett and other Nonconformist ministers called to welcome his arrival in Kennington as Bishop of Rochester. In 1902 Talbot sent Lidgett his recently published volume of sermons. Lidgett responded with his own treatise. Talbot read it while temporarily laid up by lameness, and, perhaps surprised by Lidgett's treatment of the Catholic tradition, 'wrote to say that I had rendered a great public service by sending it to him'. Lidgett triumphantly concluded his anecdote: 'When shortly afterwards, the Bishop delivered his first Charge to the clergy of the diocese, he referred them to my book'.[34] Perhaps to Talbot, as in 1909 to Professor Curtis, Lidgett's publication proved a convenient quarry for discussion. This incident, confirmed by Talbot's biography,[35] may have helped to establish Lidgett's credibility among the Anglican hierarchy as a Nonconformist theologian and public figure (in London) with whom its members could feel a rapport.

Though Lidgett never wavered in his allegiance to the Fatherhood doctrine, its defence underwent a change, particularly during and after the First World War. To follow Maurice was to be influenced by Plato, but early in 1914 Lidgett criticised Plato for being 'forced to leave his Idea of the Good in an indeterminate and variable relationship to God, and therefore to the World'.[36] His argument ran:

> If he [Plato] is able to identify the Idea of the Good with the Idea of Being, that is of Supreme Reality, both of them stand in uncertain or external relations to God, and therefore fail to assert in any adequate degree their supremacy in the realm of created existence and unfolding history.

In the same article, he wrote that the authority of spiritual and ethical perfection 'cannot reside in the bare will and sheer omnipotence of God. It springs from His inmost character, and that character is revealed in grace'.[37] These features of character and personality were far from Platonic – grace above all!

In 1907 he had considered 'judgements of value' as evidence of underlying reality and the truth of Christianity.[38] Then the First World War turned Lidgett's thought to eternal values and their link with the Fatherhood of God. His reaction to the disillusionment with God's sovereignty created by the 'holocausts of war'[39] was to tell Christianity's critics that God's prime purpose was to promote spiritual values. Amid the general loss of confidence engendered by tragic and heroic loss of life he found re-assurance in emphasising that the world pointed beyond itself to the permanence of 'Higher Values', beauty, truth and goodness. In 1915 his exposition of Ephesians, to him the final and fullest apostolic presentation of the Fatherhood of God, asserted:

> Christ guarantees the future of the universe as a whole, all the higher values that are attained in its history, and in particular all the personalities in whom these higher values are realised. The glory of God is revealed in the perfection and permanence of His work. His work can only be perfected in His Sons. Hence the whole realm of spiritual promise and blessedness rests upon the Fatherhood of God.[40]

So, Platonic influences led Lidgett to include eternal values as subsisting in

God's ultimate personality. By 1923 the first item in his list of 'essential' contents of the Fatherhood doctrine had become:

> God is the eternal and perfect realisation of those highest values which the evolution of the Universe works towards in actuality, in spiritual vision and in aspiration. He is the Archetype of the True, and Beautiful and the Good, the spring from which their manifestation issues, the guarantee of their authority and permanence.[41]

Only then did his list go on to mention personal attributes of the divine nature, such as self-giving, self-manifestation and self-realisation, his love, and his grant of independent worth and freedom to his creatures.

W. Strawson found Lidgett's thesis flawed because it rested on 'the claim that beauty, truth and goodness are unquestioned absolute values – an argument which is unstable when its Platonic substructure is removed'.[42] Lidgett would have been undeterred.

The Christian Religion, Its Meaning and Proof

The Fatherhood of God stated: 'It is impossible within the scope of this work to consider the relation between the Christian revelation and the conceptions of God and of His relationships to men contained in non-Christian religions.'[43]

The Christian Religion aimed to remedy the gap. It completed in 1907 Lidgett's response to the 1877 intimation's second command, 'Try to show that Christianity is the final and absolute Religion, taking up into itself all that is true in the rest'.[44]

His treatise[45] reflected the increased interest in world religions, fostered in the previous century by foreign missions, imperial enterprise, evolutionary ideas and anthropological research. Acceptance of evolution and Maurice's emphasis on Christ as the Head of all humanity and on Creation rather than 'the Fall' had led to the view that all religions could be seen as expressions of a common faith, and that Christians should look for good in other religious traditions. A world-embracing study gave Lidgett a further opportunity to apply the coherence and seamlessness of the Fatherhood of God doctrine beyond Britain to the community of nations.

The book demonstrated his long-standing concern for Christian apologetics. He wanted, backed by scholarship, to show that the fatherly-filial relationship revealed by Christ supplied the key to the rational interpretation of the Universe. Triumphantly, his last page concluded that:

> Revelation, religion, reflection [study of Scripture and other religions, together with philosophical reasoning], all unite in offering . . . the content of

> the Christian religion as . . . the supreme truth which verifies itself by affording the indispensable, complete and only explanation of the meaning and end [purpose] of the Universe.[46]

Over half the work was devoted to expounding Christianity and its doctrines, arguing its reasonableness and answering criticism. To Lidgett existing systems of Christian evidence had failed to accommodate changes in philosophical outlook and knowledge, establish a systematic, up-to-date alternative approach, and dispel the impressions of older teaching. After a critique of Naturalism and agnostic objections to the faith, he restated the argument from design. He then sought to show Christianity was 'the supreme expression and satisfaction of spiritual life', excelling all other religions in its capacity to explain the world as a whole.[47]

His book again dazzled readers by the number and range of authorities quoted. His intellect, and determination despite mounting pressures to keep abreast of current criticism, were manifest. He anticipated Rupp's verdict, that his book was 'addressed to a cogent contemporary apologetic too "topical" to endure'.[48] Referring to recent increases in knowledge, Lidgett wrote:

> Christian evidences, accepted at any time, are of necessity, bound up with the most congenial philosophy current at that time . . . It inevitably comes to pass that frequently the proof of Christianity is presented in terms of a philosophy which is already becoming out of date'.[49]

Lidgett sought to counter 'a reaction on the part of simple and fervid piety against any attempt to establish by reasoning the truth of the Christian religion'.[50] Yet 'exaggerated intellectualism',[51] which took insufficient account of personal conviction, had to be resisted. Lidgett wanted to stress the personal and experimental note in religion, distinctly spiritual influences and consciousness of certain definite relations to a present divine being, omitted in past explanations. Neither 'the speculative thought which seeks a theoretic explanation of the world', nor 'the practical demand for a Chief Good above the world and beyond the reach of mortal life', nor both combined, would suffice.[52] It was 'experience of immediate relationship to that Divine Other than himself, who is yet – in some sense – his true self', that enabled man to explain 'the constitution of the world'.

Though wordy, repetitive and unashamedly partisan, Lidgett's approach throughout the work was scholarly. He insisted that 'the Christian consciousness . . . should justify its peculiar claims'.[53] Before dealing with the views of Kant, Spinoza and Helmholz related to the Argument from Design, Lidgett readily admitted that 'it can only be presented in a completely satisfying form to one who is already, and on other grounds, a believer in God. It must necessarily have greater weight in confirming faith than in creating it'.[54]

Claiming[55] with some justice to have done his best to look the difficulties in the face, he argued systematically, identifying and interpreting features leading step by step to his conclusion, the supremacy of Christianity over all other religions. *The Christian Religion* was by design an academic work.

In his comments on Christianity and other religions Lidgett's strategy was first to analyse the elements that made up the nature of religion itself, perhaps the most original part of the book. He then provided an account, also soon to be dated, of leading non-Christian 'ethnic' religions, including Animism, Confucianism, Zoroastrianism, Brahmanism and Mohammedism (*sic*). Testing them by his criteria, he concluded that each one 'transgresses at one or more points the principles . . . essential to the final persistence and general acceptance of any religion'.[56] Christianity, he argued, was superior to them all: 'While supplying standards of criticism by which all other religions may be tried, Christianity finds room in itself for that which is most deeply spiritual and most broadly human in each.'[57]

For Lidgett Christianity had emerged in evolutionary terms, as 'the fittest to survive',[58] the most universally serviceable to mankind, the fulfilment of all others, giving a final explanation of the world and including 'in a perfect whole all that other religions have which is capable of becoming universal . . . in each': in sum, 'the only religion which contains the possibility of becoming universal'. Characteristically, to Lidgett 'all that God is or can be' springs out of 'the all-comprehending relationship of Fatherhood'.[59]

In writing the book Lidgett was, no doubt, indebted to two Wesleyan colleagues. The Hebraist, A. S. Geden (1857–1936) of Richmond College, had already written *Studies in Comparative Religion* in 1898 and *Studies in Eastern Religions* in 1900. C. J. Wright claimed Geden's lectures on these subjects were 'the most scientific and scholarly then given in a Methodist college'.[60] The other, known from Lidgett's Cambridge days, was James Hope Moulton (1863–1917). While a Fellow of King's College, Cambridge, he had been a friend of J. G. Frazer, the anthropologist. Appointed to Didsbury College in 1902, he subsequently became Greenwood Professor of Hellenistic Greek and Indo-European Philology at Manchester University.

Six years after *The Christian Religion*, on the centenary of the Wesleyan Methodist Missionary Society (WMMS), Moulton's Fernley lecture, *Religions and Religion: A Study of the Science of Religion, Pure and Applied* (1913), revealed an attitude to non-Christian religions astonishing in Methodism at the time, well in advance of its ministerial training even up to and during the 1960s.[61] Respect for him both as scholar and a saint explained why he escaped censure. Enthusiasm for Zoroastrianism, fed by his knowledge of Sanskrit and Iranian, led Moulton to say: 'Were I to venture to preach to Parsis, I would urge them to be better Parsis . . . I cannot think of a single doctrine that has any claim to originate from Zarathushtra which I should press a Parsi congregation to abandon.'[62] He was reported to have told a Bombay audience in 1915: 'If I can persuade you to be a proper Zoroastrian, you will be very near to Christ'.[63]

But neither in 1907 nor perhaps later was Lidgett close to this position. What he had learned from Moulton, Geden and others was the importance of studying non-Christian religions seriously and, as far as possible, objectively. He certainly did not intend to lag too long behind Geden in publishing on the subject. In the inaugural lecture of his NCEFC Presidency in 1906 he had declared that there was nothing to fear from wider acquaintance with other religions. Commending the 'more sympathetic attitude towards the nobler of the non-Christian religions', he deplored 'the desire of ascendancy, feeling of pity . . . sense of superiority, accompanied by scarcely veiled contempt not only for the religious faith, but also for the moral qualities of these races'.[64] This was the objective approach of *The Christian Religion.*

The 1906 lecture, however, had a rather patronising tone. Though not a missionary himself, Lidgett never failed to express support for WMMS, especially when, as not infrequently, it was in financial straits.[65] His mother, he proudly recalled,[66] helped to found, and eventually became President of the WMMS Women's Department. Lidgett believed the whole human race needed the faith Methodists had received, and so overseas missionary activity should not falter. His lecture was addressed to an evangelical rather than an academic audience. His whole emphasis was on conversion:

> Is it not manifest . . . that the peoples who have . . . been . . . attracted by . . . Buddha . . . will, when they are converted to Christianity, make an invaluable contribution to the fuller realisation of Christianity as the manifestation of the grace, the condescension and the gentleness of God?[67]

From Lidgett's point of view more sympathetic relationships would influence these faiths, develop in them elements most congenial to Christianity, and 'enable Christians to set forth Christianity, not as purely exclusive of all other religions, but as including, completing and harmonising all elements of truth and moral power within them'.[68] But Christianity was 'the one religion which proclaims to the world the love and grace of God, effects a full redemption from sin, and offers complete satisfaction to the infinite needs of the human heart.'

There were few concessions here. Redemption and grace were to Lidgett ineradicable 'root principles', and Christian faith need not fear contamination from being transplanted. Sympathy for non-Christians would win from them a fuller appreciation of Christ.

Lidgett had clearly not absorbed the modest receptivity of his hero Maurice, nor its reflection in Moulton's views in 1913. Among the principles Maurice advocated for the relations of the world's religions to Christianity, Cracknell discerned the conviction that 'The encounter with other religious traditions may offer correctives to Christian theological formulation'.[69] Moulton envisaged that, while other religions might be evolving into Christianity, the result might not emerge as the form of Christianity his contemporaries knew. His Fernley lecture included a chapter, entitled 'The Christ who is to be'. 'We look', he said, 'for the help of the Brahman and the Moslem, the Buddhist and the Confucian, to bring their several treasures to the feet of the coming Lord of men'.[70] Cracknell's illuminating analysis of responses to the Edinburgh World Missionary Conference in 1910 suggested that, though traditional approaches long remained in missionary propaganda at home, delegates not only recognised God's presence in every faith but also in effect admitted that contemporary Christianity did not fully reflect Christ.

No such humility marked Lidgett's sermon as retiring Free Church President in March 1907. Having in mind perhaps the outlook of his colleagues who four months later might elect him as President-designate of the 1908/9 Wesleyan Conference (his *Christian Religion* was published after the 1907 Conference), he allowed himself some rather nationalistic, even jingoistic language: 'The most thoughtful minds in the Far East are already associating the principles and ideals of Western civilisation with the name and authority of Jesus Christ, and predicting from Him a speedy world-lordship.'[71] At this point he wisely checked himself, and added, 'so far at least as the adoption and influence of the ethical ideals associated with His name are concerned'. But he continued:

> God has endowed us [the British people] with . . . unresting energy and . . . practical sympathy . . . Is it presumptuous to believe that we are an elect race, so far at least as God has fashioned alike our temper and our position in the world to enable us to realise the Catholic purposes which the twentieth century brings down from the sphere of prophecy to that of almost immediate fulfilment?

That sermon, on 'Catholicity, the Mark of Spirituality', extended its scope beyond England. Thrilled by the increasing bounds of Empire, he embroidered on the theme of 'the solidarity of mankind . . . being brought about under our very eyes'.[72] Lidgett's vision was of one religion embracing all peoples, but that religion would be Christianity as he knew it. A man of his time, he revealed its expectations of aggressive evangelism and patriotic fervour.

Lidgett always discerned implications in his theology for the wider world. But while conceding Lidgett had championed Methodism's missionary demands, Lofthouse surprisingly added that he was 'never specially interested in the cause of . . . "foreign missions"'.[73] 'Ecumenical', he said, 'meant for him the union of religious bodies within this country rather than the integration of all

Christian men and women of every race and colour in the world'. Perhaps Lofthouse meant that reunion of the English Protestant churches, though fraught with difficulties, appeared to Lidgett the priority and sooner achieved.

What cannot be contested was that to Lidgett social reform at home was urgent. But he insisted[74] it was intimately bound up with missions abroad. His 1908 presidential address to the Wesleyan Conference asked, 'What shall we offer to inquiring minds in the Far East as the practical results of our Christian profession? . . . our unemployed and unemployable, the sweated workers of the East End?'[75] For him the slum in Whitechapel was the worst enemy of missionaries in Calcutta and Tokyo. 'The victorious effort to attain a Christian civilisation at home is the necessary counterpart to a successful evangelisation', he declared.[76] For him a Christian world involved Christian civilisation. Striving for the former should not wait until the latter was achieved, nor should missionary work be hampered 'with the controversies that have vexed and sometimes divided Western Protestantism'.[77]

Reactions to *The Christian Religion* varied. Rupp suggested that though Lidgett's trilogy 'spoke acutely to the condition of the time', *The Christian Religion* seemed 'more dated that the others'.[78] Harold Roberts said that Lidgett's book 'was in its day an impressive contribution to Christian apologetics'.[79] Commenting to me, Professor Hinchliff found it 'not very interesting'. Reviewers in 1907 admired his learning and coverage, but made the by now familiar comments:[80] for one, it lacked 'the warm glow'; and for another, 'Perhaps he unbends too little . . . for the average reader . . . Not everyone can keep step with him'.

Lidgett fulfilled his intimation imperative. His book reinforced his standing as a Wesleyan scholar, but it was not his most significant work.

6

Increasing responsibilities 1892–1905

Lidgett's rise to national prominence was built on the wide range of additional, largely political responsibilities he undertook after 1890. Consciously or unconsciously he progressively found new fields to which he could apply his cherished doctrine of the Fatherhood of God. These included Poor Law Guardianship in Bermondsey; experience as an educational administrator; writing and committee work within the Wesleyan Church; and involvement in what became the National Council of Evangelical Free Churches (NCEFC). Closely interrelated, all in their different ways drew out his self-assertion, eagerness to take initiatives and shoulder responsibility, and his fierce independence of mind. His detailed knowledge and experience of social conditions and local government administration 'on the ground' commanded growing respect. Alongside his passion for justice and social dignity, he developed an understanding of others' views and circumstances which enabled him to put a case fairly and eloquently on their behalf, even when he personally did not wholly support it. Even amid colleagues' wide, at times vehement, differences of opinion he kept a cool head. The skill he showed in appraising the subtleties and penetrating to the essentials of debate, combined with an impressive command of language, caused him to be increasingly sought as a firm, persuasive, but diplomatic spokesman, committee member and chairman.

Only three months after the opening of the Settlement in 1892 the opportunity came to fulfil one of its six aims: 'to take such part in local administration and philanthropy as may be possible'.[1] The local Progressive Party invited him to stand for election as Poor Law Guardian in 'the Union of St Olave's from London Bridge to Deptford', a relatively low-level appointment in local administration, but with practical scope for acting out his central belief by serving the poor and disadvantaged. Its responsibilities, including, for example, supervision of the area's Workhouses and the Rotherhithe Infirmary, would involve him in the 'bumbledom' of vestry politics and petty disputes among the locally self-important business and tradesmen.

The invitation of 1892 was given by a political party. The duties required were, perhaps, straightforward, but the attitudes and policies behind their execution would inevitably be seen as political within the local context. To accept the post was therefore to be committed to some extent to action already roundly condemned by the Wesleyan Church principle of 'No politics in the pulpit' or outside it. But, in Lidgett's view, to achieve the improvements the community needed where the Poor Law was concerned, some Christians had to be prepared to enter public life. Though the Progressives' policies appeared to him broadly acceptable, Lidgett decided he had to consult Dr Moulton over the attendant risks. To his surprise, Moulton replied, 'Mr Lidgett, we sent you to Bermondsey to take risks'.[2] Lidgett's successful Poor Law election was to be repeated annually until 1906 when other responsibilities caused him to withdraw his candidature. He resigned once, only to be co-opted to continue his work at the Infirmary. The reputation he gained from his work led to two invitations to stand for the Mayoralty of the Borough, though he was never a member of the Bermondsey Borough Council. He felt obliged by other duties to decline the second. On the first occasion he stood as a candidate, but was unsuccessful.

Two parties dominated politics in London. *The Progressives* sprang largely from alarm among the middle class at the incidence of poverty and distress in the slums. Growing markedly since the mid-nineteenth century, these problems were brought into sharp, even stark focus notably by the publication of *The Bitter Cry of Outcast London* and the activities of such Christian Socialists as Arnold Toynbee, Samuel Barnett and others in the 1880s. This was a time, as Lidgett put it, 'of great awakening to the social responsibilities of the well-to-do'.[3] Many Londoners, not least the religious communities, including the Wesleyan Forward Movement, saw what he called the need 'of a far-reaching policy to exceed merely palliative, voluntary efforts'. There was discontent with London's then ruling party, strong Conservatives who called themselves *The Moderates*. These were perceived as reactionary or sluggish in their response, supporting decentralisation and utterly failing to adopt positive and progressive policies to tackle the capital's major problems. Dominated by vested interests, not least the owners of individual companies, they were resistant to changes which might threaten their members' influence or control. No doubt they included, like the Progressives, 'men of good-will' with or without religious affiliations, but it was the Progressives who claimed greater religious motivation and pride in their city.

Lidgett defined the aims of the Progressives as to evoke 'a new local patriotism for London'; to cause the electors 'to recognise for the first time the unity of the capital city of the Empire and the community of interests that should bind its citizens together in collective municipal efforts'; and to set the problems of local London life 'apart from and ranked higher than ordinary party politics'. Behind the words 'collective efforts' (a reference to Progressives' support for metropolitan integration and steps to correct the disabilities of London's poorer districts) can be discerned the contrast he was drawing with the Moderates' protection of disparate individual and group interests. Progressives' policies tended to be vague, paternalistic, stressing personal and social responsibility; their concern for the unprivileged was moderate, certainly not revolutionary, though it sometimes suited opponents to call them this. It was a formula, which with the dynamic Christian inspiration Lidgett, like others, brought to it, attracted a wide variety of supporters, including people of imagination, energy and ideas. Resembling in many respects a Nonconformist coalition, they laid themselves open to abuse as soft-hearted humanitarians, kill-joys, temperance fanatics and hypocrites.

Like most Progressives, Lidgett was staunchly patriotic and royalist, an Imperialist, a supporter (like H. P. Hughes) of the Boer War, and, when the First World War made them an issue, an opponent of conscientious objection and pacifism. The story is told[4] of when Lidgett was attending a Hospital Committee, Queen Mary entered a room and bade him remain seated, he nevertheless struggled to his feet, saying, 'Ma'am, even my legs are loyal!'

Progressives were mainly, but not exclusively, Liberals; though never controlled by the parliamentary Liberal Party, they developed policies broadly Liberal in tone. Some Progressives supported Conservatives in national politics, others supported Radicals. In the early days they received, he said in 1936, 'the friendly support of Labour organizations which afterwards gave birth to the present Labour Party'.[5] As with parliamentary Liberals, different views among Progressives could lead to defections, temporary or otherwise. For example, some able and powerful personalities like Sidney Webb and Ramsay MacDonald initially joined the Progressives, but later went over to Labour. Though welcoming all who supported, albeit temporarily, his party's policies, Lidgett was never at ease with Labour ideas from the time of their early percolation, as stated earlier, into Bermondsey. He was saddened when Dr Alfred Salter (1873–1945), an able medical graduate from Guy's Hospital and resident at the Settlement in 1898, whom he was instrumental in converting from atheism, could not be dissuaded from sympathies with Labour. Salter later became the Labour MP for Bermondsey West virtually throughout the period 1922–45. A later chapter comments on events which turned Lidgett from suspicious tolerance of Labour to outright hostility.

Such was the broad picture. In individual areas the situation was much more complex, featuring issues large and small, tensions between 'working men' and the Liberal élite, and the effects of changes in personalities, denominational or factional alignments.[6] Disputes between Nonconformists and Anglicans or Roman Catholics constantly bedevilled politics, and Lidgett's attempts to steer a middle path brought bitter attack.

Poor Law Administration brought Lidgett into contact with Poor Law schools and schools over a wider area: he served, for example, on the Board of the South Metropolitan District schools at Sutton.[7] He had his grandfather's interest in Elementary schools, often considered as provision for children of the poor. In the 1890s administration of such schools in London began to prove far more contentious than that of the Poor Law in individual boroughs.

There was established precedent for clergy taking part in both spheres, but schools provoked denominational disputes. Then the majority of children nationally were educated in voluntary (denominational, mostly Anglican) schools, called 'National' schools. The 1870 Forster Education Act established State or Provided schools, maintained partly out of local rates, and managed by School Boards which were set up in each area. The triennial elections to these Boards were often strongly contested between groups differing in religious motives and attitude to the two types of school. All groups were aware that the Boards' powers enabled those who emerged as the majority (ruling) group to 'protect or undermine the denominational system'.[8] Anglicans resented any state involvement and applied fierce pressures to preserve their Non-Provided schools. As their Church was the national Church, they were convinced that both Parliament and local Boards were obliged not only to give support to 'National' schools, but also to promote the teaching of Anglican doctrine in other schools. By contrast there were followers of Joseph Chamberlain (1836–1914) and others in the National Education League, for whom all denominational education was anathema. So control of a School Board could, as Machin wrote, 'secure or prevent the teaching of religion in Board-schools and . . . extend or limit expenditure on them'.[9]

On the London School Board the Moderates were the ruling party, the Progressives in opposition. Among the Board's Moderates, Anglican priests, standing as Independents, predominated, and this at a time when Nonconformist churches in London as in the rest of the country, disturbed by growing Anglo-Catholic influence on the Established Church, were becoming increasingly alarmed at what they regarded as crypto-Catholic designs on the nation's children and teachers. Detesting the growth of Ritualism, H. P. Hughes in 1890 said of the School Board election: 'If the Moderates won, England would sink to the level of Spain'.[10] A campaign to oust Moderates from their majority on the London School Board failed in 1894, but redoubled efforts in 1897 led to a large Progressives' majority on the Board.

In that election Lidgett said the cinders of what was known as the 1893 'Circular Controversy' were still hot.[11] The Circular, introduced by J. W. Diggle, Anglican chairman of the Board, abetted by the fervently Anglo-Catholic layman, Athelstan Riley, was designed to strengthen the Board's definition of biblical exposition in its schools and insist on enquiries into the dogmatic beliefs of the teachers. These 'tests of orthodoxy', of support perhaps for such detested doctrines as baptismal regeneration, sparked fears of

Romanism, and the resultant furore ensured the Circular was not enforced.[12] The *Methodist Times*[13] passionately appealed for votes against 'Diggleites' in the 1894 School Board election. In 1897 the Progressives decided the solution of the controversy was to campaign for the removal of Bible teaching altogether, but a minority of members, objecting to this secular platform, asked Lidgett to stand in support of the local Association of Christian Churches for the maintenance of biblical instruction and religious influence in schools.

Election to the School Board for the whole 'County' of London was bound to bring him into much more political prominence than the Poor Law neighbourhood post had done. Again Lidgett sought approval from Moulton, but this time also from the Settlement treasurer and the Conference Settlement Committee. They agreed. In opposition to the local party officials Lidgett had to campaign with his own election committee, but headed the poll by several thousand votes. His election, as one of the members of the Southwark Division (including Bermondsey and Rotherhithe), changed the party policy and led to rapidly increasing responsibilities within it: by 1900 he had, for example, been appointed Chief Whip, a post giving him a perspective on a wider range of issues than the schools with which he remained principally concerned. Such political involvement by a Wesleyan minister was unique, astonishing, and never fully explained. Critical colleagues would certainly have challenged it. Moulton's defence and personal encouragement again proved crucial. He had himself been associated in the launch of the Bermondsey Settlement; he accepted its experimental nature, wanted it to be given a proper trial, and acknowledged it might have unexpected results. He had, moreover, faith in Lidgett personally, and in his reasoned approach to enlarged political activity.

This can be inferred from Lidgett's words and actions at the time. He saw clearly that while valuable social work of various kinds was being carried out by individual churches in their own neighbourhood areas, social improvement had to be achieved on a much larger scale, and across a wider range of community needs, not least, but not only, in educational provision. That involved political decisions by local as well as national government on the policies required and the deployment of resources to implement them. Sermons and speeches on the principles of Christianity were important and could be very relevant to individual politicians' conduct. But they were inevitably delivered away from where parties reached detailed decisions affecting the whole community, and on specific problems they could not take interrelated issues fully into account or assess the practical scope for action; they brought only very limited discernible results. The churches themselves lacked the necessary power.

Lidgett reasoned that if Christian guidance was to be effectively given and real change brought about, some individual Christians at any rate would have to work within a party political framework; they could act in a personal capacity, and party membership would not prevent them from pursuing their Christian principles, preserving their independent integrity, and offering their own frank, individual opinions. They might not agree, but what was important was that their opinions were based on the tenets of Christianity as they perceived them. In effect Lidgett was to some extent taking his cue from the Anglicans, Gladstone, Salisbury and Balfour, as well as from fellow Free Churchmen, mainly Congregationalists like Silvester Horne, keen to apply their Christian faith within party politics.

What Lidgett said in 1938 about the London County Council, he would have claimed for the London School Board: 'It is no exaggeration to say that the policy and programme of the Council, in its formative period, were supplied by religious leaders and sustained by religious influences'.[14] Against the above background of earlier partisan debate his comment on his six 'great' years with the London School Board was surprising: 'Party considerations were never allowed to interfere with opportunities for service on the Board, where men and women came to the work with goodwill and devotion to the cause of the children'.[15] Characteristically, he admired his fellow Progressive and majority leader, the Hon. E. Lyulph Stanley (later Lord Stanley), for *constantly encouraging the suppression of party controversy*: 'for he [Stanley] always said that whenever members of the School Board, however reactionary, were brought into actual contact with the schools, they became keen in the work and reasonable in spirit'. Lidgett admitted, however, this was not always the case! As Chief Whip, Lidgett had sometimes to moderate the effects of Stanley's impetuosity and impatience on his Party and the Board of Education, but his enthusiastic leadership was supported by an able team of such outstanding figures as Graham Wallas, T. J. Macnamara, W. C. Bridgeman, Sir Charles Elliott, the Revd Stewart Headlam and Lidgett himself. Lidgett's comment was perhaps not untypical of other colleagues: 'The work is exacting. It takes me an average of 20 hours each week to discharge the work with fair efficiency, but the greatness of the issues involved is worth almost any sacrifice of time and strength'.[16]

To Lidgett the role of individual Christians in politics differed from what might be acceptable from denominations and whole churches. Any identification of the latter with a political party could be divisive and therefore unwise, since internal divisions might arise from disputes between their members about party policies or action. Lidgett, aware of division within the Wesleyan Church between Tories and Liberals, strenuously sought to prevent the Nonconformist churches, separately or together, from participating in direct, overt political action or expressing denominational differences in sectarian feuds. To him the duty of the churches was to comment on specific social and political issues only where moral and religious implications were involved.

In national politics he pinned his hopes for particular changes on the Liberal Party. Lidgett's personal political faith was 'Gladstonian'[17] from his early years;

but, turning to 'New Liberalism', he became more and more attached, as we shall see, to Lloyd George, without Nonconformity gaining any substantial legislative benefit. Liberal opinion within and outside the Connexion was often quite seriously divided. Yet amid bewildering controversy Lidgett remained politically astute. He seemed to have made every effort to understand the complexities and discern the merits of a case from whatever quarter it was made, before expressing a studied view of his own. He never engaged in invective against those with whom he strongly disagreed. His readiness to stand up to extremists and militants, however sincere, even on his own 'side', went with a strong belief in democracy and refusal to countenance any breach of the law. In general his commitment was to 'ordered progress and not . . . revolutionary methods',[18] and though he often undertook to act as a spokesman, his preference was for working behind the scenes for moderation and conciliation. He adopted a cautious, gradualist approach, steering a middle course between the type of liberal who put the pursuit of the social gospel before the salvation of the individual, and those who regarded issues of social justice as irrelevant to individual salvation.

He never had any ambition to enter Parliament, but the form he used for his Settlement Debating Society helped to familiarise his students, residents and himself with its procedure and gave up-to-date knowledge of current national issues. Casting himself always as the Speaker, he distributed ministerial portfolios and aimed to replicate Westminster debates. That experience may well have contributed to his own understanding of the legislative process, and could in part explain why he was so much at ease with politicians.

Lidgett was particularly proud[19] of the Board's achievements, and of the part he himself played in them. He had become Vice-Chairman of the School Management Committee, Chairman of the Special Subjects Committee, and a member of Committees for General Purposes, Special Schools, the Management of the Brentwood Industrial Schools, and the Teaching Staff subcommittee. To meet the needs of London's new and rapidly growing suburban populations the Board had seen its primary task to secure school places for every child of school age, both by the enlargement, where necessary, of existing schools, and the planning and erection of new ones. Assembly halls and partitions to reduce the size of classrooms 'to make effective teaching possible and lighten the strains on teachers', were provided, alongside centres for teaching boys' metalwork and girls' cookery, laundry and housewifery, and for mentally and physically defective children. Teachers' qualifications were raised, the curriculum widened, and elementary education extended: the Board's 'Higher Grade' schools, so called from their offering a higher type of instruction than in ordinary Elementary schools, were now receiving an annual intake from neighbouring schools and teaching French, physical science, music, drawing and gymnastics.[20] 'But for the work that was done . . .', he declared, 'I do not know how it would have stood subsequently with the elementary education of London'.[21] 'In short', he said,

> those six fruitful years transformed the conditions of elementary education throughout London and raised the standard for all future time. At that time it was the boast of the Progressive Party on the London School Board that almost all the improvements in *national* education that were sanctioned by successive Governments were due to the initiative and to the experiments upon which the School Board had embarked without waiting for the sanction of Whitehall and sometimes in disregard of its temporary opposition.[22]

Though much of this appraisal came from Lidgett himself, it seems reasonable to conclude that the convictions and determination of Lidgett and like-minded Progressives played a not insignificant part in the educational advance of London schools, and in turn exercised an influence on educational change nationally.

The Board, however, had had to surmount local as well as national obstacles. Adamant that high expenditure was justified to achieve such improvements, Lidgett and his friends had to face an outcry from Moderates, associations of ratepayers, clergy concerned that voluntary schools, lacking equal finance, were falling behind their provided counterparts, and the middle-class 'who complained that the rates were being used to enable children of the industrial classes to compete for employment with their own expensively educated sons'.[23] Complainants drew the attention of the Government auditor, T. B. Cockerton, in July 1899 to the very existence of Higher Grade schools and the 'extravagant' expenditure on them. School Boards across the country had in fact been limited by statute to providing elementary education only in the narrowest sense: advanced courses for senior pupils were not permitted. Not surprisingly, the resulting lawsuit in April 1901 went against the Board, and to Lidgett's intense disappointment Higher Grade schools were declared illegal. After that[24] secondary education became and remained for him an urgent priority, and he charged[25] the Board of Education with being unconcerned and unclear on the limits of and responsibility for elementary education: this could include adults who had forgotten 'arithmetic and writing' since leaving school at 14. The situation of Higher Grade schools was soon, but only partially, regularised by the Government, but the schools remained in an anomalous position until 1910 when a new policy to substitute 'Central' schools was adopted.

As a result of the 1903 London Education Act, replacing the London Schools Board with the LCC in May 1904, there was no Board election in November 1903, but Lidgett was quickly swept into the new administration, as Chapter 11 will explain. In the meantime an account of other aspects of his career calls for attention.

To return to Lidgett's Bermondsey appointment. Opponents within the Conference made it imperative for him to tread carefully: agreement had only reluctantly been given by Conference to matching other Churches' Settlements with one of its own and to terms of reference which Lidgett had stipulated and liberally interpreted. To many Wesleyans his social and educational ideas long remained suspect: this was evident, for example, in 1907 at the time of his Presidential election. His fellow members of the Wesleyan Forward Movement, activists no longer content simply to 'conserve Methodism', as Lidgett's Superintendent in Cardiff had done,[26] continued to disturb the Conference's conservative hierarchy. Attempts to reach working people alienated from local chapels and arrest membership decline were welcome, but succumbing to the 1880s Forward Movement's influence and experiment with novel presentations of the gospel in new city missions caused unease. Some Conference members, however, no doubt found comfort in seeing the Movement as an answer to resurgent Anglicanism;[27] others saw the Missions as a way to overcome class discontent which fed the growth of socialism.[28]

But there were other challenges to cause the traditionalists great unease: condemnation of the Church's existing structures and theological outlook as out of date; the call to apply Christian principles to national and international affairs; the very idea of reconstructing society, even if it was to be on the basis of justice and love;[29] the advent of the *Methodist Times* in 1885 as a weekly organ for the Forward Movement and rival to the conservative *Methodist Recorder*; and, not least, the pen of the new paper's editor, the fiery, impatient and highly controversial H. P. Hughes. Lidgett's association with *some* adherents of the Forward Movement, for example, W. Fiddian Moulton and the Wesleyans' ecclesiastical statesman, H. J. Pope, might be reassuring, but not that with Hughes. Lidgett was unrepentant, however, and prepared to follow him 'with reservations'.[30]

Evidence of such independence and his sharp analytical mind nevertheless counted in Lidgett's favour. Despite their irritation, members of the Wesleyan 'establishment' relatively quickly came to recognise his growing administrative experience, his social achievements in Bermondsey, and efforts to preserve biblical teaching in schools and resist Anglo-Catholic dogma, let alone his more than simply competent activities as a Wesleyan minister. He may have been regarded, with some justice, as an eccentric, though not an outsider. But he had undoubted abilities of which the Conference made increasing use during his first ten years in the Settlement.

On, and immediately after his Bermondsey appointment, it was logical for the Conference to elect him as a member of its Home Missions (1890), London Mission (1891) and Education Committees (1891), and in 1893 of its Social Purity Committee.[31] He became the Ministerial Secretary of the latter in 1899. Having joined the important Committee of Privileges[32] in 1894, he was elected as its Ministerial Secretary (a very responsible post) in 1899, where, as in the

Social Purity Committee, his uncle Percy Bunting served alongside him as lay secretary. In 1896 he had joined the Temperance Committee. That was the year in which he made his first noteworthy and effective intervention in Conference debates.[33] That led to membership of a committee on the Youth of Methodism, and appointment as convenor of a special committee to study the educational legislation expected after the Conservatives' General Election victory of 1895. This gave him close contact with the clash between J. H. Rigg and H. P. Hughes on school policy. Despite Lidgett's understandable apprehension about possible 'heresy' charges, no damaging criticism followed his 1897 and 1902 publications: they, in fact, established his reputation as a Wesleyan scholar. In 1902 the Conference gave him its highest honour short of the Presidency, membership of the Legal Hundred, on the proposal of James Chapman, another Forward Movement member. In 1903, when Rigg retired from Westminster College, the *Methodist Recorder*[34] noted that 'many – perhaps most – would like to have nominated' Lidgett for the post. Lidgett, however, proposed H. B. Workman, the popular choice, and Workman was successful.

The final strand plaited into Lidgett's activities in this period was that of participation in the movement for Church unity. His passion for actual and visible unity was inspired by many things: Christ's prayer that 'All may be one';[35] the vision of the Church in the Epistle to the Ephesians;[36] Wesley's evangelical enthusiasm that the world might believe; the logic of Lidgett's own doctrine of the Fatherhood of God to be proclaimed by the Church to the world; the unity of mankind; and his love of coherence and co-operation. He developed a strong distaste for denominationalism and sectarian behaviour. He abhorred, for example, wasteful duplication in church and social work in Bermondsey and the divisions of Methodism. But his desire for unity was, above all, for theological, not just practical and managerial reasons.

From the beginning of the 1890s Lidgett was associated with moves towards Church unity by a small group of Wesleyans and Congregationalists. The Wesleyan, H. S. Lunn, took the initiative of launching a monthly magazine, *The Review of the Churches*, in 1891, and a series of conferences for churchmen of all kinds at Grindelwald in Switzerland from 1892 to 1896. Lidgett spoke at one of them about his Settlement in 1893. The inclusion of an Anglican representative editor on the *Review* in 1892–6 and of major Anglican figures at Grindelwald indicated a desire for a united Protestant Church, with the Church of England alongside Nonconformists. That, and ultimately a universal Christian Church, would have been Lidgett's dream also. Pragmatically, however, Lidgett could see the need to lower the sights for the time being and aim for the lesser goal of Nonconformist unity through a National Free Church Council. But the Council was to him 'a practical instalment of that larger Reunion to which its founders had looked forward'.[37] As he wrote in 1936, 'It was never intended to keep the Free Church Council end up, as against all the world, but to lead the way for those closer relations, spiritual and otherwise, which should bind the whole body of Christians together in concord'.[38]

The NCEFC was officially launched in 1896 with Hughes formally elected as its President. In 1897 Lidgett became a member of its Executive on the proposal of C. H. Kelly, the Wesleyan Book Steward, who saw his *Spiritual Principle* through the press that year. Lidgett was soon appointed to its Education Committee. An enthusiast for the Council from the start, he was personally involved in two of the three events that marked its genesis at the beginning of the decade. H. P. Hughes commissioned for the *Methodist Times* an article by the Congregationalist, J. Guinness Rogers, recommending on 20 February 1890 the holding of an annual Free Church 'Congress', parallel to Church Congresses of the Church of England, and the NCEFC's initial title. Lidgett himself was present at a private meeting at Percy Bunting's home early in 1891 to discuss the proposal. Hughes and leading Congregationalists, Dale, Allon and MacKennal[39] attended. Bunting was another of Lunn's representative editors.

Lidgett's most significant involvement occurred in 1891 when a circular was sent to every Nonconformist minister in England and Wales by J. B. Paton and an *ad hoc* committee.[40] Lidgett was a member of the committee, and the circular had his mark upon it. It called for the establishment of 'Unions of Evangelical Churches' at town and district level to co-operate for 'social redemptive work' which should be 'thoroughly and systematically undertaken'. The finally agreed constitution of the Council reflected this. Narrow sectarianism was to be countered by promoting devotional fellowship and co-operation among fellow Nonconformists. Joint working could arise from co-ordinated responses in local councils to a variety of local social needs and from joint evangelistic campaigns. Nationally the Council's aims[41] might best be expressed as to create a forum in which the rights of the associated churches could be defended; 'the New Testament doctrine of the Church' asserted; and Nonconformist concerns on 'the application of the law of Christ in every relation of human life' aired and freely debated. But membership was based on individuals and on local councils, not on representatives of the separate denominations. Official resolutions, committing the Free Churches as a whole, were not envisaged.

The original intention was that the Council should be non-political, a policy which Lidgett, as well as the Council's major financier, the layman George Cadbury, fully endorsed but fought in vain to ensure. The action Lidgett emphasised as of particular importance for the national and local councils was that of expressing their evangelical convictions through a drive to win more converts, as for example in the Simultaneous Mission conducted in London in 1901, and generally to spread the influence of the Christian faith. This was his thesis, for example, at the Council's meeting in Cardiff in March 1901 when the radical Congregationalist, J. Hirst Hollowell, advocated direct action in parliamentary and local elections against the Government's education proposals: Nonconformist churches, Lidgett declared, should be training men rather than meddling directly in politics.

What Lidgett meant by 'training' seemed to have been efforts to improve and extend evangelism; help in developing the evangelical (and Catholic) principles of individuals, whether activists in political parties or not; and in permeating society and benefiting it through the social action those principles might inspire.[42] In the 1936 *Methodist Recorder* article mentioned above, he stressed the importance for civilisation of forming the Christian character and maintaining Christian inspiration. Lidgett saw the duty of the churches as the creation of 'a Christian Commonwealth'. In the same article he wrote:

> I fully believe that a great many of our social evils are due to *lack of education*[43] in every class of the community . . . If we were more highly inspired by Christian influence and more truly educated as members of a civilised community . . . many of our troubles would be speedily surmounted.

Lidgett saw no quick route to achieving such a community: it would evolve through steady, purposeful progress.

Motivation and priorities, however, differed among other Free Churchmen. For many the Council was an opportunity to assert the importance and strength of the Free Churches, no longer content with second-class status in relation to the Church of England, and still smouldering with resentment at battles their members had had to fight to achieve equality as citizens. Some simply wanted to assert the identity of the Free Churches and receive due recognition. At the other extreme some sought means to dislodge the Anglican Church from its privileges and established position altogether and create a single, united and powerful Free Church of England. The Liberation Society, strongly supported by some Congregationalists in particular, was dedicated to disestablishment, but its prominence and strength varied over the years.

For the majority, hostility to 'sacerdotalism' and 'clericalism' in the Established Church went on in parallel with determination by Nonconformist laymen, not least the middle class, no longer to be patronised by parson, squire and lady of the manor. Lidgett could sympathise with such complaints and support protests with sincerity. The Church of England, he saw, was not faultless; he was ready to criticise its errors, but his Anglican contacts and experience of Appleton-le-Moors[44] gave him a broader understanding and a more balanced point of view than most of his fellow activists on the Council.

The National Council itself evoked different attitudes among the Free Church denominations. Differences in history, theology, practices and structures, together with long-standing jealousies and competition between them, meant that the Council never received wholehearted support. Its work was sustained by a group of self-appointed leaders whose enthusiasm outran that of the churches from which they came: the Free Church catechism, devised in 1899 by activists, including Hughes and Lidgett, might be regarded as an attempt to demonstrate a solidarity which did not exist, or at best remained fragile.

Among the denominations, Wesleyans in particular tended to remain aloof. Individual Wesleyans had taken the lead in establishing the Council, but only a small minority were eager participants, and a significant number were openly dismissive. To some extent Wesleyans generally maintained a degree of exclusiveness, perhaps in some cases even superiority, towards other Free Churches. Their historic relations with the Anglican Church led them, despite some slackening of the old ties (seen, for example, in reduced use of the Prayer Book) and complaints they shared with other Free Churches, to shun, as already mentioned, any label of outright Dissent. The majority, it seemed, firmly opposed disestablishment. Despite the alienation caused by the 'Ritualists', a significant number still saw themselves as closely linked to the Church of England.

In the contentious issue of national education Wesleyans had voluntary schools of their own and could see the debate from a rather different perspective. To the other Free Churches, voluntary schools, the vast majority of which were Anglican, represented sectarian indoctrination and restriction of career opportunities, especially in rural districts. These concerns also affected Methodists in areas where breaches of the Cowper–Temple Clause, permitting withdrawal from religious instruction on conscientious grounds, were said to occur. Wesleyans were, however, divided on whether or not to maintain and extend their own denominational school provision. J. H. Rigg, aided by D. J. Waller (Conference President in 1895), doggedly supported denominational schools as the best guarantee of religious education's survival; he feared 'unsectarian' Board School education would become secular.[45] Conference clashes with H. P. Hughes and his Forward Movement supporters became increasingly bitter. Antagonistic towards the clericalism of Anglicans and Roman Catholics, Hughes, like other Free Churchmen, favoured School Boards and the growth of provided schools. The Conference was in fact pledged to support and protect School Boards, and it was not surprising that in 1901 Lidgett, a member of the London School Board, successfully seconded a Conference motion opposing any attempt to imperil their work.[46]

Lidgett was himself particularly well placed to appreciate the complex attitudes within his own church and outside it. As an educational administrator, he was well aware of the merits and concerns of both voluntary and provided schools.[47] Moreover, as his autobiography frankly recorded, 'My hereditary association with denominational education made me respect both the motives and the feelings of those who supported it'.[48] His personal experience of Blackheath Proprietary School, knowledge of Wesleyan schools and the work of the Conference's Education Committee, and his contacts with W. F. Moulton, Rigg and the Leys School prevented him 'from adopting the extreme hostility to denominational schools which prevailed for the most part in the Nonconformist opposition'.[49]

Balfour's 1902 Education Act, creating a dual system of national education, and allowing use of the rates to finance voluntary schools, brought that hostility to the boil, and there was predictably a spectrum of views on how to express it. After manifest Nonconformist divisions over the Boer War and Irish Home Rule, extremists like the Baptist Clifford and the Presbyterian Nicoll viewed education as an issue on which the Free Churches and Liberal Party could unite. A. M. Fairbairn, the Principal of the Congregationalist Mansfield College, a dour but very able and much respected theologian, spoke[50] vehemently against Balfour's bill and joined a deputation to him in protest. Lidgett, however, regarded the ensuing policy of passive resistance to rate payments as divisive and a dangerous precedent.[51] According to D. L. Edwards, it made relations between Anglicans and Nonconformists 'worse than they had been for a century and a half'.[52] Lidgett made strenuous efforts against opposition from powerful personalities to persuade the hesitant and often confused Council to take the same line. His preference was for negotiations, where possible behind the scenes, and for the achievement of change by democratic means and in due course. Opposition, he thought, should be conducted without bitterness and partisans with differing views should not unnecessarily wound one another.

F. C. Pritchard said that at this time of deep-seated resentment (and, one could add, even of explosive feeling), Lidgett became 'the acknowledged leader of orthodox Nonconformity, if one can so term the more moderate majority'.[53] There was, however, no such clearly defined grouping or recognised figurehead. It might be more accurate to see Lidgett as beginning between 1900 and 1903 to emerge from among the other NCEFC figures involved in public and Council debate as a fluent, well-informed and respected speaker, who could present a powerful but balanced case against injustice and advocate moderation in responding to it.

But he was, it is true, far from averse to taking initiatives and increasing his responsibilities, as three events in 1903 showed. He seems to have played a prominent part in lobbying Talbot, Bishop of Rochester, among others. His aim, he declared, was to ensure that the Education Bill for London consequent on the 1902 National Act did not apply the Act's grant of rate aid to denominational schools. In particular, and more realistically, he wanted the bill not to sanction piecemeal administration, but legislate for overall co-ordination, by directly elected councillors, which he regarded as essential for education in the capital.[54] He was elected President of the Metropolitan Federation of Evangelical Free Churches for 1904, a post which, coupled with his handling of the Free Church demonstration in the Albert Hall on 11 July 1903, and his performance on the National Council's Executive and committees, clearly helped towards his election as NCEFC President in 1906/7. But perhaps most importantly, at the Wesleyan Conference in Camborne in July 1903 he self-consciously took on the mantle of a Wesleyan leader worn by H. P. Hughes until his sudden death on 17 November 1902. That tragedy Lidgett regarded as a turning-point in his career. In effect it reinforced his ambition.

His 1928 account, however, was marked by special pleading:

> I had not felt hitherto any deep sense of responsibility in regard to ecclesiastical matters, either denominational or general . . . Now I felt that the situation was entirely altered, and that I was under an obligation to play my part in the general life and policy of the Church, as well as in special concerns.[55]

This ignored the wide array of Wesleyan Conference Committee work and debate in which he had been involved since 1892. He later said[56] that when the 1902 Conference remitted the education issue to a joint meeting of the Extraordinary Committee of Privileges and the Education Committee, he had undertaken the responsibility for the arrangements and for dealing with the meeting's decisions. His account in 1936 was in fact more misleading than in 1928: 'Until 1902 [the death of Hughes in November] I had held somewhat aloof from ecclesiastical affairs, whether Methodist or other. I had other preoccupations, and questions of organisation and Church policy were, for various reasons, somewhat distasteful to me.'[57]

Lidgett's intention was clearly to heighten the drama of the 'momentous afflatus' which came upon him as the Camborne Conference began, and led to his making what 'H. K.' in the *Methodist Recorder* Conference Diary described as 'one of the greatest speeches ever delivered in the Conference during our times'.[58] Its theme was education, the major issue of that time. To the impression it made he attributed his subsequent Presidencies, of the NCEFC in 1906/7 and of the Wesleyan Conference in 1908/9.[59]

The speech showed mastery of the issues and clarity in presenting them. He was not afraid to tell the Conference *inter alia* his frank opinion that the days of denominational schools were numbered. Wesleyans, he said, should have heeded the warning of the late Archbishop Temple against stepping onto the slippery slope of maintenance by rates: this, he predicted, would lead to public control and forfeiture of the schools' distinctive denominational character. But Lidgett's contribution to the debate was especially remarkable for steering a successful course between the various extremes of opinion. Skill in finding a compromise acceptable to all sides in complex and tense debates, evident at later times in his career, was illustrated on this occasion when, as 'H. K.' put it, he 'disavowed sympathy with Passive Resistance as a policy, whilst at the same time distinctly avowing sympathy with those individual Free Churchmen who conscientiously refuse to pay rates'. The Conference resolved accordingly.

Though during the period of national discussion Lidgett called for continued protest against the legislation, he sought to promote a calm, considered response to it. He fought hard, for example, to take the venom out of the denominational squabble. All churches, he felt, shared the belief that religious education was an essential part of the school curriculum: as in 1897, he strongly opposed suggestions that contention about its form should be solved by excluding it altogether and making provided schools purely secular. But religious education there should be, non-denominational, undogmatic, simple Bible instruction. Though aware of objections in principle and controversies that could arise from how it was taught in practice, he insisted that this policy did not endanger faith nor open it to charges of sectarian provision. He firmly rejected any proposal permitting Anglican clergy to enter Board schools to give denominational education. Voluntary schools had their place; they were entitled to give sectarian religious education to children of their own denomination. But he could not condone injustice, wherever this was identified in the treatment of Nonconformist teachers, parents and children.

While opposing unjust provisions of the Education Act, Lidgett urged[60] that attempts should be made to gain the utmost possible educational progress from it. He was not alone in his conviction that education was a national, not an ecclesiastical matter. To him it was certainly a matter for Christians. In his view a radical, national overhaul of education had long been urgently needed, and this was what the Bill, whatever its faults, was seeking to supply. The bill had taken steps to remove barriers to the progressive development of secondary education, a matter of particular importance to him: significantly, of the eight NCEFC pamphlets on the controversy, he wrote one entitled 'The Education Bill and Secondary Education'. He did not in principle object to public finance for voluntary schools: what was essential was that it should be accompanied by adequate and representative public management and control. Like other opponents of the bill, he stressed the value of School Boards and the desirability of retaining them, but despite his own pride in the London School Board, he could see the faults in the Board system as a whole.[61] He was prepared to outline its merits in public, but in private he accepted the need for reform. He often walked a tight-rope in the desire to mould, as well as represent, the views of his Nonconformist constituency.

Lidgett's shrewdness as a politician and manipulator behind the scenes was revealed by a letter marked 'Private and Confidential' which he wrote[62] on 4 October 1903 to James Hope Moulton. Referring to the recipient's correspondence (details unclear) with William Sanday, Oxford's Lady Margaret Professor of Divinity, Anglican friend of Nonconformists, it contained Lidgett's comments on a proposal to call a Conference of the Churches. This appeared to be rather like the private two-day Conference called in July 1902 by the Bishop of London, which Hughes and Lidgett had attended on the lawn of the Bishop's Palace at Fulham.[63] In his reply Lidgett said Free Churchmen were not ready for such a conference: there were too many differences between them, and it would be unwise in any case to indicate what concessions they might be prepared to make before the next General Election. He fervently hoped a Liberal Government would then emerge victorious; this would compel Roman Catholics and Anglicans to recognise the Free Churches' right to confer. In the meantime he said he was 'carefully keeping on good terms with the Archbishop of Canterbury and some of the bishops so that an approach might be possible at the right time'. Moulton was advised to act similarly: 'I wish you would keep Sanday in your line for the time when he can be useful'. Lidgett recommended no further overt action until 'the opportunity is riper and the chance of success greater'.

Lidgett's mixture of bullishness and caution should be seen against the overtly political steps the NCEFC had already taken in the same year. Though passive resistance continued, he had helped to ensure it was organised independently of the NCEFC. But the Congregationalist, Silvester Horne, not content with sustained protests and waiting for the election, proposed the Free Churches should field 100 candidates; he hoped this would guarantee an acceptable educational settlement. The Liberal Party offered to allocate 25 constituencies, and its Chief Whip promised that the first act of an incoming Liberal Government would be to amend the offending legislation. Led by its energetic Secretary, Thomas Law, the NCEFC responded with enthusiasm. Accordingly, before the summer of 1903, the Council had become entangled in the Liberal Party's election preparation.

Lidgett heartily welcomed the prospect of a Liberal Party victory and the promise to its Nonconformist allies. Though he cannot have been happy with the Council's precipitate attempt to ensure their fulfilment, he nevertheless joined Law, Munro-Gibson and Meyer in complaining to Perks that the 25 constituencies allocated to Nonconformists were 'hopeless'.[64] The principal part he played before the election was to be seen as a trusted and major advocate of the Nonconformists' case for revising the 1902 Act, ready to take advantage of Liberal success, once achieved, by advising on the consequent legislative proposals.

Part 3

Achieving prominence

The following Chapters 7–10 assess Lidgett's Free Church and Wesleyan Presidencies, the challenges he faced within and outside his own church, and some of his activities prior to and during WW1.

Calendar of main events

1906–7	Elected President of NCEFC.
1906	Met Archbishop Davidson at Sidmouth.
1907	*The Christian Religion, Its Meaning and Proof.* Appointed Editor of *Methodist Times*. Elected President of Wesleyan Conference for 1908–9.
1908–9	President of Wesleyan Conference.
1908	Licensing Bill furore.
1909	Elected to Honorary DD of University of Aberdeen.
1910	General Election. Women admitted to Wesleyan Conference. Gave evidence to Divorce Commission.
1911–12	Welsh Disestablishment discussions.
1912–13	Free Church Commission.
1913	George Jackson furore.
1913–16	Appointed to Venereal Diseases Commission.
1914	Outbreak of WW1.
1915	*God in Christ Jesus.*
1916	Accepted conscription.
1918	Death of his son, John Cuthbert Lidgett. End of WW1. Retired as Editor of *Methodist Times* at end of year.
1919	General Election.
1921	*Sonship and Salvation.*

7

National Presidencies 1906–9

Lidgett regarded the year following his inauguration as NCEFC President in March 1906 as 'in many respects . . . the most arduous year of my life'.[1] That comment may well have been valid when he wrote it: it certainly was a year packed with activity, leaving him utterly exhausted. But in no year could Lidgett have been accused of lacking energy or curtailing the range of his activity. This chapter singles out three full calendar years, as both taxing and of particular importance in his career. During 1906–9, apart from preaching twice each Sunday, administering the Settlement, serving as Alderman and member of the LCC Education Committee, and completing his draft of *The Christian Religion*, he undertook the work of two Presidencies, embarked on a journalistic career, and began a friendship with the Archbishop of Canterbury, lasting until Davidson's death in 1930.

First, his Free Church activities. The year 1906 began with election fever. Following Balfour's resignation on 4 December, Campbell-Bannerman, the Liberal leader, called a General Election in January. The NCEFC 'reached its climax of political activity' as Machin put it,[2] in the campaign. In a resounding Liberal victory some 210 Nonconformist MPs were returned. The Council had demanded a national education system under effective public control. So while a Cabinet subcommittee was preparing its promised bill, Lloyd George was deputed to keep in touch with particular church leaders, not least Clifford, the firebrand Baptist, for comment and advice. Self-importantly Lidgett recorded[3] his own contacts with politicians behind the scenes. 'Liable to receive imperative calls to confer' throughout 1906, he was drawn into confidential soundings and formal interviews with the Prime Minister and the President of the Board of Education, first as tentative proposals were drafted, and then at 'every turning point of the painful and precarious progress of the Bill in Parliament', until deliberate mutilation by the Lords caused it to be finally withdrawn on 20 December. From March 1906 onwards, while responding to these demands in private, he was expected to comment in public on the education issue in speeches as NCEFC President, a major test of his discretion.

Augustine Birrell brought the first public draft of his bill to the Commons on 9 April. Schools receiving financial aid were to be put under public control,

LEAs could opt to take over voluntary schools, and religious tests were not required of teachers. As Lidgett promised when inaugurated as NCEFC President at its annual Assembly in March, he summoned the executive by telegram to the Memorial Hall on the following Wednesday. The majority of its members, who included Lloyd George, finally accepted Clifford's resolution, giving general approval to the bill but objecting to elements of compromise, notably in religious education. This would normally be undenominational in all schools, but Clause 4 provided for 'extended facilities', daily denominational teaching, by teachers brought in from outside twice a week, at the LEA's discretion in urban schools where the population exceeded 5,000, and where four-fifths of the parents of schoolchildren were of one religious persuasion and petitioned for it.[4] The clause had been designed to win over the Roman Catholics and Irish MPs, but predictably became a bone of contention. Lidgett's account[5] of the meeting seemed mainly designed to call attention to the congratulations which he and Lloyd George whispered to one another. The latter had succeeded in diverting the extremist Hirst Hollowell from denouncing the bill as it stood into leading a hunt for omissions from it. 'What a strategist you are!' Lidgett said. 'Yes', Lloyd George replied, 'and so are you, or you would not have seen it'.

Promotion of Sunday Observance brought Davidson and Lidgett together. The initiative in calling for co-operation among all the Churches to uphold the value of the Lord's Day and secure 'a more true and wise use' of it seemed to have been taken by the Archbishop in a formal letter to Lidgett as NCEFC President at its meeting in Birmingham. Lidgett's reply of 8 March 1906 readily offering the Council's support, and Davidson's reply on 10 March, both kept in Davidson's papers,[6] were to be of wider importance than the two public meetings on Sunday Observance which followed.

At the first meeting, on 9 May at the Caxton Hall, the Archbishop took the chair, with Lidgett in his Free Church capacity on his left and the Duke of Norfolk, the leading Roman Catholic layman, on his right; other church dignitaries were also present. Referring to this unusual seating arrangement, Davidson said at the opening of the conference that he doubted 'whether he or any of his predecessors for 1,000 years had even taken part in a public meeting more remarkable in its component elements'. This comment was recorded by Bishop Bell,[7] but strangely never by Lidgett, nor by his uncle in the *Methodist Times*. The second occasion was a conference in the Jerusalem Chamber on 13 November 1906, with Davidson again presiding. Societies concerned with Sunday Observance were represented. Lidgett proposed the creation of a (National) Federated Movement to bring the interested parties together on a more formal, official basis. His prominence was indicated in a printed leaflet[8] recording the conference resolutions. Before 1906 ended, Lidgett had signed, jointly with Davidson and the Archbishop of Westminster, 'Sunday, a Message to the Nation'. This call to acknowledge the national importance of Sunday Observance went out on New Year's Day, 1907.

Lidgett's reply to Davidson of 8 March 1906 hoped their common effort on Sunday Observance 'may be blessed to enable us all to show to the world how deep and abiding are the divine influences which promote unity in spite of the real, though I think passing, causes of difference'. Lest this hint of possible rapprochement in the future be taken simply as a pleasantry within an official response, he added a personal, enticing and highly significant postscript: 'Any small service which I can personally render will always be at the service of your Grace'.

Lidgett had first met Davidson, as Bishop of Winchester, at the Bishop of London's 'private conference' on education to which Anglicans and Free Churchmen were invited in 1902.[9] There had, however, been no close intercourse between them until the private meeting which was to follow nine days after Lidgett's letter. From what Davidson said on 10 March 1906 in reply, it can be inferred that Lidgett's attempts at reconciling the warring parties over the 1902 Act were recognised, and that Davidson had already formed a favourable impression of Lidgett as a moderate Free Churchman. He had a very different opinion of the Baptist, F. B. Meyer, NCEFC President in 1904/5. During one of the fevered meetings prior to the General Election, Meyer was alleged to have told potential Liberal voters at Canterbury that they should 'hate the Church of England as I hate it'.[10] When Davidson wrote to protest on 16 January 1906, Meyer claimed the report was mistaken. He had not, it is true, used those precise words. What it seems likely he had said was:

> If you vote Conservative, you vote for the entrenchment of the priest of the Anglican Church. If you believe what you have been taught, you hate priestcraft. If you vote conservative, you vote for putting the schools in the hands of the priest.

There is little wonder that Davidson despaired of amity between the Nonconformist and Established Churches.

Davidson, however, warmed to the prospect of Lidgett's offer of extended co-operation. He replied on 10 March 1906:

> To me personally it has always seemed that the area is a very wide one, and I have been sorely disappointed (as I think you know) during the last 3 years by the ill success which has attended some of the efforts which I have tried to make. I therefore welcome the more cordially the assurance which you have given me. It is just what I should have hoped for from yourself.

His letter concluded with a request for a copy of Lidgett's inaugural address on 6 March and of 'a good report' of the NCEFC meeting as a whole.[11]

The request gave Lidgett a welcome opportunity to develop their contact further. Replying[12] on 12 March, he enclosed the proof copy of 'Alderman Lidgett's' speech and regretted that the Free Church Year Book would not be published for some time. His letter was marked 'Private', because of his personal assurances given, interestingly enough, a month before the 1906 bill was announced: 'I am most anxious', he said, 'to be used in this year of office to reduce, if possible, the acuteness of the Education controversy'. Acknowledging serious differences of principle between Davidson and himself, he admitted that the views of some Free Churchmen, whom as their President he had to represent, were further apart from the Anglican stance than his own. But he continued:

> I desire that the Education difficulty – serious as it is – may be reduced to its proper proportions by the emphasis on common agreement outside it wherever possible . . . Pray, at all times count on the very small assistance I can offer in this direction.

Davidson's letter of thanks on 13 March[13] enclosed an invitation to lunch and 'a little talk afterwards' on Saturday, 17 March. Unfortunately there is no record of their conversation, but it was to be the first of many meetings, and a growing understanding began between them.

Lidgett was proud of his inaugural address, 'The World-Wide Mission of the Christian Church',[14] and of the reception which, as editor, Bunting accorded it in the *Methodist Times*: 'one of the greatest and most comprehensive . . . given from the Chair'.[15] Bunting's comment was remarkably prophetic:

> It marked him out as destined not only for the chair of our own Conference, but for a central and commanding place in the religious, social and ecclesiastical affairs which must occupy the thought of all Churches in the country during the next decade.

Davidson was, no doubt, unaware of these comments, but his marking of passages in the text[16] indicated his interest and perhaps approval, and may have provided further reasons to invite Lidgett to lunch. Lidgett had called the Free Churches to respond to 'the transformed thought and enlarged knowledge of the present day' and adopt a 'fresh interpretation of Christ in terms of the highest modern thought and aspiration'. The relevant rhetorical question caught Davidson's eye:

> By whom can the way of such effort be better prepared than by the National Free Church Council, seeing that its chief motive lies in the endeavour to draw men away from the restrictions of a too exclusive denominationalism to the centrality of Christ, and of Christ as related to, manifested in and served by the whole range of truth and life?

Davidson also asked Forsyth for a copy of his address at the same NCEFC meeting, but no follow-up was recorded.

Debate on the 1906 Education Bill kept rumbling on. In his *Guided Life* Lidgett noted that 'Until the following Christmas I had frequent and friendly discussions with the Archbishop in regard to the serious differences that divided us'.[17] Their confidential correspondence as the Education Bill approached collapse became particularly intense: each urged the other to use his personal influence against obstruction. Davidson urged Lidgett on 12 December[18] to assure the Government both that he (Lidgett) did not agree with the extremists (Davidson had Perks and Clifford in mind) and that he (Lidgett) had support for his views. The letter ended, in manuscript: 'There is no time to lose. It is a question of hours'. Next day in reply[19] Lidgett assured Davidson he had been 'quietly active' and had spoken to two Cabinet Ministers (unspecified) who did not need convincing about the importance of reaching a settlement. At the same time, both by letter and a visit to Lambeth on 14 December,[20] Lidgett sought to defend Clifford and the NCEFC against Davidson's charge of supporting secular education: he explained that Clifford's recent letter to *The Times*, advocating a ban on distinctively denominational teaching in public schools, referred not to a resolution passed at the NCEFC Council meetings in 1904, 1905 and 1906, but to 'explanatory notes' not voted on. When, however, Davidson confronted him with Clifford's letter, Lidgett could not support it, but he still urged Davidson[21] not to provoke Clifford into 'fresh activity'.

On 22 December Davidson had clearly given up all hope of a settlement, but his letter[22] to Lidgett looked forward to devising some limited amendments in 1907 to remove a few at least of the real causes of grievance in either direction. He said that after taking counsel 'I shall venture to trouble you, in the belief that the bonds which unite us are far stronger than the forces which try to sever us'. Replying on 24 December,[23] Lidgett shared his disappointment, repeated his desire for conciliation and offered help. Aware that most churchmen favoured rejecting the Bill outright, he claimed 'some small perception of the difficulties in which the Church of England has been placed during the discussions of this year', but at the same time he felt free to voice firm, though respectful criticism of Anglican partisanship.

Davidson did not attempt to counter this. Instead, in his letter of 27 December[24] he challenged Lidgett's statement in favour of 'a completely civic as contrasted with a denominational basis for our national education'. Speaking frankly, Davidson said:

> You know, I think, that I find it difficult to get in black and white what exactly is the position of those who, like yourself, are as earnest as men can be in favour of Christian teaching, and yet speak of a civic basis being all that we can rightly ask for.

Lidgett seemed to have responded orally, but the problem Davidson raised was the major one with which Lidgett was wrestling: how to secure a national education system and preserve religious instruction within it, and at the same time uncontroversially to provide scope for legitimate denominational teaching for both Anglican and Roman Catholic children. Lidgett did not see religious instruction simply as a support for citizenship, but as something of value in itself, without which children would not gain the opportunity to appreciate that all their education was opening their eyes to the glory of God.

By coincidence Lidgett and Davidson met in Sidmouth at the end of the year. Both had gone there to rest, but they met after morning service at the parish church door. Davidson invited Lidgett for a walk together on the shore next morning[25] and in the Fortfield, Davidson's hotel. Though they had met before, Lidgett regarded these Sidmouth discussions as 'inaugurating' a friendship which became increasingly intimate over the following years. He boasted that:

> there was scarcely an occasion when the general religious interests of the nation or the common interests of the Churches were concerned that he did not call me into his counsel. Sometimes[26] when he was laid aside, these conversations were held by his bedside.[27]

In the course of reminiscences of Davidson recorded at the request of Bishop Bell, Lidgett commented that after the Sidmouth meeting Davidson had treated him in a general way as a liaison officer with the Evangelical Free Churches. As events showed, this involved no loss of Lidgett's independence, nor any brake on the frank expression, where necessary, of contrary views. Publicly they had often to maintain their formal position, but both were 'odd men out': the personal views they expressed in private by no means always reflected those of their different 'constituencies', and yet each in his own way managed skilfully to retain his public credibility.

Lidgett allowed himself only a few days' respite from his hectic presidential programme. He undertook *inter alia* nearly fifty Day Conventions all over the country. Each included an address to the ministers and church workers of the local district, a speech at a public lunch, preaching at a public service, a talk at a Tea-Table Conference, an hour-long address on the spiritual unity of the Church and the education controversy, supper with ministers of the neighbourhood, and readiness for an early start next day![28]

Moreover, before his NCEFC Presidency ended on 5 March 1907, he had to look ahead to taking over editorial control of the *Methodist Times* from Bunting, its temporary editor since the death of H. P. Hughes. The task may well have attracted him as a means of serving an even wider public than before and as a practical demonstration of his refusal to differentiate the sacred and the secular.

Lidgett had accepted the invitation in the autumn of 1906, but postponed the official date until 7 March. Plans had, of course, to be made beforehand: the weekly paper's editions of 21 and 28 February heralded expansion to eight new pages with some new contributors. That new responsibility will have been, not least initially, an extra strain: after writing for the theologically literate, he was now required to engage in popular journalism, of which he had had, he admitted, no previous experience.[29] In the event he excelled in it.

It was not surprising that the end of his Presidency[30] found him 'rather severely ill of gastric influenza . . . and . . . exhaustion'. He was, he said, 'obliged to dictate my first leader and Editorial Notes to my wife as I lay propped up on pillows in bed'. His Retiring Sermon to the Leeds NCEFC meeting had to be read out by Samuel Chadwick because he was too sick to attend the relevant session.[31] To crown it all, his Progressive Party was defeated in the LCC elections. Despite his exhaustion (he said he was hardly able to stand) he was called to appear before the new LCC to defend the Elementary Schools proposals of the outgoing régime, only to discover the victors' determination to refer them all for further consideration.[32]

Annotations by Thomas Ross on the letters[33] which Lidgett sent to him on 9 and 10 July 1907 might suggest Lidgett had undergone, not for the first time, some heart-searching about whether he should continue his work in Bermondsey. Ross had objected to a Bermondsey posting: he argued that his vocation was for 'calling sinners to repentance', not engaging in what he dubbed as social work, providing entertainments, picture shows and Greek classes under Lidgett's direction. They met in the Settlement, and Ross jotted down, in note form, his impressions of the interview.

They discussed their different approaches to the ministry and Lidgett stressed his genuine desire for a truly evangelistic ministry at Southwark Park: it was there Ross would be stationed. Ross then recorded, in his own words:

> He [Lidgett] got up from his chair, paced about, said sometimes I had serious thoughts as to whether my work is the best for me to do, but I am in it. I have this vast organisation to keep going. I am one of the authorities to consider the educational question. I am listened to more than any other men about the needs of this neighbourhood, and I feel I must go forward. Said he, 'You may be surprised I get very few Methodists to help me, Church of England, Congregational, High Church'.

Whether this was said wanly or with pride was not made clear. Dr Dale, Lidgett said, had also wished he had done differently, an unwise admission; but like Lidgett he had decided to go on. Lidgett made no reference to the prospect of being nominated for election as President Designate at the Wesleyan Conference, opening in the following week.

Lidgett admitted[34] his was the most 'controversial' Presidential election since that of Hughes in 1898. Certainly both Lidgett and Hughes were controversial candidates, and great excitement was generated in the Conference on each occasion. Hughes's battle with Rigg on education policy[35] had been reflected in Hughes's successive electoral defeats over previous years, but the 369 votes for Hughes against F. W. Macdonald's 83 (a surprising margin), coupled with the quite unprecedented outburst of sustained applause which greeted that success, were not features of the 1907 election for the Presidency of 1908/9. In fact Lidgett's majority was slender: he gained 250 votes against the 243 for William Perkins of the Mission House. Lidgett admitted 'a considerable number' of ministers regarded him as a 'dangerous person', making 'energetic efforts to postpone, if not to prevent', his election.[36] J. W. Butcher, for example, made a blatant, last-minute attempt to persuade the respected George Findlay (1849–1919), then at Headingley, to stand, but Findlay declined, saying that he was physically unequal to the challenge.

Hughes and Lidgett were very different personalities. Hughes had been charismatic, whereas Lidgett was far more complex, exhibiting a stern, even unbending exterior. As Harry Bisseker put it in 1908: 'He is a leader of men, not because of any special personal magnetism, but because of the unalterable confidence he inspires in those to whom he is really known'; and 'His power of expressing thought exceeds his power of expressing feeling'.[37]

Lidgett himself suggested several reasons[38] for the opposition: critics were saying that much of his work had been 'outside Church affairs', and within the Church he had been prepared to advocate controversial policies. The former objections may have alluded to his involvement in and outside the Settlement, in Progressive Party politics, the LCC and the Free Church Council. Lidgett's first leader of 7 March 1907 referred to many who 'feared for the integrity of Methodism' if it cultivated too intimate relations with men of other churches, and Lofthouse in 1908[39] admitted that the NCEFC was a body 'largely suspected in Methodism'.

Complaints about Lidgett's activity *within* the Church certainly included his support for the Forward Movement's pressures for internal reforms: some of his colleagues would not, for example, have applauded his championship of women's admission to Conference (finally achieved in 1910); and the length of his stay in Bermondsey (17 years so far) would have aroused jealousy, even though Conference had permitted exceptions to itinerancy rules years before. Nor was his advocacy of greater unity with the other Methodist denominations universally shared: in 1904 he had proposed a Methodist Assembly as an initial step.[40] Objections were also inevitable to Lidgett's enthusiasm for closer relations[41] with the Anglican Church as well as the Free Churches.

But hostility had been aroused within Methodism 'still more', Lidgett said, 'by the emphasis I laid on the social and even the political responsibilities of the

Church'.[42] Lidgett had shown himself unafraid to express views on current international affairs and how the Churches and Britain should react to them. He shared, for example, the concern of his aunt[43] for Armenian Christians under Turkish persecution; and his anger was aroused by the opium traffic in China, the exploitation of Chinese coolies in South Africa,[44] and the cruelties of Leopold II in the Congo.[45]

The major source of irritation, however, was not his speaking out on international issues. He had been accused of secularity in his promotion both of the Bermondsey Settlement and, more generally, of seeking to change the Church's tunnel vision on individual salvation to a focus also on the needs of society as a whole. Opposition on this count was being linked with indirectly expressed suspicions that he was 'soft' over evangelism. Even while hailing his entry into office, the *Methodist Recorder* was at pains to offer a tactfully worded warning. Acknowledging that Lidgett embodied a developing social sympathy and enterprise, the writer added: 'At the same time we need to keep clearly before us, without in any degree losing the social vision or the quickened social conscience, the great evangelical aim that must not be for one moment in abeyance'.[46]

Lidgett's association with the Forward Movement had come vividly to his colleagues' attention earlier in the year when he became editor of the weekly *Methodist Times*, founded by Hughes 'to give impetus to a modern and aggressive spirit in Christian life and effort'[47] and express social concern. The conservative *Methodist Recorder* had remained contemptuous of its younger 'sister' and conscious rival, also published on Thursdays. H. J. Pope,[48] an influential figure behind the scenes at the Conference, who had urged Lidgett to accept editorial responsibility for the *Methodist Times*, deliberately pointed up the contrast: Methodism, he insisted, needed more than one denominational paper, and one which would 'consistently advocate, with complete freedom, a thoroughly progressive policy in regard to all the concerns of the Church'.[49] At the *Methodist Times* luncheon in July 1907,[50] the retiring editor strengthened his case for maintaining a voice for 'progressive' forces in Methodism, by adding 'Reaction was always ready to spring up'. Clearly the battle against the 'Old Guard' was far from over.

Hughes had deliberately defied the gerontocracy by subtitling his paper 'A Journal Written by Young Methodists for Young Methodists'. Though Lidgett gave it a new subtitle, 'A Journal of Religious and Social Movement', the top left of his front page referred to its founding editor, and Lidgett continued to keep youthful and progressive readers, especially younger ministers, firmly in mind. It was the strong following he had among these which led the *Methodist Recorder* in 1908 to predict that Lidgett would 'probably prove a Young People's President'.[51]

Lidgett boasted that over nearly 12 years he wrote the editorial and many of the paper's 'Notes and Comments' for every week except two. This was in contrast with Bunting who quite often invited others to supply the leading article. When Bunting died in 1911, Lidgett replaced him as editor, jointly with G. P. Gooch, of the monthly *Contemporary Review*, with its Christian and humanitarian outlook. Gooch (1873–1968), a distinguished academic historian, had been Liberal MP for Bath and taught at Mansfield House, Toynbee Hall and the Working Men's College.[52] Like Bunting, who had had Paton's assistance, the new editors favoured political liberalism and social reform, offered scope for frank discussion of controversial issues, and sought to draw attention to international affairs and matters of interest in Literature, Science and the Arts. Articles in the *Contemporary* fed Lidgett with material for comment in the *Methodist Times*. The latter helped to extend his influence in religious, mainly Wesleyan, circles, and together they gave him an ever widening grasp of social, political, literary, as well as religious and theological (not just Methodist) concerns. When Sir John McDougall (1844–1917), his cousin by marriage, died in spring 1917, Lidgett became Chairman of the *Contemporary Review* Company. Lidgett's books, journalism and contacts with an increasing variety of highly placed figures will have made him a subject of envy among colleagues labouring in much less glamorous circles.

The education problem did not go away, and further attempts were made after 1906 to find a solution. The start of August 1907 found Lidgett in the Committee Room of the Lords with, among others, Archbishops Davidson and Bourne, and Lords Salisbury and Edmund Talbot, discussing how best to proceed.[53] Lidgett called on Davidson on 25 March 1908 to assure him of his readiness to repeat his words at the recent NCEFC meeting where he had 'spoken very strongly in favour of a truer recognition of the Church's rights and the Church's difficulties in the present matter'.[54] Both made efforts to promote a peaceful agreement between the various parties, but strong opposition, notably by Bishop Knox, but also by Roman Catholic and Nonconformist Churches, caused the compromise bill, introduced on 24 February 1908 by Birrell's successor, Reginald McKenna, to be withdrawn in April. It had proposed to restrict rate aid to schools providing *un*denominational religious instruction, and invite voluntary schools to 'contract out' (transfer to LEAs) or lose their aid. Lidgett pointed out[55] that finance for education was not only needed for instruction but also for scholarship schemes and essential ancillary services, such as social and medical aid, which no denomination could provide from its own resources. On 4 December another attempt, made by McKenna's successor, Walter Runciman, was also withdrawn.

Lidgett's Presidential visits indicated his priorities, notably 'the young'. By asking specifically for the help of 'younger ministers' from whom he 'selected' companions on most of his tours round the country,[56] he underlined the importance of this constituency. From its inauguration in 1896 he had supported the

Wesley Guild, a 'Young People's Society', which had adapted some educational elements from the Bermondsey Settlement for its own use. A visit to the Guild's annual Easter gathering on 12 April 1909 at 'Gravel-lane' in Manchester was one to which he would have looked forward. In fact he looked back to it with pride since his appeal there for funds to reduce the Foreign Missions deficit[57] was a great success.

Lidgett's programme in 1908/9 was bound to reflect his long-standing interest in the education of adults and children, in schools as well as in Sunday schools. He addressed the Westminster and Southlands Wesleyan Teacher Training Colleges on 28 June 1909.[58] Predictably, in reporting his seizure of all opportunities 'to come into contact . . . with all the central institutions of Methodism',[59] he instanced the theological colleges as well as the schools. His opening speech to the Representative Session of the 1908 Conference[60] drew attention to the needs of ministerial training and spoke of supplying candidates with mental as well as moral and spiritual equipment. It seemed clear that intellectual improvement was one of his important priorities. In *Reminiscences*, he criticised his Presidential predecessors: the sentence following reference to theological colleges and schools began, 'While paying special attention to such interests and activities as had hitherto come short of official recognition, though containing the promise of the future, I determined also . . . '[61]

Lidgett was conscious of Wesleyanism's wide social composition, but having already identified the multiple needs of country villages,[62] he resolved to target them in his Presidential visits.[63] The strong middle class which had helped Methodism to thrive was to be found in rural as well as urban areas,[64] and a traditional, conservative outlook could be predicted there. With Synod chairmen he made motor tours throughout their districts, and his friend, H. J. Pope, helped in arranging Conventions, perhaps similar to those of his NCEFC Presidency in 1906/7.

The aims of the message Lidgett delivered in various forms throughout his year of office were to justify his social outlook, remove former prejudices and misunderstanding, and win support. He took care first to root his social thesis in Wesley's insistence upon 'perfect love' as the ideal of true religion, and then to draw out its implications.[65] With rhetorical vigour he set out 'to enforce the unity of spiritual and social concerns in the wholeness of Christian life'. This principle was then applied specifically to 'the responsibility and importance of Methodism as a spiritual factor in the moral and social concerns of national life'.[66] If he had been looking for an example of when the Church, *qua* Church, *should* intervene in politics, the Licensing Bill incident (explained below) gave him a golden opportunity to 'expound and enforce the grave responsibility of the Christian Church when supreme moral interests are at issue in the public and political affairs of the nation'.[67]

Lidgett 'insisted upon' his social message at the three-day conference he organised in April 1909 as President of the Wesleyan Methodist Union for Social Service. WMUSS, founded as a pressure group (with S. E. Keeble as its first President) at the 1905 Conference, aimed to urge attention to social welfare, to disseminate Christian Socialist ideas, record and circulate information on social conditions throughout Methodism, but not just to 'See': its motto and title of its magazine (1906–17) was 'See and Serve'. It offered training of 'young people for positions of responsibility which they may possibly occupy in later life in private and in public'. Lidgett would have been pleased at the attendance[68] both of 'a large number of Methodist women' and 'young Methodist ministers'. In his dual presidential role Lidgett delivered his inaugural address, 'The Church and Social Problems',[69] stressing that social reform and overseas missions belonged together, since a Christian world meant a Christian civilisation. 'The Church', he said, 'as a great missionary agency, urges its heathen converts, at all risks, to become the witnesses and pioneers of a Christian civilisation'.

Keeble and the more radical WMUSS members, however, thought evangelicalism compatible with socialism and supported ideas of public ownership, the nationalisation of the means of production, distribution and exchange. This alarmed conservatives like Perks and Fowler to whom socialism was on a par with increasing secularism and 'infidelity' (decline in religious adherence). To defend the Free Churches, they founded, with Dinsdale Young, the Nonconformist Anti-Socialist Union or League in 1909. The radicals, concerned about possible disciplinary measures in Conference (which in the event did not materialise), then formed a (Wesleyan ministers') 'Sigma Club'; its 65 members included J. E. Rattenbury and Henry Carter (its first President and Secretary), Lofthouse, A. W. Harrison, J. H. Moulton and Maldwyn Edwards, but not Lidgett. As the new editor of the *Methodist Times*, he decided not to enter the current disputes himself: his paper would advocate measures 'by which . . . growing political expression will be given to the principles of righteousness and love'.[70] Defending the right of responsible citizens to state their case, three times he took issue with people who anathematised as 'Socialist' any initiative for social reform. Rattenbury was allowed space in his columns[71] to justify Sigma's attack on the Union, but Lidgett himself remained at this stage a determined moderate.

Lidgett need not have attended the annual Southport Holiness Convention on 9 July 1909. Not all Presidents, it seems,[72] undertook to address it, and it was clear from its members' concentration on individual spirituality that their fears of being undermined by the ideas of 'progressive' social reformers could result in a less than receptive audience. But Lidgett's friend, H. P. Hughes, unusually for a Holiness devotee, had, it seems, identified in the Anglican Holiness Movement 'too little recognition of the civic and virile qualities of Christians'; 'he could not accord with . . . certain traits in their conception of Christ and the kind of service that He required from men in this world'.[73] Lidgett was equally determined to challenge this weakness in the Southport equivalent as eirenically and persuasively as he could. At the same time he would have thought it essential to acknowledge Methodism's emphasis on the 'Theology of Experience', and its Holiness tradition, maintained by such ministerial colleagues as Agar Beet, Waddy Moss, Samuel Chadwick, T. Champness, C. W. Andrews and his old friend, John Hornabrook.[74] Southport also offered Lidgett a welcome opportunity to provide evidence for Bisseker's claim that 'his social enthusiasm . . . is only an outward expression of his deep spirituality',[75] a quality critics claimed was missing from his character.

But Lidgett's overriding aim was to set out his deeply felt convictions. He thought true holiness had to be expressed constantly in practical activities and personal relationships in and outside the Church. So the text he chose for his address included the words 'I sent them into the world . . . '.[76] The plea he made was for avoiding the 'spurious holiness which is separatist and censorious in spirit' and for pursuing instead 'the social life of holiness' which was 'not limited to the Church. It has its mission to the world'.[77] Lidgett argued that 'because the life of holiness is the life of love . . . it becomes pervasive in its attempt to transform all relations and interests till they serve its highest ends'.

Political intervention became the *cause célèbre* of his Presidency. It arose out of Wesleyan attitudes to 'Drink'. In 1936[78] Lidgett proudly announced he had been 'Chairman for years' (perhaps 1900–14) of the London Temperance Council, one of many such across the country. Like fellow Wesleyans, he was committed to 'Temperance' (in effect teetotalism): alcohol was seen to cloud man's spiritual perceptions and militate against disciplined life and attendance at church. The Wesleyan Conference regularly denounced 'the drink traffic' as a social evil and as a major cause of much slum degradation. Lidgett accepted this diagnosis, but like Carter he urged Temperance reformers to take a wide view. Carter thought[79] habitual drinking was often caused by other social evils. As Lidgett saw it,[80] the root problem across the country was the aimlessness of youth and lack of resources for leisure amid the 'crowded quarters of great cities' and 'the stagnant monotony . . . in the villages'. So, as in Bermondsey, the remedy he suggested was characteristically positive, through 'educational methods and the provision of healthy interests and recreations'.

Some Anglicans also supported the Temperance Movement: Archbishop Frederick Temple and Bishop Pereira of Croydon, for example. But most, while equally deploring drunkenness, disliked Nonconformist 'fanaticism' against the public house. By contrast a liking for 'drink' was associated by Nonconformists, many of whom were of lower social rank, with the upper social classes, landowners, the aristocracy and London Clubs, and so with the Establishment and the Established Church. These were all alleged to be in league with lawyers, magistrates and the armed forces for the defence of brewers' vested interests.

To combat alcohol addiction some Wesleyans advocated moral persuasion; others supported total prohibition, eventually recommended by Conference in 1917. Over the years various legislative measures were suggested, including the 'local option' which put the onus of control onto local magistrates and the power of local opinion. But Balfour's 1904 Licensing Act abolished magistrates' power over the granting of licences and offered compensation for licences which lapsed after a year. This was roundly condemned by Methodists, and it was largely their pressure for amendment that later led to Asquith's Bill in 1908. This not only aimed to curtail the number of public houses by restoring magistrates' right to renew, transfer or repeal licences at their discretion, but also included opportunities to restrict Sunday trading and provide supervision of clubs and employment terms for barmaids. Lidgett claimed[81] a million Wesleyan Methodists petitioned in its favour: the figure recorded by J. M. Turner[82] was 610,000.

Lidgett, as Wesleyan President, had successfully proposed a resolution in favour of the Bill in Conference, chaired a subsequent unofficial meeting in Wesley's Chapel, and remained undeterred by the concern expressed by George Cadbury, the NCEFC financier, that such meetings on the subject could divert the Free Churches from 'more direct Christian work'.[83] To urge the passing of the Bill, he led an NCEFC deputation to Asquith as Chancellor of the Exchequer. The Bill had in fact been passed by the Commons when Lidgett heard of a party meeting held at Lansdowne House by the Marquess of Lansdowne, the Conservatives' leader in the House of Lords, at which an almost unanimous resolution was passed to reject the Bill in the Lords on the Second Reading, with no scope for amendments in Committee.

News reached Lidgett as he was about to address the Manchester Mission's Annual Meeting in the Free Trade Hall.[84] He was outraged. 'I at once wrote a telegram to the Marquess of Lansdowne', he said, ' . . . to the effect that, should the House of Lords reject the Bill on the Second Reading, the act "would never be forgotten or forgiven by the Wesleyan Methodist Church"'.[85] These words in fact were those of a letter he sent on 25 November 1908 to the Marquess. Lidgett did send a telegram, but this was expressed in a much milder tone: 'The Wesleyan Methodist Church of Great Britain is profoundly anxious that the Licensing Bill should be passed by the House of Lords'.[86] The Lansdowne House decision reinforced Nonconformist belief that share-holding peers and the Establishment were in league with the drink trade. When Lidgett announced what had happened and his response to it, his audience cheered him to the echo.

There was, however, an opposite reaction. Letters from (he claimed) a small minority complained Lidgett's threat was political. These 'began to flood the

Methodist Recorder',[87] and a 'campaign' against him continued until H. J. Pope remonstrated against it: he warned participants it would be counterproductive, 'making him [Lidgett] irresistible'.[88] The correspondence was promptly closed, but the *Recorder* ominously made no editorial comment for nearly a month after the Lords decided the fate of the Bill. It was Lidgett's highly rhetorical outburst on 17 December 1908 which provoked the *Recorder* to break its silence on 24 December.

What Lidgett's editorial said was:

> The House of Lords must either amend its ways and make complete satisfaction for the wrong it has perpetrated, or it must become the primary public object of every Christian reformer to abolish the powers which it has abused in order to defeat what is essential to the Kingdom of God. The whole controversy is . . . taken up above the realm of party politics. If the Churches are supine, they will allow the supreme control of the nation to pass into the hands of the allied forces of Mammon, self-indulgence and misrepresentation. The Christian religion will become a pious sentiment . . . It will cease to bear its witness to the sovereignty of CHRIST . . . 'Here I stand . . . '

The *Recorder*'s response was an editorial, headed 'Politics and the Churches'. Without naming names it protested 'against much that is said about the duty of the Churches'. While agreeing that nothing could be said in favour of the Lords, it threatened that 'If there is an attempt to turn the Christian organisations into the service of the reform of the House of Lords, then there will be a mighty letting loose of the waters of bitterness'.

This stung Lidgett to fury. On 31 December the *Methodist Times*[89] declared: '*The Methodist Recorder*[90] speaks out at last. Methodism's so-called "leading" paper says, "The duty of the Churches is to mind their own business!"' This was printed over four parallel columns devoted to 'The Churches and the Lords'. The first column set out the *Recorder*'s editorial; then, alongside it, C. W. Andrews's contribution to the *Recorder* on 3 December, strongly supporting Lidgett's 'Declaration of War'; next, the resolution of the Wesleyan Conference, urging the adoption of all legitimate means to secure the passing of the Bill into law; and finally the comments on Lidgett's leader of 17 December by the *British Weekly*. Nicoll had said that Lidgett had accurately set out 'the position in which Nonconformity as a whole finds itself', and predicted 'Nonconformists will follow a bold, a wise, a daring and inspiring lead'.

This stark difference between Lidgett and the *Recorder* clearly illustrated how strongly some (unidentified) Wesleyans were opposed to him and their keenness to exploit whatever might render him vulnerable to attack. His autobiographies showed his urgent need to justify his Manchester action. In

Reminiscences,[91] the care he had taken before sending the telegram to obtain the approval of the current Secretary of the Conference was stressed, together with the nature of his demand: not that the Bill should be passed as it stood, but only that it should be carefully considered. In both autobiographies he emphasised his protest responded to intense convictions notably in the Wesleyan Church, and that his standing ovation, unprecedented in his experience, demonstrated strong support. His protest, nevertheless, was a genuine expression of principle, not intemperate outrage. Happily for Lidgett the overt opposition died away, and he said his position in the Wesleyan Church 'was strengthened and not damaged by this incident'.[92]

Lidgett's grand gesture, however, failed to achieve its object: the Bill was rejected. But he maintained that the subsequent Parliament Act, limiting the Lords' veto, was nemesis following hubris, and a triumphant vindication of his public act of defiance. In fact the Licensing Bill was not the only Bill rejected by the Lords at this period: the Education Bill was another casualty, and the last straw, the major provocation, was the Lords' blockage of Lloyd George's People's Budget. But in his own circles Lidgett still claimed a large share of the credit for focusing public attention on the Lords' iniquity. It was their earlier 'arrogant' rejection of the Licensing Bill, which, Lidgett asserted, 'more than anything else . . . emboldened the Lords and went far to compel them to reject the Budget'.[93] The Parliament Act was, in his view, largely successful, not for political or constitutional reasons, but 'because of the indignation of multitudes who would not "forget or forgive" the contemptuous rejection of a measure . . . held by them to be vital to the moral progress of the Nation'.[94]

Both the Licensing Bill incident and the run-up to the General Election of January 1910 obliged Lidgett to explain his view of the Churches' stance in politics. The social aspects of the rejected Bills gave him an ideal setting for reiterating his social message, for example, in leading articles of 4 and 11 February 1909. It was, he said, by applying the principle of love to human affairs, and by witnessing, like John Wesley, to its supremacy that Methodism should serve the State.[95] Though no social order could be identified as the Kingdom of God, that Kingdom could not come without a sustained attempt on the part of all believers to create a perfect social order, and he protested against 'any attempt to deny the sovereignty of Christ and the spiritual purpose of his world'.[96] Social reform was to him the leading issue before the nation, and national greatness and progress depended *inter alia* on the 'direct influence excited by the Christian religion in furnishing the ideals and principles by which progress, if it be real, must be governed'.[97] Aware of those who wanted to confine the Church to inculcating principles, he said a principle should be a principle of *action*; there might be times as with the Licensing Bill, he said, when 'the practical application of a principle is imposed upon the *Church* by an impression which is recognised as coming from God'.[98]

The relationship between Church and State continued to occupy his mind in the following two months, first when he addressed the NCEFC in Swansea,[99] and then the WMUSS Conference in Oxford.[100] In Swansea he was concerned with the Church's duty in regard to poverty. As he saw it, this was to 'stimulate and guide [inspire] the State by giving a specifically Christian direction to public thought and activity', and to 'render to it active assistance' through able, trained, interdenominational, *non-sectarian voluntary* workers, co-operating with public authorities; at the same time any action by the State would still need to be supplemented by the Churches' customary 'ambulance service of humanity'. In April, in Oxford, Lidgett stressed that whenever any incompatibility emerged between the principles of action in Church and State, 'the prophetic witness of the Church', fortified by 'a great increase of spirituality', was needed to call attention to it.

Though Lidgett spoke as a theologian rather than directly in the terms of Hobson and Hobhouse, 'his spiritual kinship with their [New] Liberalism', as D. P. Campbell has described it,[101] was clear. His two speeches, employing such phrases as 'collective will', 'personal liberty', 'the narrow limits of voluntary enterprise' and 'self-centred . . . competition', indirectly suggested approval for New Liberalism. Lloyd George's Budget was introduced to Parliament in March. Lidgett's April speech referred to demands for 'reform which we hold vital'. But he called on the Church to realise that 'social reform is becoming the concern of the nation, and not merely of Churches and voluntary societies', and bring 'its influence to bear upon the State' to secure 'the prevalence of Christian ideals and of the Christian temper in the national life'.

Political pressures did not abate when Lidgett's Presidency came to an end. He continued to fulminate against the obstructiveness of the Lords, and declared that vast spiritual, moral and social, as well as constitutional issues were at stake. So the question again arose as to what precise action he was advocating, and by whom. Lidgett insisted he did not want the *Churches* as such to be plunged into political strife. His call was rather to Free Church*men*:

> One of the advantages [of the establishment of the Free Church Council] is that it enables Free Churchmen to combine for necessary political purposes, without the Churches themselves being diverted from their paramount purposes or distracted by internal strife . . . No good will come, but harm, of pulpit onslaughts in services which should have a totally different spirit and aim. Principles rather than policies must be taught and enforced in the Church.[102]

Lidgett was thinking in particular of the '200' Liberal MPs, who had been seeking social reform, aiming to 'advance the cause of religious equality' and 'emphasise the moral elements of social well-being by such measures as the Licensing Bill'. He said, 'The present crisis has been largely brought about by their demands and those of the Free Churches to which they belong'. Lidgett seemed here to blur his distinction between Free Churches and Free Churchmen. He was confident that there was unanimous agreement among the Free Churches on the principles their adherents had gone on to apply in the political context. Without serious challenge his confidence appeared justified.

As the General Election drew near, and the fate of the Budget with its package of social measures was in the balance, Lidgett's stance was manifest:

> We must strive to secure a minimum of health, education and employment and sustenance for the most helpless of the community . . . Only as such efforts are made, can Christian men enjoy their property without heart-searching or even compunction. The Christian character of the nation is at stake. The social ideals of the present time represent an endeavour to create a truly Christian civilisation.[103]

Lidgett avoided Free Church criticism only to face an inter-church problem. He happily joined Lloyd George on the platform of a rally of Free Churchmen on 16 December 1909 in the Queen's Hall, but their approaches were different. Lidgett's focus was on what the Free Churches stood for in general: 'religious freedom, promotion of international peace, world-wide humanitarianism, the cause of the poorest and most helpless, and the moral tone of the community'.[104] Lloyd George, however, used his opportunity to play on Free Church animosities against the Lords and Establishment. His inflammatory speech so incensed Davidson that on 18 December he wrote privately to Lidgett 'as a trusted friend' for his 'fraternal counsel . . . which I have found so valuable before now, not once or twice'. He took exception to 'the exciting of hatred, envy and malice in the name of religion', of 'every prejudice . . . that can be inflamed by the recollection of past controversy', and to the presence, gratitude and applause of ministers and laymen 'in their religious capacity'. The incident made the Archbishop wonder whether an invitation to joint prayer for the healing of denominational divisions ahead of the Missionary Conference next year in Edinburgh would be repulsed. His postscript insisted: 'What I am referring to is in no way the political differences (between yourself and myself these would be slight), but the spirit which is being proclaimed and fostered and utilised – the spirit of *what*?'[105]

Lidgett replied immediately next day. He hastily urged him not to abandon his call to prayer, but quietly, firmly and avoiding reference to Lloyd George, defended the attitude of Free Churchmen in the coming election. It followed inevitably, he said, from their past reactions to the way the Lords had treated the Licensing Bill and to the 'Education difficulty, which we recognise would have been settled so far as your lead and influence are concerned'. Even 'the quiet men, Jowett, Munro Gibson and a host more' were, in his opinion, being provoked to rally as they had never done before. Their aim, he wrote, was not to sow discord but to remove hindrances to justice and progress. But Davidson was assured: 'We will work and pray for righteousness and goodwill, appreciating our friends of the Established Church even when we differ from them. We will realise the difficulties of their position, and we hope they will realise ours.' Lidgett went on to campaign with J. D. Jones and R. F. Morton for particular Nonconformist (Liberal) candidates.[106] His relationship with Davidson and Lloyd George remained intact.

Lidgett had many reasons to be satisfied with his Presidential year. The office conferred an important status in his own Church. It also increased his influence, as he put it, 'as one of its representatives in external relations',[107] meaning he felt he could now speak *on occasion* for the Wesleyan Church as well as for the Free Churches. Among Wesleyans, not least its 'rising ministry and laity', his seizure of opportunities during the year seemed to have helped him overcome misunderstandings and prejudices and evoke more 'effective recognition of and sympathy with the obligations of the Christian faith and influence in regard to the social responsibilities of the nation'.[108] The year, however, was a strain: the Conventions, for example, which he had requested, were additions to routine Presidential engagements. He lost his voice temporarily at the May meetings,[109] and after Conference in July took a thorough rest in his favourite Switzerland.

Perhaps, for him personally, the best moment had been on 25 February 1909. He was returning by train from a Presidential visit to Cornwall (on his way home from Taunton),[110] when he bought a newspaper, the *Daily Chronicle*, at Plymouth,[111] only to discover he was to be awarded an Honorary DD from Aberdeen University. In 1928 Lidgett claimed the degree 'forestalled the intention of another University', but he did not identify the university or supply evidence. A. S. Geden of Richmond had been awarded a DD in the year before. Lidgett was now, in title as well as in published work, able to rank himself among his academic peers. In offices and public prominence, however, he was to outdo all his Wesleyan contemporaries.

8

Progress despite conflict

His Presidencies over, Lidgett had no intention of retiring from either the Wesleyan or Free Church scene. In Wesleyan Methodism he continued to exercise an influence in Conference, in several committees (initially as ex-President) and through journalism. The Baptist F. B. Meyer (1847–1929), the NCEFC's 'travelling Bishop' since 1907, became (at first temporarily) its Hon. Secretary in 1910. Lidgett boasted[1] he was thereafter 'regularly, though informally, called upon to advise with him in regard to all the public questions that called for the Council's attention' until 1914. Meyer then, he said, made it a condition of his remaining in office that Lidgett should be officially recognised as Joint Hon. Secretary. Lidgett became sole Hon. Secretary when Meyer retired in 1920. Lidgett was already in 1910, and for years remained, on the NCEFC Education Committee, and brought a Nonconformist perspective to work with public bodies and societies promoting moral and humanitarian interests at home and abroad. Lidgett's standing steadily increased. But neither as a Wesleyan nor as a Free Church figure did he escape conflict or frustration, or avoid the need often to mediate between others and press for compromise.

Visits to two ecumenical gatherings were made by the ex-President at the request of Conference. Lidgett was one of the Wesleyan Methodists assisting in the eight International Commissions which prepared for the World Missionary Conference in June 1910 when 1,200 delegates, representing all the Reformed Churches and their Missionary Societies in Europe and America, met in Edinburgh. Comments in the *Methodist Times*[2] voiced Lidgett's familiar themes: applause for 'common counsel and concerted action'; warnings that 'denominational independency' was a barrier to evangelism of the world; and insistence that 'the strenuous . . . attempt to attain a true Christian civilisation at home' was essential for success. But the Edinburgh Conference and its significance quickly ceased to engage Lidgett's attention. It was surprisingly mentioned in neither autobiography, perhaps because the Wesleyan delegation leader was W. T. Davison, not himself. By contrast he proudly recorded[3] his commission in October of the following year in Toronto at the fourth Ecumenical Conference of Methodist Churches in Britain, Europe and

America: to set out the Conference conclusions in the encyclical letter, 'to be read in all Methodist Churches throughout the world' at the start of 1912.

Lidgett continued to speak out on matters of particular concern to Wesleyans at home. In addition to debate on the actions of the Lords, two other issues were brewing before the Conference met in Bradford in 1910. The first was again constitutional, and concerned the Declaration to be made by King George V at his accession. Catholics had been upset by the traditional wording, explicitly repudiating the Mass and transubstantiation, but proposals to remove the offending words brought angry protests by Protestants suspecting an insidious attempt to pave the way for 'a Popish monarch'. Lidgett appreciated the force of their objections, inflamed as they were by the Queen of Spain's recent vehement repudiation of Protestantism, but sought to calm tempers and (to him) unjustified fears through the *Methodist Times*. He argued[4] that introducing similarly violent language into the British King's Declaration was 'to part company in the most flagrant way with the Golden Rule'. In the Conference debate of 16 July, his influence, but perhaps principally speeches by Arthur Henderson and Walter Runciman, helped to ensure a large majority for the Government's new formula. 'I am a faithful Protestant' was its core, and Parliament accepted it.

The second related to the status of women in the Wesleyan Church. In 1909, without success, S. E. Keeble had made the first formal proposal, supported by Lidgett, that 'duly qualified and elected women' should be admitted to Conference. In the 1910 Conference debate they had to contend against powerful opposition by H. B. Workman and Dinsdale Young, but their motion was carried. W.Wakinshaw[5] paid particular tribute to Lidgett: 'The hard-won victory', he said, was largely due to his courage and 'generalship'. Like H. P. Hughes, Lidgett had always been a strong champion of women. When the suffragettes made public protests over the franchise, he supported their case, though not their tactics.

On 29 November 1910 Lidgett and W. Middlebrook, MP, were called to give evidence before the Royal Commission on Divorce and Matrimonial Causes (1909–12). The Conference was already over when Lord Gorell, the Commission President, requested the views of the Wesleyan Church. Lidgett was appointed as an official representative by a specially convened meeting of the Conference Committee of Privileges, but he had to tell the Commission that having run out of time the Conference had not discussed or pronounced on the issues.[6] He had therefore to set out informally what he regarded as a large trend of opinion; but before submitting written evidence and appearing for questioning, he took care to consult a representative number of colleagues. Divorce and separation were scarcely heard of in the Wesleyan Church, he said, and divorced people rarely applied to it for remarriage. He stood for equality of the sexes and justice for all social classes, but his contact with cases of infidelity and unhappiness caused him to oppose any extension of grounds for divorce beyond that of adultery.[7]

When the Commission declared its findings, the Archbishop of York, Sir William Anson, Sir Lewis Dibden and Lidgett submitted a Minority Report, stating that the approved extensions would lead to domestic instability, reduced regard for marriage and damage to the nation's general good. Though a more liberal line was taken by Lofthouse[8] and subsequent legislation followed the Majority Report, the majority of Wesleyans supported Lidgett's stance. The publicity Lidgett received on the Divorce Commission cannot have been irrelevant to his appointment in 1913 on the Royal Commission on Venereal Diseases.

Lidgett became known as an opponent of 'heresy hunting'. This had not died with the Beet affair, a decade before. Lidgett's involvement in a Wesleyan battle against fundamentalism, in 1913, was to be the first action in what became a guerilla war lasting well beyond 1918. In 1908 George Jackson, a Wesleyan minister, had been appointed as Professor of the English Bible at Victoria University, Toronto. His liberal theology led to conflict with a Dr Carman, but he was soon exonerated on the charge of disloyalty to Methodist standards. His Fernley lecture of 1912, however, was destined to provoke alarm among at least some of the faithful at home. *The Preacher and the Modern Mind*, calling for preachers not to be afraid of new ideas, had been favourably reviewed by E. S. Waterhouse in the *Methodist Times*,[9] but by 13 March 1913 Shepherd Allen, a prominent Wesleyan layman and former MP, had produced a pamphlet, *A Brief Review of the Fernley Lecture*, accusing Jackson of doubting the historical accuracy of the Bible. Allen and his friends pressed this charge *inter alia* to cast doubt on Jackson's suitability for taking up the pastoral theology post at Didsbury College in the autumn.

Critics pointed out that the words in the lecture attacked by Allen were in fact written by John Wesley, and the hostile *British Weekly* had to admit that the two sentences it had attributed to Jackson in a Toronto Men's Bible Class had actually been put in the mouth of an imaginary objector for Jackson to repudiate them. Undeterred, George Armstrong Bennetts (1875–1930), a ministerial friend of Allen, went ahead and published 10,000 copies of another pamphlet, *The Doctrinal Crisis in Wesleyan Methodism*,[10] berating Jackson for breaching Wesleyan doctrinal standards and reducing the authority of Scripture and the person and authority of Christ. The stage was set for a 'heresy' charge at the Plymouth Conference. In the event, when Gipsy Smith had lobbied laymen on the Sunday,[11] and not least after an hour-long, low-key, reasoned speech by Jackson himself, only 7 votes were cast in the Representative Session against Jackson's succession to the Didsbury post, and the subsequent Pastoral Session exonerated him from the doctrinal charge by 336 votes to 27. The conservative *Methodist Recorder* could only comment sourly that Jackson's over-smart journalistic style appeared to endanger fundamental truths.

In 'The Persecution of George Jackson: A British Fundamentalist Controversy',[12] D. W. Bebbington has suggested that Lidgett did most to secure Jackson's position. Quickly discerning a growing crisis, Lidgett had set out to avert it through a number of strong leading articles in the *Methodist Times* of June and July, by speeches in Conference, and lobbying (as Bebbington plausibly inferred) behind the scenes. His major aim was, as always, to persuade the Connexion, as well as (more immediately) Conference delegates, to exercise a cool, balanced, fair and informed judgement. Acknowledging the seriousness of the points at issue, he went out of his way to underline his real respect for Bennetts's sincerity, loyalty to his Lord and deep concern for the interests of the Church. But calmly and tactfully, he pointed out that in 1913 the Conference could not, in all conscience, renege on its 1912 decision to designate Jackson to Didsbury, when Jackson's views were already known not only to the Fernley Trustees but to all members of the Conference. As for biblical criticism, this had been endorsed, he said, by venerated figures of the past: H. P. Hughes, for example, had told him as long ago as 1881[13] that he accepted it. Lidgett's own support for Higher Criticism was already on record,[14] but he repeated it while defending freedom of enquiry. Instances of biblical fallibility did not, he insisted, destroy the faith of the 'truly evangelical man'. Lidgett would also have been aware that Wesley's Arminian stance was in principle opposed to fundamentalist views.

Undaunted, Bennetts continued his campaign. The WBU was formed before the end of 1913 with the support of his fellow ministers, Harold Morton and William Spiers. Whatever they thought subversive of the Bible came under attack:[15] 'Guess-Criticism', Darwinian evolution, Modernist preaching, and even international Socialism. They hoped the shock of falling membership would ensure a return to the old certainties and orthodoxy, but in vain. Steadily, not universally or suddenly, among ministers conviction was growing that biblical literalism had to be abandoned. Even Samuel Chadwick (1860–1932), Principal of Cliff College in 1913 and a champion of the Holiness Movement, came to oppose the heresy hunt, and complained that the WBU was diverting Wesleyans from the work of the gospel.[16] The WBU, nevertheless, kept up the pressure, for years enjoying support from prominent members of the Wesleyan 'hierarchy', W. L. Watkinson,[17] Silvester Whitehead[18] and the powerful preacher, Dinsdale Young.

The election of Dinsdale Young (1861–1938) as Conference President in July 1914 would have encouraged the fundamentalists. Towards the end of his address to the Representative Session of Conference he declared that the Bible:

> rightly translated and interpreted, – every sentence of it – is not a cluster of human opinions, more or less valuable, but the sure revelation of the mind and will of God. It is only in a subordinate sense that the Bible is a human book. The rock on which the Methodist Church is built is the impregnable rock of Holy Scripture.

Lidgett rose to the challenge, tactfully not in the Conference but through the *Methodist Times*.[19] Having expressed agreement with 'all the essentials' of Young's address, he then said that Higher Criticism's linguistic and documentary studies were essential if the Bible was to be 'rightly translated and rightly interpreted'. Lidgett was duly complimentary about Young's Presidency during the anxieties of 1914–15, but in his obituary for the *Methodist Recorder*,[20] he was openly contemptuous. Young, he wrote, paid little or no attention to the unsettlement of the age or the social problems of his time and place, and 'in so far as he conceived that current teachings were incompatible with the Gospel as he believed and preached it, he either passed them by, or dismissed them with a hearty, yet genial anathema'.

Before the 1914 Conference ended, Morton decided to attack Lidgett, not as leader writer, but as editor: he accused him of responsibility for publishing a favourable review of a book containing opinions which contravened doctrine on the authority of Holy Scripture. *The Chief Cornerstone*, a symposium by Wesleyan luminaries (including Lidgett), edited by Davison, had openly aimed to reconcile the older and newer elements of evangelical faith. But Morton's objections were to the essays by Findlay and, less significantly, Wilfrid Moulton, both of Headingley College and supporters of the results of Higher Criticism. Too little time was available in the Conference debate for the issue to be settled, and Morton complained through the pages of the *British Weekly inter alia* that a Conference speaker had said Lidgett was too eminent to be charged with heresy.

WBU tempers flared again over the *Methodist Times*'s 'Saturday Causerie' column by 'APG' which, on 29 October 1914, ridiculed the WBU Journal's latest number and its trio of 'shooters' at 'heresy'. After publishing a series of acrimonious letters to the editor, Lidgett intervened on 19 November to explain his view of editorial responsibility. It was absurd, he said, to imagine that he agreed with everything in the *Methodist Times*. His own views could be found in his editorial columns, but his paper was 'not a Vatican': it allowed both sides of an argument to appear, and trusted readers' 'goodwill and good sense'. He argued that the splendour of the faith 'will only be increased by permitting serious people to raise discussion from time to time as to its meaning'. The WBU seemed to him mistaken in opposing development in doctrine, claiming divine revelation had ended, and thinking freedom of enquiry was incompatible with discovery of evangelical truth and pursuit of 'aggressive' evangelism.

Bennetts was simultaneously attacking another regular contributor to the *Methodist Times*, 'Decima', for another article on 29 October 1914, prior to All Saints' and All Souls' Day. The Great War had begun to claim its casualties, and the question arose as to whether prayers for the dead were permissible. Many Protestants had thought it wrong to pray for the dead in the belief that each individual's destiny was decided at the moment of death; yet the idea that a good Father God could require eternal punishment for those who had suffered the 'Hell' of Flanders, through no fault of their own, was considered unacceptable. Reflecting this concern, Decima said all people pray both to and for the dead: 'Prayers to the Saints are forbidden, but who that has a father or mother gone to be with God does not hold with such an one fellowship which is of the very essence of prayer?' Her column provoked a virulent outburst by Bennetts, accusing her (and, in fact, her editor) of support for doctrines of probation after death, Universalism and 'Romish errors of prayers to departed saints and to the dead'.

Lidgett replied on her behalf, and also his own, on 19 November.[21] The *Methodist Times* was not committed, he said, to the pagan or medieval doctrines Bennetts had pilloried. Provided nothing was allowed 'to come between Christ and the soul', what he called 'intuition of the spirit and instincts of the heart' could be permitted 'considerable latitude'. Bennetts persisted, and Lidgett published his letter in line with editorial policy. He again tried to defuse the situation. Having begun by agreeing with several of Bennetts's points, he assured him and other readers that in the doctrine of the Communion of Saints both the departed and the living were held together in Christ.

As for the Universalist doctrine of the soul after death, it was true, Lidgett admitted, that Holy Scripture did not permit any teaching of a second probation, and put the sternest of stress on the holiness of God and the heinousness of sin. At the same time it seemed to him impossible to magnify the love and mercy of God and God's will that all might be saved too greatly, and the question had to be asked:

> When we think of the brave fellows who are rising to the heights of unselfish heroism and sacrifice on the field of battle, is it not brought home to us that God has infinite resources in and toward the human heart which our narrow thoughts are unable to measure or even explore?

The nearest Lidgett came to personal criticism of Bennetts was when he suggested that it was unseemly for those enjoying safety through the devotion of the armed forces to seek 'to define exactly the measure of mercy these men are to receive at the hands of God, our Father'. The issue did not die away. Yet with studied objectivity Lidgett reported on 20 January 1916 that WBU membership was increasing!

By 1917 the Connexion decided that the ongoing conflict over what precisely constituted Wesleyan doctrines and standards had to be resolved. A sub-committee was convened on the 'Unity of Doctrine' to examine the limits of Methodist orthodoxy. Lidgett, Davison, Workman, Maltby, R. N. Flew, Bennetts and Morton met in December 1917,[22] but without agreement; the WBU adherents were as intense and humourless as ever, and Lidgett annoyed the others by not concentrating sufficiently seriously on the issues at stake. But Conference pronounced in 1919, declaring that ministers should be expected only to give assent to 'the system of evangelical truth' contained in the Connexional standards. This was in effect a decision not to define orthodoxy, but to allow scope for more liberal attitudes to belief. Bebbington[23] has rightly concluded this indicated that the majority of the Conference had been alienated by the WBU: its fanaticism became counter-productive.[24] He could also have noted Lidgett's not unimportant part in maintaining an unruffled but firm resistance to the fundamentalist challenge.

Lidgett remained very active in Free Church as well as Wesleyan affairs. In both his autobiographies Lidgett devoted a disproportionate amount of space[25] to an isolated (and unfruitful) episode within the 25-year parliamentary battle to achieve the Disestablishment of the Church in Wales. The action he took sought to put a brake on his extremist Free Church colleagues. Fierce debate had begun when Nonconformists insisted that the Welsh Church no longer commanded the allegiance of the majority in Wales; proposals in Parliament linking Disestablishment with Disendowment added to heated arguments between opposing denominational partisans; and differences of attitude emerged among Welsh and English Nonconformist Liberal MPs and Nonconformists generally. The story Lidgett chose to tell from the period before the Welsh Church (Temporalities) Act finally became law in 1919 took place in 1911/12, but his own dating was vague and misleading, his account incomplete, and his own importance in the episode grossly exaggerated.

Lidgett approved of Welsh Disestablishment in general, as politically just and in the spiritual interests of the Welsh Episcopal Church, but he considered the 1911 Bill's proposals on Disendowment would cripple, not increase, the efficiency of the Welsh Church. Like Sir Henry Lunn, a fellow ecumenist with whom he associated himself on this occasion, he was disturbed that religion was being damaged by the ongoing controversy. He may also have been influenced by affection for the Welsh Episcopal Church resulting from his earlier friendship with Dean Vaughan of Llandaff[26] and his own wife's Welsh family connections.[27] But the motives for recording this particular incident would seem to have been the desire to illustrate his diplomatic concern for amity between all the factions involved, his enthusiastic search for compromise, his independence and courage while acting 'in a strictly personal capacity'[28] (and yet inescapably as a senior Free Church figure!, and not least the range of his contacts at the highest ecclesiastical and political level. The story revealed the man.

Lidgett claimed to have taken an initiative leading to the formation of a Conciliation Committee to suggest amendments to the 1911 Bill, and spoke as if he played a major part in its work. Having voiced concern about the divisive controversy in the *Methodist Times*, Lidgett said that he happened to meet Lunn in the House of Commons lobby, similarly engaged in gaining support from MPs for compromise amendments to the Bill; he then 'joined forces with him in the constitution and work of a special committee on the subject which he [Lunn] called into being'. Much later, in the *Methodist Times* of 29 May 1930, Lunn explained that the genesis of the idea had in fact been an appeal from Hensley Henson, then Canon of Westminster, for Free Churchmen to find a middle course between the opposing parties, and in response he [Lunn] had suggested through *The Times* forming a Committee. P. M. H. Bell[29] attributed the committee initiative only to Lunn, and made no reference to Lidgett as a significant figure, not even to his inclusion (together with Bishop Gore) in a deputation to the Prime Minister on 19 June 1912. Lunn,[30] however, did acknowledge Lidgett's membership both of the committee and the deputation, and the balanced membership of the Committee, including both Nonconformists and churchmen, clerical and lay, chimed in with the ecumenical views both men were known to share.

Lidgett was more anxious to record a breakfast meeting[31] than the deputation to Asquith later that day. Thinking he was invited to discuss conciliation, he found himself embarrassed and surprised by being caught up in a large group convened in support of the unamended Bill. Apart from members of the Government, Lloyd George, civil servants and journalists seeking a story, the group included John Massie, the Congregationalist Chairman of the Liberation Society opposed to the Established Church and State patronage. Also present was John Clifford, who had earlier written to R. Birch Hoyle[32] to attack 'the false and delusive plea of generosity towards the Anglican Church in Wales' and 'the poison of compromise' in the House of Commons. Lidgett boasted of being undeterred when Massie denounced 'weak-kneed Nonconformists' and Clifford deplored refusals to take a hard line. Unashamedly admitting to the group that he was the only 'weak-kneed Nonconformist' present, he defiantly set out the views he was to express to Asquith later that day.

This story, indicating Lidgett's independent stance within the Free Churches, was recorded nowhere else. Though the Bill finally gained the Royal Assent on 14 September 1914, the War delayed its implementation.

Once the excitement of the Constitutional crisis of 1910/11 had died down, the smouldering resentment at the Government's failure to solve Free Churchmen's educational grievances burst into flame. The heat built up so much that there were fears of an outburst of anti-government hostility at the annual NCEFC meeting in March 1912.[33] As NCEFC Secretary, Meyer persuaded Asquith to promise an Education Bill in 1913. Pressure was kept up by Clifford and the Primitive Methodist A. T. Guttery who mounted demonstrations demanding primacy for the Bill in the new session.

Lidgett's contact with Davidson had continued. On 15 May 1913 Lidgett was invited to Lambeth to discuss the educational dispute. Davidson said the Government was misguided *inter alia* in contemplating training colleges which gave no Religious Instruction, 'flooding the market with teachers quite unfit to do the very thing which the Government claims to be anxious to do'.[34] Lidgett fully agreed, but could throw little light on the situation. Complaining of unreasonable behaviour by 'the extreme folk', he attacked the vehemence of 'the Passive Resistance Party' and the narrow partisan direction of its pressure on the Government. To him the 77-year-old Clifford could not be trusted 'as a public man'.

Publicly Lidgett gave strong commendation[35] in the following month to a contribution by Sir Joseph Compton-Rickett (1847–1919),[36] a prominent NCEFC layman, to the *Contemporary Review*. The article principally appealed to all parties to compose their differences. Anglicans should, it was urged, 'learn to live with Nonconformists', their 'natural allies in the struggle against indifference and immorality'; Free Churchmen were also pressed to compromise, accepting that 'another half of the Christian World in England' had a right to be heard despite its differences in principle. The nation, he said, was tiring of religious distractions.

In the event neither Clifford's demands nor the moderates' pleas for compromise succeeded. The 1913 Education Bill was confined to increasing grants for building, and it was abandoned in August. Clifford's resultant indignation and threats led to a further promise by Asquith, offering to introduce a Bill in 1914 to meet the 'single school areas' issue. But when in June 1914 the draft Bill provoked Free Church objections, Asquith angrily withdrew it, and no further progress was made.

Pressures for Free Church unity had continued, and the desire for greater cohesiveness among its member churches led the NCEFC Council in March 1912 on Lidgett's proposal to vote for a commission. Its brief in 1913 was to inquire 'into the present condition and outlook of the Free Churches' in relation to the needs of the people and the increasing demands of the age.

The Commission met in Mansfield College, Oxford, from 25 to 28 March. Lidgett was appointed as its Chairman, Meyer as its Secretary. Its numerous representatives, meeting in seven sections in private,[37] were to produce their reports for wider discussion perhaps within two years. The news would have aroused no excitement had not Nicoll, editor of the *British Weekly*, launched an attack via a leading article headed 'Lust for Talk'.[38] His principal charges were that the Commission was for 'people who delight to rush away from the immediate duties of the monotonous field at home', and that Lidgett had been given 'an altogether disproportionate prominence in the Inquiry'. Nicoll, hardly a friend of Lidgett since 1897 (except in 1908), regarded himself as a major Free Church figure. His article was clearly a sign of jealousy.

Lidgett's response was forthright. The Commission's aim was, he said,[39] concerted *action*; if increased talk/discussion was currently being advocated for university students, the Free Churches could benefit also; and if interdenominational meetings were frowned on, then meetings of the BMA, TUC, etc. should be banned. As for Conference participants, he knew many were among the most responsible and hardest-worked people in the country, and had given up their Easter holiday to attend. He was himself, he stated, presiding at NCEFC request at a Conference he had not initiated. Lidgett's personal retaliation was brief, suggesting that there could be a 'lust for writing' as well as for talk. The *British Weekly* had, after all, hastily printed misleading reports of Jackson's Bible Class in Toronto. The dispute, however, subsided, and the Commission's work was overtaken by the outbreak of war.

But perhaps the most significant public recognition of Lidgett's standing as a Free Churchman before the War came on 1 November 1913 when he was nominated by the President of the Local Government Board as one of fifteen members of the Royal Commission on Venereal Diseases. Lidgett had been a member of the Wesleyan Social Purity Committee since 1893, and his relatives Sir Percy and Lady Bunting had helped Josephine Butler and the Rt Hon. James Stansfield in their campaign against the Contagious Diseases Acts. Lidgett had given evidence to the Divorce Commission, but his educational experience was also valued. The Commission Chairman, Baron Sydenham of Combe (1848–1943), asked him to write the Report's educational section, a responsibility of which he was clearly very proud. Coyly he reported: 'I should not mention this fact had not the chairman publicly stated it'.[40]

Education covered 8 of the Report's 35 Recommendations in 1916.[41] These included such matters as the instruction of medical students and teachers in training; instruction on moral conduct in all types and grades of education, including evening continuation schools, factories and workshops, but without detailed discussion of sexual matters in elementary schools; and designated responsibility for the literature to be used for these purposes. As expected, it was urged that the focus of instruction should not be solely on the physical consequences of immoral conduct but on moral principles and spiritual considerations. Lidgett's hand may also be seen among the Report's General Conclusions,[42] declaring that 'the growth of temperance is of great importance for the eradication of these diseases: their prevalence is also largely fostered by overcrowding'. The Report was warmly welcomed in 1916 by the Wesleyan Conference and no doubt by the NCEFC.

By the outbreak of war neither of these 'constituencies' could be in any doubt about Lidgett's prominence within them. He had taken part in major international conferences, been singled out for membership of a national VD Commission, and faced public questioning as the Wesleyan representative on Divorce. Within his own church he had dealt effectively with fundamentalist and heresy challenges, and shown courage and robust independence as a Free Churchman in opposing Welsh Disendowment. In the continuing educational dispute his search for an acceptable compromise had been maintained, and in Free Church debate he had shown realism and vision.

9

Theology and optimism before and after 1914

By 1914 the record of Lidgett's personal achievements had given him confidence in his own abilities and every ground for satisfaction. The Victorians' belief in the inevitability of world progress had become an unshakeable conviction. He was therefore optimistic about continuing social advance in England and abroad, and about growth in the churches' standing and power to influence public opinion, if not always events.

Lidgett's opening Presidential address to the 1908 Wesleyan Conference admitted that Methodist numbers[1] had fallen in the past year, but his message was upbeat, regarding the decline as temporary, a challenge and no cause for depression. When the Conference decided in 1913 to plan for an evangelistic campaign in January 1915, Lidgett gave the idea strong support.[2] A fortnight after the outbreak of war he was urging his readers to 'prepare for the new order'; he had already seen signs of 'home-sickness' for God; and to him the barrier raised against religion by current secularism and pleasure-seeking did not warrant despondency.[3] He had, nevertheless, expressed some reservations:[4] D. L. Moody's approaches to evangelism had, he felt, become 'hackneyed', and ideally a study of new methods, together with a renewal of members' inner life, should have preceded the campaign. But he remained optimistic about the outlook for the churches in general and the campaign in particular.

Lidgett's optimism was mirrored in many other church circles of the time. In 1910, for example, William Temple's collected lectures, *The Faith and Modern Thought*, sounded a typically triumphant note of confidence in the world's progress. When speaking of his theory of the Atonement as the expression of love, Temple wrote:

> remembering that the world has progressed a good deal since the earliest ages that we know, and progressed in love more perhaps than in any other quality, we shall find that it may be true that the whole world is moving onwards for ever under the impulse of the infinite love of God to a more and more adequate return of that love.[5]

Against this background, however, signs of disillusionment were beginning to appear among pre-war theologians, and Lidgett, for whom the doctrine of the Fatherhood of God never ceased to glow, failed or refused to notice its significance. As Peter Hinchliff has pointed out, R. J. Campbell in the end recoiled against the optimism of Liberal Protestantism and Idealism, and P. T. Forsyth had found 'the reductions of much contemporary theology powerless to cope with the human condition'.[6] Hinchliff has drawn attention to Neville Talbot's writing as the most striking expression of pessimism in this period, only two years after William Temple's collected lectures were published. Talbot, Chaplain and Fellow of Balliol, son of the Bishop of Winchester, supplied the Introductory contribution to *Foundations, a Statement of Christian Belief in terms of Modern Thought by Seven Oxford Men*, edited by B. H. Streeter, in August 1912. His essay on 'The Modern Situation' was a powerful analysis of the ways in which the assumptions of mid-Victorian Liberalism had been 'going bankrupt'.[7] 'The skies have darkened', he said, and 'Somehow or other the rose colour has faded out of Victorian spectacles'.[8]

His reasons derived from the state of society as he saw it, affected by economic, scientific and philosophical ideas. The Victorians, he said, thought God's Providence would 'right wrongs and check wickedness without our help'; this confidence, however, had been eroded by the results of *laissez-faire* and 'individualistic competition'; and for that the theological motto had emerged as 'Every man for himself, and God for us all, as the elephant said when he danced among the chickens'.[9]

Talbot thought people's faith in the inevitability of future progress had come from some continuous upward development in the past: that was, he argued, a false inference – they had not realised Darwin's 'struggle for existence' 'cut at the roots of the belief in the benevolence of nature to the individual'.[10] In Talbot's view, Darwin had shown men a world indifferent to their needs and interests, causing them to regard matter as dominant over mind and spirit. Talbot detected a general feeling that truth and morality were relative: nothing was thought to be absolutely right or true at any given moment, and morality was seen as 'the philosophy either of those who are paid to maintain it, or of those who can afford to be good'.[11]

After this devastating critique Talbot had to find some grounds for encouragement. Some were feeble: for example, 'If there is a crisis in the Christian faith, there is a worse one in any other'. He finally took refuge in advocating a form of cyclical philosophy to justify his assertion that the problems and doubts of the time were in themselves signs of hope. Jesus, he recalled, was always powerless with those who did not need him, and now, once again, 'a knowledge of darkness is needed to urge indolent man upon the quest after the light'. Talbot saw the original conditions coming round again: 'The questions to which the Gospel was an answer are again being asked, and Christianity as the truth of God will live again in living men'.[12] So the essay ends on a high, but perhaps not altogether convincing, note.

The *Methodist Times* paid relatively little attention to this issue in *Foundations*. The Congregationalist, Principal Selbie, invited to review the book on 6 March 1913, concentrated simply, and rather unfairly, on what he called its 'outstanding deficiencies': on its neglect of both the theology of the Reformation and of 'the more recent theological movements in Germany' (unspecified), and on the absence of a dominating philosophy. His only positive contribution called for Nonconformist and Anglican theologians to co-operate over theological reconstruction, a call that remained unanswered.

Lidgett himself, it seems, made no comment, at least directly. An indirect allusion to Talbot's as well as others' pessimism[13] might be discerned in his *Methodist Times* leader late in 1913, mentioned above, on 'The Coming Revival'. Lidgett may have echoed Talbot by recalling similar alarm at the unbelief, worldliness and corruption which pervaded the first centuries and the Renaissance; there had, nevertheless, come out of them, he said, the spiritual advances of the early Church and of the Reformation, achieved through the missionary labours of St Paul and the religious zeal of Martin Luther. Lidgett concluded: 'The overbearing tyranny of the secular at last impels the quest for the highest, awakens the inmost, and prepares men to welcome the vision of the eternal'.[14]

Lidgett refused to be downhearted. Moreover, like the vast majority of his contemporary theologians at that stage (Streeter, Burkitt and Sanday excepted), Lidgett chose in effect, as far as his own theology was concerned, to take no account of the iconoclastic intrusion of Albert Schweitzer (1875–1965) into New Testament scholarship. Schweitzer's seminal work, *Von Reimarus zu Wrede*, published at Tübingen in 1906, gained its English translation[15] in 1910, entitled *The Quest of the Historical Jesus*. The portrait Schweitzer drew was radically different from that of the idealised Jesus, whether eternal or civilised, popular among liberal theologians and philosophers of the time. To Schweitzer 'Lives' of Jesus were projections of their authors; for him Jesus was a strange, bewildering fanatic, obsessed with eschatology, going to his death to hasten the final vindicating judgement, the imminent arrival of an other-worldly Kingdom of God, but failing to achieve it and dying of a broken heart. This view was based on scholarly studies, demanding respect for their solid base in first-century Judaism and its apocalyptic outlook.

Lidgett had been fully aware of the English translation in 1910. No doubt he found Schweitzer's work too disturbing to accept, and what Lidgett may have regarded as a world-*renouncing* Jesus was in any case very far from attractive to him. His detailed criticisms, expressed in a leading article of 22 September of that year, dismissed Schweitzer's thesis as totally flawed. Schweitzer was condemned for narrow selectivity: for 'steadily ignoring the Epistles'; for discrediting all Gospels except Mark (or, rather, those parts of Mark that fitted his own hypothesis); for abandoning evidence of the Resurrection; and for failing to recognise the influence on Jesus of 'the more directly spiritual elements of the Old Testament' (Isaiah and Jeremiah for example), as well as that of 'apocalyptic features as contained in the Book of Daniel'.

Lidgett was determined that nothing Schweitzer or anyone else propounded should undermine his own unshakeable belief in the spiritual, redemptive experience of Christ and the cosmic implications of Christ's revelation of God's fatherly purpose. He drew an unfavourable comparison between Schweitzer's 'narrowly conceived interpretation of St Mark' and the Epistle to the Ephesians. Adumbrating views he was to publish in 1915, Lidgett regarded that Epistle 'as a veracious witness of a profound and far-reaching spiritual experience' and as 'a portrayal, not of a Christ of dogma or imagination, but of the historic Christ in the normal and unending exercise of his redemptive grace and power'. Moreover Lidgett was insistent on maintaining 'the purposive character of the Christian religion': 'In the purposiveness of history are involved the purposiveness of the Universe, the revelation of God as a creative Reason and Goodness. The fact of Christ and the rationality of the Universe are inseparably united.'

Lidgett's view of one aspect of Schweitzer may have changed at a later date. Lorna Horstmann wrote about Lidgett, whom she and her family often entertained: 'Like Schweitzer whom he much admired, he was mighty of intellect . . . '.[16] This comment was not amplified, but may well refer to the widespread adulation Schweitzer received for sacrificing his academic career in 1913 to devote himself to mission and the care of the sick in French Equatorial Africa. There certainly were similarities between Schweitzer and Lidgett. The actions they took at Bermondsey and Lambaréné both sprang out of their individual views on the Kingdom of God. In each case these entailed passion to find brokenness and make it whole, and determination to begin the task somewhere, even in far from attractive locations. As a significant twentieth-century theologian, however, Schweitzer did not warrant inclusion alongside Otto and Barth in Lidgett's *Guided Life*.[17]

Just after the outbreak of war with Germany Lidgett's attitude, and that of many other theologians, to Schweitzer and to German theologians in general, was deeply affected by the so-called 'Manifesto of the Intellectuals',[18] signed by Adolf Harnack and fellow German academics, attacking the British action. In 1916 Peake tried, apparently without much effect, to distinguish between potentially valuable German theology and wrong-minded German theologians. In 1917 E. S. Waterhouse took a hostile line. He predicted that 'for years to come' what he called 'intimate co-operation' between British and German scholars would not be resumed, since close relations between the two nations were essential to it, and real advantages could be gained from a rupture. British scholarship, he argued, had suffered from the 'intellectual domination' of

Germany: the Germans tended, in his view, to make one particular fact, rule or method applicable to all instances, and to prejudice critical investigations by attempts to establish a 'previously adopted theory'. In response to Germany's excessive specialisation he pleaded 'for broader culture in British education'.[19]

We now turn to Lidgett's two commentaries, one written during and the other one after the Great War. Although Lidgett said his thought 'became centred on the Epistle to the Ephesians' as early as 1909 and an exposition had been planned on travels to and from the 1911 Toronto Conference,[20] his *God in Christ Jesus* did not emerge until 1915.[21] Its timing and content would appear not unrelated to the outbreak of war.

As early as two months after war was declared Lidgett had recognised that the shock caused by the violence and horror of the war was beginning to erode among many Nonconformists their earlier convictions about the love and providence of God and the unstoppable progress of mankind. His leading article of 8 October attempted to answer the question 'What of Divine Sovereignty?', by assuring readers that God's sovereignty consisted in 'the indestructibility of the highest', 'the certain emergence of a higher order', and 'the marvellous strategy of God' in bringing triumph from disaster. In Lidgett's view, people were looking in the wrong places for evidence of God's exercise of sovereignty: God, he said, not only accepts human freedom but also achieves his purposes by permitting that freedom full scope. But Lidgett decided something less ephemeral than articles in the *Methodist Times* was needed to respond to the situation.

With this in mind, and having completed a course on Ephesians with his Bermondsey Bible Class, Lidgett may well have seen in this epistle firm foundations for optimism. His *Methodist Times* of 13 May 1915 stressed the need to sustain optimism and faith even amid the horrors of war. He recognised readers of the Epistle might conclude that its assertions were too good to be true, but he hoped the events taking place would 'send us afresh to the revelation it contains, as illustrating the most vital facts of life'.[22] These vital 'facts' [or truths] were, he was sure, 'the only way of salvation from its life's outstanding evil', and provided the eternal fulfilment of all that is promised by 'the highest and best'. Lidgett assured his readers of the truth of the Apostle's message: God and his love will triumph in the end. On the final page of his Epilogue Lidgett wrote:

> Alike the achievement to which human nature has attained, the evil by which it is afflicted, and its reaching out to a higher and larger life bear witness to the abiding purpose of God 'to sum up all things in Christ . . .[23]

This note of certainty amid a world of sudden change and upheaval was sounded throughout Lidgett's book. For comfort and support his thoughts had turned to the 'eternal verities'; his words[24] were quoted in chapter 5.

Lidgett's book on Hebrews did not appear until 1921, but the circumstances in which he wrote it seem to have been both closely related to the First World War and acutely personal. His relationship with his daughter, Lettice Mary, was said[25] not to have been very affectionate. Born on 28 October 1887, she married Gerald Henry Davy, a Settlement resident during his medical training, who later practised as a doctor variously in Hull and as a consultant neurologist in Harley Street; they had no children. In contrast, Lidgett was particularly fond of John Cuthbert, born on 18 August 1885. It appears likely that the death near Ham in France on 24 March 1918 of this only son, aged 32 and unmarried, had some bearing at least on his subsequent choice of an epistle on which to write a book entitled *Sonship and Salvation*.

Educated at St Olave's Grammar School, Bermondsey and Emmanuel College, Cambridge, John Lidgett gained a BA (Hons) in Classics and an LLB. Following his father's initially favoured profession, he was articled to Sir John Bamford Slack's firm, came second in the Final Law Examination list in 1910, and obtained a Law Society prize. He joined the army at the beginning of 1916, gazetted to the 11th Battalion of the South Lancashire Regiment. He became a full Lieutenant in July 1917, and fought in Flanders and on the French fronts. He came home on leave in February 1918, but was killed in action by a machine gun bullet on 24 March 1918. His Major told his father he had died fighting gallantly with his platoon to cover the Battalion's withdrawal, sacrificing himself for their sake. The Battalion chaplain said he could not have died a braver or nobler death.

Before joining the army his leisure time had been devoted to helping his father in the Settlement. He had taught Latin and Greek, acted as treasurer of the Settlement's large Insurance Societies and given legal advice as 'Poor Man's lawyer'. He had also taken overall charge of the Settlement's work among boys: he kept close contact with Boys' Brigade members, not only in their club life, but in the early days of the war when they had joined the forces.[26]

Lidgett wrote to Davidson to inform him of his son's death, and was touched to receive on 6 April 1918 an immediate reply.[27] After regretting that no human power could help, Davidson quoted Calvin:

> *in magnis tentationibus iuvat solitudo;*
> *sed tamen ut in propinquo sint amici.*

He then asked to 'be one of those who, in the best of all ways, are *in propinquo* just now'.

His parents were still feeling their loss deeply three years later. Emmeline's heart trouble, which contributed to her death in 1934, may well have dated from

1918: in his *Methodist Times* obituary G. H. Neal said she never completely recovered from her son's death. No doubt thinking of the strain imposed by life in the Settlement, Lettice attributed[28] her mother's death to her father. The book Lidgett published in 1921 was dedicated to their son. Its Preface was significantly dated simply 'Palm Sunday', the day on which he was killed.

This brings us to the letter to the Hebrews. Recalling their son's officer rank and fatal attempt to save his men, Lidgett found consolation in the Christ the letter described as '*archegos tes Soterias*', *the* Son and Saviour. That phrase, 'The Captain of our Salvation', was the heading Lidgett gave to his leading article in the *Methodist Times* of 28 March, four days after his son's death, and the day before Good Friday. The article chose to expound the message of the Cross from the Hebrews. It used military metaphors in its stress on discipline, obedience, comradeship, self-sacrifice and heroism: Christ, it said, not only 'restored the line' lost through sin, but 'advanced' it beyond the position to which 'his own' had been driven. To Lidgett the verse from which the quoted words were taken summed up the letter's entire teaching: 'For it became Him, for whom are all things, and by whom are all things, in bringing many sons to glory, to make the captain of their salvation perfect through sufferings'.[29] Lofthouse mentioned[30] Lidgett's wistful reply to an appreciative comment on his book: 'Yes, he was a Captain, and a Son'. Referring to his forthcoming survey and paraphrasing this verse in a letter of 21 December 1920 to his Aunt Judith Hoole, Lidgett amended the word 'sufferings' to 'sacrifice', and poignantly in the next sentence added, 'It is dedicated to Jack'.

The Easter issues of the *Methodist Times* in 1918 provide further evidence of Lidgett's own faith and courage. On 4 April he was speaking of the 'Optimism of Easter', which told 'of victory, but of victory dearly bought'. On 18 April his Leader urged the bereaved not to regard their loss as 'the mere tragic waste of promise', but as 'the sublime consecration by which civilisation will yet be redeemed'. Those who had 'the courage to enter boldly into 'the valley of the shadow of death', he said, 'find that the Divine Shepherd is with them', and they 'reach for themselves and their dearest the divine assurance, "'Tis Death is dead, not he"'. Those last six words Lidgett used again to conclude his book's dedication.

At Easter 1918 Lidgett may have recalled his own words some nine years before. Hebrews 12.2 was the text for his official sermon[31] as President of the Wesleyan Conference to the Irish Methodist Conference in Cork. 'The Comradeship and Captaincy of Faith' had described Jesus as the hero of faith, faith that was the assurance of things hoped for, a venture undertaken with vision and courage. Lidgett had also said Christianity raises the whole of human life to the heroic. His book on the letter to the Hebrews reflected his enthusiasm for it. But the notions of heroism, courage and hope Lidgett had found in the text during and after 1909 struck a particular resonance when he thought about his son after Palm Sunday in 1918.

Lidgett's previous work, *The Christian Religion*, had appeared in 1907. The publication of two more books might well have surprised Lidgett's colleagues. The tasks set by the voice heard in 1877 at Blackheath[32] had been completed. But the doctrine fundamental to all three, the Fatherhood of God, continued to dominate his thinking throughout his life.

His new works, however, differed in nature from many of the past. His studies of two particular New Testament texts were not, he emphasised, commentaries in the accepted sense, devoted to verse-by-verse exposition (making it, he thought, 'impossible to see the wood for the trees'), but surveys of the underlying messages of the epistles concerned. Lidgett and his contemporaries were tiring of detailed criticism and beginning to prefer theological exposition[33] as an alternative. He was not, in fact, starting this trend: others, Anglican and Nonconformist, notably Gore and Dale, for example,[34] had been in the field before, in relation to Lidgett's chosen epistles, and with a similar readership in mind.

Nevertheless Lidgett's Preface to his study of the Epistle to the Ephesians, *God in Christ Jesus*, declared that few predecessors had dealt systematically with the major themes of the Epistle, 'either as severally treated or as combined in a consistent and organic whole'. He gave no example or specific criticism, but he may have been thinking mainly of Wesleyan predecessors. He made no direct reference to an earlier discursive commentary on the Epistle to the Ephesians by George Findlay of Headingley College.[35] Though Wesleyans respected Findlay as a scholar, Lidgett clearly thought he could improve on his work.

The *Methodist Recorder* review of *Sonship and Salvation* was short, published a month after publication. The reviewer ('161'),[36] found in it another aspect of Lidgett's work, which he contrasted favourably with other expositions of Scripture. The problems Lidgett dealt with, he said, 'are not bookish problems, not the conundrums one generation of commentators bequeath to another. They are quick from life and contact with the currents and questions of the age.'

The *Methodist Times* reviewer, Maldwyn Hughes, called attention[37] to a contemporary theological issue, described below, which Lidgett may well have had in mind as he wrote. But it was sensitivity to the bereavements and human concerns of the time, not just a desire to provide an alternative to the traditional wrestle with 'conundrums', that should be regarded as a major cause of his writing on Hebrews after the war.

Throughout his writings Lidgett had been obsessed with the need to discern coherence and consistency, principles which enabled him to maintain optimism in the face of personal disaster and confusion both moral and political in the world around him. The consistency he found was more often than not to be seen in emphasis on the Fatherhood of God and, no doubt to no one's surprise, this proved to be the underlying motif he identified in both texts. In *Sonship and Salvation*, Lidgett found it necessary to apologise for what might seem to readers 'undue' reiteration of his 'governing and all-embracing idea'. In both works other reasons he gave for repetition included the pressures of a busy life; and *God in Christ Jesus*, together with *Sonship and Salvation*, 'brought out and made good', he claimed in 1936, 'the theological position of my previous works, as having been set forth in the Apostolic teaching of the New Testament'.[38]

Reviewing *God in Christ Jesus* in 1915, perhaps rather wearily (though under the editor's eye), Wilfrid J. Moulton reported to *Methodist Times* readers that Lidgett 'returns again and again to the subject on which he has already taught us so much – the meaning of the Divine Fatherhood'.[39] But Moulton tactfully said that Lidgett's treatment was a particularly useful corrective to any fear that the concept made Christian theology 'weak and sentimental'.

To justify his selection from the New Testament Lidgett described Ephesians as 'occupied with the doctrine of the Fatherhood of God *in its final and fullest Apostolic presentation*';[40] while Hebrews, he claimed, '*completes* the teaching of the New Testament upon this great subject by exhibiting the spiritual splendour of the Sonship, which corresponds to, and therefore manifests, the Fatherhood, with which it is eternally one'.

Such claims are clearly open to challenge. Other theologians have not discerned the same themes as dominant in the mind of the authors. Scholars would not deny, of course, that to speak of Christ as God's Son implied that God is the Father, even if they do not think the author was majoring, as Lidgett did, on that particular doctrine. Lidgett's claims are not only matters of opinion but also depend in part on technical matters of dating by expert scholars. Lidgett expressed dogmatic views about the authorship and the order, time and circumstances in which the epistles were written, but he quoted no sources for them. Writing in 1957, Rupp had to acknowledge that Lidgett's statements on these topics 'lag inevitably behind recent technical discussion in our own time'.[41] They may well have been out of date even when they were written.

But, like Harold Roberts,[42] Rupp thought highly of Lidgett's study. Rupp's overall verdict on the two books was complimentary. Though he said Lidgett's three preceding works had 'little survival value',[43] he regarded both biblical expositions as 'still well worth reading'. Rupp even suggested that a reprint might 'find a timely place in modern discussion' if the dated passages were removed. But perceptively he added that Lidgett's 'lucid English' would have to be 'broken up'! Wilfrid Moulton's review of *God in Christ Jesus*[44] quoted above, admitted Lidgett was 'not an easy writer': 'this book, like each of his earlier ones', he said, 'demands sustained attention'. In a reference to Lidgett's predecessors Moulton said he deserved praise for falling behind 'none of those who have gone before him' in warmth and enthusiasm. This compliment was followed by another which would have delighted the author (and editor!) more than any ever paid to him before: no one could read the book, Moulton said, 'without gaining fresh vision of the wonder and glory of St Paul's faith', or (the highest praise a follower of John Wesley could receive) 'without having his heart strangely warmed'. Past reviewers had found him 'cold'.

Over *Sonship and Salvation* the Methodist Press was equally tactful about Lidgett's style. Maldwyn Hughes's review in the *Methodist Times* warned: 'Dr Lidgett's methods are not those of the swallow that skims the surface of the lake'; and 'the dilettante reader and the theological impressionist had better leave this book alone'. Nevertheless Hughes spoke of the book's 'profundity', its 'masterly' coverage of the epistle's teaching in relation to the New Testament and Hellenistic thought, and how it would widen readers' 'theological horizon' and strengthen 'the foundations of their belief in Christ'.[45] The most laudatory comment appeared in the *Wesleyan Methodist Magazine* of January 1922.[46] Its Editor, unnamed, but almost certainly John Telford, the Connexional Editor, was prepared to write in his review: 'There are many noble works on the Epistle to the Hebrews, but this is one of the noblest and richest in suggestion of them all'.

God in Christ Jesus

The buoyancy with which Lidgett wrote indicated his enthusiasm for Ephesians. He warmed to the personal experience expressed by the author, and to the grounding of his theology in the Incarnation and the 'facts' of Christ's life completed in the Ascension. He praised the author's emphasis on the personality of Christ, the representative of mankind, and the focus placed both on the redemption and the spiritual life enjoyed by Christ's followers. To Lidgett unlimited horizons had been opened to mankind. The epistle's 'exuberant' language, its 'unbounded expectations' and 'enraptured wonder' appealed to him, and not least the glories promised for the Church.

Lidgett welcomed in particular the way in which, by stressing 'every true interest of a healthy human life', the Apostle had fused together the elements of mysticism and humanity, the mystical and the practical, 'a spiritual combination' covering the duties of married life, of parents, children, slaves and masters, alongside the joys of spiritual experience. The Epistle contained the doctrines on which Lidgett built his own 'high' churchmanship. It expressed the intimate connection he personally strove to underline between God's Fatherhood, the 'Sonship' of Christ and the life of the believer, both inside the Church and out in the social intercourse of the world. Lidgett derived real satisfaction from declaring, 'Fatherhood is the determining relationship upon which the whole social order is built up'.[47]

Lidgett may have seen in the Epistle a means of responding to the preoccupations, mentioned above, of at least some biblical scholars at the time with the quest for the historical Jesus. His survey seemed to imply St Paul had 'solved' their problem by a detailed exposition of what Christ meant to him. Lidgett was pleased to assert that direct spiritual fellowship with the supernatural Jesus arises from and 'brings home the meaning of the well-authenticated facts of a historic life'. In his view Christian facts and history were inseparable from Christian experience: they supported and verified one another.

The title of the study reveals the supreme importance which Lidgett found the Epistle attached to the work of Christ and his filial relationship with God. At the same time Lidgett would not have been true to his Methodist roots if he had not also brought out in his exposition the vital role of the Holy Spirit in carrying Christ's work into effect. The primacy of Christ had to be set alongside 'the experienced presence and power of the Spirit'. Accordingly, he said the Spirit was 'for St Paul conditioned by Christ',[48] and 'That which the Spirit makes effectual is from beginning to end the redemptive work of Christ and the divine purpose "in Christ"'.[49] This was, in fact, life 'in Christ', to Lidgett the central phrase in the Epistle.

Lidgett's Preface referred his readers to his previous books, *The Fatherhood of God* and *The Christian Religion*, for a systematic treatment of the epistle's doctrinal interpretation of the gospel: he clearly thought it accorded with his own. He asserted that the epistle:

> shows clearly that the whole revelation of God in Christ culminates in the full disclosure of His Fatherhood, so that His Fatherhood becomes the key to, and may be treated as the final cause of all His dealings in creating, sustaining and redeeming the world;[50]

and

> In a very real sense the whole of this epistle is only a description of the Fatherhood of God, its grace and purpose, its gift and promise.[51]

Nevertheless, despite his reference to his previous works, Lidgett felt impelled to provide within the survey summaries yet again of the relevant doctrines; Wilfrid Moulton calls the study 'a system of theology in itself'! Above all the temptation to explain how the Fatherhood of God related to his Sovereignty, and how the New Testament in this respect connected with the Old, could not be resisted. This had been one of the most insistent of Lidgett's themes, and his account of the Old Testament doctrine of the sovereignty of God over man serves as an example typical of his exposition. On this, again predictably, he wrote:

> the Old Testament doctrine of the sovereignty of God has His Fatherhood,

> though as yet not unfolded, at its heart. The creation of man is the work of divine love. It involves the gift of freedom . . . Man's freedom, disastrous as its exercise has been, is subject to a three-fold restraint and safeguard – namely, the [immanent] activity of God, the constitution of His Universe [governed by his laws], and such kinship of human nature with its Creator that entire and permanent departure from God would mean its dissolution. These saving limitations of freedom all proceed from the fatherliness of the creative sovereignty of God . . . Such appears to be in broad outline the Old Testament doctrine of the sovereignty of God over man, and it is taken over by the Apostle.[52]

To Lidgett Ephesians was perhaps of all New Testament books the most central, the one he most frequently quoted. His favourite concept of Catholicity springs out of its affirmation that God's purpose is 'that the Universe, all in heaven and on earth, might be brought into unity in Christ'.[53] To achieve this Christ had come to redeem all mankind, and in so doing reconcile its divisions. The example most ready to hand was the division between Jews and Gentiles, and if, as the Apostle declared, all men were sharers together in the promise made in Jesus Christ through the gospel,[54] then the Gentiles were 'joint heirs with the Jews, part of the same body'. In Lidgett's view the Epistle clearly showed that disunity between man and man, and between men and God, became unity when all things were united in Christ. The power to rise above discord was derived from the gospel. This was where Lidgett saw the role of the Church, as the fellowship of those who believed in Christ and gained forgiveness of their sins through him. This Church, the Body of Christ, was clearly a unity: it was inspired by one Spirit, and confessed one faith, one baptism, one Lord, one God and Father of all. This was its *Catholicity*, as Lidgett called it. Ephesians strengthened his own belief in the destiny of the united Church to go on reconciling and growing to embrace all men and nations. In this way the unity of the Church was not only to make possible but also to achieve the unity of mankind.

Here was the ground of Lidgett's optimism, never far from the surface of his exposition. Despite the slaughter then taking place, his Epilogue went so far as to speak of 'the growing humanity of modern times', a humanity 'which cannot be explained without rendering full tribute to the influence of Christ'.[55] Lidgett deplored the way 'the dictates of humanity' had been flouted 'just at the time when . . . the prospect of establishing fellowship and co-operation on the basis of universal brotherhood had come into sight'.[56] But he reiterated[57] the belief expressed in his presidential year that human solidarity ('no man lives to himself'), the co-operation among the nations, and the need and promise of a truly Catholic community were being brought clearly before men's minds as never before and offered hope for the future. There were, Lidgett suggested, parallels in Ephesians between the Church and the nations of mankind:

> Just as in the Epistle to the Ephesians the Church is seen both to transcend and to recreate the family, so we may hope that it will eventually destroy all that is sordid and divisive in nationality, and bring mankind as a whole to the apprehension and enjoyment of collective good.[58]

Lidgett saw in Christ, who was the representative of humanity and raised its status, a parallel with the heroic figures and representative personalities in the conflict. These, he said, can 'assume an attitude and . . . perform deeds which create, express and solidify the temper of whole peoples so that they take up a new position in the world'.[59] Lidgett's allusion to current events was clear.

It is remarkable how strongly the optimistic note was sounded, and how firmly he adhered to his faith in the Fatherhood of God, amid all the current glaring casualties of war, and especially later in the midst of personal devastation in his own family. His *God in Christ Jesus* went so far as to declare that war, hitherto 'treated as not only inevitable on occasion, but even desirable', was not only 'contrary to the mind of Christ', but was now being treated as remediable; and that Christian influence 'is or ought to be strong enough to render it impossible'.[60] The war was, in Lidgett's view, bringing home the need for Christ's redemptive work, and while the best to which human nature could rise could be said to foreshadow Christ (he seemed to have in mind as an example the bravery, vicarious suffering and self-sacrifice in the war), the heart 'cried out' for such a 'quickening' through Christ as St Paul described. God, in fact, was (he thought) calling men through the war to face up to Christ's challenge, showing them how futile it was to root the nation's ideals in what was contrary to his will, and pointing them to his purpose of promoting spiritual values. This was where Lidgett said that God's providence was to be sought, not where critics had been claiming that if it were a reality, it would be found.

Sonship and Salvation

This work, compared with the verve of *God in Christ Jesus*, offered 'good, solid fare'.[61] Lidgett began by criticising the commentators on the letter to the Hebrews as being so preoccupied with its 'foreground' (detailed topics such as the divinity and Incarnation of Christ, his high priesthood and sacrifice, and the relationship of his work to the Old Testament dispensation), that they missed the deeper content necessary to unify and explain them all. To them the doctrine of priesthood, in particular, was dominant. By contrast Lidgett saw the 'Master Key' to Hebrews as 'our Lord's Sonship and all that his Sonship reveals . . . in the author's mind and in the nature of Reality itself'. This, he claimed, was clear right from the opening verses, asserting that 'God . . . hath spoken unto us by his Son [Lidgett glossed this as more literally translated "one who is Son"] whom he hath appointed heir of all things, by whom also he made the worlds'.

These verses went on to mark in his view an advance on the affirmations made in the rest of New Testament Scripture: they declare the spiritual splendour of the Son,

> who being the brightness of his [God's] glory, and the express image of his person, and upholding all things by the word of his power, when he had by himself purged our sins, sat down on the right hand of the Majesty on high.

Lidgett's enthusiastic use of these words echoed the lyrical tone of *God in Christ Jesus*.

Maldwyn Hughes in his review[62] saw Lidgett's stress on this quotation as having a contemporary reference, the growing debate, perhaps a forthcoming 'storm centre', on the Person of Christ, on which Gore had stated he intended to write. This was a version of the argument about transcendence versus immanence. As Hughes expressed it, there were allegedly two stark alternatives: whether Jesus was the eternally pre-existent Son of God or One in whom God was so supremely immanent that he could have 'the value of God' for us. To Hughes what Lidgett was doing was, in the light of this controversy, to emphasise that the author of Hebrews was anxious not only to make the strongest possible representation of the 'eternal generation of the Son' but also to affirm the reality of Christ's human nature: to declare that 'the author of our eternal salvation was made in all points like unto His brethren', having a human soul, learning obedience and being made perfect through His temptations and suffering. Lidgett's contribution to the debate was, Hughes explained, to state through his exposition of this epistle that what may have seemed alternative views of the Person of Christ in fact complemented one another, and that Christ's mission and work of redemption were implicit in the nature of his Sonship.

This accorded well with Lidgett's thesis. All 'the most important Epistles', Lidgett explained, had explicitly or implicitly stated the centrality of sonship as the relationship of God into which believers are brought by faith in Christ, the Son of God. What the writer to the Hebrews had done, he said, was to focus on this relationship and provide, from his own perspective, a systematic account of it. In Lidgett's summary that account had stressed the importance of the Incarnation as the starting point, and had seen the Incarnation together with the Atonement as part of a consistent, in fact, an indivisible whole. The writer's claim, in Lidgett's view, was that the Son of God had 'fulfilled his own filial life under the conditions of the Incarnation and in accomplishing the work of salvation'[63] through the one, true and final sacrifice of the Cross. 'The sonship which men come to enjoy' was, according to Lidgett, 'bound up with the Sonship of the Son who is the eternal revelation of God'.

Lidgett summed up his interpretation thus: Jesus, the Son, constituted the universe and human nature; he became man, 'realising his Sonship in terms of manhood, and manhood in terms of Sonship';[64] his work of salvation 'superseded the Old Dispensation';[65] he 'made good his prophetic and royal High-Priesthood', and through his redemptive leadership of mankind 'at once reveals, fulfils and thereby justifies the whole purpose and process of human life'.[66] To Lidgett this constituted the global, cosmic message of the whole Epistle. He was assured that nothing could oppose the love of God, whose Son had broken the last resistance.

When the letter said that God made the Captain of our salvation *perfect* through suffering, this was to be interpreted, Lidgett advised, not as God correcting Christ, but as ensuring spiritual fulfilment not just for Christ but for mankind. Its triumphant conclusion was for Lidgett the achievement of the divine purpose of 'bringing many sons unto glory',[67] of securing the salvation and sonship of men. The two nouns in Lidgett's title signalled what he identified as the central theme of the Epistle, sonship and salvation. His book ended: '. . . and these two are one'.

While admitting Hebrews is concerned 'almost exclusively with the Son', Lidgett, entirely predictably, found that its 'outstanding theological conclusion', a conclusion unifying all the epistle's references to God, was the doctrine of God's Fatherhood, an eternal relationship in the Godhead. If the form of God's self-revelation is filial, its substance, he argued, must be fatherly. In his *Reminiscences*[68] Lidgett emphasised that his aim had been:

> to show that, even in an epistle which deals with the dominant theme of priesthood and sacrifice, the exposition and explanation are governed throughout by the conception of the Fatherly-filial relationship as the distinctive feature of the Christian Faith.

The Son's creative and redemptive work, he believed, was in unity with the Father, and the means whereby God reveals, exercises and satisfies his Fatherly love. God, he said, is both above and within the process whereby his eternal purpose is achieved: 'He can be active and interested in the process without sacrificing his perfection or becoming the means of any end outside Himself'. Because of God's fatherly love, in the last resort 'the creation, redemption and perfecting of His sons is . . . an activity within, and not outside of, His own perfect life'.[69] As Lidgett understood it, the doctrine of the Epistle accorded completely with the Gospel: 'He that hath seen me, hath seen the Father'.[70]

With words such as these, Lidgett substantiated his remark that his theological task had, from first to last, been 'concerned with the Fatherhood of God, as revealed in our Lord Jesus Christ'. *Sonship and Salvation* would be, he added, his final work.[71] Though there were other, slighter and more 'popular' booklets and many 'weighty' articles to follow, it did, in fact, prove to be his last substantial book. Both biblical studies were redolent of Lidgett's strong evangelical enthusiasm, undimmed optimism, unshaken faith and serious academic purpose. *God in Christ Jesus* was the more readable; in *Sonship and Salvation* Lidgett wrote at greater length and rather more ponderously. They served his purpose of strengthening faith and bolstering hope. But neither was a work of the highest and up-to-date scholarship, and his preoccupation with the Fatherhood of God could be said to obtrude rather than illuminate.

Nevertheless, it would be foolish to fault Lidgett for his lack of originality, repetition or misplaced optimism. He did not have to write these books, which in their different ways pose real difficulties of exegesis. The signs are that he needed them in extremely troubled times to nourish his own inner life, and that he felt driven to grapple afresh and harder with his central conviction, to test it out in new and demanding contexts. The conclusions he reaches, wrought out of disciplined study, re-established the validity of his thesis and gave him personal assurance. For him the books were a therapeutic, as well as a significant, step forward, not new or original, but valuable for their confirmation.

Barth's 1918 Commentary on Romans[72] grew out of a personal need and from a theological perception that apart from God's grace there was no hope for mankind. In a similar way Lidgett's works stem from the theological insight that, apart from the coherence and consistency brought to the human situation by the Fatherhood of God, what otherwise are the confusing, apparently contradictory, disparate, fragmented private and public experiences of human beings could provide no satisfactory explanation of the world or framework for living. Lidgett's optimism was in fact entailed by his faith in the Fatherhood of God, the Sonship of Christ, the presence of the Holy Spirit and the Communion of Saints, active everywhere and at all times. His outlook and his writings were one.

10

Spokesman, commentator and politician 1914–20

Surprisingly, few biographies of Lidgett's Free Church contemporaries mentioned his name. It did not appear, for example, in F. B. Meyer's[1] biography where at least some comment on their joint working from 1914 to 1920 might have been expected. In his journalist's survey of Free Church personalities in the early twentieth century, Arthur Porritt referred to H. P. Hughes, P. T. Forsyth, Fairbairn, Clifford and Meyer, but Lidgett only figured in a minor anecdote.[2] Biographies inevitably concentrate their attention on their subject, and especially at this time when hagiography was in vogue, but such shortages of contemporary reference might suggest his Free Church eminence can be exaggerated. General church histories make only passing references, if any, to him.

He was not the only prominent Free Churchman in this period (there were several 'prima donnas'), and the NCEFC, though unrepresentative, was inclined to an inflated sense of its own importance. The Council was, however, the only national Nonconformist body at the time, and its views had to be taken into account. The significance of Lidgett's position was that of the two Hon. Secretaries and other 'denominational heads' he became in practice the spokesman with whom the Archbishop and others in the Established Church found themselves more, and perhaps most, at home. The Wesleyan Church had had no long-standing dominant spokesman since Jabez Bunting and Osborn assumed, unofficially, such a position for themselves, and then mainly within Wesleyan circles. Lidgett's Free Church office gave him the freedom to speak, and sometimes to act, for the wider constituency.

War between two Christian nations in the twentieth century was considered unthinkable, but in July 1914 the international situation was causing anxiety. As Meyer was in America, and other leading figures on holiday, Lidgett felt he had to be ready to take whatever action on behalf of the Free Churches might prove necessary in their absence. He therefore decided not to join his wife, sister-in-law, daughter, son-in-law and over 400 other members of the Free Church Touring Guild who were setting out for Grindelwald on 28 July.

Stranded when war broke out on 4 August, the party had several very worrying weeks before reaching home on 28 August.[3]

The afternoon of Bank Holiday Monday, 3 August, found Lidgett in the House of Commons Inner Lobby waiting to receive from Sir Joseph Compton-Rickett instalments of the Foreign Secretary's speech as it proceeded.[4] As soon as it was over, Lidgett went by hansom cab to Nicoll's home, 63 Frognal, Hampstead. Both would have remembered Nonconformist and Liberal splits over the Boer War. Lidgett's relations with the editor of the *British Weekly* had been far from amicable, but Lidgett set resentment aside in an effort to ensure at this critical juncture that a Free Church 'line' in support of the Government was agreed between them in time for the issue of both papers on the following Thursday. He was, no doubt, aware that the *British Weekly* had a far wider circulation and influence than the *Methodist Times*.[5] Though Lidgett's account implied war was declared on Monday, this did not happen until 11pm on Tuesday, when German troops ignored the British ultimatum and invaded Belgium.

On Thursday the *British Weekly* was strongly jingoistic: its headline, 'United We Stand', heralded the generally patriotic stance of the Free Churches throughout the war. Lidgett by contrast retained his previously planned Leader headline, 'The Wesleyan Conference and Spiritual Advance', and reserved his reactions to the outbreak of war for his 'Notes and Comments' page. There, like Nicoll, he said the German invasion had left Britain with no alternative, but unlike Nicoll he paid particular attention to the duties of the churches in the new situation. He called for constant prayer, ministry to the distressed, sharing privations, avoidance of exploiting opportunities for personal gain, and 'stern repression of every spirit of hatred'. Lidgett's support for war was, in fact, a *volte-face*, since with Rattenbury and Perks he had earlier opposed it. Refusal to engage in the extreme war rhetoric of other Free Churchmen was again marked at the Free Church gathering at the City Temple early in November 1914. He pleaded for the Churches to match the heroism of the troops by upholding the morale of the nation and the spiritual Kingdom of God, and to maintain their obligation of Christian service to the whole family of God.

But neither Lidgett nor other Protestant churchmen escaped criticism for backing the declaration of war. Lidgett thought[6] the charges against them were unfair. They had tried to maintain the cause of peace right up to the outbreak of war. Only two days before this a Christian Peace Conference, convened at Constance, had founded the 'World Alliance for Promoting International Friendship through the Churches', and Lidgett had drafted a letter on behalf of the Free Churches for Davidson to take there. Nevertheless, the peace Lidgett advocated was not at any price. War, he wrote,[7] 'may be the indispensable means of avoiding yet greater evil', and in some circumstances to abstain from war might be 'a meaner act than participation in it'; no Christian nation bound by treaty obligations could 'buy peace by complicity with wrong'. The Christian's duty, he thought, was to seek to prevent war from breaking out, to bring it to a speedy conclusion, mitigate its horrors, and work for the triumph of moral forces.

The war gave Lidgett new scope for advocating Church unity. The churches, he urged,[8] should co-operate in helping to mould public opinion: 'to seek to create and equip a common conscience to uphold right by moral, and not military sanctions'; to promote just dealing with enemies; make alliances with the democracies of the world in pursuit of peace; and prepare the ground for international fellowship when the war was over. His theme at the NCEFC meeting in March 1915 was 'The Principles of Peace'.

Lidgett would have been pleased to be consulted with some of 'Davidson's friends'[9] on 11 September at Lambeth Palace, about a letter from German theologians, pastors and academics, led by Adolf Harnack, to their British counterparts. Their public 'Appeal to every Evangelical Christian abroad' claimed that hostility to Germany was putting Christian Europe's mission to the world at serious risk. In highly rhetorical terms it called the war 'a wanton attack' by those who had long been spinning a web of conspiracy with which to strangle Germany. This was astonishing from participants in the Anglo-German friendship movement and the 1910 Edinburgh Missionary Conference. British churchmen and theologians were outraged, more than anxious to accede to the British Government's request for a considered response. Lidgett's *Guided Life* did not mention the Lambeth discussion on 11 September, only the larger (and two-day) gathering of Anglican and Free Church leaders, convened later to draft the reply. He praised the Archbishop's skilful chairmanship in putting the most critical paragraphs into their final form.[10] Calm, firm and without anti-German rhetoric, the reply dated 23 September emphasised the obligation to treaty promises, outlined Britain's efforts to maintain peace, and asserted the need to safeguard smaller, weaker nationalities.

Of the three Wesleyan signatories the *British Weekly*[11] mentioned only Hope Moulton: it omitted reference to Wiseman and Lidgett. Nicoll, a Presbyterian, was perhaps rather more interested in nine Presbyterian and Congregational figures who wrote to Harnack on 27 August to counter the charges he was making against Britain: their names were listed in full in the *British Weekly* on 3 September. This initiative, clearly an independent, not an official or concerted Free Church response, illustrated the lack of NCEFC cohesion. The German response to the British reply was the so-called 'Manifesto of the Intellectuals', published on 4 October 1914 by the *Frankfurter Zeitung* and signed by some 93 members of the German academic establishment. *Inter alia* it alleged that the entry of German troops into Belgium had offered Britain, abetted by other Great Powers, a welcome pretext for declaring war. The weakness of its arguments met with Lidgett's scorn.[12]

Many issues exercised the churches. The German theologians' intervention only served to stiffen support for the war by British theologians of all denominations (Quakers excepted) and all schools of thought.[13] Most Anglican teachers except Gore did not see the war in terms of God's judgement, but as an unfortunate and bitter delay in the steady progress of the Kingdom of God. Many Anglican clergy regarded the crisis, Mews suggested,[14] as a welcome opportunity to reverse increasing secularisation and the decline in their own influence and prestige evident before 1914; the war would also enable them, they thought, to identify the Christian community with the nation as a whole. Winnington-Ingram, Bishop of London (1901–39), was perhaps the most extreme of the patriots, notably through his 1915 Advent sermon[15] which virtually saw the British war effort as action by the Church militant. Though some clergy and Oxford dons were deeply concerned by any encouragement to vengeance and hate, the majority supported him. Frustrated in their wish to join the battle as combatants, many priests engaged in pro-war rhetoric from their pulpits.

Free Church leaders (even Forsyth) were likewise patriotic. They too saw the war as a fight for Christianity against paganism, for right against might, for liberty against cruel tyranny, in fact for humanity itself against the Devil.[16] Similarly in April 1916 Lidgett maintained through the *Methodist Times* that triumph over Germany was essential for the progress of mankind. He could have recalled words of F. D. Maurice:

> If ever our countrymen are called upon to defend their own hearths and homes . . . I trust God will enable us . . . to say boldly that this is a duty to which God himself is calling them . . . that . . . self sacrifice is their work and privilege.[17]

Nevertheless, Wesleyan backing for the war was not entirely unanimous: M. S. Edwards[18] was right to point out Lidgett's rhetorical overestimate in the *Methodist Times*. Among Wesleyans S. E. Keeble was strongly opposed to the war, and in December 1914 Christian Pacifists founded a 'Fellowship of Reconciliation'. Even among Protestant church leaders committed to supporting the war, there were signs of uneasiness from the beginning as they found themselves simultaneously wanting peace and supporting war. This tension showed itself more clearly as the war progressed. The mood of the nation as a whole, initially marked by wild, patriotic enthusiasm, became more restrained, not least after the massive loss of life on the Somme between July and November 1916. It settled thereafter into grim determination to win the conflict.

As early as 9 October 1914 Davidson had summoned a group of ministers and laymen to the Guard Room at Lambeth Palace 'to study the deeper bearings upon our own country, Europe and the World, of this great war and the convulsion of the nations'.[19] Lidgett and other Free Church leaders were there, together with the two Archbishops, three Bishops, other Anglicans and members of the Society of Friends. The homily which Davidson composed to be read in all churches on 3 January 1915, spoke of 'no desire to see enemies crushed merely for the sake of their humiliation'; his wish was that 'we may learn to understand and respect one another . . . and be united as friends to pursue the common good'.

When the two Anglican Archbishops launched a 'National Mission of Repentance and Hope' in October 1916, they had partly in mind current fears of strife in Ireland and in industrial relations at home. But, though they affirmed the righteousness of the war, the stress they put on the need for society to repent for what was radically wrong within itself was no doubt intended at the same time to apply once again to the British people's attitude to their enemies. Davidson was ready to protest against actions by the British forces which he regarded as wrong: for example, in 1916 and 1917 the use of poison gas, and reprisals by British and French aeroplanes on Freiburg for German torpedoing of hospital ships and attacks on civilians. His plea in the Lords was that the Government should 'emerge from the war with clean hands'. Lidgett and the Free Churches supported him. Lidgett's editorials, such as 'The Futility of Force' and 'The Omnipotence of Love' in 1914,[20] had reflected much of the balance Davidson tried to maintain. Lidgett felt similar tensions but was generally more bellicose, as might be expected of one whose son had joined the army in January 1916.

The advent of conscription brought controversy. As early as 27 March 1913 Lidgett had opposed it. 'This Way Madness Lies' headed his leading article advocating adherence to the voluntary principle and opposition to anything which might promote further military efforts in Germany and militarism in England. That stance he strongly maintained throughout 1915 as the case for conscription built up.[21] But in January 1916, when the first Military Service Bill was introduced, his opposition began to crack. On 6 January he said the Bill could only be acceptable if it was strictly limited to the war and wise restrictions were put on expansion of 'our personal and military expenditure'.[22] On 11 May the *Methodist Times* announced[23] a complete *volte-face*, giving 'conclusive reasons' in favour of the Bill. It was, he said, essential that the Allies should win the war. The State, as 'the mother of us all' (a striking metaphor for Lidgett), had the right to call on its citizens in this way, and the Bill preserved the unity of the Government and the Nation.

Conscription led to the emergence of conscientious objectors, whose cases for exemption from military service were heard by tribunals set up for the purpose. In March 1916 the Free Churches petitioned the Prime Minister, requesting that these tribunals should operate fairly, making uniform, consistent decisions. Public opinion, however, despised conscientious objectors, and their claims were all too often peremptorily dismissed. A. S. Peake soon identified himself against instances of unjust treatment, while Keeble had taken up the objectors' cause as soon as individual cases became known. Lidgett, however, had little time for pacifists: despite being protected by the British fleet, they were often, he said, making unreasonable stipulations as to what non-combatant duties they would and would not undertake. He fully supported the NCEFC Committee statement in June 1916:

> We cannot admit that the individual has the moral right to decline his part in the task and burden of the community or to expect the advantages conferred by the State, while refusing to share in its responsibilities; nor can we view without grave concern the claim alleged by some on conscience grounds to be relieved of every kind of service to the nation.

When the disenfranchisement of conscientious objectors was mooted towards the end of 1917, Lidgett's view remained consistent, welcoming the Government's declaration that no man who had 'rendered satisfactory service of national importance to the State will be penalised because of his objection to military duty'.[24]

Keeble and his supporters launched in April 1916 a Pacifist manifesto demanding a Peace League, and in October a Peace Fellowship for Wesleyan ministers was formed.[25] Early in 1916, seeing conscription as a precedent for Government control of the entire economy, Keeble called for the conscription of wealth and property as well as men; and in 1917 for the nationalisation of railways and coal mines.[26] Lidgett could not endorse such extreme socialist ideas. He had, however, some sympathy with parts of the programme of the Union of Democratic Control (of which Keeble was a branch secretary), not least its plea for an international organisation to maintain peace, but he objected to attempts to play down German crimes.[27]

The Churches had their own obligations to serve the Armed Forces. As soon as wounded soldiers began to reach hospitals throughout the country in 1914, Lidgett saw the need for chaplains.[28] So he took the initiative of requesting all local Free Church Council secretaries as a matter of urgency to call a meeting of all Free Church ministers in their different areas, so that panels of voluntary (civilian) chaplains could be recruited. He asked for the names of the volunteers, and passed these on, day by day, to the War Office. By the end of the first month of the war, as Lidgett proudly recorded, nearly 500 Free Church chaplains' names had been submitted to and approved by the War Office, and the initial crisis was over.

Lidgett's involvement in chaplaincies was virtually confined to such hospital work at home. He was not a member of the Wesleyan Army and Navy Board, but the board's Emergency Committee deputed him on 6 August, as John Thompson[29] pointed out, to offer Wesleyan oversight of Baptist and Congregational soldiers 'as has always been the case . . . in the field in the past'. No doubt, as NCEFC Hon. Secretary, Lidgett would have been considered appropriate for delivering the message.

In the event both Baptist and Congregational Unions, together with the Primitive and United Methodist churches, decided to apply to the War Office for the right to nominate their own chaplains to serve their own men at home and abroad, and in January 1915 their own distinct Chaplaincy Board, the United Army and Navy Board, came into being.[30] Its Joint (in effect the dominant) Secretary was the Baptist, J. H. Shakespeare, who saw it as a symbol of the Free Churches playing their part in the national struggle. He had begun to urge the Free Church Council to form a 'Free Church of England',[31] but when the Wesleyans resisted the call for an overall Free Church Chaplaincy Board, Shakespeare had to rest content with 'the working in miniature for a specific purpose of a *partially* united Free Church of England'.[32] It seems Lidgett did not comment, but from evidence in other contexts[33] his disapproval of Wesleyan exclusiveness in this matter may be inferred.

Nevertheless, Shakespeare's efforts to implement unity in action continued. In the United Board he helped to avoid significant denominational rivalry, and was prominently involved in setting up and operating a fully interdenominational Advisory Committee on Chaplaincy Services, working alongside the denominational Boards. The Committee helped to ensure equitable treatment and maintain a continuous working relationship between Nonconformists and the War Office, never previously achieved. Referring to work on the Committee, Thompson rightly argued that Shakespeare, an intimate of Lloyd George, 'outclassed the Wesleyans in access to high places', but in the wider range of public affairs Lidgett's own contacts with Lloyd George and others among the highest leaders of Church and State were both strong and of much longer duration.

Lidgett and Davidson remained in close touch on many issues, including those concerned with chaplains to the forces. Lidgett recorded[34] one such discussion at Davidson's bedside when the Archbishop was seriously ill, but he was vague about the date. Its place in the narrative would suggest a timing late in 1917 or early 1918: 'Just at that time', he wrote, 'I was invited to confer with the Archbishop about certain questions concerning . . . chaplaincies in the war'. Davidson was confined to bed on a number of occasions, but only one of his papers recorded a visit from Lidgett about this time: this was in January 1917, when chaplaincies were apparently not discussed. There were, however, other visits in similar circumstances,[35] and it seems likely that Lidgett conflated one visit with another.

Davidson certainly faced Anglican chaplaincy problems of his own.[36] The Free Churches on their side had reasons to complain, as on the occasion when[37] it was alleged that the number of Nonconformist recruits was being understated to put Nonconformist patriotism in a bad light. Assumptions that the Church of England was the norm, entitled to the major share of appointments and promotions, and to unquestioned pre-eminence in ceremonial parades, garrison churches and cathedral chapels, were a permanent source of irritation. Issues such as maintenance of Sunday Observance, suppression of foul language, and the timing of leave trains (to prevent troops falling victim to prostitutes on London terminals overnight) would also have given Lidgett and Davidson plenty to talk about. The one strictly Wesleyan administrative issue in which Lidgett was involved within his own Church was whether Wesleyan chaplains should be permitted to hold permanent commissions: the Conference had ruled against this in 1903. As a member of the Committee which on 15 January 1919[38] successfully advised the Conference to reverse that policy, Lidgett could well have also supported the Conference decision in 1915 to accept the temporary Commissions the War Office conferred as war began.

Relief at the ending of the war was offset by deep sadness at the loss of life and the disillusionment of the troops. When the war began, the Churches saw chaplaincies as an evangelical opportunity but, far from an increase in religious fervour, bitterness and cynicism became common.[39] What did increase, however, among some chaplains and dedicated laymen, was the desire for Church unity, deriving from the comradeship and co-operation of men of all denominations under the stress of war.[40]

A revealing exchange between Lidgett and Davidson occurred over a letter from Asquith to Davidson, Cardinal Bourne, the Chief Rabbi and others on 21 October 1914. He said that French local authorities were contemplating extensive exhumation and reburial of men who died in battle, and 'qualified ministers of the great religious communions' were needed for the appropriate reinterment services. Davidson[41] thought the Anglican burial service would meet the needs of everyone except the Roman Catholics, and one or two Anglican priests would suffice. Nevertheless he courteously asked Lidgett for his opinion. After consulting ministers responsible for Baptist, Congregational, Presbyterian and Wesleyan chaplains, Lidgett agreed to the proposal on 27 October. But he said that while he had no wish to accentuate differences between the churches, the task was likely to recur at intervals and those who 'have undertaken responsibility for their adherents in the Army during life' should 'be prepared to take their share of duty to their own dead'. He suggested alternatives: joint services, or some to be taken by Anglican priests and some by Free Church ministers: the 'team' could include three clergy, plus one Baptist/Congregational, one Presbyterian and one Wesleyan minister.

Next day a dismayed Davidson reported attempts to identify the dead. Bonham Carter, for the Government, decided to request two parties of divines to operate in different fields, in practice a modification of Lidgett's ideas. By the turn of the year, however, the French withdrew permission for them to go to

France. The incident revealed Lidgett's readiness to co-operate with the Established Church as far as he could, but to put a strong Nonconformist case as well.

A further issue taxing the churches was the incidence of unmarried mothers. Within the first six months of the war, and arising from it, the incidence of unmarried mothers and provision for them and their children came to public attention. Unmarried partners and dependants of serving soldiers did not receive wives' separation allowances, and it was considered unfair for them to suffer through the men's patriotism. Some members of the public[42] went so far as to suggest that such mothers should be specially honoured, even that 'no girl of independent means . . . should shirk the risks, responsibilities and odiums of producing one well-conditioned child to the community'. Others charged the women of being spendthrift and addicted to drink. Such moral and welfare issues led Lidgett on 3 April 1915[43] to ask Davidson for an opportunity to consult him on whether concerted action by the Churches was necessary. Lidgett hoped the dimensions of the problem had been exaggerated, but when their meeting could not be arranged, he obtained[44] a few numerical statements from the Chief Lady Poor Law Inspector which revealed that the figures for Berkhamsted would, if typical, suggest a serious problem.

On 26 April 1915, Davidson announced the setting up of a small committee, convened by Mrs Louise Creighton, to investigate the nature and extent of the 'danger', and to report to a larger committee. Lidgett proudly recorded that Davidson had included him in the initial consultation.[45] On 2 June 1915 Mrs Creighton reported that the incidence of unmarried mothers was not extensive and sufficient agencies existed to deal with relevant social problems. The Government later decided that the War Office would grant allowances under certain conditions, one of which was that the dependant should be receiving a definite proportion of the pay of the soldier concerned, assigned voluntarily by himself.[46] This in effect upheld Davidson's and Lidgett's view that the distinction between the married and unmarried should be preserved.

Another topic Davidson and Lidgett would have discussed, though not reflected directly in the *Methodist Times*, was the alarming incidence of Venereal Diseases among the troops: sufferers were occupying hospital places intended for the wounded, too many men were being lost to the front line, and in particular the Army's unofficial encouragement of the use of French licensed brothels, *maisons tolerées*, was causing moral outrage in the churches, the press and both Houses of Parliament. Vehement protests by Davidson and others in late 1917 and early 1918 forced the Secretary of State for War to ban the use of all brothels by British troops. But Church leaders, Davidson in particular, were criticised for lack of flexibility towards soldiers fighting for their country in intolerable conditions.

From Davidson's papers it seemed the issue was handled for the Free

Churches by Meyer, not Lidgett: Meyer wrote to the minister, Lord Derby, and attended a meeting in the War Office. Lidgett became involved in a different but related matter. His protest via the *Methodist Times* showed his opposition, as in the past,[47] to sexual discrimination. A new regulation was being proposed under the Defence of the Realm Act, to make it an offence 'for any woman suffering from these diseases [VD] to have or to solicit sexual intercourse with any member of HM forces'. This, he said, would mean a reversion to the old Contagious Diseases [CD] Acts, with their standpoint that 'what is an offence in the woman is not an offence in the man'. The proposal was, in his view, a 'new offensive on the part of the War Office against the moral sense of the community'.[48]

An associated issue was that of drink. The Nonconformists' long campaign against alcohol received what they saw as triumphant vindication in April 1915. In the early months of the war, public concern mounted over the effects of drink, both in France and at home, on the efficiency of both the domestic workforce and the troops. Prohibition was proposed, but on 1 April 1915 Lidgett was advocating a general policy of restrictions on drink rather than an obligation on military authorities and chief constables to enforce a ban. On 8 April he was jubilant, reporting the surprising but welcome news that the King, no less, had decided to set an example of abstinence for the duration of the war. There followed a national appeal, signed by the two Archbishops, Cardinal Bourne and Sir Joseph Compton-Rickett, the first NCEFC lay President. This pressed 'the duty and privilege of bearing a voluntary part in the Nation's self-discipline and self-sacrifice by abstaining from all alcoholic drink during the continuance of the war'.[49]

Lidgett and the vast majority of his contemporaries failed to realise that the sudden escalation of pressure to condemn alcohol was in fact a ruse hastily engineered by Lloyd George. He saw in it a means to divert Welsh Nonconformists from opposing the Government's Bill to delay the implementation of Welsh Disestablishment until six months after the war.[50] The Welsh feared that if, once peace was declared, the general election returned a Conservative majority, the new Government could repeal an Act which would have had by then no time even to begin to come into force. As Mews put it,[51] Lloyd George was representing the postponement Bill 'as a bargaining counter . . . to prise temperance reform from an unwilling Tory party'. He seized the opportunity of an audience with King George V to persuade him of what he said would remedy a deteriorating situation at home and at the front. Davidson was horrified, but had to accept the King's decision and its consequences.

Lloyd George's ruse, however, did not achieve its object. The outcry forced the withdrawal of the postponement Bill by July, and the Government was left with the need to implement its drive against drink. A central Control Board was set up in 1915 to regulate the supply of alcohol initially in munition-making areas; by the end of the next year it covered the whole country except some rural districts. What was gained fell far short of what many had envisaged. Lloyd George lost interest, but his defence of the postponement Bill may well have been a significant factor in gaining for him the leadership of a coalition government in December 1916.

Lidgett had for long been mesmerised by Lloyd George's eloquence and political skills. Here, in common with the vast majority of his peers, Lidgett was deceived by his cynical and unprincipled actions. As Lloyd George privately admitted to B. C. Addison,[52] the idea that slackness and drink were the chief causes of delays in munition production was 'mostly fudge'. It would be unfair to single out Lidgett alone as guilty of *naiveté* over this incident. Equally, Lidgett should not be blamed for silence about Lloyd George's adultery with his secretary, begun in 1912: like virtually all his fellow Church leaders including Shakespeare, noted above as an intimate of Lloyd George, Lidgett never mentioned it. Michael Edwards[53] accused him of hypocrisy, turning a blind eye to immorality while at the same time upholding the Church's standards, because he believed Lloyd George seemed the Nonconformists' best hope of carrying through their policies. But Lidgett's appreciation of his political adroitness did not entail awareness of his adultery, and no such charge was ever levelled at Lidgett or other Free Church leaders during their lifetime. It is hardly conceivable that Lidgett would not have spoken out if he had known[54] of the adultery; he would have recalled H. P. Hughes's dictum that what is morally wrong cannot be politically right.

Throughout the war the Churches looked forward to its aftermath. In 1917 the Wesleyan Conference passed a unanimous resolution,[55] favouring a League of Peace to maintain a lasting peace when the war came to an end. On 9 August Lidgett, its proposer, urged his readers to focus not on *schemes* of reconstruction so much as the inspiration and enlightened sympathy needed to accompany them. On 8 November he recorded the formation of a Wesleyan 'After War Committee' to ensure that no soldier, whether disabled or not, returning from the war, was overlooked if in need of help over resettlement, employment and so on. Its aims, he said,[56] were not sectarian: it sought to stimulate Government and Parliament to take action for social well-being.

On 29 November he set out a list of what he saw to be the duties of the Churches in the coming peace. They should, he said *inter alia*, promote the claims of humanity, righteousness and freedom; withstand every tendency to hatred, revenge and inhumanity; and strive to make the war the end of war, by seeking the reconciliation of peoples and ensuring the proposed League of Peace was made effective. Predictably he called for a conference of Churches throughout the world to further these ends. By October 1918 the concept changed to the League of Nations, and again Lidgett warned people not to forget the driving force necessary for success was not machinery or structures, but religious inspiration. The post-war reconstruction Lidgett envisaged for London will be described in the next chapter.

Lidgett thought Lloyd George's call for a General Election premature.[57] He urged voters to use their vote and pleaded for responsible electioneering. On 5 December 1918 he published a Free Churches' manifesto, much of which he may have devised himself. In it, parliamentary candidates were pressed, *inter alia*, to seek the immediate establishment of the League of Nations; provision for those in need as a result of the war; effective control of the liquor traffic; an adequate policy for promoting public morality, health, housing, educational reforms and the weekly day of rest; the prevention of unemployment; and the 'complete emancipation and equipment of womanhood for service in the State'. Lidgett declared his distaste for Lloyd George's 'vulgarising vast issues',[58] making threats to exact fullest indemnities from Germany. Though Lidgett supported Lloyd George's coalition, Free Churchmen were not wholly in favour, and the split which emerged, compounding Liberal Party divisions dating from 1916, was to lead to the loss of the influence Nonconformists once had.

At the end of December 1918 Lidgett handed over the editorship of the *Methodist Times* to 'younger men', thereby removing a major source for identifying Lidgett's personal opinions before that date. The *British Weekly*, mischievous to the last, described the new editorial group, including Rattenbury, Gregory and Carter, as all warmly supporting 'the programme of the Labour Party'.

Lidgett maintained his NCEFC role. With Meyer, his fellow Secretary, he was a signatory to the churches' New Year Joint Appeal to the Nation on 10 January. In June 1921 the Liberal Lord Bryce[59] invited him, no doubt as a Free Church Liberal churchman, to join a Commission of Enquiry into alleged acts of violence by an irregular force, known as the 'Black and Tans', sanctioned by Lloyd George, against IRA guerillas. Lidgett was flattered, but the speed required for its report caused him to plead pressure of other commitments.

But the contribution Lidgett had made as a Free Church spokesman to the national political scene from 1914 to 1921 had been relatively modest, observing and commenting on events, finding the language to enable others to recognise the seriousness of the concerns he identified. Of greater importance were his educational and political activities over the years, notably in the London's County Council. To these themes we now turn.

Part 4

Pioneering in education

Chapters 11–13 recall Lidgett's educational work in the LCC, in London University, and in the cause of religious education nationally.

Calendar of main events

1903	London Education Act.
1904	LCC took over from London School Board.
1906	Liberal parliamentary majority.
1907	Municipal Reformers took over from Progressives on the LCC.
1909	Elected to Honorary DD at University of Aberdeen.
1918	Elected Leader of Progressives. 'London after the War' manifesto.
1918	Progressives lost seats at LCC election.
1922	Lidgett lost his own seat at LCC election, but elected Alderman 1922–8. Elected to University Senate.
1923	Elected to Athenaeum.
1926	General Strike.
1928	Lidgett resigned from LCC. Elected as member, later Chairman, of London University's Training Colleges Delegacy.
1929	Elected Senate representative to London University Court, and Deputy Vice-Chancellor of London University.
1930–2	Elected Vice-Chancellor of London University.
1932	Honorary DD at Oxford University.
1933	Companion of Honour. Honorary DD at Edinburgh University. Chairman of Inter-Universities China Committee.
1935	Christian Cinema Council.
1941	Leading Free Church member of Archbishop Lang's deputation to the President of the Board of Education.
1944	Education Act. Successfully advocated London University Institute of Education.
1946	Elected Honorary Doctor of Laws in London University. Retired from Senate.

11

Progressives' politician in the LCC 1904–28

Lidgett's political involvement in the London County Council related principally to education, but in line with his view of the wholeness of life, not to education alone. His LCC career was a roller-coaster, evoking both joyful satisfaction and deep disappointment.

It began when the LCC, already heavily loaded with virtually every aspect of local government from drainage to asylums, took over from the London School Board.[1] Undertaking responsibility for all the Capital's denominational schools as well as all elementary, secondary, technical and higher education was itself a mammoth task for a Council whose members had strongly objected to shouldering the additional burden and had had no previous experience in this field. But it was precisely this unified and coherent coverage of education under a single body that Lidgett and others saw as desirable when, having passed its *national* Education Act in 1902, the Government set out to legislate similarly for the County (not the very small separate City) of London. Lidgett had even lobbied Bishop Talbot for his support.

Lidgett's LCC career can be divided into four phases. The first included the years 1904–7, when the LCC became a Local Education Authority (LEA), with the Progressives being the ruling party. Arrangements for transfer were handed over to a Joint LCC/School Board Committee, with three LCC members and two former School Board members, Lidgett being one. He proudly recorded that all was ready on the appointed day. When the new Education Committee was formally constituted, five (not six, as Lidgett says)[2] members of the School Board were co-opted initially for its first two years (until March 1906). This began for Lidgett an association of 24 years. The responsibilities which the overall Education Committee gave to him showed how much it valued his experience and advice. When subcommittees were designated for the various aspects of its work, Lidgett was not only immediately elected as Vice-Chairman of its Elementary Day Schools Subcommittee, but also as a member of the Committee's General Purposes Subcommittee.[3] He became the Day Schools Subcommittee Chairman in April 1905, a year later. Before the period of Lidgett's co-option would have come to an end, the Chairman of the Council,

T. McKinnon Wood, took advantage of a resignation, and on 5 December 1905 secured his election as an Alderman for the five years remaining in the relevant term of office. Lidgett rightly regarded this as a great honour in itself. He was also flattered by its declared purpose, 'so that my services might be continued . . . and my voice on educational questions might be heard in the Council itself'.[4] But though education was now his major interest, it was not the only one. The post helped to extend his perspective across the LCC field.

'Educating the Educators' was a phrase which Lidgett used more than once in his career. In this period he had tactfully to 'educate' LCC members, many of whom were not just reluctant and inexperienced in educational administration, but prejudiced against the administrative methods of the former School Board. Two particularly difficult tasks faced the committee, not just himself, as his record implied:

1. that of persuading an aghast Chairman of the Finance Committee to accept the importance and cost of capital and maintenance expenditure on schools, as the needs of the population grew; and
2. that of helping to decide how to implement the findings of an inspection of the non-provided schools, which the LCC set in hand at the take-over. Any decisions on denominational schools were politically delicate, and especially at this early stage, when many LCC members were unsympathetic, preferring to accept only efficient schools, as the law permitted, and not to give others time to bring their buildings, for example, up to date. One sub-section of the relevant Education Subcommittee imposed structural improvements on some schools, and closed a small minority when such improvements were impossible. Amid resentment at the LEA's powers to intervene, two representatives of these national schools kept a persistent watch on everything said and done, quick to suspect unfairness and query cases, for example, where managers had proposed to appoint a teacher whom the LEA judged incompetent.

Lidgett said he chaired another a sub-section of the subcommittee, charged with the review of all the existing staff of the non-provided schools and then determining the future numbers and qualifications of teachers in relation to the size, type and organisation of each school, a lengthy and laborious task. Eventually examination of these factors 'enabled us to fix on certain principles of staffing', he wrote,[5] and these, he claimed, proved relatively durable despite educational changes over the years.

After recording this particular task as a success, Lidgett went on to mention another: 'Subsequently, as Chairman of the Elementary Day Schools Subcommittee, I presided over the section that settled the policy and planned the distribution of the *CENTRAL SCHOOLS*'.[6] These did indeed become a valuable development from the former Higher Elementary Schools in London, but the policy decision to set them up was not made until 1910; its implementation followed later. The Progressives were not in control of the LCC after 1907, nor was Lidgett subsequently chairman of the committee, but it is quite likely that the ideas behind the schools' introduction were first sketched out or elaborated by him. Possible changes for Higher Elementary and Higher Grade Schools had been contemplated on 20 July 1906, and his involvement in Elementary School committees had for long been accompanied by efforts to encourage development of secondary education.

The Central Schools provided for children not thought likely to benefit from the academic curriculum of Secondary Schools, and offered one with an industrial or commercial bias for boys and girls respectively, though without a uniform timetable. Each school served a group of ordinary Elementary Schools; children were selected at age 11 and stayed for four, occasionally five, years. A scholarship scheme was provided, helping to make the provision a success.

Percy Harris rightly called the Progressives' creation of the LCC's LEA between 1904 and 1907 'a great triumph of organisation',[7] and undoubtedly Lidgett played a major part in it. But Liberal success in the parliamentary elections of 1906 was a mixed blessing for the Progressives. Euphoria was dimmed when they found that they had lost many of their ablest LCC members. Some newly elected MPs initially maintained their membership, but the majority left altogether, a blow from which Lidgett admits 'the Progressive Party never recovered'.[8]

The Liberals' parliamentary victory stung the London Moderates into an extremely vigorous campaign for LCC control at its elections in March of the following year. The Progressives were charged with corruption, and a 'Commercial Audit' was set up; a ceaseless, virulent Press campaign was mounted by the 'Rag Press' and its halfpenny papers, against alleged mismanagement (losses on steamboats, 'defective' bricks used for building the new Norbury estate, for example), and the increase in rates necessitated by general 'extravagance'. Expenditure under attack included what was being spent on schools and on building a new County Hall, dubbed the 'Wastrels' Palace'.

Vested interests had also been threatened by what clergy called 'stingy' and 'over-exacting' treatment of non-provided schools; Percy Harris[9] thought this had much to do with the downfall of the Progressives in the election. Policies proposed by the Progressives were stigmatised as 'revolutionary'. McKinnon Wood's advocacy for taking privately run utilities, notably the generation and distribution of electricity, under municipal control was one example. Complaints were also made about the 'unfairness' of allowing foreign competition (a Belgian rails contract) under the Progressives' Open Tenders scheme which had aimed to stop jobbery! Just before the election the Moderates sought a propaganda advantage by changing their name to 'Municipal Reformers', and the Audit report, which largely exonerated the Progressives, was delayed until after the election. The public apology, made by the *Evening Standard* in the face of threatened libel action, was also too late to save the Progressives. Their control of the LCC, lost at the election, was never subsequently regained.

The second phase of Lidgett's LCC career was from 1907 to 1919 when the Municipal Reformers were in control. Immediately after the 1907 election result and his exhausting term as NCEFC President, now suffering gastric influenza and unsteady on his feet, Lidgett was called before the new ruling party to defend the Elementary School policies of the outgoing regime. He had to try yet again, albeit in different circumstances, to 'educate the educators', as every part of the Council's administration was thrown into the melting pot. Predictably, financial expenditure was the Municipal Reformers' main target, and the pace of school extension and improvement was slowed down. Angry and resentful at the Progressives' defeat, especially the way it had been achieved, Lidgett faced an uphill battle to persuade his opponents of the wisdom as well as the necessity of the Education Committee's earlier programme. But despite their reluctance to listen, he continued to insist on what he saw as priorities, and argue that educational values, as well as inescapable material provision, were at stake.

Lidgett's term as Alderman guaranteed continuity in membership of the Day Schools and General Purposes Subcommittees until March 1910. He then stood for election as LCC member for Rotherhithe, and was successful also in 1913 and 1919, the 1916 election being postponed because of the war. In 1913 he became leader of the Progressives on the LCC Education Committee and its Deputy Chairman in 1917 until 1919.[10] When Sir John Benn retired through ill heath in 1918, Lidgett reached the pinnacle of his political career by his unanimous election on 19 March as Leader of the Progressive Party in his place. This was an astonishing achievement for a Wesleyan minister, surprisingly recorded without comment in both Methodist weekly journals, but tragically marred by his son's death on 24 March, less than a week later.

Despite the initial difficulties, Lidgett claimed that 'after a short experience' the Municipal Reformers 'became converted to the maintenance and development of the enterprises, to which . . . they had been opposed'.[11] He attributed this to 'the genius of the council' and to the quality of what he and others had achieved in the past: 'The main fabric of the administration, reared by the Progressives', he said, 'survived the shock and stood the most persistent investigation'.[12] Moreover, 'A new race of administrators sprang up, and banished such of the old reactionaries as remained to the back benches'. So, encouraging progress was made, despite the change in LCC control.

Financial administration seems to have remained unchanged, and what clearly gave Lidgett particular satisfaction was that 'the claims of Education slowly but steadily awakened conviction and good-will'. He reported that 'the dignity and equipment of school buildings', denounced in 1907 as extravagant, were maintained; expansion of education went ahead (including the introduction of Central Schools); and the Non-Provided schools were, he said, put 'on a better footing, a policy of which I did not in the main disapprove'.[13] Controversy about this latter policy disappeared by 1913, though Lidgett admitted that these schools still faced recurrent financial strain.

He continued to stress the importance of provision for handicapped children, but advocacy of extending curricular breadth was more of a struggle. Always on the alert for co-operation, he joined with Sir John Gilbert, Chairman of the Education Committee, in devising and securing the adoption of a new scheme for reducing class sizes in Elementary Schools, finally implemented as envisaged, despite interruption by the war.

Central Schools marked an advance in London's secondary school provision, but for further progress Lidgett looked to the Government. When Lloyd George formed his coalition with Conservative support in December 1916, he offered Nonconformists across the country the prospect of an Education Bill ere long which would resolve their religious difficulties, and appointed H. A. L. Fisher as President of the Board of Education. Fisher's immediate priority, however, was the raising of the school leaving age to 14, coupled with part-time continuation schooling from 14, initially to 16. His bill, enacted in August 1918, had both Davidson's and Lidgett's enthusiastic support. To Lidgett[14] the principle of compulsory education was vital. In 1918[15] he had argued for the raising of the leaving age to 15 as soon as possible and in 1936 he applauded the Hadow Report of 1926 for recommending a rise 'not merely to 15, but 16 years'. So in 1918 the prospect of providing Continuation Schools in London was welcome.

Lidgett encouraged greater awareness in schools of the trades and careers likely to follow schooling, but insisted that religious and moral influences should be secured and schools' sights be set on turning out good citizens, not merely efficient 'hands' and capable clerks. While he applauded help from employers, he hoped they would be restrained from 'narrowing' pupils' education.[16] At least one Labour councillor shared Lidgett's disappointment when Fisher modified his original proposal to extend part-time education to age 18: 'In a Labour member's words', Lidgett commented, 'the scream of the factory whistle has again been allowed to drown the voice of the educational and national interests of the country'.[17] Calls for improvement in the education, especially technical education of the workforce, were widely voiced at the time, but it was characteristic of Lidgett to emphasise the wider educational perspective and to place educational advance within the overall context of post-war social reconstruction.

The co-operative atmosphere of LCC Parties in this period was conducive to discussion of a possible coalition parallel to the Government's. Sir John Benn, the Progressives' Leader since McKinnon's election as MP, supported the idea and in 1917 the Municipal Reformers agreed. To Lidgett it seemed the best way not only of securing agreement during the strains of a war still in progress but also of mounting an effective programme after the war was over.

In October 1918 the *Contemporary Review* published Lidgett's personal manifesto, 'London After The War', covering the whole field of London's needs in housing, slum clearance, transport, leisure, etc., but not least education. The practically unanimous welcome given to the Fisher Education Act (discussed below) earlier in the year had been encouraging, but to Lidgett, prolonging school attendance could not be the sole objective: it had to be accompanied, for example, by an increase in fully qualified teachers,[18] reduction in class size, improvements in school buildings and equipment, and revision of the whole scheme of elementary education, not only in its span but its aims, in the light of the change. The nub of it all was his concern for the full range of ability. His manifesto stated: 'The main equipment of life is education. Every child must enjoy its full birthright of education and opportunity.' It was this which led him to seek ample provision as well as co-ordination of all grades of education, offering the facility for able children to climb 'the ladder from mean streets to the University' and for the less gifted to gain fulfilment through a more enlightened curriculum.

Apart from education, among Lidgett's other concerns some in particular were outstanding from the past. The war had, he felt, finally brought home to the Council's conscience the need for municipal housing it had earlier disputed, and McKinnon's proposal for municipal control of electricity, rejected by his opponents in 1907, again demanded attention. In Lidgett's view the area of the LCC's administration should be enlarged to include Greater London, the relations between the Central Authority and Borough Councils revised, and the former given greater powers to perform its duties. It was a grand vision, supported by detailed proposals to improve local government efficiency and services, and promote welfare. He was certainly, *pace* D. P. Campbell,[19] 'committed to the nuts and bolts of social reform', and obviously proud of his article. Some of his proposals were adopted by the Municipal Reformers, but after the election in March 1919, confirming once more their control of the LCC, much of what he had envisaged was, he sadly reported, 'left in abeyance', and no reliance could be placed on sustained support from the ruling party.

General agreement on the essentials of post-war reconstruction, with few serious questions in dispute prior to the election, led to a low poll. It was comforting to Lidgett to have been elected for the third time as member for Rotherhithe with 'a majority of nearly two to one over my half-hearted Labour opponents'.[20] But the Labour Party's lukewarm attitude to coalition upset him. Initially, Harry Gosling, Trades Union leader and LCC's Labour Party leader at the time, expressed general approval for the coalition proposal, but then 'cautiously abstained from joining it'.[21] Lidgett regarded this lack of solidarity as irresponsible. Gosling had been the sole Labour member on the council in 1913, but the return in 1919 of 14 more members had, no doubt, boosted his confidence and offered the prospect of mounting a real challenge to the other two Parties in future. Moreover, that electoral gain had been at the expense of the Progressives, despite Lidgett, their new leader. These circumstances seem to have started the overt breach between Lidgett and Labour, which became irrevocable after the hostility shown to Lidgett personally in the 1922 election. Percy Harris commented: 'Lidgett did not like the Labour Party and showed it, and that widened the breach. Nothing would have prevented it, but we might have walked more in step and have delayed the break-away'.[22]

The period post-war from 1919 to 1922 marked the third phase of Lidgett's LCC career. Though many of his salutary proposals were implemented over the years, in this period the hard realities of post-war recovery problems, a recession, vested interests and the Council's internal rivalries combined to frustrate his idealism. In 1919 the Progressives not only remained in opposition but had also lost seats.[23] Despite the death of his son on 24 March 1918, they had a leader with enthusiasm, vigour and fresh ideas, but he was destined to face bitter disappointments.

Lidgett's Manifesto reflected the Progressives' constant desire for the co-ordination of otherwise fragmented parts of the Capital's government, and increased municipal control. Since the 1913 election, growth in London's population had caused a vast overflow into the counties of Middlesex, Surrey and Essex. Lidgett's view was that

> all the problems of traffic, transport, health, housing, water supply and drainage, electricity and education stretched out beyond the County of London boundaries, and should be dealt with as a whole, but were yet at the mercy of divergent policies of unrelated authorities.[24]

He called for a Municipal Authority 'whose area should be not less than that of the Metropolitan Police District'.[25] But the Royal Commission of Enquiry, chaired by Lord Ullswater, established by Lord Downham, President of the (National) Local Government Board rejected the case for change. The verdict infuriated Lidgett and fellow protagonists. Middlesex had been the main opponent, and the conflicting views of 150 local authorities prevented subsequent action. The result was, as Lidgett feared, the multiplication of municipal machinery in a series of separate Boards without effective popular control, uninfluenced by any general, overall policy.

Lidgett, however, derived comfort from the vast housing scheme which the LCC undertook in partnership with the Government. It aimed to relieve overcrowding, reduce insanitary areas and cater for increased population by planting housing estates beyond the County of London in places like Becontree, Roehampton, Downham (near Bromley), Edgware and Morden. Though the need was urgent, its implementation was fraught with difficulties and frustrations. For example, these estates in Greater London tended not to cater for the poor, because rents were high, and travel to and from work within the County unavoidably expensive. Moreover, some of the rehoused population disliked the flats or other unfamiliar accommodation allocated to them, and returned to their former County areas. So LCC attempts to control slum problems were to that extent frustrated. Furthermore, the Housing Acts required all the Authority's available capital to be devoted to building new houses. Some expenditure could be earmarked for Elementary Schools, but not for other types of educational institution, nor for hospitals nor public services such as sanitation and health. The Local Authorities, therefore, complained not only of these administrative burdens, but of the people 'dumped' on them who cost more than their contribution to the rates.

Nevertheless the LCC pressed doggedly on with its policy. One problem in particular annoyed Lidgett intensely. The pace of building was reduced by shortage of plasterers, bricklayers and other workmen. He laid the blame squarely on the Building Trades Union[26] (all Trades Unions and the TUC later became his *bête noir*) which stubbornly resisted Government pressure on them to allow ex-servicemen to receive intensive training in such skills. The Union feared that if any change took place in housing policy which prevented the completion of the Government's national programme, the diluted labour force would be thrown onto the Union for support.

After 1919 Lidgett remained a member of the Education Committee. He took justifiable pride in the 'far-reaching programme of Educational Advance . . . which has formed the Council's policy ever since'.[27] The Council, he said, deserved great credit for its comprehensive and continuous development of education post-war. It had caused Sir Charles Trevelyan, a Labour Minister of Education no less, to declare publicly 'that his task would have been easy were all the Education Authorities throughout the country like the LCC'.[28]

Educational advance was not, however, in the much shorter term all plain sailing. Lidgett was, it is true, successful in pressing the Education Committee to co-operate fully with the Fisher Education Act and create Continuation Schools.[29] He proudly reported that 'buildings were hired in all parts of London, additional teachers were enrolled, and the plan was carried into effect by using the compulsory power of the County Council'.[30] The first of the new schools was opened in January 1921. But the grand intentions were not fulfilled either in London or elsewhere. By the mid-1920s only Rugby was operating these schools as required by the Act.

The problems were considerable, as Lidgett sadly illustrated[31] from his

London experience. Though many major employers welcomed and co-operated with the reform, small employers were upset by the absence of young employees. Many parents thought the obligation to attend damaged their children's employment prospects. They were incensed by the inconsistent application of the law: children under the jurisdiction of the Greater London LEAs were free to be employed full-time, while those from within the County of London boundaries were not. Moreover the LCC's ambitious and expensive scheme was doomed to founder at a time of financial stringency. The economic depression of 1922 increased concern over employment and local authority budgets were cut.

Serious problems arose also from the hasty introduction of the scheme. Pupils compared their rapidly hired accommodation in unsuitable and poorly equipped buildings unfavourably with spacious Day Schools to which they were accustomed, and it soon emerged that many of the staff, hurriedly recruited and inadequately prepared for the new demands, were either unqualified or unsuitable for the task. The curriculum, as prescribed for the schools by the Act, was deliberately designed to differ from ordinary elementary education, but its insistence on pupils spending a large proportion of time on physical exercises caused working-class mothers to complain that 'they wouldn't mind if their children were learning anything useful, but they did object to their time being spent in learning dancing'.[32] It was not surprising that discipline proved unsatisfactory, when no proper classification of pupils, already poor in rural districts,[33] could be expected, diversified courses were not available to meet varied needs and abilities, there was insufficient rigour in teaching, and the final school year was often considered mere 'marking time'. Ruefully reflecting on the LCC experience, Lidgett rightly observed that the lessons learned should be taken fully into account 'if the raising of the school age is to satisfy the expectations of its supporters'.[34]

After less than two years the Continuation Schools had become extremely unpopular. Parents and employers turned against the scheme. Attendance fell from 75,000 to little more than 2,000.[35] By July 1921 the LCC felt obliged to disregard its legal obligations and reduce compulsory part-time attendance to one nominal year, ending on the pupil's fifteenth birthday. The Schools' future was clearly set to be a major issue at the elections in March 1922. The Municipal Reformers pledged themselves to closing the Schools if they were again returned to power, while the Labour Party promised maintenance grants if the Schools continued. Though disappointed and frustrated by the turn of events, Lidgett and the Progressives recognised the problems, but remained convinced of the scheme's educational value. The remedy they proposed was the taking of powers to make the curriculum more practically useful and giving pupils the choice of compulsory attendance in evenings when daytime proved inconvenient. But the general outcry against the scheme, and the personal opposition Lidgett faced at a stormy meeting in Bermondsey Town Hall when supporting the LCC's Chief Education Officer's explanation of the proposals were ominous for his election prospects, and proved a key factor in his heavy defeat at the polls. Labour, however, dealt the fatal blow.

During the 1922 LCC election campaign Lidgett's Labour opponents had tried to represent him as the enemy of the unemployed – unfairly since he was on record as having proposed the appointment of an LCC Unemployment Committee to co-operate with borough councils in finding work, 'making up the arrears caused by the war'. To reinforce their charge, they employed a stratagem he later called unscrupulous, though clever.[36] On the eve of the vote a sudden waterside dispute occurred, putting some hundreds of men out of work. The employers called it 'a strike', the dockers 'a lock-out'. Local party members saw their opportunity to reduce Lidgett's vote. Hastily calling a meeting of the unemployed in the Rotherhithe Town Hall, they accused him of 'blacklegging' on the side of the employers. Their grounds were simply that the foreman of the works was a fellow Wesleyan. On that day Lidgett was at Lambeth Palace discussing Church reunion[37] and completely unaware either of the dispute or of the latest allegations. These spread rapidly through dockland that evening, so that by the following morning Lidgett's workers had to tell him that the situation was hopeless. The bitter irony was, he said, that 'subsequently the then Conservative Member for Rotherhithe publicly took credit for having induced a number of Conservative voters to support the Labour candidates as a protest against the refusal of the Central Municipal Reform Committee to oppose my re-election'.[38]

Salt was further rubbed into the wound by the election of a Trades Union organiser, W. J. Webb, as one of the two new members for Rotherhithe, and by the increase in the Municipal Reformers' overall dominance on the Council, again at the Progressives' expense. Under Lidgett's leadership the Progressives now had 25 seats, a loss of 15 since the previous election.[39] That was clearly a major setback, but his autobiographies made no reference to it.

Efforts to preserve the Continuation Schools did not abate when the election was over. Lidgett maintained his educational case, the Schools principals' review of progress was enthusiastic, and a deputation from the bishops of Southwark, Kingston and Willesden argued strongly in favour. Nevertheless, on 3 May the LCC Day Schools Subcommittee,[40] explicitly acknowledging that the unpopularity aroused by the Government's decision not to insist on compliance by adjacent areas had proved crucial, voted to 'arrest' the scheme until the relevant clauses of the 1918 Education Act were universally applied. It agreed that the 'work' had 'already proved of inestimable benefit to the community', but regretted the need to consider the present financial condition of the country. To delay the Council's decision, Lidgett's amendment, proposing a deputation to the President of the Board to discuss the 'existing difficulties', was, to his great annoyance, decisively defeated. The Schools were closed. Eleven, later 13, were later opened on the voluntary basis.

But the Fisher Act remained on the Statute Book and influenced its successor in 1944. The focus of educational interest henceforth centred on the national scene.

The final phase of Lidgett's LCC career was the period from 1922 to 1928. The pain he suffered at the loss of his own seat in 1922 was soon alleviated by his immediate election on 14 March 1922[41] as one of 10 Aldermen, thereby ensuring his involvement in the council as Progressives' leader until 1928. He was elected to the Education Committee, and to four subcommittees, including one on unemployment. A member of the Executive Committee of the Central Council for district nursing in London[42] since December 1914, he became its Chairman from 1922 to 1928. From the early days of the Bermondsey Settlement he had had a strong interest in nursing, and the post gave him the congenial task of co-ordinating the work and supply of nurses throughout Greater London. Moreover, the opening by the King, supported by the Queen, of the new and splendidly designed County Hall in July 1922 gave him great satisfaction. It was not only a royal occasion but also a triumph for the Progressives who had been accused 15 years earlier of starting to build a 'Wastrels' Palace'. In 1923, the following year, Lidgett was delighted to be elected as a member of the Athenaeum: 'The Archbishop of Canterbury did me the honour', as he put it,[43] of proposing his name, and Dr Charles, Archdeacon of Westminster, seconded the nomination. Looking back in 1936, he commented:

> The fellowship of this distinguished club has been a source of great pleasure to me ever since, and not only a pleasure, but of practical advantage in regard to the many interests of Church, university and national life with which I have been concerned.

He was already, it seems,[44] a member of the National Liberal Club.

But these compensations were offset by a further election defeat for his party in 1925. As Alderman he had not stood for election, but only 6 Progressives gained seats, marking a loss of 19 seats since 1922. They were now reduced to the position of a third party behind Labour, now with 35 seats. The writing was clearly on the wall. By now Lidgett had become the leader of a retreating army, facing defections and with rapidly falling morale. His distaste for Labour caused him to be increasingly identified with the Right Wing Party, and this had provoked opprobrium.[45] Whether he decided in 1925 not to stand again for Rotherhithe when his aldermanic term ended in 1928, and consequently resign as Leader, is unknown, but he must have considered the possibility.

Lidgett, however, was glad to record that no acute controversy arose to spoil his remaining aldermanic term. In his view, these years were relatively peaceful and unexciting. He continued to take a very active part in the general work of the Council, and it pleased him that his colleagues there carried on the work of reconstruction after the war not only with vigour and a high level of efficiency, but with public spirit. Typically, he singled out a moral crusade as one activity which gave him great personal satisfaction. It was a privilege, he said,[46] to lead the Council in opposing the establishment of a greyhound racing track at Crystal Palace, and to find the City Corporation and neighbouring Boroughs enthusiastically co-operating in the LCC's opposition. Their success was gratifying in itself, but the achievement of 'arousing a national and parliamentary movement to put down this most demoralising evil' will have made him equally content.

The only sour note was struck during the General Strike of 1926.[47] Lidgett believed this was 'unconstitutional and dangerous',[48] and when a Special LCC Committee was formed to maintain essential services during the emergency, he took an active part, responding to the needs of schools in particular: for example, he housed some Elementary School teachers in the Settlement. The Labour Party, however, declined to co-operate in the Committee's work, 'deeming', as Lidgett wrote, 'their allegiance to the TUC to be an obligation that took precedence over their responsibilities to the citizens of London'.[49] He never engaged in personal invective, but as he bowed out of the LCC in 1928, Labour's attitude, its refusal to recognise the importance of *co-operation for the common good* (one of Lidgett's major tenets), gave him the opportunity to issue a strong denunciation of both the Labour Party and the TUC:

> It is to be hoped that the citizens of London will steadily refuse power to a Party which cannot be trusted in a crisis to set the safety and civilisation of London above the behests of outside organisations pursuing sectional aims and adopting, on occasion, revolutionary methods to advance them.

For many years Lidgett had striven to remain impartial. The bitterness and partisan organisations evident among Wesleyans and Nonconformists in 1909 seem to have faded. In 1918, when Labour adopted a new constitution, the *Methodist Times*[50] discerned the Party's increased scope for recruiting newly enfranchised women and strengthening its intellectual membership with young and ambitious thinkers, thereby paving its way before long for participation in National Government. Lidgett expressed no dismay, but privately grew increasingly uneasy about socialist ideology,[51] the hardening of Labour's policies and outlook, and its developing sophistication. His personal experience in the LCC had now turned that unease into outright hostility.

Central to his concerns when he left Cambridge for Bermondsey were the growing divisions in society. To overcome these he sought to promote social harmony and co-operation, not social equality. 'When the Labour Party came to power in Bermondsey', he said in a broadcast in 1942, 'it excluded the co-operation of all who felt unable to accept its political and economic dogmas'.[52] To him what the Capital needed was a sense of community, 'social wholeness', and the readiness of reasonable men and women to discuss great issues together on their intrinsic merits; flexibility, sharing and mutual self-giving should be encouraged. By contrast Labour had embraced division, class consciousness, the 'class self-sufficiency of the industrial majority'.

Looking back[53] ten years after leaving the LCC, Lidgett found the extreme sections of the Labour Party were reacting against 'the conception upon which the Settlements have been based'. To him Labour's 'materialist and merely external Socialism' contrasted with the views of Samuel and Henrietta Barnett set out in their volume of addresses and essays from Toynbee Hall, entitled *Practicable Socialism*: their emphasis (and clearly Lidgett's) was 'upon the sharing of the highest spiritual values and upon such reforms as would bring the treasures and instruments of these values effectively within the reach of all as the true and practicable end of human society'. Lidgett deplored the intrusion of extraneous 'outside influences' from Labour's national party interests and its party machine into the realm of local administration, the ways in which it operated through factional propaganda and the TUC, and its increasingly rigid dogma (he called it 'abstract theory'). Labour's promotion of public ownership, for example, had aroused his strong criticism in 1936,[54] when it was suggested that a London Hospital might cease to depend on voluntary subscription: 'Directly an institution becomes public', he said, 'its supporters . . . feel it means a burden instead of a social privilege'.

In his opinion Labour, trusting in what he called 'mechanism', relied on the force of mass movements directed to political action. Its aims, he alleged, were to destroy, or at any rate reconstruct the existing system of society. Writing about the General Strike,[55] Percy Harris, Lidgett's successor as Party Leader, said, 'Some', and he may well have had Lidgett in mind, 'interpreted it as a real attempt to set up a parallel force to Parliament, and, no doubt, some hotheads may have had such revolutionary aims in view'. Certainly any suspicion or mention of 'revolution' aroused Lidgett's anger. No doubt the relatively recent Russian example seemed to echo the French, and Marxist atheism was in any case anathema.

Lidgett was glad to acknowledge the influence of Methodism on the social conscience of leaders like Joseph Arch and Arthur Henderson, Labour's first Foreign Secretary (whom he called his friend), but he deplored the development of Labour's materialistic outlook and materialistic economics. The 'externality' he attacked seemed at times[56] to equate with the lack of inner spiritual motivation he now found in many Labour adherents. Some comfort came from seeing evidence of the Evangelical Revival in the industrial classes' opposition to purely secular education, despite the controversies over religious teaching. Yet the importance of the spiritual in the wider social sphere remained for him in need of constant reiteration. As he wrote in 1938,

> It remains true . . . that true progress must be spiritual in order to be truly social, and that it must be God-centred in order to call forth the best in men in fellowship with one another because they are in fellowship with God, and in partnership with His ordered purpose for mankind.[57]

Whatever strictures Lidgett expressed, Labour nevertheless was prospering. By contrast the Progressives' fortunes were declining, as is amply illustrated by the Table supplied in Appendix 3. Its eventual decline, as indicated above, was rapid. At the 1928 election, when Lidgett resigned both as Leader of the Progressives and member of the LCC, only five Progressives were returned. Percy Harris, who took over as leader of the rump, admitted that as an MP he could not give all his time to the LCC, 'but we did assert ourselves on occasions and kept alive Progressive principles'.[58] Six Progressives were elected in 1931, but none in 1934. Yet for some reason Lidgett dated the decision to wind up the Party (and hand it over to the London Liberal Federation) to 'the eve of the election' in March 1928.[59] It was a decision he understandably found unwelcome and he was 'glad to be released from participation in carrying it out',[60] but 1934, not 1928, will have marked the end of the LCC Progressive Party. Understandably he mourned the events following 1928 'which have resulted in the total extinction of the Liberal Party on the County Council'.[61]

Lidgett gave no reasons for his retirement from 'over 30 years of service in the local government of London'. By this time other fields of service, not least in London University[62] and in the moves towards Methodist Union, may have begun to prove of increasing interest and satisfaction, but there is no doubt that he was conscious of swimming against the Labour tide in the LCC. He will have been deeply disheartened by the events of the ten years since he became Party leader, and perhaps have ruminated on how far his leadership had contributed to its demise.

Lidgett's political career was not over: he was active on the national scene seven years later.[63] But as far as leadership of the LCC Progressives was concerned, his successor's tribute gave a realistic appraisal which warrants quotation *in extenso*:

> Lidgett is an able man, one of the most fluent speakers I have ever met, and had knowledge of every conceivable subject. He was a man of impeccable character and had given the whole of his life to good work, particularly in Bermondsey, where for a long time he was head of a settlement. Headlam [the Revd Stewart D. Headlam, another Progressive socially concerned and actively involved in the LCC] used to say of him that he would have made an

> excellent Bishop. Unfortunately he was not qualified, being a member of the Wesleyan Church. But for all his qualities, by the very cloth he wore and by his whole make-up, he was not cut out for a political leader. Every man to his last, and parsons do not make good politicians. Headlam was clever enough to know that, and *he* never aimed at being a political leader. He was *keen on politics*, but that is quite another matter from pretending to be a politician.[64]

Lidgett may not have '*aimed* at being a political leader', but much of this assessment rings true.

D. H. Thomas[65] quoted Beveridge as saying that Lidgett 'refused to bargain in the way politicians do'. It may be that his deeply felt religious convictions and what Labour increasingly stood for and did had made him not so much 'intransigent', as far less ready to seek compromises in LCC debates as he had been known to do in the past. Lidgett was perhaps too much of an idealist, a divine explicitly focused on furthering the Kingdom of God, and it was in that direction that he sought to channel the Progressives, believers and agnostics alike. As he himself put it, 'The very success of the Progressives in communicating their ideals to the Municipal Reformers on the right and to the Labour Party on the left has told to their disadvantage as a Party'.[66] This he called 'a triumph in the realm of ideals'. The enthusiasm which motivated the Progressives had, he admitted, exhausted itself, spread to the best representatives of the Municipal Reform Party or had entrenched itself within the Labour Party.

But his pride in London's record and his own association with it was evident. He claimed, with much justice, that the work carried on over the years by the Progressive leaders had been 'epoch-making', and that London owed the Party an 'immense debt'. He was referring, no doubt, principally to the 'golden' years when they were the ruling Party, but he would also be thinking of the years in opposition. A similar claim was made by Percy Harris who spoke of 'great things' done for London.[67] Lidgett went so far as to write, 'We had not only fashioned the structure, but had given the ideals and outlined the policy upon which the subsequent history of the LCC has been based'.[68] Here he was looking back in particular to the days of the London School Board, when 'Party considerations were never allowed to interfere with opportunities for service',[69] and to the pioneering days when initiatives and experiments were courageously undertaken, at times without Government sanction. No doubt he had in mind also the forging of an effective educational administration and the implementation of the Education Acts when the LCC took over from the London School Board; and the slow, but successful process, after the 1907 election, of enlightening the Municipal Reformers about the vital educational needs of the Capital. Long and significant service had been given in stressing both the importance of its teachers and the welfare of its children in ordinary Elementary and Special Schools. He had to fight hard for adequate expenditure. The curriculum as well as school buildings and class sizes received careful attention. He helped to improve secondary educational provision and raise standards generally throughout the Authority. He campaigned for the raising of the school leaving age. His proposals and amendments in LCC Committees were not infrequently overturned; he spent 21 years in opposition; but he was always looking for opportunities for co-operation (to him the key to progress), and never ceased to offer positive ideas and constructive criticism. His salutary and inspiring example more than outweighed his disappointments and failures.

No single or overall achievement could be attributed to him alone. But involvement on the LCC, a massive, continually growing enterprise, not only called for skills in debating and planning, but also readiness to devote considerable time to committee work, with their often weekly meetings and lengthy agendas, and to accept responsibility for major decisions on complex matters. In all its activities Lidgett had played an important and enthusiastic part. He was widely respected, even admired, as a man of principle and vision, a devoted servant of the people of London, especially its children and the disadvantaged, and one who knew its problems 'at ground level'. He had helped to widen streets, provide pure water, and give each child in London a chance of attending a good school and then university. Though education was his major concern in the LCC, his contribution was evident and his influence felt across the whole field of its administration. Indeed, in popular estimation he was regarded as having become 'Chairman of the LCC', a post he never achieved.

12

University politician and Vice-Chancellor 1922–46

Lidgett's involvement in London education extended to its university.

Though Lidgett's uncle's aversion to the older universities was not uncommon among Nonconformists at the time, his choice of the nearby University College, London (UCL), for his nephew was surprising, since unlike its rival, King's College, founded five years later in 1831,[1] it had turned its face against religion. UCL's refusal to offer a Divinity course earned it the description of 'the God-less institution of Gower Street' and C. S. Calverly's lampoon called it 'the radical infidel College'.[2] Lidgett did not argue. Though both his autobiographies[3] say he spent three and a half years there, Eric Baker was clearly correct in calculating the length of his university education after entry to the college in January 1873 as two and a half years.[4]

In terms of academic attainment Lidgett had every reason to be satisfied: he matriculated with a placing in the First Division on leaving school in 1871; at University College he gained first classes in both first and second BA examinations (an Arts degree), the former as early as 1873, the latter a year later. Both included, among other subjects, Mathematics and Science. In Branch III of the MA examination in Logic and Philosophy, he was placed fourth in a list of six students at that level. But not surprisingly he left the college in the summer of 1875 with mixed feelings. Philosophy had been his 'chief intellectual interest' there, but his studies[5] led to an 'unresolved conflict' between his religious convictions and those of his teachers, and 'years of subsequent study and reflection were needed' before he could find 'a way of escape from this deadlock'.[6]

He was, however, fortunate in the calibre of his teachers. During the period 1860–80 H. Hale Bellot said that 'except for that of W. K. Clifford in Mathematics, the work of two men alone stands out notably above the rest, that of Henry Morley in English and of G. Croom Robertson in Philosophy'.[7] Lidgett was not taught by Morley, but by Croom Robertson, appointed Professor of the Philosophy of Mind and Logic at age 24, and by Clifford, who gained the Chair of Applied Mathematics at age 26. Both were brilliant scholars, but both were opposed to the Christian religion. Clifford carried on a campaign against it, while Robertson, though making a carefully balanced presentation of contrasting arguments, strongly supported the Association

School with no time for Theism.[8] Lidgett says he gained little knowledge or illumination from Clifford, though others regarded him as an original thinker (a pioneer of the conception of non-Euclidean space)[9] and an impressive teacher.[10] Professors to whose stimulus Lidgett was particularly indebted were Croom Robertson, unusual in taking an interest in his pupils, and Dr Marks, Professor of Hebrew, noted for infectious enthusiasm and a genial, friendly approach.[11]

Well before he entered the college his interests had already shown themselves to be practical and educational as well as theological. Qualified as a Wesleyan local preacher in 1871, he had also engaged in social, philanthropic work and Sunday School teaching for his church. Even before he left school, he had founded and led a Mutual Improvement Class and given biblical and theological teaching to pupil teachers on Saturday evenings.[12] His urge to educate had no doubt developed under the influence of his grandfather, and some years after leaving college he declared that 'the prospect of becoming eventually a theological teacher began to allure me'. But the range of activities in which he was engaged before and alongside his day attendance at college explain why he 'tolerated, rather than enjoyed, academic studies, being anxious to take the plunge into practical life as soon as I possibly could'.[13]

It was Lidgett's practical life that brought him back into contact with the University and with contemporaries (or near-contemporaries) at University College. A major benefactor for the Bermondsey Settlement's work among women was, as mentioned earlier, Miss Alice Barlow of Edgeworth, sister of Sir Thomas Barlow, physician to Buckingham Palace. He was one of Lidgett's friends, and had attended the college just prior to Lidgett's arrival there. In 1904, more significantly, Lidgett met another former fellow-student, by then the Progressives' leader of the LCC, and later a member of Asquith's Liberal Cabinet, Mr (afterwards the Rt Hon.) T. McKinnon Wood. The LCC had just undertaken new responsibilities for education. Wood quickly recognised the value of Lidgett's experience and abilities for this period, and arranged for him to fill an Aldermanic vacancy.

Lidgett's concern for the cause of education had extended from elementary to secondary schools and to 'adult' education in the Settlement. His service on the LCC Education Committee from 1904 to 1928 included support for the development of the University. The readiness of the LCC to make generous financial grants to individual Colleges and Schools of the University and to the university itself and engage in debate about its future had been due at least in part to Lidgett's advocacy within the LCC's Education Committee. A cartoon in the *London Teacher* of 11 July 1914 featured him pleading for 'a great London University' at an LCC meeting.[14]

The date was significant. It was while the Committee, set up by the Government's Board of Education under Sir George Murray, was discussing how to respond to the Report of the Royal Commission, published in 1913, on the detailed future of the University. London University had undergone many changes since obtaining its Charter. Initially it was purely an examining body, granting degrees to students at individual, recognised institutions, University and King's Colleges, for example, after satisfactorily completing their terms and courses there. By the time Lidgett went to University College, the earlier insistence on attending a College had been abandoned; external candidates (matriculated students other than internal students, many studying part-time, many not at the University's Colleges) could present themselves for degrees from all over Britain and the Empire; and in 1878, soon after Lidgett left, London was the first University to grant equality to women students. In 1900 the university became a teaching, not only an examining, body. In 1907 University and King's Colleges were incorporated into it, while several other Colleges in the London area became 'Schools' of the university, offering specialist subjects such as medicine.

As the University developed, there continued to be much heated debate between those who championed the facility for external students and those who did not. In 1913, though this controversy was far from over, there were two central issues: where the University could best be sited, and what reforms were needed to its constitution to enable it to cope with its ever increasing size and complexity. The government had accepted responsibility for housing the University, but over the years its building had moved several times. Various sites were proposed, Kensington, Holland Park and Bloomsbury, and a strong lobby existed for forming a University 'quarter' within which the University's constituent buildings could be grouped. But the Great War, its aftermath, and controversy over the purchase of the Bloomsbury site postponed a decision. Yet another government departmental committee was formed in 1924. Its findings were reported in March 1926, and later that year, despite strong opposition, the University of London Act was passed, favouring the reforms and setting up a statutory commission under Mr (later Lord) Justice Tomlin to frame the requisite Statutes. The Bloomsbury site was finally chosen and paid for, and the new Statutes came into effect on 21 March 1929.

Elected in 1922 to the University Senate,[15] and regularly re-elected until his retirement in 1946, Lidgett was therefore a participant at an extremely important period in the University's development.

Lidgett was not unfamiliar with university administration. During his ministry at Cardiff he had been a member of the Court of the University College of South Wales, newly opened there in 1883 by (among others) Charles Vaughan, Dean of Llandaff.[16] In 1922, however, it was, he said,[17] with great reluctance in view of his other engagements, that he accepted nomination to fill a casual vacancy in the London University Senate on the death of Sir Albert Rollitt.

As a member of Convocation since 1875, he was eligible to stand for the

Senate as an Arts Graduate and represent the external side of the University. He was clearly well qualified. As Warden of the Bermondsey Settlement he had promoted the educational advance of students from unpromising backgrounds, eager to learn, but unable to enter a university. 'University Extension' tuition, for study 'privately' before as well as after College courses, dated from the last quarter of the nineteenth century, and was included in his Settlement programme. Quite apart from this, Lidgett had been an External Student himself at University College. Ready to innovate, and free from the alleged prejudices of colleagues educated in older, residential universities, he relished the chance to support provision for External Students against extremists wishing to abolish it. 'I believe in privileges', he remarked, 'so long as they are privileges open to anyone who is worthy of them'.[18] His membership of the University's Council for External Students ran from 1922 to 1946, and that of the Extension and Tutorial Classes Council from 1929 to 1945.

At the same time to him the future of London remained as a teaching University: he urged that everything should be done to encourage directed study in the Colleges and Schools of the University, and the highest standards of attainment everywhere. Characteristically, throughout his life he saw opportunities for reconciliation. In this instance he was involved in helping the Senate to overcome the problems of combining both internal and external provision. In 1924 the Senate instituted an Advisory Service for External Students, and in 1926 the University Act, by requiring them to register, brought them into closer contact with the University. Waterhouse was convinced Lidgett should be given some share of the credit for the system in which external and academic students in most faculties took a common examination.[19] By 1945 External Student numbers had risen to over 16,000.

Lidgett was immensely proud of London University. The problems such a body posed were daunting, but for him it was exciting to play a part in rising to the challenge. The University was expanding to a remarkable size, and bidding fair, he thought, to become the greatest as well as the largest in the British Empire and Commonwealth, indeed the world. London University was to him a vehicle for international friendship and unity, called with other universities to render services 'not only to the material well-being of the empire, but to the highest spiritual values of life'.[20] In 1935 he was boasting not only of its External and Internal sides in general, but of its 'unrivalled' opportunities for post-graduate research, scientific, medical, legal, economic and in the fields of arts and languages. Moreover, London had broken ground ahead of other, older universities fettered by tradition. Among its 'experiments', as Waterhouse[21] lists them, were: abolition of religious tests; English language recognised as essential, at the very least on a par with Latin and Greek, and made compulsory at Matriculation; a BSc offered instead of a BA for Science; women given equality with men; and London's pre-eminence among the universities in provision for teaching medical science. Lidgett delighted in all these developments, but especially in the progress of the new and imposing administrative headquarters building, as it was being built; when King George V, accompanied by the Queen, laid its foundation in 1933; and when it was finally completed in 1938.

Amid all this the work of the Senate was of exceptional importance. It is clear from his elevation in 1929 and from Waterhouse's testimony that Lidgett's contributions to its debates were widely respected. In other circumstances Lidgett could be at times tiresomely loquacious, but in the Senate a ten minute rule applied. There he was incisive: 'He spoke only when he had something to say, and he knew how to say it too',[22] and always to the point. When the time came for him to preside, he was undaunted. 'Lidgett', said Waterhouse who was present, 'was commonly thought to have no nerves. He certainly showed none, but ruled the Senate with an easy mastery on every occasion'.[23] To those like Waterhouse who knew him closely, however, he was human! He felt the stress of the great occasion, but without showing it publicly.

Once the Privy Council had approved the new University Statutes in March 1929, the Senate was formally reconstituted, and a new body, the Court, created to undertake responsibility for University finance. Represented on it were the Board of Education and the LCC, but most members were from the Senate itself. Lidgett was elected as a Senate representative from the outset, and remained a Court member from 1929 to 1943. This added to his work in the Senate.

Another effect of the reconstitution of the University was the creation of a new post, that of Deputy Vice-Chancellor, holding office for one year only. Though the office was expected to be usually a sinecure, Lidgett was proud to be unanimously appointed to it by the Senate on 3 July 1929 for the remainder of the academic year 1928/9 and for the whole of the following academic year 1929/30. The Vice-Chancellor, elected in 1928, was Sir T. Gregory Foster, Provost of University College since 1906. He, however, fell ill, and when necessary, therefore, his responsibilities fell on his Deputy's shoulders. Senate Minutes indicate Foster's absence from its monthly formal meetings only on 20 November and 18 December 1929. Lidgett claimed he deputised 'throughout the year',[24] but the extent of his commitments involved are unclear.

His conduct in office was, however, so well regarded that he was unanimously elected as the next Vice-Chancellor, not an automatic promotion. Initially for 1930/1, the post was extended to 1931/2, thus allowing him the maximum period of two years. This period of public distinction represents a high point in Lidgett's career. That it occurred as he was reaching another pinnacle of achievement, the reunion of the Methodist churches in 1932, provides a further reminder of Lidgett's capacity for working simultaneously in a variety of disparate fields and of the success and approval he gained in them.

It must, however, be acknowledged that Lidgett's London University prominence owed much to unexpected accidents: first the illness of Sir Gregory Foster and then the scandal engulfing the seventh Earl Beauchamp (1872–1938).

Lidgett said[25] that he, as the Deputy Vice-Chancellor, had installed Sir William Lygon, Earl Beauchamp, leader of the Liberal Peers, as Chancellor on the death of Lord Rosebery. This ceremony, in which Beauchamp also received an Honorary D.Litt., took place on 22 November 1929 when Foster's illness may have caused his absence. The programme for the installation speaks of installation by 'the Vice-Chancellor' (unnamed) and it was clearly unusual for a Deputy Vice-Chancellor to have to officiate at such an important ceremony, but Lidgett's statement seems likely to be accurate.

After under two years, however, Beauchamp abruptly resigned on grounds of ill-health and overwork on 1 August 1931. It later emerged that he had been exposed as a homosexual by his brother-in-law.[26] His successor was Sir Alexander Cambridge, the Rt. Hon. the Earl of Athlone (1874–1957), and Lidgett proudly recorded his 'great privilege', this time as Vice-Chancellor, in installing this, his second Chancellor, a member of the Royal family, in January 1932.[27] At the same ceremony the Earl of Athlone also received an Honorary LLD.

Referring to his period as Vice-Chancellor from 1930 to 1932, Lidgett claimed that 'During the greater portion of this time I had also, owing to unfortunate circumstances, to discharge the duties of the *Chancellor*'.[28] Yet on the following page of his autobiography he spoke of 'the short period during which I discharged the duties of the Chancellorship'. The latter seems more accurate and to allude to the 3–4 month gap between the two Chancellors. Though no ruling is now available on the division of responsibilities at that time, it would appear that a Vice-Chancellor would normally confer degrees obtained by examination,[29] whereas the Chancellor, if available, would normally officiate at any ceremonies in which honorary degrees were involved. Earl Beauchamp could have officiated on 13 May 1931 (that is before his resignation), when Lord Macmillan received an Honorary LLD. Though Lidgett praised Lord Macmillan for his chairmanship of Court, his autobiography's silence on Macmillan's honorary degree suggests he did not confer it.

Without doubt Vice-Chancellor Lidgett was acting as Chancellor in the autumn of 1931 in the conferment of honorary degrees. It was his privilege to welcome the quinquennial gathering of some 70 universities of the Empire, as well as the British Association at its centenary meetings in autumn 1931. At a ceremony (it seems especially arranged for the British Association) he said he had conferred Honorary D.Sc. degrees on five of its distinguished members, among whom was Field Marshal Jan Christian Smuts, its President for that year.[30] His welcome to the representatives of Empire universities occurred later that year, again in the period between the two Chancellors, on Foundation Day on 28 November 1931. Lidgett then conferred honorary degrees on six important figures: Sir Samuel Courtauld, Sir Edward Elgar, Baron Passfield, Baron Tomlin, M. Charlety (Rector of Paris University) and Dr Arthur Headlam, Bishop of Gloucester. Dr Thomas Masaryk, President of the Republic of Czechoslovakia, being unwell, the diploma was forwarded to him.

Curiously enough, Waterhouse mentioned[31] a further honorary degree ceremony, not recorded by Lidgett himself, when he says Lang, the Archbishop of Canterbury, knelt before Lidgett, the Free Churchman, to receive the robes of an Honorary DD. When the ceremony was over, Waterhouse went on to say that Lidgett asked him in noticeably anxious tones: 'Did I do all right?', and that he was 'able to reassure him with conviction that in my opinion both his speech and his conduct of the ceremony were faultless, and he was obviously pleased'. It seems, however, that Lang received his London University DD on 24 November 1933, that is after Lidgett's Vice-Chancellorship ceased. Moreover, there is a photographic record[32] of the Earl of Athlone conferring the degree on the kneeling Archbishop on that date. The assumption, supported by Lidgett's silence on what would have been an outstanding event for him, had it occurred, must be that Waterhouse confused two quite different occasions. Perhaps the DD conferred on the Revd Stewart D. Headlam in November two years before was in his mind. What cannot be disputed is that, whenever the need arose, Lidgett proved himself the master of the grand occasion, as well as an effective chairman and a well-informed and respected contributor to Senate and Court meetings, and their associated councils and committees of all levels of importance.[33] Nor can there be any doubt that Lidgett enjoyed receiving an honorary DD degree at Edinburgh University on 28 October 1933 on his own account and moreover receiving it on the same occasion alongside the Archbishop of Canterbury.[34]

A further event at this period pleased him. During his Vice-Chancellorship an Inter-Universities China Committee was formed to promote cultural relations between China and Great Britain, with funds allocated by Parliament for the purpose. Lidgett was prominent[35] in the committee's inauguration and as an ex-officio member subsequently. His membership ceased at the end of his term as London's Vice-Chancellor, but he was pleased to be recalled to become Committee Chairman after the Master of Balliol's resignation in 1933. He found it, as he wrote in 1935, 'a great privilege, as well as a heavy responsibility, to be charged with the development of a great undertaking which is already drawing the university students of China into close and happy relations with the Universities of this country'.[36] This chairmanship showed the regard in which he was held in British universities.

During their tenure other Vice-Chancellors sought leave of absence from their obligations elsewhere. Not so Lidgett. He relished hard and responsible work, and his acumen and stamina never failed to astonish all who worked with him. After ceasing to be Vice-Chancellor, he remained involved not only with the University's Committees, but also with the governing bodies of two constituent Colleges, Royal Holloway (for women) and Queen Mary College. Waterhouse, its Principal, also testified to his support for the Methodist Theological College at Richmond. Predictably it was Lidgett who helped to persuade the University's Finance Committee and Senate in 1934 to donate £100 for the purchase of the invaluable *Codex Sinaiticus* by the British Museum Library.[37]

Teachers in Elementary and Secondary Schools were never far from Lidgett's thoughts. As John Scott's grandson, he took especial delight in acting as Chairman of the Managing Committee of Westminster and Southlands Teachers' Training Colleges.[38] Throughout his career he had stressed the importance not only of an adequate teacher supply, but of highly qualified teachers who entered the profession as a vocation. He was convinced that if religious (Christian) teaching was to be effective, teachers should be better qualified to teach it, not just through adequate denominational and undenominational teacher training courses, but through provision for further studies after students left college. During the early 1930s he helped, for example, in London University's institution of a Diploma in Biblical Literature.[39]

To Lidgett, however, for all teachers there was something more important than training or vocation. This was *the teacher's character and personality*. These he had first singled out for special emphasis in a powerful address to Westminster and Southlands Colleges in 1909. He said:

> In every sphere of life personality is the most effective influence, but in the school it is all-important. Children are affected, one way or another, much more powerfully by contact with their teachers than in any other way. If noble suggestions and elevating ideals are to possess and mould the life of a child, it will be for the most part because they so live in the teacher as to be conveyed, both consciously and unconsciously, to the children. Each one of you is called to be a representative personality, concentrating in your character and influence the highest ideals of those who sent you forth – Christ, the Church, the nation. Much depends on what you know; more on what you are; most of all on what you are becoming. In all men character is the supreme concern.[40]

Lidgett, therefore, found teachers' status lower than they deserved. Moreover Elementary School teachers in particular had long been cold-shouldered by universities, and training colleges, however good their teaching, were bound, in his view, because they were training colleges, to lack 'the larger vision, the more profound thought, the more alive stimuli which a university provided'.[41]

An opportunity to remedy this came in 1926.[42] The Board of Education proposed to hand over the responsibility for examining teacher training college students to regional committees on which both the universities and the colleges were to be represented. The LCC's Chief Education Officer, Sir George Gates, realised that the scheme was vague and did not excite interest in London University. Taking the initiative, he approached Lidgett to act as an intermediary between the University and the LCC and its colleges in implementing it. Lidgett readily agreed and in 1928 the University's Training Colleges Delegacy was appointed with Lidgett as a member, later as Chairman, in both cases nominated by the University. The Delegacy awarded Elementary School Teachers' Certificates on the results of an examination conducted jointly by Training College and University lecturers, but hopes that it might lead to a closer relationship between the training colleges and the university, or that the gulf between Elementary and Secondary Schools would at any rate begin to be bridged, were disappointed.

A further reform was attempted as a result of the report by Sir Arnold McNair in 1944, advocating the creation of Area Training Organisations. Of the two alternative schemes mooted for these, Lidgett favoured the one to establish University Institutes of Education, thereby causing a major change in the organisation and administration of teacher training. By simply modifying the existing Joint Board system, the other in his view left the training colleges as much out of touch with the universities as before. But opinions in the crucial Senate debate to decide which scheme to adopt were evenly poised. It proved to be a dramatic occasion. Pritchard[43] described how eventually Lidgett, who had hobbled in with two sticks, struggled to his feet, and in a speech which began quietly but increased in rhetorical fervour stated the case for creating a London University Institute of Education. Waving his two sticks, he reminded the Senate of the function of a university and its absolute dependence on dedicated and highly qualified teachers 'to produce the human personalities which were the life-blood of any University'. He won the day, and the Institute, with Lidgett's help behind the scenes, in due course established its place not just in the Capital but beyond.

The University celebrated its centenary with much ceremony in 1936, but the climax of Lidgett's university career came ten years later, on Foundation Day, 28 November 1946, when he was honoured with the degree of Doctor of Laws. It marked his retirement from the Senate (he was after all 92!) and recognised his long and valued service. The custom was for only one of the honorands to speak on behalf of the others. Lidgett was chosen. His speech, Waterhouse said,[44] was short, incisive and witty, surpassing in quality the rest of the evening's oratory.

13

Educationist: The national education scene 1919–44

Lidgett's educational activities had rarely lacked a national reference, and no more so than in the controversies over religious education, arising from the 1902 Education Act.[1]

The initiative in tackling the religious difficulties at the end of WW1 was attributed by Bishop Bell[2] to Fisher as President of the Board of Education. It was certainly Fisher who on 19 June 1919 invited Davidson and Lidgett to confer with him privately at the Board of Education. D. H. Thomas,[3] however, discovered from Board of Education archives that Lidgett had written confidential letters on 5 and 21 May 1919, asking Fisher for a short interview in private: it seemed he was anxious to forestall trouble over the un-redressed Nonconformist grievances 'before the NCEFC is moved on the subject'. A minute of the Board dated 5 June 1919, quoted by Thomas, recorded his advocacy of a conference of both sides as a means of encouraging moderate Free Churchmen 'to hold aloof from the extremists'. Such a conference and the four subsequent meetings did in fact take place on and after 31 July 1919 in Fisher's office in the Board of Education. Lidgett, clearly regarded as Davidson's Free Church educational counterpart, with long and recent experience of inter-church discussion on religion in schools and the dual system, had been invited, like the Archbishop, at a meeting on 19 June, to return six weeks later, bringing six others with him. These included, among others, such earlier protagonists as E. A. Knox (Bishop of Manchester), Athelstan Riley, R. Holland (Secretary of the National Society), J. Clifford (the Baptist firebrand) and W. R. Selbie (Congregationalist). There were no Roman Catholics. Such meetings were an unprecedented procedure, and regarded as of great potential importance.

But Davidson and Lidgett seriously underestimated the strength of old fears and grudges. In fact no real progress was made. Clifford withdrew before the last session ended, and the Roman Catholics, who had been separately consulted on the five essential principles agreed by conference participants, refused their approval. On 9 December 1921 Davidson put forward a further three principles, only to find them rejected on 30 May 1923 at the Annual Meeting of the National Society which had earlier accepted them. Davidson was taken by surprise and deeply disappointed. The death of Clifford on 23 November 1923 did not advance matters. Undaunted, however, Davidson and Lidgett continued their efforts. Lidgett was convinced that the religious controversy could be solved in London and, if in London, it could be solved elsewhere. But no progress had been made when Davidson decided to resign as Archbishop on 12 November 1928.

Summing up the relationship between Davidson and Lidgett throughout the education controversy to that date, Bishop Bell commented:

> He (Lidgett) was of course thoroughly alive to the traditional Free Church point of view. At the same time he was equally alive to the great desirability of a national system being achieved which would secure adequate provision in all public elementary schools for religious observance and instruction, differentiated as far as practicable in relation to religious tenets, subject to a conscience clause. Scott Lidgett was never wanting in resolute advocacy; but he was also very much a practical man, concerned to get the best possible result in given circumstances. The two men approached the schools question from different angles, but they were both moderate and constructive. No settlement was in fact achieved. But the spirit by which each was guided had its own powerful influence on the whole educational atmosphere. It was very different from the heated days when Birrell, Runciman, and McKenna were Presidents of the Board of Education in succession.[4]

Resolution of the religious issues had to wait until the 1944 Act and its implementation. In the meantime, however, Lidgett took all the opportunities he could to maintain public and governmental awareness of outstanding problems and curb unreasonable Free Church protests. He was also active in supporting progress nationally in several ways, in moves to raise the school leaving age (again!), in the use of the cinema, and in the development of 'Agreed Syllabuses' for religious instruction.

Despite disappointment over Continuation Schools, the urgent need to raise the school leaving age remained Lidgett's constant preoccupation, but, when the issue arose again, the need to finance the requisite adaptation of existing schools and, where necessary, build new ones provoked inevitable denominational sensitivities. Again, no change was achieved, either in 1931 when Lidgett had to exercise his powers of persuasion to allay Free Church concerns, nor in 1935 when he joined a deputation to the Prime Minister.[5] There he stressed two of his major convictions: that 'the educational needs of the children must not be worsened by the religious convictions of their parents', and, above all, that 'the Churches must not stand in the way of educational advance throughout the country'.

Within the Bermondsey Settlement and the schools Lidgett had long been interested in opening students' eyes to wonder at God's creation and raising their horizons beyond their dreary surroundings through art, music, literature, history, geography, science, and the use of lantern shows and outside visits. So it was not surprising that his perspective over the whole field of education, as well as his personal standing, led to an invitation, along with some other Nonconformists, to join the 40-member strong Christian Cinema Council in 1935. Set up in 1933 originally as an Anglican body, presided over by Edward Woods, Bishop of Croydon, it aimed to 'promote the practical use and the development of the Cinema in the cause of religion, education, recreation, and social welfare at home and in our Dominions and Colonies'.[6] To Lidgett those aims were worthy of strong support. Sadly some Anglicans formed a breakaway group in 1937, and some Anglo-Catholics also in 1938, thereby reducing the Council's scope for ecumenical co-operation.

As late as at age 97[7] Lidgett was contributing to the official journal of the National Committee for Visual Aids in Education. His article praised the motor car and film as two great instruments helping to 'promote and enrich the experience and enjoyment of natural wonders'. At the same time, however, he gave a salutary warning: that pictures and other visual material should be used to inspire and enrich the imagination, not stultify it, and contribute towards the understanding by the student of what he called 'the truth, the whole truth and nothing but the truth'.

Prospects for greater agreement about the content of religious instruction in schools were enhanced in 1922 and 1924 when two highly significant documents were published by the West Riding and Cambridgeshire LEAs respectively. These, and subsequent 'Agreed Syllabuses', were the product of co-operation between the LEAs, teachers and representatives of the Anglican and Free Churches, and aimed at improving what was taught in the provided schools. Samuel Chadwick and A. S. Peake had participated in the devising of the West Riding syllabus. The *Methodist Times* greeted it warmly – and prophetically – on 22 February 1923, hoping it might 'have an influence towards a concordat on the matter of religious instruction'. This the syllabuses did, increasing awareness of how much Anglicans and Free Churchmen had in common.

By 1936 Lidgett felt able to record, no doubt over-confidently, that 'It has recently become the policy of the bishops to recommend that, wherever improved syllabuses have been brought about by this co-operation, they should form the basis of the general religious instruction in non-provided schools as well'.[8] The improvement Lidgett saw in relations between the Anglican and Free Churches over the administration of the 1902 Education Act should, he thought, be attributed to two factors: 'a growing feeling that the progress of national education must not be hindered by the scandal of sectarian . . . divisions'; and also 'to the community of conviction that the churches should co-operate as far as possible, not only in maintaining but improving religious teaching and influence throughout the schools of the nation'. He went so far as to claim that 'At all events for the present, the demand for purely secular education is dead.'

By 1942 the Cambridgeshire Syllabus was in use by over 100 LEAs. It was its growing acceptability which assisted R. A. Butler, President of the Board of Education, to make a breakthrough,[9] overcoming the opposition of the bishops of Gloucester and Oxford to reform. Numbers of Anglican school managers expressed willingness to hand over their schools to LEAs in return for Christian teaching along the lines of such an Agreed Syllabus. The Free Churches had resented the Anglican monopoly of schools in over 4,000 rural areas, and insisted on their right to invoke the 1870 Cowper–Temple Clause as a safeguard. But they could now be satisfied that their children could attend schools with an ethos and atmosphere not wholly Anglican, where the undenominational Christian teaching they had long campaigned for took place. Some Anglican schools, however, held out for continued doctrinal teaching, and the Roman Catholics similarly objected to what Cardinal Hinsley called the 'disembodied Christianity' of the Agreed Syllabuses.

It was this situation which led to Butler's proposed designation of two types of denominational schools: 'voluntary controlled' schools, in which the religious instruction was for the most part in accord with Agreed Syllabuses, and 'voluntary aided' schools where the managers maintained the right to provide and control their own religious teaching. In the former the majority of managers would be appointed by the LEA, in the latter by the sponsoring church body, which would undertake responsibility for the appointment and dismissal of teachers. These proposals became enshrined in Butler's legislation. Members of the Voluntary Bodies (Anglican and Roman Catholic) who objected to them and to such interrelated detailed measures as premises, teachers' salaries, schools' running expenses and any necessary physical reorganisation of their schools, were in due course persuaded to accept them. The Dual System remained, but in a different and much more acceptable form.

So the 1944 Education Act came into being. Lidgett could not be other than delighted by this wide-ranging reform. It was in line with what he had worked for. The place of religion in education was secured, not simply as a support for citizenship, but as something of value in itself, without which children would not gain the opportunity to appreciate that all their education was opening their eyes to the glory of God. Moreover, religious teaching was to be a statutory obligation in all schools, subject to the conscience clause; Primary and Secondary schools were to begin with a daily act of corporate worship; religious teaching could be given at any hour of the school day, to allow teachers with the relevant training to be deployed across the school; the teaching was to be subject to inspection by HMI; and religious knowledge was introduced for Teachers' Certificates at training colleges.

In 1909 Lidgett had declared, 'We will continue to strive for a completely national system of education, set entirely free from denominational tests and interests',[10] and his dream was fulfilled. In the new Act that system was to take the form of stages of schooling suited to pupils' age, aptitude and ability; Primary (no longer 'elementary') schools for pupils up to age 11; Secondary schools, for the first time guaranteed for all children, with a compulsory leaving age raised to 15 (a further extension to 16 was envisaged); part-time education available up to age 18; and grant-aided Nursery schools. John Scott's plea for the best education every poor man's children could receive was being met by the offer of equal opportunity for all.

It has, however, to be acknowledged that the path towards the Education White Paper in 1943 was far from smooth, despite Lidgett's claim of improved relations between the churches. Beneath the surface of cordiality in discussions there had remained the long-standing and still potentially explosive Nonconformist grievances, and it seems from F. C. Pritchard's account[11] that the amiable Archbishop Temple and other Anglicans had to be forcibly reminded of them by Dr A. W. Harrison, Secretary of the Methodist Education Committee, during a meeting in Leeds. Pritchard hints very strongly that by extending 'a too conciliatory hand of friendship' to the Church of England Lidgett had tended to gloss over the difficulties. Approaching the age of 90 in 1944, Lidgett had become by now in practical terms something of an embarrassment, out of touch with the blunt realities of Methodist (and indeed Free Church) attitudes with which any proposed legislation had to come to terms. 'In one sense', Pritchard rightly suggests, 'he had outgrown Methodism, possibly Nonconformity as a whole'.[12] His opposition to maintaining sectarian differences was well known, but the vigour of his ecumenical zeal, his personal friendships and frequent meetings with leading Anglican churchmen had aroused suspicion. Though he was respected as the grand old man of the Free Church Council, his Free Church friends were afraid he might 'give away too much' and sacrifice what they regarded as their educational 'rights'.[13] His considerable experience and wise guidance over many years were not in dispute. He was not, however, at any rate at this stage, the only Methodist educationist. Harrison was regarded as a negotiator more truly representative of Nonconformity, and fully *au fait* with teacher opinion. But his colleagues hesitated to make this plain.

A key meeting was held at the Board of Education on 15 August 1941, soon after the newly appointed President of the Board of Education had taken office. Among other factors at the time[14] it could be said to have jolted Butler into grasping the nettle of educational legislation, with all its religious sensitivities, once again. Leading the 33-strong deputation, Archbishop Lang set out what had emerged from previous discussion between the churches as essential for Butler to consider. The five principal points Lang made were later embodied in the 1944 Act. Lockhart, Lang's biographer, commented on the significance of the deputation's joint membership:

> For the first time in the history of English education the deputation, instead of representing division among Christian churches in England and Wales, represented their unity; for it consisted of not Anglicans only but of the leading Free Churchmen . . . This measure of unity was the result of long conferences with Free Church leaders under Scott Lidgett, who was the deputation's leading Free Churchman, and held under the auspices of the National Society.[15]

At the same time Pritchard's insight into what had occurred highlighted differences as well as agreement between the churches, as several excerpts from his account show:

> Lidgett . . . the deputation's second speaker [and leader of the Nonconformist members], claims that the Churches were unanimous in putting forward these five points. 'Unanimous' was hardly the right word, but as Lord Sankey, another member of the deputation, claimed, there was indeed a more united front being shown by that deputation than had ever appeared since the State started to interest itself in education over a hundred years before.

Cryptically, without citing his evidence and without identifying Lidgett's critics, Pritchard went on to say:

> It was shortly after this deputation had been heard that the Government was in fact warned not to listen to Scott Lidgett as the voice of Nonconformity. Nevertheless, he had to be listened to as an educationist, and it was he who, during the hearing of the five points, insisted that neither His Majesty's Inspectors nor anyone else could inspect religious teaching without considering at the same time both method and content. Some members of the deputation appeared to think they could!

Religious grievances were in fact aired at the meeting. To quote Pritchard again:

> The thoughts of many must have veered to the unhappy quarrels which had threatened the passing of the 1902 Act and caused the complete foundering of the proposed 'Birrell Act' of 1906. The President of the Board of Education voiced such thoughts as he reminded the deputation of religious tests. Scott Lidgett spoke metaphorically of 'sunken rocks', and subsequently made it clear that he did at least represent Nonconformity in regarding the chief of those rocks as the unfair amount of financial aid which Roman Catholicism and Anglicanism were obtaining from the State by comparison with Nonconformity. It was the Parliamentary Secretary to the Board of Education, Mr. J. Chuter Ede, who, using the same metaphor, said that the tide was then flowing strongly enough to carry an Education Bill over any sunken rocks that might exist.[16]

The meeting was, above all, unique in its ending: Butler's surprise decision to ask the Archbishop to close it in prayer. No Government minister had made such a request before. During the discussion it may have been borne in on Butler, as Pritchard has surmised,[17] that Christianity (embracing all denominations) had to be a main element in any legislation he might undertake. That was certainly so, but such a conclusion will have been reached despite the remaining denominational differences, not because 'he had taken Scott Lidgett's claim concerning unanimity at its face value'. Butler certainly realised at that meeting, if not before, that major changes had become imperative and the time was right for them to be made. Chuter Ede had made an accurate forecast.

The Act that followed proved a major landmark in the history of English education. Archbishop William Temple had played a significant part in the lead up to it, but considerable credit should also be given to Lidgett, less for his role in the formation of the Act itself than for his moderating influence on Anglican as well as Free Church attitudes in the turbulent years that followed the 1902 Act; for the principles he upheld; for the long hours spent in discussion with churchmen of all shades of opinion; and for his endless patience in negotiation and the search for acceptable compromises, only to find them dishearteningly abandoned. For very many years he had remained in close touch with the whole range of people involved and with the realities of Church, school, social and political life, and it was only towards the end of his long career that he could be suspected of underplaying difficulties in an attempt to realise his dream of educational harmony.

It is fair to say that few could match his experience or the *breadth* of his educational views, hammered out first in the slums of Bermondsey, rigorously derived from the doctrine of the Fatherhood of God, and thereafter consistently maintained. To Lidgett the nurture of *the personality* in the child as well as the adult was vitally important. Within the Wesleyan (later the Methodist) Church and the rest of the Free Churches he will perhaps be best remembered as the enthusiastic and yet measured diplomat,[18] who (to adapt some phrases of J. M. Turner)[19] helped in 'cushioning the more strident cries of secularists and anti-Anglicans', and sought to bring 'every child within the reach of non-sectarian religious teaching' where required, while at the same time preserving the case for Church schools, whether Anglican, Roman Catholic or Methodist. He was not to live long enough to see disappointing long-term results of the Act's religious education provision in many schools, such as perfunctory, uninspired and unqualified teaching, and poor status accorded to the subject, problems against which he had vigorously campaigned. But he will be remembered for his long and distinguished contribution to educational development not only in London but in the country at large, and for the wide educational vision and strong religious conviction which motivated all his manifold activity.

Part 5

Advancing ecumenism 1904–20

Lidgett's ecumenical enthusiasm is illustrated in Chapters 14–18. Here the moves towards Methodist union during this period are discussed alongside the pressures for unity with the Anglican and Free Churches which led up to the 'climax' of the Lambeth Appeal in 1920. These chapters help to explain the context in which Lidgett was operating and the complexity of the issues he sought to understand and interpret to his colleagues even in those circumstances where he was not personally to the fore.

Calendar of main events

1904	A Methodist Assembly proposed at Wesleyan Conference.
1907	Proposal accepted. United Methodist Free Churches, Bible Christians, and Methodist New Connexion become United Methodist Church.
1908	Lidgett made Secretary of United Methodist Assembly.
1909	United Methodist Assembly. Entry in *New History of Methodism.*
1910	Shakespeare proposed union of all Evangelical Free Churches. World Missionary Conference at Edinburgh. Protestant Episcopal Church of USA resolved to seek Conference on Faith and Order.
1911	Visit to Fourth Oecumenical Conference in Toronto.
1913	Elected to Wesleyan Conference Committee to collect information about possible Methodist Union.
1913–15	Kikuyu controversy.
1914	Faith and Order delegates arrived in England.
1916	Shakespeare's proposal repeated. Lidgett supported Enabling Bill, and proposed Council of the Churches. First Interim Report, *Towards Christian Unity.*
1917	Second Interim Report. Approaches about possible CE/Wesleyan reunion. Wesleyan Conference authorised its Methodist Union Committee to meet representatives of other Methodist denominations.

1918–19	Federal Council of Evangelical Free Churches formed.
1919	Tentative Scheme for Methodist Union. Bishop of London's plan for CE/Wesleyan Union.
1920	Lambeth Conference and Appeal. Consultation Committee formed at Geneva to make arrangements for World Conference on Faith and Order. This eventually took place at Lausanne 1927.
Later:	
1940–1	Free Church Federal Council formed, merging existing Free Church Councils.
1942	British Council of Churches formed.

14

Moves towards Methodist Union

To Lidgett ecumenism was of theological, evangelical and social importance. This chapter is especially concerned with issues of Methodist unity between 1904 and 1920.

Methodist churches had united abroad: some Americans in 1877, Canadians in 1884, Australians in 1902, the Irish in 1878 and 1902. One of the factors bringing them together had been the 'Oecumenical'[1] Methodist Conferences of 1881 (in Wesley's Chapel, London) and 1891 (in Washington, USA). In 1881 no fewer than 29 separate Methodist denominations were represented from Great Britain, the colonies and America. The Conferences, initiated by the Methodist Episcopal Church of America, were repeated every 10 years. Organic union was not part of the formal agenda in 1881: the aim seems to have been simply to share delegates' common interests and concerns; revive contact with Wesley's English 'roots'; deepen their feeling of solidarity; and emphasise the 'great' part they felt Methodism had to play in the world at large, jointly witnessing against 'Popery, paganism, pauperism, scepticism, intemperance and kindred vices'.[2] But in Canada[3] 'union sentiment' was 'quickened' by this Conference, and Canadian Methodist unity followed. Strong advocacy of such union in 1891 helped to promote Methodist unity in Australia. At the 1901 Ecumenical Conference,[4] again held in Wesley's Chapel, it was announced as imminent.

Only very slowly were the New and Antipodean World examples followed by the parent Methodist denominations 'at home'. In 1901 these included principally the Primitive Methodist Church, the Methodist New Connexion, the United Methodist Free Churches, the Bible Christians and the Wesleyan Methodist Church. Their union took place against strong opposition, and proceeded by stages until 1932. Progress was significantly boosted by discussions in the 1901 Ecumenical Conference, especially by the speech of the Wesleyan, T. B. Stephenson,[5] stressing the current wasteful competition and overlap between the Methodist churches and their missionary societies. Irritating Wesleyan colleagues at home, he argued that since in England everything possible had been done via interdenominational fellowship, the next step must be union. Three of the smaller denominations, the United Methodist

Free Churches, the Bible Christians and the Methodist New Connexion, achieved it in 1907.

In Toronto at the fourth Ecumenical Conference in 1911 Lidgett was glad to record this beginning. Simpson Johnson[6] referred to Methodist unions already completed and in prospect (New Zealand), and pointed to negotiations for uniting Methodist, Congregational and Presbyterian churches[7] in Canada. Describing the new century as 'an age of Christian reunion', Lidgett said that Methodism ought to take the lead in 'this glorious movement'.[8] That Conference was to prove the occasion of his only voyage across the Atlantic. Various invitations to the USA had to be refused owing to pressures at home, not least the schemes for union in various forms between the churches.

Ever since his first attendance at the Wesleyan Conference in 1887, Lidgett, like H. P. Hughes, had declared strong support for reuniting splintered Methodism at home. More generally, he regarded[9] the 'promotion of Christian Unity, and so far as possible of Reunion' as one of the most important activities of his life. This was evident in Conference speeches and the *Methodist Times*. His first editorial on 7 March 1907, entitled 'Progressive Methodism', set out his paper's policy, to 'hold out the hand of brotherhood and co-operation'. He sought to make the paper: 'the organ of a steadfastly progressive policy – pronouncedly Methodist, yet aiming all the while at closer relations, not only with all the Evangelical Free Churches, but with the Anglican Church as well'.[10]

'Closer relations' were an important but interim objective: unity proposals and schemes were next; visible, corporate unity of all Christendom, not only of Methodism, was the ultimate goal. In his final issue as editor he hoped the paper would long survive as an 'organ of spiritual freedom, evangelical fidelity, Christian unity, and social progress'. His reasons for seeking unity were theological, not just pragmatic.

Obstacles had to be faced. R. W. Perks, perhaps Conference's most prominent layman, had advocated Methodist unity from 1878 when laymen were first admitted, but his views were not always the same as Lidgett's. In 1904 Lidgett did not support union between the Wesleyans and the Methodist New Connexion, a scheme Perks had promoted through fear that a larger, potentially anti-Wesleyan Church might otherwise be created.[11] Unlike Perks, Lidgett and H. P. Hughes stressed 'the spiritual motives of the movement'[12] and looked beyond Methodist union. Lunn spoke of Perks's 'religious horizon bounded by Methodist frontiers on E, W, N and S'.[13]

For some Wesleyans the boundaries of Wesleyanism should never be crossed; others were prepared to consider federation or even union with the other Methodist denominations; but relatively few, it seemed, were initially keen to venture further afield. To some, re-admission to the Anglican fold was more attractive than any compromise with other Methodist traditions or other

Free Churches; but for others resentment, for example, at 'well-paid inactivity'[14] among rural clergy, and Anglicans' attitudes, past and present, gave ample reason to remain distinct. The Wesleyans' Army and Navy Board's refusal in 1914/15 to co-operate with other Free Churches, including the Primitive and United Methodist churches, for joint Chaplaincy provision amply illustrated Wesleyan self-sufficiency.

Lidgett was not afraid to criticise fellow Wesleyans in public. His first leading article included strictures on being 'far too self-contained and exclusive'. Thinking of attitudes to churches outside Methodism, he said:

> Many good souls have feared for the integrity of Methodism if its people cultivated too intimate relations with men of other Churches. Thus we have been told to hold aloof from the Free Church Council Movement . . . and from the Established Church . . . [But] when exclusive, we have become barren and unfruitful.

That view was constantly reiterated, and during his final year as editor with particular force. On 7 March 1918, for example, he charged Wesleyans with 'stiff exclusiveness' and seeking 'sham respectability'.[15] Their anxiety to win social position, he said, was making them keener to count up Privy Councillors, MPs, millionaires, even mayors, than either saints or converted sinners. Craving for respectability, he said, 'eats out the very life of evangelical experience, theological exploration, prophetic ministry and spiritual effectiveness'. As for Church architecture, he argued it was Wesleyans' 'feeble imitativeness' that had led them to adopt 'dissenting Gothic', which offended true art 'by its cheap pretentiousness'.

What Lidgett had to counter was the result of the growth of Wesleyan prosperity in the nineteenth century. The denomination had developed its own momentum. There were now Wesleyan schools, a strong church departmental structure, Wesleyan newspapers, journals and 'Bookroom' publishing. Wesleyanism could stand on its own. Pride in such progress had led to denominational self-assertiveness, and talk of change via reunion or even federation or closer relations threatened vested interests. There seemed to be little sense in change when increases in congregational sizes were giving them confidence. They were unaware that these had not kept pace with the virtual quadrupling of the population within the previous hundred years. Contacts with other denominations were in any case not strong; there appeared no need for them to be otherwise.

Lidgett recalled Wesley's description of Methodists as 'friends of all and enemies of none'. Unhappily, in Lidgett's view, their friendship was 'so tepid' that they were 'hardly on speaking terms with other denominations'. He was probably referring to the legacy of past attacks by Congregationalists and Baptists who believed in the entirely self-governing local church and regarded the Wesleyan Connexion as autocratic and unscriptural. Methodism would not survive, let alone flourish, Lidgett thought, if fear of entering into fresh combinations or closer union with other branches of Christ's Church was not overcome. He was convinced no church could survive 'on a merely sectarian basis'. Half-hearted approaches to Christians outside their own church excited his censure, however gently expressed: 'If the abiding witness of the great Denominations is to be maintained, this can only be secured on larger lines than those of sectarianism tempered by occasional intercourse and conventional goodwill'.[16]

In all their feeble respectability, sapping their spirit of adventure, Lidgett saw that Wesleyans were withholding the distinctive contribution they had been called to share in the universal Church. By correcting their errors, by becoming effective in their special witness, Methodism would, he declared, 'bring help to all the Churches in their pursuit of reunion'.[17] On 12 September 1918 he wrote: 'Methodism may well lead the way towards such evangelical catholicity as is imperatively required both for the spiritual prosperity and for the ultimate reunion of Christ's Church as a whole'. To Lidgett, aloofness and self-contained pride constituted Methodists' 'most blighting curse', because they breached 'our true apostolic succession'. He meant that Wesleyans were not keeping true to their Methodist inheritance by 'turning away from the glory of the past', the witness and *catholic* mission inherited from John Wesley: a divided Methodism 'contradicts the inmost law of its own life'.[18]

They were, moreover, leaving unworked, he wrote in 1918,[19] 'the rich mines of distinctive Methodist theology', and from weakness failing to apply their distinctive principles, for example, to social reform. Characteristically, Lidgett kept social issues constantly in the forefront of ecumenical as well as internal denominational discussion. For him the catholicity of John Wesley extended to a comprehensive grasp of both the spiritual and the 'organised and manifold life of men':[20] ecumenism which did not include the world, but was simply founded on 'Church' unity, was doomed to failure. Methodists were not meant to be simply inward looking: their vision was wider than that. The universalism of John Wesley included the catholic unity of the Church of God, an opposition to self-contained sectarianism, and concern for human needs not just inside the Church, but outside in society. If all churches moved 'to a more vital fellowship, expressed in and served by an outward organisation of unity', that would, he thought in 1918,[21] bring the living experience of Christ and the vigour urgently needed to tackle the 'new order', post-war.

For Lidgett the most positive incentives to unity, not least in Methodism, were: first, the theological and, second, closely linked with it and never more a priority than in post-war years, the boost which he was convinced it would give to evangelism. As early as 1909[22] he had written that 'Only a reunited Church can evangelise the world . . . We cannot afford in these days the narrowness of outlook, the friction and the isolation which weaken the influence of the Christian Churches'. That desire for the new Methodist Church to be 'such a spiritual fusion as would enable Methodism to become a greater evangelical force' remained his ambition for the union achieved in 1932. Union, he said, should be aimed not at the aggrandisement of Methodism, nor at making Methodism the preponderating force among the Free Churches: it should be for the benefit of the catholic Church at large. That was to him the truly Methodist emphasis, and a corollary of the Fatherhood of God.

Such comments called for clarity about the essentials of Wesleyan Methodism. In 1913 Lidgett analysed the constitutional principles of the Wesleyan Church in a series of leading articles each week from October to December, and he took special pride[23] in them. Though publishing elements on which Wesleyans could not compromise, he aimed to provide an agenda on which the Methodist union debate could begin, not final non-negotiable terms. What he said in the same journal earlier in that year and in later years about the basis of Wesleyanism to date reflected a consistent view. Constant repetition of ideas, albeit differently expressed, became characteristic. Unremitting demands on a weekly editor were perhaps partly to blame.

Overall,[24] his statements demonstrated awareness of both theological considerations and denominational sensitivities. Diplomatically, he avoided criticising the other principal Methodist denominations, but concentrated where he could on 'Methodism'. Though this could imply that Wesleyans thought they had preserved what was vital from the past, other Methodists would have clearly understood what he was doing, and no significant resentment arose. Among his (not solely Wesleyan) readers denominational pride, fears of losing identity, and apprehension about changes and their significance were factors he sought to recognise, accommodate and, where appropriate, overcome. He saw the need for compromise, stressing that 'principles were not necessarily satisfied' by the exact forms in which they were then being expressed. Union, he said on 12 September 1918, should 'gather up each separate inheritance', preserving what was 'of permanent value' in them all, for inclusion 'in a broader and more elastic organisation' than was being separately enjoyed.

Lidgett's article on 11 December 1913 provided a summary, listing what to him were the most important characteristics of 'the Methodist type' among the churches. These were 'its Evangelical Catholicity, its distinctive fellowship, its connexionalism grounded in the authority of the Conference, and the executive trust reposed in its ministers'.

Lidgett was concerned with Faith as well as Order. He personally believed[25] that all branches of Methodism shared essentially the same theology. Methodism, he was fond of saying, corresponded to the ideal of his favourite epistle, Ephesians: personal acceptance by God, the relationship of sonship, filial trust, assurance and self-surrender. But on 30 January 1913 his leading article, entitled 'An Unexhausted Mission', emphasised that Methodism still had work to do; it had been raised up to bear witness to timeless religious truths; and its duty was to remain loyal to the task of preaching them.

His own version of those truths was as follows:

the supremacy of holy love in God the Father, revealed through Christ, his Son;
the world-embracing nature of God's redemptive purpose;
the inclusion of all men in God's offer of mercy and salvation;
the unspeakable worth and possibilities of human life;
the call to full salvation and perfect love;
the constraining responsibility of all men to give effect to the world-embracing, world-transforming purpose of grace, and to engage in a life of personal service.

The expression of Methodism's national witness would not always be easy. Like the other essentials, it called[26] for consciousness of God and consecration to him.

Lidgett outlined what he saw as particular features of the Methodist Church, first, its *fellowship*. As a Society, Methodists stood for the importance of fellowship in principle and in practice. Proposals for unity between their separate denominations should serve to strengthen not weaken this. The maintenance of their Methodist faith was bound up with the intimate brotherhood and the spiritual and evangelical fellowship they shared. Its practical expression had been the local Society in general and the Class Meeting in particular; both were essential. The Class Meeting, he said, had proved itself as the basis of Church membership, the means of effective discipline, and a continuous supply of spiritual guidance and mutual support. Differentiating Wesleyans from other Methodists, Dissenters and Anglo-Catholics, Rigg had called it his Church's 'innermost institution', a training ground for preachers and church leaders, and a help for members to see the truth of their doctrine.[27] Pleased that its terms of membership were now more flexible than in former days, Lidgett thought it so important that, if it was imperilled, Methodist Union would have to be postponed.

A similarly crucial feature of Methodism, he declared, was its *connexional structure*. The annual Conference was central, its authority supreme, as its *ecclesia docens*. Synods, committees and meetings contributed to discussion of important issues, thereby enabling Conference to become the mouthpiece of the Church's collective convictions. Conference moderated controversies and subordinated partisan considerations to spiritual interests. Not aligning itself with political parties, it had achieved a nice discrimination between when and when not to speak out on national issues. The success of the Conference as an

1. Nos 7&8 The Paragon. No. 8 (on the right) was Lidgett's family home 1868–1880 in Lewisham, now Greenwich.

2. John Scott (1792–1868), First Principal of the Westminster College, President of the Wesleyan Methodist Conference in 1843 and 1852.

3. W. B. Pope (1822–1903), President of the Wesleyan Methodist Conference in 1877, Lidgett's mentor.

4. Hugh Price Hughes (1847–1902), Leader of the 'Forward Movement', President of the Wesleyan Methodist Conference in 1898.

5. John Scott Lidgett outside the Bermondsey Settlement.

6. Archbishop Randall Davidson (1848–1930), Archbishop of Canterbury 1903–1928.

7. W. R. Nicoll (1851–1923), Presbyterian editor of the *British Weekly* 1886–1923.

8. David Lloyd George (1863–1945), Liberal politician and Prime Minister (painting by Sir William Orpen 1927).

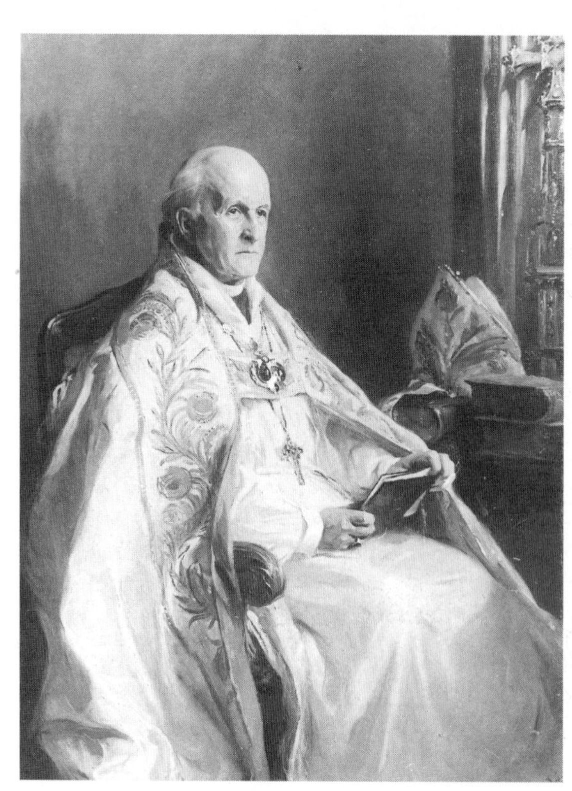

9. Archbishop Cosmo Gordon Lang (1864–1945), Archbishop of Canterbury 1928–1942.

10. A. S. Peake (1865–1929), Rylands Professor of Biblical Criticism and Exegesis at Manchester University 1904–1929.

11. John Scott Lidgett at the signing of the Deed of Methodist Union in 1932.

12. John Scott Lidgett and Mrs Emmeline Lidgett at one of the 1932 Conference Garden Parties.

institution was evident, he thought, from members' loyalty in accepting and implementing its decisions. Other Methodist Churches, however, with their looser structures, were not easily won over to Wesleyan restrictions on local autonomy.

The *authority of the ministry*, Lidgett insisted, should also be preserved. Excessive authoritarianism had, he acknowledged, caused problems in the past; he welcomed democratic ideas and the powers of the laity, growing since their admission to Conference. But he said the Church had to 'avoid the extremes of an exaggerated ministry and a fettered ministry'. The ministry transmitted ministerial office, maintained pastoral care and discipline, and exercised leadership, externally to the world, and internally to church members. Many responsibilities were shared, and ministers acted in union with and on behalf of the whole body. But if they were to represent the Church adequately, a strong position must, he asserted, be reserved for them: 'executive conditions in which their pastoral responsibilities could be effectively discharged'. Though Lidgett appears not to have argued for retaining election to the élite Legal Hundred, already somewhat of an anachronism, his words would have been intended to reassure his own ministerial colleagues. Fear that their role and status might be reduced to mere representatives in a union with denominations putting more emphasis on the laity proved a brake on progress towards agreement in 1932.

A very important element in ministers' status was their role in the Conference. Since the Conference 'Pastoral' Session, made up entirely of ministers, in some respects duplicated the work of the preceding 'Representative' Session for ministers and laity, Lidgett accepted some reform might be necessary. But he was adamant that, whatever changes or compromises were agreed, a Session reserved for ministers must be retained. He was, however, interested in a proposal by his friend, H. J. Pope, whereby a 'Pastoral Assembly' would precede a 'Legal Representative Conference' and be subject to its confirming vote. Pope, he pointed out, not least to Primitive Methodist readers, was no sacerdotalist.

Despite his assertions Lidgett recognised that all denominations had to make sacrifices – though Wesleyans no more than the rest! He was aware[28] that while Wesleyans would want to 'stiffen' any proposed future constitution, the other Methodist denominations would seek to 'broaden' it. Generous statesmanship was needed to overcome 'the temptation to treat our preferences as principles' and for justifying 'sluggishness that jogs along the old ruts'.

He admitted there was, as yet, far from real unanimity among the different churches about Union. It was 'easier to formulate a scheme than get it accepted, much less demanded'. All Methodists should be strongly in favour[29] of any scheme before it was implemented: subsequent disputes would then be unlikely. Unity needed the appropriate driving force for success. It should derive from a spiritual impetus, not engineered or hustled on business or utilitarian grounds.

Lidgett set out his priorities in the *Methodist Times* of 11 December 1913. In his view Methodist denominations should begin the unity process 'at home', among themselves; this was reiterated on 2 May 1918 when he insisted that Methodist Union would soon become 'the main issue in Methodist practical politics'. If, however, Methodist unity could not be achieved, he tended to favour a form of federation. On the wider scene, he thought that if federation among non-episcopal churches were to be established, this might pave the way for federation between episcopal and non-episcopal churches. But he decided, pragmatically, that no precise sequence could be advocated for bringing the churches together and, if the process was to be successful, it could not be hurried: unity movements could take place on several fronts simultaneously.

For example, on 2 May 1918, he stressed that acceptance of Free Church Federation would not stand in the way of two other schemes (Anglican and Methodist) currently under discussion. He was himself '*intensely in favour*[30] of closer relations with the Anglican Church and also of Methodist Union'. On 9 May he said there were not three mutually exclusive ways of achieving unity:

> Adoption of one scheme would not be detrimental, but advantageous to the promotion of the rest . . . By all means let there be one Methodist type and one Federation of Evangelical Free Churches to enter into yet larger fellowship with Anglicanism. Let us not do things by halves, still less by thirds.

He was equally anxious for the realisation of all three.

His arguments for Union never centred on the necessity to respond to the decline in membership which had begun in 1907. In other contexts he constantly called attention to the decline: efforts to reverse it, he urged, should be redoubled. But, for example, on 18 July 1918, he was not above citing the decline simply as background to the forthcoming discussions of the Wesleyan Conference, when Methodist Union, Free Church Federation and closer relations with the Church of England were on the agenda. To him positive progress towards unity was urgent, and he was then showing signs of increasing impatience. Yet the part he determined to play himself, though scornful of 'merely' friendly contacts with other churches, was to lie in establishing relationships, constantly reminding everyone of the overriding principle of Catholicity, and applying pressure whenever appropriate opportunities arose.

We turn now to the initial moves towards Methodist unity. After the death in 1902 of H. P. Hughes, the best-known advocate of Methodist Union within the Wesleyan Conference, in ecumenical conferences, and especially through his *Methodist Times*, Lidgett was seen as his successor in this cause as in many others. In 1904 at the Wesleyan Conference Lidgett proposed the holding of a 'Methodist Assembly', to involve representatives of all the Methodist denominations, 'for united devotion, and with a view to mutual counsel and concerted action in regard to the spiritual tasks which are laid upon Methodism, excluding all questions of polity and party politics'. The proposal, at first unsuccessful, was finally accepted by Conference in 1907, and then put to the other Methodist denominations. Though the initiative came from the largest denomination, the others received it well. Initially Lidgett was appointed as convenor of the relevant Committee, and then in 1908 as Secretary of the United Methodist Assembly.

The Assembly finally took place on 4–6 October 1909 in Wesley's Chapel, and 'remarkable unanimity'[31] was achieved. Lidgett, then Wesleyan ex-President, chaired one session; the others were chaired by representatives of the Primitive, United, Independent and Wesleyan Methodist churches, and the Wesleyan Reform Union. As Lidgett intended, it helped to underline the unity of Methodism in its doctrinal and evangelical faith. When Lidgett reported its success at the 1910 Conference, a second Assembly was agreed for the autumn of 1914, but war intervened.

In 1909 Lidgett had also been a co-editor of the *New History of Methodism*.[32] Under 'Methodism Today' his own contribution was (unsurprisingly) entitled, 'Fundamental Unity'.

Before the Methodist Assembly, negotiations had been taking place independently among three of the smaller denominations. In 1907 the United Methodist Free Churches, the Bible Christians and the Methodist New Connexion merged into one, becoming known as The United Methodist Church. Lidgett approved this title because he had in mind 'The Methodist Church of Great Britain' as the title for overall Union. His *Methodist Times* leader headline on 26 September 1907 was 'A Great Instalment', and he rejoiced that the new church's constitution had been so devised as to take into account the possibility of a wider reunion.[33] To him the union of the three churches was of practical, not just theological, importance. Along with C. H. Kelly and Dinsdale Young, he represented the Wesleyan Church at the uniting conference in Wesley's Chapel on 17 September.

In his *Guided Life*,[34] Lidgett claimed, enigmatically and with not a little conceit about his influential friends, that when the Uniting Bill reached the Commons, he was 'enabled to bear a small part' in assisting its passage. He may have given some advice or reassurance behind the scenes particularly to Sir Henry Fowler, then a prominent Wesleyan MP, perhaps on the choice of the new church's name and the proposal (in relation to doctrine as well as discipline) to give it power to revise its Trusts from time to time. Fowler had in fact given formal notice of opposition to the Bill, after it had already been accepted by the Lords. So Lidgett hastened, diplomatically, to assure readers of the *Methodist Times* on 13 June 1907 that this was not because Fowler was hostile to the measure, but because, being 'a master of parliamentary procedure', he decided this tactic would secure sufficient discussion of the issues involved.

Lidgett would have been delighted if he had seen the Archbishop's letter on 10 September 1907[35] to the new church's President designate, expressing support for 'the diminution of unnecessary divisions among the soldiers of Christ'.

The first tentative move towards uniting the major remaining Methodist denominations, Primitive, United and Wesleyan, was made in 1913. A motion, proposed by Perks in the Plymouth Wesleyan Conference, invited the other churches to discuss whether 'Methodist Union was not a practicable policy'.[36] A committee of inquiry was appointed to collect information, with E. Aldom French (1868–1962) as its secretary. French sent out on 28 October a Questionnaire on constitution and doctrine for the Methodist churches to answer.

Lidgett's hand had been clearly visible in the steady progress towards unity, but he scorned the idea of simply 'collecting information'. What was needed much more, he thought, was to engage in face-to-face discussion to discover how strong was the desire for unity, and what were in practice the principal obstacles to progress. Understandably Lidgett was not elected to the Committee. It was then he decided that he could best help his colleagues prepare for future negotiations with Primitive and United Methodists by attempting to define what he saw as the essential characteristics of Methodism inherited from John Wesley and the distinguishing features of the Wesleyan Church.

The outbreak of war impeded further progress in Methodist unity until 1917.[37] Unity discussions among other Protestant churches, however, soon caused reverberations within Methodism. By 1917 French's Wesleyan Committee on the practicability of Methodist Union had almost lost significance, but on a motion by French and Perks it was re-appointed, enlarged and (significantly) authorised to meet representative committees of the other Methodist denominations. It began by sending them 28 questions devised by a subcommittee. According to Currie[38] the revised and strengthened Committee represented an unexpected decisive change, caused by the threat which Perks and French thought was posed by Free Church Federation proposals[39] on one side and proposals for Wesleyan absorption into the Anglican Church on the other. Mews suggests it was these alternative visions which were responsible for 'breathing new life into the dormant proposals for the Union of . . . Methodism'.[40] This time Lidgett gained a place.

Crucially, strong support was forthcoming from Professor A. S. Peake on the Primitive Methodist side: he shared Lidgett's conviction that disunity impeded both social witness and evangelism. Both argued on theological and ecumenical grounds that corporate, not federal union, and not of the Methodist churches alone, was the will of God. Methodist Union was to them a necessary stage in the union of Christendom.

Representatives of the three churches, who reflected differing attitudes to

Union, met in autumn 1917 and January and October 1918,[41] constituted a 'United Committee' and appointed three subcommittees, with French, the Primitive Methodist Samuel Horton (1854–1949) and the United Methodist David Brook (1854–1933) as convenors. Assigned to the subcommittee dealing with constitutional questions, Lidgett insisted on the importance, proved by later events, of reaching a thorough understanding with the other churches on doctrine related to the pastoral office and the sacraments before unity could be achieved.

Progress was reported to the three Conferences in 1919. As requested, the United Committee made proposals[42] for a 'Tentative Scheme' and formally submitted them to the Conferences of 1920. The scheme was published in an annotated pamphlet,[43] containing the Conferences' official responses and legal opinion on Wesleyan Trust Deeds. Progress towards unity had been made, but over a decade of argument, analysed in a later chapter, was to be needed for its consummation.

Lidgett's position was clear, but from 1917 onwards he and other enthusiasts for Methodist Union had to face strong and organised opposition from fellow Wesleyans, ministerial and lay. Attitudes in all three churches were complex, and their views ranged widely. Some were concerned that union with overtly Dissenting Methodists would prevent future union with the Church of England; others guessed that the Anglican Church would consider uniting with one united church more happily than with three; others detested the Anglican Church and feared any breach with the Free Churches; others again objected equally to any form of union between Methodists or the Free Churches.

There were broadly four objections to Union. The first centred on conservative dislike of change, in particular the likely break with long-cherished doctrines and practices of the three denominations, and the implicit 'threat' to long-standing attachments to families and friends in chapels, however small. J. E. Rattenbury fanned this fear by asking:

> Are you willing that your chapel should be closed? Do you think that if your chapel or one of the other Methodist Churches were closed, you would gather under one roof all the people who belonged to the two chapels? If you think so, experience is quite against your conclusion.

Some Methodists feared a 'satanic' destruction of hallowed beliefs in a Gadarene rush to union and encouragement of critical enquiry. There were allegations that obsession with organisation and worldly structures had overridden the more urgent (and truly Methodist) priority of deepening spirituality. The fourth obstacle was prejudice, even hostility between denominations. Defection of the Primitives in the last century was still keenly felt by some Wesleyans. Some Primitives thought Wesleyan attitudes and practices outdated, especially in regard to the ministry, while some Wesleyans objected to what they saw as the 'excessive' prominence of Primitive laymen and a 'flabby' doctrine of the Holy Spirit. The rarely acknowledged tendency of some Wesleyans to think of themselves as higher in the social scale than non-Wesleyans was, however, undergoing a significant decline.

Opposition to Union was met by equally enthusiastic supporters of it. Many saw opportunities to meet such urgent imperatives as arresting decline in membership (which some regarded as God's judgement on Methodism's quarrelsome past) and the national drift into secularism. It was also argued that Union would be following national trends: the tendency towards groupings or monopolies in industry and commerce, in the Federation of Free Churches or in proposals for a League of Nations. Moreover, some supporters of Union perceived indications of an emerging consensus of belief after the narrow loyalties of the past century and a growing desire to break with deadening (biblical and doctrinal) inheritances, make a fresh start and regain a sense of progress. By 1917 in particular the idea of a new Church for a new post-war world had become an attractive prospect. In 1918 the League of Nations concept gave Lidgett a strong argument. In addition to the gift Methodism made to the whole Church in proclaiming Wesley's universalism and Catholicity, he discerned[44] the obligation of Methodism to search for international peace with unity. His words were scathing: he called it 'cheap for the Church . . . to exhort the nations to compose their differences while it tolerates its own'; the Church was denouncing pride and self-sufficiency 'when these same vices in subtler form are a fatal obstacle to its own unity'.

Many Methodists were sensitive to the mystification and taunts of outsiders to whom evidence of disunity was plain to see in the overlapping of chapels, central departments, newspapers and ministerial training colleges. Unionists recognised that structures and procedures of the three denominations were not dissimilar, and though differences in financial systems existed, there was clearly scope for rationalisation and savings. To Lidgett, though not to many others, there were far from insuperable differences in doctrine and its interpretation. In 1909[45] he had said of Methodism, 'The theology of all branches is identical', a view Currie[46] ridiculed as naïve, wishful thinking in the light of the obstacles doctrinal factors later posed to agreement. In the event, however, as discussions progressed and successive drafts were refined, the disparate views represented in the United Committee steadily came to converge. In 1924 Lidgett insisted that the former schism had been healing since 1913, the original difficulties had passed away, and Conference should see the Primitive/United Methodist (if not Wesleyan) agreements to date as 'an instalment of the fulfilment of the prayer that "they may all be one"'. If he was guilty of exaggerated optimism or *naïveté* in doctrine, so were many Unionists in anticipating that elimination of unnecessary chapels would soon follow the achievement of Union. One other argument which some advanced was the prospect they perceived of a revitalised Methodism gaining greater political and social influence and making a greater moral impact on the nation. Perks even dreamed of a United Methodism becoming the major Free Church and then causing Anglicanism to fragment, with its 'Protestant' section breaking off to join Methodism. To him the Anglican 'Romanising' element constituted a threat to Protestantism as a whole, and so by causing a new alignment the Union of Methodism would be a 'great advance' and help to 'save' the country.

The story of the debate is resumed in Chapter 23.

15

Methodism and the Church of England

Lidgett thought it important for unity discussions to set out how he saw the Anglican Church from his current perspective as a Wesleyan Methodist.

We have earlier noted Anglican contempt for 'enthusiasm', allegedly incompatible with reason, and Lidgett's own developing rapport with churchmen prominent in public life. Although he longed for unity with the Church of England, reunion was to him unrealistic until the legacy of past attitudes and, for many on both 'sides', currently poor relationships could be overcome. He preferred, if possible, to bring the Free Churches, including a united Methodist Church, with him. But loyally he insisted that in any future schemes of union Methodism could not, and should not, disavow its own past: the Methodist 'type' should not be lost. The visible unity of the Church Catholic never ceased to be his predominant aim. When Methodist Union was discussed at the 1918 Conference, the *Methodist Recorder* quoted him as saying he had 'only a moderate degree of enthusiasm for any union short of the much wider union than that now under consideration'.

In the latter half of the nineteenth century Nonconformist struggles for recognition and the growth of Anglo-Catholic 'ritualism' had driven Methodists into ever closer association with Nonconformist Dissent. Growing membership overall had, moreover, encouraged Methodists to begin to see themselves as rivals to the Church of England. Claiming status implied separation, all the more when Anglicans constantly referred to all Nonconformist denominations patronisingly as 'bodies' and not Churches. But despite the resentment this caused, interest in and sympathy for the Anglican Church as a whole remained, and Wesleyans in particular could never forget their origins. So in what he wrote about Methodism, Lidgett felt obliged to define where the differences lay between them. Lidgett was aware of the dangers of caricature, but his own evangelical convictions, and the image which many Anglicans all too frequently presented in his readers' personal experiences, impelled him to be critical. He sought to be honest and outspoken without being abrasive.

Among other factors his analysis mentioned contrasts in Catholicity. Lidgett admitted there were Methodist ministers and laymen who had 'arrears to make up' in their observance of the distinctive, notably the spiritual, features of their inheritance. But when Methodism was compared with the Church of England, the latter as a Church overall appeared to Lidgett deficient. Many Anglicans, he said, seemed often to lack the personal faith and evangelical experience of the true Methodist: the regenerate life of love; the power to foster and communicate the gifts of God;[1] and the constant striving to help all men see and share on equal terms the spiritual privileges of Christian 'sonship'. By contrast with Wesley's Catholicity the Church of England seemed exclusive.

The concept of 'Catholicity' was, of course, commonly used in church circles. Henry Rack[2] has drawn attention to Lidgett's distinctively Methodist interpretation. Lidgett warned, Rack said, against two faulty ways of viewing it: 'as a system of dogmatic truths imposed by the ministry' and with 'the Church seen as the sphere within which authority is exercised for dispensing ordered and external means of grace'. What Lidgett advocated was 'inward Catholicity', namely, the 'fellowship of a great experience' and 'fellowship with the saints through common access to God'. In effect this was where Lidgett discerned an important contrast between Methodists and Anglicans. But a full account of his 'Catholicity' would have included reference to the world.

A related ground of difference was the legacy of the 'Anglican revival'. To Lidgett this had 'beautiful' features, but also 'sacerdotal features which are in the long run fatal to evangelical freedom'[3] and were still too prevalent. A Royal Commission on Ecclesiastical Discipline (1904–6) had only subdued Anglo-Catholic 'extravagance'. As recorded above,[4] Lidgett personally had a genuine interest in the *writings* of Newman and Liddon and maintained good personal relations with individual Roman and Anglo-Catholics, but he was opposed to their distinctive doctrines. Alongside the lack of toleration for the Roman Catholic Church which he had absorbed from his Wesleyan childhood, Lidgett had personally developed a distaste for Anglo-Catholic ceremonial, and strongly objected to 'pseudo-Roman Catholics' betraying the ethos of Protestantism to which they all belonged. This view he, like Rigg, combined with support for the Church of England 'as by law established'. Lidgett had proposed the Conference resolution in 1901 opposing changes in King Edward VII's Declaration to Parliament which would have weakened its repudiation of Roman Catholic practice and guarantees of the Protestant succession. When the issue rose again in 1910, he was at pains to be tactful,[5] arguing against giving unnecessary offence to Roman Catholics and for focusing on essential support for the Protestant succession. He thought opposition to Roman Catholicism could go too far.

To Lidgett it was not just Anglo-Catholic priests, but the Anglican clergy as a whole who were affected by the evils of clericalism, concerned more with conservation, the Church as an institution and outward 'Order', than with inward spiritual consciousness and its application. Their unwarranted powers and authority had brought privilege and exclusiveness in their train. Lidgett thought Anglicans were preoccupied with these when they should be sharing with others 'a great spiritual experience'. He could have said it was Wesley's inclusive message that had attracted people who felt excluded from the Established Church. In making such strictures he carefully avoided reference to the Wesleyan form of exclusiveness! Nor did he mention past grievances at civic assertions of Anglican privilege, now mostly overcome.

Sacraments also gave him pause. 'Only an evangelical and personal interpretation of grace', he thought, 'could eventually rid Christendom of half-magical and materialist notions . . . which have been imported into the doctrine of the Sacraments and of their validity'.[6] But to liturgical worship and the celebration of the sacraments neither Lidgett nor H. P. Hughes, unlike some other Methodists and Free Churchmen, had any objection. Hughes had hoped the Free Church Council would help non-episcopal churches to appreciate their Catholic inheritance.[7]

Lidgett expressed further reservations, for example about the historical claims of the Church of England, and its Established status. The latter, he said, 'offends against the spiritual nature and autonomy of Christ's Church'.[8] As many evangelicals expressed it, to provide state aid for religion implied that the gospel could not attract converts unaided. H. P. Hughes had charged Establishment with tending to make 'the Church worldly, without making the world Christian'.[9] If, as Lidgett defined it, Establishment was nationalism in religion, the nation on its spiritual side, then its ideal was not catholic, and it offended against the spiritual nature and autonomy of Christ's Church. But like most Wesleyans and even Hughes, Lidgett was 'lukewarm'[10] in the matter: his dislike of Establishment did not extend to a campaign against it. He had many other, and much more important, priorities.

In this he differed from Nonconformist radicals, who at times dominated the Liberal Party, and whose 'hatred of the Church of England knew no bounds'.[11] Nonconformity clearly meant non-conforming, and from its mid-nineteenth-century foundation the Liberation Society had maintained a militant disestablishment line. Some Nonconformists dreamt of seeing the Anglican Church wither away and the Free Churches taking its place. Radical attacks on Anglicans included claims that they were inactive on 'Purity' issues, and 'undemocratic' in preference for birth and brains above character and brains. Lidgett never made such charges. He upset the Liberation Society Chairman by opposing the Welsh Disendowment proposals.[12]

Episcopacy was the major stumbling block to the union of the Anglican, Methodist and Free Churches. Though Lidgett's views were mostly expressed through the *Methodist Times*, they were not directed at Methodists alone. He wrote from his perspective both as a Methodist and as an official Free Church spokesman. But he was prepared to state his own opinion, while making clear he realised it might not be widely shared. As always, he sought an acceptable compromise which preserved (to him) the essential theological principle. Such was the opposition to the Episcopate among Nonconformists that only a qualified agreement to it would have stood any chance of consideration by them.

In the 1917 discussions it was suggested that to effect reunion between the Wesleyan and Anglican churches Wesleyan ministers should be episcopally reordained. On 5 July Lidgett firmly opposed this. It could not be a condition of reconciliation, he said, that Methodist ministers should deny their calling: anything which could be regarded as a repudiation of their past ministry would be anathema to them. Methodism's unexhausted and distinctive mission[13] should both be recognised and preserved in the united Church, not only in the spiritual interests of mankind, but also in those of Catholic Christianity as a whole.[14] Methodism, like the Franciscans, had a spirit and power to renovate Christianity, but could suffer if 'annexed' by the Anglican Church.

As for the Episcopate itself, he set out his view in the *Methodist Times* of 5 September 1918. Unity, he said, had to be sought and found 'not in any human ministry, but in the headship of Christ exercised through his living Spirit', and issues of church organisation should not be allowed pre-eminence, 'repressing the energies of faith'. If this principle was accepted by all the churches, it would then be possible, he said, 'to use and unify all ministries and methods without being in bondage to any of them'.

Lidgett declared that any scheme of union must 'both conserve and transform the manifold inheritance of the past'. This meant the retention of the episcopate *under democratic conditions*, not just because it had antiquity and prevalence on its side, but because he, like H. P. Hughes, acknowledged it had been found to be 'an effective instrument for the administration of the Church'. At the same time, retention of the episcopate must, he emphasised, be paralleled by 'the preservation and enlargement of the position of *the Presbyterate*', of *the rights of the laity* and of '*the liberty of prophesying*'. Though many Nonconformists would continue to object to episcopacy in any form, Lidgett succeeded in opening a door, hitherto firmly shut, without incurring denunciation and rejection by those he sought to represent.

Overall, his criticism of the Anglican Church appears stark and severe, but he seems to have satisfied Methodist readers and at the same time avoided alienating his Anglican contacts. On some matters he showed himself prepared to compromise or saw other priorities. His sympathy with the Anglican Church again became evident over the Enabling Bill.[15] Warm personal relations were maintained with many, including the most prominent, Anglican clergy, with whom from 1914 onwards he was almost continuously engaged in unity discussions at a high level. Davidson's undated comment[16] on Lidgett's understanding of Anglicans was confirmed in similar words by his letter of 30 October 1919[17] to the Bishop of Norwich: 'I have no fear that Lidgett and others will misunderstand us'. Lidgett gained wide respect for his sensitive understanding of ecclesiastical and public issues, and for diplomacy throughout the multiplicity of ecumenical discussions, personal and corporate.

Nevertheless, to Lidgett as a Wesleyan statesman, any unilateral Wesleyan move to rejoin the Anglican Church, a proposal being mooted during 1916–19, was out of the question without grass-roots support. His position, set out in a private conversation with Davidson at Lambeth on 9 January 1917,[18] was repeated in his autobiography.[19] Davidson, at a time of illness and depression, had asked Lidgett to tell him frankly whether he had failed to do what he ought to have done over reunion. Lidgett reassured him:

> I told him that it must not be assumed that though, because of its history, Wesleyan Methodism had closer affinities with the Anglican Church than had the other non-Episcopal Churches, therefore it could be drawn into any such partial and separate Reunion. Wesleyan Methodism, I explained, was a very powerful Church, and was deeply conscious of an unexhausted mission. The ideal of a comprehensive Reunion, I assured him, was growingly attracting the best minds throughout Evangelical Nonconformity, and Wesleyans would undoubtedly take part in any general discussions with this great object in view. But they would not move except in such general concert and under influences that were not sectional, but truly catholic.

Davidson's own memorandum on the meeting corresponded with this account, but put the nub of it more crisply: 'He did not think there was any substantial movement or desire in Wesleyan Methodism to effect at present a reunion with the Church of England.'

There were other strong reasons for regarding as misjudged any scheme such as the one being proposed. Lidgett had not mentioned the internal dissensions within the Conference at the time, too many, Mews[20] has considered, to make Wesleyan Methodism 'a worthy bride for any willing suitor'. Mews was thinking among other things of the WBU's continuing fundamentalist backlash and the bitter feeling both on doctrine and on policy over the drink question.

Lidgett could have instanced the less than enthusiastic attitude of the *Methodist Recorder* as an index of Wesleyan opinion. The *Recorder*, for years lukewarm about Church unity, had, for example, on 3 February 1910, declared its satisfaction that the Edinburgh World Missionary Conference would be barred by its constitution from considering the subject. Nor had the Wesleyan Conference offered promising prospects. At the 1913 Conference when a further advance towards Methodist reunion was discussed, Bevan Shepherd proposed an amendment that Wesleyans should look for unity not to other Methodists, but to the Anglican Church. The support it received was a mere six votes.

According to Lidgett[21] a Wesleyan minister [unnamed] encouraged Winnington-Ingram (1858–1946), Bishop of London, to consider the possibility of reuniting Wesleyan Methodism with the Church of England. Lidgett's dating of the incident was vague, 'towards the end of the Great War'. In response, Lidgett continued, the Bishop preached in St Paul's a sermon appealing for unity, and at an informal conference in London House, to which he invited several Wesleyan ministers and laymen, he set out a possible scheme. Their joint discussions, while friendly, proved not very fruitful and the scheme came to nothing.

This account, written in 1936, telescoped events from the time of the original proposal to the actual scheme suggested by the Bishop in 1919. Lidgett apparently associated his meeting with Davidson on 9 January 1917 with the occasion when the Archbishop, while 'seriously ill', had called him to his bedside to discuss issues concerning army chaplaincies. Davidson's memorandum of that date[22] confirmed the circumstances of the meeting, but the subjects discussed included a movement within the Wesleyan Methodist 'body' for rejoining the Church, not chaplaincies. Lidgett thought the scheme premature and its unidentified Wesleyan initiator 'somewhat rash'. Having recently come to recognise John Wesley's spiritual greatness, Davidson had been moved by the Bishop's appeal.[23] What had prompted the discussion on 9 January 1917 was revealed by Davidson's correspondence. The Bishop of London had on 11 December 1916[24] sent Davidson two letters 'of many similar' he had received from Wesleyan Methodists. He wanted to know if the first step towards reunion should be taken by the Church or by the Wesleyan 'body'. Lidgett was not shown the letters. Names were not mentioned, nor recorded in Davidson's correspondence: he merely spoke of such letters received by himself and others. His secretary, returning the letters to the Bishop, wrote:

> Lidgett thinks that any endeavour to act formally on the lines these letters suggest would at present be detrimental and not helpful towards the policy which he agrees with the Bishop of London in desiring to see some day followed.[25]

Lidgett had given what Davidson felt was a reliable assessment. Their discussion ranged over other issues. But Davidson was particularly interested in what Lidgett had said about: himself ('not a Dissenter, a Churchman as well as a Wesleyan Methodist'); the prospects for solving the outstanding educational problems ('bright, once the single school area issue is settled'); and Liberationism ('comfortingly on the wane'). Davidson was highly delighted with the interview: 'most satisfactory in all ways', he called it.

Debate on Wesleyan/Anglican unity was clearly very much in the air if the *Guardian* and the *Church Times* decided to comment. The *Guardian* suggested 'conditional reordination' as the means of achieving reunion. The *Church Times* proposed that the Wesleyan Church could return to the Church of England and still retain its own internal unity, but admitted it could not be a condition of reconciliation that Methodist ministers should deny their calling. In response[26] Lidgett insisted more evidence was needed for assuming the desire for unity was widespread among Wesleyans. On 19 July 1917 Lidgett warned readers against undue haste, short cuts and partial solutions. On 26 July 1917 he stressed the first necessity was for both churches to recognise more fully their common loyalty to, and life in, Christ, and that Christian education, a favourite concept, while not a speedy process, was vital in achieving this.

Winnington-Ingram was undeterred by Davidson's soundings. A 'Unity' sermon in St Paul's and a meeting consequent upon it may have occurred later in 1917, but important events also took place during the summer. Accompanied by the Bishop of Chelmsford (Dr Watts-Ditchfield), who had a Methodist background, he addressed the Representative Session of the Wesleyan Conference in July. He was well received, not least because he spoke in public of the Wesleyan Methodists as a '*Church*', not a 'Body'. No observer raised an eyebrow that the Bishop was an Anglo-Catholic. Mews[27] recalled the claim of the hostile *Methodist Recorder* on 12 July 1917 that the Anglo-Catholics were 'entirely inflexible' in essential matters, while the *Tablet* on 4 August suggested this was the very reason why evangelical Anglicans had 'welcomed Wesleyan reinforcements'.

On 2 August 1917 the *Methodist Recorder*[28] referred to a private meeting to follow up the Bishop's ideas. Though no details were given, it probably included the Bishop, fellow Anglicans and Wesleyan enthusiasts for reunion. In *Chapters from My Life*[29] Lunn mentioned that some 20 Wesleyan ministers were involved in the reunion proposal: among them, Benjamin Gregory, J. E. Rattenbury, J. Alfred Sharp and Henry Carter, but not Lidgett. Lunn said it was Gregory who first suggested to the Bishop of London that he might visit the Wesleyan Conference. The leading figure, however, according to Mews[30] was Rattenbury, Superintendent of the West London Mission, in whose Kingsway Hall unofficial talks on the reunion proposal were held.

The 20 ministers, Lunn said, did not belong to the 'platform oligarchy': they were 'from the floor'. Lunn had his own personal reason for detesting what he called the 'Wesleyan Establishment': it was these old men who had driven him to resign his ministry in 1893, and who were blocking the reinstatement he dearly wanted.[31] Confirmed by Winnington-Ingram in 1911, he had long supported the Church of England and not involved himself in NCEFC activities. Welcoming Anglican/Wesleyan reunion, though 'generations ahead',[32] Lunn joined those who met the Bishop of London on 31 January 1918 and was elected, along with the Bishops of London and Chelmsford, Athelstan Riley, Gregory and Workman, to the 'Continuation' Committee, formed to seek further progress in the scheme; it met again in April and July.[33] The January meeting had also been attended by the Bishops of Oxford, Lincoln, Winchester, Peterborough and Frederickton in Canada, a former Bishop of Bristol, Canon Masterman, Carter, Sharp, Walters, Runciman and Lidgett.

To return to the Wesleyan Conference of 1917. The President made a courteous, non-committal reply to the Bishop's speech, but subsequently there was a heated debate about what formal response should be made. Perks again indicated his lack of sympathy for reunion with the Church of England. Arnaud Scott proposed that Conference would 'confer as to the best way to promote more efficient co-operation' with the Church of England. Perks's amendment simply assured the Bishops of readiness to stand shoulder to shoulder on any great moral question. It was finally resolved to give a vague assurance that the Wesleyans were 'ready at all times to co-operate with the Church of England and all other Evangelical Churches of the country in every endeavour for the furtherance of the Kingdom of Christ'.

The issue surfaced again in the Pastoral Session. Rattenbury and Carter wanted to 'create a temper' to make reunion of all the churches less remote a possibility. There was again strong opposition. Arthur Hoyle suggested[34] the Wesleyan–Anglican proposal was being promoted as a kind of counterblast, not against Methodist Union, but against the action the previous year's Conference had taken over coming into the Free Churches' unity scheme. Lidgett, sensing the general mood, accepted the need to reiterate the Representative Session's blander resolution. At the same time 'he did not believe they were following a mirage. Closer fellowship and co-operation was (*sic*) the only way to cultivate greater unity and closer trust'.[35] The Session decided to take no action.

Lidgett's views were more frankly stated in the *Methodist Times*[36] than in the Conference. While he understood the need for caution and acknowledged that 'we can neither disavow our own past nor be content to become a mere preaching order in the Anglican Communion', he regretted that nothing was added to the response of the Representative Session. References in the *Church Times* (and *Guardian*) to such matters as reordination, conditional or otherwise, were, he accepted, bound to alarm. But in his view there was a common tendency 'prematurely to discuss questions of ecclesiastical polity' instead of making a priority of seeking 'the intimate spiritual fellowship which alone will enable such vexed questions to be wisely approached'. Lidgett recalled Conference's decision that Wesleyan spiritual and theological problems should be tackled through prayerful discussion. That was the method he favoured for putting relations with other churches on a new footing.

In 1918 it was Bishop Knox of Manchester who brought his greetings to the Wesleyan Conference, but Bishop Winnington-Ingram's enthusiasm continued unabated. He was convinced that Wesleyan Methodism could offer the first opportunity to make progress in the reunion of the Churches. On 7 April 1919 he addressed Wesleyans at 'the London Wesleyan Conference'. As the annual Wesleyan Conference met in July, he must have coined a title for an unofficial meeting in London House.

Almost certainly about this time he was setting out an actual scheme (perhaps not his first) for reunion.[37] The Bishop's suggestion, in a letter to Davidson on 8 April 1919,[38] was that six Bishops should confer with the Wesleyans, declare exactly the terms under which the Church of England would enter into reunion, and throw onto them the onus of refusing the offer. He hoped Davidson would allow him to bring the proposal formally before Convocation in May before the Wesleyan Conference met, but he was persuaded instead[39] to send the report of his addresses to the Bishops privately, for informal conversation in Convocation.

The elements or stages in his plan were as follows. From a given date all future Wesleyan ministers were to be episcopally ordained by a Bishop, thereby ensuring full reunion in 40 years. All existing ministers who wished would be episcopally ordained at once, and this would be declared publicly to be no slight on present Orders. Six leading Wesleyan ministers would be consecrated Bishops *per saltum*. This solution, in essence also advocated by T. A. Lacey (Canon of Worcester),[40] would appear to have been the one favoured by some Anglo-Catholics as well as the Bishop. Under Winnington-Ingram's plan the Wesleyan Church would be regarded as an Order within the Anglican Church, with its own officers, tests, class meetings, etc. After an appointed date Wesleyan ministers, whether episcopally ordained or not, would be permitted to preach in Anglican pulpits. Episcopally ordained Wesleyan ministers would be permitted to celebrate at Anglican altars, while continuing to administer Holy Communion in their own way in their own Churches. The Bishop left for later decision the question whether or not to admit to Communion in Anglican churches Wesleyans who had passed their own tests but had not been confirmed.

His proposals, too radical for their day, did not succeed. Lidgett's appraisal, made despite his deep affection for the Church of England, was statesmanlike . . . and vindicated. His passion for the unity of Methodism, and above all for the pursuit of the catholic ideal, was consistently in evidence, yet tempered with shrewd pragmatism. His views combined frankness and courage with tact. These qualities were again shown in the parallel unity debates examined below.

16

The Free Churches and Union

Unity among the Free Churches generally and their relations with the Established Church were also a matter of lively debate between 1910 and 1920, and Lidgett was much involved.

The vision of a 'single, united, powerful "Free Church of England"' had been articulated in the NCEFC's earliest days. It had obsessed[1] Thomas Law (1854–1910), a United Methodist Free Church minister, and from 1896 the Council's first full-time Organising Secretary. Law[2] stood for variety, for co-operation between the local Councils his considerable energies had been bent to create. Unlike Alexander Mackennal, to whom technically he was responsible between 1896 and 1899, he did not seek organic union.

When recalling the Council's origins, Lidgett's approval was reserved for the dreams of H. P. Hughes and Charles Berry, who claimed that 'until we moved together with the harmony of one inspiration, England could not be won for Christ'. As early as 1895 Berry had asked, 'Has not the time come for the federation of our barred Churches into one grand Free Church?' Under the Council's aegis, Law had been pursuing an aggressively political policy. The Council, perhaps influenced by Lidgett, from 1907 onwards became disenchanted with his schemes: it began to revert to local evangelism and focus on moral and spiritual issues. Law was abruptly dismissed from his post after the NCEFC Council meeting in March 1910, and committed suicide soon afterwards. Lidgett subsequently commended his organisational effort, but made no reference to his vision of unity.

Lidgett's approach to unity had been global but realistic. In 1908, discussing the unifying of Christendom, he declared:

> Where there are no differences our watchword must be union; where they are comparatively slight, federation; where they are more serious, yet not destructive of the fundamental agreements of Christianity, co-operation in order to defend and promote the supreme interests and applications of our common Christian life.[3]

In 1910 unity was again in the air. Shortly before the NCEFC meeting in Hull, Lidgett decided an account of his own outlook on reunion and an assessment of

Free Church attitudes towards the Church of England would be timely. His editorial on 10 March, entitled 'The Problems of the Free Church Council' was, he thought, sufficiently important, despite its frank criticism of the Anglican Church, to warrant Davidson[4] being given a copy. On 21 March the Archbishop's reply expressed agreement with much of the article, but asked for further explanation of his references to Disestablishment and the Free Church catechism: how far was the latter generally in use, and whether Lidgett's view that 'the political attitude of the Free Church Council has been due much less to Disestablishment questions than to educational and temperance controversies' was justified.

Davidson was aware that Nonconformity, with or without the Liberation Society, could still pose a threat to the Established Church. Joseph Parker of the City Temple had, for example, stated in 1902 that 'Every council of Free Churches is an auxiliary of that [Liberation Society], whether nominally so or not'.[5] Disestablishment, notably but not only in Wales, was a live issue, and the leading NCEFC layman, Joseph Compton-Rickett MP, strongly supported it.

Lidgett responded that Davidson was right to query the extent of the catechism's circulation since its publication in 1899, but the importance his article had attributed to it lay rather in demonstrating the general Free Church agreement on the main 'verities' of the Christian faith. He did not admit that it arose from the self-appointed leaders' desire to prove that Free Church unity existed, and might represent views ahead of the 'rank and file'.[6]

As for what was obviously Davidson's principal concern, Lidgett freely admitted the majority of Free Churchmen still strongly favoured Disestablishment as a general principle, and viewed Welsh Disestablishment 'as a matter of practical politics and justice'. But he imagined only a comparatively small section thought of general Disestablishment as likely to become 'practical politics in the near future'; they were more disposed to emphasise educational and temperance reform. He said that apart from country districts and Wales the *Wesleyan* Church had 'not the slightest desire' to take up Disestablishment as a cause in which it should play a part as a Church: Perks had tried to raise it once, but the Conference President had ruled it out of order. Lidgett did not reveal that the Conference generally refused to take much notice of the NCEFC anyway.

Lidgett's article had sought to focus readers' minds on the larger objective of the Free Church Council, 'that Federation of all the Churches which the supreme dictates of Christian life and the constraining needs of Christian service impel us to seek'. The Council's original catchwords were, he insisted, 'Catholicity' and 'Spirituality'. 'An endeavour after the widest Catholicity', he said, 'must be the condition of achieving a truly catholic fellowship in the Free Churches themselves'. But closer Free Church union should not accentuate the differences between themselves and their fellow believers in Anglican and other Communions throughout the world.

Lidgett had candidly acknowledged what these differences were: 'a sacerdotal theory', Catholicity's 'most deadly foe', and the State establishment of religion which 'operates against those conditions of spiritual freedom and equal brotherhood by which alone the Catholic ideal can be fulfilled'. At the same time there was considerable agreement between the churches, and Lidgett urged that Free Church spirituality must not allow the course of events on Disestablishment, education, etc. to weaken their grasp of the principle of Catholicity and essential truths. 'The Union of the Free Churches', he said, 'must lead to the destruction of all the adverse influences which create exclusiveness and antagonism within the widest borders of Christian life': the spirit of love, wisdom and forbearance was required.

Lidgett's leader of 10 March also explained that in its origins the Free Church movement had hardly contemplated 'a political direction'; this had resulted from applying the principles of Christian truth to contemporary social and political issues and urgent needs. Opposition to the Conservative Party arose, he said, from Balfour's refusal to take account of legitimate Free Church concerns in the educational legislation of 1902, and from the Party's Licensing policy in direct conflict with Temperance reformers. Davidson might have commented on sacerdotalism and the education controversy, but he made no reply.

The NCEFC meeting in Hull in 1910[7] was notable for a paper by the Baptist, J. H. Shakespeare, on 'The Free Churches and National Life', advocating union of all the Evangelical Free Churches in a United Free Church of England. Lidgett warmly welcomed[8] the idea in the *Methodist Times* of 17 March 1910, but insisted: 'The movement to such a federation cannot be rushed', and 'We shall not adopt an attitude of exclusiveness towards the great Anglican Church'. Lidgett applied that adjective to the Church on other public occasions; repetition might have been designed steadily to combat Free Church prejudice against it.

Reporting the Council meeting at Portsmouth in March 1911, the *Methodist Times*[9] said Lidgett proposed and Shakespeare seconded a motion stating it was now time for the Evangelical Free Churches to come into closer alliance 'upon the lines laid down by the Rev. J. H. Shakespeare at Hull last year', and urging the executive and local councils to undertake educational propaganda to this end. While acknowledging the importance of denominational loyalties, Lidgett said that these were too often allowed to narrow the bounds of the Churches: 'We must educate our Churches until they see that the principle of unity lies at the root of their Christian consciousness'. Stress on *education* for this purpose became one of Lidgett's frequent themes, essential, he thought, for gaining the full conviction needed to carry unity proposals through to a lasting conclusion.

Shakespeare's proposal also received strong endorsement from at least one Anglican source. Herbert Ryle, Bishop of Winchester, had declined an invitation to the NCEFC's meeting, despite Davidson's cautious approval.[10] Hensley Henson (1863–1947), Canon of Westminster Abbey, however, did agree to attend as a visiting speaker. He thought Shakespeare's ideas would have a 'most happy effect on Anglican opinion'. 'Nothing', he said, 'more effectively hinders the growth among Anglicans of a juster appreciation of non-episcopal Christianity than the prevailing aspect of unchecked and irresponsible sectarianism'. Religious cohesion, he was sure, would sweep 'out of the way of our reconciliation a whole mass of hurtful, and as matters now stand, not unnatural prejudices'. In the closing session Forsyth drew attention to some of Henson's rather more startling words: 'He rightly contended that the possibility of any union between the Church of England and the Evangelical Free Churches must depend on the repudiation of sacerdotalism by the Established Church and acceptance of "the evident logic of its situation as a Reformed Church"'.

Before the Free Church Commission of Inquiry[11] held its first major meeting, Lidgett saw a necessity to remind his fellow Free Churchmen, both at the Newcastle NCEFC Council meeting in 1913 and in a leading article of 13 March, that the 'ideal' of the Council was wider than that of unity between the Free Churches. The narrower target was the one at which they had then to aim, but in his opinion what they wanted was not confined to the Free Churches: it was the outward, visible expression of spiritual unity in Christ. The Council's original promoters, he declared, had sought to realise the true Catholicity of the whole Church of Christ by vindicating and expressing the Catholicity of the Free Churches, but the nation was imperilled by each denomination's sense of its own distinctive mission. The Free Churches were not, he said, claiming a monopoly of Catholic truth nor identifying Christianity with any single form of Church. Nor did they rate any Church office, ministerial or other, higher than was appropriate to it. For Lidgett the Catholicity of the whole Church contained and transcended all its difficulties, and only united Christendom could grapple successfully with the spiritual, social and world-wide problems of the twentieth century. His Council[12] speech reasserted his convictions: 'the only possible basis for a truly Catholic Church is not sacerdotalism, but the Evangelical Faith'; and, more boldly, that it was just as essential to him 'to see the great Church of England in prosperity as the Free Church Council'.

In 1914 Shakespeare complained that no progress had been made on his proposal 'but indifference and antagonism have been more marked than sympathy'.[13] But no effective action was taken, except on Chaplaincy provision,[14] until Shakespeare, qua NCEFC President in 1916, put forward substantially the same proposal. Voicing, consciously or not, one of Lidgett's favourite themes, he roundly declared that 'Denominationalism is a decaying idea', and the country needed a united body. The NCEFC constitution, originally devised by H. P. Hughes and Berry in 1896, had, he thought, led to an unfortunate tendency for its leaders to become 'political'; and, since the national assembly of local Free Church Councils elected the Executive, its decisions did not commit the constituent denominations. He claimed[15] the witness of the Spirit would only become really effective if the Religion of the Spirit and the Religion of Authority, hitherto in opposition, were to be fused.

Lidgett's public response[16] was enthusiastic. It was impossible, he said, to exaggerate the significance of Shakespeare's proposal: John Wesley himself would have been delighted, exclaiming again, 'What hath God wrought!'. He said Free Church union exemplified the New Testament doctrine of the Catholic Church, as 'all who partake of common life in the one crucified . . . brought in unity of Spirit into fellowship and co-operation'.

Nevertheless Lidgett remained conscious of denominational sensitivity and protectiveness: 'The great inheritance of denominations', he said, 'may be transcended and enlarged, but cannot be ignored; fulfilled, not contradicted.' On 23 March 1916 he assured his readers that federation, not fusion, was envisaged; Wesleyan doctrinal standards were untouched, and spiritual freedom, combined with the evangelical faith, remained.

Lidgett's article of 16 March was filed among Davidson's papers, along with a record[17] of a conversation between Shakespeare and the two Archbishops at Lambeth on 23 March 1916. Together they explored the financial, personal, doctrinal and political implications of his proposal. Shakespeare frankly admitted anxieties over the practical problems to be solved to make the scheme a reality: ministerial qualifications, chapel debts, unsaleable premises when closures were needed, and the NCEFC role once the scheme was in place. Shakespeare expressed a clear hope that the reunion movement would not stop at the Free Churches, though controversial topics such as the validity of Orders were not aired. He insisted he was himself 'at heart an Episcopalian', 'dead against Disestablishment', and convinced that once the United Church was working on spiritual, not political lines, pressure for Disestablishment would be immensely weakened. Davidson's record revealed close interest in Free Church leaders' thinking, not least on Disestablishment and how prospects for Nonconformist unity might relate to it. His response to Lidgett's proposal for an Advisory Council later that year illustrated this further.

What Shakespeare said privately to Davidson clearly showed[18] the United Free Church of England was to him the first step to full corporate reunion with the Anglican Church, 'including acceptance of the historic episcopacy'. The evidence also revealed this as the firm, though unspoken, longer-term intention of Shakespeare's Presidential proposal in 1916. Lidgett, however, also regarded corporate union with the Church of England as the final objective. In his *Reminiscences* he exaggerated his part in the development of Shakespeare's thinking. When Shakespeare asked for support, Lidgett said[19] he gave it, but only 'up to a point', because 'any Christian movement towards unity and reunion was intrinsically universal', and the more successful it became, the more Shakespeare's proposed restriction to the Free Churches would break down in favour of the larger ideal, complete reunion of the Christian Church. He was at pains to stress how slowly Shakespeare gained the wider vision of Church unity:

> In the end Dr Shakespeare came himself to adopt this point of view, and in the closing years of his activity . . . he devoted all his great powers to the realisation of this larger ideal. In 1916, however, he still adhered to the more limited plan.

The 'larger' vision which Shakespeare declared to Davidson in effect refuted this.

The NCEFC's response to Shakespeare's proposal was to appoint a committee and deputations to canvass opinion in the constituent Free Churches' Annual Assemblies and Conferences. In September 1916 a preliminary Conference was convened at Mansfield College, Oxford, and others in spring 1917 at the Leys School and Baptist Church House in London. Comments on interim reports, published in April 1917, were to be made at representative Conferences in the autumn. Lidgett again thought it wise in his *Methodist Times* of 23 April to allay possible fears of what was being decided. To draft a possible constitution and a declaration of faith, and study implications for Evangelism and Ministry, four committees were established, chaired by Lidgett, Carnegie Simpson (Presbyterian), J. D. Jones (Congregationalist) and G. P. Gould (Baptist), respectively.[20]

A federal structure was proposed as more practicable than fusion. For years the NCEFC had been known as the Council of the 'Federation Movement', and 'Federation' had, in fact, been used in relation to the proposal by Lidgett, Shakespeare and others since 1910. In 1916[21] Lidgett had stressed that federation, not 'complete organic union', was the aim. This federal approach, supported also by (among others) Forsyth, J. S. Banks, Arthur Henderson, and initially by Perks, found general favour. Rupert Davies[22] has plausibly argued that Lidgett would probably have been personally happier to work for a *Federal* Council than he would have been with a plan for a *united* Free Church, because of a fear that the latter might ossify and delay progress to unity with the Church of England: an earnest of wider prospects was preferable to 'one great association which shall balance the power of the Establishment'[23] in English Protestantism. Here Lidgett may have differed from Shakespeare, who was saying in 1918 that he did not regard federation as an ideal solution for the Free Churches. Whatever the distant outcome might be, the draft constitution, allowing for proportional representation by the Baptist, Congregational, Presbyterian, Moravian and Methodist churches, was considered, and agreed.

The Federal Council accordingly came into existence in October 1919, alongside the existing National Council. These two Free Church Councils were not to amalgamate until the creation of the 'Free Church Federal Council' on 16 September 1940; organic union was in fact never achieved. But in the meantime, despite some overlapping of function, they co-operated with one another without friction. Many of the same people were active in both, and a 'Nexus Committee' was formed to harmonise their activities.

The NCEFC had a looser structure than the Federal Council of Evangelical Free Churches (FCEFC). It had always been ready to express its view of Free Church opinion across the country, but never aimed to be in any strict sense responsible to member churches. The Council could advise, not order or control its constituent local councils or Regional/County Federations. As indicated above, the NCEFC consisted essentially of individuals advertising their Nonconformist identity.

In contrast, the Federal Council provided specifically for representatives of its constituent denominations and sent them an annual report, but they were not, even so, committed to implement its decisions, only to consider them carefully. In this sense the Council was not Federal! Despite strong advocacy by Lidgett, Banks and Henderson, the 1918 Wesleyan Conference hesitated, deferring its decision about joining the Federal Council for a year. Though Perks withdrew his support, the Conference finally agreed, and representatives attended the Council's meeting in 1920. Lidgett was to be elected as its Moderator for 1923–5.

The Federal Council participated in unofficial discussions prior to the Lambeth Appeal and in the later official conversations with representatives of the Church of England. Rupert Davies[24] thinks that Lidgett's role was then as a representative of the *Federal* Council, but immediately after as well as prior to the 1920 Lambeth Conference Lidgett was officially acting as the Hon. Secretary, assisted by T. Nightingale, General Secretary, of the *National* Council. Though lacking the powers federation might have implied, the Federal Council proved its value as more representative than the NCEFC over the Lambeth Appeal. It could, Lidgett said, 'focus the mind of all the Free Churches upon the subject, and could undertake, without prejudice to the rights and responsibilities of the constituent denominations, a preliminary investigation of the issues that were raised'.[25]

During the excitement of discussion on Free Church union in 1916, Lidgett supported what was known as the Enabling Bill to increase self-government in the Anglican Church by slackening the control exercised by Parliament. This exposed him to attack from Free Churchmen keen to take every opportunity to denounce the Church and its Establishment.

Nonconformist opponents had argued that if a Church was to remain established, Parliament should have undiminished control over it. In a *Methodist Times* leader[26] Lidgett referred to criticism he had received from John Massie of the Liberation Society, describing him as 'possessed by an overleaping passion for unity', 'by instinct the soul of accommodating compromise, and on crucial occasions the soul of good-natured surrender'. Lidgett responded by admitting fully his concern for unity among the churches. He frankly asserted his desire to see the Established Church energised and quickened, since the Free Churches would, he thought, gain, not lose by its increased spirit and efficiency. In his view spiritual independence was 'more vital than the entire separation of Church and State'; 'If Disestablishment is to come, it had better come by demand of the Church, and not at the instance of politicians; it had better come to a Church that has been prepared beforehand to demand and to practise freedom'. As for readiness to compromise, Lidgett regarded this as culpable only if something essential was not achieved, or if some process of development was not 'assisted by the sacrifice of what is either accidental or subordinate'.

An article Lidgett published in the November *Contemporary Review* by Viscount Wolmer MP presented the case for the Bill. It was then greeted immediately by the *Methodist Times* of 2 November with applause for its substance and tone and, in Lidgett's Editorial Notes, a call to Free Churchmen to support the Bill. He agreed with Wolmer that the fact of Establishment was no bar to the grant of the increased powers which, as a spiritual body, the Anglican Church needed when Parliament was failing to deal satisfactorily with ecclesiastical legislation. Wolmer had, Lidgett was pleased to see, called for a spirit of charity in discussion between opponents and supporters of Disestablishment, and an end to the bitterness dividing the Anglican and Free Churches. Respect for one another's convictions, he suggested, would achieve 'another step toward the reunion of Christendom'.

The subsequent Enabling Act, or *The Church of England Assembly (Powers) Act*, was finally passed in 1919.[27] Under it legislative powers were conferred on the Church Assembly, and procedures laid down for preparing measures for presentation to both Houses of Parliament, which could accept or reject, but not amend, such measures. In gratitude for Lidgett's support Wolmer assured him that the Anglican attitude to Nonconformist legislation would be completely altered. The Leasehold Enfranchisement Bill was no longer opposed, and *The Places of Worship (Enfranchisement) Act* was passed in 1920. This Act remedied long-standing Wesleyan grievances, but did not only apply to Wesleyan or Nonconformist premises. It gave trustees holding leasehold interest in places of public religious worship the right to acquire freehold.

Despite friendly relations between individual Anglican and Free Churchmen, an independent NCEFC Thanksgiving Service for the end of the war was arranged at the Albert Hall in November 1918. The attendance of the King and

Queen led Clifford to speak of 'the beginning of a new day in the relations of the State to "dissent"' and 'the lifting to a slight extent of the social stigma'.[28]

In November 1916 Lidgett had put forward a scheme of his own, wider than Shakespeare's, designed to increase understanding and advance co-operation across all the Protestant churches. This proposal for a Council of Churches was set out in the December issue of the *Contemporary Review*, and the *Methodist Times*[29] gave it further publicity.

Lidgett pointed to the recent evidence of the Churches' desire for union: the Conferences on Faith and Order;[30] the 'great' proposals of Shakespeare; the Archbishops' National Mission of Repentance and Hope; the establishment of the Christian Churches' Temperance Council; and signs he detected of a less exclusive attitude to their High Church tradition by the Bishops of Oxford and Winchester. Such circumstances encouraged him to invite the Church of England to co-operate with those currently promoting a Free Church Federation so that a new (and joint) Advisory Council could be created. Bishop Bell later commented that Lidgett

> was, as far as I can trace, the first British churchman (*sic*) in this century to formulate a clear plan for a Council of Churches, small in numbers, to consist of the principal leaders of the Churches of Great Britain (apart from the Church of Rome), with the Archbishop of Canterbury as ex officio Chairman.[31]

Lidgett suggested that if the Churches were involved on a representative basis, without affecting individual Churches' autonomy, the Council would seek to develop a considered and united mind on the ways in which their Christian religion bore on national issues and events; uphold Christian interests where public legislation and administration were concerned; and enunciate the Christian principles for moral and social reform. Such a body, he thought, would provide a more effective means of organising and expressing the Churches' views than had been possible before. Lidgett sought to widen the scope of what the Free Churches were doing on their own and bring them into closer union with the Anglican Church. His aim, he stressed, was not 'to emphasise Dissent, but to make a serious endeavour after still larger Christian unity'. He called on *Methodist Times* readers to back 'well-considered efforts after closer fellowship between Christians' and 'to stretch out the hand of brotherly love' both to Anglican and Free Churchmen.

Lidgett's proposal for the creation not only of such a National Council, but also of Diocesan Councils for social as well as for religious purposes, was adopted later in the Lambeth Appeal, but only patchily implemented.[32] In the event his initiative failed, but not for want of diplomatic effort on his part behind the scenes. Conscious that Davidson should be consulted at an early stage, he sent him a copy of his article on 29 November 1916, with a covering letter, revealing again the close relationship between them. 'I know', he wrote, 'I shall have your sympathy in making the proposal'. Stressing he had tried to guard it 'from conscientious difficulties' or from involving 'the sacrifice of any principle either of faith or practice', he offered to come over to Lambeth, should Davidson like to see him at any time.[33]

On 21 December 1916 Davidson responded[34] with some warmth to Lidgett's letter. He asked if he could 'secure a quiet half-day with you somewhere within reach of London if you could come to us for a night . . . There are a good many things which I should like to talk over with you unhurriedly, and a quiet evening together would be much to me'. At the private meeting arranged on 9 January 1917[35] Anglican/Wesleyan reunion was also discussed. Shakespeare's proposal and his own were, Lidgett declared, fully consistent, supporting one another. But, from his meeting with Shakespeare on 23 March 1916 and his own assessment of attitudes in the Free Churches, Davidson was aware of NCEFC weaknesses, and that some Nonconformists strongly repudiated Free Church union already. He realised Lidgett would find it difficult in *his* scheme to make all the non-episcopal bodies cohere as a unit, and that arrangements for formal representation would pose problems for Anglicans also. It was, he thought, essential to erect safeguards against executive or administrative action or formal commitment to action by the proposed Council, but he appreciated Lidgett's realism in discussion, frankly recognising difficulties and the need for caution.

Davidson asked Talbot to raise the proposal at the Bishops' meeting on 31 January 1917. Together with the Bishops of Wakefield and Peterborough, Talbot was appointed to confer with Lidgett and Shakespeare.[36] The meeting, of which there is an unsigned manuscript account,[37] took place in Lollards tower at Lambeth on 24 May 1917. Shakespeare could not join them. Davidson was recommended to consider the creation of a Standing Council with 'no constitution, nor of any official character', meeting at intervals in Lambeth Palace. Lidgett, speaking for others, agreed the Archbishop should be in the chair. 'Representative men' were envisaged from an agreed list; Unitarians, the Society of Friends and the Roman Catholic Church were excluded, but might be invited occasionally as a given issue might warrant. The remit would not include the Education question 'in view of the contentious character of the subject in the past'. For that a special, quite separate conference, they agreed, should be held very soon.

After the above meeting Davidson wanted to arrange some sort of preliminary conference on the notion of a Standing Council. On 22 June 1917 Davidson wrote to Lidgett[38] to explain the delay while he took more bishops into counsel. Thereafter Davidson's papers are silent on why nothing further was done. His memorandum on an Educational Conference on 13 July 1917[39] records that

Anglican and Free Churchmen who attended had agreed a widely representative Conference should be called which would concentrate 'first on the educational problem, and then on questions of reconstruction and similar social and moral subjects'. The Free Churchmen advocated inviting Roman Catholics on social topics, but not on the educational issues. Education seemed to be taking the greater priority, and there was in any case no shortage of other proposals on inter-church relationships at that particular time!

Lidgett had, nevertheless, raised an issue relevant to the forthcoming Lambeth Conference. Among Davidson's papers for tabling there was Lidgett's *Contemporary Review* article of late 1916 on 'A Council of the Churches', together with another article by Lidgett, sent with the author's compliments, from the May 1920 issue of the same journal, on 'The Anglican Church and Evangelical Nonconformity'. On its penultimate page Lidgett referred again to his 1916 proposal for the establishment of Councils of the Churches, central, diocesan and local. He claimed it had met with favour in many quarters, and been carried out in Manchester 'with admirable results'. He still felt such Councils would prove indispensable 'if the Churches, as such, are to be brought into close relations with one another'.

It was never easy from 'the outside' for Davidson to assess how far the different Nonconformist leaders' views outstripped those of their differing rank and file. Throughout this period he was keen to sound out where he could, discreetly through reading the press and in private discussion, the real extent and nature of Free Church support for the differing unity proposals. Lidgett, as we have seen, was one, almost certainly the most intimate, but not the only informant. The views expressed by one such in personal contact, and by another in his journal illustrates the divisions and animosities bedevilling the progress of unity described so far.

At Lambeth on 22 November 1918[40] James Marchant, knighted in 1921, a prominent Presbyterian minister and then Secretary of the National Birth Rate Commission, informed Davidson that Nicoll had told him he was 'going to "go for" Shakespeare as a renegade . . . truckling to Episcopacy'. But Nicoll's influence, he thought, was waning: information obtained from advertising agents alleged that the *British Weekly*'s circulation had fallen from 120,000 to 15,000.[41] Support for reunion under an episcopal system, Marchant said, was growing steadily among Baptists, Congregationalists and Presbyterians. Meyer, for example, had told him 'vehemently and repeatedly' that he was prepared to see Nonconformity as such disappear in a larger unity: he thought their work as Dissenters had been done, since matters over which they dissented were no longer dominant. If Meyer felt that, then Marchant judged the younger generation felt that way far more, and

To put it in business language, you have only 15 years' purchase to pay. In 15 years' time there will be nothing to pay – you will have got the men, for the older will have disappeared or be negligible: and even now the price you have to pay is not a high one.

Davidson's memorandum on this conversation wisely notes the need for caution in accepting these judgements, though Marchant could be said to know 'the ground and the people'. Nevertheless he could agree that Garvie and Selbie were longing for unity and accepted it could only be on Episcopal lines. As for the attitude of Wesleyan Methodists, Davidson did not challenge what Marchant had said: that Perks was taking a similar line to Nicoll, and Chadwick and Wiseman were 'difficult'. Marchant was certainly right about Perks: earlier that year, opposing the creation by the Wesleyan Conference of 'Separated Chairmen', he derogatorily called them Methodist 'Bishops'; and in the 1920 Wesleyan Conference he stated 'confidentially' that he neither expected nor desired to see reunion with the Anglican Church. Winnington-Ingram had assured Marchant 'he was roping in all the Wesleyans', but Marchant thought him entirely mistaken. The Bishop's enthusiasm had 'blinded him to the obduracy of the very people he thinks he has secured'. Marchant concluded that the real strength towards unity lay in the much larger and more general group *outside* Wesleyanism.

Soon after this interview, Lidgett drew to the attention of Tissington Tatlow, Secretary of the Archbishop's Faith and Order Committee,[42] the animus Nicoll was showing against Shakespeare and what he claimed Shakespeare stood for. Writing to Tatlow in December 1918, Lidgett alluded to the alarm being exploited by Nicoll since the beginning of the month. The *British Weekly*'s editor had headed his leading article on 5 December, 'Mr Shakespeare at the Cross Roads', a pun on Shakespeare's book *The Churches at the Cross Roads*.[43] Nicoll had set out to expose the truth he claimed was concealed by deliberately vague words in the Second Interim Report on Faith and Order, advocating reunion on the basis of 'acceptance of the fact of Episcopacy'. What this really meant, he said, was revealed by Shakespeare's book: it implied, 'unmistakably', that, to achieve reunion with the Church of England, Free Church ministers would have to submit to episcopal reordination, and its author thought reunion well worth the price.

Nicoll had rounded on Shakespeare for his readiness to reunite 'on Anglican conditions' and for rejecting the inheritance which all Free Churchmen shared: he said that 'their fathers believed sincerity and liberty to be far more precious' than visible unity; 'they acted on that belief and suffered for it'; and history had shown episcopacy to be an 'inveterate foe of civil and religious liberty'. With a highly rhetorical flourish he asserted: 'The . . . martyrs of Christian liberty purchased our freedom for us: we do not propose to spit upon their graves'.

This, however, did less than justice to what Shakespeare had written.

Responding in the *British Weekly* of 9 January 1919 to the wording of the attack, Shakespeare insisted that what he had said was self-evident: reunion was impossible 'until a way is found which accepts episcopal order without involving "any Christian community in the necessity of disowning its past"'; and 'the question of re-ordination will inevitably arise'.

Shakespeare's book had earlier received very favourable comment from Lidgett.[44] It was flattering to read that Shakespeare prized his friendship 'more than I can say'. Shakespeare had described him as unsectarian, while 'a loyal Wesleyan', and as 'absolutely straight, and he never swerves from his word'. No leader, he said, 'has done more . . . to serve public causes and Christian unity'. But, more importantly, Lidgett was pleased Shakespeare's aim was not limited to Federation of the Free Churches or to one Free Church of England, and the terms he advocated for reunion with the Church of England were such 'as will not imply either surrender of the historic witness of Evangelical Nonconformity or set up an impossible and undesirable uniformity'.

Lidgett's clarion call was a major contrast to that of his old critic, Nicoll. Referring to centuries of conflict between the churches, Lidgett asked, 'Can we not rise to comradeship and sacrifice, and win by Christian love what we have failed to win by war?' On 30 January 1919 the new editors of the *Methodist Times* again praised Shakespeare: 'We trust that J. H. Shakespeare, statesman and seer, will continue to point out the path to unity in spite of all the attacks of the *British Weekly*.'

The *British Weekly*'s attacks did not abate. News of Gore's resignation as Bishop, for example, gave Nicoll an opportunity on 3 April 1919 to stress the importance of Confirmation to Gore 'and his followers': it showed 'reunion with the Nonconformists on their part' meant (1) Re-ordination and (2) Confirmation. To him the only way out was the ejection of the High Church party from the Church of England![45] The *Church Times* of 1 April 1920[46] thought it of interest to quote the previous week's *British Weekly* where Nicoll took the strongest objection to the way 'some of our leaders' had talked 'as if episcopacy must be the form of government for the future Church'. The record of the episcopate in England and Scotland, Nicoll argued, did not justify such a belief, and leaders were 'not speaking for the rank and file'.[47]

Nicoll also remonstrated against the continuation of unity conferences. He angrily – and wearily – complained that any little concession once made was soon retracted, or 'expressed so doubtfully that . . . it may mean anything or nothing', and the meetings 'have done more to separate Nonconformists from the Church than attract them'. This was only a few months before the Lambeth Conference. An account of those unity conferences provides further background to that significant stage in the whole lengthy debate.

17

Faith and Order, Anglicans and Free Churchmen 1910–20

For Lidgett, separate though related debates on uniting the Free Churches, the reunion of Methodists, and of Wesleyans with the Anglican Church were complex enough, but far from the end of the story. More unity discussions were taking place simultaneously among the Protestant churches in this period, and in these Lidgett also played a not insignificant part. Many found him directly involved or commenting from the sidelines. Others offer an important context for the scene overall.

Enthusiasm for union of the churches increased during the decade, building up to a crescendo towards the end of the War and in its aftermath, as Conference succeeded Conference, both separately within the Free Churches and the Church of England, and jointly between Free Churchmen and Anglicans. If the narrative below is confusing, it is mainly because the welter of proposals and comment *was* confusing, at times overlapping, repeating, modifying, sometimes contradicting itself. In 1920 Bishop Talbot[1] accurately described Christian reunion as a topic which, by then, 'had been worn threadbare by discussion'. The stage was then set for the Lambeth Conference to provide a virtually necessary climax and offer a way forward.

Many factors contributed to the ferment of proposals: the diversity of missionary societies, in competition, yet with very similar objectives; an increasing sense of solidarity both at home and on the battlefront; a conviction that united action by Christians could significantly improve their impact on social problems and on post-war reconstruction, internationally through the League of Nations as well as in England itself; news of unity movements in Canada and Australia; readiness by the American Episcopal Church even to contemplate a Congregational minister being confirmed, and episcopally ordained, while remaining a Congregational minister; and, not least, the burning desire among particular leaders within the churches for positive action to achieve the unity for which Christ had prayed and for which current circumstances seemed to offer a providential opportunity.

The previous chapter illustrated internal divisions among the Free Churches. But there was no unanimity within any of the churches. Colonial expatriate bishops, involved face to face with ecumenical issues, tended to be despised by some of their counterparts in England, who recognised only slowly the existence and growth of the unity movement, and had little personal contact with Nonconformists. Distinct differences (some – but not all – acrimonious) also existed, between church leaders striving persistently for unity and their church members. Lidgett's ecumenical zeal was beyond doubt, but unlike many of his contemporary enthusiasts, he knew his 'constituency', negotiated with discretion and displayed an awareness of the obstacles on all sides and realism in facing them.

The decade after 1910 was marked by the proposal for a World Conference on Faith and Order. The Edinburgh Conference of that year had been of great ecumenical significance, but the work of its Continuation Committee and the World Missionary Movement as a whole was distinct from that of the Faith and Order Movement.[2] Both were led by Americans, the layman, John R. Mott, General Secretary of the World Student Christian Federation, and Bishop Charles Brent. Mott wanted to establish a permanent framework for ecumenical co-operation in the missionary context; while Brent sought to make arrangements for a World Conference to discuss matters of Faith and Order.

The only way to bring the various bodies together at Edinburgh had been to exclude matters of Faith and Order from the agenda. Yet unity of the churches was in fact discussed there. Indigenous churches were thought likely to move towards unity in spite of the continuing disunity of their parent bodies. Federation, it was said, was not enough: a full or 'higher' unity was needed. It was the inspiration of Edinburgh that determined Brent to commit his church to action on unity. His persuasion led the General Convention of the Protestant Episcopal Church of the United States of America (PECUSA) in 1910 to resolve:

> that a joint commission be appointed to bring about a conference for consideration of questions touching Faith and Order, and that all *Christian Communions throughout the world which confess our Lord Jesus Christ as God and Saviour* be asked to unite with us in arranging for and conducting such a conference.[3]

This daring proposal, almost incredible at that time, resulted in the appointment of a commission. Its secretary was a layman, Robert Gardiner, whose tireless efforts succeeded in bringing Brent's dream into effect. The scheme reflected a conviction that unity was to be sought, not created. Its doctrinal prerequisite, italicised above, was deliberately restricted to the minimum; the Unitarian was the only Protestant church excluded. The emphasis was firmly placed on study, not negotiation. The Lambeth Quadrilateral, though bound to be raised by most if not all participants in the debate, was not mentioned.

The Quadrilateral framework was deceptively simple, capable of expression in various forms and subject to various interpretations. It was therefore often misunderstood or unconsciously misquoted. It could connote defence of Anglican principles, insistence on their acceptance, or a *search* for a common idea.

The Quadrilateral originated in 1870 from 'The Church-Idea, an Essay toward Unity', by a High Church American Episcopalian, W. R. Huntington (1838–1909).[4] Seeing a united church as a way to bring healing and unity after America's Civil War, he set out to devise the minimum framework for a Church of Reconciliation, a national, not an Established Church. He decided on four points: the Holy Scriptures as the Word of God; the Primitive Creeds as the Rule of Faith; the two Sacraments ordained by Christ himself; and the episcopate as the keystone of governmental unity. This framework he called a 'Quadrilateral' after the four fortress cities in Lombardy used by the Austrian empire to keep Northern Italy under its control. The image suited his aim to keep the Church secure from the threats of unbelief and over elaboration. But, unsurprisingly, outside PECUSA the image aroused fears of virtually explicit Anglican imperialism.

Huntington had regarded the episcopate as a virtual necessity, though at the practical, administrative level only. When in 1886 the American Bishops adopted the Quadrilateral, they reworded the fourth point as: 'A Ministry acknowledged by every part of the Church as possessing not only the inward call of the Spirit, but also the commission of Christ and the authority of the whole body'. The omission of the word 'episcopacy' might be seen either as more eirenic than the original version, or as the opposite, virtually conferring power to insist on the historic succession. But the bishops' *Declaration of Christian Unity*, in which the Quadrilateral was included, spoke of seeking unity, not creating unity: their version was advanced as a kind of surmise about the likely outcome of the search, a view that unity, when found, would contain the four points. So, against this background, a 'ministry acknowledged by all' might not have been intended as an imperialistic rewording.

However, when the American bishops took the Quadrilateral to the Lambeth Conference of 1888, it became known subsequently as the 'Lambeth' Quadrilateral, and regarded as stating the essentials for a reunited Church as laid down by the Church of England, a quasi-Anglican ultimatum, terms for corporate reunion, not a basis for discussion with a view to ultimate reunion. This confirmed the worst fears of the non-Anglican churches. In 1890 the Wesleyan Conference[5] rejected the Quadrilateral altogether: its four points, especially the last, it said, 'do not . . . provide a practical ground for the discussion of the subject', and true unity 'does not necessarily require the corporate Union'. But in the Lambeth Appeal of 1920,[6] as Hinchliff has pointed out, the version of the Quadrilateral and its context were in fact close to the original. It did not specify the Apostolic succession as essential. It introduced the four points by: 'We believe that the visible unity of the Church will be found to involve the whole-hearted acceptance of . . . '

Discussions about union between the churches after 1913 took place against the background of a dispute between the Anglo-Catholic Bishop of Zanzibar, Frank Weston (1871–1924), and two Evangelical Bishops from neighbouring dioceses. At a missionary conference at Kikuyu in June 1913, the two Church Missionary Society Bishops proposed a federation of churches in their dioceses, and celebrated a joint Eucharist on the closing day. The federation basis was to be common acceptance of the Apostles' and Nicene Creeds; recognition of common membership between its churches; the right of receiving communion in any of them; and permission for recognised ministers to preach in other federated churches. Each society would remain autonomous in its own sphere, but work towards a common form of church organisation. The scheme triggered a furious reaction from Weston, protesting to Davidson and threatening to indict his fellow bishops. The episcopacy, for example, he said, had not been taught at the Conference as the fundamental principle of Church order, nor was the sacramental system given its proper place.

In his official response on 1915 Davidson accepted that the joint communion service at Kikuyu had been a spontaneous act, but inaugurated no general policy, and clergy should, in future, abstain from such services at the close of conferences. Baptised Christians, temporarily deprived of their own churches' ministrations, might be admitted to the eucharist in Anglican churches, but Anglicans should not 'seek communion at the hands of Nonconformist ministers'. The scheme was aborted, and the reply solved very little. But it sketched out the battleground and warned future combatants of the minefields. Lidgett was understanding.[7] He praised Davidson's balanced judgement and encouragement to further thought and effort within and outside his church. He remarked nevertheless on one issue destined not to disappear: 'Proposals which stop short of intercommunion are . . . to our mind unsatisfactory and halting. No one, however, who realises the present state of things, would expect the Archbishop to pronounce in favour of such intercommunion.'

So much for the background to what became known as Joint Interim Discussions on Faith and Order. They made a faltering start.

When Brent and Gardiner's proposal reached Davidson, he appointed a committee to consider it, but no action was taken until an American episcopal deputation to the Church of England arrived on 25 June 1912. Davidson agreed to stimulate interest through his committee, chaired by W. G. Kennion, Bishop of Bath and Wells. Anglicans, he promised, would be ready to meet any duly appointed representatives of the Nonconformists in England, but the invitation to their churches to join in discussions should be initiated by their 'co-religionists' in America. Disliking rushed discussions, Davidson sought to avoid publicity likely to arouse premature expectations, polemics and controversy. This became clear when the leader of the 1914 delegation made a request to Davidson and Meyer for press announcements about the visit and about a 'Truce of God' to precede the proposed Faith and Order Conference. Robert Gardiner sought to intervene according to Davidson's wishes but it was really too late.[8]

The omens for success in 1913 were distinctly discouraging. Having called a meeting of the committee for 7 July, Kennion admitted to Davidson[9] on 2 May that his first task was to stimulate its members with a desire to work with others outside their own church before the need to communicate with them actually arose. He saw little hope of Anglicans working with Nonconformists while the latter maintained their intolerant attitude on education and Welsh Disestablishment. Tatlow (1876–1957), the Committee's Secretary, told Davidson frankly on 13 November[10] that some members wanted to do nothing. But, faced by the imminent arrival of a delegation from the USA in the New Year, Davidson gave formal permission for the committee to meet its members. Meetings with English Free Churchmen were anticipated later.

At the end of 1913 Lidgett announced[11] the deputation's forthcoming visit and its aim to gain co-operation for the proposed World Conference. To attend this Conference when it took place, the Wesleyan Conference at Plymouth in 1913 had appointed Davison and Simon as its representatives, along with two eminent laymen to be appointed by the President. The Church of England appointed what Lidgett rightly called its own 'very influential Committee' to make preliminary arrangements.

Shortly after Lidgett's *Methodist Times* article the Free Church Council appointed him, together with Meyer and A. E. Garvie (a Congregationalist, a skilled committee man and known for ecumenical enthusiasm), to act on behalf of Nonconformist churches interested in the World Conference Movement. He was very enthusiastic: 'Every conceivable interest of the Universal Church', he said, 'stands to gain by closer fellowship and co-operation between all its branches', and the British churches should respond to the initiative. In the event, the deputation was non-episcopal, since Bishop Hamilton of the Methodist Episcopal Church could not come for family reasons. Dr Newman Smyth (Congregationalist), Dr W. H. Roberts (Presbyterian) and Dr Peter Ainslie (Disciples of Christ) arrived on 8 January 1914.

Lidgett[12] and Meyer arranged for 'influential' Free Church representatives to meet the deputation, soon after its arrival, for dinner at the Hotel Metropole.[13] Over 100 attended; Compton-Rickett MP, NCEFC President-designate for 1915/16, acted as host. Replying to Archbishop Fisher at a lunch in his honour on 5 October 1949, Lidgett claimed[14] to have introduced the American delegation to 'Anglicans as well as the Free Churches'.

Kennion's Committee met the deputation officially on 29 January at Church House. The English Churches' task was to explore, ahead of the proposed World Conference, the extent of agreement among themselves on the issues of Faith and Order. Representatives from Nonconformist denominations were invited, alongside the three NCEFC nominees, to meet a subcommittee of 20 members of the Archbishop's Committee on 15 June in Westminster's Jerusalem Chamber. The questions for debate were: 'In what direction should we look for Christian unity as being hopeful? Should we look in the direction of common work or common sympathy, or should we seek to study together what is the dogmatic basis of the Church?' So many attended that they agreed to devolve discussion to a small subcommittee: five from the Anglican Church should meet five Free Churchmen to try to arrive at 'some common statement on our Faith' and assess how far they 'agreed upon matters relating to Order'.[15]

The representatives elected were Bishops Kennion, Talbot and Gore, with Tatlow and Eugene Stock on the Anglican side; Lidgett represented the NCEFC; Davison, Garvie, Shakespeare and Anderson Scott (Presbyterian Church of England) their own denominations. After meeting 'at 3 different periods' this joint subcommittee reported to the full Anglican and Nonconformist Committees on 29 October 1915. Having agreed to some verbal alterations on 26 November 1915, it published its (in fact first and brief) Interim Report, *Towards Christian Unity*, in February 1916.[16] The only dissentient on its publication was the Anglican, Dr Frere, who preferred reunion orientated towards Rome.

The subcommittee was then enlarged, on one side with William Temple and Prof. H. L. Goudge, and on the other by Principal Selbie (Congregational) and H. G. Wood (Society of Friends). Their (often lengthy) meetings were held, usually in London, but once (in January 1917) overnight at Talbot's Farnham Castle. They ended in the summer of 1917, and published the Second Interim Report in March 1918.[17]

Lidgett's account[18] conflates the findings of both reports. He said that members of the committee had reached unanimity on the faith and 'the doctrine of the spiritual nature and constitution of Christ's Church', but that they divided over whether ecclesiastical Order was essential or subordinate to the Faith. They finally agreed that, whatever scheme of Church government was proposed, it should include: episcopacy, 'purged of the evils of Prelacy'; 'the Presbyterate, substantially as held by all the Non-Episcopal Communions'; and 'full recognition of the rights and responsibilities of the laity in the government of the Church'.

The texts of the two reports reveal more detail. The first set of discussions was principally concerned with establishing agreement on the Faith, though not on a creed for subscription. Differences were recognised over the nature of the envisaged reunited visible society; on the precise conditions which made the two major sacraments effective channels of God's grace; and on whether ministerial authority was gained through episcopal or presbyteral succession, or through the community of believers.

The second report reveals a concentration on Order. There was a similar desire not to formulate a detailed basis for reunion, nor to analyse the merits of any polity (still less to indicate any preference), nor engage in abstract discussion of the origin of the episcopate historically, or its authority doctrinally. The aim was repeated: to set out grounds and ideas to be considered at the proposed World Conference, and 'secure an atmosphere congenial not to controversy but agreement'. The step forward was to state that the committee desired from the Anglican and Free Church Communions 'not grudging concessions, but a willing acceptance for the common enrichment of the united Church of the wealth distinctive of each'. The committee hoped that in a united Church each would bring its own individual contribution not only to the common life of the Church but also to its methods of organisation.

The report had to comment on the controversial issue of episcopacy. It acknowledged that churches which had not accepted episcopacy had still been used by the Holy Spirit. They had come into being through reaction from grave abuses in the Church at the time of their origin. None of the committee's proposals would involve any Communion disowning its past, and on this basis episcopacy, embraced by the greater part of Christendom, should be effectively preserved. But, following the primitive ideal and practice, episcopacy should 're-assume a constitutional form, both as regards the method of election of the bishop as by clergy and people, and the method of government after the election'. Acceptance of the fact of the episcopacy, not any theory about its character, was thought all that could be requested: only on these lines was there any prospect of agreement on reunion.

In the *Methodist Times* of 11 April and 5 September 1918 Lidgett explained the findings to readers within his own and other Free Church denominations. Tactful persuasion was required if they were to give the report a sympathetic reception. In April he assured them the legitimate freedom of the prophetic ministry would be preserved, and a greater elasticity in the organisation and work of the Church than had hitherto been known would result. Shakespeare's participation in the discussions proved, he said, that his proposals for Free Church union were intended to assist, not block the way to larger union.

In September Lidgett emphasised the value of preserving the episcopate *under democratic conditions*, 'not on the score of antiquity and prevalence, but as an effective instrument for the administration of the Church'. At the same time he reiterated his warnings against the danger of preoccupation with organisation and any human ministry. Unity, he said, must be sought and found 'in the headship of Christ, exercised through his living Spirit', thereby making it possible to 'unify all ministries and methods without being in bondage to any of them'.[19]

Much later, in 1928,[20] Lidgett observed that issues raised by the Report had prepared the way for the 1920 Lambeth Appeal. But the War caused the World Conference, for which it was intended, to be postponed. A Preliminary Conference in Geneva on 12–20 August 1920 appointed a Continuation Committee, responsible for arranging the major World Conference along the lines originally envisaged, to discuss aspects of Faith and Order important to Christian unity. Again, all churches which 'confessed Jesus Christ as God and Saviour' were invited on equal terms, with no preconditions or commitment to any intention of adopting any scheme for reunion. But the Lambeth Appeal, inviting a response from the Free Churches, preceded, and to a large extent pre-empted, the committee's work, as far as England was concerned.

In letters of 11 and 17 December 1918 exchanged with Tatlow[21] Lidgett tactfully registered surprise that the Joint Interim Committee had decided to send its report direct to the denominational commissions: coyly he said he must have left the Jerusalem Chamber meeting early. Diplomacy would have led him to propose a preliminary conference to explain its contents and avoid the potential misunderstanding and rejection arising from commissions meeting separately. This concern had increased, he said, now the *British Weekly* 'article on Mr Shakespeare' had raised the issue of reordination, and been used to spread alarm about the main proposals of the Second Interim Report.

Several joint Free Church/Anglican conferences took place in 1918, 1919 (6–8 January) and 1920 (7–9 January) in Mansfield College, Oxford. They were initiated after the Interim Faith and Order conversations had ended, not as Lidgett stated[22] during their course.

What Lidgett describes as 'an influential group of Evangelical clergy' not represented on the Interim Committee, had decided independently to approach recognised leaders of the Evangelical Free Churches for discussions, in effect duplicating the officially sponsored ones.

The 65 participants in these conferences in 1918 and 1919 represented in roughly equal numbers the Anglican Church on the one side and the Free Churches on the other. The membership was impressive. Among the Anglicans, Lidgett specifically mentioned S. H. Clark (Vicar of Tonbridge), the organiser of the meetings; F. S. Guy Warman (Vicar of Bradford, later Bishop of Truro, Chelmsford and Manchester); C. Lisle Carr (Archdeacon of Norwich, later Bishop of Hereford); J. Gough McCormick (Vicar of St Michael's, Chester Square, Chaplain to HM the King, later Dean of Manchester); and T. Guy Rogers (Vicar of West Ham, Chaplain to HM the King). Other prominent Anglican participants listed in *Towards Reunion*,[23] the symposium of papers delivered at the conferences, included: M. Linton Smith (Bishop of Warrington, later of Hereford and Rochester), C. C. B. Bardsley (Hon. Sec. CMS, later Bishop of Peterborough), and J. E. Watts-Ditchfield (Bishop of Chelmsford). The last wrote to Davidson on 12 August 1919[24] to say that the Oxford Conference Report 'more or less represented the opinions of the largest section of the Evangelical School'. With Bardsley, McCormick and Warman, his trusted friends, the bishop had in May 1918[25] been engaged in 'private conferences with leaders of all the Nonconformist bodies'. The Free Church representation included virtually all those involved in the Interim Committee, and others such as Horton, Meyer, Peake, Guttery and Rattenbury.[26]

Towards Reunion was edited by S. H. Clark, A. J. Carlyle (Chaplain of University College, Oxford), Shakespeare, and Lidgett who also contributed the introductory article, 'Re-union and the Advancement of Christ's Kingdom'.[27] The subtitle of the conference volume was modest: 'Being Contributions to Mutual Understanding by Church of England and Free Church Writers'. Each writer was responsible for his own contribution, leaving it, as the editors said: 'to the Holy Spirit to reveal the essential unity that underlies it all, believing that this spiritual element will perhaps be found to be the most conspicuous contribution we have to offer to the cause of Unity'.[28] At the same time the symposium reflected considerable consensus. Lidgett thought[29] the result of the discussions similar to that of the Second Interim Committee Report:[30] 'save that the Evangelical clergy took substantially the same view of the subordination of Church Order' as held by the Free Churchmen.

The editors predictably expressed their 'full conviction that the only Catholicity strong enough to bear the weight of the coming days is the Evangelical'.[31] They believed any Church unity to stand the test of time would be 'of complex form'. It would need, they said, to include three major features: definite rights and functions of the laity; episcopacy, 'as the emblem and instrument of unity and order, but with strict limitations, lest an unspiritual and independent autocracy once more raise its head to corrupt the Church'; and presbytery, 'with equal spiritual rights and duties, called by the Church itself to exercise its inherent spiritual functions'. They recognised that one obstacle to reunion, Church Establishment, was beyond their present scope: 'It is clear that the type of "Constitutional" episcopacy, contemplated in this volume as the only possible basis of organic Reunion, cannot be realised under the existing relations of Church and State.'

The volume's contributors were the Bishops of Durham and Warrington, Carlyle, E. A. Burroughs (Canon of Peterborough in 1917, Bishop of Ripon in 1926), J. Gough McCormick, Gresford Jones (Archdeacon of Sheffield, later Bishop of Warrington) and Guy Rogers on the Anglican side, and for the Free Churches, Lidgett, Peake, the Congregationalists Forsyth, Garvie, Vernon Bartlett and Horton, and the Presbyterian Carnegie Simpson.

The volume reprinted Carlyle's article on the 'Historic Episcopate' from the March 1918 issue of Lidgett's *Contemporary Review*. It urged the need to restore 'the primitive and constitutional character of the Episcopate, re-establishing the concert of Bishops and Presbyters' and to secure 'for the laity their full rights in Church government'.[32] Carlyle said,

> It is at least possible that many who would refuse to consider the acceptance of the Episcopate under its present conditions may be disposed to think somewhat differently of such a constitutional and representative system . . . much nearer to the real meaning of the 'Historic Episcopate' than that which has obtained during the last four centuries.[33]

Lidgett thought Free Churchmen, Methodists in particular, should welcome movement in such directions 'in the interests of the Anglican Church and also in those of Christian union, or at all events, of much closer co-operation than has hitherto been attempted'.

In much of what he wrote over the years Lidgett was impatient of detail and minutiae: he was far more at home with the grand vision, especially the vision of the Church in Ephesians. He felt that, fully grasped, this would lead to the solution of all problems. Visible unity, for example, was in his opinion clearly envisaged there. He could not 'imagine that St Paul entertained invisible unity alone', separating earth from heaven. To rest content with some kind of spiritual unity (now, he said, fortunately abandoned by Low Churchmen)[34] between separate churches was unacceptable. The only satisfactory unity, he believed, was corporate, and on the basis of mutual recognition.

His article in *Towards Reunion*, based on Ephesians, aimed to stress 'the spiritual importance of Reunion as essential to the development of true Catholicity'.[35] He meant Christ's followers needed to grasp that reunion was their spiritual duty, essential if the Kingdom of 'Our Father' was to be realised on earth through his Son, and if, beyond this, God's comprehensive, Catholic purpose was to be achieved. The destiny of mankind was, he said, to be brought into unity of life with the one God and Father through the one Christ. The world needed unity, as plans to form the League of Nations clearly illustrated.

The Church, he then argued, was the divinely appointed instrument of the unity of mankind. A divided Church hindered the object of its existence, contradicting the purpose and law of its being. The unifier of mankind must be unified herself. It was mistaken, Lidgett thought, to argue that unity would sacrifice freedom, or that divisions in the Church must be good because each had arisen from concern for the truth. Only a united Church could fulfil its evangelical responsibility and satisfy its intense desire to see the Christian faith applied to political, moral and social issues; social reconstruction, to be successful, depended on reunion.

On 17 January 1918 Lidgett asked in the *Methodist Times* whether the churches would follow the League's example, accepting mutual recognition without betrayal of their past as essential. In progress towards Church unity mutual recognition seemed the only basis for 'an agreed order which will absorb and transform the great historic forms of Church government from first to last by common agreement'. In making their distinct contributions none of the various Protestant churches, he optimistically suggested, would be lost; all would be improved. Imperfections that might be attributed to each were, he thought, owing to their one-sided development. On 24 January 1918 he insisted the ministry should exist for the whole body, not vice versa.

J. E. Rattenbury, Wesleyan enthusiast for unity with the Anglican Church, kept up the current momentum by arranging a series of Sunday afternoon conferences from 23 February to early April in 1919 in his church, Kingsway Hall. He attracted a wide range of speakers, successively the Bishop of London, Dr Orchard, Lord Hugh Cecil, Lidgett, the Bishop of Chelmsford, Selbie and Shakespeare.

A different conference of Anglicans and Free Churchmen took place in December 1919. This was attended by Congregationalists such as C. H. Dodd and Vernon Bartlett, but, as it happens, no Wesleyans were present. Anglicans included Bishop Baynes, Stuart Clark, F. A. Cockin, Guy Rogers, H. Rashdall, N. Talbot, Tatlow and the Bishop of Warrington. Their document, *Concerning Christian Unity*,[36] said the current situation (in Foreign Missions, in the creation of the League of Nations, in moves to reorder society after the war) and the fellowship for which the Church stood made visible reunion a matter of urgency, an essential item for the Lambeth Conference agenda. Preparing for union called for opportunities for instruction in each other's system, for worship and widespread interdenominational activity. A particular plea was made for a representative conference to meet to pray and reach definite conclusions. Intercommunion, they urged, should be authorised where Communion was not available in the Christian's normal church and, *pace* Kikuyu, when there were joint conferences and special occasions.

Yet another conference, in what seems to have become a January series, was attended by Anglican and Free Church representatives in Mansfield College, Oxford, from 7 to 9 January 1920. The Free Churchmen included Lidgett, Rattenbury, Brash, Peake, and United Methodist, Baptist and Congregationalist representatives. The Anglicans included J. T. Inskip (Bishop of Barking from 1919), Bishop Willis of Uganda, Arthur Robinson (Canon of Canterbury), T. A. Lacey (Canon of Worcester), O. Quick (Vicar of Kenley) and William Temple (Canon of Westminster). This represented a wide spectrum of Anglican opinion. On 17 February 1920 Temple informed Davidson[37] that he had been deputed, with the Bishop of Warrington, Carlyle, Arthur Robinson and Burroughs, to explain to the Archbishops the discussions behind the conference's unanimous resolutions.

These included such matters as the common recognition of all the churches represented and the efficacy of their ministrations; the need for outward, visible expression of unity by means (under 'due authority') of pulpit exchange, mutual admission to Holy Communion, and the possibility of authorising ministers to 'minister fully and freely in churches of other denominations'. Authorisation was not, they said, to imply reordination or repudiation of the ministers' previous status; it referred to the authority held by the denomination concerned to be the proper one for the action concerned. Accordingly, 'authorisation to minister fully and freely' in the Anglican Church would require 'the imposition of the Bishop's hands'.[38] The conference agreed the reunited Church must be episcopal, but would conserve the essential values of other historical types of Church polity. Writing to Davidson on 11 January 1920, Canon Lacey reflected the views of his fellow Anglo-Catholic, the Bishop of London: he wondered whether 'it might be possible to dispense with the diaconate, promoting the candidate [Nonconformist minister] *per saltum* to the priesthood'.[39]

In June 1920 a conference was convened in Oxford specifically to study the theological questions underlying the problems of reunion.[40] Its members were almost all teachers of theology: Anglicans, including Lacey, Quick, A. E. J. Rawlinson, Streeter and A. C. Headlam, met on 25 and 26 June 1920, and again on 29 and 30 June, this time with representatives of non-episcopal communions. The Wesleyan College theologians, W. J. Moulton, F. W. Platt, W. W. Holdsworth and Lofthouse were invited, but not Lidgett: he had no college base.

Writing within weeks of the Lambeth Conference Headlam sent to Davidson[41] on 2 July 1920 two letters, one with the conference resolutions and the other with his private comments. As often before, members had realised how largely they were agreed in all the most essential matters of faith. He said they generally accepted episcopacy would be the basis of Church order, but in a representative and constitutional form, without the meaning given to the 'Apostolic Succession'. Though High Churchmen did not consider Wesleyans as part of the Church because they had not been episcopally confirmed, this, Headlam reported, was not held by the large majority of Anglicans. The Free Churchmen were prepared to agree to reordination if it did not invalidate or put a slur on their current orders. The conference saw agreement to the Creeds as most important, but tests as less necessary or desirable. Headlam seemed to think the United Church was on the way, and if the Church of England was not to be a backwater, it should seize the initiative, becoming the leader of a reunited episcopal, not a Presbyterian church!

One particularly interesting resolution of the conference was very similar to what Lidgett had advocated earlier: to urge the creation of a representative council to express formally and authoritatively Christian opinion on national and international affairs where these touched on moral principles.

Headlam's own Bampton lectures, published only a month or so before the Lambeth Conference, made a contribution to the unity debate. *The Doctrine of the Church and Christian Reunion* acknowledged schism[42] within the Church of England as well as between the Church and other Christian 'bodies'. He suggested the Quadrilateral should be the basis of discussion, with no fixed interpretation required and no questions raised on valid or invalid ministries. H. D. Rack points out[43] that the Lambeth Appeal seems to reflect this in its promise not to question the 'spiritual reality' of Nonconformist ministries. Mutual recognition of ministries would, in Headlam's view, have to be followed, however, by invariable episcopal ordination.

The wide diversity of Anglican opinion was certainly clear from the Church's own internal debate, illustrated below. Throughout his tenure of office Davidson had sought to achieve a balance on his committees of high, broad and evangelical churchmen, but the various groupings had long been at liberty to hold meetings and conferences of their own, with or without invitations to Nonconformists.

As a NCEFC official, Lidgett's affinities lay with Evangelical Anglicans, but he was careful not to be wholly identified with them. He wanted to maintain contact with Davidson and show understanding of and sympathy with a broader church view. Much of what was being said within Anglican circles for and against unity only reached him indirectly (he kept alert for press comment), but their evidently close concern with the issue put his Free Church problems in context and afforded him some degree of encouragement.

The Islington Conference of Anglican Evangelical clergy and laity had been held annually since 1827, but in 1916 its members were invited to an additional conference by H. A. Wilson, recently installed as Rector of Cheltenham. Under his chairmanship this became an annual event in Cheltenham, except in 1918 when London was chosen as the venue. Though other items figured on the agenda, participants were much concerned to study steps to bring about closer union with the Nonconformist churches. They laid great stress on the national crisis as calling for a united front, for which co-operation on the battlefield and in overseas missions had provided a good augury.

Discussion of closer union with the Nonconformist churches led them in 1917 to declare strongly in favour of overcoming existing obstacles. According to Lidgett,[44] their September meeting considered Nonconformists were members of the Church of Christ equally with Anglicans, but even more significantly that their ministers were exercising ministries of grace equally with their

Anglican counterparts, and rightly and duly administering the sacraments like them. Moreover no proposal for reordination in any scheme for reunion was thought welcome or practicable.

The Evangelicals called for prompt and definite action. They saw one visible society of all believers as the ultimate goal, involving some form of federation rather than organic reunion. Each year they largely reiterated and amplified their recommendations. Pending consummation of visible unity, churches which could assent to the Quadrilateral's first three articles, including the Apostles' and Nicene Creeds, should be fully recognised as branches of the Church of Christ. They considered episcopacy should be accepted as a fact, without any theory of its origin. Legal barriers to inviting recognised ministers of non-episcopal churches to preach should be removed, and interchange of pulpits at Peace services was recommended. Full members of the Free Churches should be admitted to Holy Communion in the Church of England, and reciprocally Anglicans should not be discouraged from taking Holy Communion in non-episcopal churches.

Lidgett welcomed their views in 1917, 1918[45] and later. To him it was remarkable and pleasing that Evangelical Anglicans no longer favoured invisible unity. He emphasised to his readership that, while accepting the authority of the historic episcopate, they had agreed that the Free Church claim for mutual recognition was valid. But his welcome in the *Methodist Times* of 27 September 1917, for example, was expressed in characteristically well-chosen words: 'Movement throughout the Church of England on these lines would bring immense impetus'. He was a realist.

Nevertheless the Anglican Evangelicals were divided. Their findings, though generally agreed, were not unanimous. When Davidson received them, he told the Bishop of Chelmsford privately on 11 August 1919 that he thought some participants vehement and unbalanced, and the Cheltenham proposals 'indicate a strange want of appreciation of our difficulties'.[46] Lidgett would not have been surprised! The Bishop was an Evangelical himself, but like Davidson wary of extremists. Writing on 16 May 1918, he had warned Davidson about the more militant Protestants led by Wilson, and the wholesale action which might result from the Cheltenham Conference being arranged in London.[47] The Bishop wanted organic union, but without short cuts. After the 1919 conference he advised Davidson that Evangelicals were losing ground as a party: attendance had been lower than before, and participants were men of little weight except the speakers. Yet, as a school of thought, Evangelicals generally, he warned, were gaining ground.[48]

On 18 May 1918 the Archbishops set up a committee to explore 'in what ways and within what limits effect can rightly be given to the desire for co-operation in regard to Christian teaching and united prayer between churchpeople and Nonconformists': in fact to decide whether teaching and prayer could be conducted in consecrated buildings by non-members of the Church of England.[49]

The Bishop of Hereford protested[50] that 'the great twin brothers Winchester and Oxford', fellow committee members, did not 'mean anything to be done along this line!' The Bishop of Chelmsford (convenor) found[51] opposition to any recognition of Nonconformity within consecrated buildings among 'men of extreme views', but advocates were not confined to Evangelicals. In its report on 28 June 1919 the committee could not recommend exchange of pulpits, but more ample opportunities were suggested for united fellowship, conferences and worship, though outside ordinary and liturgical services, and with appropriate safeguards; and the committee was not inclined to refuse the use of Anglican churches for the purpose.[52] On 23 July Davidson saw the group of issues as raising 'an administrative question' rather than one 'of fundamental importance': they need not wait for the Lambeth Conference.

The issue of pulpit exchange did not die. On 25 June 1918 a deputation, including the former Bishop of Ripon, Wilson of Cheltenham and Tatlow, visited the Archbishops to argue that reunion should be promoted by pulpit interchange. They stressed the intellectual solidarity of Christian scholars and the increasing appreciation on both sides of Anglican and Nonconformist literary productions. Davidson recorded no comment.[53]

Just over a year later, on 29 August 1919, a letter to *The Times*, signed by Lidgett, Forsyth, Jowett, Selbie, Shakespeare, Gillie and Carnegie Simpson, applauded a sermon by Bishop Pollock of Norwich. This advocated the interchange of pulpits at the 'usual normal worship',[54] not in an unguarded way which might cause confusion, but under carefully specified conditions: preachers would need to assent to the first three articles of the Lambeth Quadrilateral; agree not to discuss Church Order unless specifically invited to do so; and gain the consent of the proper authorities. Free Churchmen welcomed this as 'one step to reunion', cautious, but definite, practical and made by a Bishop. In a letter to the Bishop[55] Davidson seemed to have been forewarned of Pollock's intention, but he had by then decided to yield 'to many of the foremost members of Convocation' and postpone discussion until the Lambeth Conference.

September 1919 saw much lively correspondence in the press over the matter. In pressing on Davidson[56] the importance, prior to the Lambeth Conference, of welcoming the opportunities which would arise from his proposal, Pollock had the support of the Bishops of Durham (Moule), Manchester (Knox), Carlisle (Diggle), Sodor and Man (Thompson), Bristol (Nickson), Hereford (Henson), Worcester (Pearce), St Albans (Jacob) and Ripon (Drury). Six of the nine were elderly: Moule and Jacob died in 1920, while Diggle, Drury, Knox and Thompson were nearing the end of their careers.

Davidson replied[57] on 30 October that Provincial debates and possible action should follow, not precede, the wider Lambeth discussions. He felt confident 'the personal friendship which I enjoy with several of the eminent Nonconformist Divines' (he referred specifically to Lidgett[58] among those who signed *The Times* letter) ensured they would not misunderstand his decision or 'suppose . . . any thought of postponing indefinitely the settlement of the practical question at issue'.

Pollock then proposed an informal meeting between himself, several bishops and Free Church leaders to emphasise friendship and fellowship, remove misunderstandings about what he meant or implied, excuse the delay and explain the response. Writing to *The Times*, Meyer, as NCEFC spokesman, congratulated the Bishop on his approach.[59] He welcomed the correction of false expectations of 'reunion' as if it involved amalgamation or absorption and implied episcopal ordination 'to which the immense majority of our Free Church people would be entirely opposed'. His insistence on the integrity of each denomination and that any interchange of preachers should be on absolutely equal terms, was, he said, consistent with what Pollock was advocating. A letter from Lidgett would have been differently phrased! The local issue faded, the national one remained.

Another, and more daring, local experiment, notable for the support of William Temple, had been proposed late in 1917 by S. M. Berry, Minister of Carr's Lane Congregational Church, and the expatriate former Bishop of Natal, then Assistant to the Bishop of Birmingham and Cathedral Rector. They proposed in a letter to Davidson dated 30 January 1918,[60] that Carr's Lane and the cathedral should be worked as parts of one Church, its members retaining existing variety in their forms and order of worship. Baynes was willing to be admitted by the usual ceremony to fellowship and office at Carr's Lane, while Berry would be admitted to Holy Orders by Confirmation and Ordination. They would exchange pulpits, and organise in brotherly equality their pastoral and congregational activities. Hoping the experiment might be made, Temple wrote to Davidson on 18 April 1918: 'The deliberations of the entire Church bodies may be greatly helped by experience gained through individual action'.[61]

Insuperable obstacles were raised by Davidson and his chaplain:[62] differences between one individual, autonomous Congregational Church and the nationally organised Anglican Church with its three orders of ministry; the contrast between Anglican and Congregational ordination, involving a congregation's 'call' to a minister; legal barriers to celebrating sacraments in any other form than the Prayer Book; and the requirement for recipients of Communion to be confirmed. Davidson decided that giving formal sanction to the experiment 'would, in the eyes of many, outdo Kikuyu fivefold!'

A major issue was that of intercommunion. Prominent Anglicans discussing this were unlikely to have forgotten Kikuyu in 1913 nor an earlier initiative in

1911 and the way Davidson reacted to it. Frankly admitting that objections to cordial intercommunion came from a clerical party in his own church opposed to the principles of the Reformation, Percival, the Bishop of Hereford, had invited members of nearby Free Churches to a special service of Holy Communion in his cathedral to celebrate the coronation of King George V.

Lidgett welcomed[63] the 'Catholicity' of the celebration, but it provoked a furious reaction from Lord Halifax. During the flurry of correspondence[64] Davidson professed himself 'largely' in sympathy with Percival's purpose, but stated:

> [Those] who are quite as anxious as either you or I can be to promote a wider unity and a closer drawing together of Nonconformists to ourselves are emphatic . . . that the particular step you took was at the present juncture unwise, and that it must set back for a long time to come the cause which was, I hoped, prospering just because of our abstention from formal acts of that sort which must crystallise our differences.

A distinction had to be drawn, he insisted, between, on the one hand, 'letting it quietly be known that we have no desire to repel any good Christian man, and the responsibility rests with the individual communicant', and on the other 'a formal Episcopal utterance specifically inviting to Communion those who . . . are not qualified to communicate'. Even moderates, not just High Churchmen, were, he said, upset by the bishop's action.

Percival apologised, but could not refrain from hoping his action might be helpful in its desire to break down the High Church party's obsolete notions concerning apostolic succession, and their conception of schism and refusal of communion to men who were as truly Christian as they were. Eleven years later Lidgett was the first Nonconformist to preach in Hereford Cathedral[65] to a crowded congregation.

Bishop Welldon, formerly Bishop of Calcutta (1898–1902), then Dean of Manchester, was invited by Lidgett in 1917 to contribute to the *Contemporary Review* on 'The Problem of Christian Reunion'. He would have come to Lidgett's notice as a Bishop with an evangelical background, known for Temperance views and, more importantly, for his desire for reunion, first with Nonconformists and ultimately with all Christian churches. But Welldon's article stressed that intercommunion required assent to episcopacy.

Lidgett had to respond. In the *Methodist Times* of July 1917, as often, he began positively. Anglicans would naturally want to argue that episcopacy might become 'a most effective expression of unity and instrument of progress'. Moreover, to him the advantages of episcopacy were unquestionable if it were to be remodelled to become 'primitive and democratic'. But why it should be a *condition* of intercommunion was far from evident. Church government was one thing, fellowship another. Progress to reunion depended on readiness to recognise a common spiritual life; 'ecclesiastical organisation is not the creator, but only the instrument' of that life. It was only when 'one body and one spirit' were recognised, he said, that 'we can secure the essential conditions of reunion and indispensable conditions of unity in Church government'.

On 24 February 1919 Tatlow, Chairman of the Anglican Fellowship Committee, urged Davidson[66] to give further thought to the Intercommunion issue. In their memorandum, reporting the views of its Conference members, including Oliver Quick, A. E. J. Rawlinson and C. E. Raven, the Committee wished to stress its concern that, while spiritual fellowship between the churches was increasing, some Christians' tendency to abstain from taking Communion to avoid breaking the fellowship effectively relegated the Eucharist to a secondary position. At the same time they did not want 'to press for action which could lead either to a shallow unity or to strife'.

This phrase was seized upon by Davidson in a strongly worded reply[67] on 3 March 1919. What they had proposed, he wrote, 'would lead not only to strife but immediate schism!'. As over the exchange of pulpits, he postponed full discussion of Intercommunion until the Lambeth Conference, but he did not regard it 'as now desirable that Anglicans should be encouraged to communicate at celebrations of Holy Communion conducted by ministers of all or any Christian Church'.

Undaunted, C. W. Emmett, the Fellowship's next Chairman, adopted on 8 June 1920 a less sensitive approach to the unity issue. He wrote to Davidson, enclosing a letter for the Lambeth Conference.[68] Recalling their earlier memorandum, the Fellowship cited their close touch with the younger generation and its enthusiasm for a new relationship between the churches, and welcomed the prominent place of unity in the Lambeth agenda.

A major intervention was made in January 1920.[69] The Bishop of Warrington and others sent a pamphlet, *Resolutions on Intercommunion*, to Davidson and all Diocesan Bishops, regretting past exclusions from Holy Communion. It stated the conviction that the Church had a duty, already being observed in many places, to admit to Holy Communion baptised believers who accepted the first three articles of the Lambeth Quadrilateral. Defying the Kikuyu pronouncement, the signatories had no objection in principle to solemn acts of intercommunion on national or special occasions. The time had come, they said, to allow Anglicans to communicate in other churches: they saw no ground in principle against intercommunion becoming reciprocal. It could be a step towards corporate unity when a really deep realisation of spiritual unity existed. They admitted, however, that interchange of ministrations between episcopally and non-episcopally ordained ministers remained an issue.

These views were shown to have considerable support: the Bishop of Warrington (M. L. Smith) and fellow signatories of the covering letter to the

Archbishop were backed[70] first by 156 and finally by a total of 1204 clergy, including Guy Rogers, Carlyle, S. H. Clark and H. A. Wilson.

Army chaplains also had expressed their views to Davidson. To the more rigid Anglo-Catholics at or near the battle front 'Comprehensive Churchmanship ("YMCA religion") was aesthetically distasteful and theologically anathema'.[71] But camaraderie among other chaplains and soldiers, acutely conscious of the war's effect on attitudes to Christianity among troops and civilians, contributed to the pressure for Church unity. After a conference on 12–14 March 1919 at the Chaplains' School in France, a pamphlet, *Resolutions on Christian Unity*, was submitted to Davidson[72] and the various church authorities. The chaplains included such Anglicans as Bishop Gwynne (Deputy Chaplain General) and Edward and Neville Talbot (the Bishop of Winchester's sons); and among Free Churchmen one Wesleyan, W. J. Moulton. They stressed the reality of their fellowship and the benefits they had received from joint conferences and retreats. Their main message was that the approach to Christian unity should begin with intercommunion, at least at joint conferences and retreats. They admitted, however, they had not all agreed on this. The Archbishop was asked for his ruling in time for their June meeting, but their proposals were routed to the Joint Faith and Order Committee, and no ruling was given.

A different request then came from Anglicans alone. On 25 June 1919 several ex-chaplains, including Bishop Gwynne, Neville Talbot and Milner-White, emphasised to Davidson the unique opportunity of the forthcoming Peace celebrations, not only to express common gratitude to God, but to stress the essential unity of all Christians. For this purpose they asked, without success, that bishops and clergy be encouraged to hold on the Celebration Sunday joint services with all ministers who wished to join them, and to invite ministers of other denominations to preach in Anglican pulpits.

During the twelve months preceding the Lambeth Conference, as the debate was nearing its end, the two extremes of Anglican opinion were starkly illustrated among the Archbishop's papers by two letters protesting against unity, and by a memorandum pressing for its achievement.

In July 1919 several Anglicans, claiming to represent widely different schools of thought, sent Davidson a memorandum[73] summarising their convictions after the series of conferences on Church union. Signatories of the covering letter included the Bishop of Warrington, but the memorandum was also signed by (among others) Bishop Baynes, Raven, W. R. Inge and H. Rashdall. Those who accepted the first three articles of the Lambeth Quadrilateral were, they believed, true members of the Church of Christ; their ministry was a true ministry, not inoperative as a means of grace, even if irregular according to historic Catholic order; and if these views were to be admitted in acts sanctioned by corporate authority as well as in words, the way would be open to a joint reconsideration of differences of Order which, they thought, would take the churches far towards organic unity.

By contrast, on 26 March the Secretary of the English Church Union confronted Davidson[74] with the hostile views of about 1,000 churchmen, meeting at Church House, Westminster, on 11 March. Their resolutions condemned proposals to allow intercommunion and Nonconformist preachers to officiate in Anglican churches. Union, ignoring 'Catholic conditions of validity' of the Eucharist, would 'inevitably split the Church of England in two', while Free Churchmen officiating in the Church of England would 'violate all Catholic order', making for 'unreality', not any 'true unity'.

The second protest, dated 29 March 1920, was from the Master of Sidney Sussex College, Cambridge,[75] enclosing a letter signed by some clergy and several laymen, threatening 'to consider *de novo* the claim of the Church of England on our allegiance' if Anglican principles were to be surrendered along the lines of the resolutions of the Mansfield College Conference of 7–9 January 1920. A printed critique of these resolutions was endorsed by the forceful, decisive Bishop Gore and signed also by Lord Phillimore and Athelstan Riley, for example.

Last-minute pleas from Free Churchmen in contrast were not in conflict with one another. In the papers concerning preparations for the Lambeth Conference, Davidson's file contained[76] among other items a letter from Vernon Bartlett on 7 July, and another from Henry Lunn on 8 July. Bartlett enclosed a letter signed by himself, Forsyth, Jowett, Lidgett, W. J. Moulton, Nightingale, R. C. Gillie, Peake, F. Platt, Selbie, Shakespeare and Carnegie Simpson, asking *inter alia* for a united witness; for occasional joint and reciprocal participation in Holy Communion (subject to episcopal permission, where spiritual unity existed); and for an official Commission of Enquiry to supplement the more theoretical work of the Faith and Order Commissions.

Lunn's letter was personal, addressed to the Archbishop of York, Chairman of the Reunion Committee. His plea was on behalf of Wesleyans like himself, who earnestly desired reunion with the Church but had no intention of deserting the Communion to which they owed their spiritual life, and in which they had been baptised and confirmed. He hoped the Lambeth Conference would agree that, having assured their parish incumbent that they accepted the Nicene Creed, those like him should be permitted to Communion in the incumbent's church. Lunn had already published a pamphlet on 17 June, *Reunion and Lambeth: John Wesley's Message to the Bishops in Conference July 1920*. In the introductory letter Lunn explained his reasons for writing: 'It is difficult for any of them [the bishops] to realise the attitude of present day Methodism to the Church, and especially the attitude of those who are nearer in sympathy to John Wesley than were the Methodists of the middle of the last century'. His own longing for reunion remained undimmed, but he made it clear he could not be persuaded to doubt or deny the validity of the ministry of his own church or that of the historic Free Churches. As its subtitle showed, the pamphlet itself was an original composition, a series of addresses composed as from the pen of the Anglican John Wesley himself.

No more could be said. Over the decade, diverse resolutions, recommendations, protests, outbursts of enthusiasm, calls for caution, some issues and protagonists constantly recurring, all had poured in to Lambeth Palace. An initiative was now awaited from the 252 bishops assembled there in July 1920.

18

The Lambeth Appeal to All Christian People, August 1920

Debates on reunion with the Anglican Church had reached such a crescendo that all Churches were looking for a lead. From hindsight Lidgett[1] wrote of 'preparatory discussions', 'preparatory approaches' and 'preparing the ground', as if conference after conference, lobby after lobby, had been orchestrated to build up to an anticipated climax. In fact, after what had happened, 'Relation to and Re-union with other Churches' had to dominate the Lambeth Conference agenda, despite Bishop Gore's advice against it.

Convinced that the 'reunionists yielded themselves to their amiable instincts and did no clear thinking',[2] Gore feared their enthusiasm would cause a schism between Anglo-Catholics and their parent Church. Anglo-Catholics had the reputation of dubbing any positive ecumenical activity as 'a sort of Pan-Protestant ploy of the Evangelicals'.[3] Gore and Talbot attended the Edinburgh Missionary Conference, but though moved by it, kept strictly to the *inter*-denominational (not *un*-denominational) 'Edinburgh lines'.[4] Edinburgh in fact had been the first time many of the Churches' leading figures had met. The various subsequent unity conferences involved further personal contacts between Bishops and Nonconformist leaders, and brought an increase in understanding.

At the Lambeth Conference a large Reunion Committee was formed, including Bishop Weston and other strong High Churchmen, with the Archbishop of York in charge. For many days it made no progress. The break-through came when its Chairman suggested a *letter*, not to other churches but all Christian people, one which might be couched in warmer, more eirenic wording than a formal, almost inevitably to some partisans abrasive, reiteration of terms and conditions of reunion. The proposal was drafted in an optimistic tone, even suggesting only a few years might be needed before implementation. It was agreed, with only four dissentients, by the whole Conference. An anonymous Bishop[5] recalled that moment. One Bishop, he said, 'bolder than the rest', called for the Doxology, which, after prayer, 'was sung as it seldom is'.

The letter took the form of an appeal to make the vision of Christ's one Church a reality, showing to the world the unity for which Christ prayed. 'We frankly desire to confess our share', the Bishops said, 'in the guilt of . . . crippling the Body of Christ and hindering the activity of his Spirit'. They called for the creation of a visible, united Catholic Church within which Christian communions, now separated, would possess in common much that had been distinctive in their worship and service.

This they considered would involve wholehearted acceptance of all four items of the 1888 Lambeth Quadrilateral. They were, however, careful to express the fourth as 'a ministry acknowledged by every part of the Church as possessing not only the inward call of the Spirit, but also the commission of Christ and the authority of the whole body'. This ministry was then described by a question instead of a blunt statement, its impact qualified by a generous assertion calculated to win Nonconformist support.

> May we not reasonably claim that the Episcopate is the one means of providing such a ministry? It is not that we call in question for a moment the spiritual reality of the ministries of those communions which do not possess the Episcopate. On the contrary, we thankfully acknowledge that these ministries have been manifestly blessed and owned by the Holy Spirit as an effective means of grace.

So the bishops, predictably, remained firm in their claim for the Episcopate as justified in history and current experience. The word 'insist' was not used, and they said the Bishop's office should be exercised 'in a representative and constitutional manner'. The Anglican Bishops and clergy would be willing to accept from the authorities of other communions a form of commission or recognition 'which would commend our ministry to their congregations as having its place in the one family life'. At the same time they hoped ministers of non-episcopal communions would accept 'a commission through Episcopal ordination as obtaining for them a ministry throughout the whole fellowship. In so acting no one of us could possibly be taken to repudiate his past ministry'. These arrangements, they declared, were not suggesting any one communion should consent to be absorbed in another.

The issues of intercommunion and interchange of pulpits were tackled in an addition to the Appeal. General schemes for these were met with disapproval, but individual Bishops remained free occasionally, at their discretion, to authorise preaching by clergy and non-episcopal ministers in churches other than those of their own denomination, and to admit to Holy Communion in Anglican Churches such baptised but unconfirmed Christians as sought it.

Lidgett's instant reaction might be said to have been ecstatic. He described the Appeal as 'the greatest ecclesiastical event . . . since the Reformation'.[6] For him,[7] writing eight years later, it 'opened a new era' in relations between Episcopal and non-episcopal churches throughout the world. 'Whatever may be the merits and prospects of the precise plan of the Appeal', Lidgett saw 'the spirit which animated it, as well as the loftiness and breadth of its outlook' as features 'which will prove epoch-making whatever delays and set-backs it may encounter'. Immediately on hearing the news on 15 August 1920, while on holiday at Sewhurst Farm, Abinger Bottom, he wrote directly to Davidson[8] to say that 'a spiritual inspiration must have come to the Conference'. His offer of assistance in following up the Appeal was unequivocal: 'You can count upon my putting my powers and influence, for what little they are worth, at the service of the movement, with what combination of zeal and discretion I can attain to'. In 1936[9] Lidgett paid warm tribute to the influence Davidson and Cosmo Lang had had on the Appeal.

Lidgett's immediate step was to commend the Appeal to fellow Wesleyans. Significantly he turned to the *Methodist Recorder*, the more conservative of the two Wesleyan weeklies, and his article was printed[10] as early as 19 August 1920. Equally significantly its subtitle was 'Recognition of Existing Ministries'. He emphasised that, by expressly stating that ministries already being exercised would not be repudiated, the Bishops had removed the major obstacle to accepting requirements for Episcopacy and re-ordination. The form in which Episcopacy was being suggested, he went on, was to be freed from 'prelacy'. The Free Churches were already sensing their need for such an office by appointing 'Separated Chairmen' and 'General Superintendents'. Episcopacy, he said, had arisen as an essential form of ministry in the Church's development, and in sheer practical terms 'could not possibly be surrendered by a large section of those who would enter into the proposed reunion'. Rhetorically Lidgett asked, 'Can any man of large knowledge and wisdom say that the price is too great to pay for a reunited Church?' He called readers to unite 'in the great endeavour' of the Appeal, 'to recover and manifest to the world the unity of the body of Christ for which He prayed'.

To allay other concerns he pointed out that the bishops were not aiming at 'an impracticable and undesirable ideal of uniformity', but attempting to safeguard the distinctive contributions of denominations for the future. Nor was there any intention, he said, of displacing the great project of Methodist Union: 'The great types of evangelical tradition must not only be preserved, but developed within the larger union'.[11] The Appeal may have been cautious over the interchange of pulpits and the acceptance of non-Anglicans at Holy Communion, but only by being cautious, he reminded his readers, had it gained practical unanimity. Progress towards unity along the lines suggested would, he argued, solve 'the great and critical missionary difficulty throughout the world', and 'achievement of such catholicity would be the best answer to Rome'. Problems remained to be solved, but

Shall the Churches that call for a League of Nations, with the sacrifices that

> are demanded if such a League is to become effective, show themselves unwilling to make sacrifices for the fulfilment of our Lord's will 'that all may be one' and for the advancement of his Kingdom?

The Appeal was also promoted through October's *Contemporary Review*. Significantly Lidgett invited Bishop Talbot to write an article parallel to his own, not so much for what he might say, as for the support for the Appeal he represented on the High Church side. The Appeal had in fact owed much to the inspiration and even the drafting of Anglo-Catholics like Bishop Weston. Much of what Talbot wrote was an eirenic, measured exposition and commendation of the Appeal, but from Lidgett's point of view his article would have proved its value when Talbot confessed[12] that Anglo-Catholics had in the past thought of other churches as 'in schism', and succumbed to 'the temptation to arrogance and self-sufficiency'. Talbot went on: 'The sin of schism, alas! is still present and active . . . shared by all. The work of the Spirit in the other communions is the evident sign that they are within the great fellowship.'

Lidgett would have applauded the bishop's final sentence, an echo (no doubt unconscious) of his own, repeated view:

> But perhaps its [the Appeal's] best work, in which men of different kinds may unite to rejoice, was that of resetting the problem, by pointing to its true goal, by calling all of us alike to enlist under the standard of Christ's own Ideal.[13]

Lidgett's own article,[14] less rhetorical than his *Recorder* contribution, was important for its realism. Aware of obstacles to future progress, he emphasised, as before, the need for a general will to succeed: 'The ideal must be *shared*, and the plan for giving effect to it must be accepted not merely by leaders . . . but by the whole body of the denominations they represent.' He hoped that Presbyterians would find the greatness of the goal ahead would overcome their own special constitutional difficulty, but all the Free Churches needed to be convinced by the terms of the Appeal. His warning was:

> Non-Episcopal ministers will only assent to this proposal [Episcopal ordination] on the express declaration of the Anglican Church that no repudiation of their past and present ministry is involved, and on the express declaration by themselves of their faith in the validity of their ministry, and in the reality of the Divine call and the Divine grace by which they have exercised it.

If this occurred, Lidgett thought it would be the duty of non-episcopal ministers to consent to the proposal, not just as part of a corporate act of reunion, but 'as the means of assuring the conscience of a large section of those with whom they are coming into full communion and fellowship'.

He appeared, therefore, to recognise some flaws in the Bishops' optimism. It might have escaped him that the way in which the Quadrilateral's four points were introduced in the Lambeth Appeal was closer to the original version and its context than in the virtual ultimata of 1888 and successive Lambeth declarations; but he certainly did not see the appeal as High Anglican imperialism, 'Anglican norms for unity . . . laid down in advance'.[15] David Edwards' judgement,[16] that the Appeal 'would not have commanded the enthusiasm of . . . the 1920 Conference had there been a definite proposal for actions more daring than the occasional opening of Anglican pulpits to other ministers', would have troubled him.

Lidgett's optimism, perhaps tempered in private, was publicly buoyant. The Bishops' Appeal had drawn the threads of previous Conference proposals together. To him it was a significant staging point, and he vowed to exploit its possibilities as far as his Free Church constituencies and his own discretion would allow. He was not to know that the Appeal would run into the sand.

Part 6

Capitalising on the Lambeth Challenge 1920–49

Chapters 19–22 summarise ecumenical developments during this period, and in particular the discussions between Anglican and Free Church representatives which resulted from the Lambeth Appeal of 1920.

Calendar of main events

1921	Free Church and CE representatives met after 300 years of schism.
1921–5	CE and RC discussions at Malines.
1923	First CE Memorandum about status of existing FC Ministry.
1923–4	Mürren Conferences.
1924	COPEC Conference in Birmingham.
1925	Life and Work Conference at Stockholm. Second CE Memorandum. Suspension of FC/CE talks.
1926	General Strike.
1927	World Conference at Lausanne.
1927–8	Prayer Book controversy.
1928	Davidson retired.
1929	*Methodism in the Modern World*, edited by Lidgett and B. H. Reed.
1930	Davidson died. Lambeth Conference.
1931	Free Church and CE representatives resumed talks.
1932	Public Appeal by these representatives.
1934	*Sketch of a United Church*.
1935	Lloyd George's Council for Peace and Reconcilation.
1936	*Outline of a Reunion Scheme*.
1937	Second Life and Work Conference in Oxford, and Second World Conference on Faith and Order.
1941–4	Framing of 1944 Education Act.
1942	British Council of Churches formed.
1946	Archbishop Fisher's *Step Forward in Church Relations*.
1948	World Council of Churches formed.

19

Anglican/Free Church discussions 1920–5

Lidgett had already been active among his Free Church colleagues before the October 1920 issue of the *Contemporary Review* had been published. As Honorary Secretary of the National Council of Evangelical Free Churches (NCEFC), he had undoubtedly been in touch also with the Federal Council (FCEFC) in time for them to consult and issue on 28 September their joint provisional response to the Lambeth Appeal.[1] It expressed a cautious welcome, admitted reservations about several proposals and asked for elucidation before pronouncing on them. Archbishop Davidson sent for Lidgett on 4 October[2] to gain his personal advice on the best way to proceed. Lidgett explained the origin and interrelation of the two Councils, and advised him that the Federal Council was the body better able, and now formally authorised, to deal with the issues on behalf of all the Nonconformist Churches. His comments on the Federal Council Committee meeting were detailed, identifying the chief speakers, the most 'difficult' and the most 'friendly', the members appointed to confer and their respective roles. Davidson was assured there had been no wish whatever to turn down the Appeal.

On 28 October an informal meeting[3] was convened at Lambeth between the two Archbishops, designated Bishops, and members of the Federal Council's Committee, to decide how to respond to the Committee's request. It was agreed that the Archbishops and Bishops would meet the Free Churches' Joint Committee representatives on 8 December after the latter had held a preliminary meeting earlier in the day. Lidgett had to explain several features of Free Church organisation to be borne in mind in future discussions: each of the Nonconformist denominations involved (Baptist, Congregational, Moravian, Wesleyan, United Methodist, Primitive Methodist, Presbyterian Church of England, Countess of Huntingdon's Connexion) would require a formal invitation from the Archbishop; the Joint Committee representatives could not commit the constituent Churches before those Churches had met in their separate Annual Conferences/Assemblies; and annually elected 'incumbents' or Presidents of denominations were not necessarily the most appropriate people for joint Anglican/Free Church conferences on the Appeal. Davidson for his part stressed that the meeting planned for 8 December should be informal and private; it was not being convened to pass resolutions nor give any appearance of planning a campaign.

On 29 October, the following day, lest uninformed rumours might spread among his own 'constituency', Davidson issued a statement,[4] emphasising equally strongly to all the English and Welsh diocesan bishops the complete informality of the meetings with Free Churchmen. He said elucidation of the Appeal was all the more necessary because of wide misapprehensions. In the provinces friendly conversations with individuals and groups would be valuable, but premature utterances by quasi-official gatherings should be strictly avoided.

Both at the December meeting, and subsequently in private correspondence, the Presbyterian Professor Carnegie Simpson from Westminster College, Cambridge, emerged as the Free Churches' fiercest protagonist, posing some blunt challenges to Davidson: 'What do you mean by the Church? Where do we in the Free Churches stand? Is episcopal ordination merely a denominational extension? That would facilitate matters for us'.[5] Neither Davidson nor Lang was ready for such basic questions at that very early stage. They replied that answers would need to be carefully qualified, respect differences of view and avoid disunion within Anglicanism itself. Lidgett announced that the Free Churchmen would be meeting on 3–5 January at Mansfield College, Oxford, to prepare memoranda for their several Churches' Assemblies later in the year.

Davidson did not have to wait long for news. Immediately, on the day of his return from Oxford, Lidgett sent him a private and confidential letter summarising their discussion.[6] It had been:

> an arduous time, but things have gone far better than I hoped, let alone than I feared . . . a frank statement of our position will be made and some serious questions asked, but all with the desire to *get forward*, and all in a spirit which will, I hope, enable progress (sure, even if slow) to be made.

In thanking him, Davidson wrote: 'I do not doubt that we owe a great deal to your wise and conciliatory words at a time of necessary difficulty.'

Lidgett was among those who drafted the lengthy Free Church statement, published as 'The Free Churches and the Lambeth Appeal' on 22 May 1921.[7] This expressed readiness to carry discussion further, but pointed to three principal issues; first, recognition of non-episcopal communions as part of the Church of Christ; secondly, recognition of their ministries as ministries of Christ's Word and Sacraments (it was made clear that *re*-ordination by the episcopate as a prerequisite would be unacceptable, as would any form of ambiguous recommissioning); thirdly, recognition of spiritual freedom, dear to the heart of all the Free Churches.

Alongside this candid agenda the Lambeth Appeal had created a friendly and sympathetic atmosphere. Significant contributions to this were made by

Lang's addresses to the NCEFC, Baptist and English Presbyterian Assemblies and the Wesleyan Conference during the summer, and by Davidson's address later to the Wesleyan Conference in 1923. These occasions were acknowledged as important and impressive.[8] In his *Guided Life*[9] Lidgett was pleased to record that for these Wesleyan Conferences both Archbishops had been 'good enough to take me into their confidence beforehand'. Shakespeare, the 1919–21 Federal Council Moderator and now its Secretary, even consulted Davidson[10] about the wording of a draft resolution for its meeting in late September 1921.

To confer with their Anglican counterparts 25 Free Churchmen were then appointed. Of these the most prominent were the Federal Council Moderators, Shakespeare (Baptist) and his successor for 1921–3, J. D. Jones (a leading Congregationalist statesman, later awarded the CH); A. E. Garvie and W. B. Selbie, Principals of New and Mansfield Colleges respectively (also Congregationalists); Professors A. S. Peake (Primitive Methodist) and Carnegie Simpson (Presbyterian); T. Nightingale (United Methodist, the NCEFC's General Secretary); Lidgett (its Honorary Secretary); and Bishop H. R. Mumford (Moravian). On the Anglican side the Archbishops nominated nine diocesan bishops: those of London (A. F. Winnington-Ingram); Winchester (E. S. Talbot); Peterborough (F. T. Woods); Ely (F. H. Chase); Chelmsford (J. E. Watts-Ditchfield); Lichfield (J. A. Kempthorne); Hereford (M. Linton Smith); Ripon (T. B. Strong); and Gloucester (E. C. S. Gibson). A tenth bishop (St C. G. A. Donaldson, Bishop of Salisbury) and two priests, A. C. Headlam, who succeeded Gibson in 1923, and the Anglo-Catholic W. H. Frere, who became Bishop of Truro, also in 1923, were added later.

The formal meeting of the two sides was held on 30 November 1921. Taking place after 300 years of schism, it was a historic event (whatever its outcome was to be) in the history of English Christianity. It proved to be the first of 22 or so meetings between 1921 and 1925, including five full conferences, and 17 subcommittees.[11] The subcommittees were composed of six representatives on each side, chosen to represent different schools of thought. They were chaired by Archbishop Lang, with G. K. A. Bell, Davidson's resident chaplain, acting as secretary.

Already within the above account can be seen in embryo features which were to hamper or promote progress later: the pivotal role of Lidgett, and the disparities of view and structure on both sides. Neither side was a unity. There were considerable differences of view among both Free Churchmen and Anglicans. Lidgett's importance lay in being fully aware of these. He had personal contacts not only with colleagues in both Free Church Councils and their Nexus Committee, but also with Davidson and, to a very much less extent in due course, with Lang, and yet, surprisingly, he earned the respect of both sides. The most crucial period of the talks, 1923–5, saw him elected as the Moderator of the Federal Council. In the early discussions he was not as vocal as Garvie and Carnegie Simpson, but he excelled in his mastery of language, not least in the skills of drafting memoranda and resolutions. His eirenic influence and sensitivity both to theological issues and the interplay of personalities within and outside the Lambeth Palace meetings proved invaluable in avoiding damaging clashes. He encouraged both sides. He was in constant touch with Davidson (for example, he had dinner with Davidson 'quietly' on 16 June 1921),[12] counselling him not to be deterred by opposition from Clifford and the *British Weekly*.[13] The suspension of talks in 1925 certainly disappointed him, but he curbed his impatience, understanding that excessive speed could be counter-productive and substantial progress would take time. Tenets central to Nonconformity, or dear to its particular denominations, could not be played down.

The Free Church representatives had to report to the Federal Council, which in turn had to report to Assemblies of eight independent denominations. These were united in hostility to sacerdotalism, Establishment and re-ordination of their ministries, but differences between the separate Churches made the Church of England reluctant to grant them *general* recognition; distinctions might be necessary. Denominations had originated in differences of view and practice. Presbyterians held particularly strong Church principles. Congregationalists and Baptists (along with some Wesleyans) distrusted the Creeds as restricting the freedom of individual interpretation; standing for the local church, they disliked ecclesiasticism, while Wesleyans favoured a Connexion and the use of lay (local) preachers for preaching and the conduct of worship, but not for the administration of Holy Communion; Primitive Methodist lay preachers, however, had the same scope as their ministers. Free Churchmen considered the Episcopate unacceptable, or at any rate perhaps only tolerable if no particular theory as to its origin or character was attached to it. The Wesleyans were closest to the Anglican Church. Lidgett, for example, proudly called attention to his own role as Chairman of a District, a quasi-Diocese, and gave his explicit assurance that Wesleyan local preachers were not permitted to administer Holy Communion. In every denomination leaders could face problems at grass-roots level. To explain the awkward stance adopted by Garvie on the Creeds, Lidgett, during 'dinner quietly' on 16 June 1921, perceptively suggested to Davidson that 'Garvie had probably been pressed by the extremer members of his Church up and down the country – a danger . . . in almost all denominations, the smaller and more rural section of the body being usually less open to reasonable understanding on these questions on large lines'.[14]

Seen from the outside, the Anglican Church was a unity. Its members all agreed that the Episcopate had to be the basis of organic union of the churches. But despite its unified structure, as is clear from Chapter 17 for example, the views of its growing Anglo-Catholic 'wing' and the English Churchmen's Union stood in stark contrast to those of Evangelicals. Among the bishops[15] Evangelicals were not well represented in the 1920s and even less so, under the Anglo-Catholic Lang, in the 1930s. In 1923, in a dramatic and defiant gesture, Bishop Weston sent the Pope a public telegram with greetings from 16,000 participants in an Anglo-Catholic congress in London, humbly praying that peace and unity would come quickly.

Anglican attitudes to the Free Churches differed markedly: some Anglicans were friendly, anxious to make progress towards reunion; others were hostile or indifferent, their interest directed elsewhere. During the talks there was almost a panic over the stance being taken in July 1923 by Bishop Gibson and F. H. Chase, the Bishop of Ely, which, until the last moment, looked likely to prevent a unified Anglican view on the Free Churches' ministry. The two Archbishops tried to make their team as representative of Anglican opinion as possible and ensure that any Joint Anglican/Free Church statement was acceptable to the Anglican Church as a whole. There was no doubt of Davidson's sincerity in declaring his personal support for the Unity movement, nor of Lang's equally sincere and conciliatory spirit in chairing the discussions. On 27 July 1922, though nothing came of it, Davidson even responded sympathetically to Sir George Hayter Chubb about the possibility of a few prominent Nonconformist ministers joining the Bishops in the House of Lords,[16] though he (Davidson) doubted whether 'the House of Lords will be really re-constituted without long discussion and much delay'.

Lang, it seems, quickly saw[17] that without establishing points of agreement discussions would soon founder. At the first full meeting[18] on 30 November 1921 Lidgett feared premature raising of the question of conditional ordination. He preferred placing the foundations for progress deeper and stronger, by focusing attention on the Creeds and the conception of the Church itself. Carnegie Simpson[19] formally proposed the creation of a subcommittee, a suggestion Lidgett had earlier made to Davidson in private.[20] When the first subcommittee met on 30 January 1922, Lidgett's priorities were agreed: members declared 'in favour of going somewhat deeply into the theological principles or doctrines – "hack at the foundations" – before proceeding to practical proposals'.[21] They set themselves to prepare memoranda on the nature of the Church, the Ministry and the place of the Creed in a united Church.

Meetings followed in the spring. Articles drafted on these topics by individual members acting jointly were then incorporated in a report drawn up by Lang. 'To his thankful surprise'[22] this was agreed by the subcommittee, and on

24 May 1922 unanimously adopted by the Joint Conference.[23] It was a great advance on anything deemed likely to prove acceptable. Lang's joy, however, was tempered by what he expressed to his brother on 26 May:

> The trouble both among ourselves and these good Nonconformists is that our Ministers and people are a long way off the new spirit which is moving in their leaders; and I have a somewhat uncomfortable feeling that the bishops did not take sufficient steps to spread the vision which they saw at Lambeth [the Lambeth Appeal] effectively among our own people so that they could share it and take it up with enthusiasm as a real call, and give it expression in constant and fervent prayer. I don't feel somehow as if we had really appealed to the imagination of the Church as we ought to have done.

This had significance for the progress of the whole unity movement.

The Assemblies of the individual Free Churches gave the report a generally warm welcome, but a number of reservations surfaced. In the Wesleyan Conference's official reply[24] the reference to the Creeds was amended to allow for 'reasonable liberty of interpretation' after prior discussions involving (among others) Lunn, Lidgett and Wiseman. The Joint Anglican/Free Church Conference had accepted the episcopate for the United Church *of the future* as a means of giving the Church's whole authority to its ministers, and had agreed that 'similarly' elements of presbyteral and congregational order (that is the council of presbyters and the congregation of the faithful) 'should be maintained with a representative and constitutional episcopate as permanent elements in the order and life of the United Church'. The Wesleyan Conference, however, reiterated concern that acceptance of the episcopate might imply *re-ordination* which 'could not be accepted by those who believe themselves to be already ministers of the Church of God'. This in effect raised the distinction between the ministry as envisaged in the United Church of the future and the existing Free Church ministry of the present who would be joining that United Church. Wesleyans were also apprehensive that they might have to turn their backs on their fellowship with other non-episcopal groups.

Such concerns led some members of the Federal Council to propose simply to receive the report and take no further action. 'To what in practice would the Free Churches be committing themselves?', they wondered. But the personal relations being established and the atmosphere of harmony and good will in the talks so far caused the Council to request that the meetings should continue: much still remained to elucidate, and a large measure of agreement on the Faith had been established. So the Council in September 1922 set out five 'practical difficulties' or questions for discussion in future conversations.[25] At the same time they declared, and often repeated, that 'Discussion of Union should be increasingly accompanied by *acts* of unity'. Intercommunion, as at SCM

Conferences in the 1890s, in particular was in their mind, but this was continually refused.

Much debate on the questions took place between the autumn of 1922 and the temporary suspension of the talks on 19 June 1925. Six documents were published that day to conclude this phase of discussions, five on the five topics, with a preliminary covering statement signed by the two Archbishops and Lidgett who, as Moderator of the Federal Council,[26] was its official spokesman.

The following summary of the outcome of the discussions is based on his article on 'The Present Position' in the October 1925 issue of the *Review of the Churches*[27] and the response of the Federal Council. The five questions and responses can be conveniently reordered and commented upon as follows:

1. What will be the relationship of the Free Churches to other communions?

This would probably remain undisturbed. The Central Council of the United Church would deal with difficulties.

2. What will be the relations between the Church and State?

The Free Churches thought the Church should have complete autonomy. The Church of England did not regard 'Establishment' as essential to the life of the Church nor as a hindrance to Union. The question of the relationship to the State would be determined by the final terms of Union. Establishment was soon to be raised as an issue in 1928 when Bishops reserved their right on occasion to exercise their *ius liturgicum* to permit use of the Revised Prayer Book, though Parliament had rejected it.

3. Will the evangelical principles of the Reformation be safeguarded?

The Principles of the Protestant Reformation were not defined by either side in the talks. To Peake[28] they would have included the priesthood of all believers, the right of private judgement, unrestricted use of Scripture, the direct access of the soul to God. The Anglicans, however, in effect insisted that the Lambeth Quadrilateral, as formulated in the Appeal, would be the basis for discussion of related matters. Issues this raised, the Anglicans stated, could not be profitably considered at that stage of the discussions.

4. Will there be a representative and constitutional Episcopate?

What was agreed here marked a very significant advance. The Federal Council accepted that the Episcopate, not of its current character but of a 'constitutional' character, would be essential in the United Church of the future. In its turn the Church of England accepted 'similarly' place being given to elements of Presbyterian and Congregational Order as equally essential in the Church Government of the future. Suggestions as to how a 'constitutional' episcopate could be reconciled with these elements were made in memoranda by Garvie and the Bishop of Truro, but neither the Joint Committee nor the Federal Council was committed to the details. Lidgett pointed out that for administrative purposes the Free Churches had been contemplating something like Episcopal leadership and superintendency already.

5. What is the status of the existing Free Church ministry?

The first Anglican Memorandum on this subject[29] on 6 July 1923 gave rise initially to profound appreciation, expressed notably by Lidgett, Carnegie Simpson[30] and Peake, and then to concern as Free Churchmen began to note the ways in which it was qualified. They were encouraged that their ministries were not termed 'valid' or 'invalid' but regarded as 'being, within their several spheres, real ministries of Christ's Word and Sacraments in the Universal Church'. Strikingly, and to the Council's great satisfaction, this went beyond the Appeal's recognition of 'the spiritual reality of non-episcopal ministries': they were now being recognised as evangelical, sacramental and not schismatic.

There were, however, several provisos. The phrase 'within their several spheres' had been suggested by Bishop Talbot[31] to assuage objections to the initially much wider ranging formulation, expressed privately to Davidson and Lang by Bishops Gibson and Chase. The Anglican statement went on to make it clear that Free Church ministries, even when regarded as real, could be in varying degrees irregular or defective, and would need episcopal ordination if they were to function in Anglican services, notably the Eucharist. This latter proviso, as J. M. Turner says,[32] effectively took away in practice what had been granted in theory. Why, the Free Churchmen asked, was it necessary to ordain men who were already exercising real ministries? Lidgett rang Davidson on 2 October 1923,[33] asking him 'not to take too seriously the rather repellent attitude' to the recent Memorandum, which the Federal Council had taken in its resolutions of 18 September 1923.[34] He assured him that attempts by Perks and Clifford to discontinue the conversations had received only minimal support, and suggested a further subcommittee meeting with the constitutional episcopate on its agenda would be valuable ahead of any future session of the whole Conference.

After further meetings at the Federal Council's request, the Anglican representatives issued their second Memorandum on 19 June 1925.[35] They made it clear that the issue was not one of spiritual efficacy (already conceded to Free

Church ministers) but of due authority. The authority of the whole Church was conferred by episcopal ordination, and the Anglican Church had 'a special trust' with regard to this principle.[36] As this was emphatically rejected by the Free Churchmen, possible concessions or modifications of the principle were then tentatively suggested:

(a) *an extended commission*, whereby a Bishop would solemnly confer authority, committed by the imposition of hands, for the office and work of a priest (or presbyter). This, however, involved a fatal ambiguity: it could be interpreted either as conferring order or simply jurisdiction. Free Churchmen greeted this with little enthusiasm.
(b) *ordination sub condicione*, whereby episcopal ordination would take place, but the act of ordination would be prefaced by a condition, words like 'If thou art not already ordained, I ordain you'. As Lidgett explained it, this was to recognise that doubt existed on one side, but would not require any acknowledgement of the validity of that doubt from the other side. He regarded this as a real advance[37] on the universal practice of the Anglican Church hitherto: Baptism *sub condicione* had been the only precedent. But the Federal Council[38] was not impressed: it saw little or no prospect of its acceptance by any non-episcopal church, and reiterated the inconsistency of requiring ordination to the ministry of men already explicitly acknowledged as being in that very ministry.
(c) *a mutually extended commission*, that is, commission which was both mutual and *unambiguously* not an ordination. This was suggested by the Federal Council for exploration in the future. Its members noted hopefully[39] that the Anglican Memorandum had not excluded it, and that it was 'the line which is being followed wherever today union between Churches is being achieved': the Church of South India negotiations were, no doubt, in mind. They tactfully recognised that the Anglican Church had particular difficulties to consider on this issue, and it was 'one which therefore is not to be pressed to an immediate decision'.

At this point, in the summer of 1925, it was decided by common consent that the discussions could not, at least for the time being, profitably proceed further: time was needed for the churches to digest what had emerged by way of agreement and disagreement, and then, if they decided, to resume. The Federal Council Resolution of 21–3 September 1925,[40] summarising its frank response to the Memoranda, concluded by expressing satisfaction that the meetings had been conducted in a conciliatory spirit and brought closer fellowship and better understanding. The individual churches took the same very firm, but friendly view. Only the Baptists rejected the whole Lambeth Appeal proposal altogether. Shakespeare had retired through ill health in 1924.

Lidgett insisted there was now a pause for reflection and preparation;[41] the door had not been closed by the Federal Council; discussions had been suspended, not broken off. There had been, he said, positive results to date. He picked out the following: the agreed statement on the Church, the sacraments, the ministry and the Creeds; acceptance that no corporate union could be achieved without a representative and constitutional episcopate (i.e. in a revised form), and that 'similarly' (a word Free Churchmen continually emphasised) a place would be found for the presbyterate, laity and congregation in the government of the United Church; and what he called 'the epoch-making declaration in regard to duly constituted non-episcopal ministers having real ministries in the Universal Church . . . made by Church of England representatives *without any division in their ranks*'.[42] He could see that sacrifices were now required on all sides: by the Free Churches uniting on the case for corporate union; by Anglicans 'generally' accepting their representatives' declaration about 'real' Free Church ministries, realising its consequences, and working them out. He frankly admitted that 'for the time being intractable difficulties in regard to the question of the Orders of non-Episcopal Churches' remained.[43] Reunion would not occur until there was conviction that 'God wills it', and there is a 'concerted desire for its achievement'.[44] In all churches, he wrote in 1925, 'the mass-*mind* must be *informed*, and the mass-*will* stirred to *desire* and *action*'.[45] The Anglican Oliver Quick had also told Bell[46] on 27 November 1923 that '*if* once *desire* is really stirred in the main body of the members of the churches, the ordination difficulty would soon be overcome'.[47]

20

Other ecumenical events 1920–9

No further formal meetings between Anglican and FCEFC representatives took place until 1930, but both before and after 1925 other contacts and ecumenical events occurred, directly or indirectly related to the Lambeth Appeal.

Between 1921 and 1924[1] the Church of England was in dialogue with the Moravian Church (Unitas Fratrum), largely, it seems, about possible reciprocal arrangements (ordinations and confirmations) in the West Indies; Bishop Gibson led the Anglican side and Bishop Mumford the Moravian. Moravian hopes for intercommunion were dashed, and the talks suspended. Contacts, made earlier with the Eastern Orthodox Church[2] and the Church of Sweden,[3] were developed and good relations established.

Perhaps the most important, and certainly the most controversial discussions were at Malines near Brussels with Roman Catholics led by Cardinal Mercier. The initiative came in 1921 from the English Churchmen's Anglo-Catholic protagonist, Lord Halifax, with his friend, the Abbé Portal, not from Archbishop Davidson.

Only with very great hesitation and caution Davidson permitted discussion to go ahead, initially privately, and then, with the 'friendly cognizance' of the Pope and himself, on what amounted to a semi-official basis. Four meetings took place, the last in May 1925, and up to five Anglicans took part: initially Halifax and Drs Frere and Armitage Robinson (Dean of Wells), and later Dr Kidd (Warden of Keble), and Bishop Gore. A report was drawn up in November 1928. There was no tangible result, but in December 1923 Davidson found it necessary to explain to the Archbishops and Metropolitans of the Church of England what was happening at that time in relation to Rome as well as the Free Churches, and to assure his colleagues that in neither case were negotiations being attempted.

Interestingly, he also took care to inform Lidgett as well, as the latter's second autobiography proudly revealed:

> The Archbishop of Canterbury was good enough to write to me to explain the sanction he had given for this conference (*sic*) . . . I stated my opinion that

> in view of the fact that the Lambeth Appeal was addressed to the whole of Christendom, such a conference . . . was both inevitable and desirable. On every ground it was well to ascertain whether the Roman Church had made any advance towards what we regard as true Catholicity since the Council of Trent.[4]

Problems, even protests, could have arisen when the talks were mentioned at the Anglican/Free Church subcommittee on 11 January 1924, but Lidgett helped to calm the fears of Carnegie Simpson and others by asserting that such talks had been impossible to avoid, and there was no cause to complain.

The Roman Catholics showed no interest in wider ecumenical gatherings such as those organised by the Faith and Order Movement. The Continuation Committee appointed at Geneva[5] prescribed theological questions for study, and set 1925 as the date for the deferred World Conference. Lang, however, on 20 July 1922 objected to Davidson[6] that 1925 was far too soon; it could interfere with ongoing Lambeth Appeal talks; and more promising results could be anticipated in very much smaller groups. Bishop Talbot was also far from enthusiastic. Davidson then sought to persuade Bishop Brent of the need for postponement. A revised date of 3–21 August 1927 was adopted and Lausanne designated as the venue. Though Lidgett thought the Faith and Order Movement was important, he did not opt to attend the Conference, nor the International Missionary Conferences at Jerusalem in 1928 and Tambaram in 1938, noted for its remarkable openness to other faiths.

The World Conference achieved very little in practice beyond the widening of contacts, greater awareness of different Churches' stances and context, and a resolve to mount an 'intensive and extensive campaign for . . . friendly discussion throughout the world'. The organisers sought to provide conditions for harmony: the doctrinal prerequisite was deliberately minimal; the aim was simply for theological study, not for negotiations for reunion; the Conference could not commit constituent Churches to anything, and delegations could only give them advice by sending back reports. Such reports, however, tended to be vague, unexciting and prone to too much ambiguity to stimulate effective action.

Lidgett would have agreed numbers were too large, tackled too many topics, and that a gap between the understanding of the delegates and that of their Church members had to be bridged. It seems that, amid his many other commitments, Lidgett saw his priorities as Church Unity Conferences at home; international gatherings abroad had to be left to fellow Methodists and Free Churchmen. The Congregationalist A. E. Garvie came to prominence within these, for which his ecumenical enthusiasm, committee and linguistic skills made him eminently suited.

Reviewing the century's Faith and Order debates, Harding Meyer[7] states that roughly three possible forms of ecumenical advance were considered: the first proposed a loose federation, in which the Churches would co-operate in promoting a more just society without surrendering their separate identities; the second saw intercommunion as the goal; while the third advocated 'organic union', within which denominational traditions would disappear in an institutional merger, perhaps resulting in a hybrid organisation. The eventual World Council of Churches favoured a 'visible union', preserving the different Churches' traditions, 'unity without absorption', a formula Lidgett would have approved.

In England itself other ecumenical events were being organised. Sir Henry Lunn maintained the momentum by organising and financing two conferences of church leaders at Mürren in September 1923 and 1924 on the pattern of his Grindelwald Conferences in the 1890s. Lidgett attended the second, notable[8] to him for receiving the Sacrament at the hands of Bishop Talbot, then recently retired. This Conference featured 12 pairs of speakers on various aspects of 'the Evangel'. Predictably, Lidgett spoke on 'Unity and the Evangel'.

Surprisingly, however, Lidgett was not involved in the first Mürren Conference, devoted to 'The Church and Social Problems', a theme of great, but not perhaps of equal priority to him in 1923 amid discussions on Methodist and Anglican/Free Church unity. There was certainly no doubt of his interest in discussions about forming a Christian Social Council. But on 16 June 1921, while he supported the proposal of such a Council, made to Davidson on the previous day[9] by Nightingale, the NCEFC's Executive Secretary, and the use of the Anglican/Free Church conversations to discuss it, Lidgett advised Davidson[10] that any formal conference on the social subjects 'when held, should be incidental to the more difficult conference about religious reunion in doctrine and system which the Lambeth Conference advocates'.

Nightingale thought unity could only be effected by the Churches working together on social matters, and a suitable way of organising this would be to take up Lidgett's suggestion in the *Contemporary Review* of 1916 of National and Diocesan Councils (on which Anglicans and Free Churchmen should serve), for religious as well as for social purposes.[11] Pressures along similar lines were being exerted by H. H. Pereira, Bishop of Croydon, and Henry Carter, Secretary of the Wesleyan Temperance and Social Welfare Department, but their proposal for a United Social and Industrial Council seemed to Lidgett fraught with too many problems. He advised Davidson on 5 July 1921, through a private letter[12] to his chaplain, that the Churches would find it difficult to express a common mind on national emergencies: the Coal Strike, for example, raised issues partly ethical, partly economic, and partly questions of business management. It would, moreover, not be easy to define a standing committee's functions, give it recognised responsibilities, or even to decide how it could be 'safely' constituted. To Lidgett a more general Council would know better when to speak and when to be silent. Davidson took this advice and refused to be rushed.

To consider how best to proceed, it was decided that a very small subcommittee of three Free Churchmen and three Anglicans (two of whom would be Bishops) would meet on the same day immediately after the Appeal subcommittee, and report back to it. Davidson made it clear to the Revd C. S. Woodward, a member of this subcommittee,[13] on 31 December 1921, that he was not in favour of a Christian Social Council whose special function would be to issue judgements on burning social issues as they occurred: it should have much wider scope, to deal with questions of social and moral welfare generally.

Lidgett was one of the Free Churchmen chosen to attend the first meeting on 9 February 1922. This recommended[14] that a Social Council, members of which would be officially appointed by the different Christian Churches, was not desirable at present, but 'united Christian councils' should be formed in all large centres of population to 'strengthen the work of the Christian Social Crusade' beyond social and industrial functions and promote united work and witness along the lines of the Manchester 'Council of Christian Congregations'. This Council with one or two others had resulted from Lidgett's suggestion in 1916, adopted by the subsequent Lambeth Conference in 1920. Writing in 1928,[15] Lidgett commented sadly that in the event 'a more general endeavour would have been made to carry it into effect had not the COPEC Conference (on Christian Politics, Economics and Citizenship) sought to bring a somewhat similar, though more limited, organization into existence'. But as COPEC's commissions included 'the social witness of the Church', the Appeal subcommittee began to liaise with representatives of its Executive. COPEC and its follow-up apparently then took centre stage until January 1929. The Christian Social Council was then finally set up as a new interdenominational body after discussions between the COPEC Continuation Committee and the Lambeth Conference Social Service Committee.

The COPEC Conference took place in Birmingham on 6–12 April 1924. William Temple, Bishop of Manchester, was both its principal instigator and chairman. Its aim was to establish a common Christian mind, 'a norm of Christian thought and action for the working out of Christian order', to discern Christ's principles for human life and make them operative in civic, social and international affairs. Topics studied included politics, property and industry, crime, war, the home, leisure, education, and relations between the sexes. Though a member of the COPEC Council in London in 1923, Lidgett did not join the Executive or attend the Conference. It fell to Benson Perkins, Lofthouse, S. E. Keeble, Henry Carter, Ryder Smith and W. R. Maltby to make Wesleyan contributions to it. These were well regarded. Garvie was made deputy chairman.

COPEC's preparatory written material and the 12 volumes it endorsed proved to be valuable works of reference for all those who went on to work for better conditions in the life of society. Machin[16] has suggested that 'COPEC's significance lay mainly in its role as an unprecedentedly wide gathering, combining Christian contributions (shown in the Reports) to the well-established movement for social reform by collectivist means'. The overall COPEC report was seen by F. W. Dillistone in his biography of Charles Raven,[17] a major participant, 'as a blue-print for the Welfare State which was before long to be established in Britain'. Overall, however, to Machin COPEC was 'only a national preparation for a wider, international Conference on the Life and Work of the Church at Stockholm in 1925'.

Issues of social morality also had an international dimension. Recalling the conference 'for a World Alliance for promoting International Friendship' which had to be abandoned at Constance on 1 August 1914, and convinced that international problems were certain to recur post-war, Archbishop Söderblom of Sweden decided action by the Churches was morally imperative: Christian influence had to be brought to bear on world affairs if peace and justice were to be maintained. Tragically, in his view, the Churches needed persuasion to recognise the urgency and overcome reluctance to venture into politically dangerous activity. Despite their national and denominational fragmentation Söderblom sought concerted, practical action, co-operation in a spirit of unity, without waiting for agreement on doctrinal statements or Church Order. The Life and Work Movement, with its World Conference at Stockholm in August 1925, was his means of making a start.

Officially appointed delegates from the Churches across the world assembled to discuss the Christian issues inherent in the situation he had identified. An international body, more powerful, substantial and prominent than an English Churches' Social Council, was envisaged. Again, Lidgett could not attend but joined the Conference's Advisory Council later. A. E. Garvie acted as Deputy Chairman or Vice-President both in 1925 and in the second Life and Work Conference, on 'Church, Community and State' which met in Oxford on 12–25 July 1937, the year in which the second World Conference on Faith and Order was convened in Edinburgh. Lidgett wrote an article for the *Contemporary Review* in 1937 on the two conferences, entitled 'Catholicity, Constructive and Corrective',[18] which underlined their aspirations. He argued (unsurprisingly) that

> What is needed for Reunion is not analysis or synthesis, but a synoptic vision which shall promote true Catholicity . . . the most important requisite is to secure that the *élan vital* . . . in the existing Churches is not reduced to a pale uniformity, that the positive contributions of the independent traditions . . .

> shall be preserved, and that Reunion shall, therefore, enrich the united Church and not impoverish it.

He certainly wanted the best of his Methodist inheritance preserved within an overall, organic, visible union.

It was in Edinburgh that a World Council of Churches was proposed. A committee met at Utrecht in 1938 to draft its constitution, but WW2 prevented its coming into being until its official launch on 22 August 1948 at Amsterdam. The British Council of Churches, however, was formed in 1942, and Lidgett was proud to be a founder member.[19] It marked a key point in his ecumenical career.

21

Results and personalities of the Lambeth Appeal

Lidgett claimed[1] that the Appeal had 'opened a new era in the relations between the Episcopal and the non-Episcopal Churches throughout the world'. Reviewing the resulting series of Conferences since 1920, Davidson stated at Christmas 1923[2] that in composition, character and purpose they had 'no precedent in the history of the Church in these islands', and the representatives had come to appreciate one another's position, showing 'a new spirit of fellowship' and 'a new readiness for understanding and co-operation'. This was echoed by the Federal Council's resolution in September 1925, adding that the conversations had been longer and conducted 'in a far more conciliatory spirit than in any previous meetings between Conformity and Nonconformity in England'. All participants, Lidgett wrote,[3] would always treasure the memory of 'the spiritual influences that attended our prolonged discussions', so that 'relations of complete mutual confidence and intimacy were established'. Carnegie Simpson confirmed this: 'Instead of talking *at*, they talked *to* one another . . . Anglicanism shed much of its superiority, and the Free Churches outgrew their inferiority complex'.[4] These claims, even allowing for some exaggeration, were genuine enough and constituted real progress on the previous situation.

So much for what *had* happened. Never ceasing to look to the future, Lidgett even predicted the relations 'would prove lasting'. This was largely wishful thinking. Because of the encouraging climate created by the Appeal itself, the discussions had begun, it is true, without the high degree of defensiveness and suspicion which could have affected Church leaders who, apart from Lidgett, had relatively little personal knowledge of their counterparts. They moved surprisingly quickly to appreciation of how the 'other side's' minds worked, understanding the jargon each used, and recognising their sincerity and loyalty in upholding long cherished beliefs. Once the talks were adjourned, however, the momentum tended to be lost, and as changes were made in the delegations,[5] new personal relationships had to be created. When the talks resumed in 1930, the impetus was never quite the same.

Friendly relations among the participants and their carefully worded

Memoranda did not excite among rank-and-file members of the churches the depth of interest for which at least some of their leaders earnestly hoped. After discussions were suspended, Lidgett remarked sadly that 'Ordinary Church members have little knowledge and imagination to care about the subject'. He was not the only one to call, in vain, for a programme of 'education' among them. Prior to, during and after talks this could have removed ignorance about the issues, increased co-operation with others 'in spiritual fellowship and practical endeavours' and, above all, stimulated burning enthusiasm for unity in place of apathy. Without such action the Free Church Council's commendation of the Anglican/Free Church documents 'to the conscience and heart of Christian people' was doomed to be empty words.

At the same time it has to be acknowledged that rank-and-file attitudes were affected by the particular stances adopted by different groups and leaders within each of the Churches. Some prominent figures, who did not participate officially in these talks, were far from enthusiastic about them. Some were sceptical, or more or less openly hostile to progress. On the Free Church side the Baptist T. R. Glover was fiercely opposed to whatever could be seen as dangerous ambiguity. Bishops Gore and Weston both took an Anglican imperialist attitude to the Appeal. They genuinely yearned for unity, but their particular vision of it was not shared by Free Churchmen. In his biography of Frank Weston[6] H. Maynard Smith admitted that few Anglican bishops showed any intention of translating into action the desire expressed in the Appeal for the exercise of the office of Bishop in a representative and constitutional manner. Free Churchmen, he thought, were also guilty of rigidity, but theirs was culpable. His attitude, and that of fellow Anglo-Catholics, was revealed when he wrote:

> Eminent Free Churchmen have been willing to sit in Conference with Anglican divines, but their various denominations have made it clear that they represent no one but themselves. Nonconformists as a whole have not understood the Appeal and have no desire for unity. They argue, 'You recognise our ministry and admire the fruits of our system. By your own showing we are all right, and if so, why should we change?'. They were cradled in individualism and have no conception of a Church.

There were, moreover, distractions on both sides. As mentioned above, the Lambeth Appeal had stimulated other ecumenical discussions. There were also internal preoccupations. Among the Free Churches negotiations for unity between the three Methodist denominations were proving hard fought. Within the Church of England Anglo-Catholic eyes were, in fact, fixed on the talks at Malines, which most of them saw as of greater priority than those with Nonconformists. The long battle for and against 'Ritualists' within the

Anglican Church was moving to its climax in the 1927/8 Prayer Book controversy.

What then was achieved? The series of published reports could be said to have established a basis for future progress towards reunion. As a preliminary survey of areas of agreement and disagreement, they had fulfilled the objective of elucidation. Lidgett was both realistic and hopeful about them. He accepted that 'grave issues remain for the present undetermined and possibly insoluble', and yet he remained optimistic that 'the positive agreements that were reached must go far to give strength and precision to a unity of heart and mind which must eventually find expression in the life and organisation of the whole Church of Christ'.

His analysis in 1925 of those 'positive agreements' was summarised earlier. In his *Guided Life*[7] he added several more. First, the talks had 'greatly assisted in bringing about international conferences, Faith and Order and Life and Work'. Secondly, they had led to 'growing frequency of pulpit exchanges in many dioceses'. He instanced his own invitations to preach or speak in 'several Cathedrals, in Westminster Abbey, and in many parish churches in London and elsewhere'. Other Free Church leaders could make similar claims: Carnegie Simpson boasted of having preached in 'at least half a dozen Cathedrals, including Canterbury'.[8] J. D. Jones had already preached in Durham and Hereford Cathedrals before doing so in Canterbury Cathedral in January 1925 in the presence of the Archbishop.[9]

Some invitations brought objections. Lidgett did not mention the strong protest against his invitation to preach in Hereford Cathedral in October 1922. The Revd Arthur Pinchard, Secretary of the (Anglo-Catholic) English Churchman's Union, sent a formal complaint both to the Bishop, Martin Linton Smith, and Archbishop Davidson.[10] To him the Bishop's action was 'illegal'; it damaged the cause of union as he saw it; and Lidgett had 'supported the Wesleyan Conference in July, shutting the door on the inclusive Episcopate and only approving the Nicene Creed on the understanding that the interpretation is to be that of private judgement'. The Bishop replied, saying *inter alia* that Lidgett had *opposed* the Wesleyan resolution Pinchard had quoted, and no more was heard of the incident. The undercurrent of hostility among some, not all, Anglo-Catholic clergy had also been illustrated by a similar protest in October 1921[11] at Bishop William Temple's invitation to 'several' (unnamed) Nonconformists to preach in his Manchester Diocese during Advent. Davidson replied firmly to Bishop Frank Weston that Temple had done nothing to contravene the Lambeth Appeal. Weston then withdrew from all connection with the Lambeth Conference.

A third positive result could, in Lidgett's view, be seen in 'co-operation in regard not only to social enterprises [perhaps a reference to COPEC *inter alia*], but to spiritual work'. This, he wrote,[12] 'is steadily becoming an ever more widely accepted policy and prospect in this country', as well as through the work of international conferences. His words, 'is becoming', 'policy' and 'prospect' were chosen carefully: they might be thought to imply that substantive action on both spiritual and social fronts had and would take place in England, but in fact it remained to a large extent at that time mainly a hope, a possibility. The Free Churches' repeated request during the talks for action, not just words, met with no response.

There was, however, one quite notable example of *social* co-operation. The General Strike provided a significant, even dramatic opportunity for this. Appeals to the Nation, signed by Church leaders, were not unprecedented, but the Appeal on this occasion aroused particular controversy, and accounts both by Bell, Davidson's Secretary at the time,[13] and Lidgett[14] are muddled over details. What follows attempts to reconstruct the likely sequence of events and indicate the political problems they raised. Three quarters of a million Trade Unionists, supporting coal miners locked out for refusing wage cuts, began their Strike at midnight on Monday, 3 May 1926. It ended eight days later on 12 May 1926.

Nationally the decision to strike was totally abhorrent to Lidgett who, like many Liberals and Conservatives, scented likely revolution, but in the Capital itself he was outraged, not least by Labour's refusal to co-operate with the LCC's emergency measures[15] in solidarity with the TUC. At the same time, in common with others, he wanted the Churches to become involved in promoting conciliation: the Strike, he thought, had been brought about by 'the failure of temper on the part of the negotiators [miners and mine owners], caused by the exacting strain of the prolonged negotiations'.[16]

The initiative in seeking the Churches' intervention was not Lidgett's. According to S. P. Mews[17] this came from Henry Carter (Secretary of the Wesleyan Temperance and Social Welfare Department) on Wednesday, 5 May: he contacted Lidgett and P. T. R. Kirk (Director of the Industrial Christian Fellowship).[18] Lidgett[19] recommended waiting until the extent of the Strike was known: 'As a wily politician – he . . . had a deep distaste for the Labour Party – he might have been hoping that his political opponents would have the chance to discredit themselves'. On 6 May COPEC's Continuation Committee[20] wrote to all clergy and ministers 'urging them to use their spiritual influence to promote conciliatory negotiations'. On that day it seems[21] a meeting took place at Kirk's office. The participants (Bell mentioned 'the Bishops of London and Southwark (C. F. Garbett), with Dr Scott Lidgett and a strong deputation of Nonconformists') nevertheless agreed that some effort at conciliation should be made. Their tentative proposals asked for prayers and assured fellow Christians that they were 'anxiously considering possible ways by which Christian opinion might be brought effectively to bear towards the grave problems of the hour'. Having received these, Davidson promised to consider them carefully and consented to an interview on the following day, 7 May.

Bell (whose account spoke wrongly of two Appeals and two meetings with Davidson, not one) stated that Davidson's interview on that Friday resulted in a lengthy discussion. The group included the Bishops of Ripon (E. A. Burroughs) and Southwark, Canon Woodward, the Revds P. T. R. Kirk and E. S. Woods, and Nonconformists Lidgett, Carter and Dr R. F. Horton (Congregationalist). In the Lords on 5 May Davidson had spoken of the 'unwisdom and mischievousness' of the Strike, but this meeting two days later convinced him of the need to express a more conciliatory attitude. Discussion centred on the issue of an Appeal and a request for resumption of negotiations. Mews[22] wrote that it was Lidgett and Carter who asked Davidson to act in the name of them all. It was then arranged with the BBC that Davidson should broadcast *The Crisis: Appeal from the Churches*, that night. The Appeal called for conciliatory action by TUC, Government and mine owners alike, 'simultaneously and concurrently': by cancellation of the Strike; renewal of temporary financial assistance to the Coal industry; and withdrawal of the new wage scales. It was not partisan, but a sincere attempt to speak to and for the nation on behalf of the Churches. The text of the Appeal went to the press in time for publication by *The Times*[23] on Saturday, the following day, but the BBC suddenly withdrew its permission for a broadcast on that Friday night. Reith, the Director General, rang to say that to broadcast the text would 'run counter to his tacit arrangement with the Government about such things'. According to Hastings,[24] Reith feared that if he gave Davidson permission to speak to the nation, Churchill would start moves to take over the BBC, if it broadcast 'anti-government' views.[25]

Undaunted, Davidson went ahead with his engagement to preach at St Martin-in-the-Fields on Sunday, 9 May. His sermon was broadcast unopposed, and reported in *The Times* on Monday, 10 May. In it he refuted the charge voiced in some quarters that the Churches had been idle. 'On Friday', he declared, 'after prolonged discussion we published a document . . . The President and Honorary Secretary of the Free Church Council [Lidgett] are with us'.

This reference was explained in Lidgett's *Guided Life* and underlined his close contact with Davidson. The Archbishop, he said, 'rang me up to enquire whether, if he made an appeal on the wireless, he would have Free Church support'. Lidgett first rang Dr H. Elvet Lewis,[26] current NCEFC President; Lewis left the decision to Lidgett who promptly telephoned Davidson to assure him of 'our support'. Though Bell made no mention of these telephone calls, they may have taken place just before or immediately after the meeting which

Davidson had called on Friday, 7 May, but not on Saturday, 8 May, where Lidgett placed them, when it would have been too late. Davidson clearly wanted assurance of official Free Church backing for what hitherto had been only personal support.

Cardinal Bourne also preached on Sunday, 9 May, and his sermon at Westminster Cathedral was broadcast that evening. To the astonishment of the would-be conciliators he took a hard line, favouring the Government's stance and calling[27] the Strike 'a sin against the obedience we owe to God . . . and against the charity and brotherly love which are due to our brethren'. Moreover, readers of *The Times*'s report of Davidson's sermon knew Davidson had been in touch with Roman Catholic authority to gain Bourne's support for the Appeal. In Bourne's (partial) defence,[28] however, it seems that in having had to send his message of approval by his secretary he had had no direct hand in drafting the Appeal. His sermon may have been motivated[29] at least partly by a desire to support the Government, to demonstrate Roman Catholic loyalty to the British constitution and prevent 'further radicalization' of the Roman Catholic working class, but he had clearly decided it was politically better, after all, to take a very different stance from Davidson's.

In the Commons on Monday, 10 May, there was such a protest against Reith's action and the Appeal's omission from the Government's London Gazette that the text of the Appeal was finally broadcast from 2LO on 11 May.[30] But Davidson's intervention failed. The Government refused to listen and insisted on capitulation. Many clergy, who had supported the Appeal, were in fact relieved. Canon Peter Green, quoted by Mews,[31] suggested they were in effect saying to themselves, 'The action of the Archbishop and the Free Church leaders was undoubtedly inspired by the Holy Spirit; and we cannot be thankful enough that Mr. Baldwin ignored it'. The Appeal had been controversial, but Bell and Lidgett agreed it brought a real change to the atmosphere. It did not of itself bring the Strike to an end, but in Lidgett's words it assisted 'in softening the asperities with which this grave conflict had aggravated the strife'. Writing to Davidson[32] on 12 May Horton said that the co-operation between the Churches 'draws us very close together'.

There was, however, according to P. A. Harris[33] a political consequence for the Liberals. Having commented that the Strike failed to achieve anything for the miners and came to an ignominious end, Harris wrote: 'The Liberals, who were not parties to the dispute, were in a position not only to have provided a constructive policy, but to have given a real lead to the nation . . . The only effect of the Strike on the Liberal Party was to make a deep fissure', presumably within it. This may have been also an indirect criticism of Lidgett's attitude as Progressives' leader at the time.

To return to the Lambeth Appeal discussions in 1921–5. Whatever may be rated as their achievements were due principally to Carnegie Simpson, Peake, Lidgett, Lang and Davidson.

Patrick Carnegie Simpson, well informed, authoritative and acute, earned the respect of both sides. A Presbyterian and Professor of Ecclesiastical History at Westminster College, Cambridge (1914–38), he came to the fore on the ecumenical scene in the period before the Lambeth Appeal and notably during the 1920s. Henry Lunn enrolled him on the editorial committee of *Review of the Churches* (second series) in 1923/4, and he became Moderator of the Free Church Federal Council 1925–7. Like Lidgett, Simpson was pleased to claim 'friendship' with Davidson, who 'more than once invited me to stay at Lambeth'.[34] Among the Free Church representatives, his strong personality gained him more prominence than Peake. He was far more abrasive and blunt, but equally strong and courteous in maintaining his principles. 'A streak of exhibitionism'[35] showed itself in his enjoyment of public speaking and argument. His penetrating interventions in discussion could reveal a sense of humour, sometimes 'pointed with ridicule', and did much to sharpen debate. In drafting complex findings also, he showed a mastery of the crisp phrase and lucid analysis. In his contribution to Simpson's obituary Lidgett said the most memorable part Simpson had played in the Conversations was in bringing Lang to admit in 1923 that ordained Free Church ministries were real ministries of the Word and Sacrament in the Universal Church, a 'crucial declaration' which to Simpson's and others' manifest frustration was subjected to qualifications and led to no 'appropriate action'. Controversy erupted over the issue later.[36]

Peake, an eminent biblical scholar, had an equally fine mind and strong convictions, but his outstanding qualities were humility and simplicity. For example, his rejection of re-ordination and insistence on reciprocal authorisation of ministries in the conversations was quietly firm. His approach throughout was eirenic, understanding that Anglicans were bound to require episcopacy in the United Church. Later, in 1928, addressing fellow Free Churchmen as Federal Council President 1927–9, he was more explicit, pointing out[37] that for Anglicans to surrender it would break one of their principal links with the Eastern Orthodox and Roman churches, and so create insuperable difficulties for relations, let alone reunion with them. The Free Churches, he urged, should show flexibility and not take a rigid attitude, 'forgetting that all life involves development, adjustment to the environment'. He saw the need to echo and rephrase the line the Council's delegates had taken at the talks and declared: 'To an Episcopacy which would be constitutional and not prelatical, there would be no objection, provided that no theory of Episcopacy as of the essence of the Church is demanded'. To make this assertion in 1928 may have indicated his sense that hostility even to this form of Episcopacy in many Free Churches remained to be overcome.

Lidgett too adopted a statesmanlike approach. This was evident in National and Federal Council debates, official discussions of the Lambeth Appeal, working with Simpson and other Free Church leaders, and privately with Davidson. His view of the Appeal and its implications, expressed in the *Contemporary Review* of October 1920, was reprinted in *God, Christ and the Church*[38] in 1927. He thought it would be the *duty* of non-episcopal ministers to consent to its proposals if the ideal of unity was shared by the whole body of the denominations concerned; if the Church of England declared that no repudiation of the Free Churches' past and present ministry was involved; and if it had faith in the validity of their ministry, the reality of Free Church ministers' 'Divine call and in the divine grace by which they have exercised it'. Only on that basis would he personally have been prepared to be reordained as a means of achieving his dearly desired goal of a united Church.

While keeping solidarity with the vast majority of his fellow Free Churchmen, he sought to mould as well as faithfully to reflect their opinions. His personal conviction remained firm, '*Deus vult*': God wills reunion, organic and corporate, and inward Catholicity was its precondition. He fervently wanted the spiritual benefit he and all concerned had gained from the talks to become widespread throughout the world. Order was to him, as always, subordinate to Faith; a common emphasis, 'the Unity of Faith', would subordinate differences and estrangements, and all our 'prophesying' would be 'according to the proportion of the faith'.[39]

Though prepared to discuss minutiae, he was always looking beyond them and focusing all who would listen to the great vision about the Church in the Letter to the Ephesians. This was the basis of his 'New Testament Principles', a lecture delivered in late 1922, incorporated into the symposium, *The Lambeth Report on Church Unity*, edited by J. G. Simpson, and published in the following year. His talk in London to the fifth Methodist Oecumenical Conference in September 1921 was unsurprisingly entitled 'The Ideal and Basis of Union'. He explained to Davidson that it was delivered to an exclusively Methodist audience, but his principal themes had been fundamentally the same as elsewhere: the ideal should be the paramount concern of all churches; it should nevertheless not entail any 'repudiation of the past, actual or implied', and its achievement depended on 'ample, careful and prolonged discussion'.

The rapport between Lidgett and Davidson was of key importance. The discussions would have quickly foundered without this. Relations between Lang (1864–1945) and Lidgett were much less close. Their contacts did not include such informal meetings as those between Davidson and Lidgett at Sidmouth, in Davidson's rooms at Lambeth Palace, or at his bedside; they seem to have been confined to the comparatively formal setting of the Anglican/Free Church Joint discussions. Younger than Lidgett by 10 years, Lang had a similarly aloof personality. They could not be said to have been friends, but they respected one another. The letter Lidgett wrote on 15 August 1920 to congratulate Lang as Chairman of the Committee which drafted the Lambeth Appeal was genuinely warm and appreciative. Though they differed both in background and over means, Lidgett recognised that Lang had a real vision of the unity of Christ's Church, and sincerely yearned to see it achieved. Lang's Presbyterian upbringing may have helped him to understand the Free Churches; he may equally well have recoiled from it. His stance was that of a prelatical, self-consciously High Churchman, proud, pompous at times; and his energies seemed in effect arguably less directed to exploring what Anglicans had, or had not, in common with the Free Churches, than to improving relationships with the Orthodox and Scandinavian churches and Old Catholics, a larger sphere. Lockhart,[40] however, considered that Lang's overall work for reunion was 'probably his most important service to the Church and Christendom', and 'What he began in 1920 he would have carried forward a further stage in 1940, if the War had not spoiled his plans and halted the whole movement'.[41]

Davidson delegated to Lang responsibility for chairing most of the 1921–5 Joint discussions, but he was always keenly interested behind the scenes. At the same time, naturally cautious, he recognised substantial progress would take time. Writing of the friendly spirit of the talks overall and the unexpected agreement on the fundamental doctrines of the faith gained from them, Bell claimed that Davidson 'made so signal a contribution himself that it is no exaggeration to say that no Archbishop has ever been so respected and revered by the whole Nonconformist world'. The warmth of his reception by the Wesleyan Conference of 21 July 1923, not just by the particular friends he had there (Lidgett and Runciman), illustrated this. His attendance at the one hundred and fiftieth Commemoration of the Dedication of Wesley's Chapel in 1928 was similarly appreciated.

The year 1923 was also that in which Davidson proposed Lidgett for membership of the Athenaeum. Lidgett was by then Moderator of the Federal Council. His name was first suggested[42] as one of the distinguished people recruited in the Club's centenary year, through 'the kind thought of my valued friend, Sir Thomas Barlow [Royal Physician]'. Seconding Davidson's proposal was Dr R. H. Charles, Archdeacon of Westminster, another sign of Lidgett's standing in Anglican circles. Lidgett found[43] great pleasure in the fellowship there with other figures in national life. It was also, he said, 'of practical advantage in regard to the many interests of Church, University and National life with which I have been concerned'.

When the factions in the Anglican Church came publicly to the fore in the Prayer Book controversy of 1927/8, Davidson privately drew a potential parallel between what had led Methodists to form new Churches and what might happen to 'Anglo-Catholics of an advanced kind' if opposition from Sir Thomas Inskip MP [the Evangelical Attorney General] and others were to result in their being forced out of the Anglican Church 'to form some organisation of their own'. His memorandum[44] of January 1929 reflected:

> Nearly everyone now says, 'Surely if the Bishops of that [time when the break with Wesley occurred] had taken a larger view, the splendid work which the evangelists have done outside the Church for 150 years might have been done inside the Church to the steadying of vagaries and the infusion of spiritual life into the Church'.

That would have pleased Lidgett, not least the reference to spiritual life. Davidson's sympathy with Methodists, notably Wesleyans, and respect for what Wesley had stood for, derived to a significant extent from contacts with Lidgett and the strong rapport between them.

As far as the Revised Prayer Book was concerned, Carnegie Simpson and Lidgett adopted 'a friendly attitude', in contrast to the strong Nonconformist opposition.[45] Simpson had nevertheless argued that if Parliament accepted the Revised Book, there should be some assurance or guarantee that it would really be made a standard or limit for Anglican usage, and not merely a stepping stone to further ritual excesses.[46] The *Church Times* interpreted this to mean a call for penalties on Anglo-Catholics to be revived. In the event, as mentioned above, though Parliament was to reject the Revised Prayer Book twice, Bishops were allowed by Convocation to exercise discretion in its use. Anglo-Catholics, having thereby gained what they wanted against the will of Parliament, did not secede; and fears of schism proved unjustified.

Davidson retired on the day of his Golden Wedding, 12 November 1928. In the group led by the Prime Minister, Stanley Baldwin, to present the Nation's gift,[47] were other members of the Tribute Committee representing the King, both Houses of Parliament, the Free Churches and 'parties' within the Established Church. They included Lang; Lords Stamfordham (Private Secretary to Queen Victoria and Kings Edward VII and George V) and Cornwallis (prominent in winning the Lords for the Revised Prayer Book), Sir Thomas Inskip, Carnegie Simpson (current FCEFC President) and Lidgett.

Lidgett was naturally devastated by Davidson's death on 25 May 1930. He will, however, have been deeply touched and greatly honoured by being invited[48] to act as one of the pallbearers at the funeral, a privilege unprecedented for a Free Churchman. He walked alongside Stanley Baldwin, Ramsay MacDonald (then the Prime Minister), Lord Stamfordham, the Earl of Selborne (a leading ecclesiastical statesman and chairman of the House of Laity), Sir Lewis Dibdin (an ecclesiastical lawyer, Dean of Arches), Sir

Frederic Kenyon (Director of the British Museum, in which Davidson had taken a close interest ever since Queen Victoria had appointed him a Trustee in 1884) and Sir Thomas Barlow. They represented all the main branches of public life. All had been Davidson's friends and had worked closely with him in the various aspects of his career.

22

Free Church/Anglican discussions resumed

Hopes that the 1930 Lambeth Conference, chaired by Lang, Davidson's successor, would give a further boost to progress seemed doomed to disappointment. A discussion was arranged between FCEFC representatives, including Lidgett and Carnegie Simpson, and the Conference's Reunion Committee, but it was held far too early in the programme to allow members of the Committee time to review the situation and decide their approach. Several bishops, from the USA in particular, had not been briefed about the joint discussions of 1921–5 and the resulting documents. Moreover, Simpson had not endeared himself in 1928 by saying[1] that Anglican flouting of Parliament's Prayer Book decision was 'hardly cricket', and it would be safer to take the Roman rather than the Anglican form of the episcopate into his system 'since Anglicanism practised a minority form of it'.[2]

The real problem at the Lambeth discussion, however, was not earlier banter of this kind. Lang told Lunn[3] privately that Simpson, using 'his great dialectical gifts and natural emphasis', quoted Anglican recognition of Free Church ministries as 'real ministries of Christ's Word and Sacraments in the Universal Church' without placing equal emphasis on the words 'in their several spheres', which qualified it. Simpson also insisted that the declaration was itself very remarkable, recognising Free Church ministries as 'sacramental and as intra ecclesiam'.[4] The result was surprise, embarrassment, and even hostility among the Anglicans. For their part the Free Churchmen complained that the more significant findings of the 1921–5 talks were given only 'a few colourless sentences',[5] or 'inadequate consideration'.[6] Lidgett[7] applauded the warm sympathy of the Lambeth Conference for the proposed scheme for Church Union in South India, but admitted no significant advance had been made in relations between the Anglican Church and the non-episcopal churches at home. Simpson objected that both the qualifying phrase and the statement that ministries, even when 'real', might be in varying degrees 'irregular', appeared in one version of the statement but not in another.

The Anglicans countered by saying the Free Churchmen's impression was imperfect and therefore wrong. William Temple[8] (1881–1944), who took over from Lang as the Anglican leader of the joint discussions, had not been present[9] at the meeting where Free Church ministries were accorded the above recognition and was ignorant of it. On 21 November 1931 Temple, by then Archbishop of York, sought to excuse his fellow bishops by saying[10] that more time had in fact been spent at the Conference on what had resulted from the 1921–5 talks than was evident from its Resolutions. Moreover, 'a diversion of interest had been caused by the maturity (*sic*) of the Scheme for Church Union in South India which . . . became the dominant concern' – a scheme which at a committee at Mürren in 1931 he had stated[11] was 'the first consideration of those who were anxious for closer union with the separated Churches'. As Simpson impatiently interpreted it, this meant that if the bishops had given more attention to the conversations with the Free Churches, this could have jeopardised their unanimous findings on South India.[12] Lang added that more time had to be spent in discussing definite proposals brought by the Orthodox Communion than it was possible to give to the Free Church delegation which had 'no authority from their Churches to make any such response'.

The Lambeth Conference had expressed the hope that talks with Free Churchmen would restart 'with the definite aim of ascertaining whether the proposed Scheme on Union, prepared for the churches of South India, suggests lines on which further advance on questions of Order can be made'. Lang made the formal invitation to the Federal Council in the spring of 1931.

There was a telling delay before its reply, such was the Free Churches' feeling of disillusionment at the Lambeth Bishops' behaviour. Guy Rogers, Canon of Birmingham, told Lang on 4 May that the 'psychological situation was not as favourable as we might wish'.[13] In contacts with Nonconformist leaders who were debating the terms of their reply, he found 'some anxiety about the composition of the Episcopal Committee which meets them'. If it were possible, he said, to include 'one or two Bishops more directly sympathetic to their general position', this would create a feeling of greater trust and confidence. It seems from the inclusion of, for example, Arthur Perowne, Bishop of Worcester (1931–8), and Edward Woods, Bishop of Croydon (1930–7), that Lang took the point.

The Free Church reply came eventually on 24 September 1931 from W. Lewis Robertson, the FCEFC Secretary. While accepting the invitation, he frankly expressed the Council's objection to its treatment at the Lambeth Conference. So the first of what proved to be approximately nine joint conferences (with up to 18 or 20 members on each side), accompanied by roughly eight or more subcommittees (7 or 8 members on each side), between 1931 and 1939 was arranged for 21 November 1931. Chairmanship of the subcommittees was delegated by Lang to Temple, as Davidson had earlier delegated to Lang.

During this period Lidgett delighted[14] in contacts outside the discussions with prominent, even High Church Anglicans and opportunities to preach in their pulpits. He was particularly proud of being invited by Neville Talbot, formerly Bishop of Pretoria, to preach the annual sermon to the University College of Nottingham in St Mary's Church in 1933. Talbot's father, formerly Bishop of Winchester, invited him to call at his home, but sadly died the night before the proposed visit.

Lang's records of the Lambeth meetings and correspondence related to them are not as full as those for the 1921–5 period, and though there were few Joint Conferences and subcommittees[15] when he was not present, Lidgett's contributions are not mentioned as frequently as before. On the Free Church side new Moderators and Executive Secretaries were coming forward. In the early thirties Garvie (1862–1945) became a very prominent figure in the Free Churches. Lofthouse, while playing a major part in Methodism's contribution to the formation of the South India proposals, was an important participant in the Joint talks.

As so often in the past, Lidgett sought to prevent potentially serious clashes between participants, admit the difficulties from the Free Churches' side, and yet at the same time firmly to emphasise their point of view. At the first full meeting on 21 November 1931[16] he stated he 'personally was not so greatly disappointed by the reference in the Lambeth Report to Reunion in England', adding 'it should not be forgotten that some of the Free Churches were by no means yet ready to accept a more definite result in so many words'. He had always seen the problem as not merely intellectual and practical, but psychological.[17] To him the divisions of three centuries could not be healed in a day: a great educational process was yet to be carried out in both Anglican and Free Churches; impatience should therefore be avoided.[18] Nevertheless he went on to reiterate the call for concerted action, not just words: 'Free Churchmen want to see something done . . . to share in the inauguration of a spiritual movement in the face of which practical difficulties will be resolved'.

Lidgett's eirenic interjection about 'Lambeth 1930' will have steadied the atmosphere. Temple had nearly upset it earlier in the meeting when he injudiciously explained that misunderstanding had arisen because the two groups 'had tended to drift apart'.[19] To soften the impact of this remark he immediately expressed the hope that 'in future there would never fail to be a group in session whose business it would be to keep the Church of England and the Free Churches in touch with one another'. When the meeting was over, he asked for the minutes to be amended to make his point clear: that when the two groups definitely decided not to meet again, they 'did drift apart, and on each side there grew up an opinion concerning what was in the mind of the other which was baseless'.[20] Lidgett agreed that the vision had faded, but that was every reason why action should be taken, for example, by putting something before the public envisaging the Church of the future.

In January 1932 he agreed to set out his views in writing on the nature and order of the Catholic Church,[21] some of which became important in later discussions. He said *inter alia* that:

1. For the Catholic Church of the future they needed to devise a ministry and Church which would gather up the best in all the various forms and functions of the past.
2. The Church had been and still was under the *continual and universally imparted*[22] inspiration of the Holy Spirit.
3. In the light of the Holy Spirit's continuing guidance of the Church, what from the human point of view once seemed a decisive breach of continuity, like the Reformation, might from the divine standpoint be no such absolute break. 'The Spirit of God can vitalise and counteract the disruptive forces of men'.[23] (Lidgett may have been thinking of the distant day when the Roman Catholic Church would be included in the United Church, but his principal purpose was to stress the need for flexibility.)
4. Similarly, though over the centuries the episcopate had come to overshadow other forms of Church order, some were now functioning with success.

At the first full meeting of the resumed Joint Conference J. T. Barkby, Primitive Methodist and then Free Church Moderator, voiced concern about the need for fuller spiritual co-operation, not simply in social work, but in evangelistic work in the winning of men and women for Christ.[24] 'Common Action' was therefore put on the agenda of the subcommittee meeting of 15/16 January 1932. Disagreement rapidly arose on what joint evangelism was feasible: it was pointed out that wide differences existed over the underlying principles of churchmanship, and conservatism and the prejudices of a lifetime affected the attitudes of the rank and file. So the proposal for a national evangelical initiative was apparently dropped.

Experience quickly showed that joint local ventures could provoke internal Anglican division also. Bishop Woods of Croydon sought to arrange a mission for all the Protestant churches in his diocese for 14–23 October 1932.[25] Denominational missions were to be simultaneous and begin with a Joint Commissioning Service, but a missioner from the (Anglo-Catholic) Society of St John the Evangelist, already attached to one Anglican Church refused, with the support of his Superior in Westminster, to enter the parish on the same terms as Missioners from other denominations. So the Bishop consulted Archbishop Lang, but incurred his strong displeasure as a result of the letters he had written to the local churches, the Anglo-Catholic Missioner, his SSJE Superior General and the parish priest concerned. Lang also objected to the terms of the proposed commissioning service. Moreover, in deference to the sensitivities of Anglo-Catholics, who, in the Bishop's scornful words, would otherwise have felt 'defiled', the overflow from the service had to be accommodated in St Matthew's Anglican Church, as well as in the Congregational Hall. Though the bishop had to apologise for 'unguarded' actions, he grew more and more incensed by obstruction until finally he told his Archbishop: 'I must confess it taxes all my powers of Christian tolerance to bear with those . . . who seem . . . so blind that they are unable to see any new and unfamiliar work of God, even though it is going on under their noses'.[26] Lang was unmoved.

At the meeting in January 1932 the Bishop of Croydon and Mervyn Haigh, Bishop of Coventry (1931–1943), together with the Free Churchmen, James Reid and Hugh Martin (1890–1964), a Baptist and SCM Press Director and Editor, had been asked to draft a Memorandum on the way forward. The proposals of this 'Bridge Committee' included *inter alia*: a form of mutual authorisation of ministries; a United Council of Churches to promote corporate thinking and action; interdenominational groups (to be called 'Friends of Reunion') co-ordinated by an unofficial but national movement; and an introductory paragraph to precede their proposed statement to stress the progress made and call for appropriate and unofficial action. The last of these proposals was finally accepted and later enshrined in the Appeal mentioned below. The 'Friends of Reunion'[27] came into being, though not in the detailed or official terms the subgroup had envisaged. But Lang and Temple angrily rejected proposals for mutual authorisation and for the 'Friends' to attend Holy Communion in both Anglican and Free Churches: they were completely out of order, unacceptable not only to Anglo-Catholics but also to 'a large part of traditional Central Churchmanship'.[28] On 11 February 1932[29] Lang had told Temple that the whole Memorandum was 'forcing the pace quicker than the public opinion of the Church is at all ready for'.

Anglican 'coldness' continued at the second subcommittee meeting on 11 March 1932.[30] Lang pointed out the 'enormous distinction' between the situation of Free Church ministers *before* and their situation *after* the Anglican and Free Churches decided to unite. He further stressed the Anglican conviction that it was 'the disunion of the denominations rather than the invalidity of their ministries which holds them apart'. The word 'invalidity', ruled out before, would have raised a few Nonconformist eyebrows! A report by the 1930 Lambeth Conference on 'The Unity of the Church' apparently had stated that 'The will and intention of Christians to perpetuate separately organised Churches makes it inconsistent for them to come before our Lord to be united as one Body by the Sacrament of His own Body and Blood'. So progress seemed stalled and the talks near breakdown. On 14 September 1932 the Federal Council's Annual Assembly had resolved:

While it is glad to learn of continued friendly spirit existing in the confer-

> ence, and that plans for co-operation are under discussion, it cannot but feel that it will hardly be possible to continue these conversations indefinitely with hopefulness or even reality if practical proposals for action cannot be agreed upon.[31]

As late as 8 October 1932[32] Temple was privately admitting that 'Many of our people . . . wish the conversations to be purely exploratory of the ultimate problems of Union'. Yet, in his view, 'This difference is rooted in the fact that our one concern is Union, whereas they, the Free Churchmen, really care more about co-operation than union, though they are sincere in desiring the latter'.

After months of delay, at the Second Joint Conference on 21 October 1932, the Anglicans finally decided to support such co-operation and Lidgett's argument[33] that now was 'most opportune for enlisting the forces that make towards unity'. The result was the Conference's agreement to publish a Joint Appeal.

Issued in the morning of 26 October 1932,[34] this Public Appeal began by explaining that the representatives were at work on the actual problem of reunion and their main effort was directed to the task of solving it, but went on to assert:

> The injury that has been done to the Body of Christ by our Divisions cannot be repaired until it becomes the concern of all His members. We therefore at this early stage of our labours issue this appeal for fuller co-operation . . . The difficulties . . . can yet be overcome if there is sufficient earnestness in the cause of Union among Christian people.

The Appeal then suggested that the world paid less heed to the Christian claim because it supposed the adherents of the gospel were far more divided about it than they really were, and some fellow citizens were almost completely detached from any form of organised religion. Accordingly, it argued, there was now an opportunity for common witness by the churches in localities to the central Christian truths. The case it developed deserves quotation *in extenso*:

> The needs of the time and loyalty to our one Lord impel us to a warmer friendship and a more concerted policy in the carrying out of those tasks for which the Christian Church exists and which can never be performed while we work in isolation. As the Churches make plans and initiate enterprises for the discharge of that common responsibility, they will rise to a new apprehension of the unity in Christ which is already theirs, and the way will be open towards the realisation of still further unity. Above all, let there be genuine friendship between Anglicans and Free Churchmen such as may worthily express the fellowship which springs from close association among those who not only serve one cause but also are one in Christ Jesus . . . If our

> labour is to bear fruit, we are sure that there is a need of a new comradeship among the members of the Churches which we represent.

This was signed by the Archbishop of Canterbury and Lewis Robertson, then FCEFC Moderator. The names of all the individual members of the Joint Conference were to be appended, but Walter Frere, Bishop of Truro (1923–35), objected that the vote had not been unanimous, and the list was omitted. On 8 December 1932, after publication of the Appeal, he told Alan Don[35] it had faced the prospect of contempt and ridicule, but in the event it had met only with contempt. He hoped their Nonconformist brethren were now pleased with themselves, and that perhaps it had succeeded in getting them 'into a better temper again'.

The next, and more substantial issue to be tackled was how 'The Three Principles', episcopal, presbyteral and congregational, could be combined. Again the Bishop of Truro objected. In his opinion on 8 December 1932,[36] Anglicans had combined them successfully in Parish Councils already; Congregationalists were 'dominated by the rule of deacons', and Free Churchmen seemed to have no real intention of acting on the matter. They simply wanted to talk, and 'I suppose we must go on and talk, however hollow it may be'.

On 20 October 1933[37] the Free Church representatives, principally Carnegie Simpson, Garvie and Martin, had contributed a detailed Memorandum on 'Recombination' for discussion. In sum it stated:

> The Free Churches emphasise the principle that the Government of the Church rests in, and should be exercised through the 'Courts' [a hierarchy of congregational, district or diocesan, and supreme general courts] in which the Church as a whole acts – 'as a whole' meaning not only the bishops and presbyters, but also representatives of the faithful people, 'the laity' . . . The acceptance of this conciliar element in government which contained elements of presbyteral and congregational order is what the Free Church representatives regard as the condition of their acceptance of the episcopal element in ordination . . . Union would not even be considered until spiritual freedom is recognised by and also secured for a United Church. Free Churchmen are glad to know that many Anglicans are at one with them in this matter . . . These Church Courts would be open to women, duly elected, on the same terms as men.

At this time impatience at the unproductive way discussions were rumbling on surfaced not only among Free Churchmen. The Bishops of Birmingham (Ernest Barnes), Ripon (E. A. Burroughs) and Leicester (C. C. B. Bardsley), several cathedral deans and headmasters of public schools among others, in disquiet at the lack of progress, decided to draft a manifesto addressed to the Free Churches of Great Britain and to the Church of Scotland. It assured them of a large body of opinion in the Church of England which desired to press on towards unity, both in general and in detail, including greater use of pulpit exchange. They referred to Free Church ministries as real ministries; to Free Church sacraments of Holy Communion as imparting divine Grace just as that of the Church of England; and to the Episcopate as of the *bene esse*, not the *esse* of the Church. Establishment was acknowledged as a difficulty for Free Churchmen, but a *modus operandi*, ensuring both the liberty of the Church and official State recognition of Christianity, was thought possible when the Anglican and Free Churches were more closely united. This Manifesto was sent privately to Lang on 22 June 1934,[38] but little more was heard of it.

To return to the 'Recombination' Memorandum. On 19 July 1934 sufficient agreement had been reached for Edwin Palmer, Bishop of Bombay, and Garvie to be instructed to draft a statement to precede the text, explaining its objects and limits. In a private letter to Lang on 23 July[39] Temple recognised the 'immense importance' Free Churchmen were attaching to it. But he protested:

> They have a complete ignorance of the way in which our Church works, when it is free to adapt its institutions, and even how it works in this country. They always have in their minds a picture of autocratic Bishops, disposing of men and matters at their will. It is a pathetic illusion, but there it is! Consequently, while the document will not help us much, it will help them a great deal, and it is very important to give it a setting [a Preface], an explanatory statement which may avoid the risk that what they welcome so exceedingly should be disowned by the Anglicans through misunderstanding.

At long last the Joint Conference on 26 October 1934 accepted the text, now called *A Sketch of a United Church*. It was published '*as a basis for discussion*' in January 1935.

Lidgett spoke[40] warmly of the document and Preface in its final form, and of its very favourable reception[41] by both Houses of the Convocation of Canterbury and York. A special meeting of the Federal Council on 22 January 1935[42] commended the document to the denominations' careful consideration. It was glad that the conciliar system of Church government had been suggested, to be representative, include the laity and give the people a 'fully effective voice' in selecting a minister of the congregation; that no doctrine of the episcopate would be part of the Church's constitution, bishops would have no final authority; presbyters would be 'associated' with bishops in the act of ordination; and that in spiritual matters the Church would be free from civil control. The Council, however, regretted more was not done: no *acts* of unity, no practical steps as envisaged in the public statement of October 1932.

At the Joint Free Church/Anglican Conference on 25/6 June 1937[43] three other documents were nearing publication, to be 'received', not adopted, but commended for debate in the Churches concerned. On 22 October 1937 they were signed by Garvie, Lang and Temple and published in January 1938. They included a paper on *1662 and Today*, drafted by Hugh Martin and the Bishop of Coventry; *An Outline of a Reunion Scheme*; and an Anglican Memorandum on *The Practice of Inter-communion and the Doctrine of the Church*.

It was made clear on publication that this last document was a preliminary enquiry, not an exhaustive treatment of the subject. It began in the early part of 1935 as *What Is the Principle of Our Divisions?*, Temple's personal attempt to explain the root principle affecting the feasibility of intercommunion, the constantly reiterated request of the Free Churches.[44]

Anglicans, he said, were justified in refusing intercommunion, but through no lack of charity or appreciation of the spiritual values preserved in other traditions. In his view, the principle at stake lay not in the doctrine of the ministry, but in the doctrine of the Church, the relation between membership in the Church as historically organised on an episcopal basis and membership of the Body of Christ. Temple insisted that Church Order provided a warning of 'the insufficiency of the mystical trend alone'. The Church of England with its episcopate desired to witness to the objective gift of grace in actual historical circumstances, mediated by successive generations through the visibly continuous life of the Church. Schism among the denominations had caused the use of other than episcopally ordained priests for the administration of Holy Communion, and, until all ministers were episcopally ordained, open communion according to the Anglican rite was impossible. If there were to be only *mutual* recognition of Free Church and Anglican ministries, schism, he said, would be left unhealed; there would be no one authority acting for the Church and directing its various activities, and no one system or principle of ministry whereby the ministry would become the accredited ministry of the whole Church. Temple added that Anglo-Catholics believed that where an episcopally ordained priest consecrated the elements, the Host was offered to communicants, but if any other minister or priest consecrated them, it was not.

In 1937, after two years' work in committee, the Methodist Church published its own document, *The Nature of the Christian Church according to the Teaching of the Methodists*. Lidgett was, no doubt, consulted, but he does not appear to have been principally involved. R. N. Flew, who was, published his own view in *Jesus and His Church* in 1938.

The Outline of a Reunion Scheme[45] was originally drafted by a Research Group of the 'Friends of Reunion', and subsequently revised by the Joint Anglican/Free Church Subcommittee. It set out the relevant documents produced by the Joint Conferences since 1920, and the scheme under discussion in South India. Its sponsors did not expect it would be carried out in the form in which it was published; little was said, for example, about what was needed between any decision to unite and the final achievement of Union. But it was a carefully framed proposal, worthy of detailed discussion. Lidgett was a co-signatory of this draft scheme, the nearest he came to the unity he had sought.

Some 19 sections covered such matters as qualification for Church membership (Baptism and Confirmation); adherence to the Apostles' and Nicene Creeds (without excluding liberty of interpretation); organisation (a General Assembly, Diocesan Synod and Congregational Council); and relation to the secular authority (freedom in spiritual matters, but not excluding some form of State recognition). The Episcopate was accepted as giving the authority of the whole body, but presbyters would be associated in the ordination ceremony, and the laity would share in the process of approving candidates for ordination. Allowance was made for various theories on the Episcopate's origin and character; the view that the Apostolic Succession determines the validity of the ministry and sacraments was neither affirmed nor excluded. Continuity of the United Church's Episcopacy with the historic episcopate of ancient times was implied, but not stated. Administration of Holy Communion was only permitted to those who had received authority for doing so.

It seems appropriate at this point to digress from the story of Anglican/Free Church discussions in the 1930s to comment on one further, but quite different, event in which Lidgett was also personally involved, though not to his great credit. A venture into politics, it was ecumenical in that the Free Churches, not the Anglican Church, became participants.

Lloyd George had gone out of office in 1922 and was seeking a 'come-back' at the General Election of 1935. Basing his campaign on a 'New Deal' policy of economic growth, he promised to halt currently serious unemployment and industrial decline, through government-sponsored public works and other measures. The international situation, he warned, threatened an outbreak of war, 'unless peace is organised, and unless those errors of policy are avoided which in the past have led to war'.[46] He formed a Council of Action, which he claimed was to be non-political and had originated with ministers of religion and social workers. Hastings called it his 'desperate way of trying to get back into power on the old Nonconformist card which in the past he had played so effectively'.[47]

This programme certainly caught Lidgett's enthusiasm. He had already[48] called for a joint declaration by the churches in favour of peace. As NCEFC Secretary, he no doubt also saw a fresh prospect of gaining from the Free Churches' 'old friend'[49] and a resurgent Liberal Party legislation relevant to their concerns, notably alcohol, Sunday Observance and the need for moral rejuvenation. Lidgett became the Council of Action's Vice-President, and

S. M. Berry, J. D. Jones, Carnegie Simpson, J. E. Rattenbury and F. Luke Wiseman joined him as Council members. The campaign's Area Conventions were modelled on the local Free Church Councils, and Lidgett performed a major role in their organisation.

Having in effect assumed NCEFC leadership, at one Convention on 1 July 1935 he vowed that NCEFC Resolutions (hitherto pigeon-holed) would this year 'be followed up and acted upon'.[50] The Methodist Conference later that month, however, was unmoved by his rhetorical call for endorsement of the campaign, and Henry Carter, Benjamin Gregory and Robert Bond withdrew their support for the 'Call to Action'. More ominously, no major politician backed Lloyd George. The election result gave him only four seats, demonstrating how slight his political influence had become. Moreover, in S. Koss's words, the Free Churches 'never again ventured corporately into the electoral arena'.[51]

Koss launched a bitter attack on Lidgett's behaviour during this episode. He was charged with being 'authoritarian', 'naïve', lacking appreciation of political subtleties and complexities, and even 'treacherous'. Lidgett had given a commitment 'to accept any and every candidate for election who might accept the policy of the Council of Action', and to urge their return at the polls. Not unreasonably, Koss says,[52] people assumed this would include any Labour candidates who endorsed the 'Peace and Reconciliation' proposals, but when about one in three Labour candidates did so, Lidgett was severely embarrassed, having prayed for divine intervention 'to stop the march of Socialism'.[53] Hoping to extricate himself, he hedged on his promise, stating in a letter to *The Times* on 11 November, three days before the election, that Labour's proposals would 'bring about such a crisis as would disable them from giving effect to the Council's policy, however well-disposed their followers might be'. Nevertheless, as Koss puts it, 'the damage was done' and Lidgett was accused of breaking his word. Long political experience might have been expected to prevent him from making his rash, unguarded promise and failing to see through Lloyd George's rosy view of his political prospects, but it did not. Then was not the time, nor was he the man, to realise Nonconformity's hopes.

The NCEFC had overestimated its own importance: traditional loyalties had not been maintained, and its influence had suffered a serious decline. In Hastings's view, 'Much of the middle-class Nonconformity of the South and Midlands, Wesleyans and Congregationalists especially, had moved . . . into the post-war Conservative Party'.[54] Koss attributes[55] Lidgett's misjudgement of the situation to his 'penchant for self-deception' and 'self-righteousness'. Certainly events in this episode proved him to have been 'out of touch with the grass roots' and guilty of naïveté. It is true that, by now aged 81, he was apt to adopt a high, dogmatic tone, but this resulted from a long-standing and patently sincere conviction that Christians need to *act* to secure Christian goals: he constantly strove to advance the Kingdom of God as he saw it.

His characteristic optimism was maintained even in defeat: the Free Churches, he said, could congratulate themselves that Baldwin and his colleagues had given firm pledges on help for depressed areas, support for peace and the League of Nations, and on raising the school leaving age. The NCEFC nationally and locally would, he promised, continue to exert its influence 'on non-Party lines'[56] in supporting the policy of Peace and Reconciliation.

Little solid progress was made on the Joint Anglican/Free Church front between January 1938 and the early years of the Second World War. The representatives' meeting on 11/12 February 1938[57] discussed the outcomes of the 1937 Faith and Order Conference, and approved a national scheme of education about Church Unity (a venture Lidgett had long advocated) to be undertaken by the 'Friends of Reunion'. Since the Baptists had 'recently refused to accept the draft scheme for reunion even for discussion', Temple[58] toyed with holding private talks between a small group of five or six Methodists (the Methodist Sacramental Fellowship, founded in 1935, attracted him) and five or six Anglicans. Nothing seems to have come of this. Unsympathetic to 'any sort of Catholic sacramentalism',[59] Lidgett was not involved. He was elected as a Federal Council delegate in 1938,[60] but Temple did not invite him on 10 February 1939 to join Garvie, Martin, Lofthouse and W. T. Elmslie (Presbyterian) in his special committee to prepare for 'Lambeth 1940'.[61] The outbreak of war intervened to retard progress.

To return to the Anglican/Free Church conversations. What had they achieved by the end of the decade? The results can be found largely in the documents listed above, none of which provided resolutions binding on either Anglican or non-episcopal churches.[62] A limited number of pulpit exchanges continued to take place. Occasional acts of Holy Communion were permitted in special circumstances, all still depending on the view taken by the local bishop or chaplain. Overall, however, it can be said that relations between the two 'sides' had greatly improved since 1920, despite the hitch encountered in 1930.

To Reunion enthusiasts this was depressingly insufficient. But Lidgett counselled against impatience. The outlook he expressed in 1936 never changed:

> Before Reunion is accomplished, all the Communions concerned must be convinced that *God wills it*, and must make a concerted demand for its achievement. This result, however, is, as yet, far from having been attained. The existing and still prevalent denominationalism is, in all the churches, an amalgam of particular loyalties, habits, and prejudices.[63]

All churches, he wrote, can join in singing with equal intensity 'Faith of our Fathers living still', but 'both the emphasis and content are in each case different, and in important respects, divergent'. Faith, he added, can connote the inheritance from the Roman Church, or the Reformers and Puritans, or John and Charles Wesley. In his view the problem, therefore,

> is not merely intellectual and practical. It is, above all, psychological. Until the enthusiasm . . . becomes concentrated upon the same content of belief, transcending the existing, but narrower, loyalties, habits, and prejudices, the result of all this fervour may well be to fortify differences rather than to promote that inward Catholicity which is the precondition of Reunion.

The amalgamation of the separate National and Federal Councils in 1941 to form one body, the 'Free Church Federal Council' (FCFC), is likely to have pleased Lidgett in itself, but not its very negative and disappointing formal response on 16 September to the 1937 documents. They had to admit[64] that after 20 years of joint conversations reunion was not equally desired by all the members of their churches. Some thought it unnecessary for the effective discharge of the functions of the Church, or undesirable as imposing outward uniformity, or not essential to exhibit inward unity; others called it impracticable as involving the loss of different traditions and customs; and many thought divisions served 'to exhibit to the world the manifold truth and grace of Christ and the diversity of the operations of the Spirit of God'. Nevertheless the Federal Council detected an increasing number in all churches which did desire a union 'which will not enforce any uniformity, but will welcome variety-in-unity, will preserve all proved values, and will enhance the authority and efficacy of the Church'. Some wanted still further exploration of the problems, while others preferred first to study proposals for reunion among the Free Churches themselves.

Outside the conversations there were three noteworthy outcomes. The most significant and substantial demonstration of Church unity lay in the efforts to improve religious education and national education more generally, resulting, to Lidgett's great delight, in the 1944 Education Act.[65]

Next was the Churches' joint insistence on the application of Christian tenets to the aftermath of war. On 21 December 1940 a letter was written to *The Times* jointly by the Archbishops of Canterbury and York, Cardinal Hinsley (Archbishop of Westminster) and W. H. Armstrong (Moderator of the Free Church Council).[66] In *A Christian Basis for Peace* they accepted the Five Peace Points of Pope Pius XII, and declared there could be no permanent peace without the principles of the Christian religion as the foundation of national policy and all social life. All nations should be regarded as members of one family under the Fatherhood of God. Drawing on papers from the 1937 Life and Work Council in Oxford, the Church leaders set out tests for economic situations and proposals: whether extreme inequality in wealth was abolished; every child had an equal opportunity of education; the family was safeguarded as a social unit; a sense of divine vocation was restored to men's daily work; and whether the resources of the earth were used as God's gift to the whole human race and with due consideration for the needs of present and future generations. Lidgett is likely to have joined in the relevant Free Church discussions. He no doubt approved of the reference to the Fatherhood of God!

The third was Archbishop Fisher's initiative, an indirect outcome of the ecumenical discussions over 36 years. Temple, Lang's successor as Archbishop, had died unexpectedly in 1944, but on 3 November 1946 Geoffrey Fisher, who succeeded Temple, and was enthusiastic about Church unity, took an important initiative with which Lidgett probably largely concurred. Dubbed 'the schoolmaster', Fisher was anxious to bring the long discussions to an end. His sermon at Cambridge, 'A Step Forward in Church Relations',[67] asked whether the Free Churches might be prepared to 'take some form of the "historic Episcopate" into their systems' to allow full intercommunion to take place. Adopting the Episcopate would secure 'a ministry mutually acknowledged by all, possessing not only the inward call of the Spirit, but also the authority which each Church in conscience requires'. The Free Churches would be free to suit the form of the Episcopate to their individual requirements. There was no intention that they should sacrifice their principles or be impelled to make unpalatable changes to their constitutions, and it was acknowledged that the Church of England itself had 'not yet found a finally satisfying use of the Episcopate in practice'. Fisher looked forward to all parties recognising each other as within the Body of Christ, despite their divisions. After some hesitation later, he repudiated the concept of organic union.[68]

By now, though he would not have admitted it, Lidgett, the 'Nestor of the Free Churches',[69] was 'winding down', and he was not personally involved in the official responses to Fisher's sermon. In April 1946 during a speech in Westminster Chapel Fisher teasingly said, 'Discussions between the Churches should be confined to people under 50 and over 90, since Dr Lidgett could not be left out'. Lidgett only half heard, but interrupted and called out, 'I'm 92!'[70]

When Lidgett finally retired from the Bermondsey Settlement in 1949, then aged 95, Fisher proposed his health at a ceremony marking the occasion.[71] It was attended by several bishops, deans, peers and the major figures of Methodism. In his speech, recalling the educational as well as the ecumenical debates of the past, Fisher paid Lidgett a sincere and generous tribute:

> He remembers very well the bitter controversies that used to take place and the damage they did to the children and the Churches. But the position is very different now, and I would say not the least of this, if not the most, is due to Dr Lidgett himself.

In his reply Lidgett reiterated his unwavering ecumenical convictions:

'Sectarianism is doomed, and neither heaven nor earth will have anything to do with it. The great keyword of our thought, our sympathy and our practice is Catholicity'. Dr W. E. Sangster[72] recalled what the *British Weekly* described as the most revealing part of Lidgett's speech. He hoped to see while he lived one 'Catholic' Church, comprehending all denominations. For such a consummation, he confessed, he would accept the Lambeth Quadrilateral, 'even the Episcopate'. 'The speaker paused', said the journal, 'and the silence was profound. Then he added, "with certain conditions", and the gasp turned to hearty laughter'.

Lidgett's conditions for accepting Episcopacy followed:

> To begin with, I will not agree with any disparagement of that heroic mission of John and Charles Wesley which saved the English-speaking peoples of the world. In the next place, no one, I think, will be foolish enough to imagine that by a uniformity which would stereotype faith can a United Church be brought about. There must be recognition of the great traditions at the back of the Churches, springing from the root of the Apostles and the Primitive Church. They all took their rise from there. A truly Catholic Church to which all can bring the riches of their inheritance – that is the ideal.[73]

Under four years later death overtook him, and his vision remained unrealised.

Before, during and after the conversations Lidgett's theology had remained consistent. Rupert Davies, writing in 1957, also described it as fully up to date:

> If we strip it of the phrases which suggest the immanentism . . . characteristic of the first part of the century, and of those which suggest a more optimistic view of human progress than subsequent events have borne out or biblical thought warrants, and come down to its real content, we shall find that Lidgett was already saying before the first World War and just after it the things which the best ecumenical theology of today is now saying, and often believes it to be saying for the first time. The Church as the foretaste of the glory that is to be revealed, that is (in the modern jargon) as an eschatological reality, the Church's God-given unity and the consequent imperative to be outwardly what it essentially is, the Catholicity of the Church as containing and transcending all its differences – all these are familiar conceptions to those who take part in the modern ecumenical conversation. Lidgett was a pioneer in expounding them . . . before the Churches were willing to hear.[74]

Part 7

Uniting Methodism

Resuming the story after 1919, Chapters 23–4 comment on the prolonged, taxing, but successful path to Methodist Union and on Lidgett, its first President.

Calendar of main events

1920	Bevan Shepherd's Manifesto. The 'Other Side' formed.
1922	Second Manifesto by the 'Other Side'. Launch of the *Wesleyan Methodist*.
1924	Agreement on need for 75 per cent vote on union.
1926	Doctrinal issues agreed. The 'Other Side' proposed 'Union by Stages'.
1927	Crisis in Wesleyan Conference Representative Session. 'Business Committee' proposed 'Three Stage policy'.
1928	The 75 per cent vote achieved for Methodist union at the Wesleyan Conference.
1932	The Uniting Methodist Conference with Lidgett as First President. Honorary DD from Oxford University.
1933	Companion of Honour. Honorary DD from Edinburgh University.
1934	Mrs Emmeline Martha Lidgett died on 12 May.

23

Progress towards Methodist Union 1920–32

The long, tortuous road to Union can be conveniently divided into three phases.

The first brought crucial issues to the fore. In articles for the *Methodist Times* Lidgett had already expressed his personal view of the essentials of Methodism. When union discussions began in earnest, more detail was needed: the stances of all three parties had to be appreciated and, where they differed, compromises proposed between them. The Wesleyans, the largest denomination, had taken the initiative, but the Primitive Methodists (PM), half their size, and the United Methodists (UM), a third, were anxious for dialogue. In the account which follows, the contrast is made between Wesleyans and Primitives, since the beliefs and practices of both non-Wesleyan denominations were broadly similar. The issues, however, were far from simple.

Though all three denominations possessed an ordained ministry, the Wesleyans put greater emphasis on their ministers' special God-given status and pastoral authority. The Wesleyan Conference was divided into two separate sessions, one reserved exclusively for ministers, and only ministers could be elected to the annual Presidency and Legal Hundred. By contrast the Primitives' Conference consisted of only one (the Representative) Session, with no Legal Hundred, less control over local autonomy, and its Presidential office open to laymen. Each denomination admitted laymen to its Representative Conference and embraced the doctrine of the priesthood of all believers, but only the Wesleyans insisted on restricting the administration of Holy Communion to ministers; after 1893 permission had been given to Wesleyan probationers if circumstances made this necessary. John Wesley's *Notes on the New Testament* and the first four volumes of his Sermons were specifically mentioned in the Wesleyan Hornabrook's list of questions in 1917 as the 'guarantees of the evangelical doctrinal position of Methodism'. Peake, however, for the Primitives and with United Methodist support, maintained that Wesley's exegesis could now be seen to contain flaws, and in his view Methodist beliefs and those of Wesley were now not always identical.

Much bargaining had clearly taken place on the nature and powers of the

Conference before the *Tentative Scheme for Union*, prepared by the United Committee (which included Lidgett), was issued. The constitution proposed for discussion revealed that Wesleyan insistence on a Pastoral, now discreetly renamed Ministerial, Session of Conference had been successful. Without its retention little support for union could be expected from Wesleyan ministers on whom so much depended. In return for this major concession Wesleyans had to accept that the Representative Session should elect the President, 'recognise' all ministers of the United Church, and gain significant control over doctrine. The Stationing Committee, responsible for the allocation of ministers to circuits, had according to Wesleyan practice been appointed by ministers only in their Ministerial Session. But now, in response to pressure from the other two denominations, it was recommended that the committee should be composed both of ministers and laymen, and that, though the final reading of Stations should continue to take place within the Ministerial Session, as before, laymen would be permitted to attend, and no changes could be made to the list without agreement by all the relevant parties.

Ministerial prerogatives were further eroded by the removal of what had hitherto been the minister's exclusive power to nominate lay officials in the Church. In return for retaining the offices of President and Secretary of Conference and District Chairmen as ministerial roles, the Wesleyans acceded to the PM/UM demand for an annual election of a lay Vice-President. His role was not important; his significance was as a guarantee of the rights of the laity. It was further agreed that the appointment of a Legal Hundred was undemocratic, outdated and should have no place in the new constitution. Continuity from Conference to Conference was, however, valued, and a system was proposed for electing a basic 'core' within the Conference membership, consisting of ministers and laymen in equal numbers who would retire and be replaced in rotation.

Doctrine was another important issue. Having, at the start of the discussions, found fault with the initial Wesleyan formulation of the doctrinal standard, Peake came to accept that 'the loyalty of the Wesleyans to their founder is such that the inclusion of the reference [to Wesley] seems imperative'. At first, in February 1919, the phrase, 'the evangelical doctrines . . . as held by the three Conferences and as *generally* contained in the Notes and Sermons' satisfied him, but at the United Committee meeting in March 1920 he arranged with the Wesleyan Maldwyn Hughes for another insertion into the formula: namely, after 'Sermons' to add 'subject to the authority of divine Revelation recorded in the Holy Scriptures'. In this way, as Kent puts it, the Bible was 'introduced as a decisive factor in the definition, leaving biblical criticism as the arbiter. Whatever can be squared with the Bible need not be squared with Wesley's Notes on the New Testament'.[1] Such an intervention was entirely natural from a liberal biblical scholar, but the debate did not end there.

As Lidgett predicted, the principal bones of contention throughout the twenties were the nature of the ministry and the sacraments. Agreement on these was essential if a final scheme for union was to be acceptable. Those who might be called 'High Church' Wesleyans adhered to the tradition whereby ministers were regarded as delegates 'from above', a view, however, which had remained vague and ill-defined. By contrast many Methodists had come to regard ministers as representatives 'from below', from the ranks of the faithful. This was particularly emphasised by the Primitives, strong on dissent from the Established Church and its priestly order. Lidgett too had spoken out against Anglican sacerdotalism. But 'High Church' ministers, horrified by the extremes to which a representative theory could be put, feared loss of status, demeaning ministers to the position of 'paid agents of the Church'. In 1921 Peake had to point out that the former Wesleyan view had been superseded, even if these Wesleyans had not realised it. He called their attention to the views set out by their own G. G. Findlay nearly 30 years before:[2] to him the minister was brother, not ruler; he existed for the sake of the Church and arose out of it; and every member of the Church had spiritual qualities and spiritual duties. This, Peake insisted, was no 'grovelling' view of the ministry. He himself held a high doctrine of the ministry because he held a high doctrine of the Church, and in his opinion that doctrine and the representative view were now shared by all three Churches. Lidgett declared the same 'high' doctrine at the 1924 Wesleyan Conference: 'I hope I hold a sufficiently high doctrine of the responsibilities of the ministry, but a call does not come independently of the Church, nor exercises ministry in independence of the whole body of the faithful.'[3]

There was much debate also on whether lay administration of the Sacrament could be sanctioned in the United Church. Non-Wesleyans had argued fiercely for such permission to be granted not only where expediency (shortage or unavailability of ministers) called for it but as a matter of principle, and it was clear that without allowing variation between the practice of the different Churches to continue no scheme would be accepted. Though many Wesleyans found lay administration psychologically intolerable, they could not justify their opposition by claiming that ministers' ordination had conferred special grace on them. They had to fall back on stressing the need for 'Order, not Orders', that is, for decency and dignity in conducting Holy Communion. This latter emphasis appealed to Lidgett and other Wesleyans who administered the sacrament with great reverence, but without regarding themselves as 'High Church Sacramentalists'.[4] The formula proposed by the Tentative Scheme read:

> The general usage of the three Uniting Churches, whereby the Sacrament of the Lord's Supper is administered by ministers shall continue to be observed. In any area where special provision for regular administration is

required, the Conference shall be responsible for the authorization of duly qualified persons set apart for the purpose.

The question remained: how far could these persons be distinguished from ministers?

Major protagonists were soon identified. Battle lines had already been forming well before the formal submission of the Tentative Scheme in 1920. Protagonists for and against union, 'Unionists' and 'The Other Side'[5] respectively, emerged within the United Committee. Though it is possible to generalise between the views of distinct 'parties', the motivation of the many individuals involved and the stances they took were not entirely consistent.

Currie described Lidgett, French and Peake as the 'At All Costs School of Unionists'.[6] This is unfair: it represents his inference from the surprising extent of the concessions proposed in 1920 and the influence these leading figures may well have had on them. It is true that Lidgett showed impatience in the speech he made to the Wesleyan Conference during its 1920 debate on the Scheme.[7] Throughout the decade that followed there was never any doubt, despite Peake's advocacy of the Primitive stance, where all three individuals stood. Passionately convinced of the project's urgency, they were all determined to push the discussion forward, where possible, but they were not extremists. Serious differences had to be treated seriously. Lidgett explicitly condemned undue rush, and insisted that a clear and passionate desire for union by the Methodist people was the fundamental priority. Even amid heated Conference debate Lidgett and French listened calmly to their opponents and replied firmly but courteously, while in Committee Lidgett and Peake patiently tried to iron out difficulties in draft after draft.

Wesleyan Unionists also included W. R. Maltby (1866–1950), F. L. Wiseman (1858–1944), Henry Carter (1874–1951) and Maldwyn Hughes (1875–1940). Alfred Sharp (1856–1932), though attracted to the Anglican Church, sought conciliation between Methodists. John Hornabrook (1848–1937) adopted a dispassionate approach which made him respected by 'the Other Side'. The most prominent laymen among the Wesleyan Unionists were Walter Runciman (1870–1949) and in particular the strong opponent of any union with the Anglican Church, R. W. Perks, whose legal expertise and connections were vital in ensuring the appropriate formulation of the Trust Deeds and the new Church's Enabling Bill and preparing for their passage through Parliament. Peake had enormous influence among the Primitives: they were proud of his expertise and trusted his judgement. The Primitives' convenor, Samuel Horton, and his United Methodist counterpart, David Brook, while insisting that non-Wesleyan convictions were recognised, carried their denominations with them in support of union, despite brief and abortive attempts by the UM 'Progressives' in 1922 and the Primitive T. R. Auty in 1923 to counter their lead. It seems very likely that the working relationship between Lidgett and Peake and their mutual respect for one another, despite differences in churchmanship, helped to make reaching agreement between and within their churches much smoother than initially expected.

Of the three denominations the Wesleyans supplied the most numerous, and certainly the most prominent, opponents of union. The conservative evangelicals among them included, for example, W. H. Armstrong and WBU[8] stalwarts G. Armstrong Bennetts and H. C. Morton. Another group was represented by the diehard R. Bevan Shepherd, one of several who opposed any action which might, as they saw it, jeopardise possibilities for Wesleyans to join a wider union in the future, not least when the Lambeth Appeal from the Anglican Church seemed to encourage this. Maltby scornfully described them as those who 'had recently shaken hands with a bishop'. Their problems were that Wesleyans in general had been moving closer to the Free Churches, and among non-Wesleyans the long-standing Wesleyan links and emotional attachment to the Anglican Church had never made any impact. 'High Church' Wesleyans seemed to have constituted a wider group than Anglican sympathisers, but included them. They were equally adamant that ministerial status had to be preserved. They opposed any reformulation of doctrine which failed to set Methodism in the context of the wider Catholic Church, omitted reference to the historic Creeds, or allowed lay administration of the sacraments which, they were sure, would keep the Anglican door firmly shut long into the future. Contemptuous remarks about the other two denominations were spread by some of their bitterest opponents: for example dubbing them as 'Ranters' and alleging that Holy Communion[9] could be a matter of 'biscuits and water'.

The strength of opposition to union was evident when Bevan Shepherd's Manifesto, published as early as January 1920,[10] had only three months later attracted the signatures of roughly one-third of Wesleyan ministers. 'The Other Side', however, came officially into being in the Kingsway Hall on 26 November 1920 as a result of the Conference debate and the furore it caused. A propaganda fund was raised, headquarters established in London and Liverpool, and secretaries began to be appointed in the Circuits. J. H. Rider, Chairman of the Cornwall District, was elected its chairman, but Rattenbury had already become its most prominent protagonist after publicly denouncing the Tentative Scheme in June 1920. Other activists came forward: Amos Burnet (President in 1924, who died in 1926), and laymen, Sir Kingsley Wood MP[11] and Sir Henry Lunn.

At the Wesleyan Conferences of 1920 and 1921 union was high on the agenda. In the 1920 Conference debate on the Tentative Scheme, Rattenbury, red-faced at the prospect of 'sacrificing our identity',[12] was clearly galled by reports of 'remarkable unanimity on all the questions asked' and 'good ground for hopes that a satisfactory basis for union could be found'. For him the United Committee's albeit tentative proposals had gone far too far, 'wrecking' the Wesleyan Church. Gall turned to fury when the Conference asked the synods to discuss the scheme, but not to vote on the fundamental principle of union itself: this was interpreted as a means of committing them to union by sleight of hand. But the Conference agreed that United Committee deliberations would continue, and the Scheme would receive further consideration at the following Conference. Perks deprecated anything which would delay progress.

Lidgett's Conference speech ran true to form, stressing high principles. The writer of 'Conference Impressions'[13] was impressed: 'The theme was lifted above trivialities. His speech had breadth, depth and a sweep both of vision and capacity not easily characterised and seldom matched'. Lidgett, he said, thought the Conference unwise to concentrate on what he regarded as comparatively unimportant details of the bare outline of a scheme. To him the one great issue before them was whether the Conference should express some measure of hope that 'the *great* scheme' might be brought to an ultimate conclusion. As the *Methodist Recorder* reported:

> He approached the subject as one who had only a moderate measure of enthusiasm for any Union short of a much wider Union than that now under discussion . . . If he believed that any vote in favour of the scheme of Methodist Union would spoil the prospect of that larger Union, he would be seriously exercised in his mind as to what vote he ought to give . . . The only Union possible was on the basis of Evangelical Catholicity . . . Who had greater opportunity to give expression to that Catholicity than the Methodist Church throughout the world and especially in Great Britain? They were asked to look at their Trust Deeds. He was anxious rather to look forward to a Church that was to be. Could they even hope for the larger Union if they refused a Union which involved so little sacrifice? Methodist Union would become the precursor step by step of that larger Union. His enthusiasm for that ultimate ideal was tempered by realistic awareness that progress would take time.[14]

After the 1920 Conferences the United Committee went ahead with propaganda for Methodist Union. There was little opposition from the PM and UM districts to the Tentative Scheme in general, but objections were raised to an autonomous Ministerial Session and to the necessity of Conference authority for lay administration of the sacraments. Unionist optimism suffered a setback when 'the Other Side' set up its formal organisation, and when the Wesleyan synods expressed such a cautious majority in favour of the scheme that voting in Circuit Quarterly meetings was postponed. This encouraged Burnet, Rattenbury and Lunn to raise the *principle* of union at the United Committee meeting in June 1921, only to be decisively defeated. From that point delaying tactics, to defer decision or replace the Scheme, became their only option.[15] Accordingly, when at the Representative Session of the 1921 Wesleyan Conference it was proposed to accept the Scheme as a basis for further discussion, Rattenbury put forward an amendment, arguing that 'The time was not yet ripe for organic Union' and that alternative proposals should be devised. Lidgett challenged this, and Rattenbury's amendment was defeated. The Conference agreed on the substantive proposal, but the number of neutral votes and the formidable minority represented by his supporters emphasised how much more work needed to be done. Moreover the importance of Ministerial Session voting was reinforced by Burnet's (albeit abortive) attempt to require its full authority before any scheme could be considered acceptable.

The publication of the Lambeth Appeal soon after the 1920 Conference was over gave Lidgett the opportunity not only to express his excitement at the prospects it gave but also to explain how Methodist Union, far from being overtaken or needing deferment (as 'the Other Side' was to allege), related appropriately to it. His article in the *Methodist Recorder*[16] contained echoes of his Conference speech:

> Shall the Churches that call for a League of Nations, with the sacrifices that are demanded if such a League is to become effective, show themselves unwilling to make sacrifices for the fulfilment of our Lord's will 'That they may be one', and for the advancement of his Kingdom? This cannot, and must not be . . . This larger proposal does not tend to displace the great prospect of Methodist Union. The great types of the evangelical tradition must not only be preserved but developed with the larger Union, and if the Methodist type is to fulfil its distinctive mission, it must be expressed through a united Methodist fellowship and organisation.

This did not satisfy Rattenbury. In his opinion proposals for Methodist Union would interfere with response to the Lambeth Appeal, not least because of the distinctiveness of the three Churches. Lidgett took the opposite view:

> Can it really be maintained that the three branches represent three distinct types in anything like the same sense and degree as Methodism as a whole is distinct from older forms of Nonconformity? The differences between the branches of Methodism have been almost exclusively ecclesiastical, and the Tentative Scheme shows how easily these differences may now be transcended. In evangelical faith and doctrine, in experimental religion and its characteristic forms of expression, as well as in Evangelical aims and methods, Methodism is *one* – its unity of type is due to linear descent from the Revival of the Eighteenth Century.[17]

For Lidgett, 'Only a united Methodism could *tell* in a Reunited Church . . .

Methodism would bring with it a united Church government, a uniform constitution, and common institutions'. The three Churches must not, he insisted, be divided among themselves, or merely held together by a redundant federation. But in his view the prospect of fusion should cause no undue alarm.

> A *gradual* reorganisation of central and local effort would follow in due course, much waste being saved thereby. Closer fellowship would grow up, and *eventually, though not for a time*, local amalgamation of Churches would be brought about – a gradual process, not revolution.

To Lidgett the important question was then, as earlier when Wesleyan/Anglican union was proposed, 'Do people urgently desire and demand it?', but in his view it was too early to answer, and unwise to anticipate the course of events. Aware of the current state of Methodist opinion overall, he went on:

> Only when presented and explained throughout the circuits of Methodism, as it has to the United Committee, will the Church be ready for the momentous answer which must then be given. For the time being, let us keep open minds and open hearts, ready to be led step by step until the final answer can be given by all the Methodist people under the guidance of our Lord.

The Lambeth Appeal was received at the Wesleyan Conference of 1921, but a formal response could not be made until the Conference of 1922. By then Lidgett had been engaged in Free Church/Anglican discussions of the Appeal,[18] and may well have helped to draft the Conference's official reply.[19] Among other things the Conference sought clarification of its terms, but gave it a cautious welcome, as did other Free Churches at a similar stage, and expressed readiness to join in exploring the issues. The reply, however, made it clear at the outset that Wesleyans adhered to the principles of the Protestant Reformation; would favour closer fellowship at the Holy Table and regulated interchange of pulpits; but would not want any limit on its freedom of fellowship with other non-episcopal churches.

It is worth pausing at this point to note the extent of Methodist democracy at work. Though discussion on important details continued up to (and beyond) the 1932 Uniting Conference, July 1928 was effectively the date at which agreement on Methodist Union was finally achieved. Debates took place in a wide variety of forums. Lidgett's precise contribution is rarely easy to identify in necessarily abbreviated Wesleyan Conference Record and Methodist Union Committee Minutes and Journals;[20] his articles and accounts of his major speeches at Conference, provided by the Methodist Press, are clearly vital in helping to fill out the picture. But the record even of his presence at such numerous meetings in an exceptionally busy life, quite apart from his chairmanship of some, shows the extent of his participation and the confidence placed in his knowledge and judgement. That busy life included, not only the Lambeth Appeal discussions, but *inter alia* work in the Bermondsey Settlement, London University, the LCC and in committees appointed by the Conference Ministerial Session for such matters as internal discipline. It is no surprise that he had occasionally to apologise for absence.

Meetings could be placed in two broad categories. The first covered Conferences, Synods and Districts. The three Churches held their own annual Conference, not at the same dates: the PM and UM Conferences with only one Session each, but the Wesleyan with two. There were also Standing Committees for all four Sessions to keep a watch over union developments between Conferences. Each Wesleyan district held synod meetings, also with Representative and Ministerial Sessions, while the PM and UM district meetings had only one Session on each occasion. At times during the union debate, 'local courts' (the Circuit Quarterly and Trustees Meetings of each denomination), were called on for views from the 'grass roots'. Lidgett was active in Wesleyan Conference Sessions (annually in July) and both of their Union Committees, and, as Chairman of his London District, in both meetings of its Synod.

The second category included the Union Committees. Representatives (ministerial and lay) of all three Churches were elected to the United Committee, which met several times each year. Lidgett was regularly elected as a Wesleyan representative. This Committee appointed from its members an Executive Committee, meeting more frequently, and this in turn appointed a variety of subcommittees to discuss particular issues as the need arose: for example, on doctrinal/sacramental clauses; stages for Union; synod, district, and departmental amalgamations; work in specified areas of the country; legal and financial matters; codification of regulations (such as Conference procedure, membership, etc.); local and area meetings for fellowship between members of the different denominations; publicity; the Uniting Conference; celebration of Union, etc. Each subcommittee reported to its 'parent' body, so that its proposals or drafts could be amended or ratified before they were passed on up the 'hierarchy' of committees and then to the Conferences of the three Churches, the final authority in each case. Lidgett was a member of, and sometimes chaired, the Executive Committee and many of its key subcommittees, and as one of those who gave evidence to the Lords and Commons in their discussion of the Enabling Bill in 1929, he acted as 'the official witness in regard to the doctrinal portion of the Scheme'.[21]

During the second phase the struggle to devise a wholly acceptable Scheme was intense, and optimism rose and fell on both 'sides'. A full account would be tedious. What follows concentrates[22] on the principal, especially the Wesleyan, stages in the debate and identifies where Lidgett was prominent in it.

In February 1922,[23] convinced that the Methodist Press, the Conference 'platform' and wealthy Methodists were arrayed against them, Rider and his 'Other Side' Committee voted for a strong campaign to oppose Union in principle. A second manifesto was issued, sponsored by Shepherd and 75 fellow ministers equally hostile to any prospect of 'fusion', and by June the number of signatories had risen to as many as 800. Peake took great exception to the text, since it implied that he regarded ministers as paid agents of the Church. Undeterred, Rattenbury pointed out major differences between the Wesleyan and the other Churches, such as their approaches to administering the sacraments, the ministry, forms of worship, even party political allegiance.

In May 'the Other Side' launched its own newspaper, *The Wesleyan Methodist*, and its confidence was further boosted by the reaction of Samuel Horton to signs of their growing strength. Impatient at the prospect of further delays in progress towards a union with Wesleyans, he threatened to promote instead a union between the 'three lesser bodies' instead, the PM and UM churches with the Wesleyan Reform Union, whose partnership had hitherto been rejected. Moreover, the results of votes in the Trustees' and Quarterly meetings after the Wesleyan Conference of 1922 indicated insufficient enthusiasm, and its 1923 Conference was a noisy, even disorderly affair. In the Representative Session Wilberforce Allen objected to the Unionists' 'All or Nothing' policy and demanded proposals for an alternative scheme. In the Ministerial Session French was constantly heckled, and Lidgett corrected Rattenbury on points of order. Though the hostile amendments were lost, the size of Conference's anti-Unionist minority had increased since 1922.

The various committees continued their work in 1923/4. Difficulties continued over the doctrinal statement and which Conference Session, Representative or Ministerial, should follow the other and be seen to have greater power or responsibility. Questions were raised again about wording on the ministerial role and lay administration of the sacraments. Agreement was reached that ministers took 'the principal and directing part' in shepherding the flock, but had 'no exclusive title to the preaching of the gospel or the care of souls'. This preserved the role of the Methodist class leader and local preacher, but made no reference to the sacraments. Wesleyan attempts to emphasise 'the general usage' (of ministers) or to look forward to 'uniformity of practice' did not satisfy the PM and UM Churches. A compromise was (temporarily) reached which neither guaranteed nor excluded lay administration: but 'the Other Side' continued to insist on the principle of ministerial administration.

The PM/UM message to their own Quarterly Meetings was upbeat, stating that the scheme as it stood in 1924 afforded a basis 'which would ensure harmonious working without sacrifice of any principle which is vital to

Methodism'. In the event, however, though voting in the Quarterly Meetings in all three Churches indicated 80 per cent or more in favour of union, the majority in Trustees' Meetings of between 69 and 75 per cent still revealed a stubborn minority, unhappy (for various reasons) with what they were offered.

Unionists were to feel further depression. At the 1924 Wesleyan Representative Session, despite strong speeches by Lidgett and Maltby, 'the Other Side' still registered a 31 per cent vote, and at the Ministerial Session Armstrong's demand for an amended Scheme gained – to Unionist alarm – a 50.2 per cent majority. Lidgett claimed that Armstrong's criticism of the Scheme lacked sufficient detail for informed voting, but it was Hornabrook's proposal that the approval of all three churches would have to be obtained before any final decision was taken which won the day. The vote for 'the Other Side' fell to 20 per cent.

Currie suggests[24] that this reduction in their support could have signalled the start of a failure of nerve, a fear that opposing union might after all be opposing the will of Christ. Moreover Rattenbury's boast that anti-Unionists were as numerous as members of the UM Church worried *both* 'sides': the prospect loomed of an open split, dividing Methodism again, even 'wrecking' it, with its leaders being unrepresentative of the whole Church and alienating one another. Sensitive to the dangers, Hornabrook, supported by Sharp and Carter, persuaded French and the bullish Perks to support a more gradual and conciliatory approach to 'the Other Side'. Unionists said they were ready to agree on the necessity of a 75 per cent vote in both Sessions of the Wesleyan Conference before legal powers could be sought to consummate Union. They reasoned that the existing 30 per cent minority could be gradually reduced by 5 per cent. 'The Other Side' accepted the proposal, as did the PM/UM Conferences on their side. Precise percentages were now crucial.

No doubt affected by the closure of the ailing *Wesleyan Methodist* newspaper, Rattenbury seemed at first inclined towards conciliation, but the mood changed, and the anti-Unionists insisted that Union could not be accepted on the basis of the existing Scheme. At the 1925 Wesleyan Conference Burnet and Rider demanded alternative proposals, but the vote went against them, and the United Committee's resolutions gained 75.8 per cent of the vote. The *Methodist Recorder*'s 'Conference Impressions' commented on the way Lidgett 'handled not so much the subject as the two speakers [Burnet and Rider]. As a skilled debater, Dr Lidgett never did better. He roused us by his passion'. The case which Burnet and Rider had made was effectively demolished: there was no substance, Lidgett argued, in Burnet's plea for an alternative scheme, and Rider's differences over doctrine and sacraments were not between the three Churches, but 'within our own ranks'.[25] The following Session, however, was much less successful from the Unionists' point of view. Despite a 'great' speech by Wiseman, the Ministerial vote for union reached only 64 per cent, thereby signalling an open breach with the Representative Session.[26] There was clearly a serious crisis.

During 1925/6 the Unionists determined to focus on the major bones of contention, the clauses on doctrine and ministerial responsibility for the sacraments. The work, which was done principally by Lidgett and Peake, marked major progress.

The doctrinal issues were finally solved at the relevant subcommittee of the Executive chaired by Lidgett on 29 January 1926 when, as he proudly recorded ten years later,[27] 'With the invaluable assistance of the late Professor Peake . . . we came to a unanimous agreement, accepted with equal unanimity by the Conferences of all three Churches'. Mention of the Creeds had satisfied 'the Other Side'. As the document, which he and Peake drafted in its final form, has stood for many years since as the doctrinal clause of the 'Deed of Union', it deserves quoting *in extenso*:

> The Methodist Church claims and cherishes its place in the Holy Catholic Church, which is the Body of Christ. It rejoices in the inheritance of the apostolic faith, and loyally accepts the fundamental principles of the historic creeds and of the Protestant Reformation. It ever remembers that in the providence of God Methodism was raised up to spread scriptural holiness through the land by the proclamation of the evangelical faith, and declares its unfaltering resolve to be true to its divinely appointed mission.
>
> The doctrines of the evangelical faith, which Methodism has held from the beginning, and still holds, are based upon the divine revelation recorded in the Holy Scriptures. The Methodist Church acknowledges this revelation as the supreme rule of faith and practice. These evangelical doctrines, to which the preachers of the Methodist Church, both Ministers and Laymen, are pledged, are contained in Wesley's *Notes on the New Testament* and the first four volumes of his *Sermons*.
>
> The *Notes on the New Testament* and the *Forty-four Sermons* are not intended to impose a system of formal or speculative theology on Methodist preachers, but to set up standards of preaching and belief which should secure loyalty to the fundamental truths of the gospel of redemption, and ensure the continual witness of the Church to the realities of the Christian experience of salvation.[28]

The document, however, had remained vague about what constituted the 'Principles of the Reformation'. Lidgett remedied this in his inaugural address as President of the Uniting Conference by declaring them to be, in his view, Justification by Faith, the completeness and all-sufficiency of our Lord's sacrifice and priesthood, and the direct access of all believers to God through Him, expressed as the priesthood of all believers.

The issue of lay administration took longer to solve. Rattenbury thought it should have been ruled out already, except under precisely defined conditions, but the non-Wesleyans insisted that it should remain, and 'not as a favour nor as temporary provision'. The list of exceptions was rejected, but pressure from Rattenbury and Rider resulted in agreement on a procedure whereby Circuits would nominate 'persons', and, once Conference had given the necessary authorisation, a certificate to this effect would be signed by the President. At Hornabrook's suggestion, the signature of the Conference Secretary was also required. This, as Currie pointed out, turned the certification 'from quasi-ordination to administrative routine'.[29] Lidgett had chaired the subcommittee which finally decided on the revised formula.

'The Other Side' now tried delaying tactics. 'Unification by Stages' was proposed: departments and colleges first; then (tongue in cheek) encouragement of local amalgamations 'where there was virtual unanimity'(!);[30] with the Enabling Act and final Union dated when 'the time was ripe', say in 1936 and 1938 respectively. These opponents derived satisfaction from the size of the minority votes on the Enabling Bill in the Wesleyan synods and from exposing a Unionist strategem[31] to bolster voting in the 1926 Conference's Ministerial Session. Lidgett will have been well satisfied with the 76.9 per cent vote for the Scheme and for Union in the Representative Session. He had made what the *Methodist Recorder*[32] called a 'powerful speech' there. Discounting preoccupation with percentages and emphasising inward spiritual principles, he had called the Conference in lyrical terms, 'to stand solid as one body of defence, not merely of the evangelical faith's abstract principles, but of its glowing evangelical light and of its great evangelical appeal to the country'. It was now time to accept the Scheme as now proposed: 'From a situation bristling with difficulties, we have advanced from agreement to agreement, until we put before you at this Conference a Scheme which has been ratified by our Sister Churches and is in conformity with the principles of our own'. But, despite a similar plea in the Ministerial Session, the vote was only 70.4 per cent.

At the beginning of the third phase of the Union saga there was concern on all sides. By this time the patience of the PM/UM denominations was virtually exhausted. Unsatisfactory minority votes were again returned by the Wesleyan synods in 1927, and, even worse, the votes of the subsequent Representative Session of the Wesleyan Conference (for the Scheme and the Enabling Bill) fell below the 75 per cent 'watershed', from 76.9 per cent in 1926 to 71.5 per cent and 70.7 per cent in 1927.

This new crisis not only affected the Unionists in all three Churches. Rattenbury had been modifying his position. He had distanced himself from the uncompromising hostility maintained by some of his colleagues on 'the Other Side', and now began to worry that their intransigence was on the verge, if the next year's vote was indecisive, not just of delaying the Scheme, but banishing the prospect of Union altogether. Such a grave responsibility seemed[33] too much to bear.

The 1927 Ministerial Session was bound to be particularly important, and Lidgett again made 'a truly great speech'. The *Methodist Recorder*'s 'Conference Impressions' said, 'Dr Lidgett always rises to a great occasion. His speeches invariably move on a lofty plane of thought'.[34] He argued[35] that the failure to reach 75 per cent might have been the result of divine guidance, providing a year of thought and prayer to be used, with God's help, to reach agreement. To him the minority deserved respect; theirs were real and serious difficulties; but their own particular type of Methodism, however precious, might shrivel in isolation. 'The best way', he declared, 'to preserve, diffuse and enlarge the type, for which we are thankful and of which we are the trustees, is to enlarge our borders and let the type exercise on the other denominations its appropriate influence'. Union, admittedly, would be costly, but

> If we are persuaded that the unity and progress of the Kingdom of our Lord Jesus Christ will best be served by our coming into the Union, I trust we shall offer on the altar of consecration the cost which it will be to us, and that the sacrifice will be transformed into triumph.

His rhetoric, however, still left 265 ministers voting against the provisional legislation, as opposed to 448 in favour of it.

The Committee of the Conference Representative Session met in September 1927 in some concern. On 21 October they appointed a 'Business Committee', chaired by Lidgett, and he was also a member of its subcommittee. Hornabrook, Carter, Rattenbury and Rider were deputed to draft the proposal which emerged. This was a three-stage policy: acceptance of the Enabling Bill in 1928 if the requisite 75 per cent majority was obtained in *both* Conference Sessions; the final vote on Union by the three denominations' Conferences in 1931; the Uniting Conference in 1932, followed by the first Conference of the United Church in 1933; and active preparations taking place in the meantime on such detailed matters as appointments, finance, Districts, etc.

These proposals led to the vital breakthrough. The involvement of Rattenbury and Rider in them proved to be decisive. When the Committee of 'the Other Side' met on 10 January 1928, these two leading figures, along with Armstrong and two others, voted against sustained opposition to Union, and withdrew from the meeting. The majority, however, decided to continue and elected Bevan Shepherd as their new chairman. The United Committee Executive met on the next day, and Lidgett explained the three-stage policy with the support of the three leading dissidents from 'the Other Side'. This evidence of a significant split in the Wesleyan opposition and the welcome being given by committee members to the new policy offered the prospect of achieving the vital percentage vote for Union. The PM/UM representatives first requested an adjournment to consider their position, and then on their return read out a lengthy statement: 'relying on what amounts to a moral guarantee of Union being consummated, we accept the basic principles of these proposals'. This, in effect, as Currie suggests,[36] 'put the three leaders (and the whole Wesleyan Methodist Church) on their honour' to carry out what was being promised. The three-stage policy was then formally put to the committee, and passed by 68 votes to 1: only J. J. Johnson voted against it. Johnson sent out circulars and a pamphlet attacking the scheme, but in an article on 24 April[37] Rattenbury wrote that Johnson was too late, and for his own part he would 'do everything I can to reduce the minority against Union which I believe will diminish'.

Unionists now held their breath for what would happen at the Wesleyan Conference in Liverpool. Had the Executive's decision begun to erode support for 'the Other Side'? In the Representative Session on 19 July[38] French and Rattenbury urged support for both the Three Stage policy and the Enabling Bill which would provide the necessary legal basis for Union. Johnson, however, argued that no application for the Bill should be made until the final scheme for Union was completed and a vote taken on it. He further demanded special financial provision for those who dissented. His intervention failed: the vote for the two motions was 86.3 per cent and 88.4 per cent respectively. All now turned on the verdict of the Ministerial Session[39] eight days later. The motion on the scheme at issue was that 'Union is now the avowed policy of the Conference', and 462 of the 616 ministers voted for it, exactly 75 per cent! One vote could have affected the outcome. The Bill gained a 77.28 per cent vote. The Unionists had 'just scraped by', but understandably there was great jubilation. Though many details, not least on Circuit amalgamations and District boundaries, remained to be settled, by 1932, Lidgett's target, and that of his dedicated supporters, had been reached. The Bill received the Royal Assent on 10 May 1929.

24

First President of the Uniting Conference

Once Methodist union was agreed, formal ratification and the election of its first President were now required.

Though conscious of almost immediate change, the Wesleyan Conference in July 1932 formally welcomed, according to its annual routine, Maldwyn Hughes as President for 1932/3 and new members to its Legal Hundred. In fact their tenure was short. The vote for the President of the Uniting Conference, who would hold office from 20 September until the first United Conference in July1933, had already been taken.[1] It had been agreed that the Uniting President should be a Wesleyan, elected by a clear majority of the votes cast in the Wesleyan Representative Session and the other two Churches' Conferences. Out of a total of 992 votes F. L. Wiseman gained 462, and Lidgett 432, but this result was indecisive since 496 votes were needed for the requisite majority. Wiseman, however, begged to be allowed to withdraw his name, pleading that 'the brother who is second on the list is much more worthy of the office'. Lidgett replied that it was for the will of God and the people, not for any one man to decide, and though Wiseman still insisted that Lidgett 'would serve Methodism with a distinction, power and grace that he could never hope to command', a second vote was taken in the Wesleyan Session, and Lidgett gained 313 votes to Wiseman's 216. As for first Vice-President, there never was any doubt of Perks's election: having made the original proposal which invited the other denominations to consider the possibility of Union in 1913, he had been thereafter almost continuously involved as a fervent (and very vocal) Union enthusiast and legal expert. Wiseman's merit, generosity and modesty were suitably rewarded at the first working session of the Uniting Conference. There he was elected by an overwhelming 858 votes as President designate for 1933/4: as with Lidgett, it was his second presidency.

The post of first President of the Uniting Church was clearly a prestigious one. Wiseman had been a worthy and much respected candidate, but his withdrawal was a genuine tribute to his rival. He had not been so continuously involved or as prominent in the prolonged discussions of Union and detailed drafting as Lidgett, and he was aware that Lidgett had played the greater part in achieving the result. In the symposium of tributes to Wiseman[2] published after his death, Lidgett suggested that Wiseman had decided to withdraw before the vote was declared, realising how many practical problems would arise in the first year of the new Church, and preferring 'like many a great batsman to go in one wicket down'. By 1932 Lidgett was well known well beyond Methodist and Free Church boundaries, Wiseman mostly within them. Moreover Lidgett had just completed his two years as Vice-Chancellor of the University of London, and his oratory at major public events was outstanding. Though Wiseman may have been better loved, Lidgett was seen as 'the man for the hour'.

But, as Eric Baker admits,[3] the claim that Lidgett had been the principal architect of Methodist union could be disputed. Others were regularly and vigorously involved: French, Hornabrook, Wiseman, Maltby, and from the non-Wesleyan churches, Horton and Brook, for example, were far from unimportant contributors. Among the lay protagonists Peake, the Primitive Methodist, was perhaps the most outstanding, a pivotal figure,[4] but he died in 1929. Obituaries by the Wesleyans, Lidgett and W. F. Howard,[5] paid heartfelt tributes to him. While stressing how serious a responsibility it would be to decide to abandon the scheme, he had with his vision, theological scholarship, wisdom, tenacity and patience not only guided those who wrestled with words but also helped 'to assuage the deep tide of feeling on both sides'.

Baker, however, maintains that, overall, Lidgett exercised greater influence than these contemporaries. He argues that if Lidgett had opposed Union (and, one could add, if he had not ceaselessly kept on hammering home the pre-eminent theological case for it), it would have been doubtful whether Union would have come about. Consummation of Methodist Union, now the largest of the Free Churches, had been a great achievement, a triumph, and to have been prominently associated with it was the highest point in his career. He was immensely and justifiably proud. But it had been 'a near thing'. The anti-Unionist minority remaining in all three Churches was not negligible: Wesleyans constituted the largest number in the new Church, but could be said in 1932 to be the least enthusiastic; and after the protracted struggle, some in each Church had, no doubt, succumbed to constant pressure, weariness and a sense of inevitability about the outcome. On his election Lidgett had said, 'Brethren, pray for me'. He would have been conscious not only of a great honour but also of a great responsibility if all his hopes were to be fulfilled.

The ceremony on 20 September 1932 in the Royal Albert Hall to mark the Uniting Conference was an impressive occasion. HM the King sent a message of congratulation, and the Duke and Duchess of York travelled down from Scotland to be present. Lidgett had invited Lang to attend, and French hoped for Lang and three other Bishops. But disappointingly neither of the Archbishops nor the Bishops of Winchester, Bristol and Chichester were free,[6] and it was finally only the Bishop of London who came to represent the Anglican Church. There was a standing vote by the delegations from each of the three denominations, the *Te Deum* (Lidgett's favourite canticle) was sung, and the Deed of Union, the legal document formally uniting the main branches of Methodism, was finally signed. The Conference then met for business on the next two days. The euphoric adulation with which Lidgett's speech (his subject was, not surprisingly, *The Catholicity of Methodism*)[7] and his conduct of business were received was reflected in successive issues of the *Methodist Recorder*:[8]

> Dr Lidgett gave us exactly what we expected. His mind is architectonic. He delights in an occasion such as this. His inaugural was spacious in conception and fitly framed together. His patron saint is the author of the Epistle to the Ephesians. His style is reminiscent of those rolling sentences in which St Paul unfolds his inspired conception of the Church which is His Body. Could any nobler manifesto be sent forth into the world than this superb utterance in which our President declared that Methodism claims a fellowship, confesses a faith and accepts a mission. This address should win its place as a classic in the literature of the Methodist Church.

W. F. Howard added:

> No expression of gratitude could possibly exaggerate our debt to Dr Lidgett for his masterly control of this unwieldy assembly . . . A Conference of 900 will not be easy to handle. But owing to the peculiar conditions under which the Uniting Conference was constituted, this was far larger than that in number. The President's mastery of the constitution, his resourcefulness when points of order were raised, his readiness to accept information from any quarter when it was accurate, his ready wit and genial humour, made us all his willing subjects.

Laughter followed Lidgett's comment on the Union Scheme: 'It has to be worked to be understood – *solvitur ambulando*.'

The honours conferred on Lidgett in 1932/3 were not unrelated to his part in Methodist Union, though other factors were certainly involved. Two months after the Uniting ceremony, on 29 November 1932, Lidgett received an honorary DD degree at Oxford. In his *Guided Life* he explained:

> I had . . . been brought into rather close association with the University of Oxford during my Vice-Chancellorship of the University of London, then recently terminated. I was also gratified to hear a mention of my theological work that was made in the Latin Address with which I was presented by the Vice-Chancellor.[9]

It was in fact that Address[10] which credited Lidgett with the *pre-eminent* contribution to the uniting of the Methodist churches, and incidentally reflected (*and* endorsed!) his constant search for *even wider* unity: 'Idem cum nuper tres illae Societates, prius dissidentes, in unum tandem coirent, *concordiae auctor prae ceteris exstitit*; quae concordia utinam concedat Deus Omnipotens ut *latius extendatur*'.

On the Archbishop of Canterbury's recommendation another honorary DD degree soon followed, awarded as part of Edinburgh University's three hundreth celebration in October 1933. But perhaps Lidgett's proudest moment was to see his name in the New Year's Honours List in January 1933 and receive from the King at Buckingham Palace in the following month the Companionship of Honour, a signal distinction, unique for a Methodist minister.

To Lidgett in 1936[11] reunion was 'enabling the Methodist Church to concentrate its efforts upon its task, without the drawbacks of sectionalism and sometimes of wasteful competition'. Unfortunately, however, the predicted 'great forward movement' in 'aggressive evangelism' did not materialise; the settlement carried no 'teeth', and while 'the purpose of Union was to close the chapels, the price of Union was to keep them open'.[12] Ironically, redundancy became even more starkly exposed. Lidgett was inevitably disappointed, but his optimism was undimmed. Still subject to 'ceaseless calls . . . on the leaders of Methodism and myself for concerted counsel', he continued to be active until retirement in 1949. But much of the promise he envisaged for those intervening years was blunted by events in society and politics, such as unemployment, the rise of Nazism,[13] the pacifism debate and the outbreak of war, and in Methodism by unforeseen retrenchment, caution, bureaucracy and membership decline. Sadly, aged 78 in 1932, and alongside several other ageing Union enthusiasts, Lidgett proved unable, against these circumstances, to supply the intellectual agility and maintain the dynamic leadership required to realise all his ambitions for his beloved, heroically united Methodist Church. Its union, however, had marked the pinnacle of his career. He could have retired, full of honours, in 1933; his wife was ailing and died in 1934; he was in danger of being considered a member of a new Methodist gerontocracy, replacing the one he had deplored over 50 years before. After the death of Archbishop Davidson his importance began slowly to decline. But he chose to press on.

Part 8

Lidgett's qualities and personality

Chapters 25–8 summarise and amplify Lidgett's characteristics as speaker, writer and Methodist minister, and assess the remainder of his written output.

Calendar of main events

This is set out in the chapters concerned. A list of Lidgett's writings, complete as far as possible, can be found in the Bibliography.

25

Speaker and intellectual

Lidgett's intellectual abilities were outstanding. Harold Roberts[1] spoke of his massive, singularly alert mind. His university training in logic was put to the fullest use throughout his career. Sharp discernment of complexities and contrasting elements in any issue was accompanied by a constant search for their resolution, for order, harmony and coherence. He faced difficulties honestly and with the utmost integrity: in fact he enjoyed what Burke called the 'friendly hostility' of opposing arguments. An exact and careful scholar, he maintained an impressive command of theology and philosophy. Though sometimes he lagged behind the leaders in these fields, he made a vigorous effort as far as possible amid his multiple concerns to keep his reading up to date. Long hours were spent in study, his memory was astonishing, and his concentration (some might compare it with tunnel vision) was phenomenal. Eric Waterhouse[2] recalled an encounter with Lidgett on the Atlantic Coast Express. Lidgett was smoking a cigar and reading a ponderous theological tome, while the meal proceeded. Waterhouse observed that to do this was difficult at any time, but especially under the prevailing conditions. Lidgett's reply was abrupt: 'Then you have not practised full mental control!' This was in stark contrast with Dinsdale Young's justification for reading an Edgar Wallace novel rather than a biblical commentary on a similar journey: 'The bow must be unbent sometimes.'

Gifted with a prodigious capacity for hard work Lidgett was active for over 16 hours a day, but never pleaded fatigue. A member of the London University staff once commented to Waterhouse: 'The man is not human, he is made of steel. No, not that! They say steel tires!'[3] Waterhouse warned[4] that he could not maintain the pace and strain for long without damaging his health, but Lidgett replied, 'I eat well, sleep well, and do not worry'. His amazing versatility brought criticism that he had 'too many irons in the fire',[5] and that he gave too much time and strength to what some opponents regarded as 'merely secular affairs'. In effect he countered such charges by asserting his ineradicable conviction of the 'Fatherhood of God as revealed by and in our Lord Jesus Christ' and his determination to follow through its consequences, namely, the *wholeness*[6] of Life, Society and the Church. It was the firm assurance of his personal call and divine mission that removed worry and gave him peace. What he said was:

> My life has *grown* through a combination of inward urge and outward opportunity, which I have regarded as indications of a providential calling. Hence the internal unity of a sense of calling and of a governing objective have saved me, for the most part, from the jarring competition of claims and from the conflicting responsibilities imposed from without. The chief strain upon me has arisen, not from manifold activities, but from the primary concern of having to bear, often alone, wearing *financial burdens* for sustaining many indispensable agencies in a very poor district out of sight.[7]

It had been tempting to 'adopt [unspecified] methods of advertisement' as a means of meeting this problem, but he had refused because they 'inflict injury on the self-respect of the poor, vulgarise the work itself, and may easily damage the spirit of those who are driven by financial pressure to advertise themselves in order to support their work'.

Lidgett had no doubts. Regularity of habits and considerable self-denial (notably in regard to 'so-called recreations which are indeed exhausting') helped, in his view,[8] to explain his long life. Paradoxically though it seems, he found the very variety of his occupations and the multiplicity of his interests acted as a tonic and recreation, providing 'rest and refreshment'! Switching his attention quickly from one type of occupation to another became for him 'a first-class preservation of mental and physical freshness'.

He developed the mental facility of preparing for successive tasks without exhausting labour and anxiety. The concentrated studies of his early ministry stood him in good stead: he was able to draw on them for rapid adjustment to the claims made on him later. He could draft sermons, speeches and articles in his head: his most successful speeches and writing had, he said, 'always burst upon me complete in outline'.[9] Twelve years of weekly editorial dictation helped him to put his thoughts rapidly into words, writing or speaking without notes, perhaps with only a few facts jotted on the back of an envelope. 'In his maturity', Rupp declared, 'Lidgett could give an extempore speech a classic form such that it might be printed forthwith, a test which few utterances of his successors could meet'.[10] Reliance on spontaneity, however, had drawbacks. Much depended, Lidgett admitted, on 'conditions of health, mood and freshness at the moment when the call to speak arises'. In practice he seemed rarely at a loss.

The key to much of Lidgett's success was his rich command of spoken language. Even if he was not always 'at the top of his form', his arguments were always well-ordered, he took great pains with his choice of words, and though his sentences were frequently long and complex, it was always rewarding to 'unpack' what he said. He could be witty and pungent sometimes, but his themes were never trivial. The *Methodist Recorder* paid tribute, for example, to his Conference speeches during Methodist Union[11] debates. Ruth Simpson also spoke of a 'nobility' of utterance that was 'rarely matched'.

A commanding presence, Lidgett could be dramatic, powerful and authoritative, as in his 1908 pronouncement over rejection of the Licensing Bill: 'Methodism will never forget or forgive'. His speeches at times could also contain vivid, imaginative, lyrical and even blunt passages. In 1935 he spoke out against those who spurned the contribution young people could make to the Methodist Missionary Society's Appeal:

'They are not crushed, they do not want cotton wool. Young people want to be called to something BIG. A stagnant Methodism stinks! The old spirit of adventure and self-sacrifice still lives.'[12]

Clarion calls for initiative, a sense of urgency,[13] and vigorous action ('virile' was a favourite word) were frequently heard. He spoke, for example, of 'Methodism's distinctive *élan* of ceaseless, collective and organised advance to win the world for Christ'. 'Methodism', he added, 'is essentially forth-giving, free in adventure. It can only fulfil its mission if this spirit prevails. Its service to other churches has been by rousing them to like-minded emulation'.

His experiences in Bermondsey enabled him to exploit emotional appeal when he needed it. When at Conference Dinsdale Young opposed the encouragement of physical activities by Methodism's youth, Lidgett intervened to great effect: 'Some of us have seen poor and ignorant factory girls called to God first by giving them healthy physical recreation'. Some of Lidgett's sentences were particularly memorable. Speaking[14] of men whose life was conditioned by 'Bermondsey's drab materialism', smothering the divine spark of the Creator, Lidgett said: 'I have seen times when the ploughshare of sorrow and adversity has broken up the hard and trampled ground, and the spark beneath, released, has leapt upward to the Eternal Fire of Love'. His spirituality was often evident. On 31 July 1913 the *Methodist Recorder* referred to his deep emotion and spirit of worship: 'One felt here is a man who knows, who has been into regions of thought and vision into which the Fernley lecture never looks, and yet is not dismayed'. His faith made him passionate about social concern. 'The superiority of the spiritual life', he said, 'is shown not in the interests it *ex*cludes, but in those it is enabled to *in*clude, purify and harmonise, within the supreme relationship of the God and Father of our Lord Jesus Christ'.[15] Words and phrases, like 'include/exclude', 'outering the inner', and 'love as both the centre and circumference of the Universe' often featured in speeches on this theme.

Many speeches, however, were scholarly, abstract and complex, reminding hearers of the first chapter of Lidgett's favourite Epistle, Ephesians, and – in the case of William Wakinshaw[16] – suggesting that if Lidgett had lived a millennium earlier, he would certainly have been one of the Schoolmen. But whatever the theme, theological or otherwise, he was known for an involved style, featuring long, entangled sentences and rolling periodic structures. Perhaps the best description was given in a *Methodist Recorder* editorial after his death:

> As great conceptions came to birth, he saw them in their completeness, as well as in the detail of their component parts. To the interested listener he was a constant provocation and delight. He would begin a sentence, and then diverge into so many subordinate clauses that to everyone but himself it seemed clear that he was irretrievably lost in an impenetrable jungle, but he had them all under control. With unerring and flawless accuracy he moved on to the predestined conclusion, not sometimes without a small indication of satisfaction, as he saw his audience release with relief the breath it had been holding, while it waited for confusion to collapse into chaos.[17]

He always emerged with both his syntax and grammar intact. His logic was faultless. Lidgett was in fact more of a reasoner than an orator. Reasoning often took priority over the arts of rhetoric which he appeared to despise, or at least consider of less importance. Nevertheless he could be a consummate orator when he chose, not least when rising to one of his favourite themes. A lunch was organised on 5 October 1949 to mark his retirement from the Bermondsey Settlement. The *Methodist Recorder*'s account of Lidgett's reply to a toast by Archbishop Fisher read as follows:

> He began to speak in the quiet, ordered way to which Methodist and wider circles have become accustomed. Then, as he deployed his theme of Reunion,[18] and the vision which he has for the churches, building up his phrases into stately periods, but never losing the word which was the keystone to the whole structure – indeed, turning back to it again and again, when a less distinguished speaker would only have entangled himself in a slough of words – his voice rang out, and the fire sprang to his eye, and his 95 years were forgotten by those who listened as he spoke of a larger Christ than most men know.[19]

Apart from their complexity, criticism of Lidgett's speeches was twofold. The first was their length. He was once taken to task at Conference[20] for his vote of thanks to the Bishop of Stepney: a colleague recalled the aphorism of an Irish minister, 'To make speeches immortal it is not necessary that they should be eternal!' During Lidgett's 1932 Presidential year his speech dedicating an equestrian statue of Wesley at Bristol[21] was so long and comprehensive that it left other Methodist dignatories present with virtually nothing else to say. The second criticism was audiences' not unusual lack of complete comprehension! It was said that Lidgett left his hearers 'breathless with admiration, but not always enlightened'. College students were described by Ruth Simpson as having had 'the experience of seeing this devout and inspiring minister of religion', but failing 'to follow all his thought'. Rupert Davies found[22] Lidgett's pioneering views on Catholicity admirable, but he commented sadly they remained unheeded. He wrote:

> Lidgett expounded them before the churches were willing to hear them . . . in oracular, resounding periods which tend rather to deaden than to enlighten the modern mind. If his words had been heeded by those who heard them and read them, it is possible that the movement toward Christian unity would have gone further than it has, and would have been brought home to a greater number of ordinary Church members.

Lidgett's debating skills[23] were impressive. Waterhouse[24] calculated that 'at least a quarter of Lidgett's working life was spent in Committee rooms of all kinds, but he never seemed lost or uninterested in this chastening form of democratic government'. In fact he greatly enjoyed the challenge of debate, talking round issues, assessing them separately and in context, sifting the strength of opposing arguments. Some observers recalled him as 'a master of rumination', preferring argument to conclusion. At times he could be exasperating and unpredictable, making it difficult to foresee what conclusion he would finally reach. But once it became clear which opinion or policy he supported, his points in favour would be set out and pursued with tenacious logic. Unpopular causes, if he was convinced of their merit, never deterred him.

Formidable in debate, he enjoyed repartee. Contrary views might sometimes be demolished with hammer blows, as argument succeeded argument, and none of those present relished his support for a case they opposed. What he said was always well informed: it was not necessarily endorsed. Those who did not agree had to listen and think, and he was never regarded with less than the fullest respect. His courtesy to others was marked. The victories he won were 'bloodless', never malicious. He knew when to stand and when to give ground, and his judgements were balanced, firm but fair. Conciliation and diplomacy were part of his nature. Quick to appreciate opponents' honest convictions, he sought to calm disputes and, where possible, reconcile disparate views. Heated debate never rattled him or made him lose his temper; he always kept his dignity. Speeches were unhurried, often beginning tactfully, expressing a debt to X, sharing a view of Y, before setting out his own case. In 1904[25] his technique was first to propose what he wanted, and then make compromises as successive contributions by others made it clear what might sway votes against him. It was such political astuteness, accompanied by skill with words, that brought him prominence as a public figure. During the Education Act furore of 1902, for example, these qualities enabled him to give a lead and, at the same time, keep the goodwill of both sides.

Watching Lidgett at work in committee, Waterhouse[26] noted that he had 'the remarkable power of following the longest and dreariest discussions with apparent interest'. While others were bored, lost or unable to unravel what was being said, 'Lidgett, gravely listening, would suddenly come out with some point which showed that he, at least, had mastered the obscurities which had all but sent me to sleep'. His flair for sensing the right moment to intervene and saying the right thing at the right time was also invaluable when a chairman. He could be incisive. He became known as a master as well as a servant of assemblies of all kinds. Whatever their size, they were kept under firm control.[27] Making himself *au fait* with every detail of the bodies he served, he had an easy command of the most complicated agenda. Swift to discern the points at issue, he could reduce apparent complexities to simplicity and skilfully sum up a discussion. Disputes in LCC committees could cause him to rephrase a motion; everyone then voted for it happily, only to appreciate its ambiguity later![28] He had been so persuasive that they felt it must be what they wanted. But no deception was intended: he had perhaps seen more clearly than most the undesirable results to which the original proposal might lead.

26

Writer, and writings since 1921

Comment has already been made on Lidgett's writing up to and including *Sonship and Salvation*, but his output did not end there. It continued for another 30 years! But before an appraisal is made of individual books from this later period, the principal features of all his written work may be briefly summarised, since these remained broadly the same after 1921 as before.

Representing his various roles as theologian, philosopher, journalist and preacher, Lidgett's publications were impressively numerous, including not only those he wrote himself but also those to which he contributed. He was, above all, a teacher, an expositor, a pleader, anxious to persuade others. His speaking in the pulpit, Conference and LCC debates, the University Senate and other gatherings helped to develop his command of language, and this showed itself also in his written work. The experience both of preaching and more particularly of journalism (to which he was abruptly introduced in 1907 as editor of the *Methodist Times*) equipped him with the facility to contribute comparatively short pieces alongside his lengthy theological treatises and articles of ponderous solidity.

But whatever he wrote, at length or relatively briefly, was marked by similar characteristics. There was, for example, little illustration, humour or irony, few digressions, 'telling asides or occasional home-thrusts'; in this he was contrasted unfavourably with contemporaries like W. L. Watkinson and Hope Moulton. 'He unbent too little for the average reader', said W. T. Davison. There were hardly any 'fireworks'. He did not sparkle. His writing was termed 'solid', 'stiff and cumbrous', demanding sustained attention and generally lacking in the 'warm glow' which evangelical readers looked for, but few found: Wilfrid Moulton[1] was a rare exception. It was clear that Lidgett found his major theme, the Fatherhood of God, exciting, but he did not expound it in an exciting way. There were few quotations; his extensive reading had been assimilated and 'reminted'[2] for his purpose. His major works tended to feature general truths, touching on contemporary problems indirectly, not explicitly. His exposition rarely flagged, but steadily forged ahead to the desired conclusions, and not everyone was equipped to keep pace with him. Those that did were impressed by his systematic arguments (often set out in numbered points), his scholarship and logical reasoning, his sentence construction,[3] and the range and deployment of his vocabulary. He would often use two words, when at first sight one would suffice, but on reflection it becomes clear that the second added to, and did not repeat, the first.

Lidgett's language was at its most vivid, as one might expect, when he spoke before an audience at moments of deep emotion, for example when he felt impelled to insist on the importance of Catholicity. Perhaps his finest piece of rhetoric is to be found in the text of his presidential address on 16 July 1908,[4] entitled 'The Catholicity of Methodism':

> We are here today, humbly yet confidently, to affirm our share in the great Catholic inheritance of the past. Who, save ourselves, can separate us from it? Its spirit is within us . . . Not a saint, a thinker, a hero or a martyr of the Church, but we can claim our share in his character, influence and achievements, by confessing the debt we owe to the great tradition which he enriched by saintly consecration, true thought and noble conduct.

Telling phrases can also be found when he wrote fervently, for example on Methodist Union or the fate of Fisher's Education Bill. Referring to opponents of the former, he criticised their habit of 'coddling denominationalisms and erecting prejudices into principles', or of 'justifying the sluggishness that jogs along old ruts by claiming divine authority'.[5] On the Fisher Bill in 1918, a year in which military vocabulary would have been on everyone's mind, he stated that 'the once impregnable ramparts of the half-time system [schooling post-14] had been caught by enfilading fire and rendered untenable'. In general, however, to the earnest, serious-minded Lidgett the first priority was to set out thoroughly, sometimes (in major works) exhaustively, what he wanted to say. Beside that, giving rein to his capacity for the lively phrase or vivid embellishments took a low second place.

The writings with which we are now concerned may be grouped into three decades, those of the twenties, thirties and forties. In 1927 some 20 of Lidgett's articles (one written in 1914, the rest between 1919 and 1926) were reprinted in a collection entitled *God, Christ and the Church*. Three had been contributions to books edited by others, or by Lidgett as joint editor. One was his statement to the NCEFC's Annual Assembly in 1924 on progress towards Church union, but of the other contributions 12 came from the *Contemporary Review* (of which Lidgett was Joint Editor), two from the *Review of the Churches* and two from the *London Quarterly Review*. One of the last mentioned drew parallels and contrasts between John Wesley and John Henry Newman in an address commemorating the Bicentenary of John Wesley's admission to a fellowship at Lincoln College, Oxford, on 28 March 1926.

Lidgett was proud to dedicate the volume to Archbishop Davidson, to whose interests all the articles were appropriate. The second of the book's two parts was headed 'The Church', and related in particular to issues raised by the Lambeth Appeal and subsequent debates on Church Unity covered above. Other ruminations by Lidgett on this subject were published elsewhere: within J. T. Smith's *Towards Solving THE Problem* in 1925 and Sir James Marchant's *Reunion of Christendom*. In the latter Lidgett commented on the Wesleyan Methodist Church.

The first part of the book, entitled 'God and Christ', contained articles on the Christian Faith, two at least sparked off by utterances of Dean Inge at the time. Lidgett said his articles provided

> a sustained attempt to show that the Meaning and End of the Universe must be found in the *Spiritual Values* revealed in Christ, and that the nature of these supreme Values determines and accounts for the methods of the Divine Government of the World.[6]

This focus on values seems to have come from Lidgett's reflections during the 1914–18 War, as previous chapters illustrate. His article on 'Religion and Psychology' is of particular interest in revealing suspicion of the growing popularity of psychology and, subsequently, of Leslie Weatherhead, a devotee.[7] He asked:

> Do the affections commission and constrain the intellect, working through the imagination, to provide for them an adequate, yet illusory, object for their satisfaction? Or does a real and divine object awaken and inspire the affections to demand a veracious and sufficient satisfaction, directing and guiding the intellect to supply it? In other words, does the divine Reality, God, so constitute the spiritual nature of man, with its emotional, moral and intellectual activity, that his intuitions, growing eventually to reasoned ideas and concepts, are the effect and the trustworthy, though imperfect, reflection of the Reality to which they respond?[8]

In 1909 Lidgett had contributed a chapter to the two-volume *New History of Methodism,* edited by Townsend, Workman and Eayrs. It was later decided that an up-to-date single volume was required, and so *Methodism in the Modern World*, edited jointly by Lidgett and B. H. Reed, was produced in 1929. Though the decisive vote for Methodist union had already been taken, the United Church was not yet a reality, and the book's drafts would have been too far advanced to warrant holding up publication until 1932. Lidgett would certainly have regretted this. His own contribution[9] was theological, entitled 'The Person of our Lord Jesus Christ'. Having expatiated on 'The Son of Man', he argued that the doctrine of God has to take into account the full meaning of Christ's humanity, the ground of his lordship.

The thirties saw several significant books. Lidgett's delight in receiving an invitation to deliver a lecture in memory of F. D. Maurice at King's College, London, in 1934 has been mentioned above. The resulting book, *The Victorian Transformation of Theology*, in six chapters, received plaudits for the depth and range of its coverage, not least in the first chapter. Henry Bett's review[10] regarded it as 'the most illuminating survey of theological thought that we have read for many a long day'. Rupp said[11] it provided 'a valuable and compressed diagnosis of the Victorian scene a century ago'. He thought Lidgett had well described 'the transformation of the whole theological climate which occurred as a result of many influences, but among which the influence of Maurice may have been the greatest single human factor'. Lidgett certainly paid eloquent tribute[12] to Maurice as a person as well as to his 'most potent and pervasive' effect on the previous century's religious life and thought. He also acknowledged his own deep indebtedness to the insights which Maurice had given him. But though his book was admired for its sense of perspective and acute discernment, critics were disappointed that only one chapter, the second, was devoted to a systematic exposition of Maurice's thinking in his own terms. The rest of the chapters were concerned less with Maurice himself, and more with the ways in which Lidgett had gone on to work out his own theological position: two chapters were on the Fatherhood of God, and one each on the Incarnation and the Atonement. Bett thought Lidgett had paid insufficient justice to the kenotic theory and Barthian theology, but otherwise the book was generally welcomed.

A slight pamphlet on *The Christian Creeds* appeared in 1936, in the Little Books of the Kindly Light series. In it the background and characteristics of the Apostles', Nicene and Athanasian Creeds were lucidly explained, and his personal love of the Nicene Creed stood out. Much more important was *The Idea of God and Social Ideals*, the Beckly Trust's Social Service Lecture of 1938. Its 111 pages provided a brief, but useful, historical survey, explained the link between Lidgett's personal theology and his public career, and illuminated his political stance. He first sought to trace the gradual development of the idea of God, and of the doctrine of his kingdom, before summing up the social implications of the Old Testament in general. His lecture then explained how the prophetic revelation was fulfilled in Christ, how the Church relates to the Kingdom of God, and how the ideals of the Church and social service have been affected in the course of Christian history. To Lidgett the individual and social gospel were two sides of the same coin – the need for personal salvation and the need for social righteousness. Readers of his previous writings, including his addresses to the WMUSS, will not have been taken by surprise. His thesis was not novel.

In fact the basis of the lecture seems to have been an article he wrote earlier, which was included among others in his collection *God and the World* in 1943.

It had virtually the same title and the message was basically the same. Speaking of Christian ethics, he wrote:

> If their principles be fully embraced and their essential presuppositions be accepted, [they] are the only means of social safety, stability and progress. They are so deeply founded in reason and reality that, instead of ossifying past traditions, they call men to the adventurous reflections that will guide and stimulate courageous endeavours to transform an imperfect and unsatisfactory civilisation in their light.[13]

Having dealt with the implications of biblical teaching and Christian theology, the Beckly Lecture argued that what in particular had driven social improvements in England was the legacy of the Methodist Revival (the Wesleys were highly praised)[14] and emphasis on the Fatherhood of God.[15] He had to acknowledge[16] the effects of Methodism on the rise of the Labour Movement, but commented sadly that 'the influence of materialist economics has tended to displace that of the prophets of the Old Testament and the guidance of the New'. As expected, tribute was paid to F. D. Maurice, the work of Christian Socialists and the Settlement Movement (manifested not least in Bermondsey), but towards the end of the lecture he returned to the attack on Labour and its class consciousness: 'The present tendency, active in the extreme sections of the Labour Party, is to react against the conception upon which the Settlements have been based'. He was still feeling sore about the way Labour had ousted him and his Party on the LCC.

God and the World: Essays in Christian Theism,[17] continued and developed the practice Lidgett began in *God, Christ and the Church* of reprinting articles he had written, in this instance wholly for the *Contemporary Review*. Though the book was not printed until 1943, many of the 17 'chapters' dated from the 1930s and related to events, controversies and lectures of the time. The subjects ranged from the celebration of the English Bible, comment on the Ecumenical Conferences in Oxford and Edinburgh of 1937, to critiques of the writings of (among others) William Temple,[18] Karl Barth, E. W. Barnes, A. N. Whitehead and Viscount Samuel. The collection represented mainly a work of apologetics, illustrating[19] 'how deep and wide and constant was his [Lidgett's] reading not only of classical theology, but of contemporary thought'. Lidgett emerges from these articles as a well-informed and acute philosopher, well placed to offer a reasoned response to contemporary challenges to the faith, and at the same time to demonstrate the cogency of the divine Fatherhood's claim to assist in understanding reality. The issues of Theism he tackled were perhaps the reason why he dedicated the book 'to the revered memory of Dr William Burt Pope'.

Lidgett's overriding preoccupation was with the relationship of God to the world and mankind, especially the serious problems made acute by two World

Wars. He attempted, for example, to give a philosophical answer to the questions, 'Why does God not intervene?', 'What is the meaning of "God is Love"?', and 'How does the Christian religion relate to the use of force?' The final article demanded that the end of WW2 should be succeeded by World Peace. He enumerated what he saw was required, not least the *outering* (a favourite word) of religious comprehension and concern. He wrote:

> The Church must be, at the least, as alive, as aware, as persistently active and eager as the most ardent political and social reformers of the State. . . . The new Crusade must proclaim to all the world, *Deus vult*, Christ means it. *Prodeunt vexilla regis*!

Apart from *God and the World*, Lidgett's writing in the forties was of much less importance than its predecessors. It aimed to provide for the average member of mainly Methodist congregations slender, relatively simple, often devotional expositions or surveys of the great truths of the Bible and Christian faith. But his characteristic density of expression kept breaking in, and he studiously avoided the sentimental approach popular with some readers of such literature. All these little booklets found new ways of expounding in his own distinctive style his already well-known tenets: there was no fresh thinking. But they gave ample evidence that he retained his enthusiasm, verve and devotion to the end. Though in 1921 he had declared that with *Sonship and Salvation* he had written his last book, he made the same statement later about many others. In fact Lidgett's last publication, *Salvation*, was written in 1952, the year before he died.

The Cross Seen from Five Standpoints, published in 1941, spanned some 55 pages and seems to have been read widely.[20] His characteristic, tightly expressed accounts of important theological doctrines would not, however, have been easy reading for everyone. *The Crowns of Jesus*, written in the same year, also contained few illustrations and anecdotes in its 77 pages, asserting the compatibility of the Gospel of John (Lidgett's favourite Gospel) with the Synoptics. In 1943 Christian belief was analysed in his slightly longer *God and Man* under eight headings, culminating in a ninth with the assertion that 'God is Love'. In 1948 the publishers had every reason to think that in writing another booklet the author had now 'completed the long series of his theological works'. But there was to be one more to follow *Jesus Christ Is Alive*, a title consciously echoing R. W. Dale's experience[21] in *his* later years. This penultimate work concluded that Christian faith and Christian experience remained the fundamental source of all social progress. Materialistic Communism, he predicted, together with the Victorian scepticism of Christianity, would collapse: the idealism borrowed from Christianity, but then forgotten and its potent source denied, would inevitably become a spent force, failing to safeguard human rights and values.

Having sketched particular doctrines of salvation which Lidgett discerned in Old and New Testament writers, *Salvation* declared that Jesus fulfilled, realised and transcended them all. Of all Lidgett's characteristics it was his forward-looking vitality that stood out most within this very last of his writings. In the Introduction, for example, he criticised Charles Wesley's hymn, 'Let us in Jesus see thy face, and die to all below'. To Lidgett 'die' cried out for correction. 'Not "die", but "*live*!"' That summed up his life.

27

Disciple, preacher and District Chairman

In 1908 Wesleyans were aware of how complex a personality had been elected as their new and controversial President of Conference. Harry Bisseker described him as

> At once apparently stern and unbending, and yet gentle and chivalrous in sympathy; strong and yet sensitive; self-confident and yet humble; a hard fighter and yet a lover of peace; the last to compromise, and yet, apart from the sacrifice of principle, the first; a statesman and yet a man of vision; one who lives and moves and has his being in the spiritual realities of his religion, and yet is best known for his insistence on its social application. Here is a combination of qualities which to some observers has proved little less than baffling.[1]

Though a brilliant speaker, Lidgett had none of the special magnetism of Hugh Price Hughes and Lloyd George; he was not a popular figure, with the devoted following of a Sangster, Soper or Weatherhead. Reactions varied. Those who came into contact with him could not fail to be impressed by his extraordinary ability and passionate dynamism, but the deep respect and confidence he inspired in some contrasted with the suspicion, even dislike and opposition aroused in others. Though married and with children, he was a private person, self-contained, seldom ready to open his heart and reveal deep natural affections; a scholar and academic in character, and yet he had created a Settlement among deprived and poorly educated people in the London dock-side slums, and continued to lead it successfully. As his national reputation increased and especially towards the end of his life, his softer, gentler qualities became more evident, but so too did his autocracy and eccentricities.

This chapter draws *inter alia* on numerous letters I received in the early 1990s, principally from people[2] who remembered Lidgett, often with amused affection, mainly in his later years. By then he had become a legend. These sources therefore offer limited coverage, but the anecdotes and oral comments of the contributors paint a picture for the most part consistent with what is revealed by his earlier career, and I am greatly indebted to them. The characteristics they reveal of Lidgett may be seen in his roles as Ascetic Disciple, Methodist Preacher and District Chairman.

With Lidgett, like his hero John Wesley, self-discipline was severe. Ever since his first appointment he had set himself a punishing programme of work and study. He seemed not to know weariness and made do with little sleep. He schooled his body to bear the strain which might have broken another man. Connexional, University and LCC responsibilities outside Bermondsey led him to walk home from meetings through the silent docklands in the early hours of the morning, only then to tackle correspondence before retiring to bed. As far as possible, he went everywhere, even across London, on foot, never by taxi, but when circumstances (or in later years, infirmity) demanded it, by public transport, 'bus, tram or train, rarely as a passenger in a friend's car. After a major service of thanksgiving for the end of WW2, he slipped out by a side door to wait for a 'bus while others left in their carriages and cars. His aim was to live, not only where, but just as 'his people' lived, travelled and could afford. Rank and position, his own and others', counted little in his order of things. He abhorred any form of snobbishness: each person was a child of God.

He had no interest in his own material welfare. His daily regime was spartan: for example, a cold bath, two slices of toast, one with butter, one with marmalade in the morning. There were few 'home comforts' in the family flat within the forbidding Settlement building. His bedroom was almost bare, containing just an iron bedstead, chair, brush and comb. His windowless study was said to be chaotic, with papers and books covering every surface including any available seating. Interviews with him were therefore short. The story goes that a young probationary minister in Lidgett's District complained to his superintendent about his living quarters and was advised to see the District Chairman. When shown into Lidgett's room, he was so struck with its austerity that he immediately thought up a knotty theological problem to raise with him. Lidgett was always pleased to discuss theological points with students or ministers, provided he could bring the other person round to his point of view! Leslie Kingsnorth recalled his own local preacher's oral examination at the Settlement as 'like a scene from Dickens'.

> Lidgett, he wrote, wore a dressing gown [almost certainly the paisley gown which had belonged to his grandfather] over his day clothes to make up for the small fire in the grate. When I hesitated in the course of answering, he filled in all the theological details at some length. The Wesley Hall Deaconess who was present said at the end of the questions: 'I propose that Mr. Kingsnorth be accepted'. The Doctor said 'No proposal is necessary. I have decided!'

For Lidgett sombre (deep black) ministerial dress was *de rigeur*: for Conference a black frock coat; for the pulpit (gowns came in later), and on other occasions, a black suit. Eric Baker[3] recalls perhaps a synod meeting when Lidgett came across a young minister wearing a light suit with a soft-collared shirt and coloured tie. 'Who are you?', he asked. 'I am X', the apparently new recruit replied, 'A minister in your District'. 'Oh, are you?' said Lidgett, 'Then all I can say is that you are suffering from ecclesiastical nudity! Good morning!' This restriction apart, Lidgett cared little about the state of what he wore, shabby and old-fashioned as his clothes progressively became. A tailor among one of his congregations once took him aside after a service, pointed to his threadbare cuffs, and begged him to have a new suit, to which he good-humouredly agreed. At Conference it was said[4] he usually wore a loosely fitting overcoat, pockets bulging with newspapers, an umbrella [his 'gamp'], an invariable companion, hooked over his arm, hat in hand. He was particularly fond of this hat, which went everywhere with him. Many observers described it as Dickensian and *sui generis*, whatever its shape had originally been: black, wide-brimmed, with the crown higher at the front than the back, becoming green with age, and in his view an effective protection against rain, sun and German bombs! The 'gamp' in particular was characteristic. Rupert Davies tells[5] how Lidgett, always cutting an odd, ungainly figure, dealt with the problem of crossing London streets by elevating it slightly and then walking across! Many of his eccentricities may well have been unconscious, arising from fierce, perhaps blinkered concentration on urgent priorities, but some doubtless became deliberate as he began to see himself as a character and live up to others' expectations.

He was inclined to walk in the middle of tramlines, with the 'gamp' held with both hands clasped right behind his back like a tail. Tram drivers would drive right up behind him, sounding their bell and making him jump. Lidgett's behaviour was perhaps an act of peevish revenge, originating in the bad fall he suffered when a tram he wanted to board began to move; he tried to hold on, and was dragged a considerable distance. The injury apparently healed, but later arthritis set into his hip and legs, causing difficulty with walking. Eric Waterhouse once[6] expressed sympathy, seeing him moving painfully forward on two sticks, only to be met with the defiant cry: 'All my life my legs have taken me where I willed that they should, and they will still do so!'. 'If you have a leg like mine', he told F. W. Clifford, 'send it to the devil, where it belongs!'

Lidgett was of around average height, under six feet. In his prime he had flashing blue eyes and a commanding voice. His hair was cropped short to save time and trouble. He had a basically strong constitution. Having rarely suffered from colds or other illnesses in early and middle life, he faced the arthritis and deafness of later years with a characteristically indomitable will to endure. His reaction to deafness was to accuse others of not speaking up;[7] to the passage of his own years to exclaim, no doubt *sotto voce*, about a colleague (in fact 30 years younger) whom he did not recognise, 'My, how old he's looking!'[8] Detesting all branches of the medical profession (and their charges!), he refused to have half-broken teeth removed and scorned the notion of false teeth in their place. It is said that he did once have some false teeth which fell out, and which he did not replace, some say during his 1908 presidential address, others at a meeting of synod. The result was that, progressively as time went on, he was reduced to two teeth which ludicrously did not meet, and eventually to only one! Some, viewing him with his characteristic mutton-chop whiskers stirring in the breeze and virtually toothless, said his facial expression had become 'monkeyish'; at an earlier stage, some spoke of it as only occasionally breaking into a genial smile, but normally grumpy, not helped by the way he peered over steel-rimmed, metal-framed, small-lensed spectacles worn well down the nose.[9] These he lost at age 92 and never replaced. He managed thereafter with the naked eye. The overall verdict of one anonymous observer was that Lidgett's spectacles, clothes and 'the look of antique severity worn by the irritable "Old Party" in back numbers of *Punch*' could present an alarming impression.

Lidgett was deeply conscious of his high calling and preaching was central to it. He was not one who sought out prestigious churches in which to conduct worship, but would faithfully attend wherever he was 'planned'. There was, however, one favourite congregation, Farringtons Girls' School, which he visited frequently in later years, not so much because he was invited as a popular figure (the Headmistress, like many others in his later years, was terrified he would fall out of the pulpit), but because he invited himself! But this was an exception to his general practice. On the first Sunday in September, 1932,[10] responsibilities as First President of the Uniting Conference saw him at Wesley's Chapel, City Road, for a civic service in the morning. In the evening, he was planned at the comparatively 'down town' Grove Mission and refused to change his appointment. Though the press reporters outnumbered the small congregation, he refused to allow photographs, saying 'I am here to celebrate the sacrament of Holy Communion'.

Preaching was still an unwavering priority 20 years later. William Motson recalled[11] a cold November morning in 1952, a few months before Lidgett's death. Motson was preparing to conduct the morning service himself when to his astonishment Lidgett arrived, pointed to an entry in his own diary and declared, 'I have promised to preach here this morning, and preach I shall. You can announce the hymns!' In the vestry, having given emphatic instructions on the conduct of the whole service, Lidgett asked the Steward about Holy Communion, which according to current custom followed morning worship. But with no such entry on the Plan no preparations had been made, and bread had to be fetched from the manse next door. Lidgett then asked Motson what he had intended to preach on as it was Remembrance Sunday. 'The meaning of sacrifice', was the answer. Lidgett's face lit up – 'My theme!' At the time of the sermon he was helped from his chair to the pulpit and produced carefully arranged notes from a long buff coloured envelope. His text was: 'For by one offering He hath perfected for ever them that are sanctified.' During the singing of the hymn 'When I survey the wondrous Cross', tears were seen falling from Lidgett's eyes as he sang 'See, from His head, His hands, His feet, sorrow and love flow mingled down.' Afterwards, he asked: 'Did that sermon commend itself to you?', to which the reply came, 'It was a spiritual feast!' Several others have commented on his reverent conduct of Holy Communion on other occasions: his insistence, for example, on keeping up his termly Communion services at Royal Holloway College in his late eighties and his readiness, even when crippled by arthritis, to struggle to kneel at the table, dragging one leg painfully, and in danger of dropping the chalice. Determination, dignity and devotion marked his life. Multiple concerns and responsibilities never affected his deep spirituality.

Lidgett was always punctual in arrival at services and meetings, and required others to be so. Sister Muriel Gage recalled his requirement that Society Stewards should be in the Vestry an hour before the service. He insisted on the practice of the Senior Steward leading prayer during that period and immediately before the start of public worship. An example of the latter was Mrs Rouse's memory of her father's experience as the Steward in the Vestry of the Central Hall, Westminster, prior to the Uniting Methodist service in 1932. Even though all the senior ministers of the Church were present, Lidgett, as President of the Conference, called on him to lead them all in prayer. It is strange that, in all other matters of preparation so punctilious, Lidgett often gave his selection of hymns very late to the organist, on arrival in the vestry. He did not have much interest in Church choirs or organists who drowned the singing or distracted attention with what he called 'twiddly bits', though he strongly supported concerts, musical and choral, in the Settlement. His dislike of chatter in the choir or congregation before the service was well known: Arthur Kelsey recalled him mimicking a chatterer, putting his hands together before his face and turning his head from side to side, muttering 'ta-ta-ta-ta, ta-ta-ta-ta'. He would usually leave the vestry to enter the Church for silent devotions five minutes before the service's scheduled time, and then, watch in hand, announce the opening hymn promptly on the stroke of the hour. At this point it is also said that his imperious cry could ring out, 'Let the doors be shut!' This was perhaps illegal where public worship was advertised!

Nothing was allowed to interfere with the planned progress of worship. A deaconess friend of F. W. Clifford said that towards the end of WW2 the Hinde Street congregation had been given instructions as to what should be done if there were an attack by flying bombs. During one of Lidgett's services the warning siren went, and there was a murmur in the congregation as they prepared to evacuate. Lidgett raised his hand and called, 'Stop! Shall the Church of God descend to the bowels of the earth? Never!' The service continued, mercifully without further incident. The deaconess, in her twenties, admitted to mixed feelings about being urged to stay in possible danger by an octogenarian! S. B. Frost recalled that when Lidgett preached at Oakley Place, Old Kent Road, worship at the Anglican church up the road had often ended before his sermon was completed. The Anglicans' drum and bugle Boys' Brigade band paraded after their service, but Lidgett would raise his voice above the din, remarking 'We will pause until these howling savages with their tom-toms have passed by.' He then sat for a few minutes, but 'when all was quiet again', Frost said, 'he carried on with his sermon for another ten minutes before announcing the merciful last hymn.'

Services were conducted with great solemnity. His strong sense of ritual became even more pronounced as he grew older. S. B. Frost's memory of services at Southwark Park around the 1926 period was to prove typical. Lidgett regularly included the singing of the *Te Deum*, which he valued for its credal structure, and at Communion he always read the full 1662 Prayer Book liturgy. There was awe in his voice when he prayed. He unfailingly stood for the Creed, especially the Nicene which he said 'interpreted' the Fatherhood of God 'made manifest in the Incarnation'.[12] Congregations were expected to sing the great theological hymns with deep understanding, and the organ to play them strongly without unnecessary ornament and 'syncopation'.

Though to Lidgett work at the Settlement offered more practical results than preaching, the latter never ceased to be a central imperative. He wrestled, and made his congregations wrestle, with strong, unhurried, doctrinal sermons which F. W. Clifford said made no concessions to the congregation 'who nevertheless deeply appreciated them'! One such sermon was commented upon as 'One of the best you have ever given'. To this he is reported to have replied, with a twinkle – 'How interesting! You see, it was word for word one of John Wesley's sermons!' He made full use of his theological scholarship. It is no surprise that his constant theme was the Fatherhood of God – of *all people*, he insisted, not just the converted. For his contribution to a symposium of sermons, entitled *If I Had Only One Sermon to Preach*,[13] Lidgett chose his sermon entitled 'The "Yea" of God', based on 2 Corinthians 1.20. Its theme was assurance that the promises of God would be fulfilled, and in it he urged our response in faith, hope and love. His obituary in the Conference Minutes spoke generally of 'ripe scholarship, with consistent loyalty to the evangelical doctrines of Methodism'. There were many Bible references in his sermons, the most frequent quotations coming from Isaiah, Ezekiel (Chapter 37, the valley of the dry bones) and Ephesians. Kelsey recalled a woman looking at the clock in one of his sermons, whereupon Lidgett remarked: 'I know, I know you find me long-winded, but it's all your fault. If you would only bring your Bibles to Church, I wouldn't have to quote and read *in toto*.' Sister Muriel Gage said that if you *did* have a Bible he would point at you and ask a rhetorical question. 'You never dared answer!' Soper,[14] never a devotee of Lidgett, described him as 'not explosive as a preacher. His sermons were clearly expressed and, perhaps, pedestrian, but mercifully exempt from emotionalism which can so often contradict theological content. He was not prone to corybantic evangelism!' Though Lidgett's exposition was generally described as 'quiet' and scholarly, Sister Lois Rands by contrast remarked on his vitality and passionate conviction in preaching: 'He proclaimed the word of God with certainty of Christ's victory stressing the absurdity of doubting the living presence of the Lord. Any atheist present might have begun to wonder if he was a bit of a fool after all'. That conviction seemed to shine through what Ruth Simpson called his 'striking old countenance in his later years . . . as if one of the prophets had come back to life' and his 'beautiful voice'. S. B. Frost had earlier described it as 'dry and rasping', perhaps the result of open-air preaching in Southwark Park in the 1890s.

The Introduction to this biography recalled one major incident illustrating Lidgett's fierce determination to proclaim the Good News, whatever the cost to his health – or voice! A similar, less publicised event had occurred about 1947, at Mostyn Road Methodist Chapel in Brixton,[15] where congregations already regarded him as 'something rare and fragile'. Here again he collapsed from exhaustion, but treated the experience as only to be expected of real preaching. He was carried unconscious by ambulance to King's College Hospital, but incredibly returned an hour later to recover his stick, Bible, spectacles and preaching notes and command the young local preacher who helped him to the door, 'If preaching doesn't take anything out of you, *don't preach!*'

The features of his sermons on which everyone commented were their length, their detailed reasoning and their complex sentence structures. As Ruth Simpson put it, he often preached for 45–50 minutes, speaking 'in long, elaborate sentences, with many subordinate clauses and formidable thought processes'. Hearing him preach towards the end of his life, Sister Muriel Gage said he then 'preached without notes, challenging, all to the point, one thought linking with another, but *long*. We heartily sang the final hymn.' But, she added charitably, 'He had so much to give. Perhaps he felt there was not much time left'. Lofthouse commented that whereas on other occasions Lidgett could sometimes be 'witty, incisive, even at times pungent, his sentences in the *pulpit* could reach a portentous length'. He could express himself in colourful phrases, as when he shocked the ladies in his congregation by speaking of 'the painted Jezebels of the modern era', but little, if any relief was provided by illustration or anecdote. As in his theological writings, Lidgett rarely allowed himself the luxury of exercising in sermons what Rupp called 'his gift of illustration, occasionally devastating power of trenchant epigram and his humour'. Glimpses of these appeared in other circumstances.

Accordingly, reactions to his preaching were mixed, ranging from awe and admiration to barely disguised boredom. For Rupert Davies Lidgett's 'oracular, resounding periods' tended 'to deaden rather than enlighten the modern mind'. Undoubtedly Lidgett preached well over the heads of the majority of his congregations, though their respect overrode their comprehension. Writing in the *Methodist Recorder* on Lidgett's retirement, an anonymous contributor may have been right to observe that Lidgett 'did his best to compromise between people who oscillated between dull piety and emotional revivalism', but he was surely wrong to say: 'Already a scholar of some stature, he can scarcely have been appreciated by those whose simple faith found hidden blessings in the genealogies of the Old Testament and a taste for sanguinary hymns'. The perhaps surprising truth is that many congregations did appreciate him, as a distinguished and learned preacher, if not for his preaching. He did not in fact regard himself primarily as a preacher. He was, nevertheless, invited to pulpits outside Methodism, in many Nonconformist and some prestigious Anglican churches, including (in 1933, after Methodist union) Westminster Abbey. In retirement at Bidborough he preached on occasion in its parish church.

As District Chairman, Lidgett was not generally popular among his District colleagues, nor his junior ministers. This was at least partly because of his incredible versatility, his omnipresence on the churches' scene, and the fearless expression of his views. He commanded such a reputation as a scholar that, to the anonymous commentator just mentioned, he appeared 'a giant among part-time interpreters of Scripture, an intimidating peak among the foothills'. This caused him 'involuntarily' to stand 'outside and above the company of his fellows'. He was not always understood, but he had often only himself to blame for insensitively 'rubbing them up the wrong way'. His considerable gifts could be admired and feared at the same time. He was formidable even in informal discussions among ministers. Several have remembered uneasily, many years later, how he clinically demolished their opposing views 'with an outstretched finger and a curious kind of inverted beckoning'. Dominating, alert, authoritative, he was capable of such devastating asides that colleagues often found themselves unable to speak freely in his presence. He always had his say: whereas Frederick Luke Wiseman would be generous to a younger minister, and encourage him by stating he had nothing to add, Lidgett, it is said, would 'continue to strike hammer blows in reinforcement'.

It seems from reports of public debates in Conference, London University and elsewhere that these crushing traits were there generally held in check.[16] They were much less so when he presided over meetings of his London District Synod. He was its Chairman for 40 years, from 1909 till 1949, in charge of 30

Methodist Circuits in South-East London. There, in front of 200–300 ministers and laymen, he relished the opportunity to conduct the oral examination of probationers and ministerial candidates. Requiring the same high standards he set himself, he insisted they lived up to the highest traditions of John and Charles Wesley. He summoned them, even in the war years, for conversation and study. Waterhouse[17] recollected complaining at a District synod about demands for booklists of much more reading than any average probationer in a Circuit could be expected to accomplish. 'Lidgett', he said, 'flattened out my objection from the chair: "Are there not twelve hours in the day?", was the imperious reply.' For Lidgett, Waterhouse commented, there were more like 16! Examinees were kept standing, and any evidence of inadequate study was met with his lashing tongue. His detailed interrogation could be so penetrating that one candidate was said by Freda Jenkins to have fainted under it, several ministers walked out in anger, and others protested that his good practical record in his Circuit should guarantee a pass.

The young Donald Soper readily confessed that in an interview 'Lidgett scared the pants off me'. The story goes that he suffered a severe reprimand, but he had only himself to blame: his lack of proper preparation had been mercilessly exposed by Lidgett's fierce questioning, he had been impertinent and answered him back, and his written papers had gained only 23 per cent. Soper's excuse was that work on his doctorate thesis had taken priority over his probationary studies. Lidgett's response was, 'Justice first, charity later!' At the end of the interview, however, he declared, 'Charity will prevail. He may go forward to ordination.'

Anecdotes tell of probationers being given tips by their mentors on what questions to anticipate and what answers would gain approval: an example quoted was, 'Where did John Wesley get his theology?', and the answer, 'The Nicene Creed'. The most intriguing story is of Dorothy Rouse's brother being asked whether he had read 'the 45 Sermons of John Wesley'. His reply, 'Only 44 of them, Sir!', left it open as to whether Lidgett had (*un*characteristically) made a slip, or (more characteristically) set a trap! His ministers did not always appreciate a significant motive behind his probing challenges. He not only enjoyed the cut and thrust of argument himself: he saw it as a means of evoking, stimulating and developing *personality*, which he was convinced was as important to them as to everyone else.[18] Few compliments were offered. When given, they had been well earned !

All ministers in the District are asked at synod whether 'they believed and preached our doctrines'. On one occasion[19] members were taken by surprise to hear the fundamentalist William Spiers reply 'No!' Spiers explained: 'I hear my brethren saying 'Yes' to this question, and I believe they are truthful and honourable men. Yet they believe and preach what I do not and will never do'. It was unusual for Lidgett to be absent: synod duties, it was said, even caused him to leave his wife's graveside! On this occasion an LCC meeting had called him away. Deputising for him, Joseph Dixon deferred the matter until his return, and Spiers's refusal was then repeated. Lidgett angrily retorted, 'This is frivolous. Put him down as saying "Yes".' Spiers, it seems, gave up the struggle.

There is no doubt that Lidgett enjoyed the prominence and power of his District Chairmanship. Synods were major occasions: the local mayor was invited to luncheon and the National Anthem was played before members sat down. After the meal Lidgett would expansively light a cigar, and then deliver a suitable, 'very correct' speech, not excluding a few humorous remarks. Reference to his own wide experience and contacts, no doubt, irritated some of his colleagues, but the pastoral addresses he gave to synod in session were regarded as instructive and inspiring, evoking genuine admiration, even among his enemies. At the same time they were aware of the powerful influence he exercised, and enjoyed, not only as their Chairman, but also as a member of the Connexional Stationing Committee.[20] Though he once jokingly explained it as 'a means of preventing ministerial unemployment', it could be unwise to cross him. Lidgett's most celebrated intervention related not to stationing a minister in his District, but to taking the lead in preventing Leslie Weatherhead, his successful fellow minister with a devoted following, from being appointed to Wesley's Chapel, City Road. His motivation and influence emerge clearly from the account provided by John Travell in his *Doctor of Souls, Leslie D. Weatherhead 1893–1976*.[21] Lidgett, he says, 'considered his [Weatherhead's] writings on sex[22] verged on indecency' and in the 1936 Methodist Conference asserted that 'he would not agree to a psychologist[23] going to Wesley's pulpit'. The vote which followed went against the appointment and was carried by 401 to 157 votes. A rebel against the Wesleyan 'establishment' in his early days, Lidgett now counted himself among the conservative Methodist majority of the time whose hostility to the expression of controversial views went with the belief that 'psychology was subversive of faith' and 'would tend to foster moral anarchy'.[24]

28

Person and pastor

Of the multiple paradoxes abounding in Lidgett's character the greatest was the contrast between his stern severity and loving concern for others, his sensitive humanity.

What may at first seem surprising in the light of the traits exemplified in the previous chapter is the depth of affection Bermondsey felt for him. They loved him as a father. This was demonstrated above all by the memorable scenes when he received the Freedom of Bermondsey.[1] The people there knew him not as an outstanding intellectual, but as a leader who had made Bermondsey his home and remained close to them in their dreary surroundings through good times and bad, even the Blitz. He had the common touch. During a celebration at Brixton Hill Methodist Church in 1939 Harold Packington's wife recalled riding round the streets with Lidgett in a coal cart, as though this was quite the natural thing to do.[2] In 1936[3] Ensor Walters, President of the Methodist Conference, recalled that once, as Lidgett made an appearance, no doubt robed, at a stone-laying ceremony, a poorly dressed cockney woman ran forward and called out from the crowd, 'Gawd! There goes *our* Dr Lidgett!' He was one of them. They admired the courage with which he spoke out for what he was convinced was just and right, his persistent efforts to remedy abuses and improve the living conditions of the people, his disinterested work for the underdog. Self-denial, readiness to face personal, material and financial disadvantages and make any sacrifice of time and energy[4] were qualities that quickly appealed to them. But what perhaps they found most impressive was the sheer dogged tenacity with which he set out to overcome his own unsuitability for work in the slums.

Moreover, flexibility and broadmindedness were not to be expected from a minister with a strict Victorian background. In Cambridge, Moulton had assigned Lidgett to work with undergraduates on the ground he was not 'straightlaced', but among Bermondsey dockers there remained much to learn. Nevertheless, to his great credit he came to accept that some, at least, of the pleasures frowned upon by narrow evangelicals should not be regarded as additions to the Seven Deadly Sins. Bermondsey valued him for this, but the best-known illustration of his flexible approach was the heated argument in the

1942 Methodist Conference over whether dancing should be permitted on Church premises. There are several versions of the debate. Strong opposition to the proposal was anticipated from the much respected Luke Wiseman; Edward Eagles had even declared that dancing pandered to carnal lust. Lidgett, however, had felt it incumbent on him to make a preliminary investigation. Eric Baker[5] recalled that as a result he 'convulsed the Conference with a graphic description of himself taking the floor with an elderly lady of about his own age'. They had had a delirious whirl in which he forgot his rheumatoid arthritis, but he found three minutes was quite enough. 'As far as I know', he concluded, 'she was not demoralised, and neither of us came to any harm'. In Baker's words, 'The opposition crumpled and the cause was won'.

The work of the Settlement clearly played a considerable part in endearing him to the local community. They were touched by the attention he gave to children and young people. Activities (cultural, physical and educational) were energetically promoted for them; facilities previously unknown to them were made available for the poor, crippled and handicapped; and vigorous assistance given to school management and local administration. Over the course of 59 years many people of all ages in and around Bermondsey and Rotherhithe would have had many reasons to be grateful for what he had achieved generally and done for them in particular. From outside the area Lorna Horstmann and Harold Packington, for example, have written to pay tribute to the personal interest he took in them and their careers. He never forgot a name.

Surprisingly, however, the evidence available reveals few instances of Lidgett's pastoral visiting and care for individuals in his own locality. Lidgett himself mentions only one. In Meldreth, near Cambridge, he met a Beatrice Dunkin, a spinal case,[6] whom he had placed in a Home near Hendon with the help of Lady Bunting. While maintaining contact with him, Beatrice learned about his work at the Rotherhithe Infirmary and the Settlement, and aroused the interest of another patient, who after her convalescence brought nearly 100 girls from the Peek, Frean & Co.'s factory to the opening night of the Settlement's Girls' Club. In tribute to Beatrice's indirect influence the Club was named after her. On his death Lidgett was remembered with great affection by the Divisional Superintendent and members of the Bermondsey branch of the St John Ambulance Brigade. In 1933[7] the national Secretary of the Boys' Brigade nationally paid tribute to Lidgett as chaplain for many years of the Bermondsey Settlement 62nd Company: 'In spite of his many duties Dr Lidgett never forgets his BB boys, and he is as much at home with them at their football matches on Saturday afternoons as he is at their Sunday evening Bible class.' There must have been many other instances of Lidgett's pastoral care and concern for individuals and groups in and far beyond Bermondsey, but his wide-ranging and progressively increasing commitments will, without doubt, have restricted the time he could devote to it.

The Settlement residents looked up to the Warden as a somewhat Olympian figure. Yet he enthused them with his Christian and social ideals, and set them to tasks they had never contemplated before they arrived. They were made to feel they belonged to the activities in hand. After his death some critics rated him as having little inspirational quality. Donald Soper (never a resident), for example, even declared, 'He never inspired any initiative in me!' That was certainly not true of the young men and women Lidgett attracted to live and work alongside him in *dis*piriting circumstances. Of all the Settlement residents over the years only Lofthouse recorded his experiences there.[8] Writing about the 1890s, he said:

> Personal relations with the Warden varied. All met at dinner; but . . . in his desire to explain his view of a speech or a public event he was apt at times to forget his duties as a carver of the joint for which a tableful of hungry men were waiting. Some of the younger residents were naturally in awe of him, though . . . he would ask at times, in genuine humility: 'Did you approve of this?', or 'Did I say the right thing about that?' He did not then talk as though he was addressing a public meeting or preaching to congregation; yet there was always something, even in his table-talk, which smacked of the lecture room. You had the impression that his ideas on every subject were astonishingly well-drilled.[9]

Lofthouse also commented:

> No one could enter into any sort of intimacy with the Warden . . . – an intimacy which, in spite of a certain ingrained shyness, he was almost pathetically anxious to gain – without being aware of the feelers for friendship and understanding which he was continually putting out.[10]

The sadness was that, except perhaps to some extent with Archbishop Davidson, he never did gain any real confidant with whom to share his inmost thoughts. This may have been due to the lack of any theological college training and the colleagueship that might have come from it. He studied in isolation. His wife's devotion, patience and self-sacrifice were greatly valued. Alongside supervising domestic arrangements in the Settlement with her sister, she helped with its teaching and women's societies, but she remained largely in the background, and of his two children only 'Jack' seemed really close to him. He felt particularly lonely in his eighties: his son had been killed, his wife had died in 1934 a few weeks short of their Golden Wedding, and many contemporaries and contacts had gone too. Some had, in any case, been alienated long ago by his strong views, whether on pacifism, women in the ministry,[11] divorce, the Sacramental Fellowship, or political activity; others by the infuriating way he would often 'sit on the fence', refusing to adopt, as in the WMUSS,[12] the aggressive leadership role some impatiently expected of him. Pretentiousness was anathema. He could be unpredictable, 'imperious in manner',[13] intransigent and cantankerous, though such volcanic outbursts as were witnessed occurred only in the privacy of his own room.[14] Fools were not tolerated gladly, and compliments were rare.

Though basically a humble man at heart, he could push his way through crowds, required deference as '*Dr* Lidgett', and stood on his dignity. The story Lidgett told of himself, when offering Bishop Bell reminiscences of Archbishop Davidson,[15] revealed both his sense of self-importance and deep regret that Methodism could not give him the honour he felt he merited. After dinner in Lambeth Palace Davidson had once arrayed him in his archiepiscopal robes before his guests.

Glimpses of a warmly affectionate and genial nature could from time to time be seen. When he could relax with a small group of people he knew well, he could be good company, seizing the opportunity for telling amusing and informative stories with great gusto. The many people he knew not only in his District but well beyond it, and the important events he had witnessed, provided him with a fund of anecdotes. People in homes across the country felt privileged in entertaining him before and after services. The disadvantage was that he always had to 'hold the floor', and everyone present had to listen! He could, though rarely, be light-hearted, joking for example with women on the 'bus, and behave flippantly with colleagues[16] in a subcommittee. The water offered to visitors or residents at meals in the Settlement he called 'our white wine'.[17] He could relate to all sorts of people, from bishops to dockers. Flashes of unsuspected humour were observed, particularly in his later years. He had always been capable of mimicry,[18] dry wit and withering repartee. Stories were told, for example, of his comment to a garrulous lady in a settlement choir, who apologised to him for losing her voice. 'That, Madam', Lidgett replied, 'only adds to your charms!'. Dr Sangster[19] was much amused by the story about Lidgett's having his photograph taken on his ninetieth birthday. The polite young photographer said 'I trust I will have the pleasure of taking your photograph, Sir, on your 100th birthday'. Lidgett, it seems, eyed him beadily and drily retorted: 'I don't see why you shouldn't. You look a very healthy young man!' A church member told how a policeman, escorting Lidgett to a tram, suddenly recognised the old man: 'I know you. I used to go to your Church', he said. '*Used* to', muttered Lidgett drily. Only once it seems were the tables turned on him. While lunching with Sangster,[20] Lidgett, always interested in matters of social wefare, expressed concern about the considerable trouble the young waitress was taking. He asked her kindly, 'When do you finish work here, my dear?' Sangster said, 'She withered him'. 'Too late for you, old cock!', was her tart reply.

It might be thought that leisure activity was foreign to him. Wilfrid Hannam wrote in 1908:

> Get him away from his usual round of labour, and he will take his revenge on you by correcting the proofs of his latest book or planning the scope and purpose of the next. He snatches an hour or two to write.

Lidgett certainly enjoyed writing, editorship and the necessary preparatory reading. Moreover, the LCC, he once said, was his 'golf'! At the same time there is clear evidence of a liking for poetry, especially Wordsworth's celebration of the countryside, and music, both choral and instrumental. Though not a performer himself, concerts, oratorios, bands, art exhibitions, lectures on literature, etc. figured prominently in his Settlement programme. After a meal in the Quarry Centre he would ask Ruth Simpson[21] and her sister to sing and play the piano. Beethoven and Schubert duets appeared his favourites. Nevertheless it is at least arguable that throughout most of his life he was fundamentally less interested, personally, in these aesthetic activities than in making them available to children and adults from whom, because of their circumstances, they had been hidden.

Two of his activities suited a loner. Sister Helen Styles, who was his amanuensis for *My Guided Life*, mentioned walking as his recreation. He would sometimes take a walking holiday with his wife in Switzerland where they had spent their honeymoon.[22] When he permitted himself the luxury of an annual holiday away from London, he would stay at Sewhust Farm, Abinger, near Dorking, and walk over the surrounding countryside. Other venues were Anglesea and Appleton-le-Moors. His practice was to retreat on one afternoon a week to his old home in Blackheath, or later to his daughter's house in Bidborough.

His other leisure pursuit was, surprisingly, the study of rail travel. To him increased facilities for travel of all kinds seemed to offer additional scope for spreading the gospel and opening people's eyes to the glory of God in creation. He took considerable pride in knowing how to get anywhere, and from this developed a keen, accurate knowledge of railway timetables. Like H. B. Workman (1862–1951),[23] Lidgett was said[24] to be an expert on Bradshaw, so much so that some young people determined to test him out with a question on how best to travel by rail to some distant and fairly obscure destination. Apparently he rose triumphantly to the challenge, by offering alternative routes, and comparing necessary changes, waiting times and times of arrival. Checked for accuracy, the advice proved correct.

Lidgett was always optimistic, even in his old age, looking forward, never dwelling on the past. F.C. Pritchard said:

> He had the capacity of absorbing the best from the past, of registering the novelties of the present . . . regrouping them in his mind and of using those that opened up new avenues of development for attaining ideals which he never forsook.[25]

At his funeral Walter Noble paid tribute to his constant encouragement of youth, keeping 'abreast of all those movements which seek to improve man's lot'.[26] As Eric Waterhouse put it, Lidgett 'never thought of himself as at the end of his life and work'. The example Waterhouse gave[27] was when, summoning up all his tact to avoid mentioning an Obituary, he approached Lidgett to let him know that the *British Weekly* had asked for the short account of Lidgett's career, supplied some eight or ten years before, to be revised 'for filing'. 'Have you done so?', Lidgett asked. When Waterhouse said he had, Lidgett's reply was, 'Then I hope you'll have to do it again later on.'

In these later years, especially when other prominent people died, he loved calling people's attention to his own longevity. It was a matter of real pride. He boasted about it. On hearing of the death of F. D. Roosevelt, for example, Lidgett declared to Dr Sangster,[28] 'This is terrible news. I haven't had such a shock since the day Lincoln was assassinated.' Lidgett himself regaled his audience at a luncheon in his honour in 1949[29] with other memories of the death of the Prince Consort, the start of the American Civil war and the days of Gladstone, Palmerston and Disraeli. Raymond George[30] remembered a Faith and Order Meeting taking place on the day George Bernard Shaw's death was announced. 'Lidgett', he said, 'came in, sat down and said with great satisfaction, "Shaw's gone first!"'

His own mental vigour remained virtually unimpaired. He went on attending committees until illness and infirmity prevented him, but even in those circumstances he wanted first to know, and then to give his opinion on what happened. He was dictating letters until a few months before his death.

Lidgett's life was marked by sadness and joy, unremitting hard work and self-denial. Throughout it all his faith in God's love never faltered or was absent from his mind. It is no surprise to discover his favourite hymn was 'Thy ceaseless, unexhausted love' by Charles Wesley. 'Holy Lamb, who thee confess', again by Charles Wesley,[31] was also sung at his Memorial Service in Wesley's Chapel, City Road. Sangster read its last verse aloud:

> Vessels, instruments of grace,
> Pass we thus our happy days
> 'Twixt the mount and multitude,
> Doing or receiving good;
> Glad to pray and labour on
> Till our earthly course is run,
> Till we, on the sacred tree
> Bow the head and die like Thee.

Other hymns associated with him are similarly poignant: such as 'Through all the changing scenes of life' by Nahum Tate/Nicholas Brady, and 'When morning gilds the skies', Anon., tr. Edward Caswall. But there can be no doubt that one Wesley hymn in particular contained his life's 'manifesto':

> Christ from whom all blessings flow,
> Perfecting the saints below . . .
> Names and sects and parties fall:
> Thou, O Christ art all in all.

Bishop Bell commented on his death: 'The Christian Church will not be the same without him. He was a saint'.

Part 9

Bermondsey and retirement

These chapters, 29 and 30, complete the story of the Bermondsey Settlement where Lidgett's major achievements began and then describe his retirement and final years.

Calendar of main events

1914–18	Difficulties experienced in the First World War.
1918	Death of Lidgett's son on 24 March.
1927	Purchase of Fairhaven, Holiday Home.
1933	Favourable report on the Settlement by LCC Inspectors.
1934	Death of Mrs Emmeline Lidgett, on 12 May, eve of seventy-sixth birthday, just before Golden Wedding Anniversary.
1939–45	Difficulties experienced in the Second World War, e.g. bombing etc.
1942	Settlement Jubilee.
1946	Chaired arrangements for the Methodist Conference in London.
1949	Retired!
1952	Granted Freedom of Bermondsey.
1953	Death of John Scott Lidgett on 16 June.

29

The Bermondsey Settlement – 2

Chapter 2 above concentrated on the Settlement's origins, philosophy and the early years of its operation. The overall pattern established then was maintained with relatively little alteration:[1] a broad spectrum of cultural and physical activities for people of both sexes and all ages, welfare agencies giving legal and medical advice, and of educational lectures and courses, alongside the evangelistic and temperance work associated with Lidgett's role as Circuit Superintendent. For the 'Warden', as he was called, flexibility was all: he responded to the needs of individuals and the neighbourhood as he saw them. Clubs, for example, changed in number, titles and clientele. A sample range of what was on offer from time to time, together with other details on the Settlement, is provided in Appendix 1.

The programme was inevitably affected also by the fluctuating number and capacities of the residents and staff he was able to recruit. The maximum time that any resident stayed seems to have been three years, but most for a much shorter period. Few gave their full time to Settlement activities: residence was intended also for what Rex Kissack called 'consciencisation' by living there, mixing in the Settlement Clubs, and seeing social problems for themselves. For much Settlement work Lidgett had to rely on a staff of almost wholly women helpers, whose idealism had led them to overcome nervous apprehension at the local circumstances as well as the cramped and unsuitable living conditions they had to face. Lidgett's wife, Emmeline, taught French and wood-carving, conducted women's societies, took part in the local management of the groups of Board Schools nearby, and organised flower shows 'to promote the cultivation of the rather dismal small gardens and backyards of the monotonous neighbourhood streets'.[2] Her principal task was to supervise the domestic arrangements with the assistance (from 1905) of her unmarried sister, Winifred Davies, who also administered the Women's and Children's Holiday Funds. Some helpers came in for the day, such as members of the Hoole family on Saturdays, no doubt to assist with the Settlement's 'educational visits' and excursions to museums, galleries and places of historical interest. They all gained inspiration from Lidgett's own personal example and leadership, and he was proud both of the dedication and subsequent careers of those who braved the slums to join him. Appendix 1 lists some of them.

Their sense of the Settlement's importance was further underlined by the impressive number of local and national dignitaries whom he boldly invited to visit, open or contribute to exhibitions and concerts, or chair major occasions.[3] For example, in 1896 when what was to become an annual event until 1914, the Settlement's Picture Exhibition, was held, it was opened by Princess Louise (then Marchioness of Lorne) and her husband, and major artists, including Holman Hunt, contributed their paintings; Lord Crewe and H. A. L. Fisher presided over concerts; the Duke and Duchess of York (later King George V and Queen Mary) opened an exhibition of the work of the 'Barrack Schools'; and Bishop Creighton and Cardinal Vaughan assisted Lidgett in receiving them.

If the Settlement was an effort to create, it proved a constant struggle to maintain. Lidgett paid tribute[4] to successive treasurers, but the task of fund raising fell entirely on him. He found routine financial administration, alongside regular appeals and related correspondence with subscribers, a permanent headache: 'Very often I have hardly known where to turn . . . to secure sufficient financial help', he wrote, 'but in every case the generosity of friends has carried me through difficulties that have been somewhat staggering'. Grants became available from 1904 when the LCC took over London's education, but costs continued to rise. Paper and printing were one example: at times the Settlement's Annual Report could not be printed. The outbreak of War and the greatly increased cost of living caused a particular crisis in 1915. Though Lidgett's 1916 Report applauded the 'many hundreds' who volunteered to join the Forces and the increased help he received from women, he lamented the absence of men from the district and the fall in his churches' collections. Mercifully, despite Zeppelin scares, no loss or injury to his people or property had occurred by that date, and he claimed, no doubt with some exaggeration, that 'the work continued unimpaired'. Subsequently, however, the Settlement suffered a double blow, damage to its premises and, much more tragically, the death of Lidgett's own son in 1918. Lidgett decided that the Memorial Fund raised to commemorate him had to be wholly devoted to repairs.

Finance continued to be a problem between the wars. Year after year Lidgett assiduously reported that 'the work was being sustained with full vigour', but his Reports always included appeals for generous subscribers. In January 1927, walking on a rare holiday from Abinger to Leith Hill, he decided on a fresh initiative, a Holiday Home for London children.[5] The LCC showed an interest in the idea as a hostel for 'School Journeys'. So, after gaining initial funding from gifts, and guidance from a local builder, he purchased a site of nearly eight acres on Leith Hill, containing a pine-wood and a meadow, and built a bungalow and dormitory for about 50 people, at a total cost of £2,300. Known as Fairhaven, the home opened in the following September and proved a great asset. Its administration, running costs and maintenance were, nevertheless, bound to make calls on the Settlement, despite revenue from LCC grants and bookings. By 1931, when reduction in the size of Lidgett's capital debt and renovation to the Settlement building had become imperative, he appealed to the Pilgrim Trust and was given £4,000. He was further delighted at the end of his Presidential year in 1933, when a private appeal by his friends, Hornabrook and Wiseman,[6] entirely cleared the Settlement and its agencies of debt, except for 'comparatively trifling loans . . . still outstanding' for Fairhaven. In the same year LCC Inspectors gave a favourable report on the Settlement's educational work. But tragically, Lidgett's wife, who had suffered from heart trouble, died aged 76, on 12 May 1934.

Bermondsey suffered severely in the intensive bombing campaign of WW2. Its docks offered an easy target at a distinctive bend in the river. The whole area was devastated, and there were many casualties. Schools and churches (Brixton Hill, for example) were destroyed. Farncombe Street, where the Settlement was situated, was razed, evacuated and boarded up. The Settlement building was severely shaken by a landmine nearby in autumn 1940, and on 10 May 1941 the Settlement's Boys' 62nd Brigade Company extinguished a fire threatening the roof.

Despite many offers of a safe haven in the country, Lidgett characteristically refused to move, determined to remain with the people of Bermondsey. He took over from the Superintendent of the South London Mission when he moved out of London.[7] He preached regularly amid air raids and blackout, travelled by 'bus to his churches, and gave them encouragement and hope. F. W. Clifford[8] saw him striding up Brixton Hill Road in an air raid, in his long black coat and shawl, and wearing his well-known, wide-brimmed, shallow-crowned hat. This he irreverently called 'John 3.16', as a verse guaranteeing he would not perish! After another air raid Lofthouse[9] found him sitting in the one habitable room, coming to terms with the fact that his wife and son had died, his daughter was married and living away, and almost all his friends[10] had gone. 'He looked at me', Lofthouse said, 'with a smile of humour and indomitable courage, and said, "The best of all is, God is with us!"' At the Settlement's Jubilee in January 1942, when telegrams of congratulation came from, among others, the Archbishop of Canterbury, the King and Queen, Lord Macmillan, Sir Kingsley Wood MP and Sir Ernest Graham-Little MP, Lidgett's comment[11] was, 'Haven't I a great deal to be thankful for! We are going on with our work for the common brotherhood of man and for the reign of freedom, righteousness and peace'. He loved his Settlement: for him it achieved more practical results than preaching. His articles for the *Methodist Recorder* during the war[12] declared his belief that Britain was fighting for spiritual as well as moral values, reason and law as opposed to brute force, and for the safety and freedom of 'little people' and minorities. To those who attributed the war to divine judgement he insisted that if this was responsible for the suffering, then mercy was at its heart; their privations should be a tonic, a stimulant, and their interior gloom should give way to 'outering' their religious conviction. Interestingly, his rallying cry came not from Scripture, but from the Chorus in Aeschylus' tragedy, *Agamemnon*, 'Let *good* prevail!'[13]

The 'good' Lidgett sought in the Settlement during the war included the maintenance of clinics for children and minor ailments, insurance societies, play centres, boys' and girls' clubs and the Boys' Brigade. He started a day school, later taken over by the LCC, for children collected from the London streets, and towards the end of the war established a Waterside Youth Centre at Alice Barlow House. During night raids the Settlement basement was opened as a shelter and rest centre, and some meals were provided. Numbers accommodated at times were over 100, but never less than 30. The intervention of responsible authorities was welcomed: the Ministry of Health removed the Settlement's Day Nursery into Surrey, while the Bermondsey Borough Council built, with the Warden's permission, an extra shelter in the Settlement garden and set up an Emergency and Supply Depot inside the Settlement premises. Inevitably the educational programme had to be suspended, but, when possible, dressmaking took place at the Settlement, and musical, dramatic and practical activities in Alice Barlow House.

According to Lidgett,[14] as much as was feasible of the former programme was resumed at the end of the war: for example, some University Extension lectures, classes in dramatic elocution and health matters, and its choral and literary societies. But numbers were very small and his account undoubtedly made much of what took place. He looked forward to the Settlement becoming one of the 'Educational Colleges for Adolescents' envisaged by the 1944 Education Act. Welfare work continued through agencies for which the Settlement acted as HQ: the Bermondsey Branch of the Women Citizens' Association, and the Bermondsey Nursing Association, now incorporating the St Olave's and Rotherhithe Districts, under Lidgett's presidency. Once wanton damage at Fairhaven, requisitioned for military occupation during the war, was repaired, the home was put into action again for conferences, school journeys and holiday parties for young people.

Lidgett shared the universal relief at the sudden end of the war. There can be no doubt that he endorsed the concerns of the British Council of Churches' report[15] about the effects and implications of the use of the atomic bomb, but he remained buoyant and optimistic for the future. His immediate preoccupations were local. In 1946, then aged 92 and increasingly deaf, he felt able to chair the arrangements for the Methodist Conference in London and upbraid much younger colleagues for failing to 'speak up'! He continued to contribute to Conference debates, proudly announcing for example the Greater London evangelical campaign being planned by the Protestant churches for 1947. His eyesight remained good: having lost his spectacles, he refused to replace them, objecting testily that 'We now live in a Doctor-ridden rather than a priest-ridden society'. He calmly ignored the passing years, as Waterhouse put it. But there were ominous signs, not least severe arthritis in his legs, that, despite his protestations, he had started to fail. Already in 1944 he was said to 'hobble to his seat with the now familiar two sticks'.[16] He had to be eased into a car or pulpit one arthritic limb at a time, and even getting him there was a lengthy process.

Throughout the country the end of the war was the cue to take stock, and it was clear from the comments of Rex Kissack, then a member of the relevant Connexional Committee, that 'the hard heads' of the Methodist Conference were 'all for closing it [the Settlement] down'.[17] This was for two reasons: first, 'The world had swept on past all that the Settlement stood for', and secondly, 'there was no money to keep it going, though Lidgett fought on'.

Kissack's account implied a third reason also: Lidgett's age and deteriorating health. Kissack mentioned one Connexional Committee meeting (undated, but likely to have been between 1946 and 1949), at which Lidgett's amanuenses, 'two ageing and most Methodist of spinsters', stood on either side to help him rise from his chair. 'When he was finally upright', Kissack wrote, 'he went straight onto the offensive: "If you have any concern for my health, let me say that within the last week my doctor has examined me and pronounced me as fit as a bell – from the waist up."'

Financial problems were Kissack's second reported reason for closure. Lidgett had himself acknowledged that repairs and renovation to the war-damaged Settlement building were bound to be a long and costly business. Despite the Pilgrim Trust's grant in 1944, he had felt obliged in the following year not only to make the Settlement a personal donation of £800, originally intended as a legacy, but to set up a Re-equipment and Extension Fund. By then many former subscribers had died. Contributions were sought from, among others, J. Arthur Rank and local enterprises like Peek, Frean & Co. and Leathersellers. When presented with a cheque for himself on his retirement in 1949, he endorsed it immediately and peremptorily instructed his successor to devote half the amount to the work at Alice Barlow House and Lidgett Hall (the Youth Centre in Paradise Street) and half to Fairhaven. Even then his fund raising did not cease: on 5 March 1950 he broadcast the *Week's Good Cause Appeal*, and intended to broadcast another on 7 June 1953, but he was too weak. He died 9 days later.

Kissack recorded an 'early' post-war Settlement Connexional Committee meeting, when Lidgett was absent, and finance was used to make 'a direct thrust . . . to oust him'. Settlement poverty had led first to a charge for his board, and then rent was required for his lodging. Kissack could not remember 'whether it was this demand or the further one of asking him to move out altogether' that led Kissack to shatter 'a smooth unanimity' by voicing a strong protest 'which stopped them in their tracks'. As a Conference representative, he registered concern 'at what the Connexion at large would think of the idea of there being no home for Dr Lidgett in the Institution he had himself created'. For the moment Lidgett was saved. The circumstances of his retirement are described in the next chapter.

The first reason Kissack gave for closure, that the Settlement had now outlived itself, chimed in with comments of Percy Harris[18] in 1947 on the London Settlements in general. He said they were still doing useful work, 'but the real need for them was not as great as it was': poor neighbourhoods had not the same desire for outside help, and public authorities were doing much more for them. Kissack's verdict had been partially anticipated some 10 years before by Lidgett himself. His *Guided Life*[19] mentioned the criticism that the Polytechnic and increased LCC provision of evening schools had put his educational work into question. His response was to emphasise the Settlement's *social* purpose: 'It provides an atmosphere, promotes a comradeship, and seeks to inspire a spirit of social service which can only be supplied, if at all, most imperfectly in the ordinary evening schools.' Though Lidgett had a far wider view of education than simply through educational courses, this could not justify their duplication. Educational work had been almost totally suspended during the war and, despite Lidgett's glowingly optimistic assertions in November 1946, had, in the view of Bishop David Sheppard,[20] 'collapsed' afterwards. As for its social provision, Lidgett boasted at his farewell luncheon[21] that 'No single feature of our up-to-date social administration had not been anticipated by the voluntary efforts of the Bermondsey Settlement'. Health and welfare were nevertheless no longer left to pioneers: provision was now made through the Statute Book. Sheppard's verdict was sharp. While paying tribute to Lidgett and his work, he said: 'He went on too long. This made it harder for the Bermondsey Settlement to review its purpose and find a new line while it was still strong'.

At a reception in Lidgett's honour on 20 October 1949, Peter Morley, his successor, tactfully spoke of the need for new methods. He stressed[22] that the key word in the future would still be 'education', but quickly went on to stress continuity through its social aspects:

> In our social work it is not now the alleviation of poverty that is our main concern . . . Our aim is rather to help the poor and lonely to take a pride in themselves, to maintain their self-respect by providing creative and worthwhile activities. In our Youth and Adult Clubs it is still the word 'Education' that matters, for our purpose is 'to draw out' the personality, to help young men and women to mix with their fellows, and above all to educate for democracy . . . Never again shall we be able to reach the heights of formal

> education that the Settlement has reached in the past, but I hope to provide for the people of Bermondsey the best in music, literature and art . . . trying to help people to make *their own* entertainment – to make music, discussion, drama, toys and so on.

In effect Morley intended to treat the Settlement as a community centre for social work, not for 'formal education'. But he had another usage in mind, one Lidgett had studiously excluded, namely, provision for regular Sunday worship through converting the former dining room into a chapel. In 1952 a Methodist Society was established there.

In 1952 the Conference decided that, while keeping its name, the Settlement building should form part of the South London Mission. Under Ronald Marshall, a new Warden in 1954, the Settlement Church became the dominant body there, with an emphasis on evangelism amid its social work. In 1957 the deterioration of the buildings was such that plans were made for building a new 'Scott Lidgett Memorial Church and Settlement', but only £30,000 of the required £70,000 was raised. The alternative was to create a new chapel in the existing building and redecorate its premises, and for a period the Centre revived with up to 27 residents. In 1966, under a lay Warden, several clubs flourished, but debts were mounting: in 1967 the outdated building was finally declared too expensive to maintain. Garth Rogers, the Circuit Superintendent, supported by the South London Mission's GP Committee, decided to sell the premises and undertake a new scheme: residents' quarters and Youth/Community premises would be built on the site of the Central Hall in Bermondsey Street, and the Centre's work transferred there. The Settlement was finally closed in 1967. In March 1969 it was sold by auction for £21,000, its building demolished, and the site developed for housing.

But Lidgett's name lives on. What is now known as Cluny Place House, which the Settlement sale helped to purchase, contains a wing called Scott Lidgett House. On 24 September 2000, Scott Lidgett's name and ministry within the South London Mission were honoured at the centenary of its opening. At the commemorative Service rededicating its new building the Scott Lidgett Room was rededicated in his memory.[23] Bermondsey itself also features a Scott Lidgett Crescent and a Scott Lidgett School. In Epsom a room had been named after him on 13 November 1954 in the Burgh Heath Centre.

30

Retirement and final years

Despite his increasing age Lidgett had given no sign of his readiness to retire as the Chairman of the London South (earlier the Third London) District. Deliberately or not, he had maintained a practice of linking the offices of Chairman and Secretary together in a single annual May Synod vote.[1] This had ensured Lidgett's election, but soon after the Second World War was over the synod members were itching to replace him, and the District Secretary, J. Edwin Reding, was the more popular choice. The stark summaries in the *Methodist Recorder* of the Synod decisions[2] tell their own story. At the 1947 Synod Edwin Reding 'was nominated for appointment by Conference to succeed Dr Lidgett', and the 1948 Synod both 'approved the appointment of a "separated" Chairman retaining overall responsibility for the District but no longer for a Circuit as from the Conference of 1948' and nominated Reding 'for appointment as District Missionary and Chairman'. But still Lidgett did not retire. It was only at the Synod in May 1949 that he took the hint[3] and 'asked to be permitted to retire from the Bermondsey Settlement and become a supernumerary minister at the next Conference'. To his great credit he graciously went on to congratulate his successor. The Synod, with relief but in genuine admiration, immediately passed a special resolution paying tribute to the one who had spent 73 years in the ministry, acted as District Chairman for 41 years, and served as Warden of the Bermondsey Settlement for 59 years. All Methodism was startled when the news broke.

On 17 June and 5 October 1949 Lidgett's lifetime's work in promoting understanding and co-operation between the churches nationally was recognised in two celebratory luncheons, the first arranged by the Free Church Federal Council[4] in Westminster Chapel, the other by the *Methodist Recorder* in the London Waldorf Hotel. Both were attended by many leaders in Church and State. Eric Baker called attention to the latter occasion.[5] There Dr Geoffrey Fisher pointed to the significance of the fact that he, as Archbishop of Canterbury, was both willing and glad to propose the toast: it signalled the cordial relations that now existed after the bitter (educational) controversies of the past and the great regard in which Lidgett was held in both Anglican and Free Church communions for his part in bringing those disputes to an end. At the earlier luncheon Lidgett had also taken the opportunity to reiterate once again his major conviction, attacking 'the old stark denominationalism', but adding that he thanked God for 'South India' and 'Ceylon' for 'their refusal to go on any longer receiving Western denominational missionaries instead of becoming truly national members of the Body of Christ'. 'Amsterdam' (the formation of the World Council of Churches), he thundered, 'must not end in a fizzle'. For him Church reunion had become absolutely essential in the face of world materialism.

His retirement was marked by great ceremony in Bermondsey itself. The Borough honoured him with a ceremony in Rotherhithe Assembly Hall on 20 October, and afterwards in a less formal reception at the Settlement when he was presented with a farewell gift of over £100 from the people of Bermondsey.[6] He promptly handed this over to his successor as Warden. It must have been a proud moment for him to receive congratulatory messages from the Prime Minister (Clement Attlee), the Bishop of Southwark, and the Chairman of the LCC. The Rector of Bermondsey, the Revd A. J. Adams, spoke and Sir Richard Hopkins, one of his early residents, came to take the chair. So many speeches in tribute were made that Lidgett said they 'had almost buried him under a memorial'. His reply summarised some of the Settlement's achievements, and characteristically emphasised that it was the highest values of truth, beauty and goodness, 'pearls of great price', which he and his first helpers had come to share with a poor and harrassed neighbourhood. 'Never suppose', he said, 'that the population of Bermondsey must be treated as stupid and only capable of appreciating inferior gifts'. Dignatories attending from outside the Settlement, just as those who came to the Jubilee in 1942, would have been left in no doubt that all his work in the School Board, the LCC, London University, etc. had sprung out of the Settlement's fundamental principles he himself had enunciated.[7]

Lidgett made very few appearances in the Borough itself after his retirement, but two further major occasions were arranged there in his honour, both in 1952. The first was the Settlement's Founder's Day on Saturday, 6 June. A fancy dress procession through the streets took place before the opening ceremony; there were displays of work at the Settlement by groups and uniformed organisations; and a concert party and carnival dance in the evening. Lidgett refused the chairman's invitation to speak seated. The *Methodist Recorder* said, 'He laid aside his panama hat and spoke in his customary resounding tones'.[8]

The second occurred on 22 October 1952 in the Central Library of Bermondsey Town Hall.[9] There Lidgett, wearing his Companion of Honour decoration, was presented with the Freedom of Bermondsey and an Illuminated Address in recognition of his 'eminent public service'. Many tributes were paid to him by young and old, civic and other distinguished persons, and members of the local population. Afterwards his car was pulled round Bermondsey in a torchlight procession to the Settlement, illuminated for the occasion. All the Boys' and Girls' Clubs gave him a letter of appreciation. The occasion was one of great warmth, affection and gratitude.

On his retirement Lidgett went to stay with his daughter and son-in-law, Lettice and Gerald Davy, at Print Style, Bidborough, Kent. Dr Davy had by now retired as a consultant neurologist. But Lidgett frequently came up to Epsom at weekends to stay at the Quarry Centre and attend some meetings in London of the Settlement Committee and the *Contemporary Review* Editorial Board. A few friends[10] visited him there.

The Quarry Centre for Psychotherapy,[11] later the Burgh Heath Centre, had been founded in 1948 by Miss Ruth Simpson and turned into a non-profit-making company. Concerned about child welfare, she made provision, with the help of parents and teachers, for young people from childhood to adolescence suffering from nervous or behavioural problems. Lidgett had come into contact with her some 18 years before the venture began. She had often visited his cousin, Lady McDougall, at Appleton-le-Moors; and Ruth's sister, Helen, as Vice-Principal of the City of Leeds Training College, had once invited him to preach the College Sermon. In 1950 he was made Chairman, presided over the opening Committee in the following year, organised the Centre's constitution and engaged enthusiastically in raising funds from his contacts in the Pilgrim Trust, etc. Ever since he had helped to inaugurate the Guild of Play at the Settlement, children had been a delight to him, although he did not find contact easy. The Centre's focus on self-expression in the arts also quickly appealed to him as an extension of his own belief in God the Maker, source of creativity, fostering the creative ability inherent in all human beings. *De*structive behaviour, he thought, could stem from suppressing a child's creative impulse and *con*structive potential. His watchword, 'Catholicity', expressed as 'We all belong together', further endeared him to the children, staff and all who worked there.

Just before Christmas 1952 he had preached at Brixton Hill, but on 29 January he had to be taken to a Nursing Home, run by a Miss J. Jackson, at 49 Ashley Road, Epsom, 'for a rest', and he died there on 16 June 1953, 55 days short of his ninety-ninth birthday. He had hoped to be able to preach on Wesley's Day in 1954, close to his one hundredth birthday, but this was not to be. He had to be content with composing a few words for Wesley's two hundred and fiftieth anniversary in 1953. His sister, Lucie Maria, died soon after, also aged 98. Alfred Edward, his brother, who lived with her, had died aged 87 in 1945. Neither had married. Longevity was clearly a family feature!

Two or three weeks before his death on 16 June 1953, that brief message for the two hundred and fiftieth anniversary of John Wesley's birth was published in the *Methodist Recorder*. His Memorial Service took place in Wesley's Chapel, City Road, on Friday, 26 June. In the absence through illness of Colin Roberts, current President of the Methodist Conference, the service was led by Dr Sangster, Conference President in 1950. He was assisted by Edwin Reding, Howard Watkin-Jones (Moderator of the Free Church Council, and Conference President in 1951), and Eric Baker (Conference Secretary). Walter Noble DD[12] gave the Address. The Settlement held its own Memorial Service on Sunday, 28 June. Lidgett's successor preached the sermon, and the Rector of Bermondsey, the Revd A. James Adams, later Bishop of Barking (from 1975 to 1983), attended (as on many other occasions in the past) to pay tribute to the strong ecumenical relationship Lidgett had established in the Borough.

Lidgett's daughter moved to a flat at Mt Ephraim, Tunbridge Wells, in 1964. She died on 11 June 1980, aged 92. Her husband had predeceased her on 16 March 1972, probably at a similar age. There were no children.

Conclusion

Summing up Lidgett's career poses all but insuperable challenges. His packed life of nearly 99 years spanned a century of considerable change; the sheer number of his roles and aspects of his career is astonishing; he was a complex personality, full of paradoxes; and the impressions given by those who from personal experience saw the eccentricities of his old age could distract from the outstanding qualities he displayed throughout the greater part of his career. Fortunately for the biographer, however, there was a marked consistency in his views and outlook: coherence, reason and logic constantly guided what he did and said. The biography provides countless examples of reiterated tenets, expressed in a variety of words as they applied to different situations, hammered home, often tediously, to audience and readership alike. An intellectual by nature and training, he refused to desert his conclusions once established to his satisfaction. His mind rarely changed on any major issue,[1] not least on the doctrine of the Fatherhood of God. He was a *homo unius doctrinae*. As he explored its meaning in theory and practice, his conviction that it held the key to all our understanding never wavered. Though adapted as time went on, it remained fundamentally unchanged. His theology virtually 'peaked' with the third of his major publications in 1907.

As far as Lidgett's career as a whole is concerned, the 'peak' for that came in 1932 with Methodist Union. It effectively began in 1890 in Bermondsey. By the late 1930s and during WW2 the Settlement had begun to lose its original significance and value, and younger men were gaining greater authority and attention. He remained a venerated elder statesman, still active, still retaining much of his old intellectual vigour, but cutting a rather anachronistic, sometimes embarrassing figure, noted for increasing dogmatism, and lacking the restraint and understanding shown in his prime. By concentrating largely but not wholly on the years when he 'flourished', a fair and balanced survey can be attempted of his characteristics, aims and achievements by which to assess his stature in and beyond his Methodist Church.

John Scott Lidgett was a person of contrasts: a rebel turned Establishment figure; a member of an itinerant ministry who stayed in Bermondsey for 59 years; a Wesleyan working among the poor and deprived who was on friendly terms with bishops, MPs, the rich, the titled and 'the Great'; a circuit minister self-taught in theology who turned theologian; a critic of the Established Church and yet the Archbishop's friend; a contributor to national debate, yet in touch with grass-roots opinion; an idealist noted for robust common sense; an activist, forthright in his opinions, who became known for diplomacy and compromise, with no wish to 'unchurch' or alienate those whose views differed from his own.

Austere, aloof, with little personal magnetism, Lidgett had a burning passion for social justice and the welfare of others. Fiercely independent, he was throughout much of his life a lone figure, with few real friends, directing his energies almost wholly to the causes he espoused. In genuine gratitude *God in Christ Jesus* was dedicated to his wife 'who through many years has patiently borne the burden imposed by partnership in an arduous life'. Uncomplaining despite constant strain, she worked in the background, with often only her sister for company, bringing up her children in one of the poorest districts of London, maintaining their home and the Settlement, often teaching there. Lidgett seems to have been much closer to his son, cruelly taken from him in 1918, than to his daughter, and Emmeline's death in 1934 left him a very lonely man.

He kept a cool head against his many critics and amid clashes of personality and opinion (political and otherwise), within and outside his Church, and refused to be persuaded to condone breaches of the law. As a democrat he was always anxious to understand others' points of view and prepared judiciously to articulate them, if needed, on their behalf. In debate, as committee member or chairman, he subjected arguments to rigorous scrutiny, and thereafter sought a balanced resolution, responding both to the validity of the points made and to the practicalities of the situation. Becoming known as a diplomat, he seemed to find compromise personally gratifying, a means of putting his profound faith into practice.

Though a public figure, constantly seen and heard both locally in London and across the country,[2] he was essentially a private person with an inner, deeply spiritual life, fuelled by much prayer, reading and social experience to sustain his multiple activities and thought. Direct, unmediated access to God in Christ was to him 'the essential experience by which Methodism was raised up',[3] its maintenance of the utmost importance amid the social problems of human life with which he insisted all human beings, Christian or not, should be concerned. Pride in his achievements was matched by inner humility. He was not driven by a sense of duty, but obedience born of devotion and understanding. A devout preacher and supporting 'aggressive' (active) evangelism, he rejected the fundamentalism, fervid emotionalism and blinkered individualism of many forebears and contemporaries. His interests in fact were wide. Conscious of the wonder of God's creation, he was open to the discovery of all truth, whether in history, science, the arts or philosophy, and the *Contemporary Review*, for example, kept him in regular contact with it.

One of Lidgett's greatest talents was his facility with words. He was much in demand as an orator, declaring his own insights, and expressing as well as moulding the opinion of others, though his lengthy, complex periods could exasperate and delight by turns. As a speaker and in company he could be witty, even pungent, but his sense of humour was rarely glimpsed in his writing. His books impressed with their thoroughness and detail, but were 'too crammed with matter to be popular',[4] dull and lacking in the warm glow of evangelical excitement. As a weekly journalist, outside his weightier articles, he could be more incisive.

Lidgett's views reflected his two major watchwords. The first was *the Fatherhood of God.* This doctrine, learned principally from Maurice, came as a blinding revelation. It taught him that the principle on which the Atonement depends was the relation of the incarnate Son to the Father. It revealed the kinship of human beings with Christ and therefore the 'brotherhood' of all men and women. As a Spiritual Principle, it enabled them to recognise their kinship and become, through Christ, God's 'sons' themselves. The consequences dominated his career. He inferred that we all belong to one another: we need co-operation, social harmony, moderating influences, and the banishment of the feuds, rivalry and sectarian exclusiveness shown in denominations.

The world was created by the Father and its dignity revealed by his Son's incarnation. The incarnation showed *nihil humani* was *a deo alienum.* As he stated in Bermondsey, the sacred should not be distinguished from the secular; people conscious of their Sonship should be prepared to undertake social and public service to improve the welfare of their fellows, advancing the Kingdom of God as purposefully as they can. He was often heard to say, 'As in heaven, so on earth', and when Donald Soper, as Conference President in the year Lidgett died, declared, 'Thank God for the Welfare State!', its members might have recalled how Lidgett had contributed to its emergence by his words and example.

Moreover, human beings, rich and poor, privileged and deprived, had minds as well as bodies and souls, and their children were entitled to a good education, as grandfather Scott had taught him. To fulfil their potential they needed education to help them to enjoy what God has created, to practise creativity, discover and apprehend the highest values of Beauty, Truth and Goodness and gain a sense of social duty and personal responsibility, the desire to serve the common good. Lidgett's drive for universal education, a national system, was a response to God's grace. The Settlement and his LCC responsibilities demonstrated his conviction that learning was God's unconditional gift, and that education was desirable for its own sake whether or not it helped to advance a person's career, brought him to recognise God behind everything, or equipped him consciously to apply the gospel so that society might be permeated by its principles.

The Fatherhood of God also led Lidgett to Church unity. Boldly at a time of Nonconformist self-assertion, *Catholicity* became a second watchword. To him all human beings were favoured with the opportunity of *inward* catholicity, the fellowship with all other believers sharing in the spiritual experience of unmediated access to God, through Jesus Christ and the Holy Spirit. This universality of experience was a feature of the *whole* Church, not any *one* Church. To Lidgett, the Church was one in its essential nature, existing already with a common faith, discipleship and loyalty, too often tragically unrecognised. Self-contained denominations, sacerdotalism and claims of superiority in structure or doctrine were obstacles to its unity. Denominations, he said, speak 'provincial dialects which betray their lack of fulfilled Catholicity'. Reunion was to him a spiritual duty, essential if the Kingdom of God, God's comprehensive purpose, was to be realised on earth in and through God's sons. Only a united Church could fulfil its evangelical responsibilities and ensure faith was fully applied to political, social and moral issues. Ecumenism, like Methodism, which did not include the world was doomed to failure.

The ecumenical ideal was Lidgett's preoccupation, not the resolution of competing organisational structures. That ideal was organic union, visible and comprehensive, to be sought not for managerial reasons or in response to numerical decline, but because it was required by God; not for the aggrandisement of Methodism or a combined Free Church, but for the benefit of the Catholic Church at large. When Lidgett sought Methodist unity or a Federation of Free Churches, he saw them as concrete expressions of the ideal of unity, as within a much wider Christian unity, including the Anglican Church and (much later) Rome. He thought nothing should be done which would harm the future realisation of one Church: any Christian move towards unity was to him intrinsically universal. It excited him that the inward and outward Catholicity he proclaimed was distinctively Methodist, John Wesley's Arminianism, 'sacred deposit' and unfinished task.

Lidgett's interpretation of these watchwords were his major legacy to the Church.

Over his career Lidgett had a number of aims. He wanted to prove himself, explore his capacities as an apologist, philosopher, teacher and practical theologian. He set out to counter the anti-intellectualism rife among some Methodists who feared learning would destroy the Spirit. His desire to educate showed itself in seeking to educate fellow ministers by opposing fundamentalism/literalism; diverting them from stress on the future life to concern for the present life and social relationships; making them aware of Maurice's inspiration and what it implied, updating their theology; avoiding the extremes of harsh dogmatism and sentimentality[5] in the Atonement doctrine. Closely linked with this was his wish to give a new lead to Wesleyan College tutors whose training of students had focused mainly on Wesleyan writings and circuit work in a denomination which, like many others at the time, had not been much interested in matters outside it. Ministers who simply conserved Methodism were 'a real Methodist peril!' Lidgett was determined to improve the status of the Methodist Church by proving it did not lack theological understanding, and counted in British society. All these aims he sought to fulfil from within the Settlement, while advertising his circuit and District responsibilities, subjecting himself, like Wesley, to ascetic discipline, and earthing his views in grass-roots knowledge of people and conditions.

Lidgett was also determined to come to terms with the considerable transition in human thought taking place during his time, even if that meant inevitable clashes with the Conference 'Old Guard', disturbed by challenges to the old orthodoxies and prone to level charges of 'heresy'. There was, however, no 'grand plan'. He did not seek power when he took initiatives and adopted new issues. He did not know where he was heading. But he *did* know, he believed, what was the key, rarely recognised, to human life and its interrelated link with God. Inexorably, perhaps often unconsciously, he kept finding new fields in which to apply his convictions: new openings, expanding more widely all the time, offered opportunities to become *in*clusive. When they came his way, he was loath to put them down, as each was a form of serving the Kingdom of God and consistent (he thought) with his calling as a Wesleyan minister. He may well have had one doctrine, an obsession all his life, but he was constantly applying, developing, testing it out, reaffirming it (sometimes after questioning), as during the Great War. He was an opinion former, but also a pilgrim.

What then did Lidgett achieve? Answers may be summarised under four of his multiple roles, those of Methodist, Free Churchman, Educationist, Theologian and Scholar, for example. Steeped in Methodism, Lidgett was initially and progressively well-connected. He was lucky in his friends and relatives; John Scott, Percy Bunting, W. F. Moulton, W. B. Pope and H. P. Hughes, for example. He had a London base. His loyalty to Methodism never wavered. He was proud of his forebears and of the way in which Methodism had, in his (often repeated) view, saved not just England but the English-speaking peoples of the world from revolution in the nineteenth century. His Methodist inheritance excited him, and he felt he could make a contribution to its future. Despite his strong views he accepted Conference decisions, its narrowness of vision for the Church and barriers to personal leadership; he was no Conference Jabez Bunting, though he believed Wesleyanism needed his much wider perspectives. Yet through his speeches and writing he was a major, though not the only figure who succeeded in changing and moulding his colleagues' attitudes, redirecting them steadily but purposefully to Wesley's social concern and ecumenical outlook. Thereby he helped to improve the Church's standing and effectiveness.

Adopting in politics New Liberal ideas, not Labour's developing philosophy, he followed in the footsteps of the major Christian Socialists, but his message never gained their national prominence. The Settlement and related preaching of his wide-ranging social concern certainly helped to increase awareness of social needs, but his personal contribution to the growth of national welfare provision was only one of many. As a social reformer he liked to appear more radical than he actually was. Radical colleagues, like Keeble and the Sigma Club, thought he never went far enough, too often sitting on the fence and acting as a brake on their proposals. Yet he showed considerable courage in standing up against charges of secularism, neglect of the gospel, desertion of literalism, liking and consorting with Anglicans. His colleagues, however, were frequently in awe at his fluency, and his capacity in debate. They gained vicarious pleasure from his ability to walk with those they felt had despised them as socially inferior; from the honour and prominence gained from his books, journalism, synod chairmanship, Conference Committee membership, Presidencies and Honorary DD degrees.

The opinions of others mattered to him. He wanted not only to be consistent and successful, but also seen to be so. He succeeded in fields (the Settlement, local, city and national politics) no other Methodist had dared to touch. Methodist unity, for which he had campaigned, seemingly unattainable for years, had been achieved. Yet for some, admiration was tinged with resentment: 'he lived in a larger world than most ever have the chance to do'.[6] He could, it is true, be regarded as a Christian before he was a Methodist, a catholic before he was a spokesman of any denomination or denominations. But it would be false to say he outgrew Methodism: his Catholicity, his altruistic, disinterested search for the common good outside the narrow interests of his church were truly Methodist; in serving the community he was conscious of serving his church.

Lidgett was a Free Churchman, not just a Methodist. Behind the creation of the NCEFC from the start, though never at ease with its political extremists, he became a major figure both within it and its Federal successor. As NCEFC President, FCEFC Moderator, Committee member and Hon. Secretary of both Councils, he could justifiably be regarded as an ecclesiastical statesman. His Anglican and political connections gave him a unique position, enabling him to act as a trusted intermediary between ecclesiastics, and between ecclesiastics and politicians. Archbishop Davidson, a close friend, rated him highly,[7] but his relations with all churches and churchmen were similarly based on mutual trust: Lidgett was known for sound advice, discretion, for being thoroughly *au fait* with the great public issues of the day, sensitive to their moral aspects and likely reactions to them. His skill was evident in explaining one 'side' to another, without compromising his own views and loyalties. Not often the instrumental figure, he enjoyed a role in the background, behind the scenes, out of the limelight, commenting on (for example, via the *Methodist Times*) rather than directing events. He was often *a* spokesman rather than *the* sole spokesman for the Free Churches, a force for moderation in the frequently venomous interdenominational disputes over education. From hindsight, his stature lay in his Catholic vision. Amid schemes for union, reunion and federalism, he was keener on ideals than minutiae, and yet he remained a realist. He understood the psychological as well as the doctrinal obstacles to Church unity, and counselled for unanimity and against haste. Moreover, no scheme, once implemented, he warned, should ever be an obstacle to the larger unity, in which *all* Christians would be bound together in concord, fulfilling the vision of Ephesians. He was excited by prospects he saw opening up in the 1920 Lambeth Appeal, but disappointments in the subsequent Anglican/Free Church discussions failed to daunt him.

To Lidgett education was paramount. The importance of education for its own sake dominated the thinking and almost all the activities of John Scott's grandson. Maurice's Working Men's College and Barnett's Toynbee Hall may have given Lidgett ideas, but John Scott was his initial and continuing inspiration. Lidgett's educational provision for young adults in Bermondsey manifestly met a need for many years. While helping to lift students' vision above their drab surroundings, the Settlement promoted the value of co-operation in the local area, the community spirit and impetus to service which he saw as the essential remedy for society's ills. Concern for education, its social as well as its religious and ecumenical relevance, helped to drive him into politics, defying his Wesleyan critics. Lidgett led from the front, both as Poor Law Guardian, Progressive politician and campaigner against sectarian Religious Instruction and a secular curriculum in the schools. Amid the ups and downs of political life, and despite his many other responsibilities, he worked vigorously as member of London's School Board and County Council for the welfare of the Capital's children and the growth of its university. The ultimately successful progress to the 1944 Education Act, its national system and acceptable form of religious education, owed much to his efforts over 40 and more years. In many fields (social welfare, encouragement of young people, provision for handicapped children, promotion of practical and physical activities and the use of leisure, for example) he was not the prime mover in national developments, but they were furthered by what he did. Convinced that the minds, souls and bodies of the children of God all had needs, he did whatever he could to meet them. It is clear that many of the people whom and with whom he served recognised this and responded with grateful affection.

Finally, Lidgett was a theologian and scholar. Within Methodism, and to a lesser extent within the Free Churches, Lidgett's books made him respected for his scholarship, command of a vast range of theology, and the ability to accommodate advance in liberal thinking without surrender of evangelical truth. He expounded to good effect the theology of Maurice and the thinking of Kingsley. Though the Bermondsey venture was not copied in Methodism, Lidgett would have been content that the social message of its existence, its 'spin-off' in the Wesley Guild, and his words, written and oral, helped to justify, extend and reinforce his and, he insisted, the Church's central message of personal self-sacrifice and social and educational concern.

Conceitedly insisting on his own insights, he nevertheless acknowledged his debt to Maurice and, on the Atonement, to Dale. Lidgett's theology was in fact in many respects already dated, trailing behind front-rank (largely Anglican) theologians. In the strictest sense he lacked originality. He was sensitive to this charge, even though it was one levelled also at Wesley himself and Nonconformity in general. Reacting to Professor Whitehead's jibe at Methodism in 1938,[8] he argued that

> the quality of *newness* extends beyond 'new ideas'. There may be a new emphasis, a new proportion, a recovery of what has been neglected and become obscure, which may effect as true and vital a revolution of thought as the importation of new ideas from without.

Rupp has leapt to Lidgett's defence. Referring to the significance across the theological world which Lidgett perceptively identified in Maurice's exposition of the Fatherhood of God, he said: '. . . this was his own discovery, not less original because it responded to new currents in his age, or because others greater and more novel than himself were pointing in the same direction, saying the same things'.[9]

Lidgett's significance as a theologian lay in Nonconformity at the time he was writing, but in the light of posterity Rupp has admitted 'there are a great many fallen leaves', 'little of survival value'. Lidgett was not, like Maurice, 'a digger', one who kept on mining newer theological truth. Though he nourished one central doctrine, he displayed great intellectual energy both in establishing and in reconfirming it in all its complexities against his own high standards. Early in his ministry he saw his career as a 'theological *teacher*'. In that ambition, though not within a theological college, he certainly succeeded – amid many other occupations. In mediating what he read and assimilated from current scholarship he had an educative influence on his fellow ministers. In Rupert Davies's view Lidgett

> saved Methodism from any sole preoccupation with the salvation of individual souls: he was committed to the total development, spiritual, mental and physical, of people, by themselves and in community.[10]

Edmondson's College survey[11] concluded: 'It was the umbrella of respectability that he gave to liberal doctrine which enabled and encouraged the growth of that doctrine within the Wesleyan Colleges'. 'What Peake did for Primitive and United Methodism through their Colleges was', he said, 'at first hand; what Lidgett did for Wesleyan Methodism' was less direct, but 'ultimately with a far wider influence'. For that Methodism should be very grateful.

Lidgett was theologically aware and cultured, scholarly, highly intellectual, an expositor but not in the narrowest professional sense a scholar. He was, however, a great many other things at the same time. In what he proudly called his '*guided*' life his range was astonishing – minister, Warden, educationalist, social reformer, politician, theologian, journalist, ecclesiastical statesman, Free Church and Methodist observer and visionary, almost all simultaneously, and all from a base in the slums. He commanded enormous respect and admiration, though not adulation. His career rightly gave him the greatest satisfaction, but he was not always as great, as prominent or as innovative as he thought he was. Yet a degree of self-importance at his achievements and influence was combined with deep spirituality and a burning desire to educate, reconcile, unite and advance his fellow human beings.

Within Methodism and the Free Churches he had become by the 1930s *primus inter pares*. No major figure had emerged among them to match his national prominence. His manifest abilities, record, appointments, honours and prestige stood for themselves. Failures and disappointments (as in the demise of the Progressives, misjudgement over Lloyd George's 1935 venture, and in the outcome of his pressure for unity of the churches) were more than counterbalanced by his very considerable achievements. His career had gained from lucky events: his accidental meeting with Davidson in Sidmouth, the outcome of Conference's Presidential voting, unexpected elevation into London's Vice-Chancellor's chair, for example. But these were used to further his already formulated ecumenical, social and educational purposes to his and other Churches' benefit. As he began to approach the age of 90, however, his vigour and significance had clearly declined, though he would never have admitted it. He could then be, and by some was, seen as belonging to a past era, perhaps principally to an Edwardian Age. Yet over Lidgett's last 10 to 15 years the length, depth and results of his experience and unremitting service led to his being regarded as 'the personification' or 'Archbishop'[12] of Methodism. On his death the *Methodist Recorder* paid this sincere tribute: 'Of all the successors in the chair of John Wesley no name will stand higher than that of John Scott Lidgett'.[13] Such a claim was redolent of the Church's very great pride and justified admiration. Whether its hyperbole remains justified in the perspective of later events, time (not this biographer) will be able to tell.

Appendix 1

Some Bermondsey Settlement details

Premises

The Settlement Building at Farncombe Street, down a dark turning off Jamaica Road, SE16, opened on 6 January 1892, included a large hall, lecture/classrooms of various sizes, games room, gymnasium [Lidgett called it 'gUmnasium'(*sic*), the Greek word], library, sitting room and asphalt yard: upstairs a dining hall, bed-sitting rooms for 15–20 men, common room, Warden's flat (with few home comforts), and caretaker's quarters. Several other houses, scattered throughout the neighbourhood, became at various times parts of the Settlement. Some changes seem to have been made over time in their names, residents and the activities centred on them, notably the work with women. The Houses included St George's House (originally 'The George' Public House, purchased in 1894); Alice Barlow (AB) House; the Women's House; Beatrice House; Lidgett Hall (a youth centre); and other small private houses bought for nurses and other women helpers, who might (or might not) carry on some Settlement-related activity in them. Outside Bermondsey there were Fairhaven, in Surrey, and the Heritage Craft Schools, at Chailey. The latter were originally the Old Heritage buildings, a disused industrial school, initially purchased by Lidgett at the suggestion of Dr and Mrs Kimmins, and later taken over, it seems, by the LCC. He remained as Chairman of the Governing Body.

Residents and staff

The following list records, largely in alphabetical order, the names of some of the more prominent people who assisted Lidgett in the Settlement and the buildings associated with it. Many details are given in note form. Further information may be found in Lidgett's *Reminiscences* and *Guided Life*; Settlement Reports; and Chapter 2 above.

Miss Alice Barlow, benefactor (with family) of AB House.
T. Chester Barratt, Rydalian, Rydal Boys' Club, legal adviser, later City lawyer.
John Borland, choral society, etc., later Music Adviser to LCC.
Miss Margaret Bretherton.
Miss Ada Brown, married Dr Alfred Salter 1900; first woman Mayor of Bermondsey.
Sir William E. Brunyate, Mrs Emmeline Lidgett's brother-in-law, drew up rules of St George's House, later KCMG 1916, CMG 1907, and Legal/Financial Adviser to Khedive's Government in Cairo.

H. Boyd Carpenter, son of Bishop of Ripon, later i/c Egypt's Education.
Miss Winifred E. Davies, Mrs Emmeline Lidgett's sister, at the Settlement 1905–35.
Gerald H. Davy, later Lidgett's son-in-law, at the Settlement 1905–9, RAMC in Mesopotamia, OBE, consultant neurologist.
Francis Dodd, teacher of art, painter of Lidgett's portrait.
Harold and Mrs Finch, Youth Centre (AB House).
Sr Grace Hannan, 1895, married Dr Kimmins 1898, crippled children, founder and later head of the Heritage Craft Schools at Chailey.
Frank Hoole, Settlement architect's son, briefly i/c Boys' Brigade after J. M. Rippon.
R. V. N. Hopkins, Approved Insurance Society wef 1911, later KCB, head of Somerset House.
W. H. Hunt, left to run Colony for Epileptics, then Colony for Unemployed.
Dr C. W. Kimmins, Science teacher, Secretary University of London Extension Society, etc.
(Major) Norman Lewis, i/c Boys' Brigade Company after Frank Hoole.
Mrs Emmeline Lidgett, Warden's wife, domestic management until 1931, pianist, taught French, wood-carving, died 1934.
John Cuthbert Lidgett, Emmanuel College, Cambridge, legal adviser, Boys' Brigade.
Revd Dr W. F. Lofthouse, 1894–6.
Mrs E. M. Lowe, help with teaching, later Chairman of LCC Education Committee.
Miss Anna Martin, sister-in-law of Prof. J. Ward, Women's Society at AB House.
Bob Mellish MP.
Miss Morgan, married J. M. Rippon.
J. M. Rippon, i/c 62nd Company, Boys' Brigade, 1893–1903.
Dr Alfred Salter, 1898ff., Settlement's Insurance Society, bacteriologist from Lister Institute, Guy's Hospital, later local doctor and MP.
Miss Mary Simmons, Women's House, 1893–1916, nursing.
Sir Kingsley Wood, legal adviser, later Kt, MP, Chancellor of Exchequer.
Lidgett's Secretaries: at various times – Miss Victoria Alice Child, Miss E. M. Elcomb, Miss Knowles, Miss Ethel M. Still, Sr Helen Styles.

Settlement activities

Activities included:
An educational institute: University Extension Lectures (some with 'limelight' illustrations), lectures on current affairs, conversaziones; classes in French, Latin, Greek, English, Elocution, Local History, Mathematics, Natural (Elementary) Science, Music, Handwork, Dressmaking, Health (First Aid, Nursing, 'School for Mothers'), commercial subjects; gymnasium activities, swimming, excursions to museums, galleries (inc. annual Art Exhibitions at the Settlement wef 1896), the countryside; holidays for children, women and e.g. factory girls.
Clubs/societies: choral, string band, concerts and oratorios (at times conducted by composers), St John Ambulance, 62nd Company of Boys' Brigade, rambling, tennis, chess, draughts, historical, debating, Band of Hope (e.g. 'United Juvenile Order Total Abstinent Sons and Sisters of Phoenix'), etc.

Appendix 1: Some Bermondsey Settlement details

Social welfare: District Nursing, Dental Clinic and Minor Ailments Centre, Poor Man's Lawyer, Sick Benefit Insurance Dividing Society, National Deposit Friendly Society, Babies' Institute, Day Nursery, Girls' and Boys' Playhours, Little Girls' Club, Guild of Joyful Surprises, Working Girls' Club, Rydal Club for Boys, Beatrice Club for Girls, Women's Club and Socials, Working Men's Club, Workhouse Girls' Help Committee, Fireside Guild for Friendless Women, St Anne's Guild for Widows, Guild of Brave Poor Things (crippled/handicapped children) which Deaconess Grace had initiated in W. London, Metropolitan Association for Befriending Young Servants, etc.
Service in the local community in addition to the above: as e.g. Poor Law Guardians, elementary school managers, members of LCC and Borough Councils.

Doggerel about the Settlement

For 'residents' to settle in such slums,
    Where toil hums,
And to dwell amidst such dirt, and noise, and vice
    Is not nice;
Bermondsey is no Eden (with such smells)
    For bland swells;
But here Culture, in the spirit of true neighbour
    Lives with Labour;
With wisdom, love and unsectarian piety
    Lends variety
To that gloom which for poor workers and their wives
    Spoils their lives.
There are lectures, classes, clubs, 'larks' not a few,
    Outings, too!
And in outdoor recreation they all share
    For their care
Is to 'chum in' with poor folk in grief or joy –
    Girl and boy.

Lines from *Punch* – quoted in *Southwark and Bermondsey Annual*, 1905, p. 201.

Appendix 2

Family trees

Introduction

The eight family trees which follow are interrelated. Where they overlap, details are repeated whenever this can assist clarity. Few of the trees are complete: some dates and details are not known or thought unnecessary for the present purpose.

Each of the family trees is provided as follows in two parts:

(a) in the conventional layout, omitting titles, days and months of the year, and
(b) in an annotated version, giving greater detail in note form.

The family tree for DAVIES (both parts, **4 (a)** and **(b)**) is based on material principally supplied by Mrs Libby Fairweather, while the other seven family trees (again both parts in each case) are derived from material provided mainly by Miss Elisabeth McDougall and partly by Mrs Elisabeth Brewer and Mrs Elizabeth Camp. Additions, adaptation and abbreviation for all eight family trees, as well as any inaccuracies or omissions, are to be attributed to myself alone.

1. (a). FAMILY TREE: LIDGETT, with Cumpston, Budgett, Hoole, Bunting

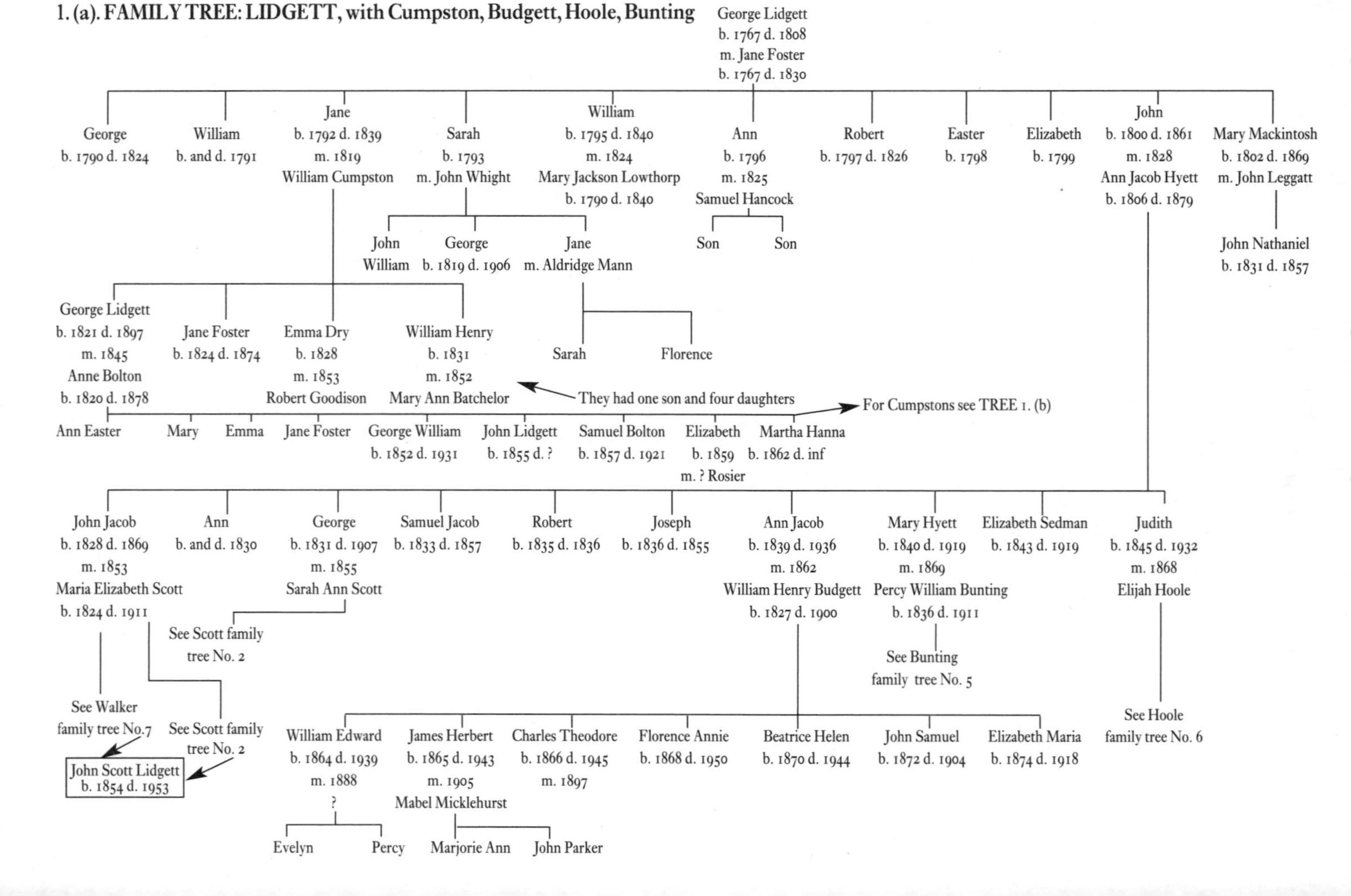

1. (b). FAMILY TREE: LIDGETT, with Cumpston, Budgett, Hoole, Bunting

GEORGE <u>**LIDGETT**</u> (Hull river pilot) b. *c.*1767 d. (pneumonia) 8 or 9 October 1808, m. JANE FOSTER d. 27 November 1830 (aged 63).

The eleven children of Jane and **George** <u>**LIDGETT**</u> were:
George b. *c.*1790 d. 12 May 1824 (unmarried).
William b. and d. 1791.
Jane b. 1792, m. 1819 WILLIAM CUMPSTON (Hull river pilot), d. *c.*1839. Four children, see below.
Sarah b. *c.*1793, m. JOHN WHIGHT of Ipswich, d.1860.
William b. *c.*1795 d. 1840, m. 1824 MARY JACKSON LOWTHORP 1790–1840.
Ann b. *c.*1796, m. 6 December 1825, in Newark, SAMUEL HANCOCK.
Robert b. *c.*1797 d. 1826 (unmarried).
Easter b. *c.*1798 (unmarried).
Elizabeth b. *c.*1799 (unmarried).
John b. 18 December 1800 d. 7 May 1861. Of Tunbridge Wells; transported Yorkshire Wesleyans emigrating to settle in Natal, on land, later Lidgetton, purchased in 1850; m. 1828 ANN JACOB HYETT b. 1806 d. 1879. Ten children, see below.
Mary Mackintosh b. 1802 d. 1869, m. JOHN LEGGATT.

The four children of **Jane** and **William** <u>**CUMPSTON**</u> were:
George Lidgett b. 1821 d. 1897, m. 1845 ANNE BOLTON 1820–1878 (went to Australia in 1852; all were Wesleyans; G. L. Cumpston's grandson (Dr Howard Lidgett Cumpston CMG, b. 19 June 1880 d. 9 October 1954) was the first Director General of the Health Department of the Commonwealth of Australia). See below for children.
Jane Foster b. *c.*1824 d. 1874 (unmarried).
Emma Dry b. *c.*1828, m. 1853 ROBERT GOODISON.
William Henry b. 1831, m. MARY ANN BATCHELOR, had one son and four daughters (unnamed).

The three children of **Sarah** and **John** <u>**WHIGHT**</u> were:
John William.
George b. 1819 d. 1906.
Jane.

There were two sons of the marriage of **Ann** and **Samuel** <u>**HANCOCK**</u>.

The ten children of **Ann** and **John** <u>**LIDGETT**</u> were:
John Jacob b.1828 d. 1869 (shipowner and shipbroker with brother George), m. 1853 MARIA ELIZABETH SCOTT b. 3 July 1824 d. 10 February 1911. Three children, see below and see **SCOTT** family tree No. 2.
Ann b. and d. 1830.

George b. 1831 d. 1907 (BA London University; JP; business partner with brother John Jacob, took over the shipping company on his death; Director of Star Assurance Society; member of Lloyds; concentration on sail, not steam, perhaps caused debt worries and strokes in final years; d. at Appleton-le-Moors), m. 1855 SARAH ANN ('Jeanie') SCOTT (see **SCOTT** family tree).

Samuel Jacob b. 1833 d. 1857 (Wrangler at Trinity College, Cambridge; preparing for the Bar; killed by cricket ball to the heart in Tunbridge Wells).

Robert b. 1835 d. 1836.

Joseph b. 1836 d. 1855 (fell from horse, accident on ice in Blackheath Park).

Ann Jacob b. 1839 d. 1936, m. WILLIAM HENRY BUDGETT JP b. 19 December 1827 d. 19 October 1900 (son of Samuel Budgett 1794–1851, founder with H. H. Budgett of prosperous wholesale grocery business in Nelson St, Bristol, and branches; William Henry Budgett, with his brothers, J. S. and S. Budgett, became Directors of the Limited Company; John Scott Lidgett's 'call' to the ministry came while on 1870 Whitby holiday with William and Ann).

Mary Hyett b. 1840 d. 1919, m. 1869 PERCY WILLIAM BUNTING 1836–1911. (Four children. See **HYETT** family tree No. 3 and **BUNTING** family tree No. 5.)

Elizabeth Sedman b. 1843 d. 1919 (unmarried; lived at Tunbridge Wells until mother died; kept in touch with family at home and in South Africa; Poor Law Guardian, St Pancras; disciple of Octavia Hill 1843–1919; wrote on Armenians).

Judith ('Jan') b. 1845 d. 1932, m. 1868 ELIJAH HOOLE 1837–1912. (Eight children, see below and **HOOLE** family tree No. 6.)

The one son of **Mary Mackintosh (LIDGETT)** and **John LEGGATT** was **John Nathaniel** b. 1831 d. 1857, at sea.

The nine children of **Anne** and **George Lidgett CUMPSTON** were:

Ann Easter.

Mary (unmarried).

Emma (unmarried).

Jane Foster (unmarried).

George William b. 1852 d. 1951.

John Lidgett b. 1855.

Samuel Bolton b. 1857 d. 1921.

Elizabeth b. 1859, m. ? ROSIER.

Martha Hannah b. and d. 1862.

The three children of **Maria** and **John Jacob LIDGETT** were:

JOHN SCOTT b. 1854 d. 1953 (see **SCOTT** family tree No. 2).

Lucie Maria b. 1855 d. 1953 (unmarried).

Alfred Edward b. 1858 d. 1945 (unmarried). Worked with George Lidgett.

The seven children of **Ann Jacob (LIDGETT)** and **William BUDGETT** were:

William Edward b. 1864 d. 1937 (continued family firm, difficulties in paying dividends in 1926); m. 1888. Children EVELYN and PERCY.

James Herbert b. 1865 d. 1943, m. MABEL MICKLEHURST. Children MARJORIE ANN and JOHN PARKER. At one period Chairman of Lidgetton, Natal.
Charles Theodore b. 1866 d. 1945, m. 1897. No children.
Florence Annie b. 1868 d. 1950 (unmarried).
Beatrice Helen b. 1870 d. 1944 (unmarried).
John Samuel b. 1872 d. 1904 (unmarried).
Elizabeth Maria b. 1874 d. 1918 (unmarried).

The eight children of **Judith** and **Elijah HOOLE** (see **HOOLE** family tree) were:
Judith Agnes b. 1865 d. 1945 (unmarried).
Violet Annie b. 1870 d. 1964, m. PERCY ZILWOOD ROUND b. 1860 d. 1934.
Elijah Basil b. 1871 d. 1954.
George Bernard Holland b. 1873 d. *c.*1960.
Elinor (?Eleanor) Saxon b. 1875 d. 1963.
Ethel Mary b. 1876 d. 1967 (unmarried).
Roger Francis (?Frank) Sebastian b. 1879 d. *c.*1960–5
Octave (?Octavia) Beatrice (? Beatrix) b. 1880 d. *c.*1965–7 (unmarried).

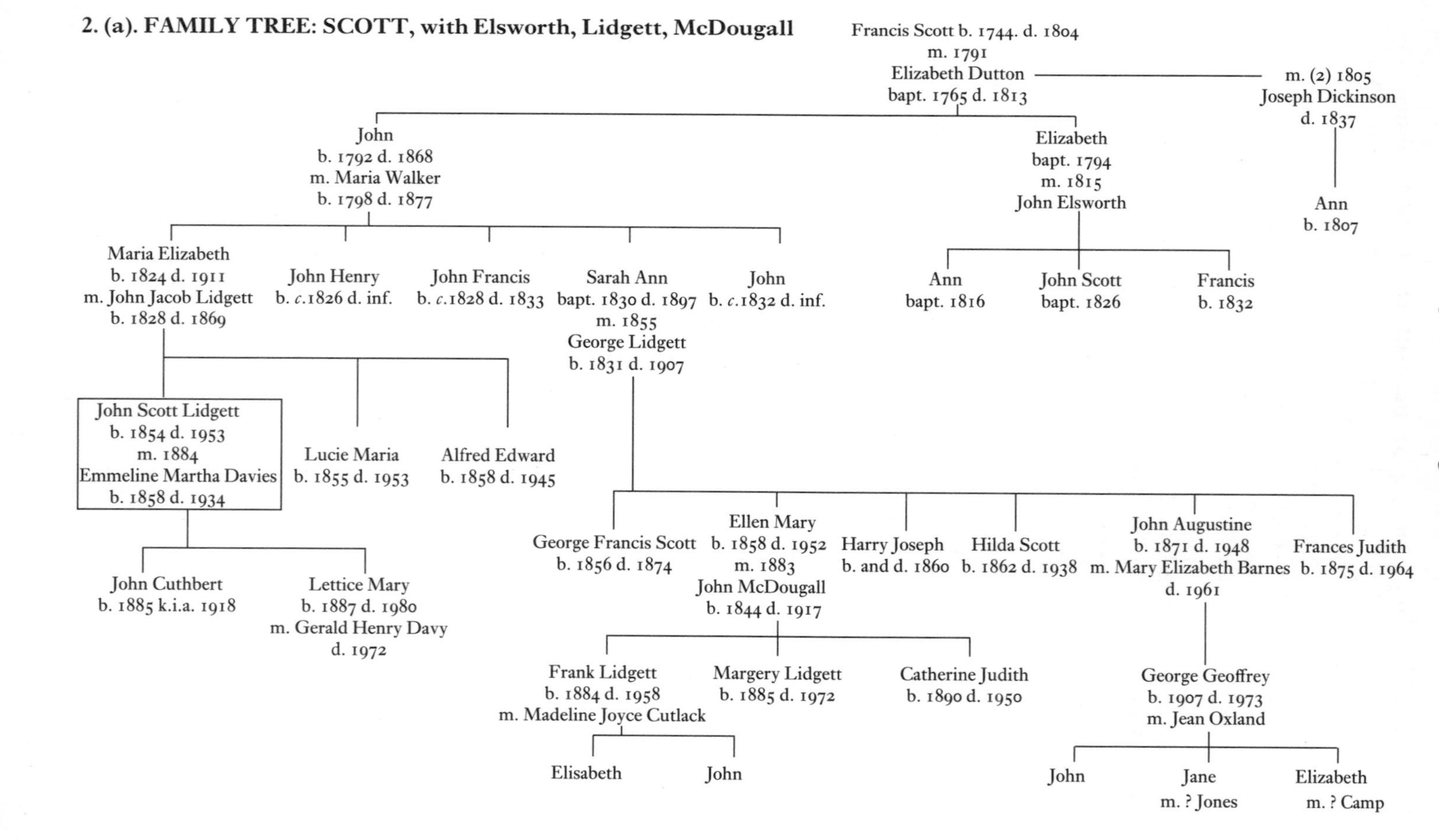
2. (a). FAMILY TREE: SCOTT, with Elsworth, Lidgett, McDougall
Francis Scott b. 1744. d. 1804
m. 1791
Elizabeth Dutton
bapt. 1765 d. 1813
m. (2) 1805
Joseph Dickinson
d. 1837
Ann
b. 1807
John
b. 1792 d. 1868
m. Maria Walker
b. 1798 d. 1877
Elizabeth
bapt. 1794
m. 1815
John Elsworth
Maria Elizabeth
b. 1824 d. 1911
m. John Jacob Lidgett
b. 1828 d. 1869
John Henry
b. c.1826 d. inf.
John Francis
b. c.1828 d. 1833
Sarah Ann
bapt. 1830 d. 1897
m. 1855
George Lidgett
b. 1831 d. 1907
John
b. c.1832 d. inf.
Ann
bapt. 1816
John Scott
bapt. 1826
Francis
b. 1832
John Scott Lidgett
b. 1854 d. 1953
m. 1884
Emmeline Martha Davies
b. 1858 d. 1934
Lucie Maria
b. 1855 d. 1953
Alfred Edward
b. 1858 d. 1945
John Cuthbert
b. 1885 k.i.a. 1918
Lettice Mary
b. 1887 d. 1980
m. Gerald Henry Davy
d. 1972
George Francis Scott
b. 1856 d. 1874
Ellen Mary
b. 1858 d. 1952
m. 1883
John McDougall
b. 1844 d. 1917
Harry Joseph
b. and d. 1860
Hilda Scott
b. 1862 d. 1938
John Augustine
b. 1871 d. 1948
m. Mary Elizabeth Barnes
d. 1961
Frances Judith
b. 1875 d. 1964
Frank Lidgett
b. 1884 d. 1958
m. Madeline Joyce Cutlack
Margery Lidgett
b. 1885 d. 1972
Catherine Judith
b. 1890 d. 1950
George Geoffrey
b. 1907 d. 1973
m. Jean Oxland
Elisabeth
John
John
Jane
m. ? Jones
Elizabeth
m. ? Camp

2. (b). FAMILY TREE: SCOTT, with Elsworth, Lidgett, McDougall

FRANCIS SCOTT (farmer) b. *c.*1744, buried at Copmanthorpe 19 November 1804, m. 21 September 1791 at York ELIZABETH DUTTON, bap. 23 June 1765 at York, d. 2 July 1813, aged 48, but m. (2nd) 9 December 1805 JOSEPH DICKINSON d. 17 May 1837, aged 84, to whom ANN was born, 24 November 1807.

The two children of **Elizabeth** and **Francis SCOTT** were:
John b. 17 August 1792 at Copmanthorpe d. 1868, m. MARIA WALKER b. 1799 d. 1877 (baptized by Dr Adam Clark).
Elizabeth b. 4 December 1794 at Copmanthorpe, m. JOHN ELSWORTH of Copmanthorpe (benefactor). Three children, see below.
The five children of **Maria** and **John SCOTT** were:
Maria Elizabeth b. 3 July 1824 d. 1911, m. JOHN JACOB LIDGETT b. 1828 d. 1869. Three children, see below and other **LIDGETT** family trees.
John Henry b. *c.*1826. d in infancy.
John Francis b. *c.*1828 d. age 5.
Sarah Ann ('Jeanie') bap. 14 February 1830 d. 19 April 1897, m. 7 September 1855 at Liverpool GEORGE LIDGETT b. 1831 d. 1907. Six children, see below and other **LIDGETT** family trees.
John b. *c.*1832 d in infancy.

The three children of **Elizabeth** and **John ELSWORTH** were:
Ann bap. 25 August 1816.
John Scott bap. 21 May 1826 at York, m. ANN ELIZABETH SIMPSON b. 1834.
Francis b. 24 September 1832, m. ELIZABETH J (?) b. 1850.

The three children of **Maria** and **John Jacob LIDGETT** were:
JOHN SCOTT LIDGETT b. 10 August 1854 d. 16 June 1953, m. 1884 EMMELINE MARTHA DAVIES b. 1858 d. 12 May 1934. Two children, see below and other **LIDGETT** family trees.
Lucie Maria b. 1855 d. 1953 (unmarried).
Alfred Edward b. 1858 d. 1945 (unmarried, bequeathes most of his estate to his sister).

The six children of **Sarah** and **George LIDGETT** were:
George Francis ('Frank') Scott b. 1856 d. 1874 (great friend of JOHN SCOTT LIDGETT, died of typhoid aged 18 in Naples, possibly visiting ELIJAH HOOLE'S architectural work there).
Ellen ('Nellie') Mary b. 1858 d. 1952, m. 1883 (his second marriage) JOHN MCDOUGALL b. 1844 d. 1917 (knighted 1902). Three children, see below.
Harry Joseph b. and d. 1860.
Hilda Scott b. 1862 d. 1938 (unmarried).

John Augustine b. 1871 d. 1948 (Leys School Accountant, Merchant Navy, Transvaal Rifles, built house at Lidgetton in 1910, managed estate until death), m. MARY ('MOLLIE') ELIZABETH BARNES d. 1961. One child, see below.
Frances Judith b. 1875 d. 1964 (unmarried).

The two children of **Emmeline** and **JOHN SCOTT LIDGETT** were:
John ('Jack') Cuthbert b. 18 August 1885 killed in action 24 March 1918.
Lettice Mary b. 28 October 1887 at Cambridge d. 11 June 1980, m. DR GERALD HENRY DAVY (Hull Mission, consultant neurologist at Guy's, RAMC in Mesopotamia, OBE, amateur artist, collector of paintings) d. 16 March 1972. No children.

The three children of **Ellen** and **John McDOUGALL** were:
Frank Lidgett b. 1884 d. 1958 (CMG 1926, set up FAO), m. in Australia MADELINE JOYCE CUTLACK. Their children were ELISABETH Mc DOUGALL (unmarried, originator of these family trees) and JOHN McDOUGALL.
Margery Lidgett b. 1885 d. 1972 (unmarried).
Catherine ('Kitty') Judith b. 1890 d. 1950 (unmarried).

The one child of **Mary** and **John Augustine LIDGETT** was:
Geoffrey George b. *c.*1907/8 d. 1973, at Leys School 1922–5, m. JEAN OXLAND. Their children are Mrs JANE JONES (now in New Zealand), Mrs ELIZABETH CAMP (now in Natal, informant re Lidgetton and lived there), and JOHN (no details).

3. (a). FAMILY TREE: HYETT, with Cowles, Warner, Lidgett

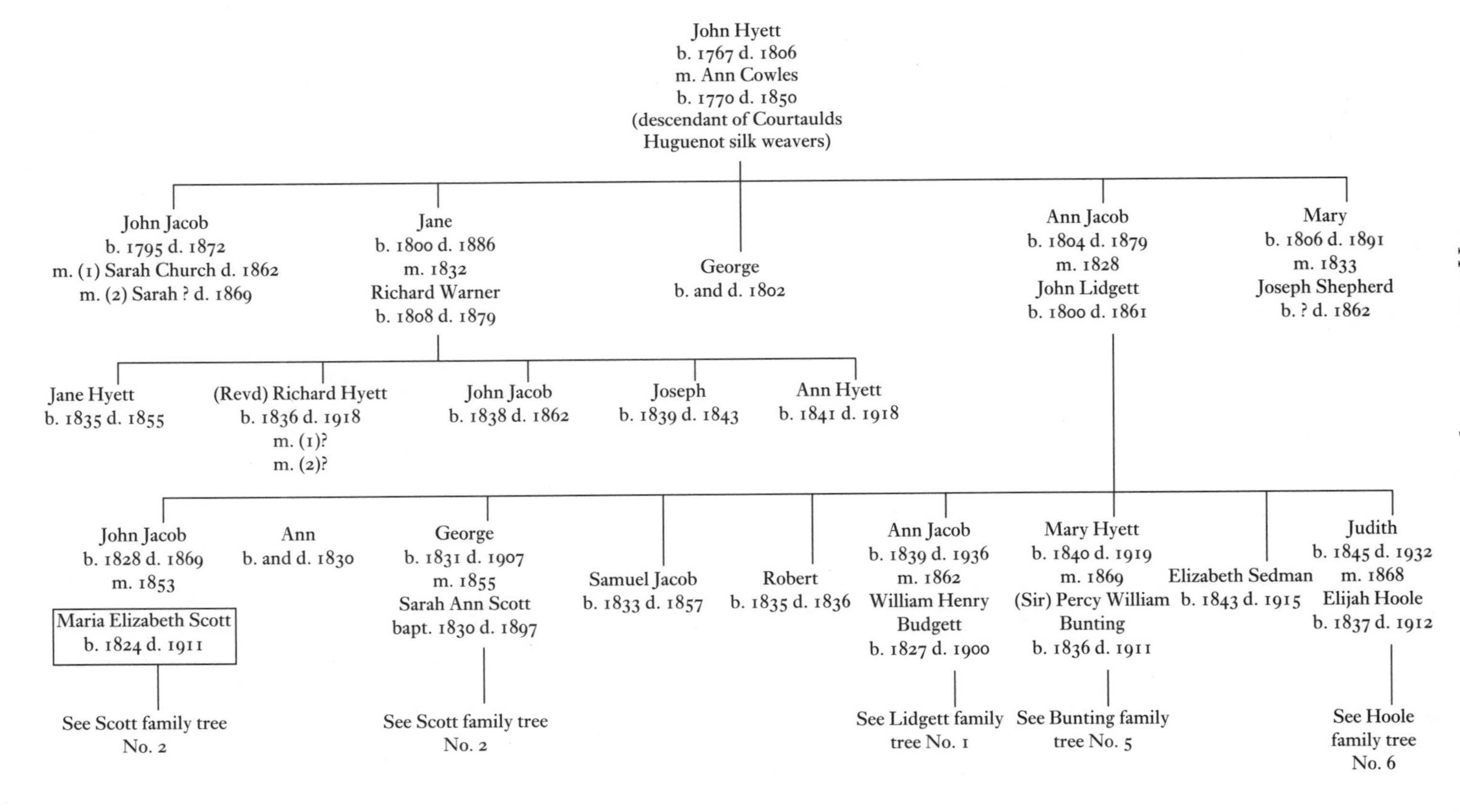

3. (b). FAMILY TREE: HYETT, with Cowles, Warner, Lidgett

AUGUSTIN COURTAULD (silk-weaving Huguenot craftsman) came to England in early 18th century. His grand-daughter, Ann Courtauld, married a **JACOB** from Metz. Judith Jacob, their daughter, married George **COWLES**, a gold and silversmith, partner of Louisa COURTAULD, 1729–1807. Their daughter was Ann COWLES, 1770–1850, who married JOHN **HYETT**, a cooper of Gloucester, of a family which had fallen on hard times. These HYETTS, John Scott Lidgett said in *My Guided Life* (p. 7), were 'my grandmother's parents'.

This **JOHN HYETT** b. 1767 d. 1806, buried in Gloucester, married ANN COWLES b. 13 September 1770 d. 23 March 1850, buried in Nunhead cemetery, London.

The five children of **Ann** and **John HYETT** were:

John Jacob b. 14 July 1799 d. 18 April 1872, m. SARAH MARY CHURCH d. 4 January 1862; he married (2) SARAH (?) d. 1869. No children by either marriage.

Jane b. 2 November 1800 d. 27 June 1886, m. 4 September 1832 RICHARD WARNER b. *c.*1808/9 d. 7 April 1879. Five children, see below.

George b. and d. 1802.

Ann Jacob (JOHN SCOTT LIDGETT'S grandmother) b. 27 April 1804 d. 2 April 1879, m. 5 February 1828 JOHN LIDGETT b. 18 December 1800 d. 17 June 1861. For nine children, see below.

Mary b. ? August 1806 d. 15 February 1891, m. 21 January 1833 JOSEPH SHEPHERD (whose father, JOHN, had married a Susannah SCORESBY); partner with JOHN LIDGETT, quarrelled, 1847–50), d. 1862. Lived at Appleton-le-Moors. No children.

The five children of **Jane** and **Richard WARNER** were:

Jane Hyett b. 9 November 1835 d. (of tuberculosis) 23 April 1855 (unmarried).

Richard Hyett (Revd) b. 2 April 1836 d. 24 July 1918. Vicar of Almeley, Herefordshire. Married twice. No children.

John Jacob b. 10 April 1838 d. 14 September1862, in army, in Barbados (unmarried).

Joseph b. 17 October 1839 d. 25 August 1843 (fell out of a window).

Ann Hyett b. 3 October 1841 d. 18 December 1918 (unmarried).

The nine children of **Ann** and **John LIDGETT** were:

John Jacob b. 1 November 1828 d. 19 May 1869, m. 7 September 1853 MARIA ELIZABETH SCOTT b. 1824 d. 1911 (see **SCOTT** family tree No. 2).

Ann b. and d. 1830.

George b. 19 November 1831 d. 18 June 1907, m. 29 August 1855 SARAH ANN SCOTT bapt. 1830 d. 19 April 1897 (see **SCOTT** family tree No. 2).

Samuel Jacob b. 22 August 1833 d. 18 June 1857 (Trinity College Cambridge).

Robert b. 1835 d. 1836.

Ann Jacob b. 17 February 1839 d. 28 October 1936, m. 10 October 1862 WILLIAM HENRY BUDGETT b. 1827 d. 1900 (see **LIDGETT** family tree No. 1).

Mary Hyett b. 17 December 1840 d. 5 October 1819, m. 1869 (Sir) PERCY WILLIAM BUNTING b. 1836 d. 1911 (see **BUNTING** family tree No. 5).
Elizabeth Sedman b. 26 August 1843 d. 8 April 1915 (unmarried).
Judith b. 5 July 1845 d. 2 January 1932, m. 2 April 1868 ELIJAH HOOLE b. 1837 d. 27 July 1912 (see **HOOLE** family tree No. 6).

4. (a). FAMILY TREE: DAVIES, with Lidgett

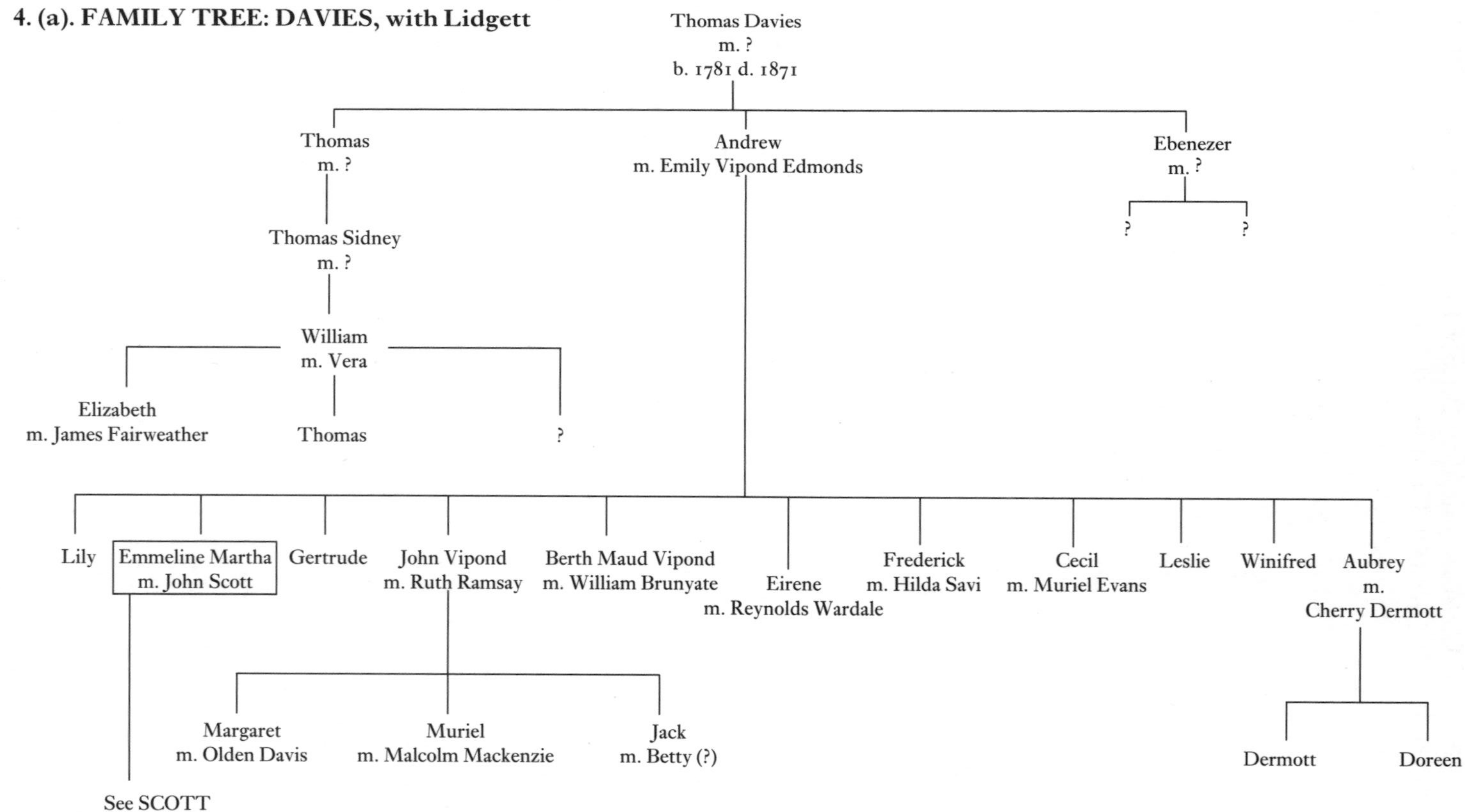

4. (b). FAMILY TREE: DAVIES, with Lidgett

THOMAS DAVIES (Head of Inland Revenue for Pembrokeshire) b. 1781 d. 1871, m. ? Had three children (see below). His grand-daughter EMMELINE MARTHA DAVIES m. JOHN SCOTT LIDGETT.

The three children of **Thomas** and ? **DAVIES** were:
Thomas Revd BA (Cantab), Rector of Llanvaches, Monmouth. One son (see below).
Andrew MD (St Andrew's and Guy's Hospital), JP, moved from Swansea to manage Varteg Hill Colliery, m. EMILY VIPOND EDMONDS. Eleven children (see below).
Ebenezer MD (Guy's Hospital, Swansea MO), m. ? Two children.

The one child of **Revd Thomas DAVIES** and **his wife** was:
Thomas Sidney Dr (Guy's Hospital), went to Australia. His son was William ('Captain Bill of the ANZACS') who married VERA ? Had three children including: Elizabeth ('Libby'), contributor to this family tree, who married JAMES FAIRWEATHER. They had two children, Sally and Jane.

The eleven children of **Andrew** and **Emily DAVIES** were:
Lily Emmeline Martha b. 1858 d. 1934, m. 1884, Cardiff, Revd JOHN SCOTT LIDGETT. Two children (see below).
Gertrude.
John Vipond Civil Engineer. Went to New York m. RUTH RAMSAY. Three children (see below).
Bertha Maud Vipond, m. Sir WILLIAM BRUNYATE, barrister associated with the Bermondsey Settlement.
Eirene, m. Prof. REYNOLDS WARDALE (Professor of Latin at Cardiff, Fellow of Clare College, Cambridge). One child (see below).
Frederick, m. HILDA SAVI. Two children.
Cecil, m. MURIEL EVANS. Four children.
Leslie d. in infancy.
Winifred (unmarried). Helped sister, Emmeline, at Bermondsey Settlement.
Aubrey MD, m. CHERRY DERMOTT. Went to Canada. Two children (see below).

The two children of **Revd John SCOTT LIDGETT** and **Emmeline Davies** were:
John ('Jack') Cuthbert b. 18 August 1885 d. 24 March 1918, killed in action.
Lettice Mary b. October 1887 d. 11 June 1980, m. GERALD DAVY MD of Hull, later of Guy's Hospital and Harley St. They had no children.

The three children of **John Vipond DAVIES** and **Ruth Ramsay** were:
Margaret, m. OLDEN (?) DAVIS.
Muriel, m. MALCOLM MACKENZIE.
Jack, m. BETTY (?).

The one child of **Eirene Davies** and **Prof. Reynolds WARDALE** was:
Norah.

The two children of **Dr Aubrey DAVIES** and **Cherry Dermott** were:
Dermott.
Doreen.

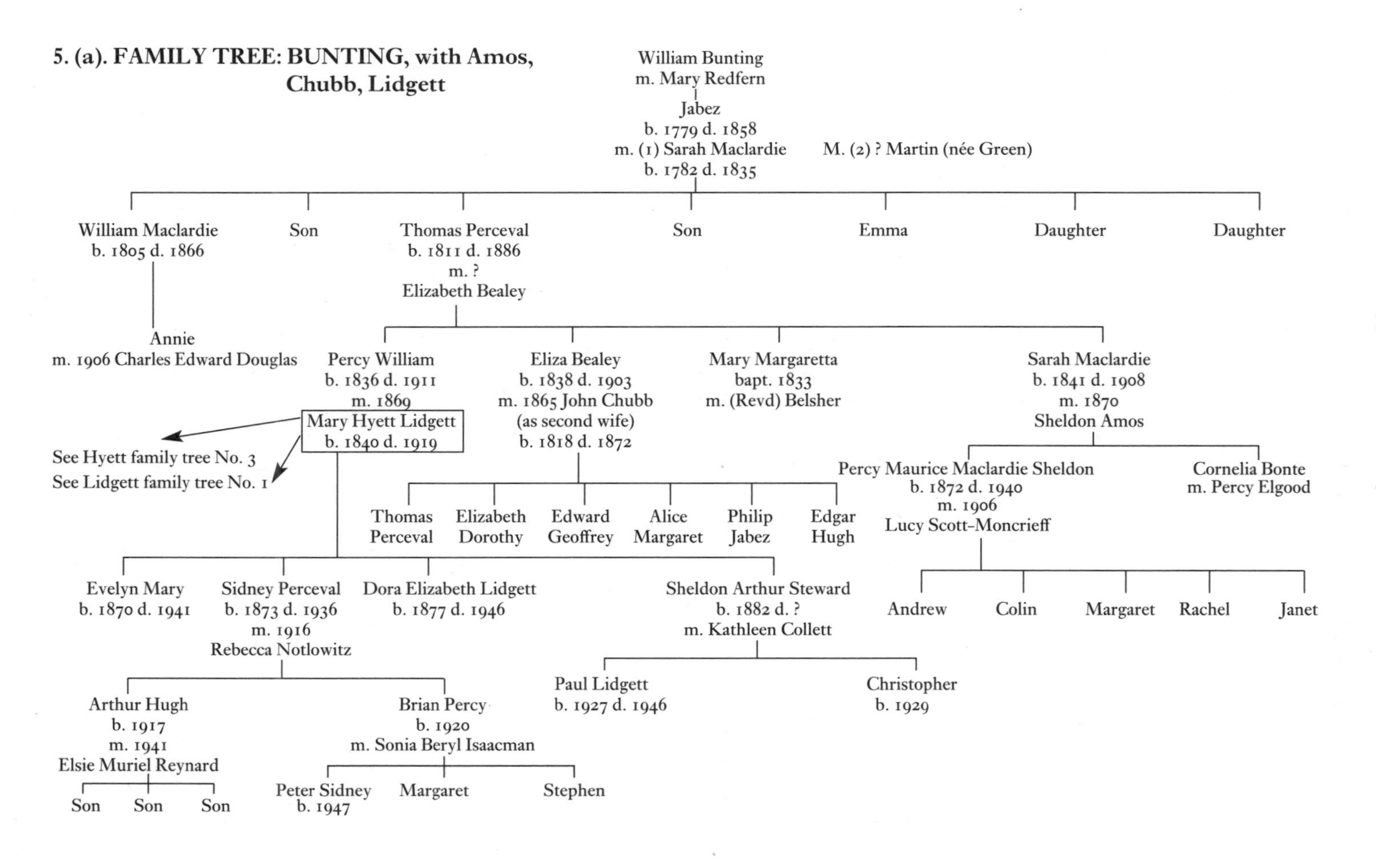
5. (a). FAMILY TREE: BUNTING, with Amos, Chubb, Lidgett
William Bunting
m. Mary Redfern
Jabez
b. 1779 d. 1858
m. (1) Sarah Maclardie
b. 1782 d. 1835
M. (2) ? Martin (née Green)
William Maclardie
b. 1805 d. 1866
Son
Thomas Perceval
b. 1811 d. 1886
m. ?
Elizabeth Bealey
Son
Emma
Daughter
Daughter
Annie
m. 1906 Charles Edward Douglas
Percy William
b. 1836 d. 1911
m. 1869
Mary Hyett Lidgett
b. 1840 d. 1919
See Hyett family tree No. 3
See Lidgett family tree No. 1
Eliza Bealey
b. 1838 d. 1903
m. 1865 John Chubb
(as second wife)
b. 1818 d. 1872
Mary Margaretta
bapt. 1833
m. (Revd) Belsher
Sarah Maclardie
b. 1841 d. 1908
m. 1870
Sheldon Amos
Thomas Perceval
Elizabeth Dorothy
Edward Geoffrey
Alice Margaret
Philip Jabez
Edgar Hugh
Percy Maurice Maclardie Sheldon
b. 1872 d. 1940
m. 1906
Lucy Scott-Moncrieff
Cornelia Bonte
m. Percy Elgood
Evelyn Mary
b. 1870 d. 1941
Sidney Perceval
b. 1873 d. 1936
m. 1916
Rebecca Notlowitz
Dora Elizabeth Lidgett
b. 1877 d. 1946
Sheldon Arthur Steward
b. 1882 d. ?
m. Kathleen Collett
Andrew
Colin
Margaret
Rachel
Janet
Arthur Hugh
b. 1917
m. 1941
Elsie Muriel Reynard
Brian Percy
b. 1920
m. Sonia Beryl Isaacman
Paul Lidgett
b. 1927 d. 1946
Christopher
b. 1929
Son
Son
Son
Peter Sidney
b. 1947
Margaret
Stephen

5. (b). FAMILY TREE: BUNTING, with Amos, Chubb, Lidgett

WILLIAM BUNTING (tailor from Monyash, Derbyshire, and Manchester), m. MARY REDFERN. Their son was:

Jabez, later **REVD JABEZ BUNTING** b. 13 May 1779 d. 16 June 1858, m. (1) SARAH MACLARDIE (of Macclesfield) b. 26 February 1782 d. 29 September 1835, m. (2) Mrs ? MARTIN, née GREEN.

The seven children of **Sarah** and **Jabez** **BUNTING** were:

William Maclardie b. 23 November 1805 in Manchester, m. ?, d. 13 November 1866.

Son ? Jabez

Thomas Perceval b. 20 January 1811 d. 1886, m. ? ELIZABETH BEALEY. Four children, see below.

Son ?

Emma.

Daughter ?

Daughter ?

The daughter of **William Maclardie** **BUNTING** and ? was:

Annie b. ?, m. 12 June 1906 CHARLES EDWARD DOUGLAS of Kirkcaldy.

The four children of **Elizabeth** and **Thomas Perceval** **BUNTING** were:

Percy William b. 1 February 1836 d. 22 July 1911 (Owens College, Manchester; Pembroke College, Cambridge, 1859; called to the Bar 1862; BA at Victoria University; knighted 1908; m. 21 June 1869 MARY HYETT LIDGETT b. 17 December 1840 d. 5 October 1919 (became Presbyterian; interest in care for prostitutes). Four children, see below, and **HYETT** family tree No. **3**.

Eliza Bealey b. 1838 d. 1903, m. 6 September 1865 JOHN CHUBB b. 1818 d. 1872, CHUBB's second marriage. Six children, see below.

Mary Margaretta bap. 1833, m. REVD DR BELSHER, d. ?

Sarah Maclardie b. 1841 d. 1908, m. 1870 PROF. SHELDON AMOS (BA Clare College, Cambridge 1859; Prof. Jurisprudence University College, London 1869–79; Judge in Egypt *c.*1882, advocate of Higher Education and political emancipation of women). SARAH had contacts with Mrs Josephine Butler, concern for Armenians in Cyprus; visited Grindelwald Conference in 1892. Two children, see below.

The four children of **Lady Mary** and **Sir Percy** **BUNTING** were:

Evelyn Mary b. 1870 d. 1941, worked on *Contemporary Review*, acted as Secretary of Lidgetton Company , at least in 1920–22 (unmarried).

Sidney Perceval b. 1873 d. 1936 (Demy of Magdalen College, Oxford; Chancellor's Latin Prize; visited Grindelwald 1892; played part in birth of Communist Party in South Africa, m. REBECCA NOTLOWITZ. Two sons, see below.

Dora Elizabeth Lidgett b. 1877 d. 1946. MD Southampton (unmarried).

Appendix 2: Family trees

Sheldon Arthur Steward b. 1882 d. ?, m. KATHLEEN COLLETT. Went to India. Two sons, see below.

The six children of **Eliza Bealey Bunting** and **John CHUBB** were:
Thomas Perceval.
Elizabeth Dorothy.
Edward Geoffrey.
Alice Margaret.
Philip Jabez.
Edgar Hugh.

The two children of **Sarah Maclardie Bunting** and **Prof. Sheldon AMOS** were:
Percy Maurice Maclardie Sheldon b. 1872 d. 1940 (Trinity College, Cambridge; KBE 1922; KC 1932; Professor of Comparative Law, London University 1932–7; m. 16 July 1906 LUCY SCOTT MONCRIEFF (daughter of Sir Colin Scott Moncrieff). Five children, see below.
Cornelia Bonte Sheldon b. ? d. ?, m. PERCY ELGOOD.

The two sons of **Sidney Perceval BUNTING** and **Rebecca Notlowitz** were:
Arthur Hugh, awarded CMG, b. 7 September 1917 d. 8 May 2002, Prof. Agricultural Botany, Reading University, m. ELSIE MURIEL REYNARD. Three sons, names unknown.
Brian Percy b. 9 April 1920 in Johannesburg, m. SONIA BERYL ISAACMAN. Three children: **Peter Sidney** b. 1947, **Margaret** and **Stephen**.

The two sons of **Sheldon Arthur Steward BUNTING** and KATHLEEN COLLETT were:
Paul Lidgett b. 1927 d. 1946.
Christopher b. 1929.

The five children of **Percy Maurice Maclardie Sheldon AMOS** and **Lucy Scott Moncrieff** were:
Andrew.
Colin.
Margaret.
Rachel.
Janet.

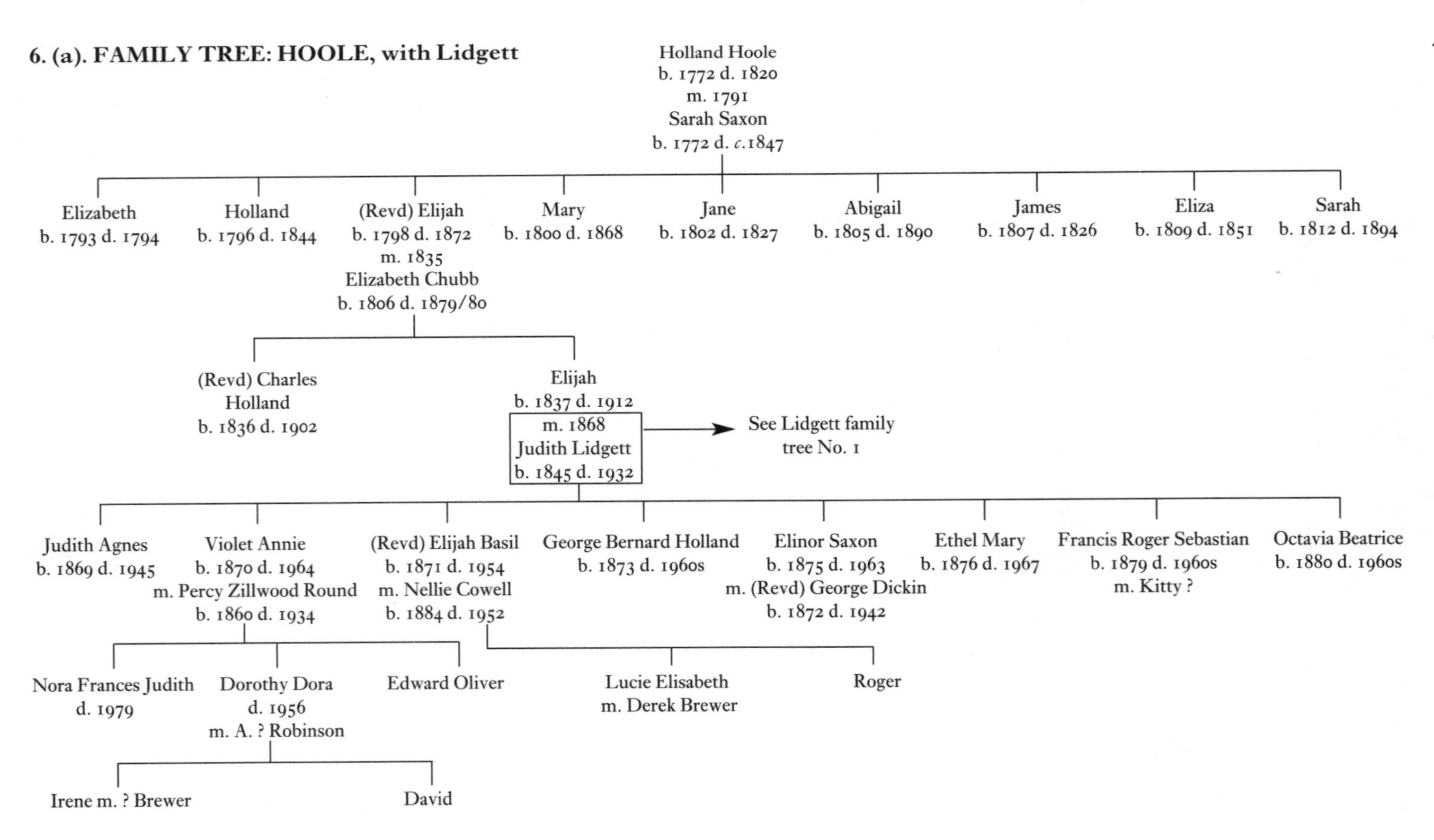
6. (a). FAMILY TREE: HOOLE, with Lidgett
Holland Hoole
b. 1772 d. 1820
m. 1791
Sarah Saxon
b. 1772 d. c.1847
Elizabeth
b. 1793 d. 1794
Holland
b. 1796 d. 1844
(Revd) Elijah
b. 1798 d. 1872
m. 1835
Elizabeth Chubb
b. 1806 d. 1879/80
Mary
b. 1800 d. 1868
Jane
b. 1802 d. 1827
Abigail
b. 1805 d. 1890
James
b. 1807 d. 1826
Eliza
b. 1809 d. 1851
Sarah
b. 1812 d. 1894
(Revd) Charles
Holland
b. 1836 d. 1902
Elijah
b. 1837 d. 1912
m. 1868
Judith Lidgett
b. 1845 d. 1932
See Lidgett family
tree No. 1
Judith Agnes
b. 1869 d. 1945
Violet Annie
b. 1870 d. 1964
m. Percy Zillwood Round
b. 1860 d. 1934
(Revd) Elijah Basil
b. 1871 d. 1954
m. Nellie Cowell
b. 1884 d. 1952
George Bernard Holland
b. 1873 d. 1960s
Elinor Saxon
b. 1875 d. 1963
m. (Revd) George Dickin
b. 1872 d. 1942
Ethel Mary
b. 1876 d. 1967
Francis Roger Sebastian
b. 1879 d. 1960s
m. Kitty ?
Octavia Beatrice
b. 1880 d. 1960s
Nora Frances Judith
d. 1979
Dorothy Dora
d. 1956
m. A. ? Robinson
Edward Oliver
Lucie Elisabeth
m. Derek Brewer
Roger
Irene m. ? Brewer
David

6. (b). FAMILY TREE: HOOLE with Lidgett

HOLLAND HOOLE b. 17 April 1772 d. 11 December 1820, m. 13 February 1791 SARAH SAXON b. 11 July 1772 d. 5 February 1847. Their nine children were:
Elizabeth b. 8 May 1793 d. 19 August 1794.
Holland b. 9 March 1796 d. 3 December 1844.
Elijah Revd Dr b. 3 February 1798 d. 1872, Wesleyan Missionary in India 1820; translator into Tamil; returned in 1834 through ill health; Wesleyan Missionary Society Asst. Sec. 1834; General Sec. 1836–72, m. 30 September 1835 ELIZABETH CHUBB of Portsea b. 2 January 1806 d. 1879/80, third daughter of Charles Chubb, lockmaker. Two children, see below.
Mary b. 22 January 1800 d. 16 March 1868.
Jane b. 18 June 1802 d. 1 February 1827.
Abigail b. 28 September 1805 d. 11 March 1890.
James b. 16 October 1807 d. 14 May 1826.
Eliza b. 7 December 1809 d. 13 March 1851.
Sarah b. 7 August 1812 d. 28 September 1894.

The two children of **Elizabeth** and **Revd Dr Elijah** **HOOLE** were:
Charles Holland b. 9 July 1836 d. 1902. Revd (Anglican; read Greek at age 3; read Classics at Christ Church, Oxford; alcoholic Oxford don; lived with his brother and sister-in-law). Unmarried.
Elijah b. 21 July 1837 d. 1912 (architect, worked on Chubb's Safe factory; also in Naples, e.g. leaning towers; for Octavia Hill, Emma Cons and others in London; constant money worries; became Anglican 'as Wesleyans were too lax'), m. 2 April 1868 at Blackheath JUDITH ('JAN') LIDGETT b. 1845 d. 1932. See **Lidgett** family tree No. 1.

The eight children of **Judith** and **Elijah** (architect) **HOOLE** were:
Judith Agnes b. 1869 d. 23 April 1945. Unmarried.
Violet ('Lettie') Annie b. 15 May 1870 d. 10 November 1964, m. PERCY ZILLWOOD ROUND b. 10 October 1960 d. 10 January 1934. Three children, see below.
Elijah Basil, Revd b. 24 November 1871 d. 2 December 1954 (began as architect; Anglican, curate at St Peter's Church, Highgate, where he met the Cowells), m. NELLIE MARGARET COWELL b. 28 April 1884 d. 6 October 1952. Two children, see below.
George Bernard Holland b. 2 August 1873 d. in 1960s (wounded in WW1; family took to Pumphouse, Gt Bardfield, nr Braintree; farmed). Unmarried.
Elinor (? Eleanor 'Nora') Saxon b. 15 February 1875 d. October 1963, m. GEORGE THOMAS DICKIN b. 1872 d. 27 December 1942 (Congregational Minister; concerned himself with Lidgetton finances).
Ethel Mary b. 13 September 1876 d. 28 March 1967. Unmarried.
Francis Roger ('Frank') Sebastian b. 6 January 1879 d. between 1960 and 1965,

m. KITTY ? (helped with Boys' Brigade Company at Bermondsey Settlement; went to Vanvouver).
Octavia (?Octave, sometimes called **'Ave') Beatrice (?Beatrix)** b. 20 August 1880 d. 1965 –7. (Lived at Pumphouse, Braintree). Unmarried.

The three children of **Violet Annie** and **Percy Zillwood ROUND** were:
Nora Frances Judith b. ? d. 1979.
Dorothy Dora b. ? d. 1956, m. ? A. ROBINSON. Two children, see below.
Edward Oliver.

The two children of **Revd (Elijah) Basil HOOLE** and **Nellie Margaret** were:
Lucie Elisabeth, m. DEREK BREWER (Master of Emmanuel College, Cambridge).
Roger.

The two children of **Dorothy Dora** and **A. ROBINSON** were:
Irene, m. ? BREWER.
David.

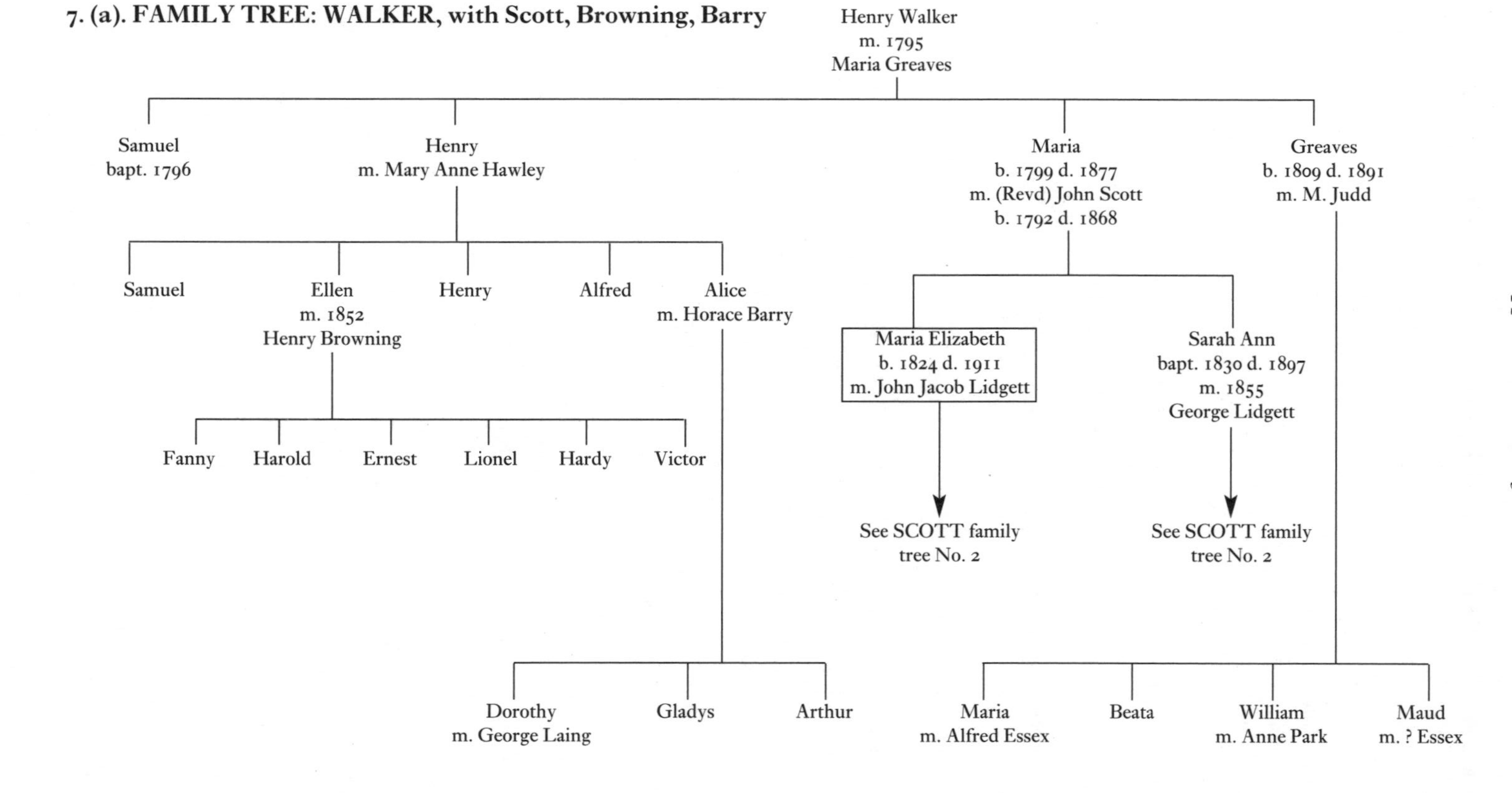
7. (a). FAMILY TREE: WALKER, with Scott, Browning, Barry
Henry Walker
m. 1795
Maria Greaves
Samuel
bapt. 1796
Henry
m. Mary Anne Hawley
Maria
b. 1799 d. 1877
m. (Revd) John Scott
b. 1792 d. 1868
Greaves
b. 1809 d. 1891
m. M. Judd
Samuel
Ellen
m. 1852
Henry Browning
Henry
Alfred
Alice
m. Horace Barry
Maria Elizabeth
b. 1824 d. 1911
m. John Jacob Lidgett
Sarah Ann
bapt. 1830 d. 1897
m. 1855
George Lidgett
Fanny
Harold
Ernest
Lionel
Hardy
Victor
See SCOTT family
tree No. 2
See SCOTT family
tree No. 2
Dorothy
m. George Laing
Gladys
Arthur
Maria
m. Alfred Essex
Beata
William
m. Anne Park
Maud
m. ? Essex

7. (b). FAMILY TREE: WALKER, with Scott, Browning, Barry

HENRY WALKER, a Sheffield plater, m. 1795 **Maria Greaves**, daughter of Samuel Greaves of Sheffield.

Their four children were:
Samuel bapt. 16 May 1796. d ? Unmarried.
Henry, m. MARY ANNE HAWLEY. Five children, see below.
Maria b. 1799 d. 1877, m. Revd JOHN SCOTT b. 1792 d. 1868. Two children, see below.
Greaves b. *c.*1809 d. 1891. Solicitor, m. M. JUDD. Four children, see below.

The five children of **Mary Anne** and **Henry WALKER** were:
Samuel.
Ellen, m. HENRY BROWNING. Six children, see below.
Henry.
Alfred.
Alice, m. HORACE BARRY. Three children, see below.

The two children of **Maria** and **Revd John SCOTT** were:
Maria Elizabeth b. 3 July 1824 d. 1911, m. JOHN JACOB LIDGETT b. 1828 d. 1869. See **SCOTT** family tree No. 2.
Sarah Ann ('Jeanie') bapt. 14 February 1830 d. 19 April 1897, m. 7 September 1855 GEORGE LIDGETT b. 1831 d. 1907. See **SCOTT** family tree No. 2.

The four children of **Greaves WALKER** and **M? Judd** were:
Maria, m. ALFRED ESSEX.
Beata.
William, m. ANNE PARK.
Maud, m. ? ESSEX.

The six children of **Ellen** and **Henry BROWNING** were:
Fanny d. aged 18.
Harold.
Ernest.
Lionel.
Hardy.
Victor.

The three children of **Alice** and **Horace BARRY** were:
Dorothy, m. 1907 GEORGE D. LAING MD, ChB.
Gladys.
Arthur.

8. (a). FAMILY TREE: CHUBB, with Hoole, Bunting, Lidgett

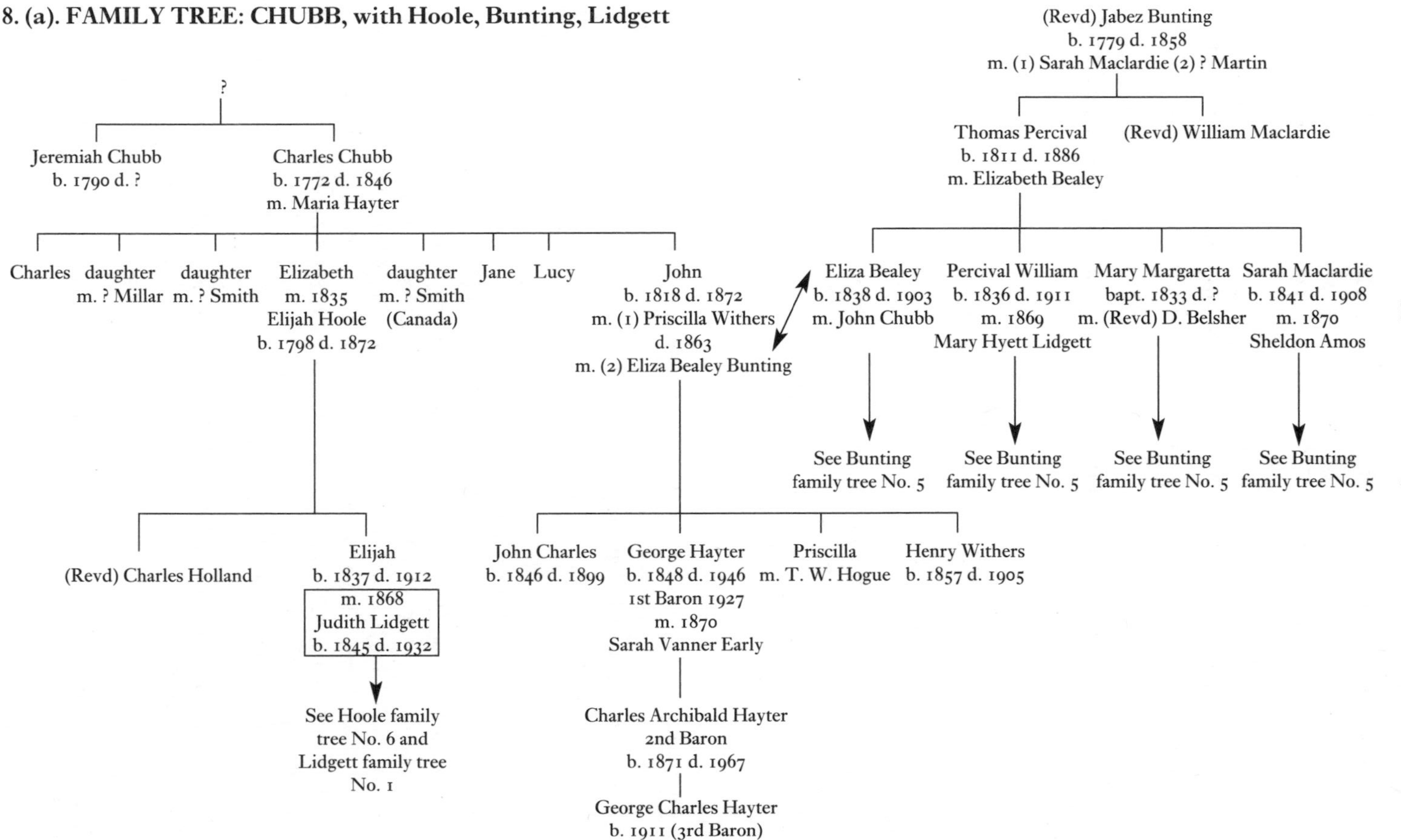

8. (b). FAMILY TREE: CHUBB, with Hoole, Bunting and Lidgett

NOTE: The **CHUBB** and **BUNTING** families come together with the marriage of ELIZA BEALEY BUNTING with JOHN CHUBB; the **CHUBB** and **LIDGETT** families through the marriage of ELIJAH HOOLE (grandson of CHARLES CHUBB) with JUDITH LIDGETT; and the **BUNTING** and **LIDGETT** families through the marriage of PERCIVAL WILLIAM BUNTING with MARY HYETT LIDGETT.

CHARLES CHUBB b. 1772 d. 1846 (the first patentee, with his brother, Jeremiah, of the Detector Lock), m. MARIA HAYTER.
JEREMIAH CHUBB b. 1790 d. ?

The eight children of **Maria** and **Charles** <u>**CHUBB**</u> were:
Charles.
daughter, m. ? MILLER.
daughter, m. ? SMITH.
Elizabeth, m. 30 September 1835 Revd Dr Elijah <u>HOOLE</u> b. 1798 d. 1872. Their second son, ELIJAH HOOLE (architect), m. JUDITH LIDGETT. See **Lidgett** family tree No. 1 and **Hoole** family tree No. 6.
daughter, also m. ? SMITH. Went to Canada.
Jane.
Lucy.
John b. 1818 d. 1872 (Lock and Safe family business, with factories in London and Wolverhampton). First m. PRISCILLA WITHERS d. 1863. Four children, see below. Second m. ELIZA BEALEY BUNTING b. 1838 d. 1903. Six children, see below, and **Bunting** family tree No. 5.

The four children of **Priscilla** and **John** <u>**CHUBB**</u> were:
John Charles b. 1846 d. 1899. Unmarried.
George Hayter b. 1848 d. 1946 (Kt. 1885 ; First Baron Hayter of Chislehurst 1927; Chislehurst Wesleyan Church Society Steward; Nonconformist Unionist Association; opponent of 'irresponsible' NCEFC; Director of Star Life Assurance Society and Chubb and Son Lock and Safe Co.), m. 1870 SARAH VANNER EARLY of Witney. Their son was Charles Archibald b. 1871 d. 1967, 2nd Baron Hayter, and grandson George Charles Hayter b. 1911, 3rd Baron Hayter.
Priscilla, m. T. W. HOGUE.
Henry ('Harry') Withers b. 1857 d. 1905.

The six children of **Eliza** and **John** <u>**CHUBB**</u>, his second marriage, were:
Thomas Percival.
Elizabeth Dorothy.
Howard Geoffrey.
Alice Margaret.
Philip Jabez.
Edgar Hugh.

Appendix 3

Party representation in the LCC

Extract from *The History of the London County Council*, Gwilym Gibbon and Reginald Bell, Macmillan 1939.

	Councillors (Elected)					Councillors and Aldermen				
	Progressives	Municipal Reform or Moderates	Labour	Independents	Total	Progressives	Municipal Reform or Moderates	Labour	Independents	Total
1889	73	45	..	..	118	91	46	..	..	137
1892	84	34	..	..	118	101	36	..	..	137
1895	58	59	..	1	118	71	65	..	1	137
1898	84	34	..	..	118	97	40	..	..	137
1901	87	31	..	..	118	101	36	..	..	137
1904	83	35	..	..	118	98	39	..	..	137
1907	38	79	..	1	118	47	89	..	1	137
1910	55	60	3	..	118	57	75	3	2	137
1913	50	67	1	..	118	53	81	1	2	137
1919	40	68	15	1	124	46	80	17	1	144
1922	25	82	17	..	124	30	94	20	..	144
1925	6	83	35	..	124	9	96	39	..	144
1928	5	77	42	..	124	6	89	48	1	144
1931	6	83	35	..	124	6	96	41	1	144
1934	..	55	69	..	124	..	64	80	..	144
1937	..	49	75	..	124	..	57	87	..	144

In the early years in particular the allocation of members to the parties or as independents is open to some question, but the table gives a generally accurate picture.

The number of elected councillors for the London County Council is fixed by the Local Government Act, 1888, as twice the number of members of Parliament returned by the electoral divisions of the county ; at present there are two members of the council for each of sixty electoral divisions and four members for the City of London, totalling 124. The number of aldermen must not exceed one sixth of the number of elected councillors, the number at present being 20.

Appendix 4

John Scott Lidgett's wills

G.H. Davy
Lettice M. Davy } Executors

A Commissioner for Oaths

101

THIS IS THE LAST WILL AND TESTAMENT of me The Reverend JOHN SCOTT LIDGETT, C.H., M.A., D.D., Warden of the Bermondsey Settlement Farncombe Street Jamaica Road Bermondsey in the County of Surrey Methodist Minister.

1. I APPOINT my son-in-law GERALD HENRY DAVY and my daughter LETTICE MARY DAVY (his Wife) to be EXECUTORS of this my Will.

2. Whereas by an Indenture dated the Twenty eighth day of July One thousand eight hundred and eighty four and made between Maria Elizabeth Lidgett of the first part myself of the second part my late Wife Emmeline Martha Lidgett then Emmeline Martha Davies of the third part and Alfred Edward Lidgett and John Vipond Davies of the fourth part being a Settlement in anticipation of my marriage whereby in the events that have happened I have a power of appointment by Will to the issue of the marriage Now I hereby appoint all the funds and property subject to the trusts of the said Settlement to my daughter Lettice Mary Davy absolutely And whereas by an Indenture dated the twenty eighth day of July One thousand eight hundred and eighty four and made between me of the one part my said wife Emmeline Martha Lidgett then Emmeline Martha Davies of the second part and the said John Vipond Davies and Alfred Edward Lidgett of the third part being a Settlement made on my marriage whereby in the events which have happened I have a power of appointment by Will to the issue of the marriage Now I hereby appoint all funds and property subject to the trusts of the said Settlement to my daughter Lettice Mary Davy absolutely.

3. I bequeath the following pecuniary legacies free of legacy duty :-

(a) One hundred pounds to my Secretary Victoria Alice Child of 11 Cavendish Road Sutton in the County of Surrey

(b) Seven hundred and fifty pounds to the aforesaid Bermondsey

1

101

Settlement (if it shall still be carried on under private management at the date of my decease) as a memorial to my wife's devoted services to the said Settlement I direct that my Executors shall have power to decide whether it is so carried on and I further direct that the receipt of the Treasurer or other proper officer of the said Settlement shall be a full and sufficient discharge to my Executors

(c) One hundred pounds to Sister Helen Styles Wesleyan Deaconess at present serving at Brixton Hill Methodist Church

(d) Fifty pounds to Margaret Murrell of the aforesaid Bermondsey Settlement if she shall still be in the employ of the aforesaid Bermondsey Settlement at my decease.

I DEVISE and BEQUEATH the residue of my real and personal estate whatsoever and wheresoever to my said daughter Lettice Mary Davy absolutely.

Lastly I revoke all testamentary instruments heretofore made by me.

IN WITNESS whereof I have hereunto set my hand this Ninth day of February One thousand nine hundred and forty

SIGNED by the said JOHN SCOTT LIDGETT the testator as and for his last Will and Testament in the presence of us who being present at the same time and at his request in his presence and in the presence of each other have hereunto set our names as witnesses

J. Scott Lidgett.

44, QUEEN VICTORIA STREET, LONDON E.C. 4.
SOLICITOR

Clerk to Mr Munro

C.A. Davy
Lettice M. Davy } Executors
[illegible]
A Commissioner for Oaths

101

I The Reverend John Scott Lidgett C.H., M.A., D.D. Warden of the Bermondsey Settlement Farncombe St. Jamaica Road Bermondsey in the County of Surrey Methodist Minister declare this to be a first codicil to my Will which Will bears date the ninth day of February One thousand nine hundred and forty

WHEREAS by Paragraph C of Clause 3 of my said Will I bequeathed to Sister Helen Styles Wesley Deaconess then (and now) serving at Brixton Hill Methodist Church the sum of One Hundred Pounds free of duty now I hereby increase the said legacy to the said Helen Styles to the sum of Two hundred and fifty pounds free of duty

In all other respects I confirm my said Will

In witness whereof I have hereunto set my hand this twenty-fourth day of September One thousand nine hundred and forty two

Signed by the said JOHN SCOTT LIDGETT as a Codicil to his Will which bears date the ninth day of February One thousand nine hundred and forty in the presence of us both being present at the same time who at his request in his presence and in the presence of each other have hereunto subscribed our names as witnesses

J. Scott Lidgett

Ernest H Pooley
Drapers Hall
London E.C.2
Barrister-at-Law

F. R. D'O. Monro
116 Fitzjohns Avenue
London, N.W.3
Solicitor

3

Letticeth-Davy } Executors

A Commissioner for Oaths

101

I The Reverend JOHN SCOTT LIDGETT C.H., M.A., D.D., LL.D., Warden of the Bermondsey Settlement Farncombe Street Jamaica Road Bermondsey in the County of Surrey Methodist Minister DECLARE this to be a Second Codicil which I make this Thirteenth day of May One thousand nine hundred and forty-eight to my Will which bears date the Ninth day of February One thousand nine hundred and forty and the former Codicil to which bears date the Twenty-fourth day of September One thousand nine hundred and forty-two.

WHEREAS by sub-clause (B) of Clause 3 of my said Will I bequeathed to the aforesaid Bermondsey Settlement (if it were still carried on under private management at the date of my decease) the sum of Seven hundred and Fifty pounds and WHEREAS this sum has been received by the said Settlement from me during my lifetime

1. I HEREBY REVOKE sub-clause (B) of Clause 3 of my said Will.

2. IN ALL OTHER RESPECTS I confirm my said Will as altered by the said former Codicil thereto.

IN WITNESS whereof I have hereunto set my hand the day and year first above written.

SIGNED by the said JOHN SCOTT LIDGETT as and for a Second Codicil to his Will which bears date the Ninth day of February One thousand nine hundred and forty in the presence of us both being present at the same time who at his request in his presence and in the presence of each other have hereunto subscribed our names as witnesses.)

John Scott Lidgett

Ethel Mary Still.
Bermondsey Settlement. S.E.16.
Secretary of the Settlement.

Gladys Elizabeth Bawden
Womens House
Bermondsey Settlement. S.E.16.
Voluntary Worker.

Appendix 5

John Scott Lidgett's death certificate

OFFICE COPY

VALID ONLY IF BEARING IMPRESSED COURT SEAL

In the High Court of Justice.

The Principal Probate Registry

BE IT KNOWN that JOHN SCOTT LIDGETT of Print Stile Bidborough Tunbridge Wells Kent formerly of The Bermondsey Settlement Farncombe Street Jamaica Road Bermondsey London

died on the 16th day of June 1953 at Ewhurst? Nursing Home Ashley Road Epsom Surrey

AND BE IT FURTHER KNOWN that at the date hereunder written the last Will and Testament with two codicils thereto

(a copy whereof is hereunto annexed) of the said deceased was proved and registered in the Principal Probate Registry of the High Court of Justice and that Administration of all the estate which by law devolves to and vests in the personal representative of the said deceased was granted by the aforesaid Court to GERALD HENRY DAVY physician and his wife LETTICE MARY DAVY daughter of deceased both of Print Stile aforesaid the executors named in the said will

And it is hereby certified that an Affidavit for Inland Revenue has been delivered wherein it is shewn that the gross value of the said estate in Great Britain

(exclusive of what the said deceased may have been possessed of or entitled to as a Trustee and not beneficially) amounts to £2609 – 13 – 10

and that the net value of the estate amounts to £2531 – 15 – 6

And it is further certified that it appears by a Receipt signed by an Inland Revenue Officer on the said Affidavit that £70 – 9 – 8 on account of Estate Duty and interest on such duty has been paid.

Dated the 19th day of November 1953

[illegible] Forbes.
Registrar.

Probate

Extracted by [illegible]
4 Drapers Gardens
Throgmorton Avenue London E.C.2

Bibliography

Unless stated otherwise, publication took place in London.

Primary sources

A. Unpublished primary sources

1. Personal letters to Alan Turberfield

Bishop J. Adams: on 4 June 1993.
Mrs Elisabeth Brewer: variously 1993–6.
Mrs Irene Brewer: variously 1993–6.
Professor A. H. Bunting: on 5 April 1993.
F. W. Burkhardt: on 28 November 1994.
Mrs Elizabeth Camp: n.d., during 1993 and variously to 2003.
Revd M. S. Edwards: on 31 July 1992.
Mrs Elizabeth ('Libby') Fairweather: variously 1993–6.
Harold Finch: on 24 October 1992.
Revd Stanley B. Frost: on 27 August 1992.
Revd Raymond George: on 18 August 1992.
Revd R. R. Kissack: on 27 July 1992.
Mrs Elisabeth McDougall: variously 1992–6.

2. Private Collections, shown to Alan Turberfield by kind permission of the owners

Mrs E. Brewer: letters in Hoole Papers to/from various, including letter from J. S. Lidgett to Judith Hoole on 21 December 1920; diary of Judith Hoole (née Lidgett).
Mrs E. Fairweather: letter from W. Davies RFC (ANZACS) to Mr and Mrs T. W. Davies on 23 January 1917; Davies family trees.
G. Hobbs: letter from Marshall Randles to W. L. Watkinson on 25 May 1902.
Mrs E. McDougall: family trees; newspaper cuttings.

3. Monographs

Privately printed biographical accounts (n.d.) of the lives of Mrs Josephine Butler and Lady Mary Bunting, kindly loaned by Mrs E. Brewer in 1993–4.
'A Bit about the Natal Lidgetts', a MS account by Mrs E. Camp in an (undated, but during 1993) letter to Alan Turberfield.

A sketch of Mrs Joseph Shepherd, by Elizabeth S. Lidgett (n.d.), kindly copied to Alan Turberfield by Mrs S. A. Brooke on 18 April 1999.

4. London: British Library

Letter: from Lidgett to Sir George Hill on 17 January 1934 (Add. 68923.f205).

5. London: British Library of Political and Economic Science (LPES)

Charles Booth, *Notebooks/Papers* (District 33): A46, Work of the Churches 33(12), p. 4 about Wesleyan Bermondsey Settlement, visited 5 May (no year stated) when Lidgett absent; and A47, Misc. Notes (33), CXVII.11, pp. 5ff., with B283, Misc. 33, pp. 11–21, notes of interview with Revd J. Scott Lidgett on 7 February 1900, the former a summary, the latter in more detail and enclosing cuttings (n.d., but early February 1898) from the *British Weekly*.

6. London: Greenwich Local History Library and Lewisham Local Studies and Archives

Local Records about addresses of the Lidgett family *c.*1850–*c.*1900.

7. London: Lambeth Palace Library

Bell Papers: correspondence between Bp Bell and Rupert Davies in April 1956, about Symposium on J. S. Lidgett, and letter from J. S. Lidgett to Bp Bell on 21 January 1931, about reminiscences of Davidson.

Davidson Papers: correspondence between Abp Davidson, J. S .Lidgett and others, 1906–28 *passim*.

Lang Papers: correspondence between Bp (later Abp) Lang and others, 1920–40 *passim*.

W. Temple Papers: correspondence between Bp (later Abp) W. Temple and others, 1930–44 *passim*.

Tissington Tatlow Papers: correspondence between J. S. Lidgett and Tissington Tatlow, 11 and 17 December 1918.

8. London Metropolitan Archive

Final Report of the School Board for London 1870–1904.
LCC Education Committee Minutes.

9. London: University of London Archive

Archives 1929–33: Scrapbook (Archive FG 5/1), Photographs (Archives F/G 5/3, 5/4, 5/5), Programme (Archive, 22 November 1929), F/G 5/4.

10. Manchester: John Rylands Library

J. S. Lidgett: letter to J. H. Moulton on 4 October 1903, and letter to Thomas Ross on 9/10 July 1907, with comments on back of letter; and various other personal letters of Lidgett himself.

Methodist Union Committees: Minute Books 1918–32.

Wesleyan Methodist Conference Journal 1920–8.

H. S. Lunn: letter to J. S. Lidgett on 22 July 1917.

11. Oxford: New Bodleian Library

Viscount Bryce Papers 1921.

12. Southwark Local Studies Library

See below under Printed Primary Sources.

13. Tape Recordings

Extract, kindly donated to Alan Turberfield by Mrs Lorna Horstmann, from a BBC tape-recorded interview of J. S. Lidgett by Paul Rowntree Clifford on 30 March 1950.

Tape-recorded interview of Mrs Lorna Horstmann by Alan Turberfield on 21 September 1992.

Tape-recorded interview of the Revd the Lord Soper by Alan Turberfield on 24 September 1992.

14. Interviews (not tape recorded)

For persons and dates see under Acknowledgements.

15. Family trees

Family trees of Bunting, Lidgett, Scott, Hyett, Walker, Chubb and Hoole, kindly donated to Alan Turberfield (later annotated by him), by Miss Elisabeth McDougall.

Family tree of Emmeline Martha Davies and the Davies family, kindly donated to Alan Turberfield (later annotated by him) by Mrs Libby Fairweather.

B. Printed Primary Sources

1. Letters

(i) Letters to and from J. S. Lidgett

G. K. A. Bell, *Randall Davidson, Archbishop of Canterbury* (Oxford 1935, 1938 and references to third edition 1952): letters from Archbishop Davidson to J. S. Lidgett on 10 March 1906 and 18 December 1909, and from J. S. Lidgett to Archbishop Davidson on 19 December 1909.

(ii) Letters to and from others in biographies, etc.

These are found included within the secondary sources listed in Section 2.A below, and also e.g. in Standish Meacham, *Toynbee Hall and Social Reform 1880–1914*, Yale, 1987, p. 53, quoting Ernest Aves in Charles Booth Papers, Notebook 8, Library of Political and Social Science (LPSS), p. 227.

(iii) Letters to and from E. B. Pusey

Edward Bouverie Pusey, *A letter to the Archbishop of Canterbury*, Oxford, 1842.
Thomas Jackson, *A Letter to E. B. Pusey, a vindication of the tenets and character of the Wesleyan Methodists against his misrepresentations and censures*, 1842.

2. Autobiographies by J. S. Lidgett

Reminiscences, 1928.
My Guided Life, 1936.

3. Theological works by J. S. Lidgett

The Spiritual Principle of the Atonement, 1897.
The Fatherhood of God in Christian Truth and Life, Edinburgh, 1902.
The Christian Religion, Its Meaning and Proof, 1907.
Apostolic Ministry, Sermons and Addresses, 1910.
God in Christ Jesus, Study of Epistle to Ephesians, 1915.
Sonship and Salvation, a Study of Epistle to the Hebrews, 1921.
God, Christ and the Church, reprinted articles, 1927.
The Catholicity of Methodism, Presidential address at Uniting Conference 1932, 1932.
The Victorian Transformation of Theology, 1934.
The Christian Creeds, Little Books of the Kindly Light No. 2, 1936.
The Idea of God and Social Ideals, 1938.
The Cross, as Seen from Five Standpoints, 1941.
The Crowns of Jesus, 1941.
God and the World, reprinted articles, 1943.
God and Man, 1944.
Jesus Christ Is Alive, 1948.
Salvation, as Proclaimed by Prophets, Apostles and by our Lord Jesus Christ, 1952.

4. Contributions by J. S. Lidgett to other books

'Settlements and the Administration of the Poor Law', in W. Reason (ed.), *University and Social Settlements*, 1898, pp. 63–70.
'Charity in relation to Social Reconstruction', in S. E. Keeble (ed.), *The Citizen of Tomorrow: A Handbook*, 1906, new edn 1915, chapter 4, pp. 71–82.
'The Church and Social Problems', Inaugural Address, in S. E. Keeble (ed.), *Social Science and Social Service, Oxford Conference Essays*, 1909, pp. 9–26.
'Fundamental Unity', in W. J. Townsend, H. B. Workman and G. Eayrs (eds), *A New History of Methodism*, 2 vols, 1909, vol. 2, ch 6, chapter 1, pp. 417–42.

'The Social Teaching of the Writings of St John', in S. E. Keeble (ed.), *The Social Teachings of the Bible*, Wesleyan Methodist Union for Social Service (WMUSS), 1909, chapter 9, pp. 173–87.

'Introduction: The Modern Social Problem', in J. B. Paton, Sir Percy Bunting and A. E. Garvie (eds), *Christ and Civilisation*, 1910, pp. 3–42.

Introductory (WMUSS Presidential) Address, in H. Carter (ed.), *The Social Outlook*, WMUSS, 1910, pp. 3–10.

'The Fatherhood of God: The Biblical Doctrine', in W. T. Davison (ed.), *The Chief Cornerstone*, 1914, reprinted in J. S. Lidgett, *God, Christ and the Church*, 1927, Pt I.i., pp. 138–56.

'Reunion and the Advancement of Christ's Kingdom', in A. J. Carlyle, S. H. Clark, J. S. Lidgett and J. H. Shakespeare (eds), *Towards Reunion*, 1919, pp. 1–26.

'Sir Joseph Compton-Rickett as Public Man', in A. Compton-Rickett (ed.), *Joseph Compton-Rickett, a Memoir*, Bournemouth, 1922, pp. 50–6.

'New Testament Principles', in James Gilliland Simpson (ed.), *The Lambeth Joint Report on Church Unity, a discussion by Cosmo Gordon Lang, Archbishop of York, et al.*, 1923, pp. 86–104.

'Purity and Efficiency', in Bp J. Taylor Smith (ed.), *Towards Solving THE Problem* (pamphlet), 1925, pp. 7–10.

'The Master Key', in Sir James Marchant (ed.), *British Preachers, second series*, n.d., but *c.*1925/6, pp. 273–81.

'The Yea of God', in Sir James Marchant (ed.), *If I had only one sermon to preach*, 1928, pp. 139–49.

'The Person of Our Lord Jesus Christ', in J. S. Lidgett and B. H. Reed (eds), *Methodism in the Modern World*, 1929, pp. 55–76.

'The Wesleyan Methodist Church', in Sir James Marchant (ed.), *The Reunion of Christendom*, 1929, pp. 151–68.

'Christ's Self-Giving Love', in Anon. (ed.), *The Christian World Pulpit*, n.d.

Chapter 5, in R. G. Burnett et al., *Frederick Luke Wiseman, a Commemorative Record*, 1954, pp. 46–55.

5. Journals and newspapers

These sources are largely located in the Bodleian Library, Oxford. Some are to be found, not least when there are gaps in the Bodleian sequence of issues, in the British Library's Newspaper Library in Colindale, or in the Library of the Wesley Studies Centre in Westminster Institute, Oxford.

Where precise issues are not mentioned, the journals and newspapers have contributed to general background reading.

Lidgett's own writing is mainly to be found: (a) in the editorials and most of his 'Notes and Comments' of the week in the weekly newspaper, the *Methodist Times*, which he edited from March 1907 to December 1918; (b) in the reports and magazines of the Bermondsey Settlement, located in the Southwark Local Studies Library; and (c) in articles for the *Methodist Recorder*.

Southwark Local Studies Library: *The Aims and Work of the Bermondsey Settlement*,

1891; Annual Reports, September 1892 and following; *Monthly Record/Magazine of the Bermondsey Settlement and St George's Social Club*, January 1895, and following; *The Bermondsey Settlement in the War and since*, November 1946.
BBC History, May 2001.
British Journal of Nursing, July 1953.
Bristol Mercury Supplement, 27 October 1900.
British Weekly, 2 September 1897; 24 December 1908; 10 April 1913; 30 July, 6 August, 3 September and 1 October 1914; 5 December 1918; 9 January and 3 April 1919; 24 March 1920.
Church History, American Society of Church History, June 1970.
Church Quarterly Review, 1897; 1898; 1968.
Church Times, August–October and December 1897; June 1917; April 1920.
Contemporary Review, 1897; September and November 1902; and *passim*. 1911–43.
Daily Chronicle, continuation of *London Daily Chronicle* and *Clerkenwell News*, 10 January 1914.
Epworth Review, January 2000.
Expository Times, 1891; 1897; and 1898.
Free Church Chronicle, November 1919.
Guardian, an Anglican religious weekly, June 1917.
Hereford Times, 19 June 1953.
History Today, October 1995; May 2001.
Holborn Review, 1930.
Illustrated London News, 6 August 1881, p. 126.
London Quarterly Review, October 1897; January 1899; April 1901; January 1921; 1921–30; April 1956, p. 137.
The Methodist, 1884.
The Methodist Magazine, June 1891; 1892; 1897; 1900; February 1903, pp. 155–6; 1904; 1905; 1909; 1912; 1922; January 1933, p. 5.
Methodist Recorder, 1901–84.
Methodist Times, 1888–1932.
Methodist Times and Leader, March 1933.
Methodist Weekly, 15 November 1900.
The Record, 15 January 1904, p. 97.
Review of the Churches, 1891–1930.
Review of Reviews, 1890.
South London Press, various and 18 June 1953.
The Thinker, 1892.
The Times, 1910–50.
Wesley Bible Union, March 1915; April 1917; August 1920.
Wesleyan Methodist Historical Society Proceedings (various dates).
Wesleyan Methodist Magazine, in 1932.
And a variety of other newspapers across the country which recorded Lidgett's death in 1953.

6. Documents

G. K. A. Bell (ed.), *Documents on Christian Unity I, II, III, IV*, OUP, 1924–48.

7. Pamphlets

Minutes of Evidence Taken before the Royal Commission on Divorce and Matrimonial Causes, Vol. III. cd. 6481, HM Stationery Office, 1912.

J. T. Smith (ed.), *Towards Solving THE Problem*, 1925, pp. 7–10.

8. Minutes and directories

Checklist of British Methodist Periodicals, E. A. Rose, WMHS Publications, 1981.

Congregational Union Year Book, 1902.

Crockford's Clerical Directory, 1914–20.

Free Church Year Book, Unwin Bros. Ltd, Gresham Press, 1902–19.

Dictionary of National Biography, 1870–1960.

Dictionary of Methodism in Britain and Ireland, ed. J. Vickers, 2000.

LCC Education Committee Minutes, 1904–28, London Metropolitan Archive.

London School Board Report, 1903/4, London Metropolitan Archive.

London University Calendar, 1952/3.

London University Senate Minutes, 1928–34.

Methodist Who's Who, 1910–15.

Oecumenical Methodist Conference (Eighth Conference) *Proceedings*.

Oxford University Gazette, 9 December 1932.

Wesleyan Methodist Conference Minutes (Minutes of Several Conversations), 1888–1953.

9. Books

Anonymous. See 'A Nonconformist Minister' below.

Arthur, William, *Tongue of Fire, or The True Power of Christianity*,1856, 1902.

—— *On the Difference between the Physical and Moral Law*, Fernley Lecture, 1883.

—— *Religion without God, and God without Religion*, 3 vols, 1885, 1905.

Ballard, Frank, *Christian Reality in Modern Light*, 1916.

Banks, J. S., *Manual of Christian Doctrine*,1887, 8th edn revised and partly rewritten, 1902.

Beet, Joseph Agar, *The Last Things*, 1897, 3rd edn 1898.

—— *The Immortality of the Soul: A Protest*, 1901.

—— *A Manual of Theology*, 1906.

—— *The Last Things in a Few Words*, 1913.

Blatchford, R., *God and My Neighbour*, 1903.

Booth, Charles, *Life and Labour of the People in London*, with Maps of London Poverty, 1889; vols 1, 2 and 3, 1892; vol. 4, 1893; vols 5 and 6, 1895; vols 7 and 8, 1896; vol. 9, 1897; Third Series: Religious Influences, 1902.

Brown, James Baldwin, *Divine Life in Man*, 1859.

—— *Doctrine of Annihilation*, 1875.

Bushnell, H., *The Vicarious Sacrifice*, 1866.

Campbell, J. McLeod, *The Nature of the Atonement, and Its Relation to the Remission of Sins and Eternal Life*, Cambridge 1856; London 1853, 1866, 1873.
Campbell, R. J., *The New Theology*, 1907 and Popular Edition 1909.
Cook, T., *New Testament Holiness*, 1902.
Dale, Robert William, *Lectures on the Atonement*, 1875, 9th edn 1884, 25th edn 1909.
Dallinger, William Henry, *The Creator, and what we may know of the method of Creation*, Fernley Lecture, 1887.
Davison, W. T., *The Christian Conscience: A Contribution to Christian Ethics*, Fernley Lecture, 1888.
Davison, W. T. (ed.), *The Chief Cornerstone*, 1914.
Denney, James, *Death of Christ*, 1902.
——*Atonement and the Modern Mind*, 1903.
——*Jesus and the Gospel*, 1908.
Erskine, T., *Unconditional Freeness of the Gospel*, Edinburgh, 1828.
Fairbairn, Andrew Martin, *The Place of Christ in Modern Theology*, 1893.
Farrar, Frederic William, *The Eternal Hope: Five Sermons*, 1878, 18th edn 1901.
Findlay, George G., *Epistle to the Ephesians*, 1892.
——*Christian Doctrine and Morals viewed in their connexion*, Fernley Lecture, 1894.
——*The Church of Christ as set forth in the New Testament*, 1892.
Flew, R. N., *Jesus and His Church*, 1938.
Forsyth, Peter Taylor, *The Charter of the Church*, 1896.
——*Positive Preaching and the Modern Mind*, 1907.
——*The Person and the Place of Jesus Christ*, 1909.
——*The Work of Christ*, 1910.
Garbett, Edward, *Evangelical Principles*, 1875.
Geden, Alfred Shenington, *Studies in Comparative Religion*, 1898.
——*Studies in Eastern Religions*, 1900.
Gore, Charles (ed.), *Lux Mundi*, 1889.
——*The Incarnation of the Son of God*, 1891.
Green, T. H., *Prolegomena to Ethics*, Oxford, 1883.
Grotius, H., *Defence of the Catholic Faith*, 1661.
Headlam, A. C., *The Doctrine of the Church and Christian Reunion*, 1920.
Horton, R. F., *Inspiration and the Bible*, 1888.
——*Dissolution of Dissent*, 1902.
——*Autobiography*, 2nd edn 1918.
Hughes, D. P., *The Life of Hugh Price Hughes*, 1904.
Hughes, H. P., *Social Christianity*, 3rd edn 1890.
Illingworth, John Richardson, *Personality Human and Divine*, 1894.
Jackson, George, *The Preacher and the Modern Mind*, Fernley Lecture, 1912.
Jowett, B., *Epistles of St Paul to the Thessalonians, Galatians and Romans*, 2 vols, 1855.
Jowett, J. H., *The Transfigured Church*, Edinburgh, 1910.
Keeble, Samuel Edward, *Industrial Daydreams: Studies in Industrial Ethics and Economics*, 1896.
——*Towards the New Era: A Draft Scheme of Industrial Reconstruction*, 1919; and see 'Contributions by J. S. Lidgett to other books' above.

Liddon, H. P., *The Divinity of our Lord and Saviour, Jesus Christ*, Bampton Lectures, Oxford, 1867, 8 edns to 1890.
Lidgett, Albert (Lidgett's brother), *Petroleum*, 1910, 1919, 1928/9; and contributor to J. H. Van Stone, *The Raw Materials of Commerce*, a descriptive account of the raw material products of the world and of their commercial uses, 1929.
Lidgett, Elizabeth S., *An Ancient People: A Short Sketch of Armenian History*, 1897.
Lofthouse, William Frederick, *Ethics and the Atonement*, 1906.
——*Altar, Cross and Community*, Fernley Lecture, 1921.
Maurice, J. F. D., *Theological Essays*, Cambridge, 1853.
——*Sermons on the Sabbath Day*, 1853.
Mearns, A., and W. C. Preston, *The Bitter Cry of Outcast London*, 1883.
(See below also A. S. Wohl (ed.), text and collected articles, 1883; with Introduction, Leicester and New York, 1970, p. 22.)
Moberly, Robert Campbell, *Atonement and Personality*, 1901.
Moulton, James Hope, *Religions and Religion: A Study of the Science of Religion, Pure and Applied*, Fernley Lecture, 1913.
Moulton, Wilfrid J., *The Life Everlasting*, 1915.
Mozley, J. K., *Doctrine of Atonement*, 1915, 1923 and 1927.
Newman, John Henry, *Sermons, chiefly on the theory of religious belief, preached before the University of Oxford*, 1843.
——*Apologia pro vita sua*, 1864, New York, 1865.
A Nonconformist Minister, *Nonconformity and Politics*, 1909.
Olver, G. W., *Life and Death, the sanctions of the Law of Love*, 8th Fernley Lecture, 1878.
Oman, J., *War and Its Issues*, Cambridge, 1915.
Osborn, George, *The Holy Spirit, His Work and Mission*, 1st Fernley Lecture, 1870.
Peake, Arthur Samuel, *Christianity: Its Nature and Its Truth*, 1908.
——*The Bible: Its Origin, Its Significance and Its Abiding Worth*, 1913.
——*Prisoners of Hope: The Problem of the Conscientious Objector*, 1918.
——*Plain Thoughts on Great Subjects*, n.d.
Platt, F. W., *Immanence and Christian Thought*, 1915.
Pope, William Burt, *The Person of Christ: Dogmatic, Spiritual, Historical*, Fernley Lecture, 1871, 1875.
——*Compendium of Christian Theology*, 2 vols, 1875; revised as 3 vols, 1879.
Randles, Marshall, *For Ever: An Essay on Eternal Punishment*, 1871, 3rd edn enlarged 1878; 4th revised edn 1895.
——*After Death, Is There a Post-Mortem Probation?*, 1904.
Rashdall, Hastings, *The Idea of Atonement in Christian Theology*, 1919.
Rigg, James Harrison, *Modern Anglican Theology*, 1857, 1859, 1880.
Ritschl, A. B., *Christian Doctrine of Justification and Reconciliation*, trans. by H. R. Mackintosh and A. B. Macaulay, Edinburgh, 1900.
Rogers, J. Guinness, *An Autobiography*, 1903.
Schweitzer, Albert, *The Quest for the Historical Jesus, Its Progress from Reimarus to Wrede*, Tübingen, 1906 (English translation by W. Montgomery, 1910).
Shakespeare, J. H., *The Churches at the Cross Roads: A Study in Christian Unity*, 1918.
Stead, W. T., *Maiden Tribute of Modern Babylon*, 1885.

Streeter, B. H. (ed.), *Foundations: A Statement of Christian Belief in Terms of Modern Thought by Seven Oxford Men*, 1912.
Tasker, John Greenwood, *Spiritual Religion: A Study of the Relation of Facts to Faith*, Fernley Lecture, 1901.
Temple, William, *The Faith and Modern Thought*, 1910.
C. H. Vine (ed.), *The Old Faith and the New Theology*, 1907.
Walker, George, *Methodist Ritualism, or a Few Thoughts on the Methodism of Today, by an old-fashioned Methodist*, 1885.
Walker, William Lowe, *The Cross and the Kingdom*, Edinburgh, 1902.
Watson, Richard, *Theological Institutes, or A View of the Evidences, Doctrines, Morals and Institutions of Christianity*, 3 vols, 1829.
—— *The Works of Richard Watson*, 12 vols, 1834.
Waugh, Thomas, *When Jesus Comes*, 3rd edn 1904.
—— *'The Clarion' or the Bible*, 4th edn 1908;
—— *The Christian Church and the Present Outlook*, 1909.
Weston, Frank, *The One Christ*, 1907.
Westcott, Brooke Foss, *Victory of the Cross*, 1888.
White, Edward, *Life in Christ*, 1846, 1875, 3rd edn rev. 1876.
Winnington-Ingram, A. F., *The Potter and the Clay*, 1917.
Wohl, Anthony S. (ed.), *The Bitter Cry of Outcast London*, by Andrew Mearns and W. C. Preston, text with articles from the *Pall Mall Gazette* and by Lord Salisbury, J. Chamberlain and F. Crozier, 1883, and Introduction, Leicester and New York, 1970, p. 22.

2. Secondary sources

A. Unpublished secondary sources

Bartlett, Alan, 'The Churches in Bermondsey 1880–1939', Birmingham University PhD thesis, 1988.
Campbell, Donald P., 'Methodism and Social Problems in the Inter-War Period 1918–39', Oxford University MLitt thesis, 1987.
Chadwick, R. E., 'Church and People in Bradford and District, 1880–1914', Oxford University DPhil thesis, 1986.
Cheetham, Carl Wade, 'Social Christianity: A Study of English Nonconformist Attitudes 1880–1914', Vanderbilt University DPhil thesis, 1982.
Clement, Mark, 'Sifting Science: Methodism and Natural Knowledge in Britain 1815–1870', Oxford University DPhil thesis, 1996.
Cracknell, Kenneth, 'The Pioneering Work of J. H. Moulton', lecture at Conference on the Contribution of Methodists to the Academic Study of Religions, Westminster College, Oxford, 1994.
Crewes, Frederick Ronald, 'An Evaluation of the Contribution to Education of the Revd Dr J. Scott Lidgett, with Special Reference to His Work at the Bermondsey Settlement', London University MA thesis, 1973.

Dunlap, E. Dale, 'Methodist Theology in Great Britain in the Nineteeth Century', Yale University DPhil thesis, 1956.

Edmondson, J. J. W., 'Doctrines of Hell and Judgement, and the Need for Personal Conversion, as an Index to the Development of Liberal Theology within the Theological Colleges of the Methodist Church in England 1907–1932', Durham University MA Theology thesis, 1990.

Edwards, Michael, 'S. E. Keeble and Non-Conformist Social Thinking 1880–1929', Bristol University MLitt thesis, 1969.

Field, Clive Douglas, 'Methodism in Metropolitan London 1850–1920: A Social and Sociological Study', Oxford University DPhil thesis, 1974.

Gwyther, C. E., 'Methodist Social and Political Theory and Practice 1848–1914, with particular reference to the Forward Movement', Liverpool University MA thesis, 1961.

Hopkins, Mark Thomas Eugene, 'Baptists, Congregationalists and Theological Change: some late nineteenth century leaders and controversies', Oxford University DPhil thesis, 1988.

Mews, Stuart P., 'Religion and English Society in the First World War', Cambridge University PhD thesis, 1973.

Richards, Edgar, 'The Nature of the Free Church Ministry, with special reference to the writings of A. M. Fairbairn, J. Oman, P. T. Forsyth, and J. S. Lidgett, and recent Reunion proposals', London University PhD thesis, 1967.

Sheen, M. J., 'The Wesleyan Education Committee and Elementary Education 1870–1902', London University MA thesis,1982.

Smith, J. Thomas, 'The Influence of Wesleyan Methodism on Elementary Education in England in the Period 1849–1902, with particular reference to the work of Dr. J. H. Rigg', Hull University PhD thesis, 1995.

Standing, Roger, 'The Relationship between Evangelicalism and the Social Gospel, with special reference to Wesleyan Methodism 1875–1914', Manchester University MPhil thesis, 1992.

Thomas, D. H., 'J. Scott Lidgett (1854–1953) and the Education of the People', London University PhD thesis, 1960.

Thompson, John H., '*The Free Church Army Chaplain: 1830–1930*', Sheffield University PhD thesis, 1990.

Wellings, Martin, 'Aspects of Late Nineteenth Century Anglican Evangelicalism: the response to Ritualism, Darwinism and Theological Liberalism', Oxford University DPhil thesis, 1989.

Wood, Stella M., 'Nonconformity, Theology and Reunion 1870–1910', Oxford University DPhil thesis,1995.

B. Published secondary sources

Books

Acton, J. E. E. D., *Historical Essays and Studies*, 1907. See J. N. Figgis below.

Addison, B. C., *Politics from Within: 1911–1918*, 2 vols, 1924.

—— *Four and a Half Years*, 1934.

Altholz, Josef Lewis, *The Religious Press in Great Britain 1760–1900*, New York and London, 1989.

Arthur, William, *The Successful Merchant: Sketches of the Life of Mr S. Budgett*, 1852.

Atkinson, J. Baines, et al. (eds), *To the Uttermost, commemorating the Diamond Jubilee of the Southport Holiness Convention 1885–1945*, 1945.

Baker, Derek, *Partnership in Excellence, the Leys School, Cambridge*, Cambridge, 1975.

Balleine, G. R., *A History of the Evangelical Party in the Church of England*, 1933 and 1951.

Battiscombe, Georgina, *Shaftesbury: A Biography of the Seventh Earl, 1801–1895*, 1974.

Beasley, John, *The Bitter Cry Heard and Heeded*, South London Mission, Bermondsey St, London SE1 3UJ, 1989.

Bebbington, D. W., *The Nonconformist Conscience, Chapel and Politics 1870–1914*, 1982.

—— *Evangelicalism in Modern Britain, 1730s–1980s*, 1989.

—— *Victorian Nonconformity*, Headstart History Papers, Bangor, 1992.

Bell, G. K. A., *Randall Davidson, Archbishop of Canterbury*, Oxford, 1st edn 1935, 2nd edn 1938 and references to 3rd edn 1952.

Bell, P. M. H., *Disestablishment in Ireland and Wales*, 1969.

Bellot, H. Hale, *University College, London, 1826–1926*, 1929.

—— *University of London: A History 1890–*, 1969.

Bennett, G. V., and J. D. Walsh (eds), *Essays in Modern English Church History*, 1966.

Bentley, M., *The Liberal Mind 1914–1929*, Cambridge, 1977.

Bernbaum, G., *Social Change and the Schools 1918–1944*, 1967.

Besier, Rudolf, *The Barretts of Wimpole Street*, 1930.

Binfield, John Clyde G., *So down to Prayers, Studies in English Nonconformity 1780–1920*, 1977.

Bolton, A. J., *The Other Side*, a pamphlet of World Wesleyan Methodist Historical Society, 1994.

Bradley, I., *The Optimists*, 1980.

Bradley, W. L., *P. T. Forsyth: The Man and his Work*, 1952.

Brash, W. B., *The Story of our Colleges 1835–1935*, 1935.

Brash, W. B., and C. J. Wright, *Didsbury College Centenary, 1842–1942*, 1942.

Briggs, Asa, and Ann Macartney, *Toynbee Hall: The First 100 Years*, 1984.

Briggs, J., and I. Sellers, *Victorian Nonconformity*, 1973.

Brockway, Archibald Fenner, *Bermondsey Story, the Life of Alfred Salter*, 1949 and 1951.

Brown, Elizabeth Baldwin, *In Memoriam: James Baldwin Brown BA*, 1884.

Brown, Kenneth D., *A Social History of the Nonconformist Ministry in England and Wales 1800–1930*, Oxford, 1988.

Bunting, T. P., *The Life of Jabez Bunting D.D.*, vol. 1, 1859.

Burnett, R. G., et al., *Frederick Luke Wiseman, a Commemorative Record*, 1954.

Butler, R. A., *The Art of the Possible*, 1971.

Carswell, Donald, *Brother Scots*, 1927. (This includes a chapter on 'Claudius Clear', like 'Man of Kent' a pseudonym of W. R. Nicoll. See also Darlow below.)

Carter, David, *James H. Rigg*, Foundery Press, 1994.

Chadwick, Owen, *The Victorian Church*, 2 vols, 1966.
Collini, Stefan, *Public Moralists, Political Thought and Intellectual Life in Britain*, Oxford, 1991.
Cox, Jeffrey, *English Churches in a Secular Society, Lambeth 1870–1930*, New York and Oxford, 1982.
Cracknell, K., *Justice, Courtesy and Love*, 1995.
Cross, F. L., and E. A. Livingstone (eds), *Oxford Dictionary of the Christian Church*, 3rd edn revised, Oxford, 1997.
Cumbers, F. H. (ed.), *Richmond College 1843–1943*, 1944.
Currie, R., *Methodism Divided*, 1968.
Dale, A. W. W., *The Life of R. W. Dale of Birmingham*, 1898.
Dangerfield, G., *The Strange Death of Liberal England*, 1935, 1966.
Darley, Gillian, *Octavia Hill: A Life*, 1990.
Darlow, T. H., *William Robertson Nicoll, Life and Letters*, 1925. (See D. Carswell above.)
Davies, A. Emil, *The Story of the LCC*, Labour Publishing Co., 1925.
Davies, Daniel Horton Marlais, *Worship and Theology in England*, vols 3, 4, 5, Princeton, London and Oxford, 1961–5.
Davies, J., *Reforming London: The London Government Problem 1855–1900*, Oxford, 1988.
Davies, Rupert E. (ed.), *John Scott Lidgett: A Symposium*, 1957.
——*Methodism and Unity*, 1962.
——*Methodism*, 1963.
Davies, Rupert E., E. Gordon Rupp and A. Raymond George (eds), *A History of the Methodist Church in Great Britain*, vol. 1, 1965, vol. 2, 1978, vol. 3, 1983, vol. 4, 1988.
Dillistone, F. W., *Christian Understanding of Atonement*, 1968.
——*Charles Raven*, 1975.
Drummond, James Siddall, *Charles A. Berry DD*, 1899.
Edwards, David L., *Christian England*, 1984.
Edwards, Maldwyn Lloyd, *The Coming of the Kingdom*, 1930.
——*Methodism and England 1850–1932*, 1943.
——*S. E. Keeble, Pioneer and Prophet*, 1949.
Edwards, Michael Stone, *S. E. Keeble, the Rejected Prophet*, Wesley Historical Society, 1977.
Ehrenstrom, N., and W. Muelder (eds), *Institutionalism and Church Unity*, 1963.
Elliott-Binns, L. E., *English Thought 1860–1900: The Theological Aspect*, 1956.
Figgis, J. N., and R. V. Laurence (eds), J. E. E. D. Acton, *Historical Essays and Studies*, 1907.
Findlay, George G., *William F. Moulton, Methodist Scholar*, 1910.
Freeden, M., *The New Liberalism: An Ideology of Social Reform*, Oxford, 1978, reprinted with corrections 1986.
Fullerton, W. Y., *F. B. Meyer: A Biography*, London and Edinburgh, 1929.
Gairdner, W. H. T., *Edinburgh 1910*, Edinburgh, 1910.
Gibbon, G., and R. Bell, *History of the LCC, 1889–1939*, 1939.
Glover, Willis B., *Evangelical Nonconformists and Higher Criticism in the Nineteenth Century*, 1954.

Gregory, Benjamin, *The Thorough Businessman: Memoirs of Walter Powell, Merchant*, Melbourne and London, 1871.
—— *Sidelights on the Conflicts of Methodism*, 1899.
Gregory, J. R. (ed.), *Benjamin Gregory D.D., Autobiographical Recollections*, 1903.
Grensted, L. W., *A Short History of the Doctrine of the Atonement*, Manchester, 1920.
Grigg, J. E. P., *Lloyd George: From Peace to War 1912–1916*, 1985.
Harris, P. A., *London and Its Government*, 1913, rev.1931.
—— *Forty Years In and Out of Parliament*, 1947.
Harte, Negly, *University of London 1836–1986: An Illustrated History*, 1986.
Harte, Negly, with J. North, *The World of University College, London, 1823–1978*, rev. to 1990, 1991.
Harwood, W. Hardy, *Henry Allon DD, Pastor and Teacher*, 1894.
Haselmayer, Louis A., *Lambeth and Unity*, 1978.
Hastings, Adrian, *A History of English Christianity 1920–1990*, 1991.
Hastings, J. (ed.), *Encyclopedia of Religion and Ethics*, Edinburgh, 1912.
Hempton, David, *Methodism and Politics in British Society 1750–1850*, 1984.
—— *Religion of the People and Popular Religion 1750–1900*, 1996.
Higham, Florence M. G., *Frederick Denison Maurice*, 1947.
Hilton, Boyd, *The Age of Atonement: The Influence of Evangelicalism in Social and Economic Thought 1785–1865*, Oxford, 1988.
Hinchliff, P. B., *Jowett and the Christian Religion*, Oxford, 1987.
—— *God and History*, Oxford, 1992.
'H.K.', *Hugh Price Hughes, Leader of the Forward Movement*, 1903.
Hughes, D. P., *Life of Hugh Price Hughes*, 1904.
Hughes, H. M., *The Kingdom of Heaven*, 1922.
Hughes, Hugh Price, *The Atheist Shoemaker*, 1889.
—— *The Revival of Oxford Methodism*, 1903.
Humphrey, Stephen, *Southwark, Bermondsey and Rotherhithe in Old Photographs*, 1995.
Hynes, S., *The Edwardian Turn of Mind*, 1968.
Inglis, K. S., *The Churches and the Working Classes in Victorian England*, 1963.
Jasper, Ronald Claud D., *George Bell, Bishop of Chichester*, 1967.
Jeffs, Harry, *Press, Preachers and Politicians*, 1933.
Johnson, Dale, *The Changing Shape of English Nonconformity 1825–1925*, 1998.
Johnson, Mark D., *Dissolution of Dissent*, New York and London, 1987.
Johnston, J. O., *The Life and Letters of H. P. Liddon*, 1904.
Jones, Peter d'Alroy, *Christian Socialist Revival 1877–1914*, Princeton, 1968.
Jones, R. Tudur, *Congregationalism in England 1662–1962*, 1962.
Kent, John, *Holding the Fort: Studies in Victorian Revivalism*, 1978.
Kingsley, Frances Elizabeth, *Charles Kingsley: his Letters and Memories of his life, by his wife*, 2 vols, 1877.
Kissack, R. R., *Church or No Church?*, 1964.
Koss, Stephen E., *Nonconformity in Modern British Politics*, 1975.
Langford, T. A., *Methodist Theology*, 1998.
Lockhart, J. G., *Cosmo Gordon Lang*, 1949
Lunn, Henry Simpson, *Chapters from My Life, with special reference to Reunion*, 1918.
—— *Reunion and Lambeth*, 1920.

——*Nearing Harbour*, 1934.
—— *United Christian Front*, 1938.
Lynch, M., *Lloyd George and the Liberal Dilemma*, 1993.
Macfadyen, Dugald, *Alexander MacKennal, Life and Letters*, 1905.
Machin, G. I. T., *Politics and Churches 1869–1921,* Oxford, 1987.
—— *The Churches and Social Issues in Twentieth Century Britain*, Oxford, 1998.
Maclure, S., *One Hundred Years of London Education 1870–1970*, 1970.
Mais, S. P. B., *Fifty Years of the LCC*, Cambridge, 1939.
Mansbridge, Albert, *Edward Stuart Talbot and Charles Gore*, 1935.
Marchant, Sir James (ed.), *British Preachers*, 1925/6.
——*British Preachers*, second series, n.d.
——*Dr John Clifford: Life, Letters, and Reminiscences*, 1924.
——*If I Had Only One Sermon to Preach*, 1928.
Maurice, F., *The Life of F. D. Maurice*, chiefly told in his own letters, edited by his son, 2 vols, 1884.
Maurice, F. D., *The Doctrine of Sacrifice deduced from the Scriptures: A Series of Sermons*, Cambridge, 1854.
McKibbin, Ross, *Classes and Cultures*, 1998.
McLeod, Hugh, *Class and Religion in the Late Victorian City*, New York, 1974.
Meacham, Standish, *Toynbee Hall and Social Reform 1880–1914*, 1987.
Mews, Stuart P. (ed.), *Modern Religious Rebels*, 1993.
Meyer, Harding, *That All May Be One*, Grand Rapids, 1999.
Morris, Margaret, *The General Strike*, 1976.
Moss, Richard Waddy, *The Revd W. B. Pope DD: Theologian and Saint,* 1909.
Moulton, W. Fiddian, *William F. Moulton – a Memoir*, 1899.
Munson, James, *The Nonconformists: In Search of a Lost Culture*, 1991.
Nicholls, David, *Deity and Domination*, 1989.
Nicholson, Peter P. (ed.), *The Political Philosophy of the British Idealists: Selected Studies*, Cambridge, 1990.
Norman, E. R., *Church and Society in England 1770–1970*, Oxford, 1976.
—— *The Victorian Christian Socialists*, Cambridge, 1987.
Obelkevich, James, *Religion and Rural Society (S. Lindsey) 1825–1875*, Oxford, 1976.
Page, I. E. (ed.), *J. Brash, Memorials and Correspondence*, 1912.
Pals, D. L., *Victorian 'Lives of Jesus'*, San Antonio, 1982.
Parsons, G., J. R. Moore, et al., *Religion in Victorian Britain*, Manchester, 1988.
Paton, J. Lewis, *John Brown Paton: A Biography*, 1914.
Peake, Leslie Sillman, *Arthur Samuel Peake: A Memoir*, 1930.
Penman, G., *I Remember*, 1916.
Pope, Robert Martin, *The Life of Henry J. Pope*, 1913.
Porritt, Arthur, *The Best I Remember*, 1922.
——*John Henry Jowett*, 1924.
Pritchard, F. C., *The Story of Westminster College 1851–1951*, 1951.
Rack, Henry D., *The Future of John Wesley's Methodism*, 1965.
——*Wesleyanism and 'The World' in the later Nineteenth Century*, Wesley Historical Society Lecture 43, WHS Proceedings, 1979.
Raleigh, Mary (ed.), *Alexander Raleigh, Records of his Life*, 2nd edn, Edinburgh, 1883.

Ramsey, Arthur Michael, *F. D. Maurice and the Conflicts of Modern Theology*, Cambridge, 1951.
——*From Gore to Temple, 1889–1939*, 1960.
Read, Donald, *England 1868–1914*, 1979.
Robbins, Keith (ed.), *Protestant Evangelism: Britain, Ireland, Germany and America c1750–1950*, Essays in honour of W. R. Ward, Oxford, 1990.
Rogers, Travers Guy, *A Rebel at Heart*, 1956.
Rubinstein, W. D., and H. I. Rubinstein, *Philosemitism 1840–1939*, 1999.
Rupp, Ernest Gordon, *Thomas Jackson, Methodist Patriarch*, 1954.
Saint, Andrew, and Gillian Darley, *Chronicles of London*, 1994.
Sangster, Paul, *Dr Sangster*, 1962.
Scoresby-Jackson, Robert Edward, *The Life of William Scoresby*, 1861.
Sheppard, David, *Built as a City*, 1974.
Simpson, Patrick Carnegie, *Recollections, mainly ecclesiastical and sometimes human*, 1943.
Simpson, Ruth, *John Scott Lidgett: A Portrait in His Old Age*, the Burgh Heath Centre for Psychotherapy, Epsom, printed in Leicester by John Culpin, 1962.
H. Maynard Smith, *Frank H. Weston*, 1926.
Smith, J. T., *Methodism and Education 1849–1902*, Oxford, 1998.
Southport Holiness Convention, *To the Uttermost*, 1945. (See J. Baines Atkinson et al. above.)
W. T. Stead, *Josephine Butler – a Life Sketch*, 1888.
Steckel, Karl, and G. Ernst Somner (eds), *Geschichte der Evangelisch Methodisticher Kirke*, Stuttgart, 1982.
Stephenson, A. M. G., *Anglicanism and the Lambeth Conferences*, 1978.
Stephenson, Gwendolen, *Edward Stuart Talbot*, 1936.
Taylor, A. J. P., *English History 1914–1945*, Oxford, 1965.
Telford, John, *The Life of James Harrison Rigg DD 1821–1909*, 1909.
Thompson, F. M. L., *The University of London and the World of Learning 1836–1986*, 1990.
Tice, Frank, *A History of Methodism in Cambridge*, 1966.
Townsend, W. J., *The Story of Methodist Union*, n.d., ?1906.
Townsend, W. J., H. B. Workman and G. Eayrs (eds), *A New History of Methodism*, vol. 2, 1909.
Travell, John, *Doctor of Souls, Leslie D. Weatherhead, 1893–1976*, Cambridge, 1999.
Turner, F. M., *Between Science and Religion*, New Haven and London, 1974.
Turner, J. Munsey, *Conflict and Reconciliation: Studies in Methodism and Ecumenism in England 1740–1982*, 1985.
——*Modern Methodism 1932–1998*, 1998.
Unwin, Mrs G. (Frances Mabelle), and J. Telford, *Mark Guy Pearse*, 1930.
Vickers, J. A. (ed.), *A Dictionary of Methodism in Britain and Ireland*, 2000.
Vidler, Alexander Roper, *The Theology of F. D. Maurice*, 1948.
——*20th Century Defenders of the Faith*, 1965.
——*F. D. Maurice and Company*, 1966.
Wakefield, Gordon S., *Methodist Devotion 1791–1945*, 1966.
——*Robert Newton Flew 1886–1962*, 1971.
Waller, P. J., *Town, City and Nation: England 1850–1914*, 1983, 1991.

Ward, W. R., *Introduction to the Early Correspondence of Jabez Bunting, 1820–1829*, Camden Society 4th Series, II, 1972.
Weatherhead, Leslie, *Psychology in the Service of the Soul*, 1929.
—— *The Mastery of Sex through Psychology and Religion*, 1931.
Weston, F. H., *History of the Ancient Parish of Lastingham*, Leeds, 1914.
Wilkinson, Alan B., *The Church of England and the First World War*, 1978.
Winer, J. G. B., *The Grammar of New Testament Greek* (ed. and trans. by W. Fiddian Moulton), Edinburgh, 1870.
Wood, H. G., *Belief and Unbelief since 1850*, Cambridge, 1955.
Young, David, *F. D. Maurice and Unitarianism*, Oxford 1992.

2. Pamphlets

Association for Moral and Social Hygiene, Josephine Elizabeth Butler Society, *Manifesto on Report of Royal Commission on Venereal Diseases*, 1916.
Bolton, A. J., *The Other Side*, a pamphlet issued by the Wesleyan Methodist Historical Society, 1994.
Barnes, The Hon. H. Gorell, and J. E. G. de Montmorency, *The Divorce Commission, Majority and Minority Reports summarised*, 1912.
French, E. Aldom, Samuel Horton and David Brook (eds), *Methodist Union*, an annotated edition, prepared at the direction of the United Committee appointed by the Wesleyan Methodist, Primitive Methodist, and United Methodist Churches, of the tentative scheme for the union of the Three Churches, submitted to the Conferences of 1920, 1920.
White, Douglas, *Synopsis of Final Report on Royal Commission on Venereal Diseases*, authorised by the Royal Commission Chairman, National Council for Combating Venereal Diseases, The Shield, Association for Moral and Social Hygiene, reprint from issue of April 1916, 1916.

3. Articles

Altholz, Josef L., 'The Mind of Victorian Orthodoxy: Anglican Responses to Essays and Reviews 1860–1864', *Church History*, 51, no. 2, June 1982, pp. 186–97.
Anonymous, 'The Women's Settlements in London', *The Sunday at Home and Oversea*, New Series, Pt 41, Religious Tract Society, March 1898, pp. 317–19. (Southwark Local Studies Library, Bermondsey Settlement file, or British Library.)
Ashley, Percy, 'University Settlements in Great Britain', in G. F. Moore, W. W. Fenn and J. H. Ropes (eds), *Harvard Theological Review* IV, Harvard University, Cambridge, MA, 1911, pp. 179–203.
Bebbington, D. W., 'The Persecution of George Jackson: A British Fundamentalist Controversy', in W. J. Shiels (ed.), *Studies in Church History 21 (Persecution and Toleration)*, 1984, pp. 421–33.
Bell, G. K. A., S. W. Carruthers, J. S. Lidgett, 'Obituary Recollections of Patrick Carnegie Simpson', in *The Journal of the Presbyterian Historical Society*, no. 1, vol. 9, 1948–52, May 1948, pp. 3–9.
Brown, K. D., 'Nonconformist Evangelicals and National Politics in the Late Nineteenth Century', in J. Wolffe (ed.), *Evangelical Faith and Public Zeal*, 1995, pp. 138–54.

Carter, D., 'Joseph Agar Beet and the Eschatological Crisis', in *Proceedings of the Wesley Historical Society*, October 1998.
Christensen, Torben, 'F. D. Maurice and the Contemporary Religious World', in G. J. Cuming (ed.), *Studies in Church History 3*, Leiden, 1966, pp. 69–90.
Edwards, D. L., '101 years of the Lambeth Conference', in Gordon Wakefield and Michael Perry (eds), *Church Quarterly* 1, 1968/9, p. 32.
Garnett, Jane, 'Evangelicalism and Business in Mid-Victorian Britain', in John Wolffe (ed.), *Evangelical Faith and Public Zeal*, 1995, pp. 59–80.
Goodman, N., 'The Established Church – Hindrance to Progressive Thought', *Theological Pamphlets*, Nonconformist Association in Manchester, Manchester, 1873.
Healey, F. G., 'Patrick Carnegie Simpson, a Man of Style 1865–1947', *Journal of the Presbyterian Historical Society of England*, Vol. 14, No. 5. May 1972, pp. 178ff.
Kent, J., 'Methodist Union in England 1932', in N. Ehrenstrom and W. Muller (eds), *Institutionalism and Church Unity*, 1963.
——'Hugh Price Hughes and the Nonconformist Conscience', in G. V. Bennett and J. D. Walsh (eds), *Essays in Modern Church History*, 1966.
Mews, S. P., 'Kikuyu and Edinburgh: The Interaction of Attitudes to Two Conferences', in G. J. Cuming and Derek Baker (eds), *Studies in Church History 7 (Councils and Assemblies)*, Cambridge, 1971, pp. 345–59.
——'Spiritual Mobilization in the First World War', in G. R. Dunstan (ed.), *Theology*, 74 no. 612, 'The Humanity of Christ', June 1971, pp. 258–64.
——'Puritanicalism, Sport and Race: A Symbolic Crusade of 1911', in G. J. Cuming and Derek Baker (eds), *Studies in Church History 8 (Popular Belief and Practice)*, Cambridge, 1972, pp. 303–31.
——'Neo-orthodoxy, Liberalism and War: Karl Barth, P. T. Forsyth and John Oman 1914–1918', in Derek Baker (ed.), *Studies in Church History 14 (Renaissance and Renewal in Christian History)*, Oxford, 1977, pp. 361–75.
——'Urban Problems and Rural Solutions: Drink and Disestablishment in the First World War', in Derek Baker (ed.), *Studies in Church History 16 (The Church in Town and Countryside)*, Oxford, 1979, pp. 449–76.
Nash, D., 'Foote and the Freethinker', *History Today*, 45, October 1995, pp. 13–19.
Nettleship, L. E., 'William Fremantle, Samuel Barnett and the Broad Church Origins of Toynbee Hall', *Journal of Ecclesiastical History*, 33, 1982, pp. 564–79.
Randall, Ian M., 'The Social Gospel: A Case Study', in J. Wolffe (ed.), *Evangelical Faith and Public Zeal*, 1995, pp. 155–74.
Thompson, D. M., 'The Emergence of the Nonconformist Social Gospel in England', in K. Robbins (ed.), *Studies in Church History*, Subsidia 7, 1990, pp. 255–80.
D. M. Thompson, 'The Christian Socialist Revival in Britain: A Re-appraisal', in J. Garnett and C. Matthew (eds), *Revival and Religion since 1700*, 1993, pp. 273–95.
Turner, J. M., 'Lidgett, John Scott (1854–1953)', in T. A. Hart (ed.), *The Dictionary of Historical Theology*, Grand Rapids and Carlisle, 2000, pp. 320–2.

Notes

Introduction

1. *M.Rec.*, 13 September 1951, p. 6.
2. *M.Rec.*, 25 June 1953, p. 6.
3. Eric Baker, in *Symp.*, p. 36.
4. *M.Rec.*, 13 September 1951.
5. Letter to Alan Turberfield, dated 27 July 1992.
6. *Symp.*, p. 36.
7. Dr Sangster, in Paul Sangster's *Dr Sangster*, 1962, p. 167.
8. *Symp.*, p. 36, n. 4.
9. cf. Chapter 27.
10. Letter to Alan Turberfield, dated 18 August 1992.

1 Background 1854–90

1. See Terms.
2. *Rem.*, p. 12.
3. *Rem.*, p. 8.
4. Royal Historical Society, Camden Fourth Series, vol. 11, 1972, p. 9, and cf. Adrian Hastings, *History of English Christianity 1920–1990*, 1991, p. 216.
5. Letter dated 27 August 1992.
6. *Rem.*, p. 12.
7. *Guided*, p. 74.
8. I am indebted to Miss E. McDougall, Mrs E. Fairweather, Mrs E. Brewer and Mrs E. Camp for these.
9. *Guided*, p. 41.
10. *Guided*, p. 106.
11. *Guided*, p. 112. To Charles Booth, in *Descriptive Map of London Poverty*, 1889, Bermondsey was one of the most deprived areas, worse than Westminster.
12. For photographs of the area at the time see Stephen Humphrey, *Southwark, Bermondsey and Rotherhithe*, esp. Sections 11 (Housing), 13 (Leather Manufacturing) and 15 (The Surrey Docks and Rotherhithe Riverfront).
13. Comments on Lidgett's early life follow later. For more detail see *Rem.*, pp. 11–13, and *Guided*, pp. 20–41.
14. *Guided*, p. 6; undated (*c.*1993) letter to me from Elizabeth Camp, enclosing her account, 'A Bit about the Natal Lidgetts'; letter to me from Prof. A. H. Bunting, on 5 April 1993.

15. Jane Garnett, 'Evangelicalism and Business in mid-Victorian Britain', in J. Wolffe (ed.), *Evangelical Faith and Public Zeal: Evangelicals and Society in Britain 1780–1980*, 1995, pp. 59–80, shows how evangelicals' exhortations and example helped to preserve and make attractive personal integrity amid the pitfalls of commercial life.

16. *Guided*, p. 22.

17. D. W. Bebbington, *The Nonconformist Conscience*, 1982, pp. 94–5, and J. S. Vickers (ed.), *The Dictionary of Methodism in Britain and Ireland*, p. 66.

18. Bebbington, *Nonconformist Conscience*, p. 94.

19. Quoted in James Munson, *The Nonconformists: In Search of a Lost Culture*, 1991, p. 215.

20. *Dissolution of Dissent 1850–1918*, 1987, pp. xxii–xxiii.

21. 'Baptists, Congregationalists and Theological Change: Some Leaders and Controversies', unpublished Oxford DPhil thesis, 1988, p. 8, n. 7.

22. See below and Chapter 3.

23. Edmondson, 'The Doctrines of Hell and Judgement, and the Need for Personal Conversion as an Index to the Development of Liberal Theology within the Theological Colleges of the Methodist Church in England 1907–1932', unpublished MA thesis, Durham, 1990, pp. 12–13.

24. The National Society, founded in 1811, set up schools for the education of the poor in the principles of the Established Church.

25. *Guided*, pp. 24–5. See Chapter 7 and elsewhere.

26. *Guided*, p. 23.

27. *Guided*, p. 146.

28. *Rem.*, p. 14.

29. *Guided*, p. 146.

30. *Rem.*, p. 14.

31. *Guided*, pp. 37–8.

32. *The Eternal Hope*, 1878, 18th edn, 1901.

33. *Life and Death, the Sanctions of the Law of Love*. For 'Fernley' see Terms.

34. R. Currie, *Methodism Divided*, 1968, p. 119.

35. *Guided*, p. 26.

36. cf. I. E. Page (ed.), *John Brash: Memorials and Correspondence*, 1912, pp. 28–9. Another Wesleyan, the Revd Frank Ballard, quoted by R. Currie, *Methodism Divided*, p. 120, in 1890 attacked 'hell-fire' preaching and God pictured as 'a merciless Shylock, exacting the last throb of agony from an innocent and helpless victim'.

37. *Guided*, pp. 24 and 151, and the father image in Lidgett's *Spiritual Principle*, 1897.

38. 1907.

39. *Guided*, p. 22.

40. *Guided*, p. 20.

41. *Guided*, p. 100.

42. *Guided*, p. 30.

43. *Guided*, p. 39.

44. *Guided*, p. 40.

45. D. W. Bebbington, *Victorian Nonconformity*, Headstart History Papers, Bangor, 1992, pp. 76ff., and cf. Lidgett's *Fatherhood of God*, p. 279, and *Guided*, p. 152.

46. *Guided*, p. 22.
47. *Guided*, p. 144.
48. *Guided*, p. 144.
49. 'Fundamentalist' and 'fundamentalism' strictly refer to 'association with a fundamental dogmatic position', but are often used loosely to connote belief in the literal interpretation of the Bible. In this passage, and where not distinguished subsequently, both meanings are intended.
50. *Guided*, p. 149.
51. *Guided*, pp. 25–6.
52. *Guided*, p. 46.
53. *Guided*, p. 55.
54. *Guided*, p. 49.
55. Letter to the Archbishop of Canterbury, Oxford, 1842.
56. For full details of his early ministry, see *Guided*, Chapter 7.
57. *Guided*, p. 147.
58. *Guided*, p. 72.
59. Oxford, 1867.
60. *Spiritual Principle*, p. 384, n. 2. References henceforth are to *SP*.
61. Letter dated 4 June 93.
62. *Worship and Theology in England 1850–1900*, Oxford, 1962, p. 251, n. 20.
63. Lidgett, confirming (*M.Rec.*, 11 June 1936, p. 7) the use of the Anglican liturgy at Blackheath in his early days, spoke of marked differences between worship in suburban, industrial and country areas at the time.
64. *Guided*, p. 77.
65. 1902, p. 269, henceforth abbreviated to *FG*.
66. cf. *Guided*, p. 26.
67. See Chapter 12 on London University.
68. *Symp.*, p. 198.
69. *Guided*, pp. 40–1.
70. *Rem.*, p. 13.
71. Edinburgh.
72. See Terms.
73. *Guided*, p. 72.
74. *Guided*, p. 156.
75. See Chapter 12.
76. *Guided*, p. 43.
77. *Rem.*, p. 16.
78. *Guided*, p. 161.
79. 1833–91.
80. Foote had been sentenced in 1883 to 12 months in prison with hard labour for the aggressively blasphemous comments and cartoons in his *Freethinker* magazine (D. Nash, 'Blasphemy in Victorian Britain: Foote and the Freethinker', *History Today*, October 1995, pp. 13–19). Lidgett was a friend of H. P. Hughes against whom Foote was continuing to wage a vendetta, calling Hughes's *Atheist Shoemaker*, 1889, 'A Lie in Five Chapters'. See D. P. Hughes, *Life of Hugh Price Hughes*, 1904, pp. 295–8.

81. *MT*, 25 July 1907, p. 632.
82. 'The Communion of Saints', *London Quarterly Review*, 1956, p. 137.
83. *HistMethGB3*, p. 230.
84. *Rem.*, p. 16.
85. *Rem.*, p. 18.
86. *The Victorian Church*, Part II, 1970, pp. 23–4.
87. Quoted by D. Read, *England 1868–1914*, 1979, p. 80.
88. J. E. Rattenbury, in W. B. Brash and C. J. Wright, *Didsbury College Centenary 1842–1942*, 1942, p. 97.
89. M. Clement, 'Sifting Science: Methodism and Natural Knowledge in Britain 1815–1870', unpublished Oxford DPhil thesis, 1996, pp. 128–54, 225ff., etc.
90. *HistMethGB3*, pp. 185–7.
91. *SP*, pp. 330–3. *Christian Religion*, pp. 320–1, 343–51, etc.
92. *Guided*, p. 87.
93. *M.Rec.*, 9 July 1903, p. 4.
94. *Guided*, p. 71.
95. *HistMethGB3*, p. 139.
96. *God and the World*. Increasing mental depression led Pope to resign his post in 1886: see *MT*, 9 July 1903, p. 468.
97. *Symp.*, p. 86.
98. Torben Christensen, 'F. D. Maurice and the Contemporary Religious World', in C. J. Cuming (ed.), *Studies in Church History 3*, Leiden, 1966, pp. 69–90. On p. 79, Christensen said that Rigg's *Modern Anglican Theology* (1857) was 'the most penetrating treatment of Maurice's theology' at that time.
99. *Rem.*, p. 19.
100. F. H. Cumbers (ed.), *History of Richmond College 1843–1943*, 1944, p. 112, and see J. Vickers (ed.), *Dictionary of Methodism*, p. 344.
101. Letter to me from Friedmann W. Burkhardt on 28 November 1994.
102. *MT*, 9 July 1903, p. 468. He translated Stier, Dorner, Ebrard and Haupt.
103. R. M. Pope, *Life of H. J. Pope*, 1913, p. 44.
104. See Chapter 3.
105. *Rem.*, p. 19.
106. *M.Rec.*, 11 June 1936, p. 7.
107. Didsbury's R.Waddy Moss (1850–1935), fearing the Conference examiner, insisted his students should not modify the notes of 'unimpeachable' orthodoxy which he dictated, however freely he had talked in the lecture room (W. F. Howard, in Brash and Wright, *Didsbury College*, p. 119).
108. *MT*, 19 June 1913, p. 3. Lidgett's first visit to the Wesleyan Conference was *as a representative* in 1887.
109. Handsworth was not opened until 1881.
110. W. B. Brash, *The Story of Our Colleges 1835–1935*, 1935, pp. 93–4.
111. Brash and Wright, *Didsbury College*, p. 97.
112. Cumbers, *Richmond College 1843–1943*, 1944, pp. 64–5 and 69.
113. *Guided*, p. 145.
114. *M.Rec.*, 11 June 1936, p. 7; *M.Rec.*, 6 February 1947, p. 9; and cf. K. S. Inglis, *The Churches and the Working Classes in Victorian England*, 1963, pp. 86ff.

115. *MT*, 21 July 1910, p. 7, and *BW*, 30 July 1914, p. 460.
116. *Guided*, p. 56.
117. *Rem.*, p. 22.
118. See Chapter 5, and *Guided*, p. 158.
119. *HistMeth GB*3, p. 153, and about comparison with the Free Churches cf. R. M. Pope, *Henry Pope*, pp. 208–9.
120. H. D. Rack, *Future of John Wesley's Methodism*, 1965, p. 52.
121. *M.Rec.*, 11 June 1936, p. 7.
122. cf. Percy Bunting, in W. J. Townsend, H. B. Workman and G. Eayres (eds), *A New History of Methodism*, 1909, vol. 2, p. 486, on taking 'full account of . . . the other religious bodies . . . as its [Methodism's] members rise in the social scale'.
123. *Guided*, p. 142.
124. *Guided*, pp. 14–15.

2 The Bermondsey Settlement – I

1. For details see *Guided*, pp. 76–109.
2. Charles Booth, *Life and Labour of the People in London*, vols 1–9, 1892–7, described the whole city in detail.
3. *Guided*, p. 73, *SP*, pp. 325–7.
4. D. P. Hughes, *H. P. Hughes*, 1904, p. 134.
5. D. P. Hughes, *H. P. Hughes*, pp. 134–6.
6. *Guided*, pp. 42, 73, 148.
7. Oxford, 1883. *Guided*, p. 73; *SP*, p. 325ff.
8. For assessments of Green's influence see I. Bradley, *The Optimists*, 1980, pp. 158, 182–3, 191, 217–20; P. P. Nicholson, *The Political Philosophy of the British Idealists*, Cambridge, 1990, pp. 3–4, 164–80; S. Collini, *Public Moralists, Political Thought and Intellectual Life in Britain 1850–1930*, Oxford, 1991, pp. 82–4, 94 and 227.
9. *Guided*, pp. 72–3.
10. My italics.
11. *Guided*, p. 70.
12. *Guided*, pp. 60, 73 and 150.
13. *Rem.*, p. 22.
14. *Guided*, p. 73. My italics.
15. See *VT*, p. 10.
16. cf. *The Divine Life in Man*, 1859, e.g. p. 95.
17. 'Nonconformity, Theology and Reunion 1870–1910', unpublished Oxford DPhil thesis, 1995, p. 148.
18. See P. T. Forsyth, 'Baldwin Brown, a Tribute, a Reminiscence and a Study', in E. B. Brown, *In Memoriam: J. B. Brown BA*, 1884, pp. 133–42 (e.g. pp. 134ff.).
19. 1902 edn, pp. 133–4.
20. 1919, quoting W. Arthur, *Tongue of Fire*, 1859, pp. 125–6.
21. *Toynbee Hall and Social Reform 1880–1914*, 1987, p. 79.
22. *Guided*, p. 141.
23. *Guided*, p. 118 and 110, my italics.
24. *Rem.*, p. 31.

25. From 1909 to 1918 his superintendency included the South London Mission with five more 'centres', four more ministers, eight 'Sisters of the People' and two Lay Assistants. Becoming Chairman of the Third London Wesleyan District in 1908/9, he remained in office for nearly 40 years. See J. D. Beasley, *The Bitter Cry Heard and Heeded*, S. London Mission, 1989, p. 40, for these details.

26. *Third Annual Report*, 30 September 1894, p. 15.

27. *Second Annual Report*, 1893, p. 19. See also A. B. Bartlett, 'The Churches in Bermondsey 1880–1939', unpublished Birmingham PhD thesis, 1988, p. 272.

28. Quoted by K. S. Inglis, *The Churches and the Working Classes in Victorian England*, 1963, p. 145.

29. Charles Booth Papers, LPSS Notebook B, p. 227, quoted by S. Meacham, *Toynbee Hall*, p. 53.

30. *Guided*, pp. 117–18.

31. Local Studies Library, Southwark, pp. 5–6. For appraisal of the weaknesses of Bermondsey's Nonconformist (including the various Methodist) churches at this period see Bartlett, 'The Churches in Bermondsey', unpublished Birmingham PhD thesis, 1988, p. 253, chs 4, 7 and throughout.

32. October 1892, pp. 22–3, my italics.

33. *Symp.*, p. 55. See Bartlett, 'Churches in Bermondsey', Synopsis.

34. *Guided*, p. 140.

35. cf. Presidential Address, *MT*, 23 July 1908, p. 596.

36. *Annual Report* 1894, p. 14.

37. p. 12, my italics.

38. *M.Rec.*, 29 May 1890.

39. *Rem.*, p. 29.

40. W. F. Lofthouse, *Symp.*, pp. 51ff.

41. Mearns and Preston, *Bitter Cry*, 1883. The Wesleyan minister, T. B. Stephenson, had founded the National Children's Home in 1869, an earlier Wesleyan response to one of London's serious social problems.

42. A. S. Wohl, Introduction to Mearns and Preston, *Bitter Cry and Related Articles*, 1970, p. 22.

43. Lofthouse, *Symp.*, pp. 51ff.

44. *Minutes of Conference*, 1889, p. 304, and in 1890, p. 298. My emphasis.

45. *Guided*, p. 117, for example.

46. *Guided*, p. 111.

47. *Annual Report*, 1894, p. 7.

48. *MT*, 30 July 1896, p. 524.

49. *MT*, 4 December 1902, p. 885.

50. *Annual Report*, 1893, p. 13, my italics.

51. *Annual Report*, 1897, p. 7.

52. *Rem.*, p. 29, and Charles Booth Notebooks A47, Misc. (33), pp. 5ff., and B283, Misc. (33), pp. 11–21.

53. Lidgett, *Idea of God*, p. 107.

54. Winter 1894/5 (1895 *Report*), p. 10.

55. For a detailed account of the Settlement see Appendix 1.

56. *Rem.*, p. 27.

57. *Rem.*, p. 29.

58. *MT.*, 17 September 1891, p. 961. This includes Lidgett's terms for Settlement residents.

59. Fenner Brockway, *Bermondsey Story*, 1949, p. 43, and see Bartlett, 'Churches in Bermondsey', pp. 30–7.

60. *Guided*, p. 113.

61. 1893 *Report*, p. 19.

62. See Appendix 1 and Chapter 29.

63. *MT*, 13 October 1949.

64. See Lidgett, *Apostolic Ministry*, 1910, pp. 212–13.

65. *Annual Report*, 1898, p. 7.

66. *Rem.*, pp. 33–4, for example.

67. *Report*, 1894, p. 34.

68. *Settlement Report*, 1896, p. 19.

69. F. Higham, *F. D. Maurice*, 1947, p. 54.

70. *Guided*, p. 15.

71. cf. 'The Ideals of National Education', Lidgett's valedictory address to Westminster and Southlands College students on 28 June 1909, in *Apostolic Ministry*, pp. 151ff.

72. cf. Benjamin Jowett, *College Sermons*, 1879, pp. 157ff., quoted by P. B. Hinchliff, in *Benjamin Jowett and the Christian Religion*, Oxford, 1987, pp. 154–5.

73. *Monthly Record*, January 1896, p. 1.

74. *Guided*, pp. 110–11.

75. *Rem.*, p. 41.

76. *M.Rec.*, 27 October 1949, p. 5.

77. Lidgett was ready to offer provision for minority interests, even Hebrew (*Symp.*, p. 60); and 'He loved Greek and wanted others to share it as well', a comment at his Memorial Service by his successor as Warden, the Revd Peter Morley, mentioned by the South London Press, 30 June 1953, p. 1.

78. *M.Rec.*, 13 October 1949.

79. *VT*, p. 17.

80. *Report*, 1894, p. 14.

81. *Apostolic 'Ministry, Ministerial Leadership'*, 23 July 1908, p. 35; *MT*, 30 July 1908, p. 633; and cf. *MT*, 4 March 1909, p. 1.

3 The Spiritual Principle of the Atonement

1. References are to *SP*.

2. *M.Rec.*, 25 June 1953, p. 8.

3. *Rem.*, p. 21.

4. *Guided*, p. 56.

5. *Guided*, p. 57.

6. *Rem.*, pp. 21–2.

7. *Rem.*, p. 22.

8. *Guided*, p. 57.

9. *Rem.*, p. 22.
10. *Rem.*, p. 22; *Guided*, p. 57.
11. *SP*, pp. 4–5, and Note 'On the Recent Tendency to Regard the Nature of the Atonement as Incomprehensible', pp. 488–98.
12. *SP*, p. 491.
13. *Guided*, p. 155, and cf. *SP*, Introduction, p. 1.
14. *SP*, pp. 6–8.
15. J. E. E. Acton, *Historical Essays and Studies*, ed. J. N. Figgis and R. V. Lawrence, 1907, pp. 285–6. See also Boyd Hilton, *The Age of Atonement 1785–1865*, Oxford, 1988, p. 296, 'making amends for one's own misdeeds', and p. 318, 'doctrine of consequences'.
16. *The Person of Christ: Dogmatic, Spiritual, Historical*, the second (1871) Fernley lecture, 1875, quoted in *HistMethGB3*, p. 188.
17. E.g. *VT*, p. 76.
18. *Guided*, p. 156, and *SP*, p. 5.
19. *Guided*, p. 153.
20. *FG*, Preface, p. vii.
21. *Guided*, p. 154.
22. See his editorial on 'Fatherhood and Atonement', in *MT*, 20 March 1913, p. 3.
23. *MT*, 24 January 1935, p. 6.
24. *HistMethGB3*, p. 189.
25. *Guided*, p. 152, my italics.
26. *SP*, pp. 226–7.
27. *FG*, p. 288.
28. *SP*, p. 2.
29. *Rem.*, pp. 22–3.
30. *Guided*, p. 153, my italics.
31. *SP*, p. 155.
32. R. W. Dale (1829–95) had died before Lidgett's *Spiritual Principle* was published.
33. *Guided*, p. 148.
34. Three volumes 1870–4. The first was published in English in 1872.
35. H. R. Mackintosh and A. B. Macaulay, Edinburgh.
36. My interview with Mrs Horstmann on 21 September 1992.
37. *Methodist Magazine*, 1933, p. 6.
38. Notably Benjamin Jowett's 1855 Essay on 'Atonement and Satisfaction' in the second of his *Commentaries on Pauline Epistles*. He said the orthodox doctrine denied the ethical quality of Christ's work and the character of God.
39. Mary Raleigh, *Alexander Raleigh*, 2nd edn, 1883, pp. 281–2, a Congregationalist's attack on the gradual erosion of the evangelical faith.
40. For example see I. E. Page (ed.), *John Brash: Memorials and Correspondence*, 1912, pp. 95ff., comments of a Wesleyan circuit minister (1830–1912) at the 'grass roots'.

41. L. W. Grensted, *A Short History of the Atonement*, Manchester and London, 1920, p. vii, acknowledges a debt to Lidgett.
42. *Guided*, p. 156; *SP*, p. 2; and *FG*, p. 244.
43. *Guided*, p. 149.
44. *Guided*, p. 151.
45. *Guided*, p. 149, and cf. *SP*, pp. 330ff.
46. cf. *Guided*, p. 152.
47. *Guided*, pp. 151–2.
48. cf. *SP*, p. 2.
49. *SP*, p. 3.
50. Thomas Erskine, *Unconditional Freeness of the Gospel*, Edinburgh, 1828.
51. *FG*, p. 272.
52. *SP*, p. 152.
53. *SP*, p. 154.
54. *Guided*, p. 155.
55. *Theological Essays*, 3rd edn, 1871, e.g. p. 144.
56. Quoted in *HistMethGB3*, p. 188.
57. William Burt Pope, *The Person of Christ: Dogmatic, Spiritual, Historical*, 1871 Fernley Lecture, 1875, p. 51.
58. William Burt Pope, *Compendium*, vol. 2, p. 316. Pope's capital letters.
59. *SP*, p. 197.
60. *Nature of Atonement*, 1873 edn, p. 102.
61. *Guided*, p. 154.
62. *SP*, p. 179.
63. *Guided*, p. 154.
64. *SP*, p. 286.
65. *SP*, p. 216.
66. B. F. Westcott, *Victory of the Cross*, 1888, p. 82.
67. *SP*, p. 186.
68. See F. W. Dillistone, *Christian Understanding of the Atonement*, 1968, p. 251; cf. Westcott, *Victory of the Cross*, p. 85.
69. *SP*, p. 188.
70. *SP*, p. 189.
71. *SP*, pp. 227, n. 1, and 396.
72. Fairbairn, *Place of Christ*, pp. 444–8 and 487.
73. *SP*, pp. 377–8 and n. 2.
74. Fairbairn, *Place of Christ*, p. 482.
75. Peter Hinchliff, *God and History*, Oxford, 1992, p. 195.
76. Fairbairn, *Place of Christ*, p. 487.
77. Fairbairn, *Place of Christ*, pp. 482–3.
78. D. W. Bebbington, *Evangelicalism in Modern Britain*, 1989, p. 15.
79. *VT*, pp. 33–4.
80. *Guided*, p.150.
81. *VT*, p. 69.
82. *Guided*, pp. 156–7.

83. *Minutes*, pp. 374–5.
84. *VT*, pp.75–6, and its review in *M.Rec.*, 26 July 1934, p. 43.
85. *SP*, p. vi, and Fairbairn's book cited, p. 476.
86. W. Strawson, *HistMethGB3*, p. 188.
87. As in H. P. Liddon, *Divinity of Our Lord and Saviour Jesus Christ*, 1867.
88. *SP*, p. 380.
89. *Bermondsey Settlement Magazine* (May 1907), pp. 79–80.
90. *God in Christ Jesus*, 1915, p. 157.
91. *SP*, p. 356. Lidgett's italics.
92. *SP*, pp. 378–9. Lidgett's italics.
93. *Guided*, p. 154.
94. *FG*, p. 280.
95. *SP*, p. 6, and cf. *FG*, p. 280.
96. *Guided*, p. 155.
97. *SP*, p. 168, and pp. 155, 163. Lidgett's editorial in *MT*, 20 March 1913, objected to '*an intervention between God and man from outside*'.
98. *SP*, pp. 193–6.
99. *SP*, p. 303.
100. *SP*, p. 268.
101. *SP*, pp. 181–3.
102. *SP*, pp. 268–9.
103. *SP*, p. 301.
104. *SP*, pp. 119–120.
105. *M.Rec.*, 9 August 1984, p. 11.
106. Munsey Turner's entry on Lidgett in T. A. Hart (ed.), *Dictionary of Historical Theology*, Grand Rapids and Carlisle, 2000.
107. *MT*, 20 March 1913, p. 3.
108. *MT*, 5 August 1897, pp. 533–4.
109. *HistMethGB3*, p. 190.
110. *MT*, 16 July 1908, p. 578.
111. 'The Emergence of the Nonconformist Social Gospel in England', in K. Robbins (ed.), *Studies in Church History*, Subsidia 7, 1990, p. 265.
112. *SP*, pp. 414–16.
113. *The Age of Atonement*, Oxford, 1988, e.g. p. ix, and throughout.
114. *Church and Society in England 1770–1970*, Oxford, 1976, pp. 8–11, and generally pp. 1–14, 180–6.
115. I. Bradley, *The Optimists*, 1980, pp. 14, 44–6, 81, 251–9.
116. Torben Christensen, *The Origin and History of Christian Socialism 1848–1854*, Aarhus, 1962, pp. 218ff.
117. D. M. Thompson, 'The Emergence of the Nonconformist Gospel in England', in K. Robbins (ed.), *Studies in Church History*, 1990, pp. 255–80, and 'The Christian Socialist Revival in Britain: A Re-appraisal', in J. Garnett and C. Matthew (eds), *Revival and Religion since 1700*, 1993, pp. 273–95.
118. For analysis of Edwardian New Liberalism, see M. Freeden, *The New Liberalism*, Oxford, 1978, pp. 12–24, 65–75, 246–9, and D. P. Campbell, 'Methodism

and Social Problems in the Inter-War Period 1918–1939', unpublished Oxford MLitt thesis, 1987, Long Abstract.

119. *Symp.*, p. 69.

4 Response to The Spiritual Principle of the Atonement

1. *Rem.*, p. 23.
2. *Guided*, p. 157.
3. Randles, *For Ever: An Essay on Eternal Punishment*, 1895. See Chapter 1.
4. He was remembered for asserting that as asbestos would stand any amount of heat, so might the soul (Brash and Wright, *Didsbury College*, p. 98). According to J. M. Turner, *Conflict and Reconciliation: Studies in Methodism and Ecumenism in England 1740–1982*, 1985, p.175, Randles said the Devil used asbestos in hell.
5. *MT*, 14 July 1904, p. 482.
6. *Guided*, p. 157.
7. *Guided*, p. 158.
8. *Guided*, p. 23.
9. *M.Rec.*, 12 August 1897, p. 653.
10. *MT*, 5 August 1897, pp. 533–4.
11. *MT*, 5 August 1897, p. 547.
12. *LQR*, October 1897, p. 151.
13. *The Idea of Atonement in Christian Theology*, 1919. Lidgett was mentioned only on the last page.
14. Beet, *Last Things*, 1897, Preface dated 13 September, pp. vi and 227.
15. See T. H. Darlow, *William Robertson Nicoll, Life and Letters*, 1925.
16. *BW*, 2 September 1897, pp. 321–2.
17. *Rem.*, p. 23.
18. *Symp.*, p. 68.
19. *Wesleyan Methodist Magazine*, CXX, 1897, pp. 796–8.
20. Moberley, *Atonement and Personality*, 1901, pp. 382–96.
21. *M.Rec.*, 12 August 1897, p. 653.
22. *LQR*, October 1897, p. 150.
23. Maurice, *Manual of Christian Doctrine*, 8th edn, 1887, p. 173.
24. *MT*, 5 August 1897, pp. 533–4.
25. *The Christian Conscience – a Contribution to Christian Ethics*, Fernley Lecture, 1888, pp. 161–2.
26. *M.Rec.*, 24 September 1936, p. 10.
27. *M.Rec.*, 24 September 1936, p.10.
28. *Guided*, p. 158.
29. *M.Rec.*, 25 June 1953, p. 8.
30. *HistMethGB3*, p. 314.
31. Dillistone, *Christian Understanding of the Atonement*, 1968.
32. *HistMethGB3*, p. 190.
33. Dillistone, *Christian Understanding of the Atonement*, pp. 252–3.
34. *Symp.*, p. 97.
35. *Wesleyan Methodist Magazine*, January 1933, p. 5.

36. *The Record*, 15 January 1904, p. 97.
37. James Denney, *Death of Christ*, 1902, revised 1911; *The Atonement and the Modern Mind*, 1903; and *Jesus and the Gospel*, 1908.
38. Moberly, *Atonement and Personality*, pp. 139, 382–96, e.g. 394–6.
39. Hastings Rashdall, *Idea of Atonement in Christian Theology*, 1919, p. 496.
40. A. M. Ramsey, *From Gore to Temple 1889–1939*, 1960, p. 49.
41. *Christian Religion*, Preface, p. viii.
42. *HistMethGB3*, p. 215.
43. *MT*, 1 November 1906, p. 730.
44. Lofthouse, *Ethics and Atonement*, p. 106.
45. Lofthouse, *Ethics and Atonement*, p. 214.
46. Peake, *Christianity*, pp. 282–3.
47. Peake, *Christianity*, p. 278.
48. Peake, *Christianity*, pp. 284–5.
49. Edmondson, 'Doctrines of Hell', p. 57.
50. R. J. Campbell, *New Theology*, 1907, p. 76.
51. Campbell, *New Theology*, pp. 172–3.
52. Campbell, *New Theology*, pp. 168–9.
53. C. H. Vine (ed.), *Old Faith and New Theology*, 1907.
54. Hastings, *History of English Christianity*, p. 108.
55. *MT*, 28 March 1907, p. 217.
56. Vine (ed.), *Old Faith*, p. 56 .
57. Peter Taylor Forsyth, *The Work of Christ*, 1910, pp. 146–7.
58. Peter Taylor Forsyth, *Positive Preaching and the Modern Mind*, 1907, p. 182.
59. Peter Taylor Forsyth, *The Person and Place of Jesus Christ*, 1909, e.g. pp. 349–50.
60. *MT*, 25 August 1910, p. 3.
61. *MT*, 25 August 1910, p. 3.

5 The Fatherhood of God and The Christian Religion

1. T&T Clark, publishers of much conservative theology in the late nineteenth century.
2. Preface, p. viii.
3. Rupert Davies, *Methodism*, 1963, p. 177.
4. Preface, p. vii.
5. *FG*, p. 277.
6. *FG*, p. 138.
7. *FG*, p. 141.
8. *FG*, excerpts from pp. 85–7.
9. *FG*, p. 92.
10. *Guided*, p. 157.
11. *M.Rec.*, 4 December 1902, p. 23.
12. *FG*, p. 267ff.
13. *FG*, p. 145. My italics.
14. *FG*, p. 270.

15. *FG*, p. 332.
16. *FG*, pp. 268–9.
17. *FG*, p. 336.
18. *FG*, p. 268.
19. *FG*, p. 272.
20. *FG*, p. 278, my italics.
21. *FG*, p. 317.
22. *FG*, p. 315.
23. *Guided*, p. 151.
24. *FG*, pp. 276–7 and ff.
25. *FG*, p. 343.
26. *Wesleyan Methodist Magazine*, February 1903, pp. 155–6.
27. *MT*, 11 December 1902, p. 898.
28. *Guided*, p. 160. D. P. Hughes, *H. P. Hughes*, pp. 645ff.
29. Letter from Randles to Watkinson, dated 25 May 1902, shown by G. Hobbs to me on 18 February 1994.
30. Beet, *Immortality of the Soul: A Protest*, 1901.
31. See D. Carter, 'Joseph Agar Beet and the eschatological crisis', Proceedings of Wesleyan Historical Society, October 1998.
32. Brash and Wright, *Didsbury College*, pp. 119–20.
33. *MT*, 7 August 1902, p. 572.
34. *Guided*, p. 231.
35. G. Stephenson, *Edward Stuart Talbot*, 1936, pp. 189–90.
36. His 'Fatherhood of God' article in W. T. Davison's symposium, *The Chief Cornerstone*, p. 148.
37. 'Fatherhood of God', p. 151.
38. *Christian Religion*, 1907, pp. 254ff.
39. Lidgett, *God in Christ Jesus* (*GCJ*), 1915, p. 371.
40. *GCJ*, p. 367. cf. Lidgett's collected articles, *God, Christ and the Church* (*GCCh*), 1927, p. 122.
41. *GCCh*, p. 122.
42. *HistMethGB3*, p. 211.
43. *FG*, pp. 10–11.
44. *Rem.*, p. 21.
45. Title henceforth abbreviated to *CR*.
46. *CR*, p. 510.
47. *CR*, p. 95.
48. *Symp.*, p. 97.
49. *CR*, p. 61.
50. *CR*, p. 4.
51. *CR*, p. 9.
52. *CR*, p. 86.
53. *CR*, p. 8.
54. *CR*, p. 376.
55. *Guided*, p. 161.

56. *CR*, p. 222.
57. *CR*, p. 246.
58. *CR*, p. 247.
59. *CR*, p. 509.
60. F. H. Cumbers (ed.), *Richmond College 1843–1943*, 1944, p. 113.
61. K. Cracknell, *Justice, Courtesy and Love*, 1995, p. 281.
62. J. H. Moulton, *Religions and Religion: A Study of the Science of Religion, Pure and Applied*, Fernley Lecture, 1913, pp. 94–5.
63. K. Cracknell, 'The Pioneering Work of J. H. Moulton', an unpublished lecture at Conference on The Contributions of Methodists to the Academic Study of Religions, Westminster College, 1994.
64. 'The World-Wide Mission of the Christian Church', *Apostolic Ministry*, XIV, 1910, p. 253.
65. For example, *MT*, 15 April 1909, p. 2, and 28 November 1912, p. 3, and *Apostolic Ministry*, p. 68.
66. *Guided*, p. 18.
67. *Apostolic Ministry*, p. 256.
68. *Apostolic Ministry*, p. 255.
69. Cracknell, *Justice, Courtesy and Love*, p. 53, quoting F. D. Maurice.
70. Moulton, *Religions*, pp. 95–6; Cracknell, *Justice, Courtesy and Love*, p. 282.
71. *Apostolic Ministry*, p. 276.
72. *Apostolic Ministry*, p. 274.
73. *Symp.*, p. 69.
74. *MT*, 22 April 1909, p. 1, reflecting his address to the Wesleyan Methodist Union for Social Service (WMUSS) meeting in Oxford on 13 April 1909.
75. *MT*, 23 July 1908, p. 596, and *Apostolic Ministry*, pp. 23–4.
76. *MT*, 7 October 1909, p. 2.
77. *MT*, 28 November 1907, p. 1029.
78. *Symp.*, p. 97.
79. *DNB* 1951–60: Lidgett.
80. For example, *MT*, 14 November 1907, p. 983.

6 Increasing responsibilities 1892–1905

1. *Rem.*, p. 37.
2. *Rem.*, p. 37.
3. *Guided*, pp. 225.
4. By Mrs Elizabeth Camp in her MS to me, 'A Bit about the Natal Lidgetts'.
5. *Guided*, p. 226.
6. For detailed accounts of the scene in Bermondsey and Lambeth, see Bartlett, 'Churches in Bermondsey', pp. 360, 364 and Chapter 10. See also J. Cox, *English Churches in a Secular Society*, New York, 1982, Chapter 5, e.g. pp. 159 and 173. Cox sketches the policies of Progressives and their opponents, and what they thought of one another, mainly but not only in Lambeth. Lidgett's writing did not repeat or rise to abuse.
7. *Rem.*, p. 38.

8. G. I. T. Machin, *Politics and the Churches in Great Britain 1869–1921*, Oxford, 1987, p. 38.
9. Machin, *Politics and the Churches*, p. 38.
10. Lidgett in *M.Rec.*, 6 February 1947, p. 9.
11. *Rem.*, p. 39.
12. Machin, *Politics*, p. 219.
13. *MT*, 15 November 1894, p. 777.
14. *The Idea of God and Social Ideals*, 1938, p. 101.
15. *Guided*, p. 177.
16. *Symp.*, p. 129, source unknown.
17. *Guided*, p. 40.
18. *M.Rec.*, 24 September 1936, p. 10.
19. *Guided*, pp. 174–5.
20. See *Final Report of the School Board for London 1870–1904*, in the London Metropolitan Archive, and *Guided*, p. 175.
21. *Guided*, p. 174.
22. *Guided*, p. 175. My italics.
23. *Guided*, p. 176.
24. Machin, *Politics and the Churches*, p. 229.
25. *M.Rec.*, 1 August 1901, p. 6.
26. *M.Rec.*, 6 February 1947, p. 9.
27. Currie, *Methodism Divided*, p. 178, and *HistMethGB3*, p. 139, n. 49.
28. H. D. Rack, *HistMethGB3*, pp. 137, 140. See Bartlett, 'Churches in Bermondsey', pp. 92 and 266.
29. H. P. Hughes, *Social Christianity*, 3rd edn, 1890, p. viii.
30. *Rem.*, p. 48.
31. See Terms.
32. See Terms.
33. See comment on Dinsdale Young in Chapter 2.
34. *M.Rec.*, 18 June 1903, p. 3.
35. John 17.11.
36. cf. *Guided*, p. 245.
37. *Rem.*, p. 45.
38. *M.Rec.*, 24 September 1936, p. 10.
39. *M.Rec.*, 24 September 1936, p. 10. J. Siddall Drummond in *C. A. Berry DD*, 1899, p. 113, recorded that date and Berry's absence.
40. Munson, *Nonconformists*, p. 169.
41. For example, in *Free Church Year Book, 1902*, p. 341.
42. R. E. Chadwick, 'Church and People in Bradford 1880–1914', unpublished Oxford DPhil thesis, 1986, p. 338, wrote that the majority of Christian social reformers envisaged a two-fold rule, the 'prophetic office' and the duty to educate, prepare and enjoin individual Christians to act in a personal capacity.
43. My italics.
44. See Chapter 1 about Anglican connections.
45. J. T. Smith, 'The Influence of Wesleyan Methodism on Elementary Education

in England in the Period 1849–1902, with Reference to the Work of J. H. Rigg', unpublished Hull PhD thesis, 1995, p. 64, and see J. T. Smith, *Methodism and Education 1849–1902*, Oxford, 1998.

46. *M.Rec.*, 1 August 1901, p. 12.
47. *Rem.*, p. 44.
48. *Rem.*, p. 48.
49. *Guided*, p. 185.
50. *Guided*, p. 184.
51. *Rem.*, p. 46.
52. D. L. Edwards, *Christian England*, 1984, vol. 3, p. 347.
53. *Symp.*, p. 135.
54. *Rem.*, p. 47. For background to London Government issues, see J. Davis, *Reforming London, the London Government Problem 1855–1900*, Oxford, 1988, and A. Saint and G. Darley, *Chronicles of London*, 1994.
55. *Rem.*, p. 48. The gap in the quotation in the text can be completed by reference to what was quoted earlier in this chapter, inserting: 'but had been content to follow, with reservations, the lead of Mr Hughes. Now I felt . . .'
56. *Guided*, p. 185.
57. *Guided*, p. 64.
58. *M.Rec.*, 23 July 1903, p. 33, and *Symp.*, p. 20.
59. *Rem.*, p. 49.
60. *MT*, 1 January 1903, p. 3.
61. *Rem.*, p. 44.
62. Rylands Library, MOU.III. 397.
63. *Guided*, p. 252.
64. S. Koss, *Nonconformity in Modern British Politics*, 1975, p. 59.

7 National Presidencies 1906–9

1. *Rem.*, p. 57.
2. *Politics and the Churches in Great Britain 1869–1921*, 1987, p. 275.
3. *Guided*, pp. 187–8.
4. Cf. Machin, *Politics*, p. 285.
5. *Guided*, pp. 191–3, omitted from *Reminiscences*, published in 1928.
6. RTD 120:356 and 358–9.
7. *Randall Davidson*, Oxford, 3rd edn, 1952, pp. 506–7.
8. RTD 493:134–5.
9. *Guided*, p. 252.
10. RTD 118:141–54.
11. RTD 120:358–60.
12. RTD 120:360–1.
13. RTD 120:367.
14. *Apostolic Ministry*, pp. 229–63.
15. *MT*, 15 March 1906, p. 165.
16. RTD 120:362.
17. *Guided*, pp. 252–3.

18. RTD 312:84.
19. RTD 312:102.
20. RTD 312:132–6 and 125–6.
21. RTD 312:135.
22. RTD 312:162.
23. RTD 312:169–70.
24. RTD 312:173.
25. *Bell Papers* 225ff.:181. *Guided*, pp. 190–1.
26. Davidson frequently retired to bed because of illness.
27. *Guided*, p. 253.
28. *Rem.*, p. 57.
29. *Guided*, p. 162.
30. *Rem.*, p. 63.
31. *MT*, 7 March 1907, p. 148.
32. *Rem.*, pp. 55–6. See Chapter 11 on the LCC.
33. Rylands Library, Lidgett's letters file, MAM.PLP.69.38.45–6.
34. *Guided*, p. 238.
35. J. T. Smith, 'Influence of Wesleyan Methodism on Elementary Education 1849–1902', details how Rigg, aided by Waller (Secretary of the Conference Education Committee), fervently supported denominational education, while Hughes upheld the Nonconformists' attack on the dual system and Anglican schools.
36. *Rem.*, p. 65.
37. *M.Rec.*, 16 July 1908, p. 3.
38. *Guided*, p. 238.
39. *MT*, 16 July 1908, p. 577.
40. See Chapter 14.
41. *Guided*, p. 163.
42. *Guided*, p. 238.
43. Elizabeth Sedman Lidgett (1843–1919) wrote *An Ancient People: A Short Sketch of Armenian History*, 1897.
44. For example, at the NCEFC meeting reported in *MT*, 8 March 1906, p. 149. See also *MT*, 15 September 1910, p. 2.
45. For example, *MT*, 1 August 1907, p. 662. Lidgett proudly told Bishop Bell (*Bell Papers* 225:184) that Davidson had congratulated him on his speech at the public meeting on 19 November 1909.
46. *M.Rec.*, 9 July 1908, p. 3.
47. *Guided*, p. 162.
48. *Rem.*, p. 68–9.
49. *Rem.*, p. 63.
50. *MT* report on 1 August 1907, p. 680.
51. 16 July 1908, p. 3.
52. Gooch was made an FBA in 1926, a CH in 1939 and gained the OM in 1963.
53. RTD 313:324.
54. RTD 314:255.
55. *Symp.*, p. 141.

56. *Rem.*, p. 66.
57. *Rem.*, p. 66.
58. *Apostolic Ministry*, pp. 130–56: 'The Ideals of National Education'.
59. *Rem.*, p. 65.
60. *Apostolic Ministry*, p. 19.
61. *Rem.*, p. 65.
62. *MT*, 21 March 1907, p. 193.
63. *Rem.*, p. 65.
64. Turner, *Conflict and Reconciliation*, p. 173.
65. *Rem.*, p. 65.
66. *Rem.*, p. 65.
67. *Rem.*, p. 68.
68. S. E. Keeble, editing WMUSS Conference Report, *Social Science and Social Service*, 1909, Preface, p. v.
69. *Apostolic Ministry*, p. 174.
70. *MT*, 14 November 1907.
71. *MT*, 9 December 1909, p. 6.
72. *MT*, 10 July 1913, p. 8.
73. D. P. Hughes, *H. P. Hughes*, 1904, p. 250.
74. *Guided*, p. 143.
75. *M.Rec.*, 16 July 1908, p. 3.
76. John 17.15–23.
77. *Apostolic Ministry*, pp. 227–8.
78. *Guided*, p. 234.
79. D. P. Campell, 'Methodism and Social Problems in the Inter-War Period 1918–1939', unpublished Oxford MLitt thesis, 1987, p. 33.
80. *MT*, 21 November 1907, p. 1005.
81. *Guided*, p. 239.
82. *HistMethGB3*, p. 354.
83. D. W. Bebbington, *The Nonconformist Conscience*, 1982, p. 158.
84. *Guided*, p. 240.
85. *Rem.*, p. 67.
86. *MT*, 26 November 1908, p. 948.
87. *Rem.*, p. 67.
88. *Rem.*, p. 68.
89. *MT*, 31 December 1908, p. 1043.
90. *M.Rec.*, 24 December 1908, p. 3.
91. *Rem.*, p. 67.
92. *Guided*, p. 240.
93. *MT*, 3 March 1910, p. 3.
94. *Rem.*, p. 68.
95. *MT*, 11 February 1909, pp. 1–2.
96. *MT*, 4 February 1909, p. 2.
97. *MT*, 4 March 1909, p. 1.
98. *MT*, 4 February 1909, p. 2, my italics.

99. *Apostolic Ministry*, e.g. pp. 210–13. *MT*, 11 March 1909, p. 1.

100. *Apostolic Ministry*, p. 178, and *MT*, 15 and 22 April 1909.

101. Campbell, 'Methodism and Social Problems in the Inter-War period 1918–1939', pp. 4, 15–16. *MT*, reporting Lidgett on 30 July 1908, p. 644, said: 'As a Union [WMUSS], they did not seek their principles from any political party'.

102. *MT*, 2 December 1909, p. 2. 'A Nonconformist Minister', writing *Nonconformity and Politics*, had already in 1909 objected to corporate Church involvement in politics, but supported individual participation. See also *MT*, 4 February 1909, pp. 1–2.

103. *MT*, 9 December 1909, p. 3.

104. *MT*, 23 December 1909, p. 4.

105. Bell, *Davidson*, 1952, pp. 598–602.

106. Koss, *Nonconformity*, 1975, p. 106.

107. *Guided*, p. 238.

108. *Guided*, p. 239.

109. *MT*, 20 May 1909, p. 3.

110. *MT*, 4 March 1909, Personalia, p. 3.

111. *Rem.*, p. 69.

8 Progress despite conflict

1. *Guided*, pp. 233–4 and 241.

2. For example, *MT*, 23 June 1910, p. 2; 20 and 27 October 1910, both p. 3.

3. *Rem.*, p. 71.

4. *MT*, 23 June 1910, p. 3.

5. *MT*, 21 July 1910, p. 19.

6. *Minutes of Evidence Taken before the Royal Commission on Divorce and Matrimonial Causes*, vol. 3, 1912, Cd. 6481, reporting minutes taken on 29 November 1910, paras 39.718–80.

7. *MT*, 1 December 1910, p. 3.

8. *MT*, 5 December 1912, p. 2.

9. *MT*, 1 August 1912, p. 2.

10. *MT*, 26 June 1913, p. 3.

11. W. F. Howard in Brash and Wright (eds), *Didsbury College Centenary*, pp. 127–8.

12. W. J. Shiels (ed.), *Studies in Church History 21, Persecution and Toleration*, Oxford, 1984, p. 430.

13. *MT*, 19 June 1913, p. 3, and see *MT*, 17 July 1913, p. 3.

14. For example, *MT*, 23 May 1907, p. 409.

15. Ten heresy charges were made against Wesleyan ministers between 1913 and 1920 by Morton alone, as recorded by S. P. Mews, 'Religion and English Society in the First World War', unpublished Cambridge PhD thesis, 1973, p. 310.

16. Bebbington, 'Persecution of George Jackson', p. 429.

17. President 1897, died 1925.

18. President 1904, died 1917.

19. *MT*, 23 July 1914, p. 17.

20. *M.Rec.*, 27 January 1938, p. 4.
21. *MT*, 19 November 1914, p. 8.
22. G. S. Wakefield, *R. N. Flew*, 1917, pp. 41–3.
23. Bebbington, 'Persecution of George Jackson', p. 433.
24. See also 'A Londoner's Notebook', *MT*, 18 July 1918, p. 3.
25. *Guided*, pp. 234–8. *Rem.*, pp. 73–5.
26. *Guided*, p. 95.
27. Her father was 'an active member of the Established Church' (*Guided*, p. 96).
28. *Guided*, p. 235.
29. Bell, *Disestablishment in Ireland and Wales*, 1969, p. 245.
30. Henry Simpson Lunn, *Chapters from My Life with Special Reference to Reunion*, 1918, pp. 299ff. and 302.
31. *Guided*, pp. 236–7.
32. Letter of 4 April 1911, quoted in J. Marchant, *Dr John Clifford*, 1924, p. 60.
33. D. W. Bebbington, *The Nonconformist Conscience*, 1982, p. 151.
34. RTD 318:99–100.
35. *MT*, 5 June 1913, p. 2.
36. See Lidgett's eulogy in A. Compton-Rickett (ed.), *Joseph Compton-Rickett*, Bournemouth, 1922, pp. 50–6.
37. *MT*, 27 March 1913, p. 2.
38. *BW*, 10 April 1913, p. 25.
39. *MT*, 17 April 1913, p. 2, and 24 April 1913, p. 3.
40. *Guided*, p. 200.
41. Douglas White's Synopsis of the Final Report, authorised by the Royal Commission Chairman, National Council for Combating Venereal Diseases.
42. Douglas White's Synopsis of the Final Report, p. 59.

9 Theology and optimism before and after 1914

1. Numbers in the Methodist Churches overall peaked at 894,179 in 1907, thereafter slowly but steadily beginning to fall (Edmondson, 'Doctrines of Hell', Table 2).
2. *MT*, 3 July 1913, p. 2.
3. *MT*, 20 August 1914, p. 4.
4. *MT*, 18 December 1913, p. 3.
5. W. Temple, *The Faith and Modern Thought*, 1910, pp. 136–7.
6. Hinchliff, *God and History*, p. 223.
7. Neville Talbot, in B. H. Streeter (ed.), *Foundations: A Statement of Christian Belief in Terms of Modern Thought by Seven Oxford Men*, 1912, p. 7.
8. Talbot, in Streeter (ed.), *Foundations*, pp. 7 and 9.
9. Talbot, in Streeter (ed.), *Foundations*, p. 8.
10. Talbot, in Streeter (ed.), *Foundations*, p. 6.
11. Talbot, in Streeter (ed.), *Foundations*, p. 8.
12. Talbot's Essay Synopsis, p. 2, referring to pp. 22ff.
13. Fr J. N. Figgis uttered similar warnings.
14. *MT*, 18 December 1913.
15. Trans W. Montgomery.

16. *M.Rec.*, 8 August 1974, p. 11.
17. *Guided*, pp. 152–3.
18. See next chapter.
19. *MT*, 2 August 1917, p. 9, reporting the *Contemporary Review* of August 1917.
20. *Rem.*, p. 69.
21. Not 1925, as Rupp in *Symp.*, p. 98.
22. *GCJ*, p. 379.
23. *GCJ*, pp. 379–80.
24. *GCJ*, p. 367.
25. Interview on 14 August 1993 with Mrs Libby Fairweather who visited Lettice in her final years.
26. *Guided*, pp. 131–2; *M.Rec.*, 11 April 1918, p. 5, *MT*, 11 April 1918, p. 4.
27. Enclosed in letter to Bishop Bell (*Bell Papers*, 225ff.:176–191) on 21 January 1931.
28. Reported to me orally by Mrs Fairweather on 14 August 1993.
29. Hebrews 2.10.
30. *Symp.*, p. 68.
31. *Apostolic Ministry*, pp. 73–88, preached on 20 June 1909.
32. *Guided*, p. 56.
33. See Rupp, *Symp.*, p. 98.
34. For example, T. C. Edwards, *Epistle to the Hebrews*, 1888; G. Milligan, *Theology of the Epistle to the Hebrews*, 1899; R. W. Dale, *Lectures on the Ephesians*, 1900; C. Gore, *St Paul's Epistle to the Ephesians*, 1898 and 1907; W. R. Nicoll (ed.), J. Parker, *The Epistle to the Ephesians*, 1904.
35. G. Findlay, *Epistle to the Ephesians*, 1892.
36. *M.Rec.*, 17 November 1921, p. 13.
37. *MT*, 20 October 1921, p. 3.
38. *Guided*, p. 161.
39. *MT*, 8 July 1915, p. 7.
40. *S&S*, Preface, p. 8. My italics.
41. *Symp.*, p. 98.
42. 'Lidgett': *DNB 1951–60*.
43. See Chapter 1, n. 82, and *London Quarterly Review*, April 1956, p. 137.
44. *MT*, 8 July 1915, p. 7.
45. *MT*, 20 October 1921, p. 3.
46. *Wesleyan Methodist Magazine*, January 1922, p. 5.
47. *GCJ*, p. 95.
48. *GCJ*, p. 242.
49. *GCJ*, p. 243.
50. *GCJ*, p. 73.
51. *GCJ*, p. 75.
52. *GCJ*, p. 105.
53. Ephesians 1.10.
54. Cf. *Symp.*, pp. 187–8.
55. *GCJ*, p. 374.

56. *GCJ*, p. 369.
57. *GCJ*, pp. 375–8.
58. *GCJ*, p. 378.
59. *GCJ*, p. 376.
60. *GCJ*, p. 374.
61. Rupp, *Symp.*, p. 99.
62. *MT*, 20 October 1921, p. 3.
63. *S&S*, p. 259.
64. *S&S*, p. 269.
65. *S&S*, p. 259.
66. *S&S*, p. 269.
67. *S&S*, p. 259.
68. *Rem.*, p. 81.
69. *S&S*, p. 255.
70. John 14.9.
71. *S&S*, Preface, p. 8.
72. Barth is mentioned in chs 10 ('Religion and Reason') and 15 ('The Spiritual Basis of Natural Law') of Lidgett's *God and the World*, 1943, and Otto in ch. 10.

10 Spokesman, commentator and politician 1914–20

1. W. Y. Fullerton, *F. B. Meyer: A Biography*, London and Edinburgh, 1929. For Meyer's pietist-cum-activist representation of the Social Gospel see I. M. Randall, 'The Social Gospel: A Case Study', in John Wolffe (ed.), *Evangelical Faith and Public Zeal*, 1995, pp. 155–74.
2. *The Best I Remember*, 1922, p. 241. Nor is there any reference to Lidgett in Darlow's biography of W. R. Nicoll.
3. *MT*, 3 September 1914, p. 5.
4. *Rem.*, p. 75.
5. A. J. P. Taylor, *English History 1914–1945*, Oxford, 1965, p. 28, n. 3; Munson, *Nonconformists*, p. 75; Edwards, *Christian England*, vol. 3, p. 271.
6. *Rem.*, p. 76.
7. *MT*, 1 October 1914, p. 4.
8. *MT*, 29 October 1914, p. 3.
9. Bell, *Davidson*, p. 741.
10. *Guided*, pp. 253–4; Bell, *Davidson*, p. 743.
11. *BW*, 1 October 1914, p. 5.
12. *MT*, 21 January 1915, p. 8.
13. Hinchliff, *God and History*, p. 247.
14. S. P. Mews, 'Spiritual Mobilisation in the First World War', *Theology*, June 1971, pp. 259–60.
15. A. F. Winnington-Ingram, *The Potter and the Clay*, collected addresses, 1917, IV, e.g. p. 42.
16. *HistMethGB3*, p. 357.
17. F. D. Maurice, *Sermons on the Sabbath Day*, 1853, pp. 94–5, quoted by Mews, in *Theology*, June 1971, p. 260.

18. *S. E .Keeble, the Rejected Prophet* (Wesley Historical Society, 1977), p. 39.
19. Bell, *Davidson*, p. 744.
20. *MT*, 10 December 1914, p. 3, and 17 December 1914, p. 3.
21. He compared the German attitude to the State unfavourably with that in England: evangelical pietism in Germany 'has never safeguarded the rights of individuality against the omnipotence of the State'; as 'the servant and not the critic of State authority', it has 'supplied the Court preacher, not the prophet of the people' (*MT*, 11 February 1915, p. 3).
22. *MT*, 6 January 1916, p. 8.
23. *MT*, 11 May 1916, p. 8.
24. *MT*, 13 December 1917, p. 6.
25. M. S. Edwards, *S. E. Keeble*, 1977, p. 40.
26. Edwards, *S. E. Keeble*, pp. 40, 43.
27. Edwards, *S. E. Keeble*, p. 41.
28. *Rem.*, pp. 76–7.
29. John Thompson, 'The Free Church Army Chaplain 1830–1930', unpublished Sheffield PhD thesis, 1990, to which I owe many details given below.
30. Thompson, 'Free Church Army Chaplain', pp. 293–9.
31. See Chapter 16 on 'Free Churches and Union'.
32. Thompson, 'The Free Church Army Chaplain', p. 301.
33. For example, Chapter 14, and *MT*, 7 March 1918, p. 3.
34. *Guided*, p. 255.
35. *Guided*, p. 253.
36. For example, Thompson, 'The Free Church Army Chaplain', p. 314ff., and, e.g., Edwards, *Christian England*, vol. 3, p. 359.
37. Thompson, 'The Free Church Army Chaplain', pp. 305–8.
38. Thompson, 'The Free Church Army Chaplain', pp. 439–45.
39. Cf. the 1919 reports of five Anglican Committees of Inquiry, and the YMCA-financed report, 'The Army and Religion', mentioned by Edwards, *Christian England*, vol. 3, pp. 362ff.
40. See Chapter 17.
41. RTD 377:200–18.
42. RTD 358:290ff.
43. RTD 358:191.
44. RTD 358:207.
45. *MT*, 29 April 1915, p. 8.
46. Bell, *Davidson*, pp. 749–50.
47. For example, in Bermondsey; on Divorce; Conference membership, etc.
48. *MT*, 28 March 1918, p. 6.
49. Bell, *Davidson*, p. 749.
50. S. P. Mews, 'Drink and Disestablishment', in *Studies in Church History*, vol.16 (1979), pp. 449–76.
51. Mews, 'Drink and Disestablishment', p. 470.
52. B. C. Addison, *Four and a Half Years*, 1934, vol. 1, p. 73.
53. Michael Edwards, 'S. E. Keeble and Nonconformist Social Thinking

1880–1939', unpublished Bristol University MLitt thesis (1969), e.g. p. 271, and Michael Edwards's letter to me on 31 July 1992.

54. Cf. Munson, *Nonconformists*, p. 218; J. E. P. Grigg, *Lloyd George: From Peace to War 1912–1916*, 1985, p. 84; and Hastings, *History of English Christianity*, p. 122.

55. *MT*, 2 August 1917, p. 5.

56. *MT*, 8 November 1917, p. 6.

57. *MT*, 12 September 1918, p. 6.

58. *MT*, 12 December 1918, p. 6.

59. Viscount Bryce's Papers, New Bodleian Library, Oxford.

11 Progressives' politician in the LCC 1904–28

1. See Chapter 6.
2. *Guided*, p. 180.
3. LCC Education Committee Minutes 27 April 1904, p. 723. This chapter draws on the Minutes of the LCC, its weekly meetings principally of its Education Committee and subcommittees, as deposited in the London Metropolitan Archive, which are then checked against Lidgett's autobiographies.
4. *Guided*, p. 183.
5. *Guided*, p. 182.
6. My italics.
7. Percy Harris, a fellow Progressive, *London and Its Government*, rev. edn, 1931, p. 79.
8. *Guided*, p. 208.
9. Harris, *London and Its Government*, 1913, p. 70.
10. LCC Education Committee Minutes, 3 April 1917, p. 308.
11. *Guided*, p. 210.
12. *Rem.*, p. 56.
13. *Guided*, p. 211.
14. *MT*, 13 June 1918, p. 6.
15. *Guided*, p. 196.
16. Thomas, 'J. Scott Lidgett', p. 367, and *Free Church Chronicle*, November 1919.
17. *MT*, 13 June 1918, p. 6.
18. *MT*, 14 February 1918, p. 6.
19. Campbell, 'Methodism and Social Problems 1918–1939', p. 27.
20. *Rem.*, p. 83.
21. *Guided*, p. 212.
22. Harris, *Forty Years*, pp. 88–9.
23. Detailed LCC election figures are given in Appendix 3.
24. *Guided*, p. 212.
25. *Rem.*, p. 83.
26. *Rem.*, p. 85.
27. *Rem.*, p. 83.
28. *Guided*, p. 221.
29. See below.
30. *Guided*, p. 197.

31. *Rem.*, pp. 86–7; *Guided*, pp. 197–8 and 221–2.
32. *Rem.*, p. 87.
33. *MT*, 14 February 1918.
34. *Guided*, p. 198.
35. Gibbon and Bell, *History of the LCC*, 1939, p. 111, n. 1.
36. *Rem.*, p. 88.
37. See Chapter 19.
38. *Rem.*, p. 88.
39. See Appendix 3 for election figures.
40. LCC Education Committee Minutes, 3 May 1922, pp. 503ff.
41. LCC Minutes, 14 March 1922, p. 333.
42. Vice-President 1948–53 (*British Journal of Nursing*, July 1953). In the 1920s he also became Chairman of the Central Council for the Social Welfare of Women and Girls in London. He was replaced as late as 8 November 1949.
43. *Guided*, p. 272.
44. *Guided*, p. 138.
45. Harris, *Forty Years*, p. 90.
46. *Rem.*, p. 89.
47. For ecumenical aspects see Chapter 21 on the 'Results and Personalities of the Lambeth Appeal'.
48. *Guided*, p. 257.
49. *Rem.*, p. 90.
50. *MT*, 28 February 1918, p. 6.
51. See Chapter 22 about Council of Action and Lidgett's attitude to socialism.
52. South London Press on 18 June 1953.
53. See Chapter 26 and *The Idea of God and Social Ideals*, 1938, pp. 107 and 109.
54. South London Press, 19 June 1953, p. 8.
55. Harris, *Forty Years*, p. 102.
56. Lidgett, *Idea of God*, p. 109.
57. Lidgett, *Idea of God*, p. 109.
58. Harris, *Forty Years*, p. 90.
59. *Guided*, pp. 224–5.
60. *Guided*, p. 225.
61. *Guided*, p. 226.
62. See Chapter 12.
63. See Chapter 22.
64. Harris, *Forty Years*, p. 88. My italics.
65. D. H. Thomas, thesis, 'J. Scott Lidgett', p. 266.
66. *Rem.*, p. 89.
67. Harris, *Forty Years*, p. 90.
68. *Guided*, p. 227.
69. *Guided*, p. 177. Percy Harris ascribed the Progressives' retention of power in the LCC until 1907 to their overall unity, avoiding serious sectional differences (*London and Its Government*, p. 48).

12 University politician and Vice-Chancellor 1922–46

1. Both colleges received a Charter as the University of London in 1836.
2. *Symp.*, p. 168.
3. *Rem.*, p.13; *Guided*, p. 42.
4. *Symp.*, p. 13.
5. *Guided*, pp. 42–3.
6. *Rem.*, p. 14.
7. H. H. Bellot, *University College, London, 1826–1926*, 1929, p. 323. See also Bellot, *University of London: A History 1890–*, 1969.
8. Lidgett said two conflicts raged at the time (*Guided*, p. 148). The Association School was overthrown later by Neo-Hegelianism through T. H. Green and the Cairds. Robertson Smith played the most prominent British part in the other (violent) controversy over Higher Criticism.
9. Negly Harte and John North, *The World of University College, London, 1823–1990*, 1991, p. 106. See also Harte, *University of London 1836–1986: An Illustrated History*, 1986.
10. Bellot, *University College, London*, p. 323.
11. *Guided*, pp. 42–4.
12. See also Chapter 1.
13. *Guided*, p. 46. *Rem.*, p. 14.
14. Harte, *University of London 1836–1986*, p. 195.
15. *Guided*, p. 200. The major source for Lidgett's career in the Senate, apart from those supplied by the autobiographies and the Senate Minutes, is the essay by Eric Waterhouse, formerly Principal of Richmond College, Surrey, in Rupert Davies's *Symposium*. Waterhouse, appointed to the Senate to represent the university's teachers of Divinity in 1928, is therefore both an invaluable, though not infallible, eyewitness of its proceedings and a well-informed commentator on the development of the university in general. Both his and Lidgett's statements have been amplified and checked by the Senate Minutes, notably about 1927–33 (2/2/44, 45, 46, 47, 48, 49), the University Calendar 1952/3, and other records in the University of London Archive.
16. *Guided*, pp. 91, 94–6.
17. *Guided*, p. 200.
18. *Symp.*, p. 173.
19. *Symp.*, p. 174.
20. *Guided*, p. 202.
21. *Symp.*, p. 171.
22. *Symp.*, p. 176.
23. *Symp.*, p. 177.
24. *Guided*, p. 201.
25. *Guided*, p. 201, and University of London Archive FG 5/4.
26. Harte, *University of London 1836–1986*, p. 218.
27. *Guided*, p. 201.
28. *Guided*, pp. 201–2.

29. For Lidgett's involvement in such a ceremony, see photograph taken at the annual Founder's Day on 28 November 1930, included in the University of London Archive FG 5/3.
30. *Guided*, p. 202.
31. *Symp.*, p. 177.
32. University of London Archive FG 5/5.
33. These are listed in *Symp.*, pp. 180–1.
34. Lunn in Lang Papers, 120:233.
35. *Guided*, p. 205.
36. *Guided*, p. 205.
37. British Library, Add.68923.f205, Lidgett's letter to Sir George Hill on 17 January 1934.
38. *Guided*, p. 206; *Symp.*, p. 179.
39. *Guided*, p. 196.
40. *Apostolic Ministry*, p. 151.
41. F. C. Pritchard, in *Symp.*, p. 145.
42. *Symp.*, pp. 143–4.
43. *Symp.*, p. 146.
44. *Symp.*, p. 176; *M.Rec.*, 12 December 1946, p. 13; and see Chapters 25 and 26.

13 Educationalist: The national education scene 1919–44

1. See Chapter 6 above.
2. Bell, *Davidson*, pp. 1125–6.
3. Thomas, 'J. Scott Lidgett', p. 369.
4. *Symp.*, pp. 200–1.
5. *Guided*, p. 199.
6. G. I. T. Machin, *The Churches and Social Issues in Twentieth Century Britain*, Oxford, 1998, p. 78.
7. F. C. Pritchard, in *Symp.*, pp. 113–14.
8. *Guided*, p. 195, cf. *Symp.*, pp. 147–8.
9. Cf. R. A. Butler's *The Art of the Possible*, 1971, pp. 99–100.
10. *Apostolic Ministry*, p. 71.
11. *Symp.*, p. 150.
12. *Symp.*, p. 149.
13. *Symp.*, p. 150.
14. See *Symp.*, pp. 148–9.
15. J. G. Lockhart, *Cosmo Gordon Lang*, 1949, p. 368.
16. *Symp.*, pp. 151–2.
17. *Symp.*, p. 152.
18. See references to Archbishop Fisher in Chapters 22, 25 and 30.
19. Turner, *Conflict and Reconciliation*, p. 142.

14 Moves towards Methodist Union

1. Hereafter called 'Ecumenical'.
2. Quoted by H. D. Rack, *The Future of John Wesley's Methodism*, 1965, p. 40.
3. Townsend, Workman and Eayrs (eds), *New History of Methodism*, vol. 2, p. 221.
4. Townsend, Workman and Eayrs (eds), *New History of Methodism*, vol. 2, pp. 469–70.
5. Wesleyan Conference President 1891. W. J. Townsend, *The Story of Methodist Union*, *c.*1906, pp. 126–36, summarised speeches in 1891 and 1901.
6. Wesleyan Conference Secretary 1910–16, President 1917.
7. *MT*, 26 October 1911, p. 3.
8. *MT*, 2 November 1911, p. 4.
9. *Guided*, p. 228.
10. *Guided*, p. 163.
11. *HistMethGB3*, p. 325.
12. *Guided*, p. 263.
13. Lunn, *Chapters from My Life*, p. 325.
14. Mews, 'Religion and English Society', p. 308.
15. cf. D. Edwards, *Christian England*, vol. 3, comment on H. P. Hughes on p. 268.
16. *MT*, 18 July 1918, p. 3.
17. *MT*, 10 October 1918, p. 3.
18. *MT*, 10 October 1918, p. 3.
19. *MT*, 7 March 1918, p. 3.
20. *MT*, 7 March 1907, p. 145.
21. *MT*, 18 July 1918, p. 3.
22. *MT*, 21 October 1909, p. 1.
23. *Guided*, p. 163, and *M.Rec.*, 24 July 1924, p. 6.
24. The summary reflects Lidgett's views over several years, including their often forthright expression.
25. Townsend, Workman and Eayrs (eds), *New History of Methodism*, vol. 2, p. 421.
26. *MT*, 6 March 1913, p. 3.
27. D. Carter, *James H. Rigg*, 1994, pp. 25–6.
28. *MT*, 12 September 1918, p. 3.
29. Cf. also *M.Rec.*, 21 April 1921.
30. My italics.
31. *MT*, 7 October 1909, p. 3.
32. Esp. vol. 2, pp. 417ff.
33. *Guided*, p. 264.
34. *Guided*, p. 264.
35. RTD 132:212.
36. *Guided*, p. 264.
37. I am indebted here and in Chapter 23 to R. Currie in *Methodism Divided*, 1968, for much helpful comment.

38. Currie, *Methodism Divided*, p. 252.
39. See Chapter 16.
40. Mews, 'Religion and Society', p. 309.
41. *HistMethGB3*, p. 337, and see *MT*, 10 October 1918, p. 4.
42. Currie, *Methodism Divided*, pp. 253–8, provides more details on the evolution of the 'Tentative Scheme of 1920', and J. M. Turner in *HistMethGB3*, pp. 333ff. helpfully surveys the whole debate.
43. *Methodist Union*, 1920.
44. *MT*, 10 October 1918.
45. Townsend, Workman and Eayrs (eds), *New History of Methodism*, vol. 2, p. 421.
46. Currie, *Methodism Divided*, pp. 165–6.

15 Methodism and the Church of England

1. *MT*, 25 November 1915, p. 3.
2. Rack, *Future of Wesley's Methodism*, pp. 46–7.
3. *MT*, 30 January 1913, p. 3.
4. For example, Chapter 1.
5. For example, *MT*, 19 May 1910, p. 2. See Chapter 8.
6. *MT*, 2 December 1915, p. 3.
7. *HistMethGB3*, p. 220.
8. *MT*, 11 November 1915, p. 3.
9. Quoted by D. P. Hughes, *H. P. Hughes*, p. 483.
10. *HistMethGB3*, p. 154.
11. Munson, *Nonconformists*, p. 255.
12. Chapter 8.
13. cf. *MT*, 30 January 1913, p. 3.
14. *MT*, 28 October 1915, p. 3.
15. Chapter 16.
16. *Guided*, p. 25, and Chapter 1.
17. RTD 261:288.
18. RTD 261:92, and Bell Papers 225:185–6.
19. *Guided*, pp. 255–6.
20. Mews, 'Religion and English Society', p. 309.
21. *Guided*, p. 255.
22. RTD 261:92.
23. *Guided* p. 256.
24. RTD 261:90.
25. RTD 261:93.
26. *MT*, 5 July 1917, p. 6.
27. Mews, 'Religion and English Society', p. 307. Currie, *Methodism Divided*, p. 252.
28. *M.Rec.*, 2 August 1917, p. 9.
29. Lunn, *Chapters from My Life*, p. 322–3.
30. Mews, 'Religion and English Society', p. 306, and Currie, *Methodism Divided*, p. 251.

31. Letter to Lidgett on 22 July 1917 (Methodist Archives in Rylands Library, PLP 71.14.1).
32. Henry Simpson Lunn, *Nearing Harbour*, 1934, p. 162.
33. Lunn, *Chapters from My Life*, p. 344. See also Lunn, *Nearing Harbour*, p. 162.
34. *M.Rec.*, 2 August 1917, p. 9.
35. *M.Rec.*, 2 August 1917, p. 5.
36. *MT*, 2 August 1917, p. 9.
37. RTD 261:196.
38. RTD 261:194.
39. RTD 261:198.
40. Chapter 17.

16 The Free Churches and Union

1. Munson, *Nonconformists*, p.173.
2. D. W. Bebbington, *The Nonconformist Conscience*, pp. 69–70, 80.
3. *Apostolic Ministry*, pp. 15–16.
4. RTD 162:381–5.
5. *Congregational Union Year Book, 1902*, p. 19.
6. Munson, *Nonconformists*, p. 174.
7. Lidgett's autobiographies give an incomplete account: *Rem.*, p. 77, referring to 1913, confused Shakespeare's proposal with the 1913 Free Church Commission; *Guided*, p. 241, referred solely to 1916.
8. *Symp.*, p. 206, dated Lidgett's support to 1912.
9. *MT*, 16 March 1911, p. 6.
10. RTD 162:386–9.
11. See Chapter 8.
12. *MT*, 20 March 1913, p. 10. Cf. Report in *Free Church Year Book* (*FCYB*), 1913, pp. 91–5.
13. *FCYB*, 1914, p. 15.
14. See Chapter 10.
15. *Rem.*, p. 77.
16. *MT*, 16 March 1916, p. 3.
17. RTD 261:69–72.
18. J. M. Turner, in *HistMethGB3*, p. 343, and *Conflict and Reconciliation*, p. 176.
19. *Rem.*, p. 77.
20. *Rem.*, p. 78, refers to two (the first-mentioned) committees.
21. *MT*, 28 September 1916, p. 3.
22. *Symp.*, p.206.
23. The Wesleyan/Anglican Lunn called such a hardened dualism 'the pathway . . . to war' (*Chapters from My Life*, p. 336).
24. *Symp.*, p. 206.
25. *Rem.*, p. 78.
26. *MT*, 17 August 1916, p. 3.
27. *Guided*, pp. 163–4.
28. A. Wilkinson, *The Church of England and the First World War*, 1978, p. 263.

29. *MT*, 7 December 1916, p. 3.
30. See Chapter 17.
31. Bell Papers 214:179ff.
32. *Rem.*, p. 79.
33. RTD 261:81–8.
34. RTD 261:91.
35. Chapter 14.
36. RTD 261:96.
37. Bell Papers 190:151–5.
38. RTD 318:369.
39. RTD 318:392–5.
40. RTD 261:164–5.
41. But see Munson, *Nonconformists*, p. 75, for a different view.
42. Chapter 17.
43. J. H. Shakespeare, *The Churches at the Cross Roads*, 1918; *BW*, 5 December 1918, p. 1.
44. *MT*, 7 November 1918.
45. *BW*, 3 April 1919, p. 3.
46. *Church Times*, 1 April 1920, p. 343.
47. *BW*, 25 March 1920, pp. 566–7, esp. p. 567.

17 Faith and Order, Anglicans and Free Churchmen 1910–20

1. *Contemporary Review*, October 1920, p. 466.
2. I am indebted in this and the following section to unpublished lectures by the late Professor P. B. Hinchliff; A. M. G. Stephenson, *Anglicanism and the Lambeth Conferences*, 1978, p. 84; H. G. G. Herklots, *Church Quarterly Review*, 169, 1968; L. A. Haselmayer, *Lambeth and Unity*, New York, 1948.
3. My italics.
4. J. F. Woolverton, *Church History*, American Society of Church History, June 1970.
5. *Minutes*, 1890, pp. 302–3, a letter written by W. F. Moulton as President of the Wesleyan Conference that year.
6. See Chapter 18.
7. *MT*, 29 April 1915, p. 8.
8. RTD 270:265, 270–3, 274–6, 285–7.
9. RTD 270:180–1.
10. RTD 270:198–200.
11. *MT*, 18 December 1913, p. 2.
12. *Rem.*, p. 78.
13. *Daily Chronicle*, 10 January 1914, p. 5.
14. *M.Rec.*, 13 October 1949, p. 3.
15. RTD 270:299–302.
16. Kennion's letter to Davidson, RTD 270:299, on 18 November 1915.
17. RTD 270:308–10.
18. *Guided*, pp. 243–4.

19. *MT*, 5 September 1918, Editorial.
20. *Rem.*, p. 79.
21. *Tatlow Correspondence* 1912–1937, vol. 1794, Lambeth Palace, 185, 188.
22. *Guided*, p. 244, mistakenly adding meetings in London to those in Oxford.
23. 1919.
24. RTD 261:253.
25. RTD 261:129.
26. Despite *Guided*, p. 245, T. R. Glover (Baptist) was not involved.
27. Later reprinted among Lidgett's articles, *God, Christ and the Church*.
28. *Towards Reunion*, p. xix.
29. *Guided*, p. 245.
30. Printed as Appendix to *Towards Reunion*.
31. Quotations in this paragraph are taken from *Towards Reunion*, pp. xvi–xviii.
32. *MT*, 14 March 1918, p. 6.
33. *Contemporary Review*, March 1918, pp. 295–300, especially p. 300.
34. *MT*, 20 June 1918, p. 3.
35. *Guided*, p. 245.
36. RTD 261:166–7.
37. RTD 261:314.
38. RTD 261:315.
39. RTD 261:309.
40. RTD 261:354–7.
41. RTD 261:357 and 360ff.
42. The Bishop of Birmingham told Davidson (RTD 261:404) on 30 October 1920 that Anglicans should be fostering union within *their own* Church.
43. H. D. Rack, *Future of John Wesley's Methodism*, 1965, p. 49.
44. *MT*, 27 September 1917, p. 6.
45. *MT*, 20 June 1918, p. 3.
46. RTD 261:246.
47. RTD 261:129.
48. RTD 261:250.
49. RTD 261:132.
50. RTD 261:133.
51. RTD 261:243.
52. RTD 261:222–6, and 233.
53. RTD 261:138–49.
54. RTD 261:163.
55. RTD 261:289, dated 30 October 1919.
56. RTD 261:283–4.
57. RTD 261:289–90.
58. RTD 261:288.
59. RTD 261:295, n.d.
60. RTD 261:97–100.
61. RTD 261:123–5.
62. RTD 261:116 and 125.

63. *MT*, 6 July 1911, p. 2.
64. RTD 261:46–8, 60–4.
65. *Hereford Times*, 19 June 1953, p. 6.
66. RTD 261:174–7.
67. RTD 261:178.
68. RTD:LC 134:248.
69. RTD 261:170–2 and 321.
70. RTD 261:321.
71. A. Wilkinson, *Church of England and the First World War*, 1978, p. 325, n. 58.
72. RTD 261:180–91.
73. RTD 261:160–2.
74. RTD 261:333.
75. RTD 261:335–7.
76. RTD:LC 134:221–9, Lidgett on the Council of the Churches, *Contemporary Review*, December 1916; 236–41, Lidgett in *Contemporary Review*, May 1920; 234–5, Federal Council Statement; 299–300, letter from Vernon Bartlett; 304–5, letter from Henry Lunn.

18 The Lambeth Appeal to All Christian People, August 1920

1. *Guided*, p. 245.
2. Quoted in *Symp.*, p. 206.
3. Hinchliff's phrase.
4. Talbot's words.
5. *M.Rec.*, 19 August 1920, p. 5.
6. *Contemporary Review*, October 1920, p. 472.
7. *Rem.*, p. 80.
8. RTD VI.58.
9. *Guided*, pp. 245–6.
10. *M.Rec.*, 19 August 1920, p. 5, and see 16 September 1920, p. 5 (account of Lidgett's talk at Guildford).
11. See also *M.Rec.*, 21 April 1921, article on 'Synods and Methodist Union'.
12. *Contemporary Review*, October 1920, p. 469.
13. *Contemporary Review*, October 1920, p. 472.
14. Quotations all from *Contemporary Review*, October 1920, pp. 474–5. My emphasis.
15. *HistMethGB3*, p. 345.
16. *Church Quarterly*, 1, 1968–9, p. 32.

19 Anglican/Free Church discussions 1920–5

1. Bell, *Documents*, vol. 1, Oxford, 1924, pp. 118–20.
2. RTD 261:372.
3. RTD 261:379–89.
4. RTD 261:390.
5. RTD 262:9–16, 28.

6. RTD 262:49.
7. Bell, *Documents*, 1920–4, vol. 1, 41, pp. 120–41.
8. For example, RTD 262:132.
9. *Guided*, p. 246.
10. RTD 262:143.
11. Bell, *Davidson*, p. 1116–7.
12. RTD 262:112.
13. RTD 264:337.
14. RTD 262:112–114, on 16 June 1921.
15. Hastings, *History of English Christianity*, p. 200.
16. RTD 201:130–1.
17. Lockhart, *Cosmo Gordon Lang*, p. 275.
18. RTD 262:242.
19. RTD 262:228.
20. RTD 262:160.
21. RTD 262:328.
22. Lockhart, *Cosmo Gordon Lang*, pp. 275–6.
23. Bell, *Documents*, vol. 1.44, pp. 143–51.
24. See also Chapter 23.
25. RTD 263:131, and Bell, *Documents*, vol. 1.45, pp. 151–5.
26. Bell, *Documents*, vol. 2.120, pp. 73–7.
27. RTD 264:343.
28. Peake, *Plain Thoughts on Great Subjects*, n.d., p. 50.
29. Bell, *Documents*, vol. 1.46, pp. 156–63.
30. *Journal of Presbyterian Historical Society*, 9.1, 1948–52, May 1948, pp. 3–9.
31. Stephenson, *E. S. Talbot*, 1936, p. 261.
32. Turner, *Conflict and Reconciliation*, p. 187.
33. RTD 264:55.
34. Bell, *Documents*, vol. 1.47, pp. 164–9.
35. Bell, *Documents*, vol. 2.121, pp. 77–85.
36. Bell, *Davidson*, p. 1121.
37. RTD 264:349.
38. RTD 264:338–41.
39. RTD 264:338–41.
40. Bell, *Documents*, vol. 2.126, pp. 98–102; and RTD 264:338.
41. RTD 264:349–50.
42. Lidgett's emphasis.
43. *Guided*, p. 247.
44. *Guided*, p. 249.
45. My italics.
46. RTD 264:83–4.
47. The italics are mine.

20 Other ecumenical events 1920–9

1. Bell, *Documents*, vol. 2.
2. Bell, *Davidson*, pp. 1104–14.
3. Bell, *Davidson*, p. 1015, note.
4. *Guided*, p. 246.
5. See Chapter 17.
6. RTD 270:369–71.
7. Meyer, *That All May Be One*, Grand Rapids, 1999.
8. *Guided*, p. 232.
9. RTD 262:109.
10. RTD 262:115.
11. *Rem.*, p. 79.
12. RTD 262:123.
13. RTD 262:322.
14. RTD 262:374.
15. *Rem.*, p. 79.
16. Machin, *Churches and Social Issues*, p. 33.
17. Dillistone, *Charles Raven*, 1975, p. 120.
18. Published in his collected articles, *God and the World*, cf. pp. 82–3.
19. *Symp.*, p. 201.

21 Results and personalities of the Lambeth Appeal

1. *Rem.*, p. 80.
2. Bell, *Documents on Christian Unity: A Selection 1920–1930*, XX, p. 131.
3. *Rem.*, p. 80.
4. Simpson, *Recollections*, p. 81.
5. *Guided*, p. 247.
6. H. Maynard Smith, *Frank Weston*, 1926, pp. 239 and 241.
7. *Guided*, p. 251.
8. *Recollections*, p. 78.
9. *The Times*, 19 January 1925.
10. RTD 201:117–27.
11. RTD 267:16.
12. *Guided*, p. 251.
13. *Randall Davidson*, pp. 1306ff.
14. *Guided*, pp. 257–8.
15. *Rem.*, p. 90, and see Chapter 12.
16. *Guided*, p. 257.
17. Mews, 'The Churches', in M. Morris (ed.), *The General Strike*, 1976, pp. 318–37, see p. 325.
18. An evangelical Anglican Society founded in 1919.
19. Mews, 'The Churches', p. 325.
20. Machin, *Churches and Social Issues*, p. 38.
21. *Guided*, p. 257.

22. Mews, 'The Churches', p. 326.
23. Headlined 'Appeal of the Churches. "A Possible Concordat"', p. 3.
24. Hastings, *History of Christianity*, pp. 186–7.
25. See K. Laybourn in *BBC History*, May 2001, pp. 21–3.
26. 1860–1953. He too was later made a CH.
27. Bell, *Davidson*, p. 1312.
28. Mews, 'The Churches', p. 330.
29. Mews, 'The Churches', p. 333.
30. *The Times*, 12 May, p. 3.
31. Mews, 'The Churches', p. 337.
32. RTD 6:108.
33. Harris, *Forty Years*, p. 102.
34. Simpson, *Recollections*, p. 82.
35. Quotations about Carnegie Simpson and comments on his character are derived from contributions to an obituary by Bishop Bell, Lidgett and S. W. Carruthers in *The Journal of Presbyterian Historical Society*, 9.1, 1948–52, May 1948, pp. 3–9.
36. See Chapter 22 below.
37. Turner, *Conflict and Reconciliation*, pp. 187–8, and *HistMethGB3*, p. 347.
38. See *God, Christ and the Church*, pp. 241–51.
39. *Guided*, p. 250.
40. In his biography, *Cosmo Gordon Lang*, p. 456.
41. Lockhart, *Cosmo Gordon Lang*, p. 456.
42. *Rem.*, p. 91.
43. *Guided*, p. 272.
44. Bell, *Davidson*, p. 1355.
45. Bell, *Davidson*, p. 1341.
46. *Recollections*, p. 87.
47. Bell, *Davidson*, p. 1369.
48. Bell, *Davidson*, p. 1380, n. 1.

22 Free Church / Anglican discussions resumed

1. Simpson, *Recollections*, p. 91.
2. Turner, *Conflict and Reconciliation*, p. 189.
3. Lang Papers 120:233.
4. Simpson, *Recollections*, p. 78.
5. Simpson, *Recollections*, p. 80.
6. Lang Papers 61:2.
7. *MT*, 21 August 1930, the leading article.
8. For relations between Temple and Lidgett, see n. 58 below.
9. Lidgett's comment in tribute to Simpson in *The Journal of Presbyterian Historical Society*, 9.1, 1948–52, May 1948, pp. 7–8.
10. Lang Papers 61:29–30.
11. Lang Papers 120:236.
12. Simpson, *Recollections*, p. 80. Advice on the South India proposals was sought

from Lidgett, Flew, Harold Roberts and Lofthouse (Wakefield, *R. N. Flew*, pp. 209–10).

13. Lang Papers 191:105.
14. *Guided*, pp. 232–3.
15. *Pace* A. C. Don, Lang's Secretary (Lang Papers 62:15).
16. Lang Papers 61:27.
17. *Guided*, p. 249.
18. Lang Papers 61:41.
19. Lang Papers 61:40.
20. Lang Papers 61:45.
21. Lang Papers 61:55.
22. My italics.
23. Lang Papers 61:50.
24. Lang Papers 61:40.
25. Lang Papers 117:360–413.
26. Lang Papers 117:368.
27. Hugh Martin was its Joint Honorary Secretary 1933–43.
28. Lang Papers 61:71.
29. Lang Papers 61:66.
30. Lang Papers 61:79.
31. Lang Papers 61:180.
32. Lang Papers 61:185.
33. Lang Papers 61:195.
34. Lang Papers 61:197.
35. Lang Papers 61:219.
36. Lang Papers 61:219.
37. Lang Papers 61:304.
38. Lang Papers 62:19.
39. Lang Papers 62:48.
40. Lang Papers 62:58.
41. *Guided*, p. 248.
42. Lang Papers 62:61.
43. Lang Papers 62:213–15.
44. Cf. *Guided*, p. 229.
45. Bell, *Documents*, 3 Series 1948, VII.175, pp. 71ff.
46. S. Koss, *Nonconformity in Modern British Politics*, 1975, p. 191.
47. Hastings, *History of English Christianity*, p. 266.
48. *Methodist Times and Leader*, 23 March 1933, p. 1.
49. Lidgett had, however, reservations about Lloyd George's theology. See *MT*, 29 August 1935, pp. 1 and 8.
50. Koss, *Nonconformity*, p. 201.
51. Koss, *Nonconformity*, p. 216.
52. Koss, *Nonconformity*, p. 211.
53. For Lidgett's views on socialism, see Chapter 11.
54. Hastings, *History of English Christianity*, p. 267.

55. Koss, *Nonconformity*, pp. 216 and 214.
56. Koss, *Nonconformity*, pp. 216–7.
57. Lang Papers 62:247.
58. Lang Papers 62:263, dated 4 April 1938. Temple's intellect and social concern earned Lidgett's praise, but his obituary in *M.Rec.*, 2 November 1944, p. 6, revealed differences of opinion. Somewhat patronisingly, he found fault with Temple for becoming in his early years 'a megaphone for advancing programmes and inflicting criticisms upon public issues, mostly administrative, which he had not taken sufficient pains to understand. Yet, when corrected . . . no man was readier to acknowledge mistakes'! Lidgett goes on to boast that when he offered 'serious criticism' of Temple's Gifford Lectures 'on one important point' (unspecified), Temple replied 'frankly and generously to say that he thought I was right'.
59. Hastings, *History of English Christianity*, p. 216.
60. Lang Papers 62:276–7.
61. Lang Papers 62:279–80.
62. *Guided*, p. 248.
63. *Guided*, p. 249.
64. Lang Papers 62:285–95; and Bell, *Documents III*, 177, pp. 102–19.
65. See Chapter 13 for details.
66. Bell, *Documents*, 3 Series, 1948, IX.185.
67. Bell, *Documents 4*, IV, 236, pp. 47–50.
68. *HistMethGB3*, p. 373.
69. Maldwyn Edwards, in *The Christian World*, 9 July 1953.
70. G. S. Wakefield, *Robert Newton Flew*, 1971, p. 230.
71. *M. Rec.*, 13 October 1949; and see Chapters 13 and 30.
72. As recorded in *Dr Sangster*, the biography written by Paul Sangster, his son, 1962, p. 163.
73. *Symp.*, p. 6.
74. *Symp.*, p. 197.

23 Progress towards Methodist Union 1920–32

1. J. Kent, 'Methodist Union in England 1932', in N. Ehrenstrom and W. G. Muelder, *Institutionalism and Church Unity*, 1963, pp. 207–8.
2. G. G. Findlay, *The Church of Christ as set forth in the New Testament*, 1893.
3. *M.Rec.*, 24 July 1924, p. 6.
4. J. Ernest Rattenbury and Soper, not Lidgett, joined the Methodist Sacramental Fellowship, founded in 1935.
5. See A. J. Bolton, *The Other Side*, Wesleyan Methodist Historical Society pamphlet, 1994.
6. Currie, *Methodism Divided*, p. 255. I am greatly indebted to Currie's account of the whole drawn-out debate.
7. *M.Rec.*, 22 July 1920, p. 8.
8. See Chapter 8.
9. Currie, *Methodism Divided*, p. 259. See also *M.Rec.*, 15 April 1920, p. 5.

10. *MT*, 5 February 1920, pp. 10–11.

11. As Mr Kingsley Wood, the first of several qualified lawyers to give free legal advice at the Settlement.

12. *M.Rec.*, 22 July 1920, pp. 8 and 16.

13. *M.Rec.*, 22 July 1920, p. 16.

14. *M.Rec.*, p. 8.

15. Kent, *Methodist Union*, p. 210.

16. *M.Rec.*, 19 August 1920, p. 5, and 16 September 1920, p. 5.

17. *M.Rec.*, 21 April 1921.

18. For Lidgett's involvement in these, see Chapters 19–22.

19. *Minutes of Conference 1922*, pp. 85–9.

20. The John Rylands Library holds these Wesleyan records and those of the union committees.

21. *Guided*, p. 266.

22. For more detailed coverage, see Currie, *Methodism Divided*, pp. 253–89.

23. *M.Rec.*, 16 February 1922, p. 15.

24. Currie, *Methodism Divided*, p. 273.

25. *M.Rec.*, 23 July 1925, pp. 4–5.

26. *M.Rec.*, 30 July 1925, pp. 4–7.

27. *Guided*, p. 265.

28. Clause Four of the 'Deed of Union'.

29. Currie, *Methodism Divided*, p. 280.

30. *M.Rec.*, 27 May 1926, p. 14.

31. *M.Rec.*, 29 July 1926, pp. 4–5.

32. *M.Rec.*, 22 July 1926, p. 5.

33. Currie, *Methodism Divided*, p. 284.

34. *M.Rec.*, 28 July 1927, p. 17.

35. *M.Rec.*, 28 July 1927, pp. 5–6.

36. Currie, *Methodism Divided*, p. 285.

37. *M.Rec.*, 26 April 1928, p. 7.

38. *M.Rec.*, 26 July 1928, pp. 3–5.

39. *M.Rec.*, 2 August 1928.

24 First President of the Uniting Conference

1. *M.Rec.*, 28 July 1932, p. 7.

2. R. G. Burnett et al., *Frederick Luke Wiseman, a Commemorative Record*, 1954, pp. 46–55.

3. *Symp.*, pp. 30–1.

4. *HistMethGB3*, p. 178. Note Peake's contribution to the Deed of Union and influence over doubters in his own Church.

5. *Holborn Review*, 1930.

6. Lang Papers 112:291–310.

7. Published in 1932.

8. 22 September 1932, an unsigned comment, and 29 September 1932, Lofthouse's tribute.

9. *Guided*, p. 271.
10. *University Gazette*, 9 December 1932. The italics are mine.
11. *Guided*, pp. 267–9.
12. Currie, *Methodism Divided*, pp. 197–8.
13. Lidgett actively supported the outcry against Nazi antisemitism in the thirties. For example, he was named as 'a Beilis protest veteran' among prominent non-Jews at a protest meeting on 27 July 1933 who supported the resolution proposed by the Archbishop of Canterbury. There he represented the Free Churches, but apparently acted in his own right that same year when he joined the Archbishop and others in launching the German Refugees Assistance Fund. See W. D. and H. L. Rubinstein in *Philosemitism*, 1999, pp. 83–4 and 87–98.

25 Speaker and intellectual

1. *DNB, 1950–1960*.
2. *Symp.*, p. 178.
3. *Symp.*, pp. 177–8.
4. *Symp.*, p. 159.
5. *Rem.*, p. 92.
6. My italics.
7. *Rem.*, p. 92. My italics.
8. *M.Rec.*, 11 June 1936, p. 7.
9. *Reminiscences*, p. 24.
10. Rupp, in *Symp.*, p. 101.
11. Chapter 23.
12. *M.Rec.*, 18 July 1935, p. 29.
13. For example, *M.Rec.*, 12 October 1939, p. 5.
14. *Symp.*, p. 161.
15. *M.Rec.*, 31 July 1913.
16. *M.Rec.*, 31 July 1913, p. 18.
17. *M.Rec.*, 25 June 1953, pp. 6 and 8; cf. *Symp.*, p. 35.
18. See also Chapters 22 and 30.
19. *M.Rec.*, 13 October 1949, p. 3.
20. *MT*, 25 July 1907, p. 641.
21. *MT*, 23 February 1933.
22. *Symp.*, pp. 197–8.
23. See Chapter 12.
24. *Symp.*, p. 162.
25. *MT*, 28 July 1904, p. 538.
26. *Symp.*, pp. 161–2.
27. As in the unwieldy Methodist Uniting Conference of 1932.
28. *Symp.*, p. 166.

26 Writer and writings since 1921

1. See Chapter 9, on *God in Christ Jesus*, note 44.
2. Maldwyn Hughes's review of *Sonship and Salvation*: *MT*, 20 October 1921, p. 3.

3. See Chapters 3 and 25.
4. *Apostolic Ministry*, 1909, pp. 12–13.
5. NHM ii. 417ff.
6. Preface. My italics.
7. cf. Chapter 27.
8. *GCC*, pp. 84–5.
9. Part I, chapter III.
10. *M.Rec.*, 26 July 1934, p. 43.
11. *Symp.*, pp. 99–100.
12. Lidgett, *Victorian Transformation*, p. 13.
13. Lidgett, *God and the World*, p. 71.
14. Lidgett also defended Methodism (p. 81) against A. N. Whitehead's allegation that Methodism was 'singularly devoid of new ideas' and 'singularly rich in vivid feelings'.
15. *The Idea of God*, p. 83.
16. *The Idea of God*, pp. 103–9.
17. The book was enthusiastically and perceptively reviewed by R. N. Flew in *M.Rec.*, 5 August 1943, p. 7.
18. Lidgett's appreciation of William Temple in *M.Rec.*, 2 November 1944, mentioned an (unspecified) 'serious criticism' he had of 'one important point' in Temple's 'great' 1932–4 Gifford Lectures 'Nature, Man and God' (see Lidgett's review in *God and the World*, pp. 39–46).
19. Rupp, in *Symp.*, p. 102.
20. J. D. Beasley, *The Bitter Cry Heard and Heeded*, South London Mission, 1989, p. 80.
21. *Jesus Christ Is Alive*, Chapter 1, p. 11.

27 Disciple, preacher and District Chairman

1. *M.Rec.*, 16 July 1908, p. 3.
2. Sadly, too many to mention always by name here, but as far as possible included within the Acknowledgements.
3. *Symp.*, p. 32.
4. *M.Rec.*, 22 September 1932, p. 10.
5. *M.Rec.*, 9 August 1984, p. 11.
6. *Symp.*, p. 160.
7. For example, Waterhouse, in *Symp.*, p. 161.
8. See *Symp.*, p. 36, n. 5.
9. Wakefield, *R. N. Flew*, p. 169.
10. Beasley, *Bitter Cry Heard and Heeded*, p. 142. A valuable source throughout.
11. *M.Rec.*, 9 July 1953, p. 4.
12. *Guided*, p. 24. R. N. Flew much admired Lidgett's presidential address on the Nicene Creed.
13. Marchant (ed.), *If I Had Only One Sermon to Preach*. To Marchant's *British Preachers* (2nd series) Lidgett's contribution was a sermon about 'Love', called 'The Master Key', preached in Liverpool Cathedral on 25 October 1925. Another

sermon, on 'Christ's Self-Giving Love', was printed in the (undated) *Christian World Pulpit*.

14. My interview with him in September 1992.

15. Beasley, *Bitter Cry Heard and Heeded*, p. 162. The Wolverhampton *Express and Star* on 17 June 1953 says that Lidgett had conducted his first service there.

16. See, for example, Chapters 12, 23 and 25.

17. *Symp.*, p. 159.

18. As in all education.

19. *Symp.*, p. 164.

20. Lidgett may well have sought to copy Dr Henry J. Pope (1836–1912, Wesleyan Conference President in 1893) whom he admired as 'a great ecclesiastical chess-player' (*Rem.*, p. 68), acting behind the Conference scenes to further his ideas and policies.

21. John Travell, *Doctor of Souls, Leslie D. Weatherhead 1893–1976*, Cambridge, 1999, pp. 67 and 93–4. See also Eric Baker, in *Symp.*, p. 34.

22. Leslie D. Weatherhead, *The Mastery of Sex through Psychology and Religion*, London, 1931.

23. Cf. Weatherhead's *Psychology in the Service of the Soul*, 1929, and subsequent writing and speaking.

24. The quoted words come from comments in 1993 about the period 'sixty years ago' which Colin Morris made at a service commemorating the centenary of Weatherhead's birth (Travell, *Doctor of Souls*, p. 297).

28 Person and pastor

1. See Chapter 30.
2. Packington's letter to me of 16 March 1993.
3. *M.Rec.*, 24 September 1936, p. 10.
4. *Symp.*, p. 129.
5. *Symp.*, pp. 34–5.
6. *Rem.*, p. 34–5.
7. *M.Rec.*, 14 December 1933, p. 11.
8. *Symp.*, p. 39–78.
9. *Symp.*, pp. 58–9.
10. *Symp.*, pp. 53–4.
11. Lidgett told the 1945 Methodist Conference that 'Women should be entitled to complete the ministry they were exercising in the most solemn rite' (*M.Rec.*, 26 July 1945, p. 12). But women's ordination was not agreed until 1971.
12. See Chapter 7, and Lofthouse, in *Symp.*, p. 70.
13. Rupert Davies, in *M.Rec.*, 9 August 1984, p. 11.
14. *Symp.*, p. 137.
15. Bell Papers, 225:191.
16. Wakefield, *R. N.Flew*, pp. 41–3.
17. An anecdote given me orally by Rupert Davies about when he visited the Settlement as a representative of Oxford University students' John Wesley Society.
18. cf. Chapter 25.
19. Paul Sangster's biography of his father, *Dr Sangster*, p. 329.

20. Paul Sangster, *Dr Sangster*, p. 329.

21. Ruth Simpson, *John Scott Lidgett: A Portrait in His Old Age*, the Burgh Heath Centre for Psychotherapy, Epsom, printed in Leicester by John Culpin, 1962, pp. 9 and 10.

22. And e.g. on the holiday cut short by the outbreak of WW1.

23. Samuel Chadwick in *MT*, 11 October 1906, p. 690.

24. Oral information from Lorna Horstmann.

25. *Symp.*, p. 153.

26. *Symp.*, p. 153.

27. *Symp.*, p. 160.

28. Paul Sangster, *Dr Sangster*, p. 329.

29. *M.Rec.*, 13 October 1949.

30. Letter to me on 18 August 1992.

31. Methodist Hymn Book 598.

29 The Bermondsey Settlement – 2

1. For details and comment I am especially indebted to J. D. Beasley, *Bitter Cry Heard and Heeded*; to Lidgett's *Guided Life*, Settlement Reports and 1946 pamphlet on *The Bermondsey Settlement in the War and Since*; and to a variety of letters from Lidgett's contemporaries.

2. *Guided*, p. 98.

3. *Guided*, pp. 122, 128, etc.

4. *Guided*, p. 143.

5. *Guided*, pp. 138–9.

6. *Guided*, p. 143.

7. Letter from Harold Finch to me on 24 October 1992.

8. Letter to me, no date.

9. *M.Rec.*, 25 June 1953.

10. cf. *M.Rec.*, 10 August 1944, 'Bermondsey is not a place for making chums'.

11. *M.Rec.*, 15 January 1942.

12. For example, *M.Rec.*, 28 March 1940, p. 3, and 3 December 1942, p. 7.

13. Lines 120, 139, 159.

14. His pamphlet, *The Bermondsey Settlement in the War and Since*, dated November 1946.

15. *M.Rec.*, 9 May 1946.

16. *Symp.*, p. 146.

17. Letter to me dated 27 July 1992.

18. Harris, *Forty Years*, p. 17.

19. *Guided*, p. 119.

20. Sheppard, *Built as a City*, 1974, pp. 111–12.

21. Beasley, *Bitter Cry Heard and Heeded*, p. 126.

22. Beasley, *Bitter Cry Heard and Heeded*, pp. 126–7.

23. I am indebted to the Revd J. S. Lampard for notification of these details.

30 Retirement and final years

1. Detail mentioned to me orally by the late Reginald Buckmaster.
2. *M.Rec.*, 15 May 1947, 13 May 1948, 12 May 1949.
3. *Symp.*, p. 33.
4. *M.Rec.*, 23 June 1949.
5. *Symp.*, pp. 5–6; *M.Rec.*, 13 October 1949. See also Chapters 13, 22 and 25.
6. *M.Rec.*, 27 October 1949, p. 5.
7. cf. *M.Rec.*, 8 January 1942.
8. *M.Rec.*, 12 June 1952, p. 7.
9. *M.Rec.*, 30 October 1952, p. 3.
10. For example, Lady Graham-Little, widow of the MP for London University 1924–50.
11. See Simpson, *John Scott Lidgett*.
12. Methodist Conference President in 1942.

Conclusion

1. *Symp.*, p.185.
2. As well as travelling widely across the country, he broadcast on a number of occasions, as e.g. on the BBC Radio Studio Service (South London Press, 11 November 1927, p. 11). He appealed on the radio for funds for the Settlement, for example in 1942 and 1950, and was to have done so on 7 June 1953, but he was too ill and advised against it.
3. *M.Rec.*, 11 June 1936, p. 7.
4. *Methodist Magazine*, January 1933, p. 5.
5. *FG*, pp. 280 and 404.
6. *M.Rec.*, 9 August 1984, p. 4.
7. *Symp.*, p. 200.
8. See *Idea of God and Social Ideals*, pp. 82–3; and F. D. Maurice, *The Doctrine of Sacrifice deduced from the Scriptures: A Series of Sermons*, Cambridge, 1854, pp. xff.
9. *Symp.*, p. 85, and see pp. 103–5. *London Quarterly Review*, April 1956, p.137.
10. *M.Rec.*, 9 August 1984, p. 11.
11. Edmondson, 'Doctrines of Hell', p. 156.
12. As e.g. in the *Birmingham Mail* of 17 June 1953 ('He was often referred to as "the Archbishop of Methodism"'), in the *South Wales Echo* of the same date ('He was widely known as . . . '), and in many other newspapers at that time. See also Chapter 28 above which reveals that Lidgett wore Archbishop Davidson's robes at the latter's invitation on one occasion at Lambeth Palace. That story was told by Lidgett himself among the reminiscences of contacts with Archbishop Davidson which he passed on to Bishop Bell (Bell's Papers, 225:191).
13. *M.Rec.*, 25 June 1953.

Index